Sri Garib Das Oriental Series No. 356

Dialogues on the Hindu Philosophy

COMPRISING

THE NYĀYA, THE SĀṄKHYA, THE VEDĀNTA;

TO WHICH IS ADDED A DISCUSSION OF THE AUTHORITY OF THE VEDAS.

Krishna Mohan Banerjee
(1813 – 1885)

Edited by :
Amit Bhattacharjee

Foreword by :
Prof. V. N. Jha

Sri Satguru Publications
A Division of
Indian Books Centre
Delhi, India

Published by
Sri Satguru Publications
Indological and Oriential Publishers
A Division of
Indian Books Centre
24/4, Shakti Nagar,
Delhi-110007
India

Second Revised Edition: Delhi, 2014

ISBN 817030928X

Printed at: Dynamic Printers, Delhi

Krishna Mohan Banerjee
(1813 - 1885)

Foreword

It gives me immense pleasure in writing this Foreword to this volume edited by Dr. Amit Bhattacharjee. What a coincidence! This book is being published in this year 2013 in which the Bengal Theosophical Society is going to celebrate 200th birth anniversary of Rev. Krishna Mohan Banerjee. This publication is a great tribute to that great intellectual of Bengal who for the first time attempted to understand and compare the illustrious Indian dialogical heritage with that of the Greek tradition. It is a pity that thereafter no attempt has been made to go deeper into this topic. I, therefore, would like to congratulate Dr. Amit Bhattacharjee for editing this invaluable study of Rev. Krishna Mohan Banerjee and making it available to the lover and admirers of Indian Intellectual Heritage. I also thank Indian Books Centre for coming forward to publish this book.

Even a cursory look at the huge Sanskrit literature handed down to us from Vedic times up to the medieval period, embracing every aspect of human life, can tell us how much deeply engaged the Indians were in the study of language, literature, philosophy, art, architecture, dance, drama, music and culture, to name a few.

The structual depth of enquiry into truth was acquired only through dialogue traces of which can be found right from the Ṛgveda, the earliest available literary record of human beings in this world. Scholars all over the world admire the structural depth of Indian Epistemology. This was possible only because the Indians enjoyed freedom of thought and expression all through our intellectual history. There were inter- and intra-systemic dialogues. It was possible to interpret a text in more than one way. That is why we do not have only one system of Vedānta, but many systems of Vedānta. Even the Advaita Vedānta is not one, but many. Pūrvamīmāṁsā developed into three schools : Bhāṭṭa, Prābhākara and Murāri. Examples can be multiplied. All this could happen only because there were interdisciplinary and multi-disciplinary dialogues. Bhartṛhari, the celebrated language philosopher of 6th Century A.D. expressly writes that the dialogical mode of enquiry is the only way which can enrich human understanding. In his words :

Prajñā vivekaṁ labhate bhinnair āgama-darsanaiḥ/

Kiyād vā śakyam unnetum svatrkam anudhāvatā?//

'A knowledge is transformed into wisdom, when one is exposed to number of thoughts. If a man decides to depend upon his or her own power of inferencing how much can one conjecture?'

Man is a limited being, and therefore, engaging in a dialogue is the only way to take him or her to better understanding. That is why, the sages in the Upaniṣads opined that one should first listen (śrotavyaḥ). I would like to interpret it as 'listen to others'; then one should reflect (mantavyaḥ) critically and conclude and then concentrate on what has been concluded. This is the only scientific and democratic way to enquire into 'truth' and our forefathers were practising this method.

The history of development of all philosophical systems upto the medieval India bears testimony to this. Raghunātha Śiromani of Navadvīpa wrote Padārthatattvanirūpaṇa, a fresh reflection on the Nyāya-Vaiśeṣika Categorization of the universe where he offered constructive criticism to the traditional doctrine. He was aware of this fact and so at the end of his book he writes the following :

'I invite you to criticise me; but only after you understand my heart. And even after that if you find there is scope for criticism, I am least perturbed.'

I think we need to revive that democratic tradition of dialogue for which Indians were so much appreciated world over. I am hopeful that the publication of this book : *Dialogues on the Hindu Philosophy* of Rev. Krishna Mohan Banerjee will be a positive step towards that direction. I congratulate Dr. Amit Bhattacharjee once again and expect many more such useful volumes from him.

I also believe that the volume will receive with joy by the inquisitive readers and researchers of Indian Intellectual traditions.

Prof.V N Jha,
Former Director,
Centre of Advanced Study in Sanskrit,
University of Pune,

Pune.
20/05/2013

INTRODUCTION

I am happy in editing the book named *'Dialogues On The Hindu Philosophy'* which is divided into ten dialogues written by Rev. Krishna Mohan Banerjee in 1861 A.D. For the said book reveals our own contributions to dialogical heritage. It is striking that as far back as 1861, i.e. almost over one hundred fifty years ago the inquisitiveness of K.M. Banerjee was drawn to the inter and intra systemic dialogue. The writer of this book deserves grand salutation from those readers who are interested in understanding our rich cultural heritage in modern context. Preface of this book was written on 29 June, 1861 from Bishop's College. I pay my grand homage to the writer.

Krishna Mohan Banerjee (1813-1885 A.D.) was one of the 19th century Indian thinkers who attempted to rethink Hindu philosophy, religion and ethics in response to the stimulus of Christian ideas. Krishna Mohan was born in a Brahamin family on 24th May 1813 A.D. at Shyampur, Kolkata, Bengal, in the house of his maternal grandfather, Ramjay Vidyabhusan, the court-pundit of Santiram Singha of Jorasanko. The name of Krishna Mohan's father was Jibon Krishna Banerjee and mother was Sreemati Devi. He was the first president of the Bengal Christian Association and was a prominent member of Henry Louis Vivian Derozio's young Bengal group. In 1852 A.D. Krishna Mohan was appointed a professor of oriental studies at Bishop's College, Shibpore, Kolkata.

Krishna Mohan was the author of several rare works viz (i) 13-volume English-Bengali encyclopaedia 'Vidyākalpadrum' (1846-1851), (ii) Dialogues on the Hindu philosophy (1861), (iii)

The Arian Witness (1875), (iv) Upadeśkathā and (v) The relation between Christianity and Hinduism (1881). It was he who for the first time accumulated dialogues from almost all of the Hindu philosophy, containing an elaborate discussion on the art of dialogues.

The question is the first groping step of the mind in its journeyings that lead towards new horizons. It may be well at this point to remind ourselves that when someone likes to raise question he obviously must want to know the unknown. So question and answer, problem and solution are always used in philosophical discourse to make the clean enviroment of the dias. Large number of knotty problems are being solved by adopting certain rules of questioning.

Ever since Nalanda dialogue started in the year 2005 A.D. and I was invited almost at every dialogue I thought earnestly in writing our dialogical heritage. Indian philosophical schools have proved marvellously stimulating to the intellect. They are the product of profound, acute and restless minds. We may at least boast of having more dialogues, which may be considered as intellectual productions that can vie with those of Europe. Democratic readers are stunned after listening the discourses for the quest of truth. This book adequately will fulfil the long-standing need of our mission as it bears an intensive study of certain facets of dialogical heritage. This book throws up an hmazing variety of conflicting ideologies and opinion, some of which are being placed together.

The dialogues in this book are both self-contained and thematically linked to each other. I firmly believe that the reader will detect some inner unity in the fact that this study begins and also ends with a discussion on significant issues related to dialogue. So the name of the book is highly appropriate. Diacritical marks are put properly, though those were not seen in the original text.

In elaborating dialogues Krishna Mohan Banerjee mentioned the name of Kaṇāda, Kapila, Patañjali, Vyāsa, Jaimini, Gotama,

Śaṅkara, Vātsyāna, Buddha, Rāmānuja, Probhākara, Rāmānanda and Rammohan Roy etc. In this regard, I also wonder, when during argumentation, Tarkakāma said that Plato's argument was almost identical with Gotama's (p. 97). I heave a sigh of relief having seen unification of thought. It is remarkable to say that in describing dialogues of Hindu systems side by side the author had cited Greek doctrine, Plato's doctrine (dialogue-III) that may sufficiently prove versatile erudition of the author.

Actually Krishna Mohan Banerjee was a wonderful genius born in our province. There is not another discourse in Indian philosophy like the *'Dialogues on the Hindu philosophy'*, no mistake in that ; and it is difficult to come across a book like that in the whole of Indian philosophy. He began to explain lucidly the arguments and conclusions about the difficult points in all philosophies. In course of the conversation he did not forget to highlight modernity.

There is no iota of doubt that this 'Dialogue' is really a pioneer work in front of us to fulfil our dream in reality. Towards the last stages in editing this book, I was benefited greatly from the occasional exchange of views I had with professor V.N. Jha. Such dialogues, I am happy to say, have emboldened me to offer certain arguments that I would have been otherwise reluctant to do.

As for example Bankim Chandra Chattyopadhyay also had sharp exchange of words with Rev. K. M. Banerjee (September-November 1882). Although the book dealt with the Nyāya, the Sāṅkhya, the Vedānta and above all the Bauddha but the writer did not carry out his benevolent design without going through another course of temptation i.e. the temptation of christanity (Christ). In spite of that, I myself, am proud enough as a Bengalee that the earliest authentic account of 'Dialogues On The Hindu Philosophy' was first written by an intelligent observer who also was a Bengalee by birth. A fair inference may be founded that Brāhmanism and Buddhism existed side by side in India.

Dialogues are nothing but conversation that are being expressed through languages. As the book contains philosophical discourses, the readers may not expect here daily usage or colloquial languages. Differences of opinion are expressed through dialectics. It must be borne in mind that the rules of discipline are properly maintained by both the disputant and opponent. During dialogue truth is established on examination by experts and on proof by reasons. Readers would wonder to find that India has such heritage where much difference of opinion prevails, and yet democratic norms are not violated. India had glorious past when opponents could raise their voice without fear.

Philosophers would prefer questions as because philosophy survives only by questions. The whole foundation of philosophy is questioning. One of the important methods of acquiring knowledge is said in Śrimad-Bhagavad-Gīta that we should try to acquire knowledge through searching questions 'Pariprasńena' (4.34). This contribution continued up to the period of Raghunā th Śiromaṇi, the great celebrated logician of Navadwip of medieaval period. The importance of query does not only indicate the mark of interrogation in the negative sense, rather it reflects inquisitiveness. Kena Upaniṣ ad was begun through such query viz. Directed by what agent the mind goes towards its own object etc (1.1). We have found that in Praśna Upaniṣad venerable Pippalāda asked Sukeśā, Satyākama, Kauśalya and Kabandhī to have put questions, with regard to anything that anyone of them may desire to know. The intention of Pippalāda was that in accordance with the desire each of them might entertain. He also reminded them if he knew, what they ask, he would obviously explain. And all of us know that subsequently six questions are raised and categorically replied by Pippalāda. Needless to say, that Śrimad-Bhagavad-Gītā also was written in dialogical form. Someone may cite an example of Katha Upaniṣad and say that the wisdom is not to be attained through dialectics (1.2.9). It is remarkable to point out for them that Kaṭha Upaniṣad also holds dialogue between Yama and Naciketā

. Questioner like Naciketā is always welcome : त्वादृङ्नो भूयान्नचिकेतः प्रष्टा' (1.2.9).

Dialogical materials are large and abundant in all the philosophical texts. They exhibit a characteristic feature of human being viz. to study and enquire about himself and one's own mind. This is common to men of the past as of today. Examples are many : (a) Bhagavan Kutaḥ ha vā imāḥ prajāḥ prajāyante (O Venerable sir, from what indeed are all these beings born?) (b) Bhagavan kati eva devāḥ prājam vidhārayante, katare etat prakā śayante, kaḥ punaḥ eṣām variṣṭhah (Adorable sir, how many infact are the deities that sustain a creature? Which among them exhibit this glory? Which again, is the chief among them?) (c) Bhagavan Kutaḥ eṣaḥ prāṇa jāyate, Katham āyāti asmin śarīre, ātmānam vā pravibhājya katham prātiṣṭhate, kena utkramate, katham bāhyam abhidhatte, katham adhyātmam (O Venerable sir, from where is this Prāṇa born? How does he come into this body? How again does he dwell by dividing himself? How does he depart? How does he support the external things and how the physical?

Regarding the dialogues in the Dīgha-nikāya and the Majjhima-nikāya Rhys Davids has observed 'In depth of philosophic insight, in the method of Socratic questioning often adopted, in the earnest and elevated tone of the whole, in the evidence they afford of the most cultured thought of the day, these dialogues constantly remind the reader of the dialogues of Plato. But not in style. They have indeed a style of their own; always dignified and occasionally rising into eloquence. (Encyclopaedia Britannica, 11th edition, p. 746).

Actually most of the suttas are in the form of a dialogue, where an introductory passage relates the occasion (nidāna) : a person comes to visit Buddha, or Buddha comes across a person. Then begins a dialogue followed by a discourse by Buddha or, in some cases, by one of his disciples. The Milindapañha or the questions of Milinda, the Indo-Greek king Menandros or Menander of the 2nd century B.C. is a dialogue between the king and the Buddhist monk Nāgasena, which may have been an historical event. The king asks a host of questions to which the monk gives suitable replies. However, the king is not easily satisfied, and the dialogue becomes quite animated at places. The work has been compared to the upaniṣads, but while in the upaniṣads the princes are carried away by the discussions, king Milinda does not concede defeat, though he admits Nāgasena's adroitness and the value of his doctrine to which he is most probably converted.

Although Winternitz observes 'the method of argumentation in our suttas can by no means be compared with that of Plato. And as dialogues only a few suttas can stand comparison with the Platonic dialogues. No doubt Karl Fries (The Philosophical dialogue from Hiob to Plato, P. 65) has pointed out a number of remarkable parallels between Indian and Greek dialogues. But there is no similarity in just the most essential points. And they are certainly not conspicuous enough to compel us to think of any mutual influence. The majority of the suttas are not "dialogues" in the proper sense of the word, but they are rather speeches of a chief speaker (usually the Buddha) which are interrupted by the other speakers only through a "yes" or "no" or expressions of approval or applause. But even the best of the real dialogues in the Nikāyas will seldom remind us of the dialogues of Plato. On the other hand they will again and again remind us of those Itihāsa-dialogues which we have come across in the Mahābhārata' (A History Of Indian Literature, Vol. II, p.-74).

But in this context it may be pointed out that we do find the forms of dialogue popular since early ages, namely the pure dialogue as well as the Ākhyāna or the ballad, in which the stanzas of dialogues alternate with those of narration, and finally we find the Ākhyāna forms, a mixture of prose and verse which we have already seen in the old Brāhminic and epic poetry. The purpose may vary and models of raising questions perhaps may be changed and added to satisfy the minds of modern people.

But steps can be linked up easily. Actually dialogue supplies a pattern of introspective analysis of mind.

Summary of each dialogue (I-X) has briefly been expressed as follows. The author deals with the dialogue in all its aspects historically, analytically and comparatively. Dialogue I holds 'A Brahmin to a Brahmin'. The main portion of dialogue I is entirely philosophic in content and actually represents rationality. The characters of Satyakāma, Tarkakāma, Āgamnika, Daṇḍī, Yogī, Ādhunika are all imaginary. But debatable issues are raised and clarified so explicitly that readers do not at all get time to consider opponent and disputant as author's own imagination. One debator tries to topple another. Since time immemorial people want to know the meaning of *Swadharma*. Satyakāma observed although there is no enternal *Sanātandharma* but *Iṣṭadevatā* has had great position within one's own conscience. From the speech of Āgamnika it is clear that one may even give up one's caste for Hari. Sectarian attitude is ignored through dialogue. Readers become cheerful having listened from Tarkakāma that the sectaries are a set of ignorant fanatics—dupes of cunning and ambitious leaders. If people's mind had been enlightened by the teaching of Indian Philosophers they would not have been so unsteady. In the long run, one can very well understand whose cause they espouse. By the art of argumentation, it was clear that participants sought justice. Meeting had focussed the methodology of dialogue. In brief, dialogue I treats of Indian discources which comprise as it were all the topics of *Vādamārga.* The intention of the author was to establish doubt *(saṃśay)*, confutation *(tarka)*, certainty *(nirṇaya)* and tenets *(siddhānta)* etc.

Dialogue II represents an interesting problem of social speculation. Due to lunar eclipse the debator could not attend in time—it really reflects grief. During proposed conference every invited should be punctual or it shows disrespect to the dialogical institution. Side by side the author expressed his anguish asking how few had read Vedānta Sūtra, Vaiśeṣika Sūtra, Sāṅkhya Sūtra and Yoga Sūtra! So stress was given on reading original sūtras. Unless one reads thoroughly and carefully the *sūtra-granthas* minds may not be freed from bondage. People have come to know that progress of Nyāya may prevent progress of heresy. Being born within the society why Śūdras were eliminated and why they had lost their human rights—having raised the said questions the author really became a dynamic person, and, I believe, he had worked for the nation's development too.

Dialogue III produces a firm belief by evidence. It is really convincing. Readers will read on and on and consider how magnificently Tarkakāma approaches regarding the necessity of future births which were also the causes of our bonds. Sterk truth was revealed in saying that each person of the world is by birth in a state of bondage. The author obviously had disclosed that the study of any philosophical school invevitably demands certain pre-requisites and that these pre-requisites include a fairly correct understanding of the historical inter-relationship gaining among the various philosophical systems of India. Hair-splitting analysis is found about *adṛṣṭa* (desert). We may explain *adṛṣṭa* by the following example. An effect proceeds from a cause. If there had been no interdependence of a cause and its effect, the latter would have been found always and everywhere. But an effect is only occasional and hence it is dependent on a cause. Therefore our happiness and misery are dependent on a cause called *adṛṣṭa*. Categorically Nyāya, Sāṅkhya and Vedānta views are simplified. Exploring doctrine of transmigrations, doctrine of causation and above all God Himself is dependent on *adṛṣṭa*. The author deserves respect. In this context it should be pointed out that Revd. K. M. Banerjee had side by side profound knowledge in western thought also. Otherwise he would not be able to cite Greek doctrine of pre-existence and to compare Plato's doctrine of reminiscence similar to Gotama's. Plato was born in 427 B.C. and became a pupil of Socrates 407 B.C., remaining with him until the latter's death (399 B.C.). Plato was a poet and mystic, as well as a philosopher and dialectician. Of the writings transmitted under his name are 35 dialogues. Even question-answer formula is remarkable when one speaks that he is not at all satisfied by the reply.

Dialogue IV treats elaborately *adṛṣṭa*. Though literally it means 'unseen' yet our author reminded us Vaiśeṣika sūtra (6.2.12). Kaṇāda attributes the soul's departure from one body and adoption of another, to the agency of *adṛṣṭa* while Gotama ascribes it to *karma* and meaning of the both is same. To glorify *adṛṣṭa* Śrīharṣa, Kālidāsa, one of the commentator of Nyāyakusumāñjali, Kaṅāda and Gotama all are quoted. From the discource of Satyakāma one may be able to realise that the term *adṛṣṭa* actually implies yantra or instrument and it is dependent on God's will. Therefore supreme being may be addressed as Yantrī or the user of the instrument. One may recall the song of Rāmprasad : 'Tumi yantrī āmi yantra/yemmi chālāo temmi chali.' Having listened the art of argumentation raised by Tarkakāma, Satyakāma, Nyāyaratna one understands clearly why the schools of Nyāya and Vaiśeṣika are called samā natantra. During philosophical discource, flying off from one point to another is not at all appreciable—it also has been mentioned. Readers come to know how a congenial debate (anuloma sambhāṣā) may be continued. When being charged by Tarkakāma, Satyakāma replied to pardon him and he would say something the other day on the same subject—then readers cannot conceal their pride. The author's intention is that one must express regret for the lapse of one's own tongue during dialogue. The character of Nyāyaratna is appreciable as from his discource one may know even Sir Isaac Newton was a follower of our Kaṇāda. Theory of Śaṇkarācārya and the notion of pañcīkaraṇa are also explained in this context. In brief, exploring the theory of creation the author is totally successful. But he reminded us *śuṣka tarka*, i.e. dry and unprofitable debate should not be encouraged. Reason is the attribute of the human being manifested in understanding, evaluation, discernment and judgement.

Dialogue V contains several important discourses. No doubt it is more miscellaneous and is a mine of information. Readers get an inkling about the dialogical condition of ancient India. On the banks of the river the same party except Nyāyaratna namely Āgamika, Satyakāma and Tarkakāma assembled for coversation. One of the important principal subjects treated in the Nyāyasūtra is pramāṇa. Tarkakāma categorically had mentioned four-fold pramāṇas of Nyāya viz. perception, inference, analogy and affirmation (verbal testimony). In delivering his lecture Tarkakāma would not forget to mention that Gotama's intention was to teach the art of reasoning and as all reasoning depended on proof, Sūtrakāra perfectly laid the greatest stress on pramāṇa. No hesitation was found in comparing five member syllogism and Grecian syllogism. If one asks which was simpler, answer was given analysing Gotama's view and he was described as a teacher of mankind. Satyakāma wanted to know how the accurate knowledge of Gotama's sixteen categories or six of Kaṇāda could lead emancipation! People are obviously able to know through the art of argumentation about the nature of paramapuruṣārtha. It also was established that in no way one could undervalue the study of logic. When Tarkakāma requested Satyakāma not to exhaust his energy on mere verbal criticisms, readers can not conceal their pride. Culture as revealed in śāstras is necessary to uphold human life. Through the dialogues held between Āgamika and Satyakāma, someone may know the resemblance of orthodox Gotama and heterodox Gotama. Emancipation and nirvāṇa both are alike but difference lies only in dialectics. Reality was expressed by Tarkakāma that some kind of truths can only be realized by the feeling not by the metaphysical and logical speculation. All Buddhists are not to be entitled as atheists as some of them acknowledged a self-existent Deity whom they call Ādi Buddha. Tarkakāma reminded Satyakāma to take facts as they are. Quoting from Taittirīya Brāhmaṇa Satyakāma tried to explain what does the word heaven (suvarga) mean. It only indicates the good society. At last it may be said that during debate Āgamika's muscular motion on his face was indescribable indeed. Therefore platform of dialogue was nicely built up.

Dialogue VI bears an interesting topic which is related to cosmology. To sharpen our thinking this chapter deserves esteem. Here is a typical instance of philosophers' inquisitiveness. Readers may want to know how the universe is composed. Actually one of the oldest intellectual defences of theism is the cosmological argument. The argument runs as follows. Every event must have a cause. Therefore there must be a first cause, and this first cause is God, the initiator of all changes in the universe. Since a non-intelligent cause cannot produce its effect without the superintendence of an intelligent spirit, it is to be admitted that there is a supreme Agent called the All powerful God who bestows on us pleasure and pain as the effects of our activities. Here Kāpila was a representative of Sāṅkhya system and Satyakāma, a representative of Śaṅkara. Satyakāma's arguments are among the most challenging in the history of dialogue. Everyone will readily allow that there is a considerable difference between the theory of Sāṅkhy and Vedānta. So commotion was created through the dialogue as Satyakāma was determined to establish the existence of an intelligent author. He cited that habit is also produced by intelligent training. Readers will find that Satyakāma was modern in nature. So giving glaring example no doubt reflects his modernity : "the power of steam is no doubt wonderful as we see it daily in the train that passes from Rajmahal to Howrah. But can you forget the mental exercise involved in the projection of the Railway scheme—the vast preparations making for years by skilful engineers, the making of roads and bridges, the laying of the rail, and the daily labour bestowed by intelligent workmen on the guiding of the train? The railway is no doubt a brilliant triumph of science, but science implies intellectual exercise, not the blind force of nature." Satyakāma charged kāpila in saying : "Do you think the locomotive moves from Rajmahal to Howrah without the intervention of intelligent engineers"? No doubt, Satyakāma was excellent. Here disagreement in attitude determines what beliefs are relevant to the argument. Question-answer forms are really fantastic. Sāṅkhya view was refuted by Śaṅkara in Brahma-sūtra-bhāṣya (2.2.1) where he said that there are some people of dull intellect who on noticing the great scriptures of the Sāṅkhyas and others, may conclude that these too are to be accepted as a means to right knowledge. Their interpretations are mere fallacies and not the correct explanations.

Dialogue VII exhibits that on the occasion of the wedding Tarkakāma, Āgamika, Satyakāma, Buddhist, Bhāgavata, and Vaiyāsika are invited and assembled. As usual argumentation also was started among them. Buddhist was an erudite scholar who had tried utmost to show the supremacy of Śākyasiṅha. Quoting from Bhāgavata, Bhagavad Gītā, Muṇdaka, Taittirīya, Aitareya, Kena and Brahma-sūtra-bhāṣya he tried to establish that he alone had a consistent doctrine whereas every philosophical school has made a convenience of his gods and Vedas. In most of the cases, whimsically, each of the schools has defended or condemned gods and Vedas. Buddhist found a series of inconsistencies in all philosophical schools and firmly believed that every school has somehow borrowed some of his ideas about the bondage of works and the means of samādhi and nirvā ṇa. In brief, Buddhist retorted and succeeded in achieving so. All on a sudden readers faced a hot debate between Satyakāma and Tarkakāma. Satyakāma called a spade a spade to Tarkakāma that view of Advaita-vedānta implied pantheism which was nothing but practical atheism. Here I may quote Tarkakāma to explain the gravity of the situation : 'I think, Satyakāma, you rely too much on English reviewers. If you adopt them as your masters, no wonder you will vilify the doctrine of the Vedānta as practical atheism. Like teacher like pupil. But you can not expect me to be much influenced by the language of your English masters'. Satyakāma pacified Tarkakāma in saying that he was not influenced by any English reviewer. But it was prescribed by Cirañjīva in his Vidwān-moda-taraṅgiṇī "if the universe be in your opinion unreal, then why unnecessarily invent your Brahma? Without form, without agency, what can he be doing in the world"? Satyakāma logically proved reality of the world citing Nyāyasūtra of Gotama.

There is another point. Western philosopher Berkeley was named in this dialogue. We know that George Berkeley (1685-1753 A.D.) was born in Ireland. Berkeley made use of the basal empiricism of Locke to establish idealism and thereby refute materialism and atheism. He believed that there must be some cause of the sensations or ideas in our mind. This cause must be an active substance. It can not be a material substance, for there is no such thing. Therefore it must be an incorporeal, active, active substance or spirit. A spirit is one undivided, active being. We cannot perceive the spirit itself, but only the effects which it produces.

Tarkakāma found a similarity between the doctrine of Berkeley and the ontology of Vedānta. He explained, as Berkeley admitted the existence of spirit and denied matter so Vedānta did the same. Although from the speech of Satyakāma we are able to know that 'Berkeley was unfortunately destitute of the light of the Vedas, and ignorant of our grand doctrine of unity'. Therefore Indian readers may be happy. Simultaneously unification of thought is praiseworthy.

Dialogue VIII contains an ornate version. The Buddhists believes that the doctrines of māyā and mukti are borrowed from them. Buddhist system is older than that of Vyāsa or Gotama. In this regard it was cited that all our philosophical schools aimed at the refutation of Buddhism as one of their chief objects. Buddhists thought that before the birth of Śākyamuni vedic seers would only preach rites and ceremonies and their primary aim was to pave the way of heaven. Buddha was the first to teach earth and heaven are transient and illusory. External world is nothing but a phantom, a māyā. Vedic seers only fought for the pleasures of life. To achieve external bliss after death they wrote their scriptures. Millions of people are attracted by Lord Buddha's principles, yet in the long run, orthodox schools banished them influencing party-spirit. The original Vedas didn't say anything regarding māyā, miseries of life, apavarga, nirvāṇa and mukti. Buddhist categorically cited the name of śvetā śvataropaniṣad that quoted the term māyā by which they can easily prove the doctrine of māyā to be post-Buddhistic. The doctrine that identifies God with the universe was inculcated in Vedānta sūtras. Satyakāma raised a pertinent question that may convince orthodox schools too. "Śākya was brought up under the influence of Brāhminism, and if Brāhminism has taken lessons from his school, it is simply the tutor learning in his turn from a smart pupil." Readers do find through the whole 8th dialogue a sign of anuloma sambhāṣā (congenial discussion). It shows a sense of fitness or decorum. But in this chapter readers may also know that pantheism spoils moral consequences. If God and man be identical, then there can be no relation in life to give rise to the notion of duty. So God is different from the individual being. It has been said that spiritual pantheism is nothing but a written accusation.

Dialogue IX accounts strictly existence of God. As a non-intelligent cause cannot produce its effect without the superintendence of an intelligent spirit, so it is to be admitted that there is a supreme Agent called the All-powerful God who bestows on us pleasure and pain as the effects of our desert. Daṇḍī appreciated Satyakāma's debatable method but subsequently reminded him if we call the world an illusion, we cannot argue from it as a reality. Satyakāma defends himself from the attacks of Daṇḍī by saying that his view of the Vedānta appears to be derived from foreign sources. Through dialogue one is able to know that to deny the world is to deny the power and wisdom of God. The term heaven was analysed and explained too. Swarga may have been derived from suvarga (good company) as swarṇa (gold) is from suvarṇa. Yogi did not like to carry on a debate in that assembly and as a result of it he left the place. Although this book focuses attention on the dialogues of the Hindu philosophy, simultaneously it records the Brāhma-Dharma and how the school of Rammohan gradually gives up the orthodox interpretation of śāstras. It was this rational scrutiny of ancient scriptures that led Rammohan to extricate the original Hinduism from a morass of illogicality and superstition.

Dialogue X argues the authority of the Veda and analyses what the Vedas can be. This dialogue is comparative and is included in order to make it clear that the Bible is the true record of God's will. It has not been definitely proved either by perception or by the the Vedas that the Vedas have no author. A sentence is composed by a person since it is a combination of words. Therefore how can we say that the Vedas are eternal, i.e, they have not been composed by a person? This appears to me as something of an anomaly, because the concept of the eternity of the Vedas is refuted. Mention might also be made of the standpoint adopted in the essay. Āgamika wanted to know from Satyakāma where his true coin was. Satyakāma replied that the true coin he believed to be the Bible. It had strong external evidences for its being composed under divine inspiration. Both the writers of the Old and New Testaments obtained knowledge by divine inspiration. After much discussion Āgamika also had felt that if there be truth in the world, it must be found in the Christian Scriptures. Here arises an interesting problem of dialogical speculation. Although readers do not find a heated controversy on this question.

I have not however seen anything which would make me revise the standpoint adopted here, though some details might need modification here and there. The book is an excellent piece of dialogical writing, both with regard to the range of problems covered and the delightful manner of presentation.

I have made every effort to make this edition an attractive one, and hope that it would be a welcome to all lovers of dialogue. In transliteration I have followed the international diacritical mark system with which the readers are familiar. I am grateful to Indian Books Centre for bringing out this invaluable edition.

I must mention also a very remarkable moment here. It was a nice morning of 18th November, 2012 when my revered Sir

Prof. V.N. Jha stayed in my house and began to disclose his mission of spreading dialogical studies of India throughout the world. I showed him the rare of the rarest xerox copy of this monumental work. For the art of argumentation or the art of dialogue that was presented by our Indian philosophers always beckon me. According to my Guru's advice I promise to edit it. Therefore, I bow down to him who not only had encouraged me to bring out this volume into public and also expressed his firm faith in me. He readily agreed to write Foreword of this book that will extend the periphery of this edition.

In this context it is pertinent to point out that we have taken a grand project on 'Dialogical tradition' as revealed in India. Contents of the project are almost prepared. Project has been divided into five volumes respectively :

Vol-I	:	Narratives of dialogue from Ṛgveda to Sūtra period (approximately 5th B.C.).
Vol-II	:	Organised structure of dialogue.
Vol-III	:	Dialogue through commentaries.
Vol-IV	:	Language of discourse.
Vol-V	:	Contribution of Bengal to the dialogical discourse.

In course of time, we would like to develop the said thought, although preliminary structure has been written almost. It is a matter of pride that basic material is already provided by Rev. Krishna Mohan Banerjee in this respect.

Amit Bhattacharjee

Calcutta
24.05.2013

TO

JOHN MUIR ESQ., D.C.L.

LATE OF THE BENGAL CIVIL SERVICE,

WHO FOR A LONG SERIES OF YEARS

HAS CONTRIBUTED

BOTH BY HIS PURSE AND HIS PEN

TO THE VERY OBJECTS HEREIN AIMED AT,

THIS WORK IS INSCRIBED

AS A SMALL TRIBUTE

OF THE AUTHOR'S RESPECT AND ESTEEM.

PREFACE

सत्यमेव जयते ॥

THE objects aimed at in the following dialogues are, *first,* to give a correct and authentic statement of the doctrines of Hindu philosophy, and, *secondly,* to suggest such modes of dealing with them as may prove most effective to the Hindu mind.

Our first object we have attempted to ensure by citing the original authorities, and letting the old Ṛṣis speak for themselves. The second we have endeavoured to attain by availing ourselves in some measure of the arguments which the advocates of contending schools have used against each other. We have thus impressed Kaṇāda, Kapila, Rāmānuja, to do battle for us against the Vedānt, and taken advantage of Śaṅkarācārya's powerful battery against the Nyāya and the Sāṅkhya.

There was a time, not full fifty years ago, when politicians and statesmen expressed the most extravagant admiration of the Hindu philosophy, both in official documents and in speeches delivered in the parliament of Great Britain. In defence of the policy of excluding Christian missions from the country, reference was made to "her philosophers, lawyers, and moralists who have left the oracles of political and ethical wisdom, to restrain the passions and awe the vices which disturb the commonwealth[1]." The panegyrics passed on the Hindu systems by politicans are no doubt to be referred in part to the temporary excitement and consequent bias under which they were written or spoken. But writers are still not wanting who affect to be amazed at the transcendental excellency of the Hindu philosophy, and who do not hesitate to declare that however much the undoubted excellency of the system may be mixed up with possible errors, it would be impossible without profane violence to the one to refute the other.

The difficulty of the task we freely admit.But our endeavour has been candidly to recognize what we have found to be true, and courageously to condemn what we have discovered to be false.

What, it may be asked, is to be the test of truth and error in these discussions? We say, in the language of the Royal proclamation,—the only document through which the Queen has ever spoken to her Indian subjects and in Indian languages,—that "firmly relying ourselves on the truth of Christianity, and acknowledging with gratitude the solace of Religion, we disclaim alike the Right and the Desire to impose our convictions," on any of our controversial opponents. The Christian religion itself, which recognizes "the work of the law written in the hearts" of men, forbids unfairness of argumentation in discussions, voluntarily undertaken, with the full understanding that the parties argued with are not Christians. We have no right therefore in this argument to appeal to that which we believe to be the primary standard of truth, and the highest authority in all controversies to which it is applicable.

That authority, however, as we have just hinted, recognizes another authority—the authority of conscience—limited indeed in its range, but still a sufficient authority within its own province. Now the questions discussed in these pages certainly fall within that province. We have to deal with those who profess to discriminate between *dharma* and *adharma*, between right and wrong. Our test of truth and error in these discussions is accordingly the same which writers on moral philosophy and natural theology are in the habit of observing. It is substantially the very test to which the founders of the Hindu philosophy themselves appeal.

But do not the founders of the Hindu philosophy appeal also to the positive authority of the Vedas which they look upon as a revelation from God? This is only partially true, for most of the schools maintain that their doctrines are superior to the Vedas, and as to the few which profess to deduce their tenets from the authority of texts, they certainly do not say that the texts contain a revelation of God's will. Some of them say nothing at all about the existence of God, and all deny that the Vedas had any author, human or divine. (See below pp. 485, 486). We have discussed their tenets on these points, and the final appeal remains therefore to *the work of the Law written in the hearts of men.* One of the staunchest of the defenders of the Vedas allows that even their authority could not sanction what involves an absurdity or a contradiction.

It is generally believed by the modern followers of Brāhminism that the Vedas contain a revelation from God, and under this impression they implictly submit to their spiritual guides; whose authority they think may be traced to the teaching of the Vedas, and through them to the declaration of God's will. It is only justice to all parties to say that those founders of Brāhminical systems who were considered must orthodox did not propound the Ṛik 'Yajush, Sāman and Atharvan as given by God in any sense of the term.

It is also a popular belief among the Hindus that the great Ṛṣis, who founded their schools, and whose teaching they consider to be infallible, were themselves men of superior sanctity that had laboured to counteract the atheistic teaching of the Buddhists by zealously and skilfully arguing for the existence of a Supreme Intelligence, the Author and Governor of the universe. This is what living Paṇḍits say, and their unlearned followers believe. That nothing can be a greater delusion will appear from the following pages. It is much to be regretted that the delusion has in some respects been sanctioned even by Christian authors writing on the Hindu philosophy. The accounts given by living Paṇḍits and the representations contained in popular elementary treatises have been too unsuspectingly received. Perhaps we may say that no writer since the days of Colebrooke has endeavoured to test the correctness of the popular representations by a careful examination of the original Sūtras themselves. The popular delusion has consequently been widely spreading without any thing to rectify it.

The following broad facts may be advanced without much fear of contradiction. Neither of the two Ṛṣis of the Nyāya school, Gotama and Kaṇāda, has argued at all for the existence of a Supreme Intelligence as the Author and Governor of the universe. Kaṇāda, again, positively accounts for the construction of the world without the intervention of any Supreme Intelligence[2], while the principles of Gotama with reference to life and emancipation are almost identically the same as those of the Buddhists. The principles on which Kapila (if indeed he was the author of the Sāṅkhya sūtras) denied the existene of God, he held in common with all the other Ṛṣis, and so far the elements of atheism exist in all the schools. Patañjali, the author of the Seśwara or theistic Sāṅkhya, though he acknowledged a Supreme Being, did not declare Him to be the creator of the universe. Jaimini, the author of the Prior Mīmāṅsā, has never argued for the existence of God, and if he ever said any thing of a Supreme Being, it was only to deny His providence and His moral government of the world. His dscription of the Veda, as a *śabda* or infallible teaching without a teacher, involved atheism in the coneption of some of his eminent followers; who have not hesitated to argue on his principles against the possibility of a God to create the world or teach the Veda. Vyāsa the author of the Vedānt sūtras did certainly argue for the existence of a God, but he taught that the universe is identical with Him, and consequently that there is no God above the world.

It is also believed among those who admire the transcendental doctrines of the popular Vedānta that the universe is but an illusion, a Māyā, a phantom.The discussion of this question will be found in the following pages. Here we would only ask the advocates of Māyāvāda to remember that their favourite theory was first propounded by the founder of Buddhism, and that the Brāhmins had probably learnt it from those very schools on which they continue to this day to affix the stigma of heresy.

We say that the Brāhmins had probably borrowed their transcendental doctrine of Māyā from Buddhist schools, because,when they first settled on the fertile plains of Hindustan, they were far from pronouncing the world to be a phantom, or sensuous life to be an essential evil. In their earliest literature, the *Mantras* of the Vedas, we do not see any traces of such doctrine. Every thing is there natural—nothing transcendental. We see hymns and prayers addressed to divinities. The things prayed for are all such as belong to our common everyday life. Offspring, cattle, lands, houses,—such are the boons which the gods are requested to bestow on their votaries. No impatience of life, no description of the world as an assemblage of evils,—much less as a mere phantom or māyā,—no aspirations after release from corporeal existence, are found there.

Nor do we descry any decided advance toward the transcendentalism of the ṣaḍ-Darśanas in the *Brāhmaṇas* of the Vedas. Hindu society was then regularly formed,—the institution of caste was matured,—the Brāhmins were recognized as the repositories of learning, and ministers for the performance of rites and ceremonies. Rules had been formed for their initiation in theology. The learned among them were teahers of their order. Young Brāhmins would be broguht up in the houses, and under the watchful eyes, of their preceptors. They would take lessons on the Vedas. Clever pupils would be allowed to ask questions on speculative science, and the tutors would resolve their doubts. In these conferences between teachers and pupils, metaphysical questions would naturally be debated. The prospects of the soul after death would often become the subject of catechetical instruction. But these instructions and speculations, so far as appears from the Brāhmaṇas, had nothing decidedly transcendental in them. They were for the most part ethical and ritualistic. We do indeed see occasionally certain aspirations after union with the divinity, but these are rare and exceptional. We also notice a tendency toward identifying the universe and deified impersonations with the Supreme Brahma.But we do not see any marked condemnation of the world because of the evils of disease and death. We do not see it denounced as an assemblage of essential evils incapable of remedy. We do not find any impatience of life and embodied existence. We do not hear of the necessity of getting rid of transmigrations. We are not told that supreme felicity consists in the separation of the soul from body and mind, or that the functions of body and mind inevitably lead to misery. We do not learn that *pravṛtti* or activity is an evil in itself—or that our chief good can only be found in a state in which the soul will be deprived of its capacities of thought, feeling and action.

The transcendental notions, now the fundamental principles of Hindu philosophy, had no existence in the Mantras and Brāhmaṇas. When,then, were they first broached, by whom, and how?

The Upaniṣads, as will be seen from the following pages, do not give a satisfactory account of the origin of the doctrine of Māyā. The Buddhists, on the other hand, do supply us with what must be admitted to be at any rate a plausible explanation of its origin. The incidents of their founder's life are all we require for this purpose. They say the father of Śākya Muni had been apprized from the beginning that his son would soon take to the life of an ascetic. When the boy was twelve years old, the king assembled his Brāhmins and asked them to state the cause for which the prince would renounce his home and his kindred. They told him that the boy would see four things–decrepitude, disease, a dead body, and a recluse, which would induce him to leave the palace and retire to the forest. The king commanded that those four sights should always be kept at a distance from him, and that care should be taken to prevent his ever coming across them. But these precautions were all in vain. The gods themselves were impatiently waiting for the happy moment when Siddhārtha would enter on his high calling. One day therefore when he was resolved to go out on a drive–and when by the king's orders all unseemly sights had been removed from the town, the gods exhibited in his way the appearance of a decrepid old man, humpbacked, with broken teeth, grey locks, wrinkled, leaning on a staff, and walking slowly with tremoulous steps. Wondering, aghast, at the wretched spectacle, the prince inquired of the coachman, who the person was? "An old man, my Lord, answered the coachman, bent down by age, his strength and energy gone, his senses worn out, and he himself destitute and disabled." Struck by the coachman's answer, the prince asked again, "Is such a wretched existence peculiar to the race or tribe of which this unhappy person is a member, or is that the common lot of the whole world? Do tell me the truth quickly."

The coachman replied : "It is not a peculiar misfortune, my Lord, of this poor man–or of his family, or country. Youth and old age are incident to all, nor can your highness expect to be free from it. No one can escape decrepitude."

The prince was so overwhelmed with the conception of the world's misery, that he immediately ordered the coachman to turn the carriage homeward, and he came back in a most melancholy mood of mind.

When the prince on another ocasion was driving out with a large retinue, a leper, full of sores, unable to move, and breathing with difficulty, fell in his sight–and from the enquiries he made of the coachman, he concluded that disease was another evil to which all were subject. A third drive brought him the sight of *death* in a similar manner, and another addition again was made to his knowledge of the evils of life. A fourth drive revealed the sight of a mendicant Brahmachāri, absorbed in meditation with subdued mind and senses. Buddha was at once convinced that this was the only mode of living by which earthly perils could be avoided.

The dreaded sights produced the effects which the Brāhmins had foretold. The prince began to cry *shame* on life and existence. "Fie on youth", said he, "almost in the very grasp of decreptitude!Fie on health, soon to be overpowered by disease! Fie on life, running headlong into the jaws of death[3]."

This legend is found in the traditions of all Buddhists, whether of China, Nepaul, or Ceylon. Divested of the romantic ornaments, the story means that certain sights of woe had produced in young Buddha a feeling of disgust with life and earthly existence, which he characterized as an assemblage of decrepitude, disease, and death, a māyā, a mirage. The Brāhminical philosophers use the very same expressions with reference to the evils of life, but they cannot produce a hero, as the original teacher of the doctrine. When they say this doctrine was taught by the Creator to the Sun, by the Sun to Manu &c., it is simply a confession that they know not how to account for it, —for their own Vedas show that the doctrine was unknown in the period of the Mantras, and they themselves declare that the doctrine was *lost* by the lapse of time, until it was restored in the *Bhagavad-gītā*[4]. But the Bhagavad-gītā, is clearly a *post-Buddhistic* work, and we cannot admit Kṛṣṇa's claim to the doctrine taught by Śākya. It is singular that, on Kṛṣṇa's own confession, the transcendental doctrine should have remained with the *kings,* instead of Brāhmins.

We have in the following pages suggested a historical consideration of the relation between the Brāhminical philosophy and Buddhism. What appears to us most strange is the occurrence of two names, Gotama and Kapila, in the Buddhist tradition of the origin of the race from which their leader sprang. The following is the Tibetan version of a tradition held in common by all Buddhists :

Śākya, is the name of that tribe or family of Śākya Muni, belonging to the Kṣatria caste. According to Buddhist traditions, this race descends from *Ikṣwāku,* a prince of the solar line and founder of the royal race of Ayodhya, or Oude. The name however does not appear in the genealogical lists of Hindus, as that either of a tribe or of a people.

* * He had two sons, GOTAMA and BHARADHWAJA. The former took the religious character, but *Gotama* being afterwards accused of the murder of a harlot, was unjustly impaled at *Potala,* and the latter succeeded to his father. He dying without issue, the two sons of GOTAMA inherit, who were born in a praeternatural manner; from the circumstances of their birth, they and their descendants are called by several names; as, *Yan-lag-s,kyes;* (S. Angiras), *Nyimahignyen,* (S. Surya Vaṇśa), Gautama, *Bu-ram shing-pa,* (S. Ikṣwāku.) One of the two brothers dies without issue, the other reigns under the name of IKṢWĀKU.

"To him succeeds his son, whose descendants (one hundred) afterwards successively reign at *potala Gru-hadsin.* The last of whom was Ikṣwāku Virudhaka, (or Videhaka.) He has four sons, and after the death of his first wife, he marries again. He obtains the daughter of a king, under the condition that he shall give the throne to the son that shall be born of that princess. By the contrivance of the chief officers, to make room for the young prince to succession, the king orders the expulsion of his four sons.

"They taking their own sisters with them, and accompanied by a great multiude, leave *Potala,* go towards the Himalaya, and reaching the bank of the *Bhagirathi* river settle there, not far from the hermitage of CAPILA the *Ṛṣi,* and live in huts made of the branches of the trees. They live there on hunting; and sometimes they visit the hermitage of CAPILA the Ṛṣi. He observing them to look very ill, asks them why they were so pale. They tell him how much they suffer on account of their restraint or continence. He advises them to leave their own uterine sisters, and to take themselves (to wife) such as are not born of the same mother with them. O great Ṛṣi! said the princes, is it convenient for us to do this? Yes, Sirs, answered the Ṛṣi, banished princes may act in this way. Therefore, taking for a rule the advice of the Ṛṣi, they do accordingly, and cohabit with their non-uterine sisters, and have many children by them. The noise of them being inconvenient to the Ṛṣi in his meditation, he wishes to change his habitation. But they beg him to remain in his own place, and to design for them any other ground. He therefore marks them out the place where they should build a town; since the ground was given to them by CAPILA, they called the new city *Capilavastu*. They multiply there exceedingly.The gods seeing their great number, show them another place for their settlement. They build there a town, and call it by the name of *Lhas-bstan,* (shown by a god).

"Remembering the cause of their banishment, they make it a law, that no one of them hereafter shall marry a second wife of the same tribe, but that he shall be contented with one wife.

"At *Potala* the king IKṢWĀKU VIRUDHAKA, recollecting that he had four sons, asks his officers, what has become of them. They tell him, how for some offence His Majesty had expelled them, and how they had settled in the neighbourhood of the *Himalaya,* and that they have taken their own sisters for their wives, and have been much multiplied. The king, being much surprised on hearing this, exclaims several times : *śākya! śākya!* Is it possible! Is it possible!(or O daring!O daring!) *phod-pa,* and this is the origin of the *Śākya* name[5].

The Singalese legend is more circumstantial as to names and personalities. The Ikśwāku Virudhaka of Tibet is Okkaka the third of the Singalese, otherwise called Amba. He had five-principal queens, one of whom Hastā bore him four sons and five daughters.

After the death of Hastā, the king promoted one of her maids to the rank of queen and was by her persuaded to send Hasta's sons out of the kingdom—who accordingly went away, as exiles, accompanied by their five sisters. Wandering in quest of a site to a build a new City,they fall in with the Ṛṣi Kapila, who was the Bodhisat of the age, and who was afterwards to become Gotama Buddha. Kapila had his habitation on a charmed spot where hares over-awed the jackal, and frogs struck terror into the naya or snake. This site he presented to the princes for the building of a town which he requested them to name after him. This was built according to the advice they received, and was called after the name of the sage. The princes then said to each other, "If we send to any of the inferior kings to ask their daughters in marriage, it will be a dishonour to the Okkaka race; and if we give our sisters to their princes it will be an equal dishonour; it will therefore be better to stain the purity of our relationship than that of our race." The eldest sister was therefore appointed as the queen-mother and each of the brothers took one of the other sisters as his wife. In the course of time each of the queens had eight sons and eight daughters, or sixty-four children in all. When their father heard in what manner the princes had acted he thrice excalimed, the princes are indeed *able* (Śakya), the princesses are indeed *very able* (Śakya)[6] !

Such is the Buddhistic account of the origin of Kapilāvastu and of the tribe of Śākya. It is singular that the Buddhists should cherish a legend which assigns an incestuous origin to the race from which their leader was descended, and that they should perpetuate, in the surname of Śākya Sinha, the very term which was derived from the daring moral impurity by means of which that tribe had sprung. And it is not the less remarkable that the person who took the lead in protesting against the pride of caste, should himself bear an appellation expressive of the extreme jealousy of *clan* and family dignity, to which his progenitors did not scruple to sacrifice all other ideas of domestic virtue and propriety.

Whether there is any connection between the character Kapila, mentioned in the above legend, and that to which the Sāṁkhya sūtras are attributed, it is impossible to determine with any accuracy. There is nothing improbable in the idea of Buddhists claiming the name of an old Ṛṣi as a friend and adviser of the progenitors of their founder, nor is it unlikely, on the other hand, that the Brāhmins would deeply resent such a proceeding, and claim him in their turn as the founder of one of their great schools.

But whatever be the historical relation between the two, the intelligent Hindu can scarcely fail to recognize the analogy in point of doctrine between the conflicting systems. Their difference is only in name and in the personalities of the two parties. If the Hindu philosophy be true,Buddhism cannot be far in the wrong; and if Buddhism be false, Hinduism cannot have much truth. This consideration alone ought to stimulate the inquiry whether there is saving truth in either of the systems? And, if both be found equally barren in this respect, the question must follow, WHERE IS SUCH TRUTH TO BE LOOKED FOR?

BISHOP'S COLLEGE :
29th *June*, 1861.

*** The author must here acknowledge his obligations to his senior in office, the REVD.DR. KAY, to whose remarks and suggestions, while the work was passing through the press, is mainly owing any merit that may be accorded to the following pages.

References

1. Speech of Mr. Charles Marsh in the House of Commons in Capt. Kaye's *Christianity in India, p.* 280.

2. To prevent misconceptions we feel it right to explain that the aphorism in which Kaṇāda asserts the authority of the Vedas as His word, is considered by some succeeding writers as a proof of his theism. An author who could account for the origin of the universe without God, can hardly be called *theistic* for any thing he may say on other points. But the natural, rendering of the aphorism would be, 'The Veda is of authority, because it is its declaration," (*tadvachanāt*), the antecedent of "its" being *Dharma* mentioned in the previous aphorism. *It is of authority because it is the declaration of Dharma.* It is after the same fashion that most Brāhminical writers have argued. We did not question the other rendering in Dialogue x,because the point at issue being the authority of the Veda,we were unwilling to clog the discussion with other matters.

3. Lalita Vistara.

4. इमं विवस्वते योगं प्रोक्तवानहमव्ययं। विवस्वान् मनवे प्राह मनुरिक्षाकवेब्रवीत्॥
एवं परम्पराप्राप्तमिमं राजर्षयो विदुः। स कालेनेह महता योगोनष्टः परन्तपः॥
स एवायं मया तेद्य योगः प्रोक्तः पुरातनः॥

5. Notes, in the Pilgrimage of Fa Hian.

6. Hardy's Manual of Buddhism.

References

1. Speech of Mr. Charles Marsh in the House of Commons in Capt. Kaye's *Christianity in India*, p. 280.

2. To prevent misconceptions we feel it right to explain that the aphorism in which Kanada asserts the authority of the Vedas as His word, is considered by some succeeding writers as a proof of his theism. An author who could account for the origin of the universe without God, can hardly be called *theistic* for any thing he may say on other points. But the natural rendering of the aphorism would be: "The Veda is of authority, because it is its declaration," (*tadvachanát*), the antecedent of "its" being *Dharma*, mentioned in the previous aphorism. *It is of authority because it is the declaration of Dharma*. It is after the same fashion that most Brahmanical writers have argued. We did not question the other rendering in Dialogue I, because the point at issue being the authority of the Veda, we were unwilling to clog the discussion with other matters.

3. Lalita Vistara.

4. [illegible]

5. Notes in the Pilgrimage of Fa Hian.

6. Hardy's Manual of Buddhism.

CONTENTS.

DIALOGUE II.

DIALOGUE III.

DIALOGUE IV.

DIALOGUE V.

DIALOGUE VI.

DIALOGUE VII.

DIALOGUE VIII.

DIALOGUE IX.

DIALOGUE X.

DIALOGUE I

FROM A BRĀHMIN TO A BRĀHMIN

You wonder at the doings of the Kali Yuga. The late mutiny in the Bengal army gives a plausible appearance to your wonder. You quote the Śāstra that the Kali Yuga will be followed by the return of the Satya Yuga; you say the terrible scenes you have witnessed are only a prelude to the Mahāpralaya, for which you are now looking. But the mutiny is over, and there are no signs of a Pralaya.

How do you know that the renovation is not to be brought about by the gradual progress of opinion without any violent catastrophe? The manifestation of Viṣṇu, which the Brāhmins expect at the end of the Yuga, may prove to be nothing more than the general dissemination of truth and knowledge. That circumstances are tending towards a new order of things cannot be doubted by the most superficial observer.

You say that your fellow Śāstris in the holy city show now-a-days a freedom of speculation which would have surprized Gotama and Kapila. You may consider *that* as one of the signs of the times. But such plain speaking is not confined to the city of Śiva. I have witnessed occasional instances of it in lower Bengal.

After my departure from the North-West, on the breaking out of the rebellion, I had many a narrow escape from the violence of the soldiery, and at last arrived safe in Bengal.

Some time after finding lodgings in this town, I paid a visit, in the cool of a lovely morning, to my old friend Satyakāma. I found him standing at the gate on the side of the road. You have no doubt heard of the movement in his mind. He no longer bows to the high-sounding names of your Ṛṣis. Notwithstanding the tender cry of the Veda against being subjected to the arguments of heretics, he feels no hesitation in controverting some of its fondest doctrines. "Quarter," says he, "must indeed be given to parties when they ask for mercy, provided they submit at discretion;—but while a party continues rampant, and issues orders that you must not attack him, the mandate is a threat, not capitulation."

While the Tilangas have been so fiercely plying their *Śastra* (weapons) in the North-West, the puṇḍits in Bengal have been equally zealous in the exercise of their Śāstra—some of the latter manifesting no greater fidelity to the systems of their order, than did the Sepoys to the Government which so long protected and patronized them. Of the Sepoys' doings you have had enough in your own province. I will tell you something of the Puṇḍits' doings here.

I have already said I paid a visit to Satyakāma. We were talking on the events of the day, when two middleaged persons, from whose neat appearance I concluded they were Brāhmins, even before I saw their thread, approached the house. They were both *nearly* as devoid of artificial decorations as the poet represents the peasants of Oude[1], perhaps with this difference,that they took pains religiously to wash and clean themselves every morning, which was more than your rustics care to do.

If there be any truth in the common saying, that externals form an index of the internal[2], one of the new comers was certainly a guileless candid Brāhmin, though the physiognomy of the other was somewhat ominous.

While they were yet at a distance, Satyakāma appeared to eye them very intently, paying little or no attention for the moment to what I said. As soon as they were near enough to be spoken to, "Obeisance, Āgamika," said he, "Obeisance, Tarkakāmạ! What an unexpected pleasure to see you both together after so long a separation. It is like the nectareous moonbeams on the thirsty Chakar!"

While uttering these words, he beckoned to them with his hands to enter the house.In his eagerness to show attention to his new (as I then thought, but, as I afterwards learnt, his old) friends, he almost forgot that I was in the company. I followed them however into the house, curious to know who the new comers were. As we were walking in, one of them, Āgamika, pleasantly remarked, "I am glad to find, Satyakāma, you can refer in such good humour to our sacred adages. I, too, am delighted to see you, as indeed I am, to see all who were the companions of my youth under the happy roof of our common preceptor."

I soon learnt who the new arrivals were. They were old friends of our host—no way pleased with his recent change of opinion, but very kind and respectful. In the course of conversation, Āgamika, though naturally cheerful, said with an air of melancholy; "The only painful reflection which crosses my mind whenever I think of you, Satyakāma, (and believe me it does so, with the sharpness, no less than the swiftness, of an arrow,) is, that after all the instruction you had received from our venerable Ācārya, and the various tokens of affection he had heaped on his pupils, you should, by embracing foreign opinions, have frustrated the hopes once entertained of you. Never did a father contemplate, more joyously, the birth of his first-born, procuring him *absolution from the debt*[3] *he owed to his ancestors,* than did our holy tutor, the gradual development of our minds under the discipline of the Vedas and others Śāstras. His benevolence and love of literature had persuaded him, that besides the obligations which the Śāstras entailed on the whole of the *twiceborn* order, there was a fourth debt[4] which he owed to posterity. The success with which he had mastered the oracles of inspiration, and had traversed all the arcana of a philosophy, which had exercised the minds of countless sages, anxious for liberation from the bonds of transmigration, called upon him to communicate what he had learned to intelligent pupils, that, through their instrumentality, myriads, yet unborn, might be supplied with the treasures of knowledge, and thus a recurrence of that fearful catastrophe, the loss of the Veda, which had once rendered necessary an incarnation of the divine Viṣṇu, might be averted. He was accordingly overjoyed at the prospect of discharging what he owed to succeeding generations, by bequeathing, through his pupils, those invaluable remedies for the perils of our nature, which had come down from the age, when the four heads of Brahmā produced the Ṛk, Yajus, Sāman, and Atharvan. Oh what a disappointment have you inflicted on him! Have all his labours come to this, that you should become a scoffer at the Vedas, renounce the Sandhya[5], forsake that which the illustrious son of Vasudeva said, was the *most excellent* for you, and adopt a foreign system, which the same sacred authority emphatically pronounced to be fraught with TERROR.[6] Who could have imagined that you would bring on your preceptor the disgrace of betraying divine learning to a future enemy, notwithstanding its tender appeals for protection.[7] Why even the Mahometan imposter Feizi, a very type of the demon who had made off with the churned-nectar in disguise, turned to a better use the Vedic learning he had unblushingly stolen.[8] But perhaps you could not help it; there was no contending against *Adṛṣṭa* (fate)!"

The Brāhmin paused—evidently overcome by conflicting feelings. But scarcely had he stopped, when his companion broke forth in a tone which presented a remarkable contrast to the melancholy gravity of Āgamika.

"Yes, said he, "if idiosyncrasy be Fate!" "Our friend," continued Tarkakāma, "has so strong a predilection for what is singular, that he must needs forsake every thing that accords with the common sense of his countrymen."

Satyakāma had listened very attentively to Āgamika, but he was vexed at the sneers of his other friends.

"My beloved friend Āgamika,"said he, "has greatly misapprehended my doctrines and practice.I hope to explain both before we part. I cannot help meanwhile expressing my surprise at Tarkakāma's taxing me with singularity, and rebuking me for my deviation from the track marked out by the common sense of our counrymen. Such a censure might have been expected from the poetical Kālidāsa, who never allowed his mind to be distracted with the intricacies of science and philosophy, and who lauded the king and people of Ayodhia, for *not* deviating from the path chalked out ever since the days of Manu[9]. But I must confess I was not prepared for such a lecture from my philosophical friend Tarkakāma. One who never for himself pretends to bow to common sense, but is always in chase of *bright* ideas, dazzling to ordinary intellects, should not condemn another on the scrore of *singularity*. Nothing satisifed this Ācārya that is not transcendental. Nothing is of any value that is not above popular sense. The teaching of the Veda fails to come up to his mark. The whole town talks of the eloquence with which he repeats and expounds Kapila's and Īśwarkṛṣṇa's open declarations of the shortcomings[10] of the Veda. Human society is to be improved, and its highest interest secured, not by the application of means which are open to ordinary men, but by something that even the majority of the learned fail to apprehend; not by adherence to the precepts and injunctions of the Vedas, but by something which will be above the Vedas—something of which Madhuchhand,Viśwāmitra, and other old sages were all equally ignorant, – which it was reserved for a Gotama or Kapila to expound for the edification of the wise.To be taxed with singularity by one who is so regardless of established systems, is itself most singular."

Tarkakāma seemed somewhat uncomfortable under the rebuke which his own sneers had provoked. He was anxious to drop a subject he had indiscreetly introduced, and yet he was unwilling to appear vanquished by allowing his opponent to have the last word.

"My friend Satyakāma," said he, "is eager to take every thing wrong. May it not be allowable in a person to speculate on grand truths, so long as he does not practically deviate from the duties of his class? I do not blame you for *thinking* above the level of ordinary intellects. A philosophic mind cannot help doing so. Nor do I cavil at your diverging in thought from Vedic teaching, which certainly has not exhausted the topics of rational inquiry. I am not charging you wih *mental* heresy. What I find fault with you for is your *practice*. You do not tell the Sandhyā. You mix and fraternize with barbarians. You are for placing the unholy on the same level with the holy, the race that proceeded from the feet, with that which issued from the mouth of the Creator.[11] Already has our discipline been sadly relaxed by the ascendancy of barbarian rulers. Already are the worst anticipations of ancient sages realized in the insolence of the lower classes, and the depression of the sacerdotal office. But if your principles prevail, there will be an end to whatever still remains of peace and order. Social anarchy, added to political humiliation, will fill the cup of our misery up to the brim. The family will share the fate of the state. Vile Śūdras and apostate barbarians, still under the ban of maledictions that cannot fail, will arrogate equality with gods-of-the-earth[12]. Nay matrimonial alliances will be unblushingly propsoed without distinction of high and low. Our females, now scarcely accessible to the solar rays, will be exposed to the gaze of barbarian eyes; and consequences, still worse than those which were so graphically depicted by the son of Kuntī[13], will be the result of disregarding the honor and dignity of our race."

The debate now grew warm. Principles and practices were called in question, and though the parties were never forgetful of the respect they owed to one another, each was eager to defend his own point.

"I hope to satisfy you by and bye," replied Satyakāma, "that neither my practice nor my principles are justly chargeable with any evil tendency. But allow me to express my wonder at the distinction you have drawn between your innocent speculations and my noxious example. If I understand you rightly, your philosophy treats with perfect contempt the very institutions which you blame my practice for ignoring. You laugh at the rites and ceremonies to which our countrymen are so much attached. The pride of caste stands neither the test of your dialectics, nor of your most favourite texts of the Vedas. You claim for your system the moral dignity of inclucating sympathy with all God's creatures. But it appears your maxims are intended only for fine essays and eloquent speeches. It is not your purpose that they should be realized in practice. This is a nice discrimination in which I much confess my inability to follow you. I am accustomed to believe that what is really good in theory cannot be evil in practice. If you admit the maxim that one should look on all creatures as on himself[14], then do not find fault with your more consistent neighbour, for *placing the race that proceeded from the feet on the same level with that which issued from the mouth of the Creator.*

"I might go further and say, that such censure is the more inconsistent on the part of those who are fond of saying, not only that the rites and ceremonies of the Vedas do not,as remedies,sufficiently meet the disease with which mankind is afflicted, but that they are *impure*—because they enjoin sacrifices involving injury to the animal creation. *From pain can only proceed pain, nor is a feeling of chillness removed by the affusion of water*[15]; how then can the shedding of blood, while it makes the victim writhe with pain, procure blessings for the slaughterer? Such is the reasoning of some of your philosophers. Do you not see that they are animated by the very spirit of Buddhism which they profess to detest? What more needs an open enemy say to throw discredit on the whole Brāhminical system. Whatever the origin of the Vedas may be, it is easy to see the inconsistency of calling them the word of God, and at the same time charging them with encouraging impure practices. If the Vedas were really revealed as the way to supreme felicity, they cannot be superseded by the mere theory of a mortal. If on the other hand the Vedas do not teach what is necessary for our lasting interests, let them not be paraded as eternal repositories of truth. Let their high pretensions in such a case be at once and for ever repudiated. There is something not only irreverent, but immoral, surely, in saying that the Veda contains a revelation of God's will, and yet that the means of salvation, therein propounded, are futile—and I appeal to Āgamika himself, whether my open disregard of the Veda is not at least more consistent, than the professed allegiance of one, who nominally acknowledges its authority, but in reality laughs at the provisions it has made for final emancipation."

Tarkakāma betrayed many tokens of uneasiness while listening to this plain-spoken address. But he patiently heard it out, and replied in a somewhat subdued and faltering voice : "I do not see any inconsistency in the position that the Vedas exhibit an inferior, but nevertheless, a real road to felicity. The felicity to which that road leads may fall short of reaching the utmost limits of human capacity and human aspiration; but still it is felicity. There many be two ways, both real, but differing in character, and suited to men of different abilities. The Vedas do not ignore the dispairty which exists in the capacities of men. Some persons there are, capable of greater mental abstraction, and fitted for higher roads than others, to whom every passage that does not keep to the level of their gross sensibilities, appears uphill work."

"Oh," rejoined Satyakāma, "then there are exceptions to the dogma that *pain proceeds from pain*. You think the aphorism is not of universal application. But be that as it may, since the candidates for this transcendental knowledge are manifestly few, it does not appear to me particularly modest to condemn the largest portion even of learned Brāhmins, to a state of deplorable ignorance of the more excellent way. But do you really mean to adopt this distinction? The Vedas you say teach a real but an inferior way, suited to men of small capacities. Yet these Vedas in fact constitute the peculiar inheritance of the twice-born classes. The Brāhmin is especially enjoined to study them, while the servile order, in common with the female sex, is excluded from the privilege of even hearing them read[16]. The Vedic ritual can only be used by the higher classes. Whom then do you mean by the persons of gross sensibilities for whom the Vedas are intended? It can be no other than the Brāhmins themselves. What becomes now of the dignity of the exalted race, that sprang from the noblest member of Brahmā's body? Their high pretensions can have no solidity, if their class privileges turn out to be of such questionable worth. Their especial inheritance, the right to read and expound the Vedas, has after all but a nominal value. To obtain a real superiority, they must still qualify themselves as disciples of Gotama and Kaṇāda. They must, by a more successful cultivation of their intellects, exhibit a higher proof of their second birth than the mere possession of their sacred thread, or they will be left in a position scarcely more to be coveted than that of barbarians and *once-born* Śūdras. They will still be excluded from the beatitude which awaits the adepts in the Nyāya and Sāṅkhya. They must know how to define terms and classify ideas. They must enter the lists and choose their sides in the philosophical controversies which have divided Gotama, Kapila, Kaṇāda, and Vyāsa. They must decide whether sound is eternal or not, whether proofs, or *instruments of right knowledge,* are in number four, three, two, or one. Failing in these and other like distinctions, they must find themselves—in company with barbarians and Śūdras, as aliens from the society of emancipated saints. And so, alas! Tarkakāma, you too bring down the exalted race that proceeded from the mouth, to the same level with those that issued from the feet, of Brahmā.

"But I have yet weightier matters against you. What right have your philosophers to assert that fallible men can teach a way which Śāstras of God cannot teach? Can the teaching of finite minds be superior to that of the Infinite? Supposing you can surmount this (to me insurmountable) difficulty, another at once presents itself. These your guides are not only *fallible,* they are *discordant.* How then am I to choose? I should still reqire an infallible monitor to teach me which of these fallible guides (if any) is to be followed."

Tarkakāma.—"The infallible monitor you reqire is provided for you in the Veda. The Veda may not teach the highest way to felicity. It is nevertheless an infallible touch-stone of truth—and herein consists its dignity. Whenever great Ṛṣis are discordant, the Veda steps in and reconciles them. The final appeal with all of them is to the *Śruti.* You can easily understand what an elevated position I am allotting to the Veda,when I am declaring it to be the highest authority in the decision of controversies. It is our Sudder Court of appeal in philosophical disputes—"

Satyakāma.—"And a pretty Sudder Court you make of it! I suppose Gotama, Kapila, and others, are your Moonsifs and Deputy-Magistrates.Your Sudder Court is so obliging that it upholds all their decisions, however discordant and mutually conflicting. But what do you think would be the fate of a Moonsif that set at naught a construction of the Sudder Court, by maintaining that justice could not flow from its descisions, any more than the *relief of chillness from the application of cold water?* An English philosopher said that while man has the exclusive privilege of forming general theorems, he has also a monopoly of the *privilege of absurdity,* to which no other living creature is subject. *And of men,* he added, *those are of all the most subject to it that profess philosophy.* Excuse my presumption, but it strikes me that in India this monopoly is in the hands of those who profess to adhere to the Darśanas. All these systems are right in their eyes, notwithstanding their mutual inconsistencies[17]. Which-ever system they happen to take up is for the time supreme. This is your philosophy. The fact is you hardly know your own minds. You care little for the objects of science, and you have no hearty belief in the Vedas.You cannot persuade yourselves that offerings of twigs, steeped in butter, and thrown over a blazing fire, will really procure heaven, and yet the fear of being branded as heretics deters you from expressing your contempt for the Mantras.Nor have you the courage to test the correctness of philosophic results,which may have been arrived at by teachers of established reputation. And you virtually set the Veda at naught, when you receive with admiration the aphorisms of your sages. It is chiefly when an honest thinker, who candidly speaks and follows out his sentiments, is to be rebuked,that you fall into a paroxysm of loyalty for the Śāstras."

While this animated conversation was going on, Āgamika appeared to be labouring under great perturbation of mind. Attached as he was, devotedly, to the ritual system of Brāhmanism, he had much clearness of mental perception and great honesty of purpose. He oberseved with unexampled candour; "In justice to Satyakāma I must say that he has reason to inveigh against your positions, Tarkakāma. I quite agree with the English philosopher's remark. After the Vedas have laid down your duties, it is highly arrogant in you to speculate on a more excellent way. I do not question your liberty to expound, illustrate, and declare the sense of the Vedas. That is in truth the study and peculiar privilege of our class. Jaimini, in his Sūtras of the Mīmāṅsā, has indeed conferred a benefit alike on learning and theology. I do not deny that, in his eagerness to defend the institutions of the Veda, he has made use of expressions, at least seemingly at variance with the reverence due to Him who *breathed* it out. But I am very jealous of Gotama, Kaṇāda, and even Vyāsa, though the latter professes to base his system almost exclusively on the authority of the Śruti. What respect could Gotama entertain for the Vedas when he introduces terms and definitions on which the sacred oracles are wholly silent, and declares their investigation to be necessary for emancipation? The Vedas then must fall short of securing that object. The wisdom inspired by Brahmā must then be inferior to that of the husband of Ahalyā! And as to your Kapila, though I can never deny the tribute of veneration to a name honourably mentioned in the vedas[18], yet I consider his system as scarcely disguised Buddhism. If you can go the length of Kapila, I really cannot see how you may not go further. If you can be justified in openly declaring that the means of salvation revealed in the Vedas are insufficient, how can I blame Satyakāma for reducing your maxims to practice? You are both impugners of the Vedas.If we tolerate the one, while we exclude the other, we shall be following neither Menu nor reason. You may differ ever so much from each other, what have we to do with that? If the supreme authority of the Vedas be attacked, it matters little what particular line of approach the rebels adopt. As to the distinction attempted to be drawn between theory and practice, if there be any difference it is rather to the credit than the discredit of Satyakāma."

Tarkakāma appeared quite amazed at the tone in which his friend spoke. He never expected such a rebuke from that quarter. He was at a loss what to say in reply. After a short pause –

"What, said he, "is it all the same to you whether a person follows a system that originated in the country itself, the Āryāvarta of Menu, called also Puṇyabhūmi by the lexicographer, or whether he becomes an adherent of foreign novelties hatched in the defiled land of Mletchas?"

The remark was accompanied by a misanthropic sneer which certainly did not enlist my sympathy in its behalf. Satyakāma however, only observed, good humouredly –

"It seems as if the spirit of your philosophy ceases to inspire you directly you begin to think of the poor Mletchas. Does not your admired aphorist say that time and place[19] cannot affect the *eternal* soul. Truth cannot suffer from the place where it is recognized, any more than the sun[20] from the disorders of the eye that beholds it.What is right in itself is right in all places, and at all times. Truth may confer a distinction on a site otherwise of no importance, but it is impossible for any place, however unholy, to cast a slur on truth. If what you call a Mletcha region has received the light which truth sheds, you must not say that the truth is thereby defiled. You should,on the contrary, correct your vocabulary, and find a better term for such a country."

To Āgamika the turn which the discussion had taken did not seem to augur well at all. He was trembling lest his polemical friend might, in the heat of the debate, take up positions which would do not credit to his order. He was hardly more anxious that the controversy should be dropped, than that Tarkakāma himself should renounce his attachment to logic and metaphysics.

"You see, Tarkakāma," said he, "your dialectics will not do. You had better submit with becoming humility to the teaching of the Vedas, without affecting wisdom superior to Brahmā's. Unlearn, as fast as your can, the restlessness which probably the aphorisms of Gotama and Kapila have produced in you. Remember an unsettled state of mind is not the characteristic of a wise man, nor is there any moral dignity in continually seeking to split straws. Keep to the duties enjoined in the Veda, and eschew your philosophy. Remembr how hopeless it is to arrive at truth by means of controversy. Listen to what Śaṅkarācārya says: 'Arguments, founded on human speculation alone, and not derived from the Śāstra, are interminable, because there can be no limits to mere speculation. The arguments which some clever disputants may bring forward, after much thought, may be refuted by others broached by cleverer heads; those again may be cut up by still sharper intellects.It is impossible to bring a discussion to a close, because of the diversity of human thought. Nor can one hope for finality in a discussion, by resting on arguments, approved by some eminent teacher of established reputation, such as Kapila; because we see that the opinions even of Kapila, Kaṇāda, and other *saintly* sectaries of acknowledged eminence, are mutually conflicting.'[21] Thus said Śaṅkarācārya. I hope this will satisfy you how dangerous it is to depend on the precarious results of human philosophy."

Satyakāma.—"Though it is not directed against any of *my* positions, I must not allow your sweeping attack against philosophy to pass without a remark. It is but just that we should hear what Śaṅkarācārya says on the other side of the question :—'It cannot be urged that no argument is allowable. Even where the sense of the Vedas is opposed, it is only by logically refuting such false interpretation that the true sense can be made out. Manu, too, thought on this wise.' The Commentator of the Vedānta then quotes the author of the Institutes to uphold the lawfulness of argumentation[22]. Of course neither Vyāsa nor Śaṅkarācārya will on the whole tolerate an argument on matters revealed in the Śāstra (*Āgama.*) But what if we be disagreed (as indeed *you* and I are,) which is the real *Āgama*—the true record of God's will? You cannot expect me to be silenced by the authority of that which I do not allow to be an authentic statement of the Divine law. The question necessarily admits of fair discussion. Then again, though I believe with you that God has spoken, it may yet be possible that there are provinces of thought in which scientific speculation is not only allowable, but highly laudable. Human philosophy cannot of course, as I have contended, teach a more excellent way than Divine revelation. But there are various questions, connected with our earthly improvement, on which the Divine law is silent, because they fall within the range of human investigation. Whatever it is within the power of reason to discover, does not need the assistance of revelation. Such questions are left to be determined by the light of nature. Though not necessarily connected with the well-being of the soul in another world, they are subjects justly demanding our attention.

"Such philosophy, it must be remembered, can never be opposed to God's will; for one fact can never contradict another fact, the book of nature cannot contradict the book of revelation—nor the works of God be otherwise than conformable to His word. The primary duty of man is to inform himself of what is required of him in the World and, that he may do so as intelligently as possible,his next duty is to cultivate his mind to the utmost extent of his opportunities and capacities. It is not the least of a man's privileges to read, as deeply as he can, the book of nature, so full in its delineation of the power and wisdom of his heavenly Father. The Bhāṣā poet[23] gives a description, as true as it is beautiful, of the influence of material vestiges on human sensibility, when he represents Bharata as deriving, from the foot-prints of an absent brother, all the joy of a personal interview in the charming forests of Chtrakūta. The pious heart may in like manner derive the unalloyed delight of a communion with his unseen Maker, by recognizing the vestiges of His wisdom and beneficence in the creation around him.

"The success which has manifestly attended the cultivation of natural and experimental science in Europe, is a sufficient index of God's will in this respect. Is it possible that the Supreme Being had created the elements, and adapted their properties in such a manner, that water should, by the application of heat, produce a power capable of propelling vessels on the great deep, and dragging trains of carriages on the dry land, without wishing that man should, by the exercise of his intellect, discover the secret? Can a cultivated mind treat with scorn the science which, by the agency of steam, has connected the very antipodes of the globe, as if they were no further off from each other than Calcutta and Agra—and which will one of these days turn Puruṣottama itself into a single *manzal* from Kāsī? Is it possible that the application of certain acids to certain metals should generate a power by which men, separated by hundreds of miles, might communicate with one another as if they were conversing in the same room; by which the priests of Viśveśvara can ask a question, and get the reply in a minute from the Paṇḍās of Jagannāth; and the Creator of the Universe not will that men should avail themselves of such a power? The most rapid communication, which the poetical genius of Kālidāsa could conceive, was by the flight of a cloud from the verdant peak of Rāmagiri to the genial atmosphere of Alakā; but he put forth the idea only to condemn it as the reverie of a mad sentimentalist[24], smarting under sentence of separation from the wife of his bosom. Science has however carried facts beyond the fictions of poetic imagination. What would Kālidāsa have said to a line of electric telegraphs connecting Bengal with England, and carrying messages with a velocity that may anticipate the very steeds of the sun? Is it possible to decry the study of science after such triumphs?

"Of course the systems of philosophy which have prevailed among us for centuries justify much of your apprehensions. They have produced no results on which the mind can dwell with complacency. The misfortune is that our leading Ṛṣis, instead of patiently investigating facts, and thence deducing general principles, laid down certain dogmatic aphorisms, to be received without controversy, or, if discussed at all, to be discussed after the manner of a paid advocate. The way again in which physics, ethics, and theology were blended (or rather, confounded) did service to none of those sciences, but propagated and confirmed errors in them all. Such a process is apt to alarm all inquirers after truth.

"But, because a Gotama or Kaṇāda has staked the soul's salvation on a precise knowledge of his own categories, and imposed his aphorisms on posterity, with the understanding that they were to be received, not reasoned against; it is not necessary that every teacher of science should follow the example. Śaṅkarācārya says, 'there is no reason whatever that one should himself be a fool, merely because an elder was a fool.'[25]

"It must also be remembered, in justice to the founders of our philosophy, that their eminence in learning, and intellectual activity, necessarily earned for their writings an authority to which their successors implicitly submitted. They could not help their own greatness.

"The rules of philosophical investigation which Gotama and Kaṇāda, more especially the latter, propounded, were no doubt fundamentally correct. If they had followed out those rules themselves, and encouraged their followers to do the same, we could not have had much to complain of. The pity is that they hastily entertained, and dogmatically inculcated, principles,which cannot stand the tests of their own logic.

"Still though a man may, without endangering his soul's welfare, remain ignorant, not only of Gotama's own ideas of the properties of water or air, but also of the real facts, as unravelled by the patience and industry of experimental philosophers in Europe, yet human society has undoubtedly benefitted much by philosophical investigations of physical and mental phenomena, in the East no less than the West. The definitions of our predecessors have unquestionably contributed to precise expressions of truth.

"As to scientific speculations in general, you cannot refuse assent to the maxim of your own Veda, that the ignorant are *murderers of their souls.*[26] Those who wilfully throw away opportunities of mental improvement, and of philosophical investigation, certainly do great injustice to themselves."

Āgamika was a good deal affected by the above speech. He on his part had not calculated on hearing the names of Gotama and Kaṇāda mentioned with any degree of approbation by Satyakāma. "It is impossible for me," said he, "to make a hasty statement on all the points that you have advanced.I can only promise to think on them. But, Satyakāma, you said a little while ago—that I greatly misapprehended your doctrines and practices, and that you would explain both before we parted. I am ready to hear you now."

Our host had now a delicate task to perform. He had to satisfy his guests that the cry raised against himself had no foundation. When men differ in opinion on points of practical philosophy or theology, it is no easy work for them to understand each other. Staykāma endeavoured to make out that men who freely speculated among themselves, regardless of the authority of the Vedas, had no just ground of complaint against him—and that his guests had no more right to find fault with him than with one another.

"The regrets you have expressed," said he, "at my disappointing expectations formed of me, I accept, not as reproaches, but as compliments—not as tokens of disregard, but as proofs of kindness and affection. I fear, however, I am in your estimation a godless person, without those tender sensibilities, which you think are not compatible with the rejection of the Vedas, and neglect of the duties they enjoin on Brāhmins. The pictures, which a large portion of our literature has drawn, of the doctrines and practices of those, who, in former times, impugned the Vedas, readily present themselves to your imagination. You cannot believe that one can reject the Vedas, without being a Bauddha, Jain, or Cārvāka, or a demon incarnate, such as Kaṅsa or Rāvaṇa was. Now will you allow me to say that, whilst I pronounce no opinion at present as to the correctness of the portraits that Śaṅkarācārya and Vyāsa have given of their heretical opponents, I do most unhesitatingly repudiate (and with no less depth of feeling than you yourself, Āgamika, would,) the supposition that I hold anything akin to the atheistical and sensual doctrines attributed to Bauddhas and Cārvākas. Let me assure you that, although my opinions have changed since I was young, I have not unlearnt a particle of the horror which we all entertained for God-denying and voluptuous principles. You are astonished at this? And yet is it not possible that two things may differ from a third, and yet be very far from identical with each other? This is all that I have any right to demand of you now:—but so much I may without impertinence demand.

"I must embrace another opportunity of explaining in full the doctrines which at present guide my conduct. But allow me, once for all, to relieve your anxiety on my behalf, by satisfying you that not one of the doctrines and practices which haunt your imagination, when you think of me, has any countenance from myself. You charge me with forgetfulness of spiritual duties, because I have ceased to tell the Sandhyā three times a day. It is not from thoughtless indolence that I have given up that form of devotional exercise. My maxim still is—'*Evening, and morning, and at noon-day, will I pray.*' It is only because I have found a more excellent way that I do not make use of the *Sandhyā.* I do not indeed invoke blessings from the *waters of dry and marshy lands, from natural and artificial pools*[27], nor call upon the sun, and the elements, *to take away in the morning sins committed in the night;* but it is my practice to call daily upon Him, who made the waters, the sun, and the elements, to confess before Him, morning and evening, both what I have done and what I have left undone, and to ask His pardon for sins, of *thought, word, and deed,* whether committed at night or in the day.

"You have also charged me with abandonment of my Swadharma. Now do not consider it a mere cavil, if I ask you, what do you mean by *Swadharma?*"

"Why, *your own religion*", said Tarkakāma, rather impatiently.

"Pardon me," said Satyakāma, "if I repeat the question—What is *my own religion?*"

"The Hindu religion to which you were born—the religion of the people of India. That is plain enough as a definition."

"The Hindu religion! Does such a term or idea occur in any Śāstra? Will you cite a passage of Śruti or Smṛti, giving such a definition of Swadharma?"

Tarkakāma paused for a moment—when Āgamika remarked, "Yes! it is singular the term *Hindu* is not found in our sacred language, and yet we speak of the Hindu religion. I wonder how we got such a term. I fancy we got it from the Mohammedans."

Satyakāma.—"The oldest writing in which the word, or something very like it, occurs, is a portion of the Hebrew scriptures[28]. The Greeks appear to have got it from some eastern country, and rendered it '*India,*' and the Arabians and Persians '*Hind*'. We received it no doubt from the Mohammedans."

"Whatever the origin of the word may be," said Tarkakāma, "here we have it—and by the Hindu religion we mean the religion of the inhabitants of this country. I mean the rightful inhabitants of our Puṇyabhūmi, excepting of course such men as the Mohammedans, Parsees, and other foreigners who have recently settled here."

Satyakāma.—"But where do you find the religion of the rightful inhabitants of the country?"

Tarkakāma.—"You are putting questions after the manner of Vakeels in the courts;—of course, in the Veda and other Śāstras."

"Pardon me again," said Satyakāma, "I mean no offence; but I am not aware of any system inculcated in the Śruti and the Smṛti which may be called the religion of the rightful inhabitants of this country. Nor is it easy to determine who *are* the rightful inhabitants of our Puṇyabhūmi. The Vedas speak of the *Āryas,* and it is supposed by many learned persons that the Āryas were emigrants from the other side of the Indus. But whether they were emigrants or aborigines, they certainly did not form one community with the Dasyus, spoken of also as inhabitants of the country—and there could be no system which might be called their common religion. And there were Rākṣases, also inhabiting the country, whose *Swadharma,* or religion, as you have expounded the term, consisted in acts which it would not be safe in us to encourage, though Rāma Candra himself did not deny it was their *Dharma*[29]."

"But the Rākṣases never pretended to be any other than enemies of Brāhmins."

"Very true—but they were nevertheless rightful inhabitants of the country. All I contend for, is that there is no system in the Śāstras, which may be called the common religion of all Hindus."

"But the Rākṣases were not *Hindus.*"

"I do not know that you can deny them the right of

occupation in the country. But I will not dispute that point with you. You acknowledge the Śūdras as Hindus —do you not?"

"Certainly. If we were to discard the Śūdras, *twelve annas* or more of our community would be lopped off—The Rajah, our own Zemindar, would himself be excluded. And we should lose almost all patrons of our religion."

"Well:—do the Śāstras inculcate any common *Dharma* for Brāhmins and Śūdras? I suppose you cannot answer the question in the affirmative. The Brāhmins have to study and meditate on the Vedas—Śūdras only to do service to the twice-born. 'Only one duty,' says Manu, 'has the Creator ordained to the Śūdra—to serve the three superior orders.' And this is his *swadharma*.

"Granted—what then?"

"Swadharma, then, means the duties proper for one's class. I only wish to understand the precise nature of the charge against me. I suppose I may expect that you will not encourage the vulgar clamour in this respect. People ignorant of the Śāstra think that all Hindus have a community of Dharma—a word by which they understand religion, when, as we have just seen, it more properly means class-duty. The word Hindu is unknown in the *Śruti* and *Smṛti,* and there is no other term by which the whole body of rightful occupiers of our *puṇyabhūmi* may be designated. If there were a community of religion, there would surely be a name whereby to designate it."

Tarkakāma.—"Āryāvarta is synonymous with Puṇyabhūmi. I should say the word *Ārya* would be a common designation."

"But," said Satyakāma, "Ārya cannot possibly include Dasyu, with which it is plainly contrasted in the Vedas, and I believe it excludes Śūdra. 'The Brāhmin is a caste divine; the Śūdra from *Asuras* or demons[30].' You would hardly be disposed to call the Śūdra an Ārya."

"But why all this discussion? Granted, Swadharma means the peculiar duties of one's own class. Can its observance be the less binding for that?"

"Let it be understood then, that I am to be put on my trial on a charge of deviating from the duties of my class. Will you tell me what those duties are?"

"Manu's summary," said Tarkakāma, "is no doubt the best. "To Brāhmins he assigned the duties of reading 'the Veda, teaching it, of sacrificing, of alluring others to sacrifice, of giving alms (if they be rich), and, if indigent, of receiving gifts[31].'"

"You cannot easily convict me," said Satykāma, "of habitual neglect of all these duties,unless I voluntarily plead guilty of doubting the inspiration of the Veda."

"Well," said Tarkakāma, "there can be no difficulty in showing that you have not been particularly careful in abstaining from acts forbidden in numerous texts of the Śāstras, such as the following : 'The Brāhmin is not to dine with the Śūdra[32].'"

"You have not given the full meaning of that text, as expounded by Ṛṣis. The brāhmin is not to take any food supplied by a Śūdra. Even raw materials[33] such as ghee, and unprepared rice, given personally by a Śūdra, are forbidden to him. Is that not the teaching of the Śāstras?

"It is," said Āgamika. "There can be no doubt about it."

"Well then," said Satyakāma, "although on my trial, allow me to suggest another rule, which may further strengthen the cause of the prosecution, whenever a Brāhmin is arraigned before you for breach of duty. *The Brāhmin is prohibited to cook for the Śūdra,—to perform religious offices for him—to follow the profession of arms—or to live by his pen or by selling his learning*. Is that not the dictum of the Śāstras[34]?"

"There can be no doubt about it," said Āgamika.

"Hear now my defence"—said Satyakāma. "You have lamented over me as an apostate from my Swadharma. We have seen that the observance of our Swadharma means the observance of all the rules we have just cited, and many others which we have not cited. Do you not see that if I am to be lamented over as an apostate, there are myriads of others who are as fitting objects of your compassion. If my friend Tarkakāma condemns me, I find myself condemned in very good compâny. Whosoever, being a Brāhmin, follows the occupation of a paid professor of our sacred language, in a College or School, whosoever officiates as a village priest, or at poojas in the houses of Śūdras, whosoever accepts from Śūdras offerings of any thing eatable, whosoever enlists in an army, or works for his livelihood as secretary or clerk, is as much an object of your compassion, as one that may have given up the Sandhyā, or renounced his Dharma, as the vulgar would say. How many Brāhmins do you think there are who can stand a searching investigation on these poins? You have no doubt heard of a society called the Dharma Sabhā; you will recollect who its president was—a Raja of the Śūdra caste, while the Secretary was a Brāhmin."

"What could we do under the circumstances?" said Tarkakāma. "No Brāhmin could be found possessing sufficient influence to be fit for the President's office. We were glad to accept the assistance which the Rajah rendered, though a Śūdra. We have no longer Kṣatriya princes.There would be none to defend our Dharma, if we did not allow Śūdra zemindars to support it."

"They support your Dharma by really *destroying* it. It is like the visit of congratulation which Śani paid on the birth of Gaṇeśa—*the infant's head dropping off from his neck; the moment the visitor's eyes fell on it*[35]. The Śūdra that puts himself at the head of a society, having Brāhmins for its members, breaks through his *Swadharma,* by placing himself in such a position—and the Brāhmins, who are members, break through *theirs,* by humbling themselves before those who ought to be their servants. What they then defend is neither the spirit nor the letter—but the *carcase* of their

Dharma, strangled to death by the Sabhā itself."

Tarkakāma.—"It would be impossible to maintain our real position over the Śūdras at a time when we have no Kṣatriyas to defend our Dharma, or to make public provision for our maintenance, and the Śūdras have risen to such power as Rajahs and landholders."

Satyakāma.—"I am rather surprised Takakāma at your defending deviations from *Swadharma* on the part of men, like the domestic priest of our Śūdra zemindar, while you are still eagerly condemning me for *my* departures. You say, there are no Kṣatriya patrons of Brāhmins—no provisions for them from the public revenue—how are they to mainain themselves? They are compelled to accept service from Śūdra patrons. I do not wish to contradict your position. Let me however remind you of what the Śrī Bhāgavat says : 'While there is the bare ground, why labour for beds? While there is your own arm, why labour for a pillow? While the palms of your hands may be joined, why trouble yourself for dishes and platters? While there are barks on trees, why labour for raiment? And—are rags never found on the high way? Do not hospitable trees give alms? Are rivers dried up? Are caves closed up? Besides—does not the Lord support all who seek his protection? Why then do the wise serve those who are blinded by the pride of wealth[36]?" You may admit this reasoning if it please you. But if you persist in saying that hard necessity has driven the stipendiary professors of our Colleges, the domestic priests of our Śūdra nobility, the Brāhmin clerks of our public offices, to a deviation from the rules of *Swadharma,* then it is a confession, that the obervance of *our own religion is impossible* in these days. Do not then insist on its observance, since it is impossible to maintain it in its integrity. Scarcely a single Brāhmin keeps to the prescribed rules of his class. You confess it would be impossible to observe them all in these days. But Kapila says rightly, *what is impossible is no rule—though enjoined, it is no injunction.*[37]"

Āgamika here heaved a deep sigh, and said, "Alas for

the humiliation of our Sanātana (eternal) Dharma in this Kali Yuga!"

"You need not grieve, friend Āgamika," said Satyakāma, "for there is no such thing as an *eternal* Dharma to be deduced from the Śāstras. Class rules, now called *swadharma,* do not seem to have existed from the commencement of Indian society. There are no traces of them in the oldest Mantras of the Vedas. And it is said in the *Mahābhārata* itself, that *there was at first no distinction—the whole universe was of Brahma*[38], *the distinction arose subsequently from different occupations.* The caste rules, then, could not have existed at that time. They were formed long after in the age of the Purāṇas—and if they are not strictly observed in the present day, it is because the castes have been much modified under new influences. Surely there is no *sanātana,* or eternal, Dharma in all this. Our *swadharma,* as we have been speaking of it, may have existed in the medieval period of Hinduism—but certainly it had no existence in the Mantra period, and, as you see, it has very much changed in the present era of foreign domination."

Tarkakāma.—"But I cannot allow that one becomes an apostate by officiating for Śūdras, or accepting gifts of eatables from them. A Brāhmin's dignity may be somewhat compromised thereby, but he does not cease to be a Brāhmin."

Satyakāma.—"Many texts inveigh as strongly against such degrading acts, as they do against any other delinquency which you may call more heinous. While other texts again speak of the indelible character of the Brāhmin's sanctity, so that he can never forfeit his superior station, how gross so ever his delinquency may be. But you will not deny, Tarkakāma, that some of the Śāstras, at least, not only tolerate, but highly applaud a total renunciation of caste, or, in other words, our *own Dharma.*"

Tarkakāma.—"What do you mean?

Satyakāma.—"I mean when a person joins any of the sects[39], and devotes himself to some peculiar *iṣṭa devatā,* whether it be a form of Viṣṇu or of Śiva."

Takakāma.—"Ah, but then, he renounces the world for his *iṣṭa devatā,* and, with the world, all its occupations and pleasures—every thing appertaining to it—and, consequently, its Duties also.'

Satyakāma.—" So may one, for aught you know to the contrary, that gives up his *swadharma* for the sake of some other *iṣṭa devatā.* At any rate the renunciation of the world by a sectary does not mean that he may not marry and keep house. For such persons are not infrequently *exhorted*[40] to lead "household" lives, and yet they are absolved from the bondage of *swadharma.* Nor are shortcomings in point of personal character considered a disqualification for such liberty, for, it is added, that if a person, giving up caste from religious motives, *fails* in attaining his end, he suffers no harm thereby."

Āgamika—"That is only when one gives up caste for Hari, *i.e.* Viṣṇu."

Satyakāma.—"Very true, but the principle of abandoning *one's own religion* (as the vulgar understand by Swadharma) for something more excellent—some *iṣṭa devatā* to which the mind is devoted, is recognized, may applauded, in the *Śāstra.* Whether I have found a more excellent way to justify my act, is a point on which I will not offer evidence now;—and, indeed, according to Indian custom, one ought not to *pry* into another's *iṣṭa devatā,* that being a pure question of conscience with him. But if occasion should offer, and you desire it, I, for my part, shall have no scruple in laying before you the grounds on which I adhere to my Lord and Master."

Tarkakāma.—"But to what extent so ever a person may deviate from his *Swadharma,* we have never heard him say he does not reverence the Vedas. All Hindus, including Śūdras and Sectaries, bow to the authority of those oracles of inspiration."

Satyakāma.—"The Śūdras *cannot* know any thing of the

Vedas, because they are not allowed even to hear them read—and there can be no *real* reverence for a Scripture without knowing something about it. As to the sectaries, they are glad enough to seize on any passage that may be tortured into an approval of their opinions, but it is evident they care little for texts of the Vedas when opposed to their sentiments. And it is notorious they have fabricated many Upaniṣads in order to beguile the unwary. Such a vague and questionable reverence, producing the most opposite doctrines and practices, cannot be recognized as a bond of union in Hinduism, for even the Jesuits of Madura exhibited some *such* reverence. You may have heard of their forgeries."

Tarkakāma.—"The sectaries are a set of ignorant fanatics—dupes of cunning and ambitious leaders. If their minds had been enlightened by the teaching of Gotama, Kapila, and others, they would not have been so unsteady."

Satyakāma.—"Some of the sectaries have ideas of Divine love, and are animated by sentiments of devotion to the Supreme Being, which they would fast unlearn, under the teaching of Gotama and Kaṇāda. And as to Swadharma, those doctors would make quick work of it."

Tarkakāma.—"You must be greatly mistaken. I wonder the more at your mistake, because even foreign scholars profess the greatest respect for the schools of philosophy, though they despise our rites and ceremonies. I should like to disabuse your mind by pointing out in detail the excellencies of those systems, and refuting your objections."

Satyakāma.—"I shall be very happy to listen to your explanations."

Tarkakāma was going to commence his explanations, when Āgamika, having no great relish for them, and perceiving that the son of Kaśyapa had already driven the solar car nearly over our heads, proposed that we should stop this intellectual repast, however pleasant, and look for something more material, which, whatever his philosophical friends might say to the contrary, he, for his part, particularly felt the need of at the moment; promising, if it pleased the company, to come some other morning to listen to Tarkakāma's explanations. All assenting to the proposal, the meeting was adjourned to Monday week.

Such, my learned friend, was the conversation I witnessed between the parties I have already named. The whole occurrence was so novel—almost startling—that I could not forbear sending you this full account. If any thoughts strike you after reading it, pray let me have the benefit of them.

References

1. आहार्य्यशोभारहितैरमायैरैक्षिष्ट पुंभिः प्रचितान् स गोष्ठान्॥
2. आकारैरिङ्गितैर्गत्या चेष्टया भाषणेन च। नेत्रवक्त्रविकाराभ्यां ज्ञायतेऽन्तर्गतं मनः। (Hitop.)
3. एष वा अनृणो यः पुत्रीति श्रुतेः *He who has begotten a son is absolved from his debt. Veda in Mallinātha.* The Hindus are of opinion that the happiness of those who have departed to another world depends in a great measure on the performance of certain ceremonies by their descendants. A man is accordingly considered to be in debt to his forefathers as long as he has no son—the hope of the family,—as of the living so also of the dead.
4. The Vedas speak of three debts in which the Brāhmin is involved from his birth.

   जायमानो ह वै ब्राह्मणस्त्रिभिर्ऋणैर्ऋणवान् जायते ब्रह्मचर्य्येण ऋषिभ्यो यज्ञेन देवेभ्यः प्रजया पितृभ्यः॥

"A Brāhmin is born to three debts—he owes studentship to the Ṛṣis, sacrifices to the gods, and offspring to his forefathers."' Veda quoted in the Nyāya Sūtra Vṛtti.

5. The prayers which the Brāhmins have to repeat three times a day are called the Sandhyā. They are generally free from references to the more recent legends of a directly idolatrous nature. They are held in the highest estimation. A Brāhmin forfeits his position, not only by practically neglecting, but even by theoretically disregarding them. "Whosoever," says Śatatapa, does not honor it, is not esteemed a Brāhmin" यस्य नास्त्यादरस्तत्र न स ब्राह्मण उच्यते।

The Purāṇas are full of eulogies of the Sandhyā. I shall give only one passage from the *Brahma-Vaivarta* यावज्जीवनपर्य्यन्तं यस्त्रिसन्ध्यं करोति च। स च सूर्य्यसमो विप्रस्तेजसा तपसा सदा॥ तत्पादपद्मरजसा सद्यः पूता वसुन्धरा। जीवन्मुक्तः स तेजस्वी सन्ध्यापूतो हि यो द्विजः॥

6. श्रेयान् स्वधर्म्मो विगुणः परधर्म्मात् स्वनुष्ठितात्। स्वधर्म्मे निधनं श्रेयः परधर्म्मो भयावहः॥ Bhagavad Gītā III. 35.

7. It is said in the Vedas that Divine Learning went to a Brāhmin begging protection against unworthy candidates for instruction. विद्या ह वै ब्राह्मणमाजगाम तवाहमस्मि त्वं मां पालय अनर्हते मानिने नैव मादा गोपाय मां श्रेयसी तेहमस्मि।

8. "Not all the authority of Akbar could prevail with the Brāhmins to reveal "the principles of their faith. He was therefore obliged to have recourse to artifice to obtain the information which he so much desired. The Emperor, for this purpose, concerted a plan with his chief Secretary, Abul Fazil, to impose Feizi, then a boy, upon the Brāhmins, in the character of a poor orphan of their tribe. Feizi, being instructed in his part, was privately sent to Benares, the principal seat of learning

among the Hindus. In that city the fraud was practised on a learned Brāhmin, who received the boy into his house and educated him as his own son." —*Dow's History of Hindustan*. While Feizi was carrying on his studies in disguise, a secret attachment grew up between the preceptor's daughter and himself. The Brāhmin was easily persuaded to make him his son-in-law. But Feizi's conscience smote him. He could not any longer practise the deception without incurring to guilt of swindling. He discovered himself to his benefactor, and craved pardon for what he had done. The Brāhmin was thunderstruck. From the mortification he felt in communicating the Vedas to an unclean barbarian, he could think of no other relief than instant death. He drew his knife to stab himself. Feizi fell down at his feet, beseeching him not to lay violent hands on himself. The Brāhmin consented to live only on the Mahometan's solemnly promising not to translate the Vedas, nor to reveal the Brāhminical creed to his fraternity.

9. रखामात्रमपि क्षुणादामनो वर्त्मनः परं। न व्यतीयुः प्रजास्तस्य नियन्तुर्नेमिवृत्तयः॥ Raghuvaṅśa.

10. Sāṁkhya Sūtra I. 83. नानुश्रविकादपि तत्सिद्धिः साध्यत्वेनावृत्तियो-गादपुरुषाथत्वं॥

Kārikā, II. दृष्टवदानुश्रविकः सह्यविशुद्धिक्षयातिशययुक्तः।

11. The Śāstras speak of the Brāhmins having been produced from the mouth, and the Śūdras from the feet of Brahmā.

12. भूसुराः भूदेवाः॥ So the Brāhmins are called.

13. कुलक्षये प्रणश्यन्ति कुलधर्म्माः सनातनाः। धर्म्मे नष्टे कुलं कृत्स्न-मधर्म्मोऽभिभवत्युत। अधर्म्माभिभवात् कृष्ण प्रदुष्यन्ति कुलस्त्रियः। स्त्रीषु दुष्टासु वार्ष्णेय जायते वर्णसंकरः। संकरो नरकायैव कुलघ्नानां कुलस्य च। पतन्ति पितरो ह्येषां लुप्तपिण्डोदकक्रियाः॥ Bhagavad Gītā, I. 35-37.

14. आत्मवत् सर्व्वभूतेषु यः पश्यति स पण्डितः॥

15. दुःखाद्दुःखं जलाभिषेकवन्न जाड्यविमोकः॥ Kapila Sūra, 1. 84.

16. स्त्रीशूद्रद्विजबन्धूनां त्रयी न श्रुतिगोचरा॥

17. "The puṇḍits of the Benares College were one asked the following questions : "As the three systems of philosophy which you have studied in the College professedly dispute each other's positions, and cannot therefore all be entirely in the right, tell me whether you adopt any one of them to the exclusion of the others: or, provided you really have formed any opinion of your own at all, whether you adopt, eclectically, something from each? The answers were generally to the effect that all the three systems were reconcileable with Scripture, and that what appeared in any of them to be a deviation from the truth, was, in reality, only an accommodation to the weakness of the human understanding, which renders it necessary in the first instance to communicate the truth under the garb of error, just as a mother, in pointing out the moon to her child, speaks of it as the shining circle at the end of her finger, which is intelligible to the child, while the mention of its being distant by thousands of leagues would have hopelessly bewildered him." —*Synposis of Science,* vo. I, pp. vii, viii.

18. ऋषिं प्रसूतं कपिलं यस्तमग्रे ज्ञानैर्बिभर्त्ति जायमानञ्च पश्येत्॥

Śwetaśwatara Upaniṣad.

19. न कालयोगतो व्यापिनो नित्यस्य सर्व्वसम्बन्धात्॥12॥

न देशयोगतोऽप्यस्मात्॥13॥ Sāṁkhya Sūtra :

20. सूर्य्यो यथा सर्व्वलोकस्य चक्षुर्न लिप्यते चाक्षुषैर्वाह्यदोषैः॥

Kaṭhopaniṣad.

21. निरागमाः पुरुषोत्प्रेक्षामात्रनिवन्धनास्तर्का अप्रतिष्ठिताः सम्भवन्ति उत्प्रेक्षाया निरङ्कुशत्त्वात् तथाहि कैश्चिदभियुक्तैर्यत्नेनोत्प्रेक्षितास्तर्का अभियुक्ततरैरन्यैरा-

भास्यमाना दृश्यन्ते तैरप्युत्प्रेक्षितास्तदन्यैराभास्यन्त इति न प्रतिष्ठितत्वं तर्काणां शक्यं समाश्रयितुं पुरुषमतिवैरूप्यात् अथ कस्यचित् प्रसिद्धमाहात्म्य कपिलस्य अन्यस्य वा संमतस्तर्कः प्रतिष्ठित इत्याश्रीयेत एवमपि अप्रतिष्ठितत्वमेव प्रसिद्धमाहात्म्याभिमतानामपि तीर्थकराणां कपिलकणभुक्प्रभृतीनां परस्पर-विप्रतिपत्तिदर्शनात्।

Commentary on Vedānta, II. i. 11.

22. नहि प्रतिष्ठितस्तर्क एव नास्तीति शक्यते वक्तुं। श्रुत्यर्थविप्रतिपत्रौ चार्थाभासनिराकरणेन सम्यगर्थनिर्धारणं तर्केणैव वाक्यवृत्तिनिरूपणरूपेण क्रियते मनुरपि चैवमेव मन्यते प्रत्यक्षमनुमानञ्च शास्त्रञ्च विविधागमं त्रयं सुविहितं कार्य्यं धर्म्मशुद्धिमभीप्सतेति आर्षं धर्म्मोपदेशञ्च वेदशास्त्राविरोधिना यस्तर्केणानुसन्धत्ते सधर्म्मं वेद नेतर इति च ब्रुवन्।

Com. Vedānt. II. i. 11.

23. हर्षहिं निरखि रामपद अङ्काः। मानद्धं पारस पायेउ रंका॥ रज शिर धरि हियनयनन्हवालवहिं। रघुवर मिलन सरिस सुख पावहिं॥

Toolsedass's Rāmāyaṇa, Ayodhyā Kāṇḍa.

24. धूमज्योतिःसलिलमरुतां सन्निपातः क्व मेघः सन्देशार्थाः क्व पटुकरणैः प्राणिभिः प्रापणीयाः। इत्यौत्सुक्यादपरिगणयन् गुह्यकस्तं ययाचे कामार्ताहि प्रकृतिकृपणाश्चेतनाचेतनेषु। Meghadūta.

25. नहि पूर्वजो मूढ़ व्यासीदित्यात्मनापि मूढ़ेन भवितव्यमिति किञ्चिदस्ति प्रमाणं।

26. असूर्य्या नाम ते लोका अन्धेन तमसावृताः। तांस्ते प्रेत्यभिगच्छन्ति ये के चात्महनो जनाः। Iśopaniṣad.

आत्मानं घ्नन्तीति आत्महनः के ते येऽविद्वांसः कथं ते आत्मानं नित्यं हिंसन्ति अविद्यादोषेण विद्यमानस्यात्मनस्तिरस्करणात्।

Śaṅkara's Commentary on Ditto.

27. शन्न आपो धन्वन्याः शमनःसन्तु नूप्याः शन्नः समुद्रिया आपः शमनः सन्तु कूप्याः * * * सूर्य्यश्च मामन्युश्च मन्युपतयश्च मन्युकृतेभ्यः पापेभ्यो रक्षन्तांयद्रान्त्र्या पापमकार्षं मनसा वाचा हस्ताभ्यां पद्भ्यामुदरेण शिश्ना अहस्तदवलंपतु॥ Sandhyā.

28. Esther.

29. अघ्नो द्विजान् देवयजीन्निहन्म: कुर्म्म: पुरं प्रेतनराधिवासं। धर्म्मोह्ययं दाशरथे निजोनो नैवाध्यकारिष्महि वेदवृत्ते॥ धर्म्मोस्ति सत्यं तव राक्षसायमन्यो व्यतिस्ते तु ममापि धर्म्म:। ब्रह्मद्विषस्ते प्रणिहन्मि येन राजन्यवृत्तिर्धृतकार्म्मुकेष:॥ Bhaṭṭi.

30. दैव्यो वै वर्णो ब्राह्मण: असुर्य्य: शूद्र:। Taitirīya Brāhmaṇa.

31. अध्यापनमध्ययनं यजनं याजनन्तथा दानम्प्रतिग्रहश्चैव ब्राह्मणानामकल्पयत्।

32. नाद्यात् शूद्रस्य विप्रोन्नं।

33. शूद्रान्नं तदपि स्मृतं। अपि शब्दात् साक्षाद्दत्तघृततण्डुलादि।

34. शूद्राणां सूपकारी च शूद्रयाजी च यो द्विज:। असिजीवी मसीजीवी विषहीनो यथोरग:। यो विद्याविक्रयी विप्रो विषहीनो यथोरग:।

35. सव्यलोचनकोणेन ददर्श च शिशोर्मुखं। शनिश्च दृष्टिमात्रेण चिच्छेद मस्तकं मुने॥ Brahma Vaivarta.

36. सत्यां क्षितौ किं कशिपो: प्रयासैर्वाहौ स्वसिद्धे ह्युपवर्हणै: किं। सत्यञ्जलौ किं पुरुधान्नपाया दिग्वल्कलादौ सति किं दुकूलै:। चीराणि किं पथि न सन्ति दिशन्ति भिक्षां नैवाङ्घ्रिपा: परभृत: सरितोऽप्यश्रुष्यन् रुद्धा गुहा:। किमजितोऽवति नोपपन्नान् कस्माद्भजन्ति कवयो धनदुर्मदान्धान् II, 2.

37. नाशक्योपदेशविधिरूपदिष्टेऽप्यनुपदेश:। 1.9.

38. न विशेषोस्ति वर्णानां सर्व्वं ब्राह्ममिदं जगत्। ब्रह्मणा पूर्व्वसृष्टं हि कर्म्मभिर्वर्णतां गतं॥

39. त्यक्त्वा स्वधर्म्मं चरणाम्बुजं हरेर्भजन्नपक्वोथ पतेत् ततो यदि।
यत्र क्व वाभद्रमभूदमुष्य किं कोवार्थ आप्तो भजतां स्वधर्म्मत:॥

40. भयं प्रमत्तस्य वनेष्वपि स्यात् यत: स आस्ते सहवट्सपत्न:। जितेन्द्रियस्यात्मरतेर्वुधस्य गृहाश्रमं किं नु करोत्यवद्यं॥

DIALOGUE II

FROM THE SAME TO THE SAME

Pursuant to the arrangement of the previous week, I went to Satyakāma's as early as I could on Monday, hoping, though not sanguinely expecting, to witness the conference proposed by Tarkakāma. We had all made a grand mistake in appointing that morning for the discussion. On the day of the first conference, we did not remember that our almanacs held Out the threat of an eclipse to the beautiful moon, which had been waxing for several nights past. The giant was right earnest in verifying the threat. Nearly a third of the splendid orb which rose in the evening, shedding its nectareous beams on a delighted world, was in the ruthless demon's grasp for more than two hours after midnight. The excitement produced by the event turned night into day. Every lane and alley was crowded by men, women, and children, some begging, others giving alms, and all in breathless haste moving towards the river. For Àgamika to think of rest in such a night was impossible. The ceremonies, usual on such occasions, occupied him nearly till the close of the third watch. He could hardly have any sleep after that. It was not to be expected that he could take part in a conference on speculative subjects after the fatigue and excitement of a sleepless night. He did not make his appearance at all.

Nor was Tarkakāma punctual in coming. It is not probable that a mere lunar eclipse could have disturbed the repose of an admirer of Bhāskarācārya, but he did not wish to appear singular in his practice, and was resolved not to show any disrespect to the institutions which governed the conduct of his countrymen.

"Our friends are not yet arrived," said Satyakāma, "perhaps they find it inconvenient to come this morning, because of last night's eclipse."

"I have no doubt," said I, "that is the cause of their absence. But I am not sorry your conference is postponed. As I never paid much attention to the dogmas of the schools, the discussion will not be the less interesting to me, if meanwhile I can revive my knowledge of the Sūtras. The fact is we generally receive our ideas of the Nyāya and other systems at second or third hand. Few of us ever read the Sūtras themselves. The Bhāṣāparichheda and the Vedānta Sāra are text books with most of us. The Sūtras of Gotama are indeed studied to some extent. But how few have read even the Vedānta Sūtras. How still fewer are those who have seen, (to say nothing of *reading*) the Sūtras of Kaṇāda, Kapila, Patañjali and Jaimini. And yet we all talk of the Vaiśeṣika, Mīmāṅsā, and Sāṅkhya, as if we were quite familiar with them. I should be glad to know something definitely of them. But what puzzles me most is that the different schools are supposed to discuss one another's views. We hear of Gotama replying to Kapila, and Kapila to Gotama; of Vyāsa assailing Kaṇāda, and Kaṇāda Vyāsa. How could the earlier philosopher reply to the later? Or are we to suppose that they knew one another's opinions by supernatural vision, and that the earlier sage replied to the later by *anticipation?* A mystery seems to hang over the whole question. Is it quite impossible to trace the gradual formation of the various schools?"

Satyakāma.—"It is perfectly true, as you have said, that Brāhmins often talk of the opinions of Gotama and Kaṇāda without caring to read their Sūtras for themselves. They thereby give circulation to erroneous opinions on the subject. It is commonly believed, is it not? That while Kapila discarded the idea of a Supreme Intelligence creating the universe, Gotama and Kaṇāda repudiated such atheistical views, and laboured hard to prove the existence of an Almighty and Intelligent effcient cause who arranged the universe."

"Of course" said I, "that is the traditional account we have of those eminent Ṛṣis' doctrines."

"The Sūtras do not bear out the tradition," said Satyakāma. "I will show you the Sūtras on some future occasion. With reference to the order in which the various schools were formed,—that is a question which has often exercised my thoughts. Last night I put some ideas on paper on the subject, which I would have read to you, but that I fear they are very crude and undigested."

"You have no doubt studied the subject," said I, "though it seems you have not drawn the right conclusions. Such, however, is my desire to enlarge my general knowledge of the question, that I shall gladly hear what you have written. Do therefore read your paper."

Satyakāma accordingly read as follows :—

"It is very difficult to trace the origin of Hindu philosophy. Our ancient writers have left no records which can be properly called historical. The charms of poetry, by which their minds were captivated at an early period, maintained their power to the last. Not only in the department of subjective theology (where the facilities which poetry lends to devotion cannot be denied), but in historical narratives, in science and philosophy also, the genius of poetry had absolute sway. The metaphysics of Iśwara Kṛṣṇa, and the astronomy of Bhāskarācārya are both in verse. Pleasant reading it was, no doubt, to have the fascinations of poetry along with the dry facts of history, and the stern principles of science. But nothing can be had in the world without a price. If history and science were made to contribute pleasures and amusements which they were not bound to supply, it has been at the expense of their proper tributes—truth and exactitude. The exchange has been no benefit, but rather the reverse. When the annals of kingdoms, and the definitions of science, are given in poetry, it is obvious that the labour required for conducting critical and inductive investigations will be in constant danger of being supplanted by the comparatively more agreeable exercise of the imagination and fancy.

"And as to chronology nothing can be a more heterogeneous compound of *possibilities and impossibilities.* You have the same Viśwāmitra, putting Hariścandra to the trial of his faith, and afterwards conducting Rāma Candra to the palace of Janaka. You have the same Vaśiṣṭha at the courts of Dīlipa and Dsaśaratha.

"Accordingly we are left to grope our way in the dark as we best may. All our writers were poets. Facts are so blended in their compositions with fictions, that it is impossible to disintegrate them."

"But," added he, folding his paper with some diffidence, "I am afraid what I am reading is irrelevant to your question. You probably do not care about the early history of the Brāhminical intellect, nor the way in which the various schools of philosophy arose." "Pray go on," said I—"Let me hear what you have written. I feel much interested in the question how these several systems originated;—which was the earliest, and which the most recent."

"I do not pretend to unravel that mystery, but perhaps some light will be thrown by a consideration of the Sūtras themselves." Satyakāma then continued to read : "In the midst of the obscurities in which the want of historical records has left us, one thing we may assume as certain, that the Brāhminical mind was formed in the mould of the Vedas. Indian scholars were from the earliest times possessed with the highest notions of reverence for those writings. In all questions, whether political or religious, dogmatic or philosophical, the authority of the Vedas was conclusive. None dared to contradict, what *they* inculcated. No appeal to reason or experience lay from their verdict.

"But the Vedas are for the most part known to our countrymen, now, by name only. Probably not one of our contemporaries has read the whole of them—or even seen them in their integrity. European enterprise has given portions of them to the world, but few of us think it worth our while to procure or peruse them. The small tracts, distinguished by the name of Upaniṣads, are alone familiarly known to any of us. Nay it appears that our standard authors on theology and physics confined their attention to those tracts, for it is but seldom we meet with Vedic passages, quoted in their writings, which may not be traced to some Upaniṣad or other.

"The division of our Vedas, it is well-knwon, is twofold, into Mantras and Brāhmaṇas. The former may generally be considered devotional, the latter ceremonial and dogmatic. As for the short treatises called Upaniṣads, they are, with a few exceptions, appendices to the dogmatic parts, and, like codicils of wills, are held to be the most recent, and therefore the most matured, expositions of the authors' minds. They profess to be repositories of *parāvidyā,* or superior knowledge, and look down on the great bulk of the Vedas, as *aparā,* or inferior. They contain some rude indications of philosophic thought, and, like the twinklings of stars in a dark night, may occasionally serve as guides in a history of Hindu philosophy. They do not however exhibit any great attempt at method, arrangement, classification, or argument. Even there the poetry predominates over the logic. Bold ideas abruptly strike your fancy, but you find no clue to the associations which called them forth in the author's mind, and search in vain for the reasons on which they were based. Sublime thoughts are not wanting, but they resemble sudden flashes, at which you may gaze for a moment, but are, immediately after, left in deeper darkness than ever. Nor are they free from those irregular flights of the imagination in which poets, with vitiated tastes, delight to indulge, setting at defiance all rules of decency and morality[1].

"The Upaniṣads appear from their language and style to

have been the latest, and the Mantras, the earliest of Vedic compositions. It may be a delicate question, but it is one which ought not to be unfairly suppressed, whether the authors of the earliest compositions, the Mantras, profess to have written them down as inspired records. You are fond of saying that they were breathed out by Brahmā at the time of the creation, and yet you speak of the *Ṛṣi* of each *Mantra*. The *Mantra* itself is such that its *Ṛṣi* may well be supposed to have composed and chanted it, and there is nothing as to matter and style which could possibly require divine illumination.

"That our ancestors looked on the Vedas with such reverence is no marvel. The Vedas were the first national efforts in the department of literature. In the infancy of literature, the ignorant, who did not know how to read or write, would naturally look upon those mysterious talents as divine endowments, as especial instances of Saraswati's grace. They would accordingly feel a sort of religious veneration for such gifted and highly favoured persons, and consider their writings as divine inspirations.

"The Mantras again were hymns. Those who could not read, would listen to their recital with the greater devotion, and learn to rehearse them in moments of leisure. And those, who could read, would go over them as religious exercises.

"Rhythmical phraseology is always favourable to the sentiment of devotion. The fine versification of the Mantras, their excellent adaptation for chanting and music, were charms which could not fail to impress both readers and hearers. They accordingly considered them as the voice of God. No wonder that in the language of poets even birds and beasts should be subject to the spell of Vedic recitations.

"The reverence, first accorded to the Mantras, was easily extended to the whole Vedas. Their interpretation was held a secondary point. It was received as tradition handed it down. No one dared to expound the Veda in a novel way. The faith and practice of one generation were quietly followed by that which succeeded it. Indeed the question with the generality of men in all countries has been, not, What says the law? But, What says practice?

"The Vedas formed from the first the peculiar inheritance of the learned, who were honoured under the title of Brāhmins. Originally all who could, were allowed to read them. This appears to be the meaning of the tradition in the Mahābhārata, that there was no distinction of castes in the beginning, and that the distinction arose subsequently from diversities of occupations—and, it may be added, of talents. The learned were then classed in a separate order—the Brāhmins—who became the priests of the whole nation, charged with the duty, and endowed with the privilege of *tapasyā,* or divine meditation, for the benefit of themselves and of the whole community. The fact is attested by the Rāmāyaṇa, the oldest of epic or Pourāṇic poems, which says that, in the Satya-yuga, devotional exercises were not allowed to any but Brāhmins[2]. And indeed some such spiritual privilege must have been the monopoly of the priestly order, when Viśwāmitra and Janaka, excluded therefrom by their birth, made such strenuous efforts to partake of it.

"That the right of engaging personally in hard religious exercises was not considered an empty privilege, will appear from a story, related in the oldest epic poem, just named[3]. After Rāma had returned home from his expedition to Laṅkā, and commenced a happy and prosperous reign in Oudh, a Brāhmin came to his door, bitterly complaining of the untimely death of a child, only five years old, and attributing the tragical event to some curse under which the kingdom lay, owing to the king's want of watchfulness. Rāma, listened to the Brāhmin's invectives with self-reproach, and could not, with such a humiliating fact before him, gainsay the Brāhmin's conclusion. Advised by ministers and Ṛṣis, he proceeded, sword in hand, to search out the unknown cause of the national sin. By the side of a tank he discovered a man absorbed in deep and austere devotion. Challenged by the king, the devotee gave his name (Sāmbuca), and confessed his race (Śūdra). For a servile man to seek admission to the society of gods by such religious exercises, was an iniquity, which sufficiently accounted for the national calamity. With one stroke of his sword, the king severed the Śūdra's head from his body. Indra and the other gods fell into ecstasies of delight at the promptness with which the son of Daśaratha exterminated such a crying evil, and immediately sent down a perfumed shower of celestial flowers, acknowledging at the same time that the stop, so effectually put to the aspiring Śūdra's attempt to obtain a footing in heaven, was a service done to themselves. And Rāma was then assured that the moment the wretched man's head dropped from his neck, life was restored to the Brāhmin's son.

"Although the Kṣatriyas were afterwards (in Tretāyuga, says the Rāmāyaṇa[4]) admitted to the privilege of devotional exercises, they were only allowed to read the Vedas for themselves. They were forbidden to teach or expound them. That still remains the exclusive privilege of Brāhminical scholars, to whom implicit obedience was paid when they laid down any doctrine.

"This implicit obedience appears to have been cheerfully accorded to them in the Vedic period. The whole community entertained such high notions of their learning and sanctity, that none dared to dispute their authority. Between that period and the age of the Darśanas, however, a tremendous revolution had taken place in the opinions of men.

"From extreme credulity to extreme infidelity the transition is easy. Those who were called upon to render implicit obedience to the Brāhminical college, began to question the very foundations of sacerdotal authority. The Brāhminical hierarchy had become so powerful, as to set the sovereignty of kings and princes at defiance. The fear of incurring their malediction—an anathema, the effects of which would be felt for countless generations,—would haunt the priest-ridden minds of Kṣatriyas by day and by night, if ever they set themselves in opposition to Brāhmins. The legend of Hariścandra, who consented to sell his queen and his only son, and submitted to the vilest of servitudes, rather than incur the consequences of a Brāhmin's resentment, bears conclusive evidence of the fact. At length, however, a prince arose in the royal line of Ikṣwāku, (to which Hariścandra himself belonged,) determined to dissolve the charm by which the minds of men were held in servitude to the Brāhmins. Śākya Muni imposed on himself the task of reforming the religion of his country. He cared not, like Viśwāmitra, for promotion to the Brāhminical College—nor, like Janaka, for occasional participation in their exclusive privileges—nor yet for inflicting such temporary humiliation on the priestly order, as was implied in Rāmacandra's triumph over Paraśurāma. Disgusted, when young, with the evils of disease and death, he renounced the pleasures of dignity and royalty, and went about preaching every where on the necessity of seeking for Nirvāṇa, or release from transmigrations, as the only remedy for the evils of life. He pronounced the rites and ceremonies of the Veda to be idle sports, and the exclusive privileges arrogated by the Brāhmins, to be empty pretensions. He assailed the authority of the very books on which those pretensions were founded. He declared that the division of castes was a mere human invention, and invited all ranks to assemble under his banners on a footing of equality. The Brāhmins add that he also denied the immortality of the soul, and pronounced the expectation of a future world to be a vain reverie.[5] Whether Buddhism was really liable to the charge of materialism preferred against it by the Brāhmins, or not, it certainly had no divine revelation to plead for its support, nor could it appeal to any tradition in its favour. It could only stand on its *rational* pretensions. The study of philosophy and metaphysics was therefore absolutely needed for its very existence. So long as men believed in the infallibility of the Veda, they could appeal to its texts for the decision of controversies and the solution of doubts. But when revelation was ignored, disputes could only be settled by the verdict of *reasons*. The necessities of Buddhism rendered the cultivation of logic and metaphysics absolutely indispensable, and thus were the first attempts at philosophy called forth in India. Hence it was that the terms *Haituka* and *Hetu-Śāstra* were applied to the heretical systems.

"Buddhism however failed to maintain its ground against the Brāhmins. It was driven to seek refuge in regions whither the Brāhmins did not care to pursue it, and where it found as firm a footing as Brāhminism itself had on the plains of Hindustan.

"But though expelled from India,Buddhism left strong traces of its anti-Vedic rationalism on the field it abandoned. It had infected the Brāhminical mind itself. It had sown the seeds of heresy in the very camp of orthodoxy, and fostered among the champions of the Śāstra themselves, a spirit of discontent with its ritual. Hence it is that so little of reverence for the Veda is found in the systems of philosophers. All the Darśanas are branded in the Padma Purāṇa as equally pernicious with Buddhism, and equally destructive of the rites and ceremonies of the Veda. Śiva openly confesses to his wife Pārvatī that he had himself taught those doctrines of *darkness,* in the forms of Kaṇāda and others, with a view to bring about the destruction of the world[6].

"Of our six Darśanas, or schools of philosophy, two, however, those of Jaimini and Vyāsa, are generally considered orthodox—while the other four are looked upon with great suspicion by the Brāhmins themselves.[47] I think that the Darśanas of Jaimini and Vyāsā, (called the Former and Latter Mīmāṅsas, or deciders,) were written with a view to correct the errors of their predecessors, and were of more recent dates than the rest.

"The Nyāya and the Sāṅkhya are in fact a sort of compromise between Brāhminism and Buddhism. They contain as much of the Buddhist element, as could be held without danger to Brāhminical supremacy. The authors *profess* to uphold the Veda, because experience had taught them that the dignity of their order could not be maintained without the Veda—and they inculcate the reality of future states of life against the Buddhists. But the spirit of their teaching is quite as hostile to the ritual of the Veda as that of Buddhism.

"I believe therefore that the Nyāya and Sāṅkhya were among the first fruits of the Brāhminical intellect, when it sought to enlist the aid of rationalism in the service of the Brāhminical order. As to the question of priority between the two systems themselves, the fact of one of the Sāṅkhya Sūtras making plain reference to the Nyāya, and speaking of its *sixteen* topics, may be considered as decisive proof in favour of the Nyāya. Such evidence, it is true, is far from being conclusive, because there have been many interpolations;—but the Nyāya is the least controversial among the systems, and there is no reason of any cogency for rejecting the authenticity of the Sāṅkhya Sūtra in question. The Nyāya may therefore be considered the first production of Brāhminical philosophy after the overthrow of Buddhism in India.

"The prevalence of Buddhism had convinced the Brāhmins of the use of metaphysics in conducting controversies, and especially in refuting objections—and of the risks, they ran, of incurring the contempt of the community by confining their attention to the simple ritual of the Vedas. The Nyāya with its orderly array of scientific terms, its physics, logic, and metaphysics, *was manifestly fitted to train and quicken* the intellectual powers.

"While heresy had been rampant, the vast majority of the Brāhminical order were unable to think for themselves, or unlearn prejudices already instilled into their minds. The reasons for which Śūdras were relieved from the task of intellectual exercises, were becoming more and more applicable to the twice-born classes. Traditional teaching, and the prescribed ritual, received with implicit submission, were fast incapacitating them for vigorous mental labour. If the servile tribes had a routine of duties made ready for them, the higher grades had also *their* routine, not indeed of servile attendance on human superiors, but of endless rites and ceremonies, no less enslaving to the mind. As far as intellectual activity was concerned, the distinction between Brāhmins and Śūdras had become almost nominal.

"The author of the Nyāya would no doubt have the satisfaction of believing that his new system would arrest the progress of heresy, and prevent the gradual decline of the orthodox intellect. If the Brāhmin's mind continued to be stinted by the discipline of the Vedas, in the same manner as the Śūdra's was by the authority of the twice born, what real difference would there remain in point of mental freedom between the highest and the lowest tribes? Implicit submission of intellect was exacted from both. Was it at all wonderful then that heresy stalked abroad, and that many Brāhmins had themselves fallen into the snare? Could minds of any activity acquiesce in the above restrictions? Must they not meditate on the wonders of the creation, except as the antiquated Vedas directed them? And must they always interpret the Vedas in the *monotonous* way taught by the old Ṛṣis?

"Orthodox philosophers accordingly came forward to supply the craving of the Brāhminical mind, without endangering the stability of the Brāhminical order. They did not seem to think very highly of the Vedas, but were unwilling to renounce those time-honoured compositions. The Vedas had indeed charms to which Gotama and Kapila themselves, however sceptically inclined, could not be insensible. And besides the real interest they might take in the fine hymns of the Sāman, and in the theological enigmas of the Upaniṣads, there was another point to be considered. A slur cast on the Vedas might prove dangerous to the Brāhminical order, and would be enjoyed as a triumph by the vanquished Buddhists. It might also lead to radical changes in the constitution of society. The improvement of the Brāhminical intellect could not indeed be safely attempted, unless revolutionary agitations among the Śūdras were at the same time jealously guarded against, and unless the twice-born themselves maintained inviolate their respect for authority.

"To conservative considerations, such as the above, we may fairly attribute the notable fact, that, in most of the systems of Brāhminical philosophy, we find the authors not only addressing a select few, by means of enigmatical Sūtras, instead of the public at large, in language understood by all,—but also maintaining the authority of the Veda, without caring much for its doctrine and ritual, and, while introducing mere physical and metaphysical subjects, promising to their pupils nothing less than the final emancipation of the soul as the reward of their intellectual labour.

"That the Brāhminical philosophers taught initiated scholars only, and that their systems were thoroughly esoteric, is evident, not only from the jealousy with which they excluded the inferior castes, but also from the mode in which they committed their lectures to writing. It is related of the great Alexander, who invaded our country more than two thousand years ago, that when his tutor Aristotle published his physical lectures, the monarch wrote him to the following effect : "You have not done well in publishing these lectures; for how shall we, your pupils, excel other men, if you make that public to all which we learnt from you." To this Aristotle is said to have replied, "My lectures are published and not published; they will be intelligible to those who heard them and to none beside[48]." The authenticity of this anecdote may be reasonably questioned, but the very fabrication of it would show the difficulty which the world experienced in comprehending the lectures of Aristotle. Now if lectures which, however abstruse, had their sentences complete, and their subjects and predicates expressed, could still be so obscure that their publication was held to be no publication, how little was the chance of an uninitiated mind's understanding the Sūtras of *our* philosophers! Their sense was couched in sentences often incomplete, with subjects or predicates in the minds, not in the language, of the authors, with arbitrary *anuvṛttis,* or ellipses,—and the reasoning but obscurely hinted at. Sūtras, without commentaries, are proverbially sealed books.

"The peculiar construction of these sentences could not have been accidental. We cannot suppose that Gotama and Kapila were not competent to write more intelligibly, nor can we entertain the idea that they would, without a motive, write what no one could read. The obvious inference is, that they were unwilling to speak but to a select body of pupils, for the edification of whom, and of none others, the Sūtras were composed. They were not intended for the public. The Śūdras certainly had no right to them.

"Nor does it appear that our philosophers had a real belief in the Vedas. Āgamika was not far in the wrong the other day, in saying that Gotama and Kaṇāda could not entertain much respect for the Vedas, when they set forth categories and topics, wholly unknown to those Śāstras, as absolutely necessary for Emancipation. And yet they never formally denied their authority. On the contrary, they professed the highest reverence for them as oracles of truth, as if they really constituted (to use the homely illustration of Tarkakāma), a Sudder Court of Appeal. This appears still more clearly from the way in which some have endeavoured to reconcile these inconsistencies. They divide the Veda into the *Karma Kāṇḍa,* or the Chapter on Works, and the *Jñān Kāṇḍa,* or the Chapter on Knowledge. The former, they say, were intended for the ignorant, the latter, for the enlightened. We might have known how to understand them, if they had maintained that the *Chapter on Works* was revealed in the infancy of human society, when the minds of men were not prepared for a higher knowledge of divine things, and that the Chapter on knowledge was communicated in a more enlightened age. But their theory is, that the Vedas were, in their entire form, produced before the origin of human society. And the division into the chapters on works and knowledge is altogether arbitrary. For the *Jñān Kāṇḍa* itself contains directions for ritual observances!

"The most striking instances of such spasmodic fits of reverence for the Veda is found in Kapila. In the 82nd Sūtra of the 1st Chapter, he maintains that the provisions in the *Śruti* are insufficient for the final cure of the threefold evils of life, and in ther 83rd Sūtra, he appeals to the Veda itself for the truth of that assertion, thus citing it as a witness against its own incompetency, and extorting a confession of its own imbecility. The fact is that while our philosophers were glad enough to make a convenience of the Veda, they entertained little or no respect for it absolutely.

"Probably they conceived that, as some external respect for the Vedas was necessary to conciliate the feelings, and command the attention of even their own pupils, the division mentioned above, would be the most sagacious device for inculcating a more rational doctrine than that of mere ritualism. The Brāhmins were far too devoutly attached to those writings to listen to teachers who openly attacked them. Of course this mode of teaching involved a sort of *chhala,* or deceit, which did not credit to the teachers; but if Gotama and Kapila did not act altogether innocently in adapting their doctrine to the prejudices of their contemporaries, the spirit of the age in which they lived would be some palliation of their conduct.

"The same desire of humouring the prejudices of the times led them to promise supreme felicity as the reward of philosophical speculation. Nothing short of the *summum bonum* was considered a sufficient recompense for the trouble it imposed. That the sentiment of religion predominated in the minds of our ancestors is evident from the spirit of our ancient literature. It indicates a feeling of dependance on supernatural powers, which is equalled only by the contempt the authors expressed for the perishable objects of the world. Philosophers perhpas imagined that whether they treated on the highest truths which could concern human nature, or merely speculated on the qualities of earth and water, they could never find an audience, unless they held out hopes of everlasting welfare as the *prayojana,* or end, of their investigations. In the estimation of their contemporaries, no inferior boon was worth the trouble.

"The offer of such spiritual rewards on the part of philosophers, for investigations chiefly physical, at best metaphysical, though it must be accepted as a pleasing testimony to the religious feelings of our predecessors, was productive of consequences very much to be regretted. Physics, metaphysics, and theology, were confounded in one mass. While the most trifling points of inquiry (whether, for instance, *upamāna,* or "comparison," was a distinct class of proof, and, whether the body was a compound of one, three, or five elements,) were prosecuted with some feeling of religious awe, questions of really vital importance, which regarded the existence and attributes of God, and the permanent interests of the soul, were necessarily robbed of their due solemnity. Theology and physics being placed on the same level, the former could challenge no greater degree of attention than was accorded to the latter. The degradation of the one, and the undue exaltation of the other, were the natural consequences"–

"I do not quite comprehend the drift of your observations–" said I, interrupting the essayist.

"I mean," said Satyakāma, "our philosophers considered the investigation of the elements of which the body was composed, and the inquiry into the source whence the world was produced, and into duties on which our everlasting welfare depends, as of equal importance, thus unduly exalting the one, and virtually degrading the other branch of human inquiry. If we did not know the precise nature of our corporeal composition, we could not lose much by our ignorance; but we might be in eternal peril by our ignorance of the duties we owe to our Maker. Things of time were placed on the same level with things of eternity. That which might be called the one needful thing for all persons, and which might therefore *justly* engross our chief attention, was set on a footing of equality with other questions of far less importance."

Satyakāma continued; "Gotama, appears to me to have led the way in the career of Brāhminical philosophy. The name must be familiarly known to all students of Vedas and Purāṇas. My namesake in the Chāndogya Upaniṣad, the son of Jabalā, had a *Gotama* for his patron and preceptor. It was a *Gotama* too (I cannot determine whether he was identical with the son of Haridrumat of the Chāndogya,) whose domestic happiness was marred by the lascivious prince of the gods, himself punished with the natural consequences of the Brāhmins' indignation. Various other Gotamas are also celebrated in the Śāstras. There was one of that designation, the spiritual preceptor of the Paṇḍavas. There was another too, famous in the legends of the Buddhists, and corrupted in extra-Gangetic India into Gaudma. Which of these, or whether any of them, was the author of the Sūtras, which claim the same name for their author, is more than I can say.

"The author of the Nyāya Sūtras has been otherwise called Akṣapāda. The *Sarvadarśana-Saṅgraha* styles him so. Vijñāna Bhikṣu, the commentator of the Sāṅkhya, gives him the same appellation. There are various stories current among the learned as to the reason for which this surname was given him. One of those stories has been thus communicated to me. Gotama, they say, used to go about in such a state of abstraction, pondering the figments of his system, that his ordinary eyes quite forgot their office, on which Viṣṇu was so good as to plant a pair of optics in his feet, hence Akṣapāda or *eye-footed*. Hemcandra however gives the word Naiyāyika as synonymous with Akṣapāda, the etymology of which is given differently in a manuscript lexicon, the *Śabda-muktā-mahārṇav*[49].

"Gotama aimed at the promotion of scientific and metaphysical researches, as the best mental discipline for the Brāhmins. An idle dependance on the authority of the Veda, and a blind adherence to the ritual therein enjoined, had not proved a sufficient protection against heresy. When Buddhists made their appeals from the authority of the Vedas to that of reason and conscience, Brāhmins were almost silenced. Many were evn converted, to the no small triumph of the enemy[10]. It was high time that Brāhmins should know how to wield the weapons of logic, and not allow their opponents to make a monopoly of *hetu,* or arugument.

"Gotama accordingly directed the attention of the Brāhmins to the several branches of human knowledge, which he thought were calculated to strengthen the intellect, and enable it to conduct polemical discussions with advantage. He classified them under sixteen topics, which he enumerates in his first aphorism. It is singular that, unlike Brāhminical authors in general, he commences his work without any *maṅgalācaraṇa,* or auspicious introduction. The aphorisms of all the other schools commence with the word *atha,* supposed to be an auspicious particle. The sixteen topics proposed by him certainly embrace a wide range of human research and speculation; but as the Brāhmins in general cared little for intellectual and physical inquiries, not founded on the Veda, he endeavoured to gain them over by proclaiming that the final liberation of the soul depended on the study of his topics.

"I have supposed Gotama to be the earliest of Brāhminical philosophers. My reason for doing so is that his system, while it combats many opinions advanced by teachers of heresy, contains nothing that may be considered as levelled against doctors of other orthodox schools. He notices and answers numerous objections, (some of a most fanciful description,) which cannot be traced to any work or system now known; but there is no evidence of his contending against Vedāntism, or even the Sāṅkhya. The commentator recognizes a few skirmishes against Kapila in some of the Sūtras, but in no Sūtra does any characteristic doctrine of the Sāṅkhya school appear to be the point of attack.

"Gotama appears, as I have said, to have laboured to introduce among the Brāhmins the study of logic and physics, and although in consequence of the great variety of topics which he undertook to discuss simultaneously, he did not arrive at any great results, the rules he laid down for correct reasoning, and especially for the detection of fallacies, have done great service to posterity. He taught in its elementary form the very method of syllogism with which the name of Aristotle is associated in Europe—a name which many of us have heard from the Omla of our courts, and from others who have carefully studied the literature of the Mohammedans. If Gotama's system of logic were amended by succeeding scholars, not bound by the authority of their immediate teachers, we might expect the same success in India which has crowned the efforts of philosophers in Europe.

"But in order to ensure that success it would be necessary to allow fair discussion—unrestrained by the dictum of authority, and unhampered by the dread of incurring popular obloquy, when errors, and defects required to be corrected by careful experiment and investigation. To perpetuate those errors and defects, instead of rectifying them by the light of new discoveries, is in reality not reverence to the memory of that eminent philosopher, but injustice to the truths with which the errors are mixed up. It was a great thing that he taught the rules of correct reasoning, and a system *capable of improvement*—and if he did not succeed in rightly applying those rules in many points, it is incumbent on his successors to follow them up, and supply the deficiency. But to perpetuate the errors alongside the truths, is like an obstinate refusal to wipe off the mildew on a beautiful picture, and like wilfully thrusting a great piece of art on the notice of posterity in an unclean and disfigured state."

Satyakāma paused for a moment here to decipher some scrawls in his paper. I took the opportunity of asking what he meant by errors in the system of Gotama. "Ṛṣis," said I, "cannot err. We must have very cogent reasons, indeed, if we be called upon to abandon that long-cherished maxim." "I will not enter now," said Satyakāma, "into the question of the specific errors of Gotama. We must have a conference on the subject sooner or later. But the fact of the various Ṛṣis, who founded schools of philosophy, having disagreed among themselves, is sufficient evidence against your long cherished maxim. Where two persons hold conflicting opinions, one must be in the wrong—because truths cannot be conflicting."

"But perhapas," said I, "they only misunderstood each other—perhaps their opinions were only *seemingly* conflicting."

"Śaṅkarācārya," replied Satyakāma, "understood them to be *really* conflicting. Āgamika cited a passage to that effect the other day. But even if they misunderstood each other, the misunderstanding itself was an error."

Satyakāma resumed his discourse :—"I should be inclined on general grounds to place Kapila as the immediate successor of Gotama, but the express mention of the *six categories,* and 'the Vaiśeṣikas' in the 25th Sāṅkhya Sūtra presents a difficulty. A comparison of the Sāṅkhya and Vaiśeṣika does not countenance the supposition of that Sūtra being an interpolation. I must therefore name Kaṇāda as our second philosopher in order of succession.

"Kaṇāda's system is considered a branch of the Nyāya. His theory is what we call the atomic—a theory which was simply hinted at by Gotama. The founder of the Vaiśeṣika school took up "the less than the least," as the author of the Nyāya Sūtras had defined an atom, and produced the theory, which has earned for him and his followers the nickname of *feeders on small particles.* The name Kaṇāda itself has that meaning, and was evidently given him by his enemies. His real name appears to be unknown.

"His first three Sūtras form an extraordinary introduction to his work. As if by way of making a mere confession of faith, he begins by defining Dharma[11], and declaring the authority of the Vedas, though we hear nothing on religion or ethics in the first chapter, and but very little in any other part. His categories and his classification of causes bear a singular resemblance to those of the Greek philosopher

Aristotle, while his mode of accounting for the origin of the world, by the combination of atoms, is almost identical with that of a sect of ancient European philosophers, the Epicureans, as represented by Lucretius. He does not indeed betray the diffidence with which the Latin poet asserts the necessity of a small, the smallest possible, inclination in the motion of falling atoms, nor is he afraid of introducing the theory of oblique motions[12], but he boldly attributes to *adṛṣṭa, four* things, which he conceived to be necessary for the first start of his world, viz. the upward course which heat takes when emitted by fire, *the oblique motion of the air, and the primal action of atoms and of the mind*[13]. He does not seem to have enterained the idea of a Self-existent Supreme Intelligence creating the world."

I could not help interrupting my friend again. "Do you mean," said I, "to maintain that Kaṇāda did not allow the existence of God, or that his system is *nirīśwara?*"

"I have no knowledge of him," answered Satyakāma "except from his Śūtras, and I can safely say he makes no *mention* of God in any of them—and that he ascribes the primal action of his eternal atoms to *adṛṣṭa.* Atoms combine by actions and impulses. These are imparted by combinations already formed, and thereby fresh combinations are produced. In tracing these actions and impulses to their *origin,* he could not find any cause for the *first* impulse, except in *adṛṣṭa.* If this implies that he did not admit the existence of a God, I am sorry for it, but I cannot help it."

"Does not Śaṅkarācārya say, and is it not universally believed, even among the opponents of Brāhminism, that the Nyāya, including the Vaiśeṣika, considers atoms as the *material*, but God as the *efficient* cause of the world[14]?"

"Śaṅkarācārya certainly attributes that doctrine to the *followers* of Kaṇāda, and many of them indeed maintain it, but there is no trace of it in the Sūtras of their original teacher; and Śaṅkara thus represents *his* doctrine : 'At the creation also, an operation is produced in aerial atoms, which is dependant on *adṛṣṭa*. That operation joins its own atom with another. Then from binaries, by gradual steps, is produced the air. The same is the case with fire. The same with water. The same with earth. The same with organized bodies. Thus is the whole universe produced from atoms. The form and other qualities of binaries and other compounds are derived from those of the atoms themselves[15].' As to the opponents of Brāhminism—if thereby you mean Europeans, they have for the most part drawn their information from Colebrooke, the most learned of foreign scholars—and the very few that may have consulted native authorities, probably attended solely to modern manuals, or confided in their puṇḍits, and did not care to verify what they read or heard by a reference to the Sūtras.

"Colebrooke makes no mention of the above Sūtra, but he evidently refers to it when he speaks of the Nyāya theory of the original combination of atoms.[16] As he did not *discuss* the meaning of *adṛṣṭa,* those that followed him, without a knowledge of the Sūtra itself, did not perhaps pay especial attention to all the expressions which he used, and so missed his *real* meaning. Whether *adṛṣṭa* means destiny, or some unseen virtue in the material atoms themselves, is a question which we shall discuss afterwards. I shall for the present content myself with having given you Kaṇāda's own words, which scarcely justify an elaborate exposition of their theistical character[17], nor is there anything in Gotama calling for the same."

I was much surprized by what Satyakāma represented to be the teaching of Kaṇāda, but, reserving further discussion for a future occasion, I begged him to resume his paper. He continued; "Kapila came forward next with his remedy for the *three-fold evils* of life, which neither the Vedas nor the common sense of mankind had been able to remove. Who this Kapila was, or when he lived, is equally uncertain with the age and personality of Gotama. There is a Kapila mentioned in the Śwetāśwatara, a son of Brahmā, but some commentators explain it away by taking the word as an adjective, not a substantive. Kapila is also reckoned in the Purāṇas as an incarnation of Viṣṇu, by whom the Sāṅkhya system was revealed for the salvation of the world. He is identified with the sage, represented in the Rāmāyaṇa, as the destroyer of the unhappy sons of Sagara, who were disturbing the world in search of their stolen horse. Sagara had all but completed the wonderful sacrifce, Aśwamedha, when an envious god interrupted it by stealing the steed consecrated for the altar. Commissioned by their father, the princes, sixty thousand in number, went in all directions to trace the course of the missing animal, and when it could not be found on the *surface* of the earth, they dug out a passage to the lower regions, where the consecrated horse was seen by the side of the divine Kapila absorbed in religious contemplation. Not doubting that the apparent devotee was in reality but a thief, the princes, meditating revenge, set up a yell, which roused him from the lethargy of his devotion. Directly the sage's eyes, glowing with fury at the uncalled-for disturbance, fell on the vociferating princes, they were reduced to a heap of ashes. A nephew of the ill-fated youths afterwards recovered the sacrificial horse, and was advised to make supplications for the descent of the Gaṅgā from heaven, with a view to the future salvation of his uncles. At Gaṅgā Saugor, or the mouth of the river Hogghly, there is still a shrine dedicated to Kapila, and that is supposed to be the spot where the tragical event took place, though Saugor in central India corresponds better to the geography of the site where the sacrifice is said to have been celebrated. The Śrī Bhāgavata expresses its doubt as to the correctness of this legend, which, it says, ill accords with the excellence of a character that was at the same time an incarnation of Viṣṇu and the founder of the Sāṅkhya.

"Kapila went the length of denying, outright, the existence of the Deity. The wonder is, that he is still ranked among orthodox philosophers, and not denounced as a teacher of heresy like the Buddhists. But the Brāhmins are very forgiving, if one will humour them in their notions of superiority as *gods of the earth,* and conform to the authority of the Vedas. The 92nd and two following Sūtras of the first chapter of Kapila, may be characterized as *black aphorisms,* since therein he not only declares that the existence of a Supreme Being is not proved, but asserts it impossible for such a Being to be the Creator of the World[18].

"With Kapila there could be no real freedom if a person were subject to a desire or motive. The soul, being essentially free, is, according to his theory, incapable of volition. It is *udāsīn,* or perfectly unmindful of the external. It is a simple witness. He accordingly argues that, since no thinking agent performs an action without a *motive,* the soul could not be supposed to be the CREATOR without being subject to a motive or desire. Such subjection however would imply a *bondage,* and detract from its freedom, and, by necessary consequence, from its *power.* If it had the *desire,* it would be wanting in the *power*—and if it had the *power,* that is to say perfect freedom, it would not have the *will.* Hence a thinking agent *would* not, if he could, and *could* not, if he would, create the universe. The acuteness displayed in this argument is indisputable, but subtlety and profundity are not synonymous.

"The system of Kapila is more metaphysical than that of Gotama or Kaṇāda, and deals as much more with mere subtleties, as the latter two, with the realities of psychology and physics. But Kapila has in many respects influenced the popular mind more than Gotama or Kaṇāda. The title Sāṅkhya, accorded to his system, signifies *numeral,* implying its precision in the enumeration of first principles. It stands also for discriminative knowledge, or judgement. Although plainly denying the existence of a Supreme Being, and therefore styled *Nirīśwara,* neither he nor his system has incurred the odium which had fallen to the lot of Buddha and *his* system. The Purāṇas and Tantras, those undoubted exponents of the popular mind, have brorrowed more from Kapila's, than from any other philosopher's, system. It is a common saying that there is no knowledge equal to the *Sāṅkhya,* nor any power equal to the *Yoga*[19].

"Kapila maintained that the true remedy for the perils of life is to be found in discriminative knowledge. The instruments of that knowledge are three, perception, inference, and *śabda,* which may be rendered, the word. Gotama also had acknowledged those sources of knowledge, and had added a fourth, *upamāna,* or analogy, while Kaṇāda had reduced the number to two, by contending that the *word* was implied in Inference.

"It does not clearly appear what Gotama, Kaṇāda, and Kapila meant by Śabda, or the *word.* They defined it to be the language of *unerring authority;* but was it unerring *de jure,* or simply *de facto*? If, as is more probable, they meant the former, then by *Śabda* they understood simply the authority of the *Śāstra*—ignoring that important branch of evidence for truth, which is founded on human testimony. According to the rules of those philosophers, it would in that case be impossible to prove to a Bengali, that the sepoys of the Bengal army mutinied at Meerut and Delhi.

"The *objects* of Knowledge are, according to Kapila's arrangement, twenty-five. *Prakṛti,* or nature, defined to be the equipoise of the three qualities of *excellence, foulness and darkness,* is the first, as *Puruṣa,* or soul, is the last. The intervening twenty-three are *mahat,* or intelligence, *ahaṅkāra,* or self-consciousness, the five *tanmātra,* or subtle elements, eleven organs, inclusive of the mind, and the five gross elements. Of these Prakṛti, the *rootless root,* is the first cause of all things—while Puruṣa, or soul, is a simple witness. Both are eternal : but the former, inanimate and non-sentient, is prolific and active;—the latter, intelligent and sentient, is non-productive, because free and indifferent. Prakṛti however creates *for* the soul, and in its vicinity.

"The atheistic part of Kapila's system was rectified by a mystic Ṛiṣi of the name of Patañjalī, who unmistakably inculcated the existence of Īśwara or God, and whose system has consequently been called *Seśwara,* or theistical. It must however, be confessed, in justice to Kapila, that Patanjalī does not attribute the *creation* to his Iśwara. His definition of Iśwara corresponds exactly to Kapila's idea of the soul—viz. "untouched by troubles, works, fruits, or deserts[20]." The only difference is that Pātanjala considers him to be the *guru,* or master, of "even the elder being[21],"—thereby acknowledging one spirit as supreme over the rest. The non-acknowledgment of some such Supreme Being was a glaring inconsistency in Kapila, when nevertheless he contended for the authority of the Vedas. Who could have inspired the Vedas if there were no Supreme Being?

"Patañjalī's is thoroughly a mystical system. It consists mainly of some vague rules of *yoga,* or a sort of mental and corporeal discipline, which cannot be considered as other than chimerical. His references to *Iśwara praṇidhāna,* or divine contemplation, we must accept as a pleasing witness to that religious sentiment, which God has implanted in human nature, and which is indeed the most satifactory evidence of His existence. But we cannot set much value on the rules he has laid down for Yoga. They are only *negatives*[22]. The internal and external senses must be abstracted from the out-side world. Except the vague idea involved in the expression *Iśwarą praṇidhāna,* he suggests no realities on which the mind is to exercise itself—nothing about the doings of Iśwara, or his perfections.

"The rules again for the performance of Yoga, not only relate to various kinds of mental abstraction, but embrace peculiar corporeal practices, such as the suppression of breath, the twisting of limbs, and certain prescribed postures of the body. The system is in fact a motley compound of mental and corporeal exercises. To those exercises, extraordinary physical and intellectual powers are ascribed. By abstracting the corporeal senses from their ordinary media of communication, the Yogi is endowed with *heavenly* senses.

He may not see or hear what passes around,—he may be insensible to external impressions—but he has intuition of things which his neighbours cannot see or hear. He becomes so buoyant, or rather so *sublimated* by his Yoga, that, gravitation, or, as Bhāskarācārya calls it, the *attractive power of the earth*[23], has no influence on him. He can walk and ascend in the sky, as if he were suspended under a balloon. He can, by this intuitive process, inform himself of the mysteries of astronomy and anatomy—of all things in fact that may be found in any of the different worlds. He may call to recollection the events of a previous life. He may understand the language of the brute creation. He may obtain an insight into the past and future. He may discern the thoughts of others, himself vanish at pleasure, and, if he chose to do so, enter into his neighbour's body, and thus take possession of his living skin[24]!

"Before I introduce the names of the two remaining leaders of Brāhminical philosophy, a few remarks may not be irrelevant, on the effects produced by the dogmas of the schools already named. I am not now speaking of those dogmas in detail. But, from the open avowal, or unmistakeable insinuation, that the Vedas were not competent guides to inquirers after saving truth, and from the promise of emancipation to a mere knowledge of physics or metaphysics, it will perhaps be acknowledged that their speculations did not contribute much, either to the growth of the religious sentiment, or to any real advancement in human science. When men prescribed means for attaining supreme felicity other than the teaching of what was conceded to be a revelation from God, especially when those remedies were trumpeted forth as superior to and purer than what was "heard,"—the tendency of the doctrine must have been to foster a spirit of infidelity and of self-willed philosophy, far worse, because more insidious, than that of Buddhism; at which Āgamika's indignation, the other day, was only consistent with his avowed principles as a Vedic Brāhmin. The desultory passages in which our philosophers contended for the authority of the Vedas were probably dictated by prudential motives. They were mere manifestoes of faith, unconnected with the arguments of the Sūtras, and could not be intended for the conviction of intelligent inquirers.

"The results of philosophical speculations, which, professing to include theology, ignored every consideration calculated to magnify the glory of Him, from whom the science of theology derives its title, were not unlike the effects produced elsewhere by the writings of the earlier sages of Greece. There are but few educated Indians who have not heard of Scorates and Plato. The philosophers who preceded them had in some respects speculated, like Gotama and Kapila, on the properties of matter and mind. They were also classified into schools, such as the Ionic, the Eleatic, the Pythagorean. They propounded many theories on the origin of the world, the nature of God, the properties of matter and mind. Water, air, fire, had each its claims recognized as the primary element. Some thought that the world was evolved by the disjunction or decomposition of an infinite mass, the reverse process of the Nyāya; others, like Kaṇāda, taught that it was formed by the combination of small particles.

"The effects produced by such speculations were the unsettling of men's minds, and the mere disturbance of existing institutions. Nothing was established, every thing was shaken. Sciences, distinct in themselves, were blended together. Objects, which surpassed the limits of the human understanding, were pursued with the same confidence and eagerness with which the easiest questions were investigated. The philosophers professed to have solved problems, really out of the range of our knowledge, while they threw doubts on matters which every body believed, and which none could deny without belying his nature.

"The speculations of the Nyāya and Sāṅkhya bore a striking resemblance to those of the Grecian schools, and the results were not unlike. The topics of Gotama, the categories of Kaṇāda, and the twenty-five principles of Kapila, though they included some important points of human knowledge, proved nevertheless a failure. The authors began to dogmatize in the very infancy of philosophical speculation. They drew general conclusions before they had collected facts. They worked up their own ideas, without sufficient attention to external phenomena. They delivered obscure Sūtras to exercise the ingenuity of their followers. Their disciples were reduced to the ncessity of exhausting their talents in servile commentatorial work, without the liberty of rectifying what was wrong.

"Neither did they stop to consider the true range of human capacity, and the limits which mark off things *comprehensible,* from those that are incomprehensible. While they boldly speculated on points which man can never determine by the exercise of reason, they did not deal fairly with those inquiries for which they were really competent. No wonder that their researches were unsatisfactory.

"In justice to the founders of our schools, we must confess that the opinions which they embodied in their systems had probably long been floating in the popular mind. The Buddhist defection had no doubt produced a spirit of scepticism, from which the authors of the Sūtras were not altogether free. And they perhaps laboured to give such a shape to those sceptical opinions as might be consistent with the supremacy of the Brāhminical order. Two things, they thought, were necessary for the maintenance of that supremacy; the toleration of the Vedas, and the substitution of metaphysical speculations for the too frequent performance of the Vedic ritual. Without the first, the foundation of Brāhminical supremacy would be cut away. Without the second, the Brāhminical mind would be doomed to a state of perpetual imbecility, familiar only with ceremonial observances, and utterly unable to meet the challenges put forth by sceptical heretics on the arena of controversy.

"Not that there was much essential difference in point of doctrine between the heretical and some of the orthodox schools. If Kapila could assert the non-existence of a Supreme Being, and if Kaṇāda could attribute the primal action of eternal atoms to *adṛṣṭa,* I cannot see how there could be a marked difference of opinion between them and the heretics. And so, instead of repulsing and discouraging the enemy, they armed him with stronger weapons."

Scarcely had Satyakāma read the last words when Tarkakāma came in. After the customary salutations, "Whom were you comparing," said he, "with the heretics, and what is that long file of papers about?"

Satyakāma.—"I said that I failed to see a marked difference of opinion between Kapila, Gotama, and Kaṇāda on one side, and the heretics on the other."

Tarkakāma.—"Indeed! Then does it seem to you that the distinction between those who revere, and those who despise, the Vedas, is so extremely impalpable? To my mind it involves something like down-right antagonism?"

Satyakāma.—"I have really failed to see much devotedness to the Vedas in Kapila and others. But that was not what I meant. I meant that the opinions of the one party were very much like those of the other party on the *being and attributes of God.*"

Tarkakāma.—"Then, again, the practices of the heretics, they are unclean and unholy."

Satyakāma.—"I was not talking of practice either. In practice, the Buddhists are of course anti-Brāhminical. Their deviation from Brāhminical practice is no doubt an act which you cannot easily forget. If Buddhists had only kept up your external observances, you would not have treated them as heretics."

"But what did you mean," said I, "by asserting that the teaching of Kapila has influenced the popular mind more than that of any other philosopher?"

"I meant," replied Satyakāma, "that the cosmogony of the most popular Purāṇas is founded on the basis of the Sāṅkhya. Kapila taught that *prakṛti,* or nature, produced the world *for* Puruṣa, or soul—but without any interference on the part of soul. This is the Nirīśwara or atheistic Sāṅkhya.

The Seśwara, or theistic, Sāṅkhya of Pātañjala did not correct Kapila's theory of the creation. But other popular teachers took up the ideas of Prakṛti and Puruṣa from the Sāṅkhya, and, rejecting the doctrine of Puruṣa's inactivity and unproductiveness, attributed the creation of the world to the *union* of the two eternal principles enunciated by Kapila. This was a sort of philosophical amendment on the Nirīśwara theory of Kapila,—and it originally implied nothing more than that the creation was the joint operation of God and nature, or, in other words, that God and matter were concurrent causes of all things—a doctrine not essentially different from that of the modern Naiyāyikas. But poetic imagination found something in the ideas of Prakṛti and Puruṣa, which it did not in God and Atoms—and therefore, leaving the system of the Nyāya to its own initiated adherents, allegorized the philosophical amendment on the Sāṅkhya; and mystic theology turned Prakṛti and Puruṣa into divine personifications. Prakṛṭi was held, in the philosophic conception, to be the *passive* or material cause of the world, and Puruṣa the *active* or efficient. The one was accordingly represented in popular theology as the *female,* and the other, the *male* energy; and to the union of the two was attributed the production of the universe. Hence perhaps originated the mythological representations of male and female divinities. The Puruṣa, or male creator, was identified either with Śiva or Viṣṇu, according as the mystic theologian was himself a follower of the one or the other—while Prakṛti, or the female power, was considered to be no other than the wife of either of those gods—Pārvatī, otherwise called Śakti, or Lakṣmī. And it is in this sense that Kālidāsa called Śiva and Pārvatī the *parents of the universe*[25]."

"To this compound of metaphysical and mythological ideas is owing the reverence with which the legendary accounts of Śiva's and Kṛṣṇa's sensual indulgences are received by their respective adherents. The extent to which Kapila's theory has in this way affected the popular mind can hardly be exaggerated."

"I do not understand," said Tarkakāma, "the drift of all this. But let me not interrupt your discourse."

Satyakāma resumed his paper—"When Jaimini came forward with his *Mīmāṅsā,* or decider, he was probably desirous of meditating between the controversialists that preceded him, and hoped to determine questions which had so long agitated the Brāhminical mind. He could not fail to see that neither the Vedas, nor the institutions they supported, could stand long, if the Nyāya and the Sāṅkhya were to direct the Indian intellect. Barren speculations, he thought, had been abundantly indulged. Topics, categories, and principles, had been sufficiently discussed. What was the result? They had introduced some technical terms, and taught some controversial tactics. But they gave little or no assistance in the discovery of the truth which those terms and tactics were intended to guard. The patient was supplied with scales and weights, mortar and pestle, but the medicines to be weighed and compounded were not forthcoming. Poisons and noxious weeds were alone at hand. Jaimini stepped in to give a practical turn to what was before mere speculation. He commenced his *Mīmāṅsā* with the enunciation of *Duty*[26], the only topic he had to propound."

Tarkakāma.—"Kaṇāda, too, commenced his system in the same way—did he not?"

Satyakāma.—"He did, but, as I have already remarked, after the second Sūtra you hear nothing more of Dharma until you come to the sixth chapter—and then the only ethical instruction given is on the kind of Brāhmins among whom you are to distribute alms, and the sort of men whose properties you may accept, as well as the extent to which you may attack your neighbour in self-defence. The author throws but little light on what we absolutely owe to God and man."

Satyakāma continued; "If Jaimini had carried out his proposal of considering the nature of *duty* in a truly philosophical spirit, he might have greatly contributed to the improvement of the Indian mind. The wisest philosopher of ancient Europe had undertaken to correct the wild speculations of his predecessors in a similar way, and it is universally confessed that he created an epoch in the history of the human mind. The measure of success which crowned his efforts was doubtless owing to his powerful appeals to 'what is fixed and indestructible in man, his moral convictions.' He referred men to those ethical principles which lay within the range of their own consciousness. This was certainly treating man as his maker intended he should be treated. Had Jaimini laboured in a similar way to strengthen those moral principles which the Almighty had implanted in the human mind, he might have met with a success honourable to himself and beneficial to the nation. But a servile adherence to the Vedic ritual had unfitted his mind for such speculations. Jaimini had no other idea of duty than as *an injunction of the Śruti;* and that, apart from any notion of its Inspirer, or his Will. We have seen previously how Kapila could admit the Veda as an authority, without a Supreme Intelligence to inspire it. We observe a similar anomaly in Jaimini. He urges the consideration of DUTY, without caring for any to whom it may be *due.* He contends for the authorized Veda without an *authorizer,* for a law without a *law-giver,* a revelation without GOD. He detaches the idea of duty, not only from moral convictions, but also from the sovereign will of a Supreme Governor. It has no existence save in the texts of the Mantras and Brāhmaṇas. Bent on the vindication of the Vedas, and anxious to avoid the rock on which metaphysical authors before him had struck, he felt no scruple in devastating the province of reason, and contended for the paramount authority of the Veda, without any reference to Him from whom alone such authority could be derived. He enforced the observance of Dharma as the highest duty of Brāhmaṇs. But no term in our language is liable to greater misconceptions than Dharma. While it means duty, it means also religious merit, and hence the desert derived from the doings of a previous life. In this last sense it implies the same idea as *adṛṣṭa.* Now, while enforcing Dharma in the sense of duty, or works, he has taken no precaution to magnify Him from whose will alone the idea of *duty* could receive its highest sanction. To say that Dharma signifies an injunction of the Veda, can only be intelligible in the sense of its involving the will of the AUTHOR of the Veda. Jaimini, however, has said nothing as to its AUTHOR, nor while talking of its *eternity,* as Śabda or the word, has he made mention of any co-eternal Intelligence, uttering or revealing it. His Sūtras are so vague on this point, and on the existence and providence of God, that for any thing which may be adduced to the contrary, he may be called a *second* Kapila, maintaining the authority of the Veda, without admitting His existence without whom no composition can be pronounced to be inspired. His system has accordingly been understood by many in a *nirīśwara* sense. It is expressly stigmatized by that name in the Padma Purāṇa[27]—and the *Vidwanmoda-taraṅgiṇī* attributes sheer atheistic opinions to his follower, the Mīmāṅsaka, who is made to say *there is no God the creator or preserver of the world.*[28] Some of Jaimini's eminent disciples also took his lectures in the same sense, and taught atheistic doctrines under the title of the Mīmāṅsā. Śaṅkarācārya too, whose fairness in representing the opinions of orthodox schools is above suspicion, puts the following language into the mouth of Jaimini : 'If the Veda be authority, the relation of works and fruits (or effects), thought to be received just as it may be proved from that source. That God gives the fruit (or effect), is not deducible, because various kinds of effects cannot proceed from a cause in which there is no variableness, and because [if an intelligent author were allowed] he would be subject to a charge of injustice and cruelty, by reason of inequalities in the creation. Such a theory would render the observance of ceremonies futile. Wherefore fruits (or effects) are 'from Dharma (or works) alone[29].'

"The opinions of Jaimini are still more startling than those of Kapila—for Jaimini is the great champion of Dharma and the Veda. It is impossible to imagine how Dharma or the Veda could stand without God.

"That the Mīmāṅsā of Jaimini met with no success in settling the questions so long controverted, is no marvel. Men who had learned the arts and tactics of Gotama and Kapila were not to be silenced by the *eternity of Sound*. The human mind wanted something more substantial than the offerings and oblations of the Vedas—the authority of which was contended for without an Intelligent Author. Dharma was set forth; but there was no one in the system to whom it could be *due*, if it meant duty,—nor any who could be trusted for its fruits, or reward, if it meant works.

"Vyāsa, the well-known compiler of the Vedas, accordingly put forth a second *decider*, the Uttara Mīmāṅsā, or Vedānta, in which the old pantheistic doctrine of the Upaniṣads was reproduced. Not to give an uncertain sound like Jaimini on such a cardinal point in Theology as the existence of a Supreme Intelligence, the Creator and Governor of the universe, he propounded that as the most prominent, and the only great, idea pervading his system. But if there can be no mistake as to the idea of a GOD in his doctrine, it is neutralized, if not nullified, by the identity of that God with everything else—with the whole visible world. He inculcated the existence of one *sole essence*—manifesting or producing itself in the form of the universe before our eyes. If Brahma is the efficent cause or Creator of the world, he is also its *substance*—as the gold is of the bracelet. This identity of the universe with God precludes the idea of *duty* on the part of the creature towards the Creator, quite as effectually as does Jaimini's theory.

"Tradition will have it that Jaimini was a disciple of Vyāsa. Their Sūtras certainly show that they were contemporaries, for they refer to one another by name[30].

"The very first aphorism of the Vedānta proves that its object was to substitute *Brahma* for the *Dharma*, or "Duty," of the first *Mīmāṅsā*. Of the peculiar doctrines of the Vedānta philosophy I need not now speak more in detail. The analogy between the first and the second Mīmāṅsās ought however to be noticed. One grand feature is common to them. Both profess to be founded on the Vedas, the texts of which their authors labour to expound. Both repudiate arguments and assertions unsanctioned in, or militating against, the Śruti. But here the similarity ceases. Jaimini is of opinion that the end of the Vedas is to enforce certain practices.[31] Vyāsa thinks their ultimate object is intellectual apprehension—even the knowledge of Brahma. His effort accordingly is to discover the occult signification of passages whose obvious meaning had satisfied his pupil, and to deduce a consistent theory from conflicting texts. Jaimini takes up the sense of the Veda as he finds it on the surface; Vyāsa must dive into the depths, and collect its tenets from the bottom. He will not allow that the sentences of the Vedas are to be blindly followed. Their sense must be logically arrived at. He, therefore admits deductive reasoning as a legitimate source of knowledge, so long as it is consistent with the dictates of the Vedas. He necessarily claims greater latitude in interpreting the oracles of inspiration than Jaimini thought it proper to allow to himself. Śaṅkara gives an ingenious reason for this claim; and that reason is itself a good index to the character of the second Mīmāṅsā : 'In the inquiry after Brahma, the Vedas alone are not authority, as is the case in the inquiry after Dharma, or Duty. But here deduction too, is, as far as possible, proof; because the knowledge of Brahma is to be collected by deduction, and because it concerns an existent substance. In *duties* to be performed, there is no room for deduction; hence the Vedas alone may be the proofs. That which is to be done depends on the man for its accomplishment. A duty, whether secular or Vedic, may be (at the doer's pleasure) performed, or omitted, or gone through in a modified manner. As one may go on horseback, 'on foot, or in another way, or not go at all; so it is possible for one (to fulfil opposite injunctions of the Veda) and to receive a particular utensil in a particular ceremony, and also not to receive it; to sacrifice at sunrise, and to sacrifice before sunrise. But one cannot say alternately in the same way that a substance is thus and not thus, is and is not. Therefore proofs concerning an existent substance depend on the substance itself[32]."

"The doctrine which Vyāsa brought to light from the depths of the veda is no other than the teaching of the Upaniṣads, that this universe is God—that the things made and their Maker are identical—that the human soul is one and the same with the Divine Spirit. The doctrine is held in two different ways[33]. One way is the *Pariṇāma Vāda,* which, acknowledging the reality of the visible universe, while it identifies it with God, pronounces it to be a formation or development of Himself. The other is the *Vivarta Vāda,* which, maintaining that the one eternal essence, Brahma, manifests himself in various illusory forms, denies the *real* existence of any substance which is not God, and holds the visible world to be a mere shadow, or Māyā, such as the reflections of the sun and moon in waters. Both these views are condemned in the passage, to which I have already made reference, in the Padma Purāṇa[34]. The first is said to have been inculcated for the *destruction of the world*—and the second is stigmatized as *Buddhism in disguise.*

"All ideas of duty and responsibility are openly repudiated in the Vedāntism of Vyāsa. The human soul and the Divine Spirit, being identical, how can there be an obligation on the part of the one to the other? How or whom can one mind or despise[35]? 'Here, says Śaṅkara, there is no admission of even a smell of works[36].' Good manners and good works are however declared to be *useful* for the attainment of true knowledge.

"To this rapid survey of the schools of Brāhminical philosophy, I shall only add, that the mistakes in their various theories of the creation, were owing to a notion in which they all participated, that since every human fabric before us had a pre-existent material cause—since no architect can make a house without bricks or bricks without earth—the same necessity must be supposed in the case of the universe at the creation. Waiving therefore the question *by whom,* they confined their attention to the question *of what* the world was made. The pre-existent material must be such as to preclude the recurrence of the question, *And that matter whence?* The Upaniṣads had inculcated that Brahma or God was himself the substance of which the world is made. The Nyāya and the Sāṅkhya, rightly judging that a *spirit* could not be the *matter* of a world, nor a pure intelligence the substance of a universe full of impurities, rejected that pantheistic theory, and introduced materialistic hypotheses. The Nyāya propounded a theory of atoms less than the least, and, in their disconnected state, incapable of forming any magnitude cognizable by the senses; and the Sāṅkhya found the material of the universe in Prakṛti, or inanimate and unintelligent Nature. Neither school however properly discussed the question of an intelligent efficient Cause, to whose creative power the harmony, observable in the world, might be attributed. The Vedānta, justly condemning this omission, reproduced the theory of the Upaniṣads, and maintained that Brahma was at the same time both the material (call it substantial, if you will,) and efficient cause of the universe, which it produced from itself—after the manner of a spider forming his web from his own substance. In the controversy between the three schools, we find the Nyāya and Sāṅkhya strongly inveighing against the doctrine of a spirit being the substratum of a material world, and the Vedānta equally ardent in condemning the theory of such a beautiful and harmonious world coming into existence without the agency of a Supreme Intelligence. They were all right and all wrong—right in their exposure of opposite errors, wrong in their adherence to their favourite tenets. The controversy does not appear to have been entirely fruitless in its effects on posterity. The followers of the Nyāya subsequently brought in their existing theory of atoms as the material, and God as the efficient cause of the world. The Sāṅkhya was amended, (as I have just mentioned), by the theory of Prakṛti and Puruṣa jointly creating the world—and the Vedānta modified its pantheism by the doctrine of Māyā, pronouncing the world to be a mere reflection—a shadow—an illusion."

Satyakāma having read thus far, placed his paper on the carpet, when Tarkakāma remarked that he must protest against many points asserted in the essay, which, to say the least, would admit of much discussion.

"I have no doubt of that," said the essayist. "We hoped to see you earlier. It was the eclipse that prevented your coming in time?"

"That was the reason of my being late this morning. Will you have any objection to handing me your paper?—And then let us meet, say on Thursday morning, to discuss the points you have raised. I will undertake to inform Āgamika, if you approve of my proposal." Satyakāma cheerfully gave up his paper, and we, readily assenting to what Tarkakāma suggested, parted as good friends.

You see, my learned friend, what we are about. I will not fail to communicate to you from time to time how the discussion goes on. I hope you will also send your comments on the topics contained in Satyakāma's essay.

References

1. Thus : योषा वा अग्निर्गोतम तस्या उपस्थ एव समिल्लोमानि धूमो योनिरर्च्चिर्यदन्तः करोति तेऽङ्गारा अभिनन्दा विस्फुलिङ्गास्तस्मिन्नेतस्मिन्नग्नौ देवा रेतो जुहूति तस्या आहुत्याः पुरुषः सम्भवति।

Bṛhadāraṇyaka.

2. पुरा कृतयुगे राजन् ब्राह्मणा वै तपस्विनः। अब्राह्मणस्तदा राजन् न तपस्वी कथञ्चन॥ Uttara.

3. तस्मिन् सरसि तप्यन्तं तापसं सुमहत्तपः। ददर्श राघवः श्रीमान् लम्बमानमधोमुखं॥ राघवस्तमुपागम्य तप्यन्तं तप उत्तमं। उवाच च नृप्रो वाक्यं धन्यस्तवमसि सुव्रत॥ कस्यां योन्यां तपोवृद्ध वर्त्तसे दृढविक्रम। * * * शूद्रयोन्यां प्रजातोस्मि तप उग्रं समाश्रितः॥ न मिथ्याहं वदे राम देवलोकजिगीषया॥ भाषतस्तस्य शूद्रस्य खड्गं सुरुचिरप्रभं। निष्कृष्य कोशाद्विमलं शिरश्चिच्छेद राघवः॥ सुप्रीता श्चाव्रुवन् रामं देवाः सत्य पराक्रमं॥ सुरकार्य्यमिदं देव सुकृतं ते महामते। खर्गभाक् न हि शूद्रोयं त्वत् कृते रघुनन्दन॥ * * * यदि देवा प्रसन्ना मे द्विजपुत्रः स जीवतु। * * * यस्मिन् मुहूर्त्ते काकुत्स्थ शूद्रोयं विनिपातितः। तस्मिन्मुहूर्त्ते वालोसौ जीवने समुयज्यत॥ Uttara. 75.

4. ततस्त्रेतायुगं नाम मानवानां वपुष्मतां। क्षत्रिया यत्र जायन्ते पूर्वेण तपसान्विताः॥

5. न स्वर्गो नापवर्गोवा नैवात्मा पारलौकिकः नैव वर्णाश्रमादीनां क्रियाश्च फलदायिकाः अग्निहोत्रं त्रयोवेदास्त्रिदण्डं भस्मगुण्ठनम्।

Sarvadarśana Saṅgraha.

6. शृणु देवि प्रवक्ष्यामि तामसानि यथाक्रमम्। येषां श्रवणमात्रेण पातित्यं ज्ञानिनामपि॥ प्रथमं हि मयैवोक्तं शैवंपाश्रुपतादिकम्। मच्छक्त्यावेशितैर्विप्रैः सम्प्रोक्तानि ततः परम्॥ कणादेन तु सम्प्रोक्तं शास्त्रं वैशेषिकं महत्। गौतमेन तथा न्यायं साङ्ख्यं तु कपिलेन वै॥ द्विजन्मना जैमिनिना पूर्व्वं वेदमयार्थतः। निरीश्वरेण वादेन कृतं शास्त्रं महत्तरम्॥ धिषणेन तथा प्रोक्तं चार्वाकमतिगर्हितम्। दैत्यानां नाशनार्थाय विष्णुना बुद्धरूपिणा॥ बौद्धशास्त्रमसत् प्रोक्तं नग्ननीलपटादिकम्। मायावादमसच्छास्त्रं प्रच्छन्नं वौद्धमेव च॥ मयैव कथितं देवि कलौ ब्राह्मणरूपिणा। अपार्थं श्रुतिवाक्यानां दर्शयल्लोकगर्हितम्॥ कर्मस्वरूपत्याज्यत्वमत्र च प्रतिपाद्यते। सर्वकर्मपरिभ्रंशान्नैष्कर्म्यं तत्र चोच्यते॥ परात्मजीवयोरैक्यं मयात्र प्रतिपाद्यते। ब्रह्मणोऽस्य परं रूपं निर्गुणं दर्शितं मया॥ सर्वस्य जगतोऽप्यस्य नाशनार्थं कलौ युगे। वेदार्थवन्महाशास्त्रं मायावादमवेदिकम्॥ मयैव कथितं देवि जगतां नाशकारणात्। Cited by Vijñāna Bhikṣu.

7. अक्षपादप्रणीते च काणादे साङ्ख्ययोगयोः। त्याज्यः श्रुतिविरुद्धोंऽशः श्रुत्येकशरणैर्नृभिः॥ जैमिनीये च वैयासे विरुद्धांशो न कश्चन। श्रुत्या वेदार्थविज्ञाने श्रुतिपारं गतौ हि तौ॥ Ibid.

8. Whewell's History of the Inductive Sciences.

9. अक्षेण ज्ञानविशेषेण व्यवहारेण वा पद्यते ज्ञायत इति अक्षपादः॥

10. The following text in Manu could not be a gratuitous hypothesis of an improbable contingency : योवमम्येत ते मूले हेतुशास्त्राश्रयो द्विजः। स साधुभिर्वर्हिय्ष्कार्य्यो नास्तिको वेदनिन्दकः॥

11. अथातो धर्म्मं व्याख्यास्यामः॥1॥ यतोऽभ्युदयनिःश्रेयससिद्धिः स धर्म्मः॥2॥ तद्वचनादाम्नायस्य प्रामाण्यं॥3॥ वैं सूं॥

12. Quare etiam atque etiam paullum clinare necesse est Corpora, nec plus quam minimum, ne fingere motus Obliquous videamur, et id res vera refutet.

13. अग्नेरुर्द्धज्वलनं वायोस्तिर्य्यक्पतनमणूनां मनसश्चाद्यं कर्म्मादृष्टकारितं।

14. काणादास्त्वेतेभ्य एव वाक्येभ्य ईश्वरं निमित्तकारणमनुमिमते अणुंश्च समवायिकारणं। I.1.4.

15. ततः सर्गकाले च वायवीयेष्वणुष्वदृष्टापेक्षं कर्म्मोत्पद्यते तत्कर्म्म स्वाश्रयमणुमणवन्तरेण संयुनक्ति ततोह्यणुकादिक्रमेण वायुरुत्पद्यते एवमग्निः एवमापः एवं पृथिवी एवं शरीरं सेन्द्रियमित्येवं सर्व्वमिदं जगदणुभ्यः सम्भवति अणुगतेभ्यश्च रूपादिभ्योह्यणुकादिगतानि रूपादीनि सम्भवन्ति॥

16. "Two earthly atoms, concurring by an unseen peculiar virtue, the creative will of GOD, or time, or other competent cause, constitute a double atom of earth; and, by concourse of three binary atoms, a tertiary atom is produced; and, by concourse of four triple atoms, a quaternary atom; and so on, to a gross, grosser, or grossest mass of earth : thus great earth is produced; and in like manner, great water, from aqueous atoms; great light, from luminous; and gret air, from aerial. The qualities that belong to the effect are those which

appertained to the intergrant part, or primary particle, as its material cause : and coversely, the qualities which belong to the cause are found in the effect." Colebrooke's Essays.

17. "The Nyāya is essentially theistical. Acording to them, God is personal. He is not, as it expressly asserts, mere existence, mere knowledge, mere bliss, but he is a substance, of which existence, &c. are attributes; for it is impossible to think of existence, knowledge, &c., without referring them to a subject which exists, which has knowledge, &c. He is not the supreme soul of the Vēdānta which is the whole universe, but distinguished as well from the world as from finite spirits. He is not a mere emanation from nature, as Kapila asserted, but altogether different from nature, and self-existent.He is also not, as appears to be Pātañjali's opinion, a merely omniscient being; but he is of infinite power, the Ruler of the universe, and nature could not exist independent of a God, or could exist only without order, harmony and object. And this idea is not only a fortuitous addition to the system, but one of its chief springs; for all the substances in the world, without God, remain unconnected. There may be atoms, but they do not constitute a world, they are solitary, unconnected, without any apparent difference; of themselves they have no action, produce no effects,and not even the simplest compound of two atoms can arise from them alone, much less a compound of a certain form and for certain objects, not the world in its unity, harmony, and infinite variety of forms.There may be souls, independent of a creator, but without conscience, without enjoyment, without development, and without a final end, for they are not united with mind, the instrument, by which they are connected with the world, among themselves and with the Creator. Because this connexion exists, because there is form, because individual souls have conscience, therefore it is necessary to assume a God

who by his infinite power and knowledge is the author of this connexion, of the all-pervading harmony of the world. This argument for the existence of a deity is essentially theological or based upon final causes in nature. They deity is the creator of the world as to its form, not as to its matter." Dr. Roer—Bibliotheca Indica, Vol. ix.

One cannot help wishing that the learned expositor had added definite references to the passages of Gotama or Kaṇāda on which these remarks are based.

18. ईश्वरासिद्धेः। मुक्तवद्धयोरन्यतराभावान्न तत्सिद्धिः। उभयथाप्यसत् करत्वम्॥

19. नास्ति सांख्यसमं ज्ञानं नास्ति योगसमं वलम्॥

20. कलेशकर्म्मविपाकाशयैरपरामृष्टपुरुषविशेष ईश्वरः॥

21. स एष पूर्व्वेषामपि गुरुःकालेनानवछेदात्॥

22. योगश्चित्तवृत्तिनिरोधः।

23. आकृष्टशक्तिश्च मही तया यत् स्वस्थं गुरु स्वाभिमुखं स्वशक्तया। आकृष्यते तत्पततीव भाति समे समन्तात् क्व पतत्वियं खे। Siddhānta Śiromaṇi.

24. परिणामत्रयसंयमादतीतानागतज्ञानं। शब्दार्थप्रत्ययानामितरेतराध्यासात्सङ्कर-स्तत्प्रविभागसंयमात्मसर्वभूतरुतज्ञानं। संस्कारसाक्षात् करणात्पूर्वजातिज्ञानं। प्रत्ययस्य परचित्तज्ञानं। बन्धकारणशैथिल्यात्प्रचारसंवेदनाच्चित्तस्य परशरीर-प्रवेशः। कायरूपसंयमात्तद्ग्राह्यशक्तिस्तम्भे चक्षु प्रकाशासंप्रयोगेऽन्तर्धानं। भुवनज्ञानं सूर्य्ये संयमात्। चन्द्रे ताराव्यूहज्ञानं। ध्रुवेतद्रतिज्ञानं। नाभिचक्रे कायव्यूहज्ञानं। श्रोत्राकाशयोः सम्बन्धसंयमाद्दिव्यंश्रोत्रं। कायाकाशयोः सम्बन्धसंयमाल्लघुतुलसमापत्तेः आकाशगमनं। Pāñtanjala, Sūtra III.

25. जगतः पितरौ वन्दे पार्वतीपरमेश्वरौ॥

26. अथातो धर्म्मजिज्ञासा॥1॥ र्मी सू॥

27. See the passage cited in page 48.

28. देवो न कश्चिद्भुवनस्य कर्त्ता भर्त्ता न हर्त्तापि च कश्चिदास्ते।

कर्म्मानुरूपाणि शुभाशुभानि प्राप्नोति सर्व्वो हि जनः फलानि॥1॥
वेदस्य कर्त्ता न च कश्चिदास्ते नित्याहि शब्दा रचनाहि नित्या।
प्रामाण्यमस्मिन् स्वत एव सिद्धमनादिसिद्धेः परतः कथं तत्॥2॥
आद्यन्तशून्येऽत्र जगत् प्रवाहे क्रिया भवेत् कर्म्मत एव सर्व्वदा।
कर्म्मापि पुंसां भवति क्रियातो वीजाङ्कुरन्यायतया न दोषः॥3॥
यागादिकार्य्याहुतिभागभाजो मन्त्रात्मका देवगणा निरुक्ताः।
ब्रह्मादयः कर्म्मवशेन भोगं कुर्व्वन्ति सर्व्वेऽपि चराचरस्य॥4॥

29. श्रुतिश्चेत् प्रमाणं यथायं कर्म्मफलसम्बन्धः श्रुत उपपद्यते तथा कल्पयितव्यः। * * * ईश्वरस्तु फलं ददातीत्यनुपपन्नं अविचित्रस्य कारणस्य विचित्रकार्य्यानुपपत्तेः वैषम्यनैर्घृण्यप्रसङ्गादनुष्ठानवैयर्थापत्तेश्च तस्माद्धर्मादेव फलम्। III. 2. 40.

30. Dr. Ballantyne says in a foot-note to the 1st part of his "Aphorisms of the Mīmāṅsā" – "The mention of the name of 'Bādārayaṇa' (or Vyāsa) in the Aphorisms "goes to prove that Jaimini's work, the 'Pūrva-mīmāṅsā,' was not antecedent in "time to Vyāsa, the author of the 'Uttara-mīmāṅsā'. Mr. Colebrooke's rendering 'of the terms *Pūrva* and Uttara by 'prior' and 'later' (see Essays, vol. 1, pp. 227, "and 295), would seem to have led Dr. Ritter to suppose that Jaimini's system was "the earlier in point of time. He says, (at p. 376, Vol. IV of his History of Philosophy, – Morrison's version) that "according to Colebrooke, the adherents of this "School may be divided into the earlier and the later," – and then he goes on to "speak of "the older and genuine Vedānta:" – but in fact the terms 'prior' and "'later' refer to the divisions of the Veda which Jaimini and Vyāsa respectively "expound, the latter confining himself to the Upaniṣads, or theological sections, "which stand last in order."

Colebrooke, and after him Ritter, were not wrong in considering Jaimini's as the earlier work. At any rate it is certain that Vyāsa speaks frequently of Jaimini *by name.* (See Vedānta Sūtras I. 2. 28, 31.I. 3. 31.I. 4. 18. III. 2. 40. III, 4. 2. IV. 3. 12). The master and pupil must have revised their works after seeing one another's productions. From the nature of the subject, Jaimini's would appear to be the "prior" work.

31. आम्नायस्य क्रियार्थत्वादानर्थक्यमतदर्थानां॥ जैं. सू.॥ II. 1.

32. न धर्म्मजिज्ञासायामिव श्रुत्यादय एव प्रमाणं ब्रह्मजिज्ञासायां किन्तु श्रुत्यादयोऽनुभवादयश्च यथा सम्भवमिह प्रमाणं अनुभवावसानत्वात् भूतवस्तुविषयत्वाच्च ब्रह्मविज्ञानस्य कर्त्तव्ये हि विषये नानुभवापेक्षास्तीति श्रुत्यादीनामेव प्रामाण्यं स्यात् पुरुषाधीनात्मलाभत्वाच्च कर्त्तव्यस्य कर्त्तुमकर्त्तुमन्यथा वा कर्त्तुं शक्यं लौकिकं वैदिकञ्च कर्म्म यथा अश्वेन गच्छति पद्भ्यामन्यथा वा न गच्छतीति तथा अतिरात्रे षोडशिनं गृह्णाति, नातिरात्रे षोडशिनं गृह्णाति, उदिते जुहोति, अनुदिते जुहोति नतुवस्तवेवं नैवमस्तिनास्तीति वा विकल्पते एवम्भूतवस्तुविषयाणां प्रामाण्यं वस्तुतन्त्रम्॥

33. This is well expressed by Viśwanātha, the commentator on the Nyāya.

वदन्ति तथाहि ब्रह्मैव नामरूपप्रपञ्चभेदेन विपरिणमते मृत्तिकेवोदञ्चनादिभावेन अतएव प्राकृतरूपस्य सत्त्वस्यापरित्यागः प्रपञ्चेषु उदञ्चनादाविव मृत्तिकात्वस्येति परिणमवादः ब्रह्मैव चानाद्यनिर्व्वचनीयाऽविद्यावशान्नानारूपेण विवर्त्तते मुखमिव तत्तजलाद्यालम्बनभेदादिति विवर्त्तवादः॥

34. See the passage cited in pages 48 and 49.

35. केन कमभिवदेत् केन कं मन्वीत॥

36. तस्मात् ज्ञानमेकं मुक्त्वा क्रियाया गन्धमात्रस्याप्यनुप्रवेश इह नोपपद्यते॥

DIALOGUE III

FROM THE SAME TO THE SAME

I told you in my last that Tarkakāma took away the discourse which Satyakāma had read. He came to the appointed place of meeting on Thursday, accompanied by Āgamika. After some conversation on the events of the day, "I have read your paper, Satyakāma," said he, "but cannot report that it has convinced me of the correctness of your strictures. You evidently wrote it in a spirit of hostility to all the orthodox schools : which again you endeavoured to embroil in mutual disputes. You have studied to damage the reputations of their founders and leaders. Well, I do not regret your attempt,—and I do not charge you with artifice or unfairness; but I am confident that the honoured names of Gotama, Kaṇāda, and the other great characters will outlive your attack :—and that their memories will be all the dearer to posterity for this onslaught. They will shine the more brilliantly for all you have said against them; jsut as a mirror[1], to use the poet's illustration, becomes the clearer by the very action of the dusty hand that rudely brushes it. Two simple points, which you seem to have ignored, might have explained all the difficulties that you have found in the Sūtras, and dissolved the evil phantoms that your imagination has conjured up. You seem to have forgot that our philosophers were devising remedies by which the necessity of future briths might be obviated, and the bonds of Dharma, or works, be broken. And you appear to have ignored the fact that, since *nothing can be produced out of nothing,* our Ṛṣis were constrained to look for a material cause of the universe in their theory of the creation. The Nyāya pronounced pre-existing atoms to be the materials of which the world was made – the Sāṅkhya would not acquiesce in the theory of an infinite number of eternal entities of diverse kinds, and therefore declared Prakṛti or nature to be itself the cause of all things – while the Vedānta magnified the ineffable glory of God, by teaching that He was the sole cause – the maker and substance of the universe. There is in all this nothing that should provoke criticism, much less hostile declamations; and there is certainly a great deal to call forth our admiration."

Satyakāma. – "Confining myself to your *first* point for the present, may I ask you what you mean by the bonds of works, and the necessity of future births."

Tarkakāma. – "The necessity of future births arises from the events of previous briths, which were also the causes of our bonds – the bonds of works. Every man that you see in the world is by birth in a state of bondage. He *must* satisfy the requirements of adṛṣṭa. He *must* undergo those troubles which are the necessary consequences – the legitimate fruits – of his previous works. His deeds in the present life, again, lay the foundation of future sufferings in his next scene of existence. Philosophers have therefore merciully come forward to rescue them from that bondage. There is nothing in all this which it can be difficult to appreciate."

Satyakāma. – "You are assuming that we have all passed through a previous state of existence before the present life."

Tarkakāma. – "I am not assuming it without high authority. Have not all the schools consentiently held that doctrine as proved? And does not the experience of the world bear testimony to it?"

Satyakāma. – "I have not observed any such testimony in nature – nor have I noticed any reasoning on the subject which may not be called *Sādhya-sama,* or identical with the thing to be proved – in foreign words, a *petitio principii.*"

Tarkakāma. – "Do you mean to assert that the doctrine of the soul's pre-existence is a gratuitous tenet, for which our philsophers had no authority, and of which they adduced no proofs?"

Satyakāma. – "They certainly had no right to receive or assert such a doctrine. The proofs they adduced were no better than arbitrary assumptions. That there are reasons for not considering this as the only scene of our existence, I am far from denying. Eternity will open before us as soon as we escape from the bonds of time and sense. But no one can prove that we existed in a previous state before we were born : much less ought such a theory to be made the basis of those startling conclusions which our philosophers have drawn from it."

Tarkakāma. – "Do not the inequalities in birth, position, tastes, and enjoyments, observable in human life, prove such a prior existence? Some are very happy, namely the gods and other residents of the upper regions; some are very miserable, namely, the brute creation; while others have a middle state between the two, such as men. Śaṅkarācārya reasons most justly in attributing these inequalities of birth to works performed in a prior state, and requited in this.

"The incidents of life, again," continued Tarkakāma, "are so irregularly diversified, that the only way to reconcile them with rule or order, is by supposing them to be the consequences of past works. In the same family you will often find one member clever and sharp, a second dull and stupid, a third self-denying and virtuous, a fourth sensual and voluptuous, a fifth in the enjoyment of wealth and plenty, a sixth in penury and misery. Do not such facts prove a by-gone state of life, in which certain habits were formed, by which tastes and dispositions are influenced in this world, and certain merit or demerit acquired, regulating the present distribution of pleasure and pain, – especially when you often see the wicked prospering and the righteous suffering?"

Satyakāma.—"They do not prove your theory. As to Śaṅkarācārya's argument, we shall presently examine it. You will then see in what different tones he speaks in two different places. And with reference to the inequalities of birth to which you have alluded, they do not necessarily imply a disproportion of happiness or misery. How often do we find the high-born man in greater misery than the low-born! A Persian poet has well said, 'While a poor man has only to seek a morsel for himself, and when he has got that, sleeps as soundly as if he were an emperor, a prince is troubled with the concerns of a whole world.'

"As to diversities in intellectual and moral habits, they do not require to be accounted for by the supposition of a previous life. Man is in a state of probation. The development of his character depends on the way in which he makes use of his *opportunities,* and profits by his external circumstances.

"Diversities of enjoyments and sufferings, again, may in a great measure be traced to virtuous or vicious conduct in *this very world.* Virtue, as such, naturally procures considerable advantages to the virtuous, and vice as such, naturally occasions great inconvenience and even misery to the vicious, in very many instances. The immediate effects of virtue and vice upon the mind and temper are to be mentioned as instances of it. Vice, as such, is naturally attended with some sort of uneasiness, and, not uncommonly with great disturbance and apprehension[2]. Our success in life also is much dependent on ourselves. You will frequently find that the man whom the world calls fortunate, has made a better use of his time, his talents, and his abilities, than he who has proved unfortunate. The fortunate man has perhaps been industrious, attentive, honest, courteous; the unfortunate, on the contrary, may have been inactive, lazy, imprudent, dishonest, ill-mannered, or rash. Public-honors too, and advantages, are the natural consequences, are sometimes at least the consequences in fact, of virtuous actions; of eminent justice, fidelity, charity, love to our counry, considered in the view of being virtuous. And sometimes even death itself, often infamy, and external inconveniences, are the public consequences of vice as vice[3].'

"The facts to which you have adverted, Tarkakāma, in order to prove a prior existence, may be, in a great measure, accounted for by differences observable in the world itself, in the actions of men.

"It is not necessary for any to blame Destiny, after the fashion of the *ignorant*[4], for what his *own* acts bring on himself; neither is it philosophical to seek an *unseen* cause in 'adṛṣṭa,' where there are visible causes before you to explain the mystery. I do not of course mean that all the inequalities in life can be accounted for in this way. I admit that you will find a large residuum which, after your have solved the far greater portion in the manner suggested above, will still continue a difficulty in one's way."

Tarkakāma.—"I admire your candour. I was going to say you could not in that ingenious way explain away all the inequalities in the world. Well, how can you account for the residuum without admitting a previous life?"

Satyakāma.—"That, Tarkakāma, only shows that we cannot consider this as our only stage of life. It forces us to look forward to another. It does not however necessarily force our eyes *backward* to a previous state."

Tarkakāma.—"So you wish to get rid of what you call an arbitrary assumption of our Ṛṣis, in order to make room for *an arbitrary assumption* of your own?"

Satyakāma.—"I am not contending for any arbitrary assumption. But I can safely say that the doctrine of a prior existence is the very worst way of accounting for inequalities in life. You say they are the results of peculiar habits and works in a previous scene of existence. But you thereby only remove your difficulty one single step, for the question will recur, *Whence those peculiar habits and works,*—and,

Whence the inequalities *in that life?* You will say with your philosophers that those inequalities were owing to the acts of *another* previous life. You will then refer to *another still older,* and so on, until you are forced to conclude, as indeed the Ṛṣis before you did conclude, that the world had in reality no beginning! Thus your theory involves difficulties far greater than any it is intended to remove. Your remedy proves worse than the disease. One obvious disadvantage is the false security on the one hand, and the despair on the other, which it is calculated to produce. And it precludes that wholesome discipline which hopes and fears of a *future retribution* must exercise on the mind."

Tarkakāma.—"How can our theory preclude the wholesome discipline of hopes and fears? We do not say that man has no control over his future lot. Why should there be any false security or despair? We only account for his present *condition* in life by a reference to his prior existence, and to *adṛṣṭa.* He has still the power of self-determination, and there is every room for hope and fear. Indeed the actual experience of the effects of his previous acts will add strength to his hopes and fears, and so deter him from repeating wicked deeds. He will *feel* that there is such a thing as retribution in the world."

Satyakāma.—"But you do say—I mean philosophers and authors of Śāstras, have said in several places—that no one can resist the power of Destiny, or adṛṣṭa, which not only determines the conditions, but also guides the actions, of men, and imparts the motions under which the body and its members perform their functions[5]. The condition itself often influences actions, and affects the interests of futurity. Eminent sages have also frequently excused heinous acts of their own perpetration, by laying them at the door of *daiva* or *adṛṣṭa*—that is to say, Destiny[6]. Some have also extenuated offences committed by their neighbours by attributing them to the same influence[7]; which others, again, have held as a good reason for not putting forth any efforts for the improvement of their circumstances[8]. These views of your doctrine can exercise no good moral influence on men—nor give rise to salutary motives. Why then introduce a gratuitous theory so replete with evil?"

"Of such inequalities as may not be explained by men's virtuous or vicious conduct in this very world, a simpler, and far more satisfactory, account may be found in the doctrine of a *future* state of final rewards and punishments; for which the present is a mere preparation. Are you puzzled on seeing honest men suffering in the world without any fault of their own? Do not aggravate the infliction by telling them that it is the consequence of vicious acts done in a former life, and for which there is now no remedy! The suffering may be intended as a discipline, only to enhance their future happiness. Have you not heard, Tarkakāma, of king Hariścandra? The story may be a mere fable, but it beautifully illustrates what I mean. You see there a good man and a great man reduced to a condition, the very recollection of which floods your eyes with tears. Must you say he suffered for his previous crimes? Do you not see what the end was? How it compensated for his past sufferings! Think you that the good king regretted what he had undergone when he had received the fruition of the glory that awaited him? He did not. Thus it is that 'virtue is often militant here; and various untoward accidents contribute to its being often overborne : but it may combat with greater advantage hereafter, and prevail completely, and enjoy its consequent rewards in some 'future states. Neglected as it is, perhaps unknown, perhaps despised and oppressed here, there may be scenes in eternity, lasting enough, and in every other way adapted to afford it a sufficient sphere of action; and a sufficient sphere for the natural consequences of it to follow in fact[9].'"

Tarkakāma was for a moment silent, when Āgamika interposed a remark—"What you say, my long-tried friend, suggests a most important consideration. That I will not fail to give to the question. But is it not true, (I have at least heard so from many friends learned in Mohammedan lore,) that the most eminent philosophers among the Yavanas held the doctrine of the soul's pre-existence? Is it fair, is it modest, so summarily to condemn a doctrine that has approved itself to the reasons and consciences of so many races of men?"

Satyakāma. – "Had that doctrine not been productive of so much undeniable mischief in our country, I could not have denounced it in strong terms. It is truth which constrains me to say that this is a question on which philosophers had for a long time groped in the dark, even in Europe. That the soul was immaterial, and distinct from the body which it animated, they understood easily enough; not indeed from the necessity of thinking charitably of those who performed pious offices toward the dead, as Gotama would have it[10], but from its peculiar independent functions, of which each individual was conscious in himself. That the soul was unaffected by those causes of decay to which the body was subject, they also comprehended. But, like our own ancestors, they had (apparently, without discussion) adopted a maxim, that whatever had a beginning must have an end. Those who could not allow that the soul died with the body were driven to the conclusion that it had no beginning. Until nearly two thousand years ago, when *life and immortality were brought to light by One who spake as never man spake,* (of whose teaching I shall embrace an opportunity on some future day of saying something), men could not understand that the soul could be immortal without being also uncreated. They accordingly pronounced it to be eternal. They stopped not to reflect on the consequences involved in such a theory; they did not consider that it robbed the Supreme Being of some of His most glorious titles which even their own poets had accorded to Him, in common with other writers of more than human authority. If all souls were eternal, then there could be no *Creator* of souls, no *Father of spirits.* As most of those philosophers also held that matter, too, was eternal in some shape or other, their doctrine obviously involved the denial of a real creation, and consequently of a Creator."

"You refer to the philosophers of Greece. Your Mohammadan friends are right in saying they held the theory of the soul's pre-existence. We should however consider how they deduced it, before attaching much value to their conclusion.

"Among the arguments which Plato uses in his celebrated dialogue on the Immortality of the Soul, one is the deduction of its eternity from its past and future existence. Its past existence is deduced from his well-known dogma, that all learning is reminiscence. He proves this point by assuming that a spectator often associates a truth he had never before soon or perceived with some fact just presented to his senses. From this mental association, which is carefully explained in another dialogue (the 'Meno'), as well as from his theory of general ideas, the philosopher deduced his maxim, that knowledge is nothing but reminiscence;—which of course involved the pre-existence of the soul."

Tarkakāma.—"Plato's argument is almost identical with Gotama's, and that is what I meant by the experience of the world. I wonder how you can still resist the doctrine. You may account for the unequal distribution of pleasure and pain, by the supposition of a future state of retribution, but how can you account for peculiar capacities and habits in men equally circumstanced. Gotama's argument is unanswerable."

Satyakāma.—"Is it so? Will you state the argument in detail."

Tarkakāma.—"Gotama, you must remember, was demonstrating the eternity of the soul, and so he proves that it never began, nor shall ever cease, to be. The former point, from which the latter followed as a matter of course, he thus attempts to make good. He says (III. 19.) 'Because of the manifestation of joy, fear, and grief, in him that is born, from the memory of previous habits.' The commentator expounds the meaning of the Sūtra in the following words : 'The rise of joy and other feelings in the infant that is born, while the occasions of those feelings are yet not apprehended in this birth, can only be accounted for by his recollection of previous apprehensions. Thus the successive prior stages of the present soul being shown, it is proved to be without beginning. And what is without beginning can have no destruction. Thus is its eternity demonstrated[11].' Can any one conceive a possible objection to this argument?"

Satyakāma.—"It seems Gotama himself could conceive an objection to his argument; at least he notices one in the next Sūtra.—'The changes (on the child's face) may 'be like the opening and closing of the lotus.' (III. 20.) The commentator thus expounds the objection. 'Joy and other feelings in the infant are inferred from changes 'on his face. They may be produdced by some especial 'unseen virtue, as in the opening and closing of the lotus'[15]."

Tarkakāma.—"But Gotama furnished a ready reply to the objection. 'No! for causes of changes in things 'composed of the five elements, are heat, cold, rain, 'season[16]."

Satyakāma.—"The reply is not satisfactory. The objection is neither worded nor expounded as clearly as it might have been. It may fairly be thus paraphrased. Gotama says that certain internal emotions are indicated by changes on the child's face, and that those emotions are proofs of a prior existence. The objector does not disallow the premises, but he disputes the conclusion. He admits the existence of the internal emotions, but he contends they are occasioned by external impressions *after* birth. He contends that the *first* instances of joy and fear are owing to outward causes surrounding the child. Of the changes on its face, those emotions may be the *proximate* causes; but the external impressions, by which the emotions themselves were excited, must be recognized as their *remote* causes. The changes on the child's face may accordingly be compared with the expansion and contraction of the lotus. You say the expansion and contraction of the lotus are caused by heat and moisture. Granted. But it would be more accurate to say that the heat and moisture are neither their *immediate,* nor *only* causes; that the expansion and contraction have the flower's *own organism* as their proximate cause, and that the external heat and moisture are *remoter* causes acting on that organism : for without the intervention of that organism the flower would no more be affected by the atmosphere, than the wax or light-wood lotus which your children value so much as a toy. The analogy between the child and the lotus, therefore, stands good. External circumstances act on something internal in each case, and *thereby* occasion certain visible changes. That the organism is in the one case only physical, in the other both physical and intellectual, does not affect the analogy.

"It cannot therefore be said, in reply, that the changes on the child's face are independent of external causes. That would be a begging of the question. The child is exposed to certain outside impressions from its very birth, and these impressions excite certain mental emotions which are indicated by change of countenance. The case of the lotus is an example in point. The child has a mental constitution by virtue of which external circumstances are able to call into action certain internal feelings. The lotus, too, has an organism of its own, by virtue of which the action of the atmosphere occasions the expansion and contraction of the flower. In both cases certain effects are produced by virtue of internal organisms, through the action of external impressions. The child may be *afterwards* capable of pure internal impulses, not depending immediately on the external. But you cannot prove that, previously to the reception of its *first* impressions from without, any of its internal capacities are in active exercise; much less that such exercise is conscious and deliberate. The indications of joy and sorrow on the infant's face do not, therefore, demonstrate the fact of previous habits acquired in a prior state of life, but are simly proofs of the *capacities,* in the mental constitution of human nature, for certain emotions which are *put in exercise* by impressions from without; and the analogy of the lotus stands good, inasmuch as the lotus has also an organism in its tender stalk, by virtue of which its flowers open and shut when acted upon by heat and moisture."

Tarkakāma. – "I am not convinced that Gotama's argument is invalid. But that is not his only argument. He has another : – 'From the desire for milk, after dying, caused by the habit of taking food.' (III. 22.) The commentator gives the following scholium on it – 'After 'dying, or rather having died, means being just born, 'after the dissolution of the previous body[14].'"

Satyakāma. – "Neither is this argument above the possibility of asault in the author's estimation, for he anticipates an objection. 'The child's spontaneous approach 'to the mother's breast may be like that of the iron to 'the magnet.'" (III. 23).

Tarkakāma. – "That only shows the author's candour. But see how he repels the objection. 'No! because there is no motive, elsewhere.' (III. 24). That is to say, as the scholiast renders it, 'the child is moved only to suck the milk. The rule does not hold good in the other case. Why? Because there is in reality no motive in the other 'case *i.e.,* in that of the iron. Motive is deduced from effort, not from a mere act[15]. Hence the argument is not vitiated.'"

Satyakāma. – "I do not deny that the child, being endowed with intellectual and active powers, is capable of an effort of which inanimate iron is incapable. But this fact does not prove the soul's pre-existence. But as Gotama has another argument yet, let us hear it before we discuss the reasons he has adduced for and against his doctrine."

Tarkakāma. – "'From not seeing any one, born without desire[16].' The innate affections of human nature are proofs of a previous state of existence, in which their germs were planted."

Satyakāma. – "The author is again candid enough to anticipate an objection. Its birth is like the production of a substance with inherent qualities[17].'"

Tarkakāma. – "He refutes it too. 'No! for desire and other affections are occasioned by intelligence,' *i.e.,* deliberation[18]."

Satyakāma. – "I say again the answer is not to the point. With reference to the second argument, facts do not warrant the conclusion that the infant, previous to afterbirth experience, is moved, or makes a deliberate effort, to approach the breast. All that you can say is, that when the breast is applied, it sucks. But it will suck any thing that is presented to it. It sucks its own fingers. The fact only proves that it has a capacity and an inclination for sucking, just as the magnet has the capacity of attracting iron. If the infant *afterwards* indicates a discriminative knowledge on the subject, *that* is owing to *its experience after birth.* The three arguments of Gotama may be compressed into one. He contends that men exhibit from their infancy certain habits and inclinations, passions and affections, which cannot be accounted for without assuming a previous state of existence; and, as that state, again, must, for the same reasons, have another antecedent to it, you must carry the argument successively backwards, and pronounce the soul to be eternal. Is not this his argument?"

Tarkakāma. – "I do not object to your construction of his argument; but what can you say in reply?

Satyakāma. – "I can say something by quoting one of his own texts, by opposing Gotama to Gotama. He had asserted in his definition of the soul, that 'Desire, Aversion, Volition, Pleasure, Pain, and Knowledge, are its characteristics. (i. 10).[20]' If then the infant exhibits external indications of those mental operations, *the phenomenon simply proves the existence of a soul in him.* Those characteristics have nothing to do with the soul's pre-existence. The examples cited in the objections, are not fairly met by his answers. It is a characteristic of the soul to think, feel, desire, shun; to desire that which imparts pleasure, to avoid that which communicates pain. If the infant spontaneously takes to sucking, it is because that is an effort natural and agreeable to him; and indeed every effort is then agreeable, which affords exercise to his physical or mental capacities, without actually imparting pain. There is not the slightest necessity for assuming that his involuntary motions are the results of habits acquired in a previous state of existence, or that they are reminiscences of past associations."

Tarkakāma.—"The argument is not merely that the infant evinces desire and inclination, but that he evinces inclination for *particular* objects, as if known by previous experience to be agreeable to the taste; and hence Gotama contends that it is proof of a previous life."

Satyakāma.—"Here the premise is incorrect. It is not true in fact that the infant evinces a taste for particular objects, *prior to experience in his existing state.* It makes an effort to suck whatever is presented to its mouth. Among some nations it is usual to give the oil of *Reṇḍi* (castor-oil) as the first food for an infant when it is born—and it takes the oil as promptly as it does milk. And it would suck either liquid with the same readiness, even if it contained arsenic. You cannot say it had found oil and arsenic to be so agreeable in a prvious life.

"These involuntary efforts in the infant are exactly what you would expect from human nature. You need not form a theory of pre-existence in order to account for them. Since light and heat are characteristics of fire, if you make a piece of iron red-hot, it will naturally both shine and burn. Would you say it is owing to habits of previous state? Of course you would not. You would simply recognize the natural property of fire already ascertained. So, when the child only manifests the characteristics of the soul that animates his body, you have simply to accept the fact as a verification of your own aphorism on the nature of that soul. You have no room for bringing in a new theory. You cannot do so without stultifying your own *Sūtra.* The child does what you would expect from his soul. If the case were otherwise, if the child gave no more indication of internal sensibility than a wooden doll, you should have to revise your aphorism. You have no phenomenon before you, but what is fully explained by your previous premises. Your argument is redundant, and your theory of a pre-existence unnecessary."

Tarkakāma.—"Even if Gotama's argument were inconsistent with his definition of the soul, still how would you account for such natural dispositions in the infant? Who taught him the way to take food at an age when he is incapable of learning from those around him?"

Satyakāma.—"The natural dispositions of the infant are to be accounted for in the same way in which you might account for the natural properties of other substances. Who gave the *champā* its fragrance, the lion its courage, and the sun its refulgence? Answer my query, and, I warrant you, the same answer will explain who taught the way of taking food at an age when the infant is incapable of communicating with his neighbours. The same great Being, Tarkakāma, is the giver and the teacher in both instances. His Maker instructed the infant to desire food, to take it in the way best suited to his state, to give forth signs of pain when he misses his sustenance. Do not stare at what I say, as if it were something uncommon. The natural law which instructs and guides the infant governs the whole of the animal and vegetable creation. The same fiat which bestowed on the peacock its beauty, the swan its gloss, the *kokila* its voice, the *chakwa* its sentiment, the elephant its strength, conferred on man the nature he exhibits even in infancy. The babe is taught how to suck, by Him who instructs the bird how to build her nest when the comforts of her offspring require it; who commands the *mālatī* to entwine itself round the tree that supports it, the lotus to open by day, and the *kumuda* by night; who admonishes trees, herbs, and creepers to germinate in the way best suited to their organism, and animals to seek the nourishment best adapted for their constitution."

Tarkakāma.—"What you say may be a fine theory in itself. But it does not *disprove* Gotama's doctrine. The phenomena you have mentioned may be accounted for equally well on the supposition of a previous existence."

Satyakāma.—"Neither do the reasons adduced by Gotama *prove his theory;* which indeed reaches much further back than simple pre-existence. He contends that the various stages of previous lives may in like manner be proved from those immediately succeeding them, and thus the soul demonstrated to be uncreated and eternal, and that not merely in a spiritual state, unconnected with body and mind, but in an embodied and intellectual state. See then the length to which the argument carries you. If man has existed without beginning, sucked milk, taken food, there must have been vegetable life, co-existent with him. How could he otherwise be sustained? Even if he lived on nothing but animal matter, still the animals which supplied that matter must have required vegetable sustenance. And if animal and vegetable life be uncreated and eternal, so must inorganic matter be too; for it is from inorganic matter that vegetables draw the sap which sustains them, the gas which supports them, and the heat which vivifies them. If you allow the validity of Gotama's argument for the pre-existence of the soul, and extend it, as he has done, to times without beginning, you must then maintain the eternity of every thing around you; and that, in an atomic state, but collected in masses. And if the universe be uncreated and eternal in a perfect state of development, how can you, on your own theory, contend for the existence of God? Since the theory of a previous life, and the principles of Gotama drive us to this extremity, how can you say that the supposition of a pre-existence explains the facts before us, *equally well* with that for which I am contending?"

Tarkakāma.—"But granting that the argument, based on the infant's spontaneous efforts, is inconclusive, because there is nothing to preclude the supposition of their being natural to him; how can you, still, get over the *moral* argument, or withhold your assent from the doctrine, when you consider the marked inequalities in the circumstances and positions of men? How can you reconcile with the justice and equity of God the fact of some men being in the enjoyment of honor and wealth, others pining in penury and misery,—except by considering their various conditions as the consequences of their own works in a past world? Human happiness or misery, you said, may be traced to virtuous or vicious conduct in this very world. I do not deny it may be so in some cases—but surely you do not mean to stigmatize every poor man as a monster of wickedness. To vindicate the justice of God, and to save the credit of men, it is necessary to look to the events of a prior existence for an explanation of the difficulty, especially when you consider that many are born with diesase and infirmity which they could not have brought on themselves by their own acts, but which nevertheless render them miserable for life."

Satyakāma.—"That a portion of our happiness or misery is owing to our actions in this life, you seem to admit.

"So far then we are agreed. As regards differences in race and birth they are not, (I have already said,) necessarily connected with corresponding diversities in enjoyment or suffering. The elephant is of a different species from the lion, the peacock from the deer, the bull from the horse. Does it necessarily follow that the deer is less happy than the lion, or the horse than the elephant? By no means. Is it then impossible to vindicate the justice of God without supposing a prior existence regulating the differences in their species? Each may be amply endowed in its own way, and each bears testimony to the wisdom and beneficence of the Creator. The same may be predicated of races of mankind. There is a variety in the creation which, while it indicates the inexhaustible riches of the Divine intelligence and goodness, does not for a moment suggest a want of equity in the Author of our being. No one had an antecedent right to be created in a particular manner, or of a particular race. He that was free to create in His own way, has so performed his work that there should be symmetry, variety, and happiness, in the universe. And that there is. The smallest insect that crawls on the ground contributes to the beauty and harmony of the world in its own way, as the lofty elephant does in *his* way. How could there be order if there were no variety? Is that symmetry, or that harmony worthy of the name, where there is no plurality of different, but proportional, substances? Inequalities are in themselves no proofs of injustice, or culpable partiality.

"I will not deny, what I have already admitted, that there is a large residuum of worldly inequalities which may still remain to be accounted for. That account, however, is found more satisfactorily in my theory than in yours–I mean, in the supposition that this is a state of probation and trial preparatory to another and a better world. Probation itself demands difficulties. The gold cannot be tried without being placed in the heated crucible. The child is not trained for the purposes of life without passing through the ordeal of a school. This world may be to us a preparation for a better. There is nothing in this idea which is derogatory to the justice and goodness of God."

Tarkakāma.–"You called the doctrine of a prior state an arbitrary assumption. Is your doctrine of probation and trial, preparatory to a better world yet to come, any thing better? You cannot prove it either."

Satyakāma.–"Storng presumptive evidence you know is proof in cases which do not admit of mathematical demonstration. The theory I propose accounts for our difficulties, without giving the lie to our moral convictions. Your theory, on the contrary, is nullified by its own vagueness, and, instead of justifying the ways of God, has a tendency to cast doubts on His very existence. Witness the argument of Śaṅkarācārya; 'What is the want 'of equity (on the part of God)? He makes a distinction between souls, high, low, middling. Hence 'exhibiting partiality and prejudice, and other infirmities, 'he might be proved to be like ourselves, and therefore 'no God[21]." The question is accordingly one of vital importance in theology. Śaṅkara, I may say, has given two solutions of the problem which are apparently inconsistent with each other. In one place, at least, he strongly inveighs against the way in which you propose to account for it.

'If it be said,' he continues, 'that the above distinctions 'are owing to the past works of the souls themselves, and 'that consequently there can be nothing wrong in the 'existing inequalities; the solution will not stand : for 'works being motions, and God the mover, there will 'still be the fault of [cause and effect resting on] reciprocal support [as in a vicious circle]. If you say 'there has been a series of works without a beginning, 'then, as in the present world, so also in past states, the 'same fault must be found of reciprocal support, [each 'cause producing, and also being produced by, its own 'effect] and it will be after the manner of a troop of blind 'leading the blind[22].'

"I do not cite Śaṅkara approvingly, but I wish simply to remind you that he does not here countenance your theory of past works justifying present distinctions. It will drive us from one world to a second, from that again to its predecessor, until, as in Gotama's theory, you are compelled to hold the eternity of the world before us."

Āgamika. – "But if so many philosophers of the west and east held the doctrine of the soul's pre-existence, is it, I ask again, modest to treat it as a mischievous thoery?"

Satyakāma. – "I have myself only said that our philosophers have drawn from it the most startling conclusions. It would hardly be worth one's while to combat the doctrine, if it were held as a mere opinion, and if no inferences, subversive of the interests of religion and morality, were deduced from it.

"In Plato's system the theory of the soul's pre-existence holds a very subordinate place. It is not pushed to any extreme conclusion, destructive of religion or morals. The doctrine appears to have had a feeble hold on his mind. In the arguments brought forward there is nothing which corresponds to the force usually attached to Socratic sayings. The immortality of the soul is his great theme. Its past existence is insisted on for the purpose of demonstrating that theme. As your Arabic and Persian scholars constantly parade the name of Plato in connection with the doctrine under consideration, let us, once more, consider that philosopher's reasoning.

"Plato's opinion of the soul's pre-existence appears somewhat abruptly in the conversation which Socrates last held with his friends before his death. The philosopher was there joyously contemplating the happiness that awaited his submission to the cruel sentence of his countrymen. He did not grieve at a prospect which to his friends appeared so melancholy, but looked without the least concern for the fatal cup preparing for him. As a reason for this indifference, he stated his belief that he was going to a happier world, where he should find a better community. The scepticism of his friends leads him to a philosophical discussion of his hope of immortality. He assumes as an axiom, what his friends admit without difficulty, that in all things which are produced, the process is no otherwise than opposites issuing out of opposites. So that when a thing becomes greater, it is from having been less. Life proceeds out of death, and death out of life. Thus he concludes that souls exist in Hades after death. The pre-existence of the soul is involved in this reasoning, which is founded on the gratuitous assumption, so frequently observed in our Indian Śāstras—that whatsoever, is born must necessarily die, and whatsoever dies must as necessarily be generated again[23]. Birth succeeds death, no less than death birth. The soul when it is born is only re-manifested after a previous death—and consequently after an anterior existence. In the course of the above reasoning, he refers to an old tradition, that souls, dying, go to Hades, and, being born, return from the dead. That this old saying had influenced Plato more than any reasons by which the doctrine itself was supported, would appear from the assertion of Aristotle that the ancient philosophers were afraid of nothing more than this one thing, that any thing should be made out of nothing pre-existent. To say that the soul was created would of course invovle the dreaded predicament.

"Then again Plato's opinion of knowledge being mere

reminiscence, necessitated the doctrine of the soul's pre-existence. Socrates calls up an untaught slave boy, and, by a string of leading questions, makes him enunciate the rule for the duplication of a square. I am not sure that any catechizer, short of a Socrates, would succeed in drawing, from the lips of an uninstructed clown, a statement of the truth, that in a square, the square of "what professors of science call the diagonal" is equal to twice that of one of the sides. But even if every teacher of youth had the tact and ability with which that great philosopher catechized the boy, just referred to, what would the fact prove? Nothing more than this, that the human mind was so constituted that some ideas should be suggestive of others. The truths of geometry have been successively deduced by that very mind. What wonder then that a clown, under the tuition of such an interrogator, should gather some of those truths, though never before instructed. The notions which, from the constitution of our minds, are generated within us by external sensation and internal reflection need not be considered as stamps of previously existing ideas. Whatever those ideas be in Plato's system, there is no reason why we may not at once assume the present as a world of reality in which our ideas are for the first time learnt.

"Plato likewise concluded that the soul was uncreated and immortal from its being an independent ever-moving principle. 'Every soul is immortal, for that which is in ceaseless motion is immortal. But that which moves another, and is moved by another, as it stops in motion, stops in life. If then there be nothing 'which moves itself but the soul, it necessarily follows 'that the soul is a thing uncreated and immortal[24].'

"Plato you will observe did not deduce or persist in any conclusions from that doctrine opposed to the glory of God or the interests of man. In truth Socrates himself propounds it with diffidence in the *Meno*. He positively refuses to make any other use of it than that of encouraging men to persevere in intellectual pursuits. He thought people would be more manly and less idle, if they were persuaded they were once endowed with knowledge, and could consequently regain it with facility, than if they believed they were never blessed with knowledge, and that what they had never known, it was neither possible nor necessary to inquire after. If you were once possessed of ideas, now forgotten, it is evident you may recall them without difficulty. You should not then indulge in idleness as if it were impossible for you to improve your mind. This is the sort of exhortation in which that philosopher delighted. But it is evident there was no necessity for postulating the pre-existence of the soul with a view of this. It were quite sufficient to say the soul is naturally capable of intellectual acquisitions, and that therefore earnest endeavours after knowledge must be successful.

"If he made any other practical use of his doctrine, it was to enforce the observance of morals, by holding out the terrors of a future world to the wicked and ungodly. 'Whosoever passes his life justly, afterwards obtains a 'better lot, but who unjustly a worse one. Those who 'are timid and unjust are changed into women in their 'second generation.'"

Tarkakāma.—"What other conclusions could *our* philosophers, either, have drawn from the doctrine of the soul's pre-existence? They too insisted on good behaviour as a necessary qualification for future happiness."

Satyakāma.—"I see I have not yet succeeded in explaining my views to you, notwithstanding several attempts. I think it is not too severe a remark to say that they have all drawn from it conclusions which militate against our conceptions of the divine attributes, and which tend to the subversion of good manners. Such conclusions may be called mischievous, may they not, Tarkakāma?"

"Of course, if they really involved notions scuh as you describe."

"Well, then, one great conclusion that our philosophers have drawn from the doctrine of the soul's pre-existence is that this world is a scene of reward or punishment according to works performed in a previous state. Whatever happens now is owing to *adṛṣṭa,* or the 'unseen' merit or demerit of past works, otherwise called *daiva*[25]. Our thoughts, feelings, and actions are all fettered by the events of a life already passed. It is impossible even for God to help us except as far as *adṛṣṭa* will allow. He cannot get over this difficulty any more than he can produce rice out of wheat seed, as Śaṅkarācārya says. On the immoral consequences of such a doctrine of necessity, I need not expatiate."

Tarkakāma. – "But adṛṣṭa simply regulates our *condition* in life as the reward or punishment of past works. I repeat, it does not diminish our control over ourselves."

Satyakāma. – "The *condition* itself is in your system almost every thing. If a person is degraded by adṛṣṭa to a Śūdra's condition, he is precluded from every aspiration which may be called noble – for according to the Śāstra he should be engaged solely in doing service to the *twice-born.* He may, by a lucky stroke of *daiva,* get up to the surface again, but he cannot calculate on such a chance, nor guide himself by such a hope.

"Then, again, although some parts of the Śāstra, with a view no doubt to stimulate human efforts, limit the operation of adṛṣṭa[26], and magnify man's freedom of will and action, thereby enhancing his responsibility, there are other parts equally, – I may say, more, – decisive in establishing the paramount influence of *daiva,* and extending it without bounds to all actions and events.[27] The very exceptions that are solemnly mentioned prove its absolute sovereignty as a rule. Philosophers maintain that by true knowledge one can cast off the bonds of works, and sectarians contend that by devotion to their *iṣṭa devatā*[28], or favourite god, one can get over the effects of *daiva*, or Fate; both thereby admitting its uncontrolled potency in ordinary cases. And it is not denied by those who would limit the influence of *daiva* that it extends over every event – only that it requires the concurrence of human efforts."

"But I do not see," said Tarkakāma, "what great evil would arise from the doctrine of *adṛṣṭa* or *daiva,* supposing that it does imply a restriction on men's actions."

Satyakāma. – "If you admit the extreme view of its power, by which for instance the Brāhmin, already adverted to[29], excused an unnatural act of severity against his own sons, it amounts to a doctrine of fatalism. Now suppose a fatalist to educate any one from his youth up, in his own principles; that the child should reason upon them; and conclude, that since he cannot possibly behave otherwise than he does, he is not a subject of blame or commendation, nor can deserve to be rewarded for, or punished : imagine him to eradicate the very perceptions of blame and commendation out of his mind, by means of the system to form his temper and character and behaviour to it; and from it to judge of the treatment he was to expect, say, from reasonable men, upon 'his coming abroad into the world, as the fatalist judges from this system, what he is to expect from the Author of nature, and with regard to a future state. I cannot forbear stopping here to ask, whether any one of common sense would think fit that a child should be put upon these sepculations, and be left to apply them to practice. And a man has little pretence to reason, who is not sensible, that we are all children in speculations of this kind. However the child would doubtless be highly delighted to find himself freed from the restraints of fear and shame, with which his play-fellows were fettered and embarrassed; and highly conceited in his superior knowledge so far beyond his years. But conceit and vanity would be the least bad part of the influence which these principles must have, when thus reasoned and acted upon during the course of his education. He must either be allowed to go on and be the plague of all about him, and himself too, even to his own destruction : or else correction must be continually made use of, to supply the want of those natural perceptions of blame and commendation which we have supposed to be removed; and to give him a practical impression of what he had reasoned himself out of the belief of, that he was in fact an accountable child, and to be punished for doing what he was forbid[29].'

"Our best security against this mischievous theory of *adṛṣṭa* is in those principles of conscious responsibility which the Supreme Being has implanted in our minds, and which we cannot wholly unlearn, notwithstanding all that philosophers may say to the contrary. Hence it is that poets have often censured an idle dependence on *daiva,* and inculcated a firm resistance of its power. But the *power itself is not denied*[30]."

Tarkakāma.—"What is *daiva* but the inscrutable will of God? Is it not right that man should not presume too much on his power or freedom, but be constantly reminded of his dependence on the will of God?"

Satyakāma.—"Certainly. If *daiva* or adṛṣṭa signified the inscrutable will of God, there could be no objection to extending the range of its operation. The impression that we are under the power of God's will, can never discourage efforts in the right direction, nor diminish our sense of responsibility. Indeed it would rather heighten both. But neither *daiva* nor its synonyms *dṛṣṭa, adṛṣṭa, bhāgya,* can be so construed. They are defined by philosophers, poets, and lexicographers, all, to mean the luck, desert, habit, or disposition which depends on, and is derived from one's own acts in a previous life[31]. To be under the influence of such luck is not to be under the guidance of an all-wise and beneficent Intelligence—but to continue subject to a blind influence, the nature and extent of which are obscure and indefinite. I do not wonder at men's impatience under such a supposed bondage, and their eagerness to escape from its trammels.

"The theological errors deduced from this theory of the soul's pre-existence are equally grave. How does Gotama for instance account for the creation? He introduces a *pūrvapakṣa,* or a primā facie opinion, different from his own, to the effect, that 'God is the cause (of the universe) for the (previous) works of men are found to be unfruitful' (iv. 19). He then replies, 'No; for there can be no fruit without (previous) works' (iv. 20.). The *obvious* meaning here is that the works of a previous life, not God, *produced the world.* The scholiast does his best to explain away this apparent denial of God, by contending that the author only denies the material, or *sole,* causality of God, teaching thereby that God and adṛṣṭa were joint causes of the Universe[32]. Even if this explanation were accepted, it would still, by associating Him with Fate or Luck, be an avowed abridgement of the Creator's power, already curtailed by the admission of atoms. But this is not all. How could there be a Fate or Luck, dependent on prior works, at the *original* creation? If then, there could be *no fruit without such works,* the world could never have been really created. That this is not a mere speculative inference drawn by myself from his principles, but expresses his real opinion, is evident from his argument for the Soul's pre-existence and eternity already considered[33].

"The Vaiśeṣika leader Kaṇāda, too, drew a similar inference from the theory of pre-existence and adṛṣṭa. He boldly asserted that the primal action of atoms is caused by 'adṛṣṭa,' to which was also owing the *first act of mind* (manasaśca.) So that if there be a Supreme Being, still He cannot have moved without adṛṣṭa.

"In Jaimini's system, again, every thing is *works,* that is to say, works in the sense of adṛṣṭa. It is by virtue of 'works' that the affairs of the world are conducted. Works procure merit, and merit regulates events. This succession of works, and their consequent events, has gone on from eternity like seed and plant. The seed produces the plant, and the plant again yields the seed. Works regulate events, and events lead to works. They thus form a chain of inter-dependent links.

"It is adṛṣṭa, too, which affords refuge to the atheistic Sāṅkhya. The arrangement of the world and the regulation of human affairs might have driven him to the necessity of acknowledging a Supreme Intelligence, but the doctrine of adṛṣṭa furnished him with an escape. 'The distribution of fruits could not be by a divine cause, for it is determined by works[34].' This, as we have seen, was likewise the opinion of Jaimini, Śaṅkarācārya being witness.

"As to the Vedānta, although, as I have shown before, it does not consider the doctrine of previous works as a sufficient explanation of the diversity observable in human condition, yet it draws in other places conclusions equally subversive of the Creator's independent agency. As Śaṅkarācārya always states his opinion with great perspicuity, I shall read his words in full. Commenting on Sūtra II. i.[34], the object of which is to show that God creates the world out of regard to human works, It may be objected,' he says, 'God is then proved not to be 'the cause of the universe. Why? From the visible instances of injustice and cruelty. Some he makes very happy, i.e., the gods' some very miserable, the brutes, &c.; some middling, men, &c. As the author of such an 'inequitable creation, He is proved to be subject to passions like other persons, that is to say, to partiality and prejudice, and therefore His nature is found wanting in the spotlessness which is set forth in the Śruti and Smṛti. And by dispensing pain and the ruin of all creatures, He is chargeable with a malicious cruelty, deemed culpable even among the wicked. Hence, because of the visible instances of injustice and cruelty, God cannot be the cause of the universe.' 'To this,' continues Śaṅkara, we thus reply : 'Injustice and cruelty cannot be charged upon God. Why? Because he did not act independently. If God, alone, had, independently, created the world of inequalities, then these faults of injustice and cruelty might indeed be attributed to Him. But one, who is not independent, cannot be charged with the act of creation. God, being dependent, creates this world of inequalities. If you ask on what is He dependent? We reply, He is dependent on Merit and Demerit. That there should be an unequal creation, dependent on the Merit and Demerit of the souls created, is no fault of God. God is to be looked upon as the rain. As the rain is the common cause of the production of 'rice and wheat, but of their specific distinctions as rice and wheat, the causes are the varying powers of 'their respective seeds; so is God the common cause, in the creation of men, gods, and others, but of the distinctions between gods, men, and others, the causes are the varying works, inherent in their respective souls. Thus God, being dependent (on works), cannot be charged with injustice and cruelty[35].'

"Śaṅkarācārya then shows that the Vedas inculcate the same view, and proceeds to expound the next Sūtra, in which is answered the objection, how could there be *previous* works at the original creation? The objection itself is thus represented : 'This, beloved, was one, without a second, at the beginning. Hence, as there could be no distinctions before the creation, there could be no works, in dependence on which inequalities might be created. *After the creation* there may be works dependent on corporeal distinctions, and corporeal distinctions dependent on works : this reciprocal inter-action may *then* be made out. God may be dependent on works *after* the distinctions are made. But before those distinctions are made, there could be no works caused by varying instruments, and therefore we ought to find a uniform creation.'

'If this objection be urged,' continues Śaṅkara, 'it does not vitiate our doctrine, because THE WORLD IS WITHOUT 'BEGINNING. It would vitiate our theory, if the world had a beginning. But the world being without beginning, nothing can prevent works and unequal creations continuing in the states of cause and effect, like the seed 'and its plant[36].'

"Consider, friend Tarkakāma, the mischievous consequences that have resulted from the theory of the soul's pre-existence. Our philsophers resort ot *adṛṣṭa* in order to account for certain difficulties in the world, and *adṛṣṭa* compels them to fly from stage to stage, until they are forced to declare, that the world was never created—that it is without beginning, that it is eternal. And that which is eternal, is, in their conception, again, not dependent on a cause[37]. How can our philosophers, consistently find fault with the Cārvākas who deny the necessity of an intelligent First Cause, when they themselves pronounce the world to be without beginning?"

While this conversation was going on between Satyakāma and Tarkakāma, Āgamika and myself behaved with exemplary patience. We did not once interrupt the disputants. But I was now irresistibly led to express my wonder how Śaṅkarācārya could hold such an opinion after ridiculing the idea of an eternal succession of works and creations, as a troop of blind leaders of blind.

"Both passages are before you," said Satyakāma, "you can judge for yourselves. If I were to hazard a conjecture, I should say that his object, in the passage I quoted first, was to uphold the material causality of God against a whole host of antagonistic philosophers, such as the Vaiśeṣikas, the Māheśwaras, the followers of the Sāṅkhya and the Yoga. He maintained against them all that it was necessary, no less from moral considerations than from regard to the authority of the Veda, to acknowledge God to be both the material, or substantial, and the efficient cause of the universe, and consequently to be identical with the world. Without that supposition, he thought the inequalities, in the world could not be satisfactorily accounted for. Unless God and the world were identical, how could He escape a charge of injustice and cruelty, when manifestly there are so many inequalities in the creation? The idea of an eternal succession of works and worlds depending on each other, he ridiculed by comparing it with a troop of blind leaders of blind. But in the passage I have just read, he is facing the question of inequalities in opposition to the atheistic followers of Jaimini, who had on that ground argued for the non-existence of a Creator; and he takes refuge in the very supposition of an eternal succession of works and worlds, which he elsewhere ridicules."

"Very strange self-contradiction!" said I. "Is it not possible to reconcile the two passages?"

"That," replied Satyakāma, "must be left to the diplomatic abilities of friend Tarkakāma."

Tarkakāma said nothing. We waited a minute or two to hear how he would reconcile such a seeming contradiction. At length Āgamika asked, whether by arguing against the soul's pre-existence, his friend meant to deny its eternity *both ways,* and pronounce it to be perishable with the body. "Most certainly, *not,*" replied Satyakāma. "The soul, though it had a beginning, as indeed all *creatures* must have, is imperishable. That whatever had a beginning must have an end, may be a favourite theory with some philosophers; but they can never prove it. The soul may be immortal without being eternal. The Greek philosopher who argued for its pre-existence, in order to prove its immortality, had given reasons for the latter which did not depend on the former, and which human nature cannot gainsay. 'Good hope have I,' said he, 'that something is in reserve for the dead, and that (as I said long ago) the good shall fare far better than the bad.'"

"This," continued Satyakāma, "together with the soul's essential independence of the body, which he also asserts afterwards, ought to convince the incredulous that there is another and a better world reserved for us, where our soul's aspirations will find their corresponding objects, and where that which we now but partially understand will be clearly apprehended. Do not think, Āgamika, that I deny the future glories of the soul. I have reasons for believing in them, still higher than the teaching of mere philosophy,—on which we may converse some other day. I believe that the righteous will meet with rewards in another state of which the present world can afford but faintest fore-shadowings. It is the supposition of a previous life, and the consequences deduced from it, that I protest against. Those consequences I have already mentioned in detail, and I may add that as a further corollary from the theory of the soul's pre-existence, our philosophers also held the doctrine of its successive transmigrations. The Nyāya, Sāṅkhya, and Vedānta equally teach that the souls of the deceased remove for a time to heaven or hell, to receive the due rewards of their actions. Those rewards do not however exhaust their merit or demerit, which still adheres to them, 'as greasy substances stick to the pot, even after it has been emptied'.[38] They accordingly return, and are again born with such bodies as are suitable to their previous lives. The new circumstances in which they appear, and the new works which are developed in them, influence their destinies in the next succeeding age. In this manner their souls transmigrate as gods, men, or animals, until the dissolution of the world, which again is followed by a second creation and by their re-appearance agreeably to their previous works. This succession of creations and briths, in which the events of each cycle are regulated by those of its predecessor, is considered by our philosophers an intolerable evil. They were thoroughly disgusted with this idea of a puppet life, in which rational beings were irrevocably committed to conditions and impulses, not according to their own will, but as they were, by the verdict of adṛṣṭa, declared to have merited them, by reason of works of which they were not themselves conscious; and hence they looked upon existence as a burden, and enjoyment itself as a task. To a certain extent I cannot help sympathising with them. If indeed we were subject to the sort of transmigrations taught in the Brāhminical philosophy : if our circumstances were so fixed by the events of a previous life, that we were mere toys for the sport of Fate; if a hard, unsympathising, impersonal, *adṛṣṭa* must necessarily govern our deliberations, and, in a manner, supersede our judgments, then no man of any energy could submit to such an infliction. Bitter complaints would escape the lips of the most forbearing. All would naturally wish they had never been born. No wonder, then, that existence should be considered an evil, and that men should pant for *mukti,* or release from this servile bondage to *adṛṣṭa.*"

Āgamika, – "Well, Satyakāma, you have spoken out your mind. We are glad at least to have some insight into the mental process you have gone through. We can only promise to think on these points."

Tarkakāma.—"Yes, thinking is man's great prerogative. We must think on what our friend has said. But (turning to Satyakāma) you have overlooked one main point. In your essay you condemned the theories of all the schools about creation. Is it possible that the universe could proceed *out of nothing?* Every effect must have a cause."

Satyakāma.—"I do not deny that every effect must have a cause. But we probably assent to the maxim in very different senses. Let us see how the theory of causation is treated in the schools. It is commonly understood that the Nyāya philosophy acknowledges three sorts of causes, substantial or inherent, non-substantial or exterior, and a third which might, perhaps, be conveniently styled the *operative* cause. The modern followers of the school do indeed entertain such a view, as is evident from the *Bhāṣā parichheda* in which we find a neat expression of that view[39]. The founder of the system, however, does not clearly inculcate that doctrine. In truth, the most prominent, if not the only, idea of causation which pervades his Sūtras, is that of a material or substantial cause. This, possibly, was the reason of his abridging God's act in the work of creation. Kaṇāda indeed speaks of a multiplicity of causes, and may be considered as an authority to which the Naiyāyikas may appeal for their theory of a threefold causality. But while his ideas coincide with those of the moderns as to the first two, his view of the third cause does not quite correspond to that of an intelligent efficient agent, such as the potter is of the jar, a favourite example with the school in our days. His operative cause implies simply an action *tending* to a result, but not the action of an intelligent agent *aiming* at a certain end; and the examples given by his commentator are those of heat in the process of decoction or cremation, and of texts of the Vedas inducing the observance of sacrifices[40]. Neither of the great authorities of the Nyāya appears to have taught the idea of an intelligent *efficient* cause of anything.

"The Sāṅkhya school, too, presents little or no trace of the idea of efficient causation. The material or substantial cause is what it maninly, if not exclusively, recongnized. The 79th Sūtra states plainly that a substance cannot be made of no substance[41]. (Ex nihilo nihil fit.) The author repeats in another Sūtra that there must be a material for every thing[42]. But while so careful in his recognition of the material cause, he says scarcely any thing, even by implication, of an efficient cause. He adds in his definition of destruction that it is mere resolution into the cause[43], and maintains that production is nothing else than the manifestation of that which pre-exists in the cause[44]. The statue, already existent in its cause, the stone, is only *manifested* by sculpture. The oil already existent in its cause, the *sesamum,* is only *brought out to view* by pressing. The rice, already existent in its cause, the paddy, is only educed by beating[45]. Cause and effect stand to each other like the seed and its germ[46]. Hence arose the godless conclusion that since the created universe consists only of inanimate and irrational substances, (the rational principle, or soul, being uncreated and eternal)—it could have no other than an unintelligent cause such as nature; her products having as common characteristics, 'the three qualities, and want of thought and animation[47].'

"The Vedānta did certainly *not* ignore the theory of an intelligent efficient cause; but the idea of a material cause, which it received from the Upaniṣads and held in common with the other Schools, completely vitiated its philosophy, and, what is still more unfortunate, its theology.

"While reasoning against the Sāṅkhya, Śaṅkarācārya does not fail to expatiate on the intelligence of the First Cause; and, without committing himself to a decided assertion of the necessity of an efficient agent, points out the impropriety of hunting for a material cause to the exculsion of an efficient agent. 'There is no necessity, says he, for seeking an original, such as earth or other material of the same substance (as the effect,) instead of an exterior cause such as the potter or other artificer different from it. The idea of cause and effect is founded on the skill with which beds, chairs, and other articles are manufactured. Nor is it possible to deduce from the idea of cause and effect a common irrational substratum of external and internal diversities[48].' The prominence here given to intelligent agency stands in marked contrast to the examples elsewhere made use of to express God's causality of the universe. He is to the external world what the yarn is to the cloth, what milk is to curds, the earth to a jar, the gold to a bracelet, the iron to a nail-parer. The very passage of the Upaniṣad, (the basis of the 2nd Sūtra,) which declares the universe to be the product of God, presents the cause (*Yatas*) in the ablative case; which, says Śaṅkara, is alone sufficient to show that the creator is spoken of as the substantial cause *out of which,* not the efficient cause *by which,* the universe was formed. This proves that the idea of material causation was uppermost in Śaṅkara's mind."

Tarkakāma.—"But where is the error, and where the danger, in this idea of causation? Gotama, Kapila, and Śaṅkara may not have thought it necessary to expatiate on the efficient cause. Will you not allow an author to choose his own subject? Can you show that they have not accurately represented what they *did* undertake to explain?

Satyakāma.—"A fair issue. I say, they did not. It is not quite philosophical prominently to connect the idea of causality with the *material of a thing*. That is the *substance* of which, not the *cause by* which, an article is made. It would sound rather strange to say that the rim of your spectacles has *gold* for its cause. The idea of substance is to my mind very different from that of causality. Would it not be a truism to connect cause and effect in this way? Kapila virtually confesses this when he says a product is identical with the cause[49]. And Śaṅkara, I have shown, admits that the radical idea of causation is that of intelligent agency."

Tarkakāma—"I suppose you mean to read a lecture to our philosophers on Grammar and Rhetoric:—they have not chosen the best term for the substance of a thing. If that be all, it is a small offence, hardly deserving of criticism, except from unrazored lips within the walls of a school, though even there, neither Pāṇini nor Vopadeva will assist you in deriving an intelligent efficient agent from the word *Kāraṇam* (cause). And a most celebrated philosopher of ancient Europe, I am told, held exactly the same view of causality as the Naiyāyikas."

Satyakāma.—"You mean Aristotle. He did not hold exactly the same view, but one very analogous to it. He inculcated a quadruple causality. The fourth or 'final' cause does not appear in the list of *Kāraṇas* in the Brāhminical philosophy. I would not object to the use of the term, *material* or substantial cause, in a secondary sense of the word cause, and in reference to works of human art; but when we come to the grand question about the universe I do object to its use. Human agents cannot work without materials. The carpenter wants his wood, the weaver his yarn, the jeweller his gold. But we have no reason for thinking that the great Artificer of the universe stood in similar need. It is by no means philosophical to attribute to One, whom we acknowledge to be Omnipotent, the imperfections and weaknesses of agents of limited capacities. Śaṅkarācārya[50] himself acknowledges that the work of creation is not to be classed in the same category as human acts in the world. The prominence given to the material cause has a tendency to make men forget this distinction, and hence my jealousy of it.

"As for Aristotle, I would remark that he employed his fourfold division of cause chiefly as a guide to the inquiries of the *physical* philosopher; who was thus directed to inquire into (1) The internal physiological character of a thing : (2)Its form, or logical definition as a species : (3) Its history : (4) Its uses. He did not profess to rescue men from misery by discovering to them the cause of the Universe; he only proposed to investigate the nature of things, because man's nature urged him to pursue "THE TRUE;"—and since in the course of this investigation man's own nature came to be examined, and on examination turned out to be pre-eminently *moral,* he taught men to seek for happiness by the practice of virtue.

"With reference to the grammatical formation of the word *kāraṇam,* of course the affix *anat,* as Vopadeva calls it, does not indicate the agent. Neither does it signify the *substance* of which a thing is made. It properly means the instrument by which an action is done. But the custom of philosophers of making it the correlative of *kārya* (act) does certainly point to the agency of the efficient as the most important of the causes. Now tell me candidly, Tarkakāma, what did you admire most, when you saw a watch for the first time; the metal, the combinations, or the inventor's skill?"

Tarkakāma stared.—The question seemed to throw some new light on the theory of casuation. The metal, the combinations, and the inventor's skill were of course the substantial, the non-substantial, and the operative causes of the watch in the vocabulary of the Nyāya.

Tarkakāma said, not without changing colour, "Of course I admired the inventor's skill the most."

"The idea foremost in your mind as to the causality of the watch was the inventor's skill, was it not?"

"I should think so."

"The metal was quite a secondary idea. Your admiration of its excellence as a *time-piece* would hardly lead you to ask what the particular metal was. You would think chiefly, if not solely, of the inventor's skill as regards its causality. Would you not?"

"Very probably I should."

"You would at once conclude that an intelligent architect must be the *kāraṇam* of such a *kārya.*"

"I suppose I should."

"Well; you have passed setence yourself on the theory of causation in the Brāhminical philosophy. You would think first of a cause which Gotama and Kapila do not recognize at all, which Kaṇāda speaks of somewhat obscurely as the last in the series, and which the Vedānta strangely mixes up with the substance of the manufacture."

Tarkakāma. – "What do you mean by saying that Gotama and Kapila do not recognize the cause which, in the case of the watch, would be foremost in my mind?"

Satyakāma. – "An intelligent efficient cause is not found in Gotama's and Kapil's lists. The latter certainly ignored the necessity, in the formation of the world, of such an Agent directing the operation of *prakṛti,* or nature, *the rootless root of all things,* which acted independently, 'like milk turning into curds;' though the example was singularly inappropriate, since milk would never turn into curds without the action of the atmosphere. You would not say, would you, that gold or silver turned into a watch, like milk into curds."

Tarkakāma gave no answer, but put a question; "Admitting that the term material or substantial cuase is an unfortunate expression, and that it ought not to have been put forth prominently in the theory of causation, what are those dangerous consequences of which the theory is productive? Why this appeal to our fears?"

Satyakāma. – "I have already answered this question. By calling the substance of a thing its *cause,* our philosophers introduced the most dangerous theological errors. Whatever has a direct tendency to obscure the majesty of God, and curtail our sense of His power, may well be denominated dangerous. The theory which makes the material the most important of the causes, led people to rest satisfied with speculating on the *material* cause of the Universe. That no man can work without materials is denied by none, simply because man is not omnipotent, and has not creative power.

But when one looks at an exquisite production of art, he is so lost in admiration at the skill of the artist, that he almost forgets the minor question of the material. And yet so banefully has the theory of material causality worked among us that the mental energy of our philosophers has found most active exercise not *in the exclamation,* how wonderful is the arrangement of the universe! But *in the interrogation,* Of what pre-existing substance is all this made? Nay they have been so lost in that worse than useless question, as to forget that a Creator of infinite power and perfection needs not, like weak and imperfect man, to stop for materials, but can make materials by the mere fiat of His will. If the natural instincts of the human soul lead us to believe in the existence of an All-powerful and Perfect Being, if the irresistible arguments of the Vedānta itself drive us to the conclusion that the Universe was created by a God, infinite in wisdom and contrivance; then there can be no possible necessity for speculating on the *material* of the world : then the most philosophical course is to consider the objects originally created by such a God as at once the *matter and form* of the world. To assume the eternity of some gross material, existing side by side with an intelligent and all-perfect God, is not only unnecessary, (and therefore unphilosophical,) in as much as it assumes two principles, where one is amply sufficient to account for all we see; but it is inconsistent with the idea of perfection which we must attribute to the Deity. If He had some material to work upon, previously existing independent of Him, then there was nothing peculiar in His agency; then it was of the same species as that of a human architect; then He was our creator in no higher sense than that in which a potter is the maker of a jar. The Vedāntist, on the other hand, placed himself in a false position, by seeking in a spiritual essence, the substance of such a world consisting of pure and impure, intelligent and unintelligent, rational and irrational, animated and inanimate creatures.

"The fact is that if the Supreme Being could not really create this world without pre-existent materials, it would be no easy task to answer the arguments of the godless Sāṅkhya. Since then, this peculiar theory of causation has driven our philosophers to the sad strait of virtually abridging the power of God, and, in some cases, of even ignoring His operation and denying His existence altogether, I suppose I am justified in stigmatizing it as a dangerous error.

"It was," continued Satyakāma, "these two cardinal errors, that of the soul's pre-existence and this of material causality, which betrayed the Brāhminical Intellect into gross mistakes in philosophy and theology. Few philosophers in any country were possessed of the acuteness, the patience, and the industry which distinguished our ancestors; but, under the baneful influence of those two errors, the excellent qualities of their minds produced much evil, and little good.

"You seem to contend, Tarkakāma, that the conclusions of our philosophers are based on the two theories we have been discussing. *This fact I concede to you once for all.* Granted that many of their conclusions are deducible from those theories; what then? Are we tamely to submit to such startling conclusions because of those gratuitous assumptions? By no means. We are rather to be the more jealous of them because of their leading to those conclusions. Let us not resist our moral intuitions, nor, because of arbitrary hypotheses hastily adopted, run headlong into errors that would limit the range of Almighty power, and deprive the world of the only Being to whom the mind spontaneously betakes itself for help and refuge when appalled by danger and difficulty.

References

1. इस्त इव भूतिमलिनो यथा यथा लङ्घयति खलः सुजनम्। दर्पणमिव तं कुरुते तथा तथा निर्मलच्छायम्॥ Vāsavadattā.
2. Butler.
3. Butler.
4. विषमां हि दशां प्राप्य दैवं गर्हयते नरः। आत्मनः कर्म्मदोषांस्तु नैव जानात्यपण्डितः। Hitopadeśa.
5. अदृष्टाकृष्टैरेव शरीरेन्द्रियादिभिस्तद्भोगजननात्। Haridāsa Bhaṭṭa's Commentary on the Kusumāñjali.
6. दैवमत्र परं मन्ये धिक् पौरुषमनर्थकं। अकार्य्यं कारितो येन बलादहमचिन्तितं॥ Mārkaṇḍeya Purāṇa.
7. अपराधः स दैवस्य न पुनर्मन्त्रिणामयं कार्य्यं सुघटितं यत्नात् दैवयोगाद्विनश्यति। Hitopadeśa.
8. सम्पत्तेश्च विपत्तेश्च दैवमेव हि कारणं। इति दैवपरो ध्यायन् नात्मानमपि चेष्टयेत्। Hitopadeśa.

   सुखदुःखहेतुश्चादृष्टं। Prabhākara Mīmāṃsā.
9. Butler.
10. शरीरदाहे पातकाभावात्। Nyāya Sūtra, III. 4
11. पूर्व्वाभ्यस्तस्मृत्यनुबन्धाजातस्य हर्षभयशोकसम्प्रतिपत्तेः॥

    जातस्य बालस्य एतज्जन्माननुभूतेष्वपि हर्षादिहेतुषु सत्सु हर्षादीनां सम्प्रतिपत्तिः उत्पत्तिस्तस्याः पूर्व्वपूर्वानुभवाधीनास्मृतिसम्बन्धादेव सम्भवात् इत्थञ्चेदानीन्तन-स्यात्मनः पूर्वपूर्वसिद्धौ तस्यानादित्वमनादेश्च भावस्य न नाश इति नित्यत्वसिद्धिरिति भावः॥
12. पद्मादिषु प्रबोधसम्मीलनविकारवत्तद्विकारः॥20॥

    बालस्य हर्षादयो मुखविकासादनुमेया न च तत्सम्भवः पद्मादीनां प्रबोधादिवददृष्टविशेषाधीनक्रियावशादेव तदुपपत्तेरिति भावः॥
13. नोष्णशीतवर्षाकालनिमित्तत्वात् पञ्चात्मकविकाराणां॥

14. प्रेत्याहाराभ्यासकृतात् स्तन्याभिलाषात्॥

प्रेत्य मृत्वा जातमात्रस्य। Scholia.

15. अयसोऽयस्कान्ताभिगमनवत्तदुपसर्पणं॥

नान्यत्र प्रवृत्त्यभावात्॥

स्तनपान एव बालः प्रवर्त्तते नत्वन्यत्रेतिनियमः कथं स्यात्। वस्तुतस्तु अन्यत्र अयसि प्रवृत्त्यभावात् प्रवृत्तिर्हि चेष्टानुमितालिङ्गं नतुक्रियामात्रमतो न व्यभिचार इति भावः॥

16. वीतरागजन्मादर्शनात्॥

17. सगुणद्रव्योत्पत्तिवत्तदुत्पत्तिः॥

18. न सङ्कल्पनिमित्तत्वाद्रागादीनां॥

19. इच्छाद्वेषप्रयत्नसुखदुःखज्ञानान्यात्मनो लिङ्गं॥10॥

20. किं पुनरसामञ्जस्यं हीनमध्यमोत्तमभावेन हि प्राणिभेदान् विदधत ईश्वरस्य रागद्वेषादिदोषप्रसक्तेरस्मदादिवदनीश्वरत्वं प्रसज्जेत।

Commentary on Vedānta Sūtra II. ii. 37.

21. प्राणिकर्म्मापेक्षत्वाददोष इति चेन्न कर्म्मेश्वरयोः प्रवर्त्यप्रवर्त्तयितृत्वे इतरेतराश्रयदोषप्रसङ्गात् अनादित्यादिति चेन्न वर्त्तमानकालवदतीतेष्वपि कालेष्वितरेतराश्रयदोषाविशेषादन्धपरान्यायापत्तेः। Ibid.

22. जातस्य हि ध्रुवो मृत्युर्ध्रुवं जन्म मृतस्य च। Bhagavad Gītā.

23. स्वमेव कर्म्म दैवाख्यं विद्धि देहान्तरार्जितं। Matsya Purāṇa.

24. दैवमेव विजानन्ति नराः पौरुषवर्जिताः। Matsya Purāṇa.

25. दैवाधीनं जगत् सर्व्वं जन्म कर्म्म शुभाशुभं। संयोगाश्च वियोगाश्च न च दैवात् परं बलं॥ Brahma Vaivarta.

अरक्षितं तिष्ठति दैवरक्षितं सुरक्षितं दैवहतं विनश्यति। जीवत्यनाथोपि वने विसर्जितं कृतप्रयत्नोपि गृहे न जीवति॥ Hitopadeśa.

26. दैवं वर्द्धयितुं शक्तः क्षयं कर्तुं स्वलीलया। न दैवबद्ध स्तद्भक्तश्चाविनाशी च निर्गुणः॥ Matsya Purāṇa.

27. See Foot note 7, page 94.
28. Butler.
29. न दैवमपि सञ्चिन्त्य त्यजेदुद्योगमात्मनः। अनुद्योगेन तैलानि तिलेभ्यो नाप्तुमर्हति॥ उद्योगिनं पुरुषसिंहमुपैति लक्ष्मीर्दैवेन देयमिति कापुरुषा वदन्ति। दैवं निहत्य कुरु पौरुषमात्मशक्त्या यत्ने कृते यदि न सिध्यति कोत्र दोषः॥ Hitopadeśa.
30. अदृष्टं जन्मान्तरीयसंस्कारे। Śabda-muktā-mahārṇava.

    तत्र दैवमभिव्यक्तं पौरुषं पूर्व्वदेहिकं। Mātsya in Ditto.

    अदृष्टस्य प्राक्तनशुभाशुभकर्म्मणः। Premachandra on the Naiṣadha.

    पूर्व्वजन्मकृतं कर्म्म तद्दैवमिति कथ्यते। Hitopadeśa.
31. ईश्वरः कारणं पुरुषकर्म्माफल्यदर्शनात्। न पुरुषकर्म्माभावे फलानिष्पत्तेः। पुरुषकर्म्मणोपि सहकारितावश्यकी॥
32. It must be confessed that a few commentators, of no great celebrity, take a different view of the *sūtras* quoted above. The question will be again mooted in the next Dialogue.
33. नेश्वराधिष्ठिते फलनिष्पत्तिः कर्म्मणा तत्सिद्धेः। Kapila Sūtra,v. 1.
34. नेश्वरो जगतः कारणमुपपद्यते कुतः वैषम्यनैघृण्यप्रसङ्गात्। कांश्चिदत्यन्तसुखभाजः करोति देवादीन् कांश्चिदत्यन्तदुःखभाजः करोति पश्वादीन् कांश्चिन्मध्यमभाजो मनुष्यादीनित्येवं विषमां सृष्टिं निर्मिमाणस्येश्वरस्य पृथग्जनस्येव रागद्वेषोपपत्तेः श्रुतिस्मृत्यवधारितस्वच्छत्वादीश्वरस्वभाव विपरिलोपः प्रसज्येत तथा खलजनैरपि जुगुप्सितं निर्घृणत्वमतिक्रूरत्वं दुःखयोगविधानात् सर्व्वप्रजोपसंहरणाच्च प्रसज्येत तस्माद्वैषम्यनैर्घृण्य-प्रसङ्गान्नेश्वरः कारणमित्येवं प्राप्ते ब्रूमः वैषम्यनैर्घृण्ये नेश्वरस्य प्रसज्येते। कस्मात् सापेक्षत्वात् यदि हि निरपेक्षः केवल ईश्वरो विषमां सृष्टिं निर्मिमीत स्यातामेतौ दोषौ वैषम्यं नैर्घृण्यञ्च। न तु निरपेक्षस्य निर्मातृत्वमस्ति। सापेक्षो हीश्वरो विषमां सृष्टिं निर्मिमीते किमपेक्षत इति चेत् धर्म्माधर्म्मावपेक्षत इति वदामः। अतः सृज्यमानप्राणिधर्म्माधर्म्मापेक्षा विषमासृष्टिरिति नायमीश्वरस्यायापराधः ईश्वरस्तुपर्ज्जन्यवदद्द्रष्टव्यः। यथा हि पर्जन्यो

व्रीहियवादिसृष्टौ साधारणं कारणम्भवति व्रीहियवादिवैषम्ये तु तत्तद्वीजगतान्येवासाधारणानि सामर्थ्यानि कारणानि भवन्ति एवमीश्वरो देवमनुष्यादिसृष्टौ साधारणं कारणं भवति। देवमनुष्यादिवैषम्ये तु तत्तज्जीवगतान्येवासाधारणानि कर्म्माणि कारणानि भवन्ति। एवमीश्वरः सापेक्षत्वान्न वैषम्यनैर्धृण्याभ्यां दुष्यति॥

35. सदेवसौम्येदमग्र आसीदेकमेवाद्वितीयमिति प्राक्सृष्टेरविभागावधारणान्नास्ति कर्म्म यदपेक्षा विषमा सृष्टिः स्यात्। सृष्ट्युत्तरकालं हि शरीरादिविभागापेक्षं कर्म्मकर्म्मापेक्षश्च शरीरादिविभाग इतीतरेतराश्रयत्वं प्रसज्येत। अतो विभागादूर्ध्वं कर्म्मापेक्ष ईश्वरः प्रवर्त्ततां नाम प्राक् तु विभागाद्वैचित्र्यनिमित्तस्य कर्म्मणोऽभावात्तुल्यैवाद्या सृष्टिः प्राप्नोतीतिचेन्नैषदोषः अनादित्वात् संसारस्य भवेदेषदोषो यद्यादिमानयं संसारः स्यात्। अनादौ तु संसारे वीजाङ्कुरवद्धेतुहेतुमद्भावेन कर्म्मणः सर्गवैषम्यस्य च प्रवृत्तिर्न विरुध्यते॥

36. सदकारणवन्नित्यं॥ Kaṇāda.

37. स्वर्गार्थस्य कर्मणो भुक्तफलस्यावशेषः कश्चिदनुशयो नाम भांडानुसारिस्नेहवत् यथा हि स्नेहभाण्डं रिच्यमानं न सर्वात्मना रिच्यते भांडानुसार्य्येव कश्चित् स्नेहशेषोवतिष्ठते तथानुशयोपीति। Vedānta Sūtra, Com. III. i. 8.

38. अन्यथा सिद्धिशून्यस्य नियता पूर्व्ववर्तिता। कारणत्वं भवेत्तस्य त्रैविध्यं परिकीर्त्तितं॥ समवायिकारणत्वं ज्ञेयमथाप्यसमवायिहेतुत्वं। एवं न्यायनयज्ञैस्तृतीयमुक्तं निमित्तहेतुत्वम्॥ यत् समवेतं कार्य्यं भवति ज्ञेयन्तु समवायि जनकं तत्। तत्रासन्नं जनकं द्वितीयमाभ्यां परं तृतीयं स्यात्॥

39. संयुक्तसमवायादग्नेर्वैशेषिकम्। Sūtra.

अग्नवैंशेषिकं विशेषगुणं औष्मसंयुक्तसमवायात् पाकजेषु निमित्तकारणं। Śaṅkara Miśra.

40. नवस्तुनो वस्तुसिद्धिः। I. 79.

41. उपादाननियमात्। I. 116.

42. नाशः कारणलयः। I. 122.

43. नाभिव्यक्तिनिबन्धनौ व्यवहाराव्यवहारौ। I. 121.

कार्य्योत्पत्तेर्व्यवहाराव्यवहारौ कार्य्याभिव्यक्तिनिमित्तकौ अभिव्यक्तित उत्पत्तिव्यवहारोभिव्यक्त्यभावाच्चोत्पत्तिव्यवहाराभावो नत्त्वसतः सत्तेत्यर्थः॥

44. यथा शिलामध्यस्थप्रतिमाया लैङ्गिकव्यापारेणाभिव्यक्तिमात्रं तिलस्थतैलस्य च निष्पीडनेन धान्यस्थतण्डुलस्य चावघातेनेति॥

45. पारम्पर्य्यतोऽन्वेषणाद्वीजाङ्कुरवत्॥

46. न च मृदाद्युपादानस्वरूपव्यपाश्रयेणैव धर्म्मेण मूलकारणमवधारणीयं न वाह्यकुम्भकारादिव्यपाश्रयेणेति किञ्चिन्नियामकमस्ति। कार्य्यकारणभावस्तु प्रेक्षापूर्व्वनिर्मितानां शयनासनादीनां दृष्टः। न कार्य्यकारणभावाद्वाह्याध्यात्मिकानां भेदानामचेतनपूर्व्वकत्वं शक्यं कल्पयितुं।

Com. Vedānta Sūtra II.ii. 1.

47. यत इतीयमपि पञ्चमी यतो वा इमानि भूतानि जायन्त इत्यत्र जनिकर्त्तुः प्रकृतिरिति विशेषस्मरणात् प्रकृतिलक्षणएवोपादाने द्रष्टव्या।

Com. Vedānta Sūtra I.iv. 23.

48. कारणभावाच्च। I. 119.

49. न लोकवदिह भवितव्यं। Com. Vedānta Sūtra I. 4. 27.

DIALOGUE IV

FROM THE SAME TO THE SAME

After long expectation I have at last received your letter of the 20th Chaitra, commenting on the conferences that are going on here. You say 'it is a great pity that, life 'being short in the Kali Yuga, Brāhmins can now-a-days scarcely read one-twentieth of what they ought to study, and that is the reason why so few are familiar with the texts and aphorisms on which our philosophy and theology are based. We begin our course of study early enough, and we certainly keep it up as long as we can, but it is a drop only from the inexhaustible ocean that we are able to sip. As soon as a boy attains the age of five, we *put the chalk* into his hand, and guide it to form letters. The smartest lad must be allowed two or three years for learning to read and write in the vernacular. When he is seven or eight, he commences his education 'in the Śāstras. He takes a year or two to commit the Sūtras, or rules, of Grammar to memory. Then the rules 'are explained to him. The study of the Grammar with the *Gaṇa,* or list of verbs, and the lexicon, or list of nouns, must occupy him, perhaps, till he is sixteen. He must then learn some of the poems in order to perfect his knowledge of the language. He can hardly be expected to take up theology or philosophy before he is eighteen or twenty. If he commences the Nyāya, he goes cursorily over a manual such as the *Bhāṣā parichheda,* with or without its commentary the *Muktāvalī,* and then he takes up works treating on Anumāna, or deduction. A careful study of these occupies him for many years, and then he can no longer continue in the state of a student. He has by that time perhaps become a father, and the duties of a house-holder, the second stage in his life, press upon him. He has studied the *Anumāna Khaṇḍa,* or the Chapter on deduction, and made himself familiar with the rules of syllogism, but he has learnt nothing else. *Pramāṇa,* or proof, is but one of Gotama's sixteen topics, and *Anumāna,* or deduction, is but one of the four sub-divisions of proof. So that he has mastered but $\frac{1}{64}$ of Gotama's teaching when he quits College for the cares and anxieties of a house-holder. And as to the Sūtras, or aphorisms, of either of our leading teachers, he has not in all likelihood even seen them. A controversy on the Sūtras must therefore be something foreign to his habits and study. This appears to be the secret of your friend Satyakāma's 'success in some of his attacks against Tarkakāma.

'Satyakāma', you continue to remark, 'represents a new school of Brāhmins altogehter. These are raised in the Colleges established by the English—and their course of study is regulated by the maxim, *something of every thing,* without caring for *every thing of anything*. They learn the Sūtras; they read foreign literature too; and they obtain in a short time a general survey of all the systems. They are up to all kinds of discussion, and it requires more than ordinary tact to deal with them.'

Your remarks, my learned friend! perfectly coincide with my experience. To what a low ebb is divine learning now reduced! If Nārada had to confess he had no knowledge of the soul, notwithstanding his vast learning, how pitifully small must our knowledge be in these days!

With reference to your remarks on Kaṇāda's theory about creation, you will see what use I made of them when you hear of a conference which took place yesterday on the Nyāya.

It was the *Vāruṇi* (a holy day) and the conjuncture for bathing early in the morning, so the bank of the river was more than usually crowded. Many had come from distant villages to obtain the merit of a bath in the Gangā on such a holy occasion. Tarkakāma met several of his learned friends, and related to them the discussions he had with Satyakāma. After our ablutions were over, we all came into Satyakāma's house. We formed a pretty large circle, all deeply interested in scholastic disputations. There were some versed more particularly in the Nyāya, and among them was one who had, by his extensive reading, earned the appellation of *Nyāya-ratna.* There were others, though but few in number, whose studies had been directed to the Sāṅkhya. They too had one, more eminent than the rest, who rejoiced in the surname of Kāpila. Others again there were of various acquirements who held opinions more or less different from one another, but all entertained the highest reverence for the founders of the several schools. One of them, named Vaiyāsika, knew the Vedānta Sūtras and Śaṅkara's commentary almost word for word by heart.

The conversation at my suggestion turned on Kaṇāda's theory of the Creation to which reference was made in Satyakāma's discourse. I began with reading your remarks on that point. 'Satyakāma certainly read the Sūtra right. Kaṇāda does attribute the primal action of Atoms to adṛṣṭa, and the primal action certainly means the impulse by which the first combination took place, and that was of course the operative cause of the creation. The scholium of Śaṅkara Miśra is to the same effect. The *primal* means *before the creation.* At that time there could be no such thing as an impulse or a stroke[1].' But the question is what is adṛṣṭa? Literally, it means *unseen,* and is an adjective. Technically, in the usage of philosophers, it is a substantive, and means a power or influence inhering in things both animate and inanimate. As inherent in the former it implies an unseen power, both intellectual and active; as inherent in the latter it signifies a material power, perhaps partly the effect of previous combinations and motions. In souls embodied, it influences both thoughts and actions. Thus the poet Śrīharṣa[2] says a person often dreams by the powr of *adṛṣṭa* of things he had never seen in life. And Kālidasa[3] says that when Pārvatī commenced her 'studies, all her learning of a former life flocked into her mind, just as a swarm of cranes flocks into the Gangā in autumn, or the spontaneous brilliancy of certain drugs comes into them at night.

'And with reference to its impulses as an active power, the commentator on the Kusumāñjali[4] says that in the performance of ceremonies on which the enjoyment of heaven depends, the body and the organs are moved by adṛṣṭa. This unseen moving power in men is again the 'consequence of works done in a previous life, and hence 'it stands sometimes for *Dharma* and *Adharma* (virtue and vice) and *Karma* (works). Thus the origin of the 'world is attributed by the scholiast on Kaṇāda's Sūtras 'to *Dharma* and *Adharma*[5], after he had himself declared adṛṣṭa to be the cause of the creation. And 'Kaṇāda attributes the soul's departure from one body 'and adoption of another, to the agency of *Adṛṣṭa*[6], while Gotama ascribes it to *Karma*[7], both evidently meaning the same thing. In inanimate objects it simply signifies a material property or virtue, perhpas a sort of velocity or attraction—as in the (magnetic?) motion of stones and needles which Kaṇāda expressly attributes to adṛṣṭa[8].

'Now the point to be decided is whether Kaṇāda, who simply undertook to explain the phenomena of the world, as far as possible, by natural causes, that is to say, who would not unnecessarily obtrude a supernatural cause, excluded the divine operation, when he declared that the primal action of Atoms was owing to a power or virtue 'inhering in them. What can debar the supposition that he held the power itself to be a gift of God, who was consequently the original operative cause of the Universe, the adṛṣṭa itself being dependent on His Will? Adṛṣṭa was a mere *yantra* or instrument, while the Supreme Being was the *yantrī,* or the user of the instrument.'

Tarkakāma.—"This is an excellent solution of the difficulty raised by Satyakāma, and I trust we shall hear no more of great men's names being subjected to charges of atheism—for it is a sin to be even a hearer of such charges[9]."

Satyakāma.—"I wish I could report myself satisfied with

this explanation, but it is not in my power to do so. We seem to be pretty well agreed as to *one* meaning of adṛṣṭa. It is a power, influence, or habit based on the acts or relations of a previous existence. It is inherent in men, animals, and inorganic matter. But it has another meaning. It is not only an inherent power or habit. It is also a destiny that acts externally. The adṛṣṭa, inherent in one man, will often influence others with a view to bring about consequences which that man's merit or demerit calls for. It is with reference to this sense of adṛṣṭa that men often excuse their neighbour's delinquencies, as well as their own, by attributing them to its influence.[10]

"We have not discussed in which sense Kaṇāda used the word when he attributed the creation to adṛṣṭa. Was it an inherent power in Atoms, or an external influence?

Nyāyaratna.—"In whichever sense the word may have been used, I suppose you may admit the explanation suggested by our Benares friend in defence of Kaṇāda's theism."

Satyakāma.—"I do not see how the explanation *can* be applicable, if adṛṣṭa be taken in the sense of destiny, or a moving power, exterior to the Atoms. You must therefore make up your mind as to the meaning of the term in Kaṇāḍa's Sūtra."

Tarkakāma.—"Well, suppose we take it in the sense of an inherent power in Atoms, with which they were endowed by the will of God."

Satyakāma.—"You wish me to try, by the process of exhaustion, if, on either supposition, I can bring myself to accept the explanation above referred to. I must frankly say, I am not satisfied on either view of the meaning of Adṛṣṭa. Taking it in the sense of an inherent power, I am constrained to say, that the explanation not only fails at the very outset in its object of defending the theism of Kaṇāda's system; but is in itself vague and almost unintelligible. It fails as a defence of Kaṇāda, because Kaṇāda has never in any of his Sūtras spoken of God as the ultimate cause of all things. In truth, the word God never occurs in his work. The only aphorisms in which he may be supposed to make a remote reference to Him are those (and they are only two) in which he asserts the authority of the Veda. But we know, as in the case of Kapila, that our philosophers had a way of their own of asserting the authority of the Śāstra without acknowledging a Supreme Intelligence as the Creator of all things. To maintain that a writer, who has never spoken of God as the author of the universe, and was yet all the time accounting for the origin of that universe by a concourse of atoms, caused by a certain power or virtue of their own, was all the time meaning that the power was communicated by God, and was therefore himself a theistic teacher, is, to say the least of it, mere *Sāhasa* (boldness)."

Nyāyaratna.—"Are you not aware that *Kaṇāda's* system was only a supplement to Gotama's, and, therefore, many things, expressly asserted by his predecessor, are *implied* in his aphorisms."

Tarkakāma.—"You yourself acknowledged, Satyakāma, in your essay, that the Vaiśeṣika was a branch of the Nyāya."

Satyakāma.—"I do so still. And I am quite ready to concede that whatever is expressly asserted in the Nyāya, belongs impliedly to the Vaiśeṣika as well. But where has Gotama said any thing expressly *for* God?"

Tarkakāma.—"What do you mean by laying the emphasis on *for*?"

Satyakāma.—"Simply this, that the word Īśwara, or God, is certainly found in Gotama, but it requires commentatorial ingenuity to make out that it is used in a *theistic* sense."

Tarkakāma.—"You are mystifying still."

Satyakāma.—"Pardon me, Tarkakāma. I said something to you the other day on the same subject, and so I thought a bare reference would be sufficient. Gotama does introduce the name of God, but only to maintain that he was not the cause of the universe—that works of a previous world, (or, in other words, adṛṣṭa) were the cause. The popular scholiast Viśwanātha says that the aphorist simply meant that God was not the *sole* cause, and that the co-operation of adṛṣṭa was necessary. Supposing we accept the commentary, we can only allow that the Nyāya *hinted at* theistic doctrine, and that, still more obscurely, than at the atomic theory. If the Vaiśeṣika intended to confirm and develop that theistic doctrine, as it really did the atomic, it would only be natural to expect from it an explanation of the former, at least somewhat corresponding to its exposition of the latter. But far from exdpounding Gotama's implied idea of God, as *an associate creator with* adṛṣṭa, Kaṇāda says nothing at all about an Intelligent Creator, and only re-iterates, what Gotama had himself expressly stated, the agency of adṛṣṭa in the creation. How then can we allow the Vaiśeṣika any credit for theism based on the Nyāya? The rules of fair criticism would rather lead us the other way, to make Kaṇāda reponsible for not expatiating on that which his predecessor had so obscurely taught; if indeed we are to admit the popular commentary of the scholiast Viśwanātha."

Tarkakāma.—"Your '*if indeed*' is a very discreet addition, Satyakāma; for the 'three aphorisms' are differently explained by other commentators, of whom you have thought proper to say nothing."

Satyakāma.—"If I have said nothing of them it was because we have all along been talking of Gotama's Sūtras, as expounded by the *popular* scholiast Viśwanātha. You refer now to such commentators as Udyotakara Miśra. I did not speak of this author simply because he is so little countenanced any where. I doubt whether there are four copies of his work in all Bengal, while Viśwanātha's commentary is circulated every where in print and received by every student. Besides, we are discussing the *Sūtras,* not their modern paraphrases and commentaries, which I have repeatedly admitted are theistic. We have been referring to Viśwanātha for no other reason than because he is a scholiast rather than a commentator—and is generally intent more on the literal interpretation of the words in the Sūtras than on any exposition of his own views. Udyotakara, on the contrary, gives you little help in construing the aphorisms, and writes his own discourse after citing a Sūtra, only adding in conclusion, *such is its meaning*. But I have no objection to your calling him in as a witness—and I grant to you (what I have all along been saying with reference to modern commentators) that he understands the 'three Sūtras' in a theistic sense. But you must remember that if he is a more favourable witness for Gotama than Viśwanātha, he is a dangerous one for Kaṇāda—because in writing against the theory of the fortuitous concourse of Atoms, he evidently levels his remarks against the very aphorism of Kaṇāda now under discussion. He will allow no such explanation as has been suggested by your Benares friend. 'As to those,' says he, 'who maintain that atoms are the cause of the universe, by virtue of the works of embodied souls, (which is synonymous with Kaṇāda's adṛṣ ṭa) we tell them in reply that, if atoms are moved in that way, they ought to move incessantly; but they move dependent on especial causes and occasions[11]. 'If you rejoin,' he says again, 'that inanimate matter may move like milk; and that, just as for the nourishment of the infant, the mother's milk, though itself inanimate, comes up spontaneously, even so may atoms, though inanimate, move for the objects of animated creatures: such a rejoinder is illogical, for its involves a Sādhyasama (petitio principii). When you have to prove that atoms can move independently, you assign as a reason, 'that milk, though inanimate, moves independently! If milk moved independently, then it would do so in carcasses too, but it does not.' If therefore you wish to save Gotama, you must sacrifice Kaṇāda by the verdict of this chosen champion of the Nyāya himself.

"And you must also consider that your new witness discards the agency of Adṛṣṭa. He interprets Gotama's Sūtra IV. 21 to mean that *because of God's causing it, works (i.e.,* Adṛṣṭa) are no causes. Since Kaṇāda then brings in Adṛṣṭa as the cuase, without any mention of God, he is, according to the rendering of Udyotakara, *in conflict* with Gotama, and cannot receive any credit on the score of his opponent. The wordings of Gotama IV. 21 and Kaṇāda V. ii. 12 are singularly analogous. Both used *kārita* for caused—Kaṇāda gave Adṛṣṭa as the agent, Gotama *tat* or 'it.' If Udyotakara's comment is to be received, the *tat* of Gotama means God. If the *tat* be God, then *ahetu,* or no cause (next following), must refer to adṛṣṭa—which is therefore discarded—and Kaṇāda, by re-asserting it, must be deliberately opposing the theistic theory."

Tarkakāma.—"You say Kaṇāda makes no mention of God. You forget what he says on the *naming* and *operation* of the five elements. He attributes them directly to God. He says that the air, invisible in itself, is a matter of revelation, and that its name and operation are owing to God's agency."

Satyakāma.—"Is that not an over-statement of the fact? Kaṇāda himself attributes them, neither directly nor indirectly, to God. All he says is that naming and action are signs of *our betters.*[12] Commentatorial ingenuity discovers in these last words the occult meaning of *God and the great Ṛṣis*[13]. You must excuse my obtuyseness if I fail to find any thing decidedly theistic in the phrase *our betters.* Even atheism may admit that there are higher orders of beings in the world than man, and use those words without self-inconsistency. Kaṇāda says that names must have been given to things by certain intelligent beings, more eminent than the class to which he himself belonged; but there is nothing in this assertion to warrant the conclusion that 'the giver of names and the Author of the univese are identical'[14] in his estimation, or that by referring to the one, he necessarily admitted the other. But the most singular point is that Kaṇāda speaks, not of One being, superior to himself, as THE originator of names, but of givers of names in the plural, *i.e.,* his betters. And the commentator is obliged to confess that he speaks of 'God and the great Ṛṣis.' He does indeed speak of certain prsons who gave names to certain things, and perhaps invented human language, but he makes mention neither of *God,* nor of *great Ṛṣis* either.

And if he had heard of foreign, or as you would say, *barbarian* languages, it may well be doubted whether he would include the authors of *those* languages among 'God and the great Ṛṣis.'"

Tarkakāma.—"Will you not allow that language is of divine origin, and that Kaṇāda, when he was speaking on the subject, would not exclude the divine agency in the matter? To the great Ṛṣis he attributed the giving of such names as they were competent to give, and to God, those that none but He was competent to invent. Even the names which were of human creation were owing to God's act, for He laid down the law that the *father should give a name* to his son *on the twelfth day*[15]."

Satyakāma.—"As we are now conferring on Kaṇāda's theory about creation, we need not enter into the wide question of the origin of languages. The origin of language cannot supply a stronger argument for the existence of God, than is presented by the origin of the universe itself; unless indeed you accept the Buddhist dogma that the letters of the alphabet *are seeds of the universe*[16]. While we are discussing Kaṇāda's teaching on the greater question of the creation, we cannot be fairly called upon to admit his theism on the lesser point without decided evidence. His use of the phrase *our betters* cannot be a decided proof of theism, even if the commentator's scholium *God and the great Ṛṣis* were found in the text itself; for Kapila also admitted an inferior god although he denied his creative power[17].

"But we are flying off from our point,—which is your Benares friend's comment on the sūtra of Kaṇāda under discussion. What does he mean by suggesting, that adṛṣṭa was a power inherent in atoms *as a gift from God.* When was it given? I suppose he would not say it was *originally* given by God, for atoms are, in Kaṇāda's system, eternal and uncreated, and therefore they *could* have no origin. The inherent power then must have been imparted to them at some definite period, when they commenced action. If so, then the communication of that power was itself a stroke or impulse. If that was Kaṇāda's meaning, it is impossible to conceive why he should attribute the primal act to adṛṣṭa, and not to the divinely imparted impulse itself.

"The explanation under review, again, is opposed to the interpretation, which the scholiast of Kaṇāda put on his theory, notwithstanding his discovery of God in the phrase *our betters*. In the passage already cited, Śaṅkara Miśra says, that Merit and Demerit, or in other words, adṛṣṭa, were the *original cause* of the world[18], thereby excluding a remoter cause.

"But what appers to me conclusive against the explanation suggested by your learned friend, is, that it is directly opposed to Śaṅkarācārya's view of the Sūtra. That eminent scholar understood the aphorism of Kaṇāda in a very different sense. Here are his words[19]:

'The combining of atoms, while they are in a state of separation, must be allowed to require an action; for we see that the conjunction of yarn requires action (in the manufacture of clothes). But since an action 'involves an effect, an efficient cause must be acknowledged. If an efficient cause be not acknowledged, then there cannot be the primal action of atoms for want of an agent. And even if, being acknowledged, it implies 'an effort or a visible cause, such as a stroke, the primal action of atoms would still be impracticable, because of the impossibility of such effort or stroke. In that state (*i.e.*, before the creation) there could not be an effort which is a quality of the soul, because of the absence of a body. When there is a mind residing in a body, 'the connection of the soul with the mind may bring about an effort which is a quality of the former. The same may be said of a stroke, or other visible cause. All these come in after the creation; they cannot be the cause of the primal act. If it be said, let adṛṣṭa 'or destiny be the cause of the primal act; that must be inherent either in the soul or in atoms. But on neither supposition can the action of atoms be attributed to destiny, for destiny is inanimate. We have already said, while examining the opinions of the Sāṅkhya, that an inanimate thing, unconnected with an animated one, can neither be self-moved nor move another.

"The soul too, continues Śaṅkara, is at that time itself *inanimate,* for its animation is not then yet produced. Nor can the supposition of a destiny, inhering in the soul, turn it into a cause of atomic action, for there is no relation (between the two). If you say, 'there is a relation between the soul endowed with destiny, and atoms, that relation being permanent, there 'would be permanent motion too, because of the want of a separate governor. Therefore from the want of a directing efficient cause, there could be no primal 'action in atoms, and without such action there could be 'no combination ; nor without combination, the production of binaries &c.'

"You see here Śaṅkarācārya fails to discover in Kaṇāda's system any being of supreme and absolute intelligence to whose operation, in the absence of any other soul, endowed with body and mind, the primal action of atoms might be attributed. Kaṇāda left no room for such a God. Śaṅkara at least saw none."

Nyāyaratna. – "The argument appears to me to be quite irrelevant, Satyakāma. Whatever Udyotakara's ideas of the Vaiśeṣika theory may be, and in whatever sense Śaṅkarācārya may have received the words of Kaṇāda, certain it is that we, Naiyāyikas, do *not* hold that the universe was constructed by the mere action of Atoms impelled by a blind necessity. Nor can I allow, notwithstanding the evidence you have adduced to the contrary, that Kaṇāda really taught such a theory. I do not wish now to discuss the meaning of his Sūtras, but our immemorial tradition ought to determine the question. It is a fact that we do not teach any atheistic doctrine, and we have always been followers of Gotama and Kaṇāda. You say we have modified and improved on their doctrines. How could we dare do so? Can you point to any especial act of ours by which we could have introduced the theistic element into our system, if we did not receive it from our primitive Ṛṣis?"

Satyakāma. – "I think I can. Gotama and Kaṇāda, when they introduced *atmā,* or spirit, into their list of substances, did not discriminate between any two *orders* of *atmā.* Later writers of your School, finding that the original teachers said nothing of a Deity or His attributes, made room for Īśwara, or God, by classifying atmā as two-fold; *jīvatmā,* or ordinary soul, and *paramātmā,* or Supreme spirit, that is God. This was a classification which your leading doctors never thought of, or we cannot conceive how they could have omitted it, when they were so particular in their divisions and classifications, elsewhere, even on common topics."

Nyāyaratna. – "I am sure you will not consider me too sensitive if I protest against this free use of the names of our holy Ṛṣis."

Tarkakāma. – "You have yourself maintained in your essay that our original teachers spoke to initiated pupils only, and that Sūtras without commentaries are sealed books. Why then do you wish to break the *seal?* You must receive our commentary. We protest we do not receive Kaṇāda's teaching in a *nirīśwara,* or godless, sense. You must not therefore think that Kaṇāda was as atheistic as Kapila."

Scarcely had Tarkakāma uttered these last words, when the Sāṅkhya śāstri, who was listening to the conversation with deep interest, ejaculated, "Oh this Kali yuga!" Tarkakāma instantly felt as if he had given some real cause of offence, and immediately apologized for the use he had inadvertently made of Kapila's name. "No offence, Sir," answered Kāpila. "Never mind it. Kapila has left behind him too venerated a name to be soiled by your handling. I know you did not intend any offence. I only wish you had employed a little of your generous ingenuity in favour of the Sāṅkhya. You might then have easily made out that it is no more atheistic than the Nyāya."

"For what" continued the Sāṅkhya philosopher, "was Kapila's difficulty? Was it not simply this – that intelligent agency would be inconceivable without an effort, and an effort would imply a motive. The supposition of a motive in the case of a creator, would in other words be a supposition of incompetency. One could not have a motive without yielding to a desire. The same difficulty I see in the Nyāya. The founder of this system classifies *pravṛtti,* or effort, with *dukha,* or pain, *doṣa,* or fault, and other hindrances to the soul's emancipation. And he expressly defines *fault* to be a cause or effect of *effort*. How *could* he then consistently inculcate the existence of an Intelligent Creator? The author of the Vedānta and Śaṅkarācārya argue for their pantheism on this very ground. They say that if the world were not identical with God, and if He created it as a substance, separate from Himself, then, on the very principles of the Nyāya, He would be chargeable with the fault of making efforts under motives, and thus be proved to be *no God* at all[20]. The only difference between Kapila and your teachers consists in the one's frankly acknowledging his difficulty, and the other *covertly* teaching the same doctrine."

Nyāyaratna.—"As we are discussing certain points which Satyakāma had urged against the Nyāya, you will excuse us, learned Kāpila, if we decline a controversy with you on the present occasion. You have allowed, and I am sure you have done so heartily, that Tarkakāma meant no disrespect to the venerable founder of your school, and my friend has also expressed regret for the lapse of his tongue.

"But now, Satyakāma, you must not go on with your own fancies about the teaching of great Ṛṣis. You must allow us to interpret our own doctrine. We say that Atoms are the material, and God the efficient cause of the world. This doctrine I understand is much admired even in Europe. Philosophers have in all ages had recourse to it in order to account for the physical phenomena which the world presents. Even Sir Isaac Newton, I am told, was in this respect a follower of our Kaṇāda.

"Our doctrine, continued Nyāyaratna, is the same which Gotama held and Kaṇāda taught. We have no fancy of our own, no new theory. We keep to the old paths of our primitive Ācāryas. The doctrine is simply this; that God constructed the world by combining an infinite number of hard, indivisible, eternal, and indestructible particles. The primary combination was of two atoms, which we call *dvyaṇuka,* or a binary. The combination however does not become, what geometers would call, a *magnitude,* before a *trasareṇu* (tertiary), or a compound of three *dvyaṇukas* is formed.

"It is necessary to believe that matter is not divisible beyond a certain point. The point where it is no further divisible we call an atom. If infinite divisibility were allowed, than might a mustard seed be pronounced to be equal to Mount Meru[21], for it is a simple mathematical truth that all things, which are divided by *infinite,* are equal. Now unless you are prepared to combat this great theory, thus explained, you must not assail the time-honoured system of the Nyāya.

Satyakāma.—"I shall most willingly accept your own interpretation of your scholastic theory. I will give up further criticism on your original Sūtras by simply remarking that the history of philosophy requires, that there should be a discrimination between your modern explanations and the opinions of the founders of your school. We are all bound to contribute our mite to the discovery of historic truth. But I admit that the Naiyāyika doctrine of our day does not ignore an intelligent Framer of the world. Still you hold that your Atoms are uncreated and eternal, do you not?"

"Of course," said the Naiyāyika, "that is the peculiar teaching of our School, and I may say I glory in following it."

"How came they into existence?"

"We say they are eternal. They never *began* to exist."

"You maintain," said Satyakāma, "that souls are eternal, and matter is eternal. Your School then teaches that God created nothing in reality. He merely combined the Atoms and constructed the universe."

"What more *could* he do? How could he *make* Atoms? Can the artificer make his bricks if he has no earth?"

"The artificer, said Satyakāma, is a frail mortal.—He is not omnipotent. But God is. You cannot account for the wonderful arrangement which the world exhibits without assuming the existence of an Independent and Eternal Being, all sufficient and all powerful, of infinite goodness and wisdom. The supposition of dead matter, co-eternal and independent, must militate against His perfection. 'If without something distinct wholly from Himself He cannot produce any thing, then must He want some thing external; and whosoever wanteth any thing is not all-sufficient[22].'

"The theory of a co-eternal and independent material substance," continued Satyakāma, "is opposed both to our *moral convictions* and to the fundamental principles of sound philosophy. A rightly constituted mind attributes all perfection to the Deity. It is among our religious intuitions. Is it not, Nyāyaratna?"

"Of course it is."

"The mind you pronounce to be an organ of internal sensation. It must then have the same claim to our confidence as the external organs. In fact without the mind you could not have a complete perception of any object of even external sensation. In a matter of pure mental intuition, the testimony of the mind is quite as strong as the testimony of other senses in matters of external sensation. Now the mind intuitively bears testimony to a Supreme Intelligence of all perfection, the author of the universe. This testimony is as valid as the testimony of your other senses to the existence of the river Gangā, from the banks of which you have jsut returned after your morning ablution."

"I do not in the least doubt what you say."

"You cannot then without violence to the religious intuitions of your mind allow a rival material cause, existing beside God from eternity."

Naiyāyika.—"Would you say that the great Newton offered violence to our moral convictions and religious intuitions, by inculcating the atomic theory?"

Satyakāma.—"Certainly, *not.* He did not hold the Atomic theory after your manner. He did not allow that any thing could be uncreated and eternal, but God. This one omnipotent and all-knowing Creator was sufficient in his estimation for making every thing that exists. Listen to his own words. At the close of his Opticks, he says; 'All these things being considered, it seems 'probable to me that God in the beginning formed matter 'in solid, massy, hard, impenetrable, moveable particles, of such sizes and figures, and with such other properties and in such proportions to space, as most conduced to the end for which He formed them, and that these primitive particles, being solids, are incomparably harder than any porous bodies compounded of them, even so very hard as never to wear or break in pieces, no ordinary power being able to divide what God had made one in the first creation. While the particles continue entire, they may compose bodies of one and the same nature and texture in all ages : but should they wear away or break in pieces, the nature of things depending on them would be changed. Water and Earth composed of old worn particles and fragments of particles would not be of the same nature and texture now with water and earth composed of entire particles in the beginning. And therefore that nature may be lasting, the changes of corporeal things are to be placed only in the various 'separations and new associations and motions of these permanent particles; compounded bodies being apt to break, not in the midst of solid particles, but where those particles are laid together, and only touch in a few points.[23]'"

Naiyāyika.— "How could a substance be made out of nothing?"

Satyakāma.—"What can be impossible for the omnipotent?"

"We never see any thing made out of nothing," rejoined Nyāyaratna.

"Neither do you see particles without magnitude, said Satyakāma, producing by combination substances possessed of magnitude. Your atoms have no length, breadth, or thickness, and yet you allow they produce all three by combination.

"See how Śaṅkara[24] criticises your theory—which indeed is as unphilosophical, as it is repugnant to religious intuition. You say that the universe was formed by the combination of eternal atoms which are endowed with colour, but are, like mathematical points, without dimension. The measure of an atom you express by a word, which, again, you cannot explain but by the word *atomic!*[25] When two atoms combine and form a binary, you attribute to the compound a measure which you call *hraswa,* or short. You do not call it *dīrgha,* or long. And it is not until the compound you call *mahat* (great), or a magnitude, is formed, that you attribute to it the property of sensible matter. Without pronouncing any opinion on Śaṅkara's criticism, may I simply ask you, whether it can be more difficult to conceive that the universe was created, both in matter and form, by a Supreme and all-sufficient Intelligence, than that material length, breadth, and thickness arose *naturally* from invisible particles devoid of those properties? And whether it is not far more philosophical to recognize One Supreme Being alone as existing, independently, by and of himself, and to attribute to His creative power the existence of whatever else has any sort of being, than to maintain a theory of innumerable eternal entities, of which you can form no conception but by detaching from them your conception of all things that you know, or have any idea of? If God could produce magnitudes out of *no magnitude,* why could he not also call into existence that hypothetical entity of *no magnitude* out of a state of absolute non entity?

"The original creation, Sir, under the agency of an omnipotent Supreme cause, is not to be compared with mere human manufacture. I must again refer to Śaṅkarācāray's excellent remark[26]. You must not expect divine perfection in human weakness, nor ought you to attribute human deficiency to the divine sufficiency.

"To prevent mistakes, however, let me say that I have no wish to censure Kaṇāda's doctrine of *atoms,* as such. It is simply with his doctrine of *eternal* atoms that I quarrel. European science is obliged to own that we cannot speak otherwise than conjecturally about the ulitmate constitution of matter.

"That the Vaiśeṣika view, however, has its difficulties, is evident from the notion of *Pañcīkaraṇa* braoched by some of our philosophers, and from certain other strictures of Śaṅkarācārya on your doctrine.

"The process of *Pañcīkaraṇa* is the formation of a specific Atom of one element by the combination of parts of those of others. A specific earthy Atom, for instance, is made up of ½ of a general earthy Atom, and $\frac{1}{8}$ of each of the other elementary atoms[27]. This process pre-supposes the *divisibility* of what you have assumed as indivisible.

"The Atomic theory involves another difficulty which is thus represented by our ingenious Śaṅkarācārya : 'The combination of one Atom with another must either be by entire amalgamation or by partial contact. If it be an entire amalgamation, then because of the impossibility of collective increase[28], the compound will still be an *Atom,* and an invisible substance; for it is the combination of one spacious substance with another that is visible. If on the other hand the combination be a partial contact, then the question is (virtually conceded to be) one of aggregates (*i.e.* it is no longer a combination of *indivisible* Atoms)[29].'

I do not however mean to say that I agree with Śaṅkarācārya in his objection. I think the whole matter is one that science cannot properly deal with. You may form *convenient hypotheses* about it, but nothing more. The Brāhminical philosopher has the same liberty to try to account for facts by hypotheses as any other. But our question is an entirely different one, with which experimental science has nothing whatever to do. Granted the *existence* of Atoms; *how* came they into existence?

"I must hope that as you have apparently modified your theory, so far as to introduce the idea of a supreme Intelligence as the efficient cause of the Universe, by subdividing the *atmā,* or spirit, of your original teachers into the *jīvātamā,* or ordinary soul, and *paramātmā,* or supreme Spirit, – you will continue to improve that idea until you arrive at the conclusion, which alone is consistent with sound philosophy, that having deduced the existence of an Omnipotent and absolutely independent eternal Intelligence, as the author of all things, you have no room left for the conception of any other eternal and independent principle."

Nyāyaratna. – "Your argument, Satyakāma, has, I cannot deny, some force in it, but it appears to me to prove too much. If you will not allow more than one eternal principle, how will you dispose of the human soul? Will you throw yourself into the arms of Vedāntism, and pronounce human souls to be identical with the Divine Spirit? If you do not, I cannot see how you can deny a separate eternal existence to the human soul. You cannot therefore persist in your doctrine of one eternal essence. You must acknowledge at least a second, even the human soul. Your theory will otherwise be confounded with the teaching of such Vedāntic texts (I mean as they are interpreted by Vedāntists) as the following; 'This was in the beginning a spirit like a male. He looked but found nothing else beside himself. This was in the beginning a spirit even one. All these become one here. This was in the beginning one without a second[30].'"

Satyakāma. – "There is no fear of my falling back on Vedāntism; but I do maintain, – not that this Universe was a *spirit* in the beginning, or that human souls were identical with the Supreme Being, but – that there was only ONE spirit (including, doubtless, in His own infinite nature, mysterious depths that we can never fathom, but still *one*), and *nothing else* before the origin of things. As I have already said, I allow one eternal principle alone, and that is, the Supreme Author of all things. As to human souls I cannot admit their eternity. It is easy to say the soul is eternal, but it is not so easy to define what you mean by that saying. I am afraid you are somewhat affected by Vedāntism yourself when you speak in that way. What can you mean by the soul collectively? The soul has no collective existence, no *Samaṣṭi,* except in Vedāntic vocabulary. Human souls have each an individual existence. How many souls do you call eternal. Every human soul?"

Tarkakāma.—"And what if we did say so?"

Satyakāma.—"How many souls then do you reckon to be eternal?"

Tarkakāma.—"As many as there are human beings."

Satyakāma.—"Whether in human form or not? For your mythology speaks of souls passing through the bodies of beasts."

Tarkakāma.—"All souls, those in brute forms included."

"And in the forms of gods?"

"Yes all spiritual essences, men, beasts, gods."

"And demons?"

"Yes, demons."

"But souls pass through vegetable forms too," said Satyakāma. For, says the Veda, 'some souls enter the womb for embodiment; some into immoveable bodies, (or trees)[31]. Witness the case of the two trees plucked up from their roots by the infant Kṛṣṇa. Are the souls of trees too eternal?"

"Well, suppose I say, trees too."

"So then, said Satyakāma, men, brutes, gods, demons, trees are all eternal. Can you give an estimate of the number of your eternal essence?"

"I have no doubt our Ṛṣis could have given it."

"But to cut short such a *śuṣka tarka* (dry and unprofitable debate), I appeal to you Nyāyaratna, said Satyakāma, if it be not perfectly unphilosophical, because absolutely unnecessary, and egregiously extravagant, to assume such an indefinite number of eternal essences, when one supreme essence is sufficient to account for all things, visible or invisible, material or spiritual.

"Consider again the bad morals and the bad theology which such a theory is calculated to teach. What would you say, learned Nyāyaratna, to a man who denied that God was his Maker and heavenly Father?"

Nyāyaratna. – "I should say he was exceedingly impious."

"Much more so, than if he denied his earthly parents, though that is sufficiently heinous."

"Certainly."

"Well," said Satyakāma, "I am sure you will appreciate the argument with which I mean to support my assertion that your theory of the eternity of souls teaches bad morals and bad theology. If all souls are eternal, they must be uncreated too, for, says Kaṇāda, that which is eternal is not dependent on a cause; and if uncreated, and, yet in existence, they must be self-existent. To say they are self-existent is to say they have independent existence. They need not then acknowledge God as their Maker or heavenly Father. If they are independent essences, possessed of absolute existence, they can not be rightfully called upon to acknowledge a Supreme Being as the Moral Governor of the universe. They are themselves a sort of miniature gods. Nor can any Supreme Being be especially entitled to the epithet of *Svayambhu,* or self-existent. You see the impiety to which the doctrine leads?"

Nyāyaratna. – "To confess the truth, Satyakāma, when we received our scholastic doctrine of the eternity of the soul, we never stopped to calculate its consequences. We received it as a deduction from our received tenets. But I now see that it involves, in its turn, another deduction, which is certainly absurd and impious, that every creature must have independent existence. Without countenancing Vedāntism, we cannot speak abstractedly of the soul's existence. The soul, you have truly remarked, can have no *samaṣṭi,* or collective reality. We may indeed speak collectively of the soul's characteristics, but that will imply that the characteristics are distributive, that is to say, applicable to all individual souls. I must thank you for suggesting a consideration which imparts a new aspect to our theory. If my venerable preceptor were now living I would submit my doubts, and ask him, how the soul could be eternal without being also self-existent and absolutely independent."

Satyakāma.—"I commend your candour, Nyāyaratna. But since your preceptor is no more, is it not your duty to consider and determine the question yourself? To the world you are his representative, and to God you are responsible for what you teach. You may yet save your school from the odium of inculcating a doctrine, which as you justly say, borders on impiety, and saps the foundation both of philosophy and theology. The object of philosophy is to narrow as much as possible the range of first principles and first causes. To acknowledge countless millions of eternal principles, when one supreme Author can account for them all, is a *gaurava,* a needless multiplication of causes, which is as unphilosophical as it is irreligious. It is a violence to our moral convictions and religious intuitions. The glory and perfections of God can leave no room for a second eternal and independent principle. What must be thought then of your countless millions of eternal beings, material and spiritual, standing, as it were, in rivalry with God?"

The apparent surrender on the part of Nyāyaratna of a peculiar tenet of the Brāhminical philosophy struck us all with a painful sentiment. Āgamika seemed absorbed in melancholy thoughtfulness. Tarkakāma, too, already vexed with himself for having inadvertently given offence to Kāpila, maintained a sullen silence. Not a voice was heard for some minutes. Then the meeting broke up, rather abruptly, by the company rising spontaneously, and separating with the customary civilities and salutations.

References

1. आद्यमिति सर्गाद्यकालीनमित्यर्थः॥
2. अदृष्टमप्यर्थमदृष्टवैभवात् करोति सुप्तिर्जनदर्शनातिथिं।

Naiṣadha, I. 39.

3. तां हंसमाला शरदीवगङ्गां महौषधिं नक्तमिवात्मभासः।

स्थिरोपदेशामुपदेशकाले प्रपेदिरे प्राक्तनजन्मविद्यां॥

Kumāra Sambhava.

4. See page 93 Foot note.
5. संसारमूलकारणयो धर्म्माधर्म्मयोः परीक्षा॥
6. अपसर्पणमुपसर्पणमशितपीतसंयोगाः कार्य्यान्तरसंयोगाश्चेत्यदृष्टकारितानि। V. ii.
7. पूर्व्वकृतफलानुबन्धात्तदुत्पत्तिः। III. 132.
8. मणिगमनं सूच्यभिसर्पणमित्यदृष्टकारणकम्। V. i.
9. न केवलं यो महतोपभाषते शृणोति तस्मादपि यः स पाकभाक्।

Kumāra Sambhava.

10. एवं शप्ता स्म भगवन् पित्रा दैववशात् पुरा। Mārkan. Pu.

सेयमुच्चतरता दुरितानामन्यजन्मनि मयैव कृतानां।

युष्मदीयमपि या महिमानं जेतुमिच्छति कथापथपारं॥

Naiṣadha.

11. ये परमाणुं पुरुषकर्म्माधिष्ठितत्वात् जगत्कारणत्वेन वर्णयन्ति तान् प्रतीदमुच्यते परमाणवः प्रवर्तन्त इति सततं प्रवृत्त्या भवितव्यं अथ विशेषापेक्षाः प्रवर्तन्ते। * * * क्षीरादिवदचेतनस्यापि प्रवृत्तिरिति चेत् यथापत्यभरणार्थं क्षीरादेरचेतनस्यापि प्रवृत्तिरेवं परमाणवोऽचेतनाः पुरुषार्थे प्रवर्तिष्यन्त इति तन्न युक्तं साध्यसमत्वात् यथैव परमाणवः स्वतन्त्राः प्रवर्तन्त इति साध्यं तथा क्षीराद्यचेतनं स्वतन्त्रं प्रवर्तत इति यदि स्वतन्त्रं क्षीरादि प्रवर्तेत मृतेष्वपि प्रवर्तेत न तु प्रवर्तते। Gotama-bhāṣya.

12. वायुसन्निकर्षे प्रत्यक्षाभावात् दृष्टं लिङ्गं न विद्यते। तस्मादागमिकं। संज्ञाकर्म्म त्वस्मद्विशिष्टानां लिङ्गं॥

13. अस्मद्विशिष्टानां ईश्वरमहर्षीणां सत्वे लिङ्गं॥ Śaṅkar Miśra.

14. संज्ञाकर्तुर्जगत्कर्तुश्चाभेदसूचनार्थं।

    यः शब्दो यत्रेश्वरेण सङ्केतितः स तत्र साधुः॥ Ibid.

15. यापि * * सापि द्वादशेहनि पिता नाम कुर्य्यादित्यादि विधिनानूनमीश्वरप्रयुक्तेव॥

16. See Hodgson's Illustrations, p. 60.

17. ईदृशेश्वरसिद्धिः सिद्धा। III. 57.

18. See page 141, Note 5.

19. विभागावस्थानां तावदणूनां संयोगः कर्म्मापेक्षोभ्युपगन्तव्यः कर्म्मवतां तन्त्वादीनां संयोगदर्शनात् कर्म्मणश्च कार्य्यत्वान्निमित्तं किमप्यभ्युपगन्तव्यं अनभ्युपगमे निमित्ताभावान्नाणुष्वाद्यङ्कर्म्म स्यात्। अभ्युपगमेपि यदि प्रयत्नोभिघातादिर्वा यथा दृष्टं किमपि कर्म्मणो निमित्तमभ्युपगम्येत तस्यासंभवान्नैवाणुष्वाद्यं कर्म्म स्यात्। न हि तस्यामवस्थायामात्मगुणः प्रयत्नः संभवति। शरीराभावात् शरीरप्रतिष्ठे हि मनस्यात्ममनःसंयोगे सत्यात्मगुणः। प्रयत्नो जायते एतेनाभिघाताद्यपि दृष्टं निमित्तं प्रत्याख्यातव्यं सर्गोत्तरकालं हि तत् सर्व्वं नाद्यस्य कर्म्मणो निमित्तं संभवति। अथादृष्टमाद्यस्य कर्म्मणो निमित्तमित्युच्येत तत्पुनरात्मसमावायि वा स्यादणुसमवायि वा उभयथापि नादृष्टं निमित्तमणुषु कर्म्मावकल्पेत अदृष्टम्स्याचेतनत्वात्। न ह्यचेतनं चेतनेनानधिष्ठितं स्वतन्त्रं प्रवर्तते प्रवर्त्तयतिवेति साङ्ख्यपरीक्षायामभिहितं आत्मनश्चानुत्पन्नचैतन्यस्य तस्यामवस्थायामचेतनत्वात् आत्मसमवायित्वाभ्युपगमाच्च नादृष्टमणुषु कर्म्मणो निमित्तं स्यात्। असंबन्धात् अदृष्टवता पुरुषेणास्त्यणूनां सम्बन्ध हति चेत् संबन्धसातत्यात् प्रवृत्ति सातत्यप्रसङ्गः नियामकान्तराभावात् तदेवं नियतस्य कस्यचित्कर्म्मनिमित्तस्याभावान्नाणुष्वाद्यं कर्म्म स्यात् कर्म्माभावात् तन्निबन्धनः। संयोगो न स्यात् संयोगाभावाच्च तन्निबन्धनं द्व्यणुकादिकार्य्यजातं न स्यात्।

Com. Vedānta Sūtra, II. ii. 12.

20. अपिच प्रवर्त्तनालक्षणा दोषा इति न्यायवित्समयः नहि कश्चिददोषप्रयुक्तः स्वार्थे परार्थे वा प्रवर्त्तमानो दृश्यते। * * स्वार्थवत्त्वादीश्वरस्यानीश्वरप्रसङ्गात्। Śaṅkara. Com. Ved. II.ii. 37.

21. सर्वेषामनवस्थितावयवत्वे मेरुसर्षपयोस्तुल्यपरिमाणत्वापत्तिः॥

22. Bp. Pearson.

23. Whewell's Philosophy of the Inductive Sciences.

24. परमाणवः किल कञ्चित्कालमनारब्धकार्य्या यथायोगं रूपादिमन्तः पारिमाण्डल्यपरिमाणास्तिष्ठन्ति। ते च पश्चाददृष्टादिपुरःसराः संयोगसचिवाश्च सन्तो द्व्यणुकादिक्रमेण कृत्स्नं कार्य्यजातमारभन्ते कारणगुणाश्च कार्य्ये गुणान्तरं। यदा द्वौ परमाणू द्व्यणुकमारभेते तदा परमाणुगता रूपादिगुणविशेषाः शुक्लादयो द्व्यणुके शुक्लादीनपरानारभन्ते। परमाणुगुणविशेषस्तु पारिमाण्डल्यं न द्व्यणुके पारिमाण्डल्यमपरमारभते द्व्यणुकस्य परिमाणान्तरयोगाभ्युपगमात् अणुत्वह्रस्वत्वे हि द्व्यणुकवर्त्तिनी परिमाणे वर्णयन्ति। यदापि द्वे द्व्यणुके चतुरणुकमारभेते तदापि समानं द्व्यणुकसमवायिनां शुक्लादीनामारम्भकत्वं। अणुत्वह्रस्वत्वे तु द्व्यणुकसमवायिनी अपि नैवारभेते चतुरणुकस्य महत्त्वदीर्घत्व-परिमाणयोगाभ्युपगमात्॥

25. पारिमाण्डल्यं अणुपरिमाणं॥

26. See foot note page 132.

27. द्विधाविधाय चैकैकं चतुर्द्धा प्रथमं पुनः खस्वेतरद्वितीयांशैर्योजनात् पञ्च पञ्च ते। Pañcadaśī.

28. Śaṅkara alludes to the dogma of the Naiyāyikas themselves that the measures of Atoms, each being infinitely small,cannot increase by addition. If the dimension of a binary atom were supposed to be the aggregate measure of the parts, it would, on their theory, be *still more infinitely small* as a compound : thus,

पारिमाण्डल्यभिन्नानां कारणत्वमुदाहृतं। Bhāṣāparichheda.

पारिमाण्डल्यं अणुपरिमाणं कारणत्वं तद्भिन्नानामित्यर्थः अणुपरिमाणं न तु

कस्यापि कारणं परिमाणस्य स्वसमानजातीयोत्कृष्टपरिमाणजनकत्वात् महत्त्वारब्धस्य महत्तरत्ववत् अणुजन्यस्याणुतरत्वप्रसङ्गाच्च।

Siddhānta muktāvalī.

29. संयोगश्चाणोरण्वन्तरेण सर्व्वात्मना वा स्यादेकदेशेन वा सर्व्वात्मना चेदुपचयानुपपत्तेरणुमात्रत्वप्रसङ्गोदृष्टविपर्य्ययप्रसङ्गश्च प्रदेशवतोद्रव्यस्य प्रदेशवता द्रव्यान्तरेण संयोगस्य दृष्टत्वात् एकदेशेन चेत् सावयवत्वप्रसङ्गः॥

Com. II. ii. 12.

30. आत्मैवेदमग्र आसीत् पुरुषविधः सोऽनुवीक्ष्य नान्यदात्मनोऽपश्यत् अत्र हि एते सर्व्वे एकं भवन्ति।

Bṛhadāraṇyaka. The other passages will be found elsewhere.

31. योनिमन्ये प्रपद्यन्ते शरीरत्वाय देहिनः स्थाणुमन्येऽनुसंयन्ति यथा कर्म्म यथा श्रुतं॥

DIALOGUE V

FROM THE SAME TO THE SAME

Our last conference had an abrupt termination. The regrets which Nyāyaratna expressed for having all this time been holding a doctrine from which it followed, as a legitimate inference, that every soul, and consequently every man, might claim the title of *Svayambhu,* or self-existent, produced a strong impression on us all. No one felt disposed to keep up the discussion at the time. Even Tarkakāma seemed for a moment to lose his presence of mind. So after some desultory conversation of a purely social nature, and the customary civilities, we returned each to his own home. The next morning the same party met again on the banks of the river; and when the prescribed ablutions were over, all went in a body to the scene of the conference. Nyāyaratna alone was not there. He had returned to his native village after the conference the same evening.

Āgamika began the conversation by avowing that he had been thinking all night on the consequences, which, according to Satyakāma's showing, might follow from the doctrine of the soul's eternity. "But," said he, turning to Satyakāma, "your ingenious remark against a doctrine in which all our schools are agreed admits of a conclusive reply, though it did not occur to me at the time. We say the soul is uncreated and eternal, but we do not say it can perform any functions before it is joined with body and mind. That junction is properly speaking its *creation,* and the beginning of its existence. Its previous existence is more nominal than real, because it is not competent at that time for thought or action, not having as yet obtained a body and mind. It cannot therefore be properly called self-existent, for its *real existence* is derived from something *outside itself.*"

Satyakāma.—"You say the soul's existence before it is endowed with body and mind is more nominal than real. That is not however the consentient opinion of your philosophers. The Bhagavad Gītā expressly magnifies that existence, when it says that the soul is 'neither born at any time, nor does it ever die[1].' And is it not also that very existence, without body and mind, which your doctors consider the *summum bonum,* or chief good? Do they not say that the soul's connection with body and mind is its greatest misery? Do they not teach you that *niśreyasa,* or your best interest, consists in emancipation from the bondage of births? Does not Gotama classify *birth* with *pain* and fault and the other hindrances to emancipation? Is it not separation from body and mind to which you are taught to look up as your supreme felicity? Is it not return to the original state of the soul that philosophers pronounce to be the end and object of their speculations? If God be your Creator, *only* because he caused the connection of the soul with body and mind,—the very connection which you condemn as an evil,—then He cannot have conferred any great beneift on you; nor do you show much piety when you look forward to the time when you may be able to *cast off* that benefit, and return to the state in which you were before the 'primal action of atoms and of mind.' I do not see, Āgamika, how the explanation suggested by you can exhibit the theology of the Nyāya in a more favourable light."

Tarkakāma.—"It appears to me, my dear friends, you are proceeding too fast in your discussions. Will you allow me to suggest a doubt, (I have a srong opinion myself on the point), whether you are not mistaking the province of the Nyāya? It does not profess to be a *theological* system."

Āgamika.—"I am very much of the same opinion with yourself; but the inquiries of philosophers bear *some* relation,—do they not, Tarkakāma, to the highest of all problems?"

Satyakāma.—"It is only so far as the Darśanas tend to impede the right view of divine truth, that we are concerned with them, at least for the present. However, as you, Tarkakāma, have a strong opinion, perhaps you will throw some light on the point."

Tarkakāma.—"Let us estimate every thing by the degree in which it attains its professed object."

Satyakāma.—"Certainly; its *professed* object."

Tarkakāma.—"And what is the manifest aim of the Nyāya, but to afford us an account of the methods of attaining knowledge? Its object was to teach the art of reasoning; and, as all reasoning depended on *proof,* Gotama very properly laid the greatest stress on *that,* and propounded rules which have gained the admiration even of Mletcha philosophers. He tells you that proof is fourfold—*Pratyakṣa,* or Perception, *Anumāna,* or Inference, *Upamāna,* or Analogy, and *Śabda,* or Affirmation.

"Perception he defined to be the knowledge derived from the contact of the senses with their objects. It includes internal perception, or intuition, but excludes the errors that may be based on unsound sensation. Inference is grounded on perception[2],' and is subdivided into three classes, *Pūrvavat,* on a priori, *Śeṣavat,* or a Posteriori, and *sāmānyato dṛṣṭam,* or *mixed. Anumāna* includes both induction and deduction. As this branch of evidence involves the art of reasoning, and the least flaw may induce serious errors, minute details are given of sound and unsound inferences, so that fallacies may be at once detected, and the truth recognized, even when mixed up with error. Analogy is defined to be that which helps you to arrive at the unknown by means of that which is known; and Affirmation is the teaching of unerring authority.

"With a view to promote the detection of error and the discovery of truth, the eminent founder of this great School enters into an explanation of the true nature of *doubt,* of *example,* of *demonstration,* of *argument,* direct and indirect, of *controversy,* of *objection*, of *fallacies,* of *reason,* of *confutation*—in fact of every thing which can claim a place in a system of logic.

"Men do not generally err much in their perception and sensation. It is seldom that we mistake land for water, or a house for a tank. Well has it been said in the Veda that the *eye is truth,* although *words and thoughts may be untrue.* Hence when a traveller relates a story and *affirms he has seen it*, we believe *it to be true*[3]. But we are always liable to make mistaken inferences and draw false conclusions. Gotama therefore considered the subject of *Inference* as the most important. He divided the process into five *avayava,* or members—1st. *Pratijñā,* or the statement of the question, 2nd. *Hetu,* or reason, 3rd. *Udāharaṇa,* or example, 4th. *Upanaya,* or application, 5th. *Nigamana* or conclusion.

"*Anumāna* is defined to be the instrument of *anumiti,* which means the knowledge derived from the ascertained fact of the subject possessing a property which is *pervaded,* or constantly attended, by another property. The knowledge, that such a mountain is fiery, is *anumiti;* the instrument, whereby that knowledge is produced, is the ascertainment of the fact, that the mountain has *smoke,* and that *smoke* is universally attended by *fire. Anumāna* is therefore further explained as the contemplation of the sign by which the facts of the pervading and pervaded properties may be ascertained[4].

"I should be unwilling to repeat the well known illustration of the *five members* by the mountain and fire. But I have heard it objected against Gotama that his division of an argument is unnecessarily prolix, and that the Grecian syllogism is simpler. It is therefore necessary to bear in mind that Gotama's anumāna is not identically the same with the Aristotelian syllogism. *Anumāna* is classed among *Pramāṇas,* or instruments of *pramā* is classed among *Pramāṇas,* or instruments of *pramā,* which signifies accurate knowledge, and accuracy consists in *attributing to a thing that which is in it.*[5] The object of anumāna, therefore, is not merely to test the logical correctness of the conclusion, but to investigate the *major* and *minor* premises themselves. Nor must we forget that the author was writing at a time when the minds of men were still infected with the heresies that had threatened the stability of Brāhminical institutions before his age. He was accordingly desirous of teaching the most efficacious way of dealing with error, without caring for what the ignorant might choose to condemn as *tautology.* He had shown in his defence of the Vedas[6] that the charge of tautology, preferred against them, was founded in popular error, that there was, in reality, no fault in the tautology of the sacred writings, and that what some people called tautology, was only a fuller explanation of truth in condescension to human weakness, and a more powerful enforcement of precepts in consideration of human callousness. And so he taught that anumāna consisted of five members. The first two, or the statement and reason, form what the Yavanas called an *enthymeme. The mountain is fiery; because it has smoke.* It is a convenient and concise way of stating an argument, and is generally followed by controversial writers where there is no *living* disputation. No other form is made use of in Sūtras and commentaries. But when you may have to convince an adversary before yourself, the three remaining members will be found practically useful. After you have given the statement and the reason, you may be called upon to *justify* your reason. So you have the third member, or *example* illustrating the minor premise; thus, *whatsoever has smoke has fire, such as a culinary hearth.* The fourth member is the application of the rule to your subject; *now the mountain has the same :* the fifth is the inevitable conclusion, *therefore it is fiery.* The fourth and fifth are repetitions of the second and first, calculated to carry conviction into your adversary's mind, and preclude the possibility of doubt.

"It may be said that the first, or the Proposition, is itself no part of the argument[7], being, at the time of the statement, a mere assumption without proof; and that the second, or Reason, should have been placed as the first member. But the first is simply a statement of the question under discussion, and, prior to its enunciation, the appeal to Reason would be like the production of a witness before the plaint or plea is filed. In a disputation, too, you may properly anticipate your adversary's challenge to prove a certain point, as for instance (if you have a *Mīmāṁsaka* before you), that sound is not eternal; and in such cases it is necessary, for the sake of perspicuity, that you begin with laying down the proposition which you intend to prove.

"It has been objected against the third member that a solitary example cannot lead to a universal rule. It is never pretended that the rule *relies* on the example. We say distinctly that no examples, how numerous soever they may be, no observations, how often soever they may be repeated, can *of themselves* establish a universal rule. A hundred observations may err, and therefore fail in this respect[8]. And if we ever speak of one example in point, where counter examples are not found, it is practically to illustrate, not logically to establish, the *vyāpti,* or universality of the rule.

"The fourth and fifth members again have been objected to on the ground of their not being necessary. It is said that since the third gives the universal rule, and the second the particular fact, the question is *ipso facto* demonstrated. The second however only gives the reason (*smoke*) for the inference (of fire). It is not intended, like the fourth, solemnly to identify a particular mountain as containing smoke *de facto*[9]. And with reference to the fifth member you cannot say it is useless, or that the fact is already demonstrated and the argument completed in the first four[10]; for as you are talking of a particular mountain, the argument is not really complete before you have formally concluded, without the possibility of an opposite error, whether it be one of rule or fact, that it—even the mountain you are pointing to—is, and cannot but be, FIERY.

"This is but a meagre statement of Gotama's excellencies as a teacher of mankind, but it may serve as a specimen of what I conceive to be the true point of view from which his merits should be canvassed."

Satyakāma.—"I concur with you, Tarkakāma, in thinking that the logical principles laid down by Gotama and Kaṇāda, the rules they have enunciated for the detection of error, the ideas they have broached on the origin of human knowledge (excepting, of course, their theory of the soul's pre-existence) are radically sound, and, in some points, unimprovably good. I will not undertake to decide that Gotama's four-fold classification of *pramāṇas,* as instruments of true knowledge, is not unnecessarily prolix, or that Kapila's and Kaṇāda's abridgements are not improvements; nor can I confess that his five-membered syllogism, as expounded by eminent writers on the Nyāya, is *not at all* liable to the charge which has been preferred against it. I must, however, acknowledge that there is great force in the concise explanation, which the author of the Tarka Saṅgraha, has given, of that form of syllogism, though I can find nothing in Gotama corresponding to the discrimination between *svārtha* and *parārtha*—for *oneself* and for *another*[11].

"I may add that Gotama has also done essential service to the cause of truth by exposing the quibbles of those who had denied the possibility of attaining any knowledge by perception or inference[12]; who maintained that Perception could neither be supposed anterior nor posterior to its object, nor again simultaneous with it,—for, if anterior, it would invovle the absurdity of proving an object before its existence, if posterior, it could not really be a proving of the object, and if simultaneous, there would be wanting the idea of succession between proof and its object;—who would, also, either give no room whatever for *doubt,* or open the door to universal scepticism[13]; who would further insist on having *an endless succession of proofs for the proofs themselves,* not allowing axioms or first principles[14]. Gotama correctly says that if there can be no knowledge, no truth, no perception, no proof, then the quibbler himself has no right to obtrude his own opinions, for *they* cannot be proved either. There must, again, be first principles, and first principles *are like the light of a lamp*[15]. It is a pity that the true nature of affirmation, or testimony, has not been more fully expounded by his commentators. Gotama defined affirmation to be *teaching of unerring authority.* '*Āpta,*' says Vātsāyana, 'is one, who, having had ocular proof of a certain matter, desires to communicate it to others, who thereby understand it; and this is a common characteristic of Ṛṣis, Āryas, and Mletchas. The practice of all parties is thereby regulated. Gods, men, and animals act on these proofs, and not on any other. Affirmation is of two kinds, according as the object is visible or invisible. That which is seen *here* is visible, that which appears in the *other* world is invisible. And thus are the words of Ṛṣis and ordinary men divided[16]. So far good. But we have nothing whereby to sift the testimony of 'Ṛṣis, Āryas, and Mletchas.' A great deal of unimportant discussion has been raised in the refutation of frivolous objections on the possibility of mistakes in the import of words. Language may of course be sometimes ambiguous, but it is nevertheless sufficiently explicit for all human purposes. Gotama says, accordingly, 'Reliance is placed on the contents of a statement on the strength of the affirmation of a competent person.' 'By verbal evidence[17], *I believe* this,' says the scholiast.' We do not however find much discussion on the nature and characteristics of credible testimony; nor are we taught how to discriminate between that which may, and that which may not, properly challenge our *belief.*

"I cannot follow Gotama in all he says about the composition of the body, and about the elements. You may have heard that a great many more elementary substances have been discovered than are found in his list. I do not know that the supposition of an *ākāśa* (ether), pervading all space as a *substratum of Sound* is not somewhat gratuitous. But I have no hesitation, on the whole, in acknowledging, learned Tarkakāma, that the works of Gotama and Kaṇāda lay down excellent rules for the investigation of Truth. But here the vulgar proverb is verified : *The man who holds the torch does not see for himself.* Those who inculcated such correct modes of investigating truth failed to find her themselves on some points of great importance. In spite of their care in furnishing us with the methods and instruments of thought, they left us as far as ever from a satisfactory solution of the most important problems that the human mind can propose to itself."

Tarkakāma.–"On this purely philosophical point, we may perhaps fairly expect a dispassionate discussion. What are the truths you think they failed to discover?"

"*Pramāṇa,* Sir," said Satyakāma, "is not *pramā.* The two are quite different. The first is the instrument of true knowledge; the second is true knowledge itself. A person may possess the one, without employing it to get at the other. He may have the instrument, and yet fail to make any worthy use of it. Such I believe to have been the case with Gotama and Kaṇāda. On several points of serious importance they have taught what is inconsistent with their own principles of Reasoning."

Tarkakāma.–"Do not indulge in general censures, Specify what you mean."

Satyakāma.–"I will not again refer to their theology. You say their object was philosophy. Do they not however *profess* to clear the way to final emancipation thereby? Do they not say that a knowledge of their especial topics and categories is necessary for Salvation? Gotama promises Emancipation on an accurate knowledge of his sixteen topics, and Kaṇāda on that of his six categories. What connection those topics or categories can have with the emancipation of the soul, is to me incomprehensible."

Tarkakāma.—"Does not the knowledge of truth lead to the improvement of our nature?"

Satyakāma.—"Gotama does not sepak of the *knowledge of truth,* but of the *true knowledge of his sixteen topics.*"

"You are so hard on poor Gotama," said Tarkakāma.

"An eminent Scholar, himself a Mletcha, has construed his first aphorism in a very different way. 'Gotama starts,' says he, 'with the grand question of all questions, the inquiry as to how we shall attain the *summum bonum,* the chief end of man, as the Westminster catechism literally represents the Sanskrit *paramapuruṣārtha.* The general answer to this he states in his first aphorism, where he lays down further the position that deliverance from evil can be reached only through knowledge of the truth[18].'"

Satyakāma.—"Here are Gotama's own words as, translated by that eminent Scholar himself. 'Proof (*i.e.,* 'the instrument of right notion), that which (as having 'a proof) is the subject of right notion; doubt; motive; familiar fact; scholastic tenet; confutation; ascertainment; disquisition; controversy; cavil; semblance of a reason; perversion; futility; and unfitness to be argued with:—from knowing the truth in regard to these (sixteen things) there is the attainment of the *summum bonum* (niśreyasa)[19].'

"I do not see, continued Satyakāma, what connection most of these topics can have with any such improvement of our spiritual nature, as is involved in the idea of emancipation. You will say, the second topic, 'subject of right notion,' includes every thing. So, according to the Purāṇas, did the mighty ocean, both poison and nectar. Would you then tell a person, who was longing for immortality, to go down to the sea-shore, and drink a quantity of sea water?"

"Do you then deny, asked Tarkakāma, that the pursuit of

philosophy is the highest employment in which man can engage?"

"Philosophy is a loose expression; so I cannot directly answer your question. But to say to a *mumukṣu,* or an inquirer after Salvation, that a knowledge of certain topics and categories is necessary for the soul's welfare, is like telling an invalid, who requires a remedy for the cure of fever, that anatomy and materia medica are necessary to be studied for the removal of diseases."

"But is not the mind improved by the knowledge of logical rules? And as the soul derives, through the mind, the information necessary for its welfare, it follows that the art of disputation is useful for the soul's welfare."

"You mistake me, said Satyakāma, if you think I undervalue the study of logic. That study may be as important a help in leading to right conclusions and guarding against fallacies, as the sextant is to the mariner in making his observations at sea. But the logician should not therefore set forth *Niśreyasa,* or emancipation, as the reward for studying that science."

Tarkakāma.—"But why do you exhaust your energy on mere verbal criticisms? What wrong doctrine do you find in Gotama's philosophy?"

"Let us then consider, said Satyakāma, the nature and end of human existence, as inculcated by Gotama. Your Ācārya places *janma*[20], birth, and *pravṛtti,* activity, among evils, the annihilation of which is necessary for Emancipation. He also says distinctly that birth is a calamity. (Nyāya Sūtras i. 2. and iv. 55). I appeal to you, is birth then essentially an evil[21], and activity a sin?"

Tarkakāma.—"Is it not a fact, notwithstanding what Āgamika said a little while ago, that our birth is attended with numerous sufferings, and that when the soul is born, it is born to misery and unhappiness?"

"Is it not," said Satyakāma "sapping the very foundation

of filial duty to parents, and to piety of God, to say that birth is an essential evil?"

Here I interposed a remark; "I confess it is possible to push the doctrine to an unwarrantable extreme."

"But," said Satyakāma, "has not Gotama already so pushed it? We must get rid of our births if we are desirous of Liberation. This view I know he deduced from the endless transmigrations invovled in his doctrine of a pre-existence. Those transmigrations are in spite of ourselves. We are tied hand and foot by *karma* or *adṛṣṭa*[22]. If we do good, we shall have to return to the world to enjoy our reward. If we commit evil we must still return to undergo our punishment. Tired of such transmigrations, he considered birth itself an evil. The pity is he rested so much on deductions from a theory hastily adopted, in opposition to his own principles of investigation. He did not reason inductively by regular argument from *facts*.

"Then, again, continued Satyakāma, *prvavṛtti,* or activity, is noted down as an evil, and *prvṛtti* is defined to be the originator of the functions of the voice, the understanding, and the body." (Nyāya I. 17).[23]

"I am sure, said Āgamika, you will not tax Gotama with what he has not himself said. He placed *pravṛtti* among *the things to be removed,* but did not call it an evil."

"Whatever is necessary to be removed, rejoined Satyakāma, in order to attain a good object, must be its *pratiyogī,* or something incompatible with it, and therefore an impediment in its way, and whatever is incompatible with a good object, must be an evil. But it is not by mere implication that he condemns *prvṛtti*. He has defined it to be the cause of doṣa, or fault[24]." (I.. 18.)

"I cannot deny that he does say so," replied Āgamika.

"Let us then see what this amounts to. Agreeably to

Gotama's doctrine, it is a fault to speak, think, or do anything. Can this be a true view of the nature of human existence?"

Āgamika. – "It is a fault because it is not the chief good."

Satyakāma. – "And yet, on your theory, the thought, speech, and powers of action are divine gifts; – indeed the only gifts God bestows on man; – for as regards existence, that you do not hold to be a *gift of God,* since the soul is uncreated, and has independent existence. The body and mind are only given by God, and yet, you say, it is a fault, or rather it is not for our chief good, to give exercise to our physical and mental powers."

Āgamika. – "But man has abused the gifts of God. When the nectar is converted to poison, what can you do? You must throw it away."

Tarkakāma. – "Victory to Rama! You have made a very good remark, Āgamika. I contend that Gotama has not pushed any doctrines to unwarrantable extremes, nor is it mere deductions from a 'hastily adopted theory,' that he sets forth in his work. In his representation of the evils of life, he only reasoned from facts, and there is no gap in the chain of his reasonings. Every conclusion has a *hetu,* or reason, to support it. You seem, Satyakāma, to stumble at the 2nd Sūtra in which he shows how certain hindrances to the soul's release require to be removed. I had a sort of presentiment that it might be a stumbling-block in your way, and I have brought with me a leaf from Vātsāyana (the very author to whom you have just made reference) in the hope of smoothing your passage. Now listen attentively how that excellent commentator expounds these grand ideas of Gotama, – ideas which he was the first among our Ṛṣis to embody in a short pithy sentence for the instruction of mankind. That sentence is as follows : 'pain, birth, activity, fault, false notions, – since on the successive annihilation of these in trurn, there is the annihilation of the one next before it, there is (on the annihilation of the last of them) 'Beatitude.' That is to say,

Beatitude proceeds from the annihilation of false notions as its primary cause. Vātsāyana thus expounds this sentence : 'False notions are manifold; (1) with reference to Spirit, that there is no spirit at all; (2) with reference to Matter, that it is spirit; (3) with reference to Pain, that it is pleasure; '(4) with reference to the Transient, that it is eternal; (5) with reference to No-salvation, that it is salvation; (6) with reference to Risk, that it is security; (7) with reference to the Culpable, that it is desirable; (8) with reference to the thing to be eschewed, that it is not to be eschewed; (9) with reference to Activity, that it does not involve *karma,* (deed), nor the fruits of deeds; (10) with reference to Faults, that this world is not caused by faults; (11) with reference to Renewed birth, that there is no being, soul, entity, or spirit, that dies, and, having died, is born. Birth is without cause, the cessation of birth is without cause. Renewed birth has a beginning and is without end. Being occasional, renewed existence is not the effect of *karma,* (works). Renewed birth is without soul, because of the growth and existence of the body, the senses, the understanding, and the feeling. That Emancipation is terrific. That it is in fact the cessation of all work, the disruption of every thing. That many good things are thereby destroyed. What intelligent person, then, will desire such emancipation—a state of insensibility, in which all works and all enjoyments are extinct?

'From this false notion, or ignorance, continues the commentator, proceed partiality to favourites and prejudice against adversaries. In partiality and prejudice, again, consist the faults of detraction, envy, delusion, intoxication, pride, avarice, &c. Connected with faults, and acting with a body, a person commits injury, theft, and unlawful sensualities; becomes false, harsh, and slanderous in speech; with hatred, avarice, and atheism, in the mind. This vicious activity produces *adharma,* (demerit). But to do acts of charity, benevolence, and service, with the body, to be truthful, useful, agreeable in speech, or given to reading the Veda, to be kind, disinterested, and reverential in the mind, these produce *dharma,* (merit). Now *dharma* and *adharma,* (merit and demerit), being fostered by *pravṛtti,* (activity), are denoted by the word *pravṛtti,* just as life is denoted by food which fosters it, for it is said, food is the life of living creatures. This activity is the cause of a vile, as well as of an honourable, birth. Birth, again, is connected with 'the manifestation and assemblage of body, senses, and understanding. Attendant on birth is pain. That, again, comprises the feeling of distress, trouble, disease, sorrow. The congregated attributes, beginning with Ignorance and ending with Pain, compose *saṅsāra,* '(the world).'

"Having thus described the concatenation of evils, produced by ignorance, the learned and ingenious Vātsāyana proceeds next to represent the effects of *true knowledge.* 'But when,' says he, 'ignorance is extinguished, then, by the extinction of ignorance, Faults are extinguished. By the extinction of faults, Activity is extinguished. By the extinction of activity, Birth is extinguished. By the extinction of birth, Pain is extinguished. By the extinction of pain, is the beatitude of final Emancipation. As for true knowledge, it is best explained as the contrary of ignorance. With reference to spirit, that such a thing exists. With reference to matter, that it is not spirit. And it is to be similarly understood with reference to pain, to the transient, to the no-salvation, to the perilous, to the culpable, and to the things to be eschewed. With reference to activity, that it involves *karma,* (works), and the fruit of works. With reference to faults, that the world is caused by faults. With reference to renewed birth, that it is a living soul, entity, or spirit, which, having died, is born. Birth has a cause, the cessation of birth has a cuase, renewed birth is without beginning, and continues until emancipation. Renewed birth has a cause, and its cause is activity. Being endowed with a soul, renewed birth remains 'in force until emancipation, with the restitution of the body, senses, understanding, and feeling. Emancipation, however, is the disruption of all these, the cessation of all these. A multitude of troubles, fears, and vices is thereby extinguished. What intelligent person will not desire an emancipation which is the extinction of all pain, which is separation from all pain? For it is said, food mixed with honey and poison is to be avoided; pelasure, joined with pain, is to be avoided.'"

"Such is the exposition of Vātsāyana[25]. You see how correct was Āgamika's remark, that if the nectar be converted to poison, you must throw it away. Saṅsāra is but an assemblage of ignorance and other evils. This is a matter of fact, and not a mere deduction. If you are disposed to deny the fact, then you must have a theory of *optimism,* in which it will be impossible for me to follow you. For I cannot overlook the miseries and suffferings with which the world abounds. Let us only make up our minds to call things by their right names, and then—what can we say of life in this stage of existence? Is not this the one great characteristic of our bodies, that they fall into decay and are dissolved? How can we, then, think complacently of them[26]? We may as well repose confidence in lightnings, and autumnal clouds, and fairy cities[27]. For what, indeed, is it to be born? Is it not simply—to die! Every thing, accordingly, is unstable[28]. Life is only a source of trouble, the mind being *intoxicated* with the poisoned objects of sense, and the soul being destitute of true knowledge[29]. You may speak of the beauty and symmetry of our corporeal frames, you may talk of our mental powers, you may set forth the excellencies of our understandings, and the greatness of our efforts; but is not the whole, I ask, troublesome in the extreme,—like an additional weight on the neck of a man already burdened?[30] To what is an infant born in the world? To a life of happiness? By no means. It is only to buffet the waves of *works* in the ocean of this world[31]. And, as he grows in years and attains manhood, he is exposed to temptations calculated to cause his ruin[32]. As to old age, again, it is difficult to determine which of its infirmities are the more pitiable—the physical or the moral[33]. Who, then, can desire to cotinue in this embodied state—this house of a body, in which the organs of sense, and desire, and the mind, are, as fellow-occupants, continually deluding and distressing us?[34] Of all the causes of our miseries the greatest is desire, which, like a traitor in your own house, betrays its inmates to danger and difficulty.[35] Hence we say that the renouncement of this whole assemblage of evils is our only remedy, and that they alone live happily, whose birth shall not be renewed in the world[36]!

"We do not say that there is no such thing as happiness in the world. We do not deny the possibility of dharma, or merit, but we cannot ignore the painful fact that dharma is mixed up with adharma, that pleasure is linked with pain, and that birth, when renewed, is but a renewal of misery. We do not deny the existence of pleasure, nor do we say that there is no good *pravṛtti,* or laudable activity[37]; but, since evil unquestionably predominates, we cannot help considering life, in our present stage, to be a great misfortune. Hence we denote both *dharma* and *adharma* by pravṛtti, because it produces *karma,* which is our great bondage. When honey is mixed with poison, the whole cup is called poison, and thrown away. Even so we call *pravṛtti* an evil, and look for emancipation, as our only effectual escape from the miseries of transmigration and the sufferings of life."

Satyakāma. – "If you had not said that the yellow paper[38] in your hand is a leaf from Vātśayana's commentary, and that you are giving an exposition of the doctrine of Gotama, the author of the Nyāya, I might have mistaken it for the teaching of Gotama, the founder of Buddhism."

Āgamika. – "Mahābhārat! Mahābhārat[39]! Oh Satyakāma! what do you say? Can there be any similitude between a learned Ṛṣi, who contended for orthodoxy, and the unhappy heretic, who reviled gods and Brāhmins?"

Satyakāma. – "Pardon me, Āgamika, if I have caused you pain. But the 'heretic who reviled gods and Brāhmins' taught doctrines so very much akin to those of the 'learned Ṛṣi who contended for orthodoxy,' that it is no hyperbole to say you are liable to mistake the one for the other. Indeed, the tenets of the two Gotamas, the orthodox and the heretic, bear such a strong resemblance in their features, that you may safely declare they were uterine brothers, if not twins; and, unless you studied to note their distinctive signs, you might always incur the danger of a mistake. Now mark their resemblance. The orthodox Gotama begins with the assertion that supreme felicity is derivable from true knowledge. The heretical Gotama exhorts his followers to seek it from the same source[40].

The orthodox Gotama says that Ignorance, by producing faults and activity, becomes the cause of Birth. The heretical Gotama taught the same—only enlarging the list of intermediate agencies between Ignorance and Birth. The orthodox Gotama acknowledged that the world is a compound of good and evil, dharma and adharma, pleasure and pain, and yet maintained that the whole is to be renounced, and that the only remedy for the perils of life is *apavarga,* or the complete cessation of effort and activity, and separation of the soul from body and mind. The heretical Gotama also allowed that the world contains *dharma* and *adharma, kuśala* and *akuśala,* the one being a cause of virtue, and the other of vice, and yet that there is no other salvation from the miseries of life, than the 'acquirement of the unchangeable state of *nirvāṇa*[41]." Both pronounced the world to be a state of suffering, and transmigrations to be calamities and misfortunes[42]. Both considered human life to be unimprovable, except as it tends to *apavarga* or *nirvāṇa.*

"You have heard how Gotama, the orthodox, connected birth with ignorance, and emancipation with true knowledge. Hear now how Gotama, the heretic, did the same in the following catechism;

'On what existing, do decrepitude and death come into existence, and on what do they depend?'

'On Birth taking place, decrepitude and death come into existence, and they depend on birth.'

'On what existing, does birth come to pass, and on what again does it depend?'

'On the World existing, birth comes into existence, and it depends on the world.'

'On what existing, does the world come into existence, and on what does it depend?'

'On Affection existing, the world comes into existence, and it depends on affection.'

'On what existing, does affection come into existence, 'and on what does it depend?'

'On Desire existing, affection comes into existence, and it depends on desire.'

'On what existing, does desire come into existence, and on what does it depend?'

'On Sensibility existing, desire comes to exist, and it depends on sensibility.'

'On what existing, does sensibility come to exist, and on what does it depend?'

'On Contact existing, sensibility comes to exist, and it 'depends on contact.'

'On what existing, does contact come to pass, and on what does it depend?'

'On the Six organs existing, contact comes to pass, and it depends on the six organs.'

'On what existing, do the six organs come to existence, and on what do they depend?'

'On Name and form existing, the six organs come to exist, and they depend on name and form.'

'On what existing, do name and form come into existence, and on what do they depend?'

'On Apprehension existing, name and form come into existence, and they depend on apprehension.'

'On what existing, does apprehension (vijñāna) come to exist, and on what does it depend?'

'On Ideas (saṅskāra) existing, does apprehension come into existence, and it depends on ideas.'

'On what existing, do ideas come into existence, and on what do they depend?'

'On Ignorance existing, ideas come to exist, and they depend on ignorance?'[43]

"Having thus given the succession of causes by which the sufferings of decrepitude and death, the two great evils which had struck Śākya most, are produced, he proceeds next to show how their cessation may be brought about. 'On what subsiding, do decrepitude and death 'subside, and on whose cessation is the cessation of decrepitude and death?'

'On birth subsiding, decrepitude and death subside, and on its cessation is their cessation.'

'On what subsiding, does birth subside, and on whose cessation, is its cessation?'

'On the world subsiding, birth subsides, and on the world's cessation, is the cessation of birth.'

'On what subsiding, in fine, do ideas subside, and on whose cessation is the cessation of ideas?'

'On ignorance subsiding, ideas subside, and on its cessation is their cessation. On the cessation of ideas, is the cessation of apprehension[44].'"

Tarkakāma.—"The sufferings and miseries of existence are the common lot of all men. That the Buddhists had their share is no marvel; and it is only natural that, in their deplorable ignorance of the true remedy for the perils of life, they should be somewhat uncomfortable. To place them on the same level with us, simply because they did not know how the escape from their miseries, and therefore complained of their sufferings, is certainly not fair. Our Gotama did not rest satisfied with giving us a knowledge of evil and a sight of darkness. He also taught us the way of emancipation. He showed us light. Like a benevolent and experienced physician, he told us at once what our disease was, –what its cause, –and what the treatment should be, that we might be restored to health. The Buddhists, on the contrary, only set up loud yells under their sufferings, but were lamentably ignorant of the means of escape. Their *master physician,* as they delighted to call their leader, could only tell them what the very clowns in the streets knew for themselves –that they were miserable and wretched, and that their only escape was in the extinction of their miserable existence! The great empiric could only cure souls by condemning them to–perdition. He could talk of nothing but *Nirvāṇa,* (annihilation), as if an eternal principle, such as the soul, could ever cease to exist. The founder of the Nyāya led us to look for *apavarga* or emancipation."

Satyakāma.–"But what is *apavarga?*"

Tarkakāma.–"Apavarga, or emancipation, is final deliverance from these, that is to say, from pain, birth, activity, fault, false notions, and it is a state of unmingled felicity."

Satyakāma.–"If, as you say, the soul, when emancipated gets rid of birth it must, on your theory, be separated both from body *and* mind. It cannot then have any powers of thought and action. Emancipation must accordingly be a state of torpor and of perfect insensibility. I cannot understand what *felicity* there can be in such a state, nor, in what respect, it *can* differ from the Nirvāṇa of the Buddhists."

Tarkakāma.–"There are certain truths, Satyakāma, which cannot be described by metaphysical definitions. They can only be realized by the *feeling*. I mean they are comprehensible to those alone, who can understand and *enjoy* them. I must therefore decline a discussion of the metaphysical definition of our Emancipation. I can only say that it is a state of supreme felicity, by which all evil, all suffering, all sorrow, all pain, are at once and for ever extinguished. The utmost efforts of human rhetoric cannot adequately represent—the highest flights of human imagination cannot properly comprehend—such a state of ineffable joy and of undisturbed tranquility. But do not, I pray you, commit such a grievous outrage on common sense, as to confound our Emancipation with the Buddhistic *Nirvāṇa* or annihilation."

Satyakāma.—"But Buddhists talk of their Nirvāṇa precisely in the same way as you do of your emancipation. 'The Pāli doctrinal books speak of Nirvāṇa as an exemption from old age, from decay, and from death; and as being also the acquirement of all bliss. The most celebrated of the Burman priests at Ava, in reply to inquiries made by one of the Catholic Missionaries, replied as follows : 'When a person is no longer subject to any of the following miseries, namely, to weight, old age, disease and death, then he is said to have obtained nirvāṇ. No thing, no place, can give us any adequate idea of nirvāṇ; we can only say that to be free from the four above-mentioned miseries, and to obtain salvation, is nirvāṇ[45]." Here, said Buddha, lust and anger arising from delusion, and infesting the world, are, like convicted thieves, utterly destroyed. Here that ignorance and worldly lust, which are ever productive of mischief, are burnt up from their corrupt roots, by the great fire of knowledge. Here the intractable cords of time, with lands and houses as hard knots, and consisting of the selfish discriminations, *myself and mine,* are cut down by the weapons of my knowledge. Here is dried up, by the sun of my knowledge, the violent stream of desire, which takes its rise in evil, and is fed with the waters of sight, together with avidity and all evil thoughts. The forest of troubles, slander, and detraction, together with delusion, jealousy, and envy, is here burnt up by the fire of moderation. The three-fold bonds of the world are all loosened by me on attaining emancipation by the weapon of knowledge. Here I have, by the boat of resolution, (*vīrya*), got over the ocean of saṅsāra, (the world), infested with the aquatic monster of lust, and agitated by the waves of the waters of desire, excited by an evil eye. Here I have an experience of immortality for the benefit of the world, wherein is cessation of old age, death, sorrow, and trouble, and which is 'unattainable by the followers of other doctrines. Here I have experience of that which was known to innumerable saints of yore, whose agreeable and pleasing report is celebrated in the world.[46]' "

Tarkakāma—"I cannot understand the utility of this laborious attempt to confound the teaching of the Nyāya with that of Buddhism. You are acting with a vengeance on the principles of *upamāna,* or analogy, inculcated by Gotama himself. You are exerting yourself to no purpose with a view to turn his own weapon against himself. You forget that there are certain truths, which, like the solar rays, are self-apparent to the whole world, and that although, if a desperately blind man fails to recognize them, it is no proof *against* their existence, (any more than the incapacity of certain animals for seeing by day-light is an argument against the existence of the meridian sun,) yet when men of gross sensibilities do succeed in getting glimpses of the truth, the fact is a verification not refutation of it. What if the Buddhists had understood a few fragments of the grand truth which our Gotama was the first to embody in his memorable work?"

Satyakāma.—"I do not see how you can justly say that the Buddhists had only got glimpses of the 'grand truth' which Gotama taught in the Nyāya. The followers of Śākya appear to me to have had greater reasons for saying that the *grand truth* was first inculcated by *their* leader.[47] The fact is that the thoughtful natives of India had begun at an early period to recognize the evils which existed in the world, and were not satisfied that the mere performance of the ceremonies inculcated in the Veda could give them deliverance. Such ideas had long been floating in the popular mind, and certain aspirations after higher objects than were propounded in the Mantras and Brāhmaṇas had also occasionally found entrance into it. But to say that Gotama, the founder of the Nyāya, was the first to embody them in his sūtras, appears to me to betoken no small *sāhasa* or boldness. For the age of Buddha was confessedly anterior to that of the Nyāya. Indeed you glory in saying that one great object of the Nyāya was the refutation of Buddhism. And surely the inculcation of the evils of existence and of the alleged felicity of emancipation or Nirvāṇa was more characteristics of Buddhism than of the Nyāya. What is the idea prominently suggested by the word Buddhism? Is it not (however divided public opinion may be as to its *theism*) associated with the idea of an aspiration after something called *Nirvāṇa* as an escape from the sufferings of life? 'Anitya, Dukha, Anatta, (*anāmā*), Transience, Pain and Unreality, (so the devout Buddhist mutters 'as he tells his beads) these are the characters of all existence, and the only true good is exemption from these in the attainment of Nirvāṇa[48].' What again is the prominent idea associated with the *Nyāya*? Is it not metaphysical and logical speculaion? If then the Nyāya gives a representation of the evils of life and of emancipation, which has a strong resemblance with Buddhistic teaching, the probability is that the author of the Nyāya made a concession to Buddha on these points under the pressure of existing popular opinion, or was perhaps himself infected by the doctrine of the great heretic.

"You say that the author of the Nyāya was the first to embody those ideas in his sūtras. But the founder of Buddhism had embodied them in his *personal history.* For what is his biography, but a consecutive account of acts, deeds, and speeches, all indicative of his impatience of life, because of the evils of decay, old age, and death, and of the sufferings entailed by desire and attachment, and bearing record to his idea of nirvāṇa, or final escape from these? Śākya was in this respect a *character,* such as the Brāhminical literature fails to produce in the pre-Buddhistic age."

Āgamika. – "But the divine Rāma, we find, was also disgusted with the evils of life, and panted after mukti or emancipation."

Satyakāma. – "Vālmīki, if he was really the author of the *Yogavāśiṣṭha,* has certainly attempted the personation of a character in that work, somewhat approaching to Śākya's. Nay he makes use of the identical terms (*jarā, maraṇam, tṛṣṇā,*) by which Buddha described old age, death, desire. But Vālmīki's sketch is a poor imitation of the Buddhists, and in ill keeping with the story of his own Epic. Rāma was only for a time afflicted, when a boy, with the ideas in question. The Brāhmins in the palace of Daśaratha were evidently greater adepts in the art of persuasion than those in the court of his successor Śudhodhana, for we find that Rāma had quickly unlearnt his disgust with the world. He chased the Rākṣasas, when his infantine locks were yet uncropped on his head, in the hermitage of Viśwāmitra, and then accompanied the sage to the court of Janaka, where he competed successfully for the prize of fair Ṣītā's hand. Returning home with his bride, he accepted his father's proposal for his installation as associate king, and was only prevented from assuming the reins of Government by the jealousy of his step-mother. He became a voluntary exile from his country under the necessity of vindicating his father's truthfulness, and retired to the forests in the cheering company of his wife and brother. Even there, though unjustly excluded from his home and his throne, and afterwards deprived of his wife's society by the dastardly outrage of the wicked Rāvaṇa, he does not appear to have had any relapse into his early disgust with life. On the contrary, nothing can exceed the thoroughly business-like energy, with which he proceeds to the rescue of his captive wife. We then see Rāma happily returning hom with his queen, and resuming the pleasures and responsibilities of his throne. And if we afterwards find him abandoning the world in a melancholy mood of mind, we are at the same time assured that it was to return to a life of sensuous enjoyment in heaven.

"Buddha, on the contrary, declined to accept a throne and a sceptre, the possession of which was undisputed, and betook himself to the life of an ascetic, notwithstanding the importunities of affectionate relatives, —teaching every where that life was a series of troubles and sorrows, and holding out the hope of nirvāṇa as the only effectual escape. The means adopted for reconciling his mind to the pleasures of a palace served only to increase his disgust. To the characteristic peculiarities of his life and doctrine, and to the success which attended his efforts, ample testimony is borne to this day by the history and traditions of Nepal, Tibet, Burmah, Ceylon, Siam, China and Tartary."

Āgamika. —"You seem to have a greater faculty for recognizing resemblances than differences. You are ignorning the fact that the Buddhists denied the existence of God and spirits, and reviled the Vedas and Brāhmins."

Satyakāma. —"Atheism is certainly not the common teaching of all Buddhists, for the Aiśwarikas among them acknowledge a self-existent Deity whom they call Ādi Buddha[49]. Nor do they positively deny the existence of the soul. In fact the existence of the soul cannot be practically denied by men who hold out promises and threats of future reward and punishment. The Buddhists certainly do hold out such hopes and fears. 'The sceptic,' they say, 'will be punished in one or other of these two ways. He will be born in hell or as a beast. The wise man will be rewarded in one or other of these two ways; he will be born in a deva-loka, or as a man[50].' They, again, who get a sight of Buddha are exempted from troubles for thousands of Kalpas[51].

"I do not pretend to have a clear understanding of

Buddhistic psychology. Many of their writers speak of the soul in terms that might justify your suspicion of their denying its existence. But it is impossible to charge them with such positive denial of the soul in the face of their declarations of future retribution.

"As to their 'reviling' of the Veda, it would be more correct to say that they do not enforce the necessity of the prescribed rites and ceremonies, and thus *ignore,* rather than revile, its contents. They may, under cross examination by Brāhminical controversalists, or when irritated by invective and abuse, have used strong expressions against its authority, or even denounced it as the production of impostors. But that was the language of provocation, and what a man says under provocation requires to be charitably construed, for Nārada himself poured, under irritation, blasphemous invectives on Viṣṇu[52], and yet no one would call him a reviler of gods.

"With reference to the Veda, again, has not the divine lecturer in the Bhagavad-gītā himself spoken in disparagement of it. Those who, relying on the promises of the Vedas, engage in the performance of prescribed rites and ceremonies are denounced as *fools*. The heroic son of Pāṇḍava is exhorted to rise above the level of the Veda, which propounds nothing but *objects connected with the three qualities*. 'Be thou, O Arjuna, above 'the three qualities.[3]' And since Gotama and Kapila themselves say that something else is necessary for human emancipation than the mere observance of its ritual, I do not practically see any real difference between theirs and Buddha's teaching.

"Nor do I find, with reference to their 'reviling Brāhmins,' that Buddha ever taught his desciples to denounce the sons of Brahmā on peril of their salvation. Many Brāhmaṇs had themselves enlisted under his spiritual standard. He was of course no advocate for the distinctions of caste, and received as equals all that came unto him. But he did not say, 'revile Brāhmins and be saved.' On the contrary, he virtually allowed some sort of superiority to the higher castes, when he declared that birth in a Brāhmin family was reward for merit. He taught (with reference to those who commit murder) that such persons, on the breaking up of the elements (the five Khaṇḍas), will be born in one of the hells; or if on account of the merit received in some former birth, they are born as men, it will be of some inferior caste, or if of a high caste, they will die young, and this shortness 'of life is on account of former cruelties. But if any one avoid the destruction of life, not taking a weapon into his hand that he may shed blood, and be kind to all, and merciful to all, he will, after death, be born in the world 'of the dēvas, or if he appear in this world, it will be 'as a kṣatra, or Brāhman, or some other high caste, and he will live to see old age[54].'

"He only denied the spiritual supremacy of Brāhmins. I do not know however that some of the sects, tolerated by yourselves, do not go a good way with him in this respect. The Vaiṣṇavas and other followers of special gods admit men in their respective fraternities without any distinction of caste or race. The Buddhists do the same. They do not go about teaching that salvation depends on service done to Brāhmins. They maintain that *Nirvāṇa* consists in the moral improvement of human nature with which caste has nothing to do.

"And here I will take the liberty of adding that their scheme of Nirvāṇa, notwithstanding the false view of human nature implied in it, is more consistent than Gotama's of emancipation. While they agree with the Naiyāyikas in denouncing the world as an assemblage of evils, and in considering *karma* as the cause of continuance in life, they do not say that good works present an obstruction to final bliss by requiring reward and so keeping up the transmigrations of the soul. They do not say you must get rid *both* of merit and demerit in order to escape transmigration. They agree with the Naiyāyikas in representing that Adharma, which they also call Akuśala, leads to punishments here and hereafter, and causes ignoble births, but they do not say that Dharma, or, as they more frequently style it, Kuśala, is a hindrance to what they consider supreme felicity. 'The reward of merit is according to its character, as well as its degree. When it arises from something unconnected with dharma, worldly prosperity is received, or birth is secured as a garuda, with suparṇa, or nāga. When it arises from something connected with dharma, it secures birth in a dēva-loka or brahmaloka, or an entrance into the paths[55],'—the paths being four in number, 'leading to Nirvāṇa[56].' The Buddhists accordingly felt themselves at liberty to propound an elaborate system of ethics for the moral government of their community. They enforced the practice of virtue, and held out hopes of the highest of their rewards to the meanest of their fraternity.

"The author of the Nyāya, however, could not consistently propound such a system of ethics—could not so boldly enforce the practice of virtue—because the rewards of virtue were, on his theory, opposed to the attainment of Emancipation. He does indeed advise his followers to purify their souls by 'abstinence and observance,' and recommends them to have recourse to the *Yoga*[57], but that is simply as a temporary expedient, not so much with a view to emancipation, as with the intention of preventing inveterate habits of sinfulness. For how does he dispose of the objection, cited by himself, to the possibility of Emancipation? 'There is no emancipation because of the association of one's debts and troubles and exertions[58],' or, as the scholiast expounds it, 'there can be no emancipation, because, by reason of the clinging to us of our "debts,' &c., there is no opportunity for working out our salvation :—and so it is stated in scripture 'when born, verily, a Brāhmaṇ is born triply indebted;—from the Ṛṣis, by his course of student-life; from the gods, by sacrifice; from the progenitors, by progeny;'—that is to say, one is *freed* 'from the Ṛṣis,' i.e., from his debts to the Ṛṣis, by his course of student-life; he is freed 'from the gods,' i.e., from his debts to the gods, by sacrifice; he is freed 'from the progenitors,' i.e., from his debts to the progenitors, 'by progeny,' i.e., by [his begetting] offspirng : and life passes away in the mere 'clearing off of these debts[59].' The debts or duties, thus entailed by the Śāstra, are opposed to the idea of Emancipation, – for their non-performance would be a *demerit,* and hence require punishment by renewed birth, while their performance, on the other hand, would entail *merit,* and require reward, also precisely in the same way. Well how does he dispose of the objection? Not by contending that the discharge of duty is not incompatible with salvation, – but by endeavouring to weaken the force of the injunctions, and showing that, since the words could not be literally interpreted, – for how can a child, just born, perform any duty or discharge a debt? – They must be taken figuratively[60]. And then he falls back on another rule of the Śāstra which requires a Brāhmin to retire from the world when he is old. Noticing the objection that 'even if burnt sacrifices were no obstacle, the very 'fruit of it, Heaven, must be an obstacle to emancipation,' Gotama refutes it by saying that the Brāhmin, when old, must retire from the world, and so be unable to procure the utensils necessary for a sacrifice, which cannot therefore be completed, and the enjoyment of heaven will as a matter of course be avoided[61]. Dr. Ballantyne, expounding Viśwanātha's scholium on iv. 61, says, 'when a Brāhmin, having reached the age at which he ought to retire from the world, is no longer competent to perform the regular daily duties, he must *imagine* himself performing them; – and this will free him from the bad consequences of *neglecting* them; while, on the other hand, the defect of actual fulfilment will free him from the necessity of having to undergo *reward* for the same.' 'In the case of him that possesses knowledge, the 'fruit,' i.e., Paradise, does not take place: – for burnt sacrifice implies a collection of vessels, – vessels, i.e., vessels for burnt 'sacrifice, – a collection of such, – an arrangement of them 'with respect to the members of the victim, the thing 'sacrificed, – according to the direction "In the mouth a ladle filled with butter," and so in order. These cannot be provided by a *beggar,* and therefore, the fruit of the burnt sacrifice, from the want of these things, does not take place.' Dr. Ballantyne makes the scholiast's meaning clearer, by adding, 'for it is he "that possesses knowledge" who can both perform the "constant duties," so as to avoid the guilt of their neglect, and at the same time escape the opposite Charybdis of having to *suffer the reward* of them in Paradise.'

"The scheme of emancipation in the Nyāya comes then to this—that none but Brāhmins of advanced age can possibly attain it, for all others are bound by duties, the performance of which, quite as much as their neglect, must subject them to transmigration. To the Kṣatriyas, Vaiśyas and Śūdras, and to *young* Brāhmins, the Nyāya has nothing to say—nothing to propound with a view to their final salvation. The Buddhist scheme, to say the least of it, is certainly more consistent and better arranged. Śākya could address himself to all men, and enforce the practice of virtue by holding out the prospect of supreme felicity or Nirvāṇa."

Tarkakāma.—"You are talking after a fashion which makes me suspect that Buddhism is your newly adopted faith. You must be a follower of Śākya in disguise, and are attempting to lead us, blindfolded, to the borders of his impious system."

Satyakāma.—"I can assure you, Tarkakāma, I am no Buddhist. In the midst of this controversy I will not tell you what my new faith is, for I do not wish to propound it as a rival system. If after mature consideration of the points we are discussing, you should be desirous of hearing me on that subject, I shall gladly embrace a future occasion of explaining my views. Meanwhile I must tell you that you have already been brought,—and that, blindfolded too,—by Gotama himself into the very heart of Buddhism. What a melancholy prospect you are laying before human nature when you say that life is an essential evil, that the soul must get rid of its moral powers and emotions, and return finally to the state of torpor and insensibility, in which it was before 'the primal action of atoms and of the mind;'—that the only escape from transmigrations is in that torpid state;—that this escape, again, is available to old Brāhmins only, who, being necessarily beggars, cannot have the means of completing sacrifices, and thus, not meriting heaven, may attain to emancipation, if only they be versed in the topics and categories of Gotama and Kaṇāda."

Tarkakāma.—"You seem, Satyakāma, to be ridiculing the systems of Gotama and Kaṇāda. You cannot surely be such an *optimist* as to deny the ocrruptions which abound in the world. Take facts as they are, and you will easily understand the difficulty our Ācāryas had to deal with. Here is an evil world tormenting the soul which is burdened with the *accidents* of body and mind. Its physical and mental powers are not necessary to its existence, for it eixsted before it was endowed with them, and it exists independent of them during *pralayas,* or periods of the world's dissolution. Whatever is accidental and transient is removable. The divine Vāsudeva has taught us that as the constantly existing can never cease to be, so the transient can never have constant existence[62]. The soul then is capable of final release from its bondage of life. The possibility is evident from the freedom it enjoys during periods of dissolution. Now how is the transient freedom, which recurs periodically, to be made perpetual? The question will be best understood by considering its hindrances. What is it that prevents the perpetuation of that freedom? Is it not the merit and demerit of past works?—the requital of which requires fresh creations and brings on the transmigrations of individual souls. How to procure emancipation means in other words how to prevent transmigrations. This is a question as important as it is solemn. You cannot avoid *merit* without incurring *demerit,* for we have certain duties to perform, certain debts to discharge.Are we to perform those duties and discharge those debts? If we do, we must accept merit, and be entitled to rewards, the enjoyment of which will render renewed birth necessary. But can we not avoid the merit by neglecting the duties? We may, but *demerit* will then stick to us, and require a repeated life of punishments. In this dilemma Gotama proposes that since a Brāhmin must, toward the close of life, become a mendicant, he may as well take care to remain in want of the utensils necessary for the due performance of sacrifices., Let him perform the prescribed rites in his intention, but neglect them in the act. The intention will be accepted for the deed, and guard him against punishment. The non-fulfilment, from want of the requisite vessels, will protect him from the evils of *merit,* and save him from reward. He may thus get rid of the bondage of birth, and, meriting neither reward nor punishment, be released from the necessity of transmigration. Thus will he be blessed with emancipation, like a person who sleeps soundly, and, not being disturbed by dreams, has no distress[63]."

Āgamika.—"I do not like this subtle metaphysic, Tarkakāma. It appears to me to be a piece of refinement, unworthy the character of spiritual guides and leaders of communities. And this is the reason for which I have always had a dislike of your philosophy. Why not rest satisfied with the plain injunctions of the Śāstra? *Let him who desires heaven perform sacrifices*[64]. Why not content yourself with heaven, and the plain words of the Vedas. You wish to obtain emancipation by setting one injunction against another. Because you msut be poor in your old age, you will take advantage of your poverty, and neglect to procure the sacrificial vessels, and thus leave undischarged your debts to the gods."

Tarkakāma.—"Oh Āgamika! beware of the precipice of heresy. You wish to be satisfied with heaven. Do you not know that it is equally transient with the earth, that Brahmā, Viṣṇu, and Rudra are all fast approaching their end[65]. Emancipation is our only escape from the evils of life."

Satyakāma.—"But what is Emancipation? It is a state in which the soul must get rid of its physical and mental powers, in which there can be no speech, no deed, no thought, nor any feeling or sensibility. It is, you say, a sleep without dreams.

What then is the meaning of the soul's being in the enjoyment of *felicity* in such a state of torpor? What right have you to say that the soul exists at all, when it is without its characteristics, without thought, desire, or aversion? You know it now by these characteristics. How can you say it is capable of existence without them? You have no *udāharaṇa* or instance of spiritual life in which there is an *atyantābhāva,* a necessary absence, of signs of animation and intellect. You may as well undertake to predicate of a stone that it has spiritual existence, *in a sound sleep without dreams."*

Tarkakāma. – "I have already told you that the soul exists in an emancipated state in the same manner as it did before creation."

Satyakāma. – "What is existence then? How can a spiritual essence exist without thought, feeling, desire? The very idea is incomprehensible. And if it were possible, it would still be far from desirable. The existence you attribute to the soul in such a state appears to be a mere technical deduction from certain of your maxims. But what idea can you form of spiritual existence, destitute of thought and feeling, not only without body, but also without mind? It becomes a word without meaning. You have dwelt too much, learned Tarkakāma, on the dark side of human nature. That nature is no doubt corrupt. But the picture, as a whole, is far from being so melancholy as you are representing it. That the affections of human nature, if unrestrained and misdirected, lead to evil, no one can for a moment deny. But it must be remembered, that it is useless to dream of perfect release from those characteristics without which the soul cannot possibly exist in any state. Nor must you forget that God has endowed us with the capacity of correcting and purifying our affections. True happiness consists in seeking the best way of rectifying our passions, not in vainly trying to get rid of them; for improvement does not imply annihilation or eradiction. When you improve your garden you do not pluck up every plant, and reduce your grounds to a desert.

"I say again it is useless to dream of a total release from our passions and appetites. Your venerable Kaṇāda himself maintains, that no substance can exist without action or quality. The soul is a substance. The soul must always possess some characteristic qualities. If it be, as you rightly hold,indestructible, it can never be deprived of its peculiar properties. Emancipation, such as you define it, is simply a creature of the imagination, a sky-flower, a town of Gandharva. It can have no reality.

"Then, again, you have entirely left out of consideration that we are endowed with the capacity of correcting and purifying our passions. Have you not heard of the filial piety of a Naciketas, not only cheerfully submitting to his fate, when unjustly consigned to death by an angry father, but coninuing, without abatement, the affection and reverence due to a parent? You would not surely say that the affection he exhibited was a *doṣa.* What think you again of the joy with which a Śaivyā accepted the degraded condition of a menial slave in order to absolve her royal husband, Hariścandra, from a debt, which she believed was pressing on him? Could such conjugal devotion be called an evil? I do not cite these as instances of human perfection, but I ask you if the affection and devotion therein displayed could be called *doṣa.* Perfection is not of course to be found on the earth. Desire and aversion, Love and hatred, when misdirected, are no doubt sources of misery and unhappiness. But would you call the love of good and hatred of evil, sources of misery? In classifying the active powers of the mind, the popular scholiast of Gotama has not made a fair enumeration; and of those which he has enumerated he has given the darkest definitions. He gives seven sorts of desire, and six of aversion. He speaks of *thirst after objects,* of *covetousness,* of *desiring other's evil,* &c[66]. But of those affections which bind men with men, he mentions only *Kāma,* and defines it to be *riraṅsā,* which again he renders *a desire of sensual enjoyment*. Kāma itself does not, however, exclusively imply lust, since the Upaniṣads themselves attribute it to the Supreme Spirit before the creation. 'He desired (akāmayata) let me become many.' And as to those feelings which attach parents to children and children to parents; which distinguish the amity that brothers and sisters bear to one another; which knit the hearts of friends and companions, fellow citizens and fellow subjects; which compose the links by which Society is kept together; of these lovely traits of the human character the author of the *Vṛtti* makes not the slightest mention.

"Likewise, in classifying Aversion, he speaks of anger 'which produces a redness in the eye,' of envy, malice, &c.[67] but says nothing of such feelings as resentment, indignation, and impatience of that which is wicked or evil.

"This, I repeat, is not a correct analysis of human feelings. The Upaniṣad, notwithstanding what I believe to be its fundamental error, *i.e.,* its pantheism, gives a much more correct description of the human passions. It compares them to horses which the understanding, as charioteer, guides by the reins of the mind. When the passions are left unrestrained, they become liek *bad* horses : when properly checked they resemble good steeds[68]. You would not condemn the whole breed of horses as essentially evil, because when they are not properly restrained they turn out bad. Neither ought you to pass a sweeping condemnation on human affections. Without those affections man would be incapable of piety, devotion, and charity; and, sure I am, that the pleasure and satisfaction which these feelings of duty to God and man contribute to the mind are far more cheering than your artificial notion of Emancipation which is only an imitation of the Buddhist conception of nirvāṇa. It is a satisfaction, however, to believe that there is no reason for thinking such a catastrophe to be even possible. Why spend your strength, then, on what—supposing its desirability—is yet impracticable?

"It is useless to exhaust one's energies on the achievement of impossibilities. Even if the annihilation of our passions were desirable, it is impracticable. Our wisest course is to seek the amendment of that which we cannot destroy. By amending and purifying, we may turn them into sources of unalloyed pleasure and of rational enjoyment. But by seeking their destruction we may be in danger of imparting to them a greater impetus *in the opposite direction.* A most profound writer says : 'Those who formerly aimed at this (*i.e.,* the destruction of the passions) upon the foot of philosophy, appear to have had better success in eradicating the affections of tenderness and compassion, than they had with the passions of envy, pride, and resentment[69]." How many instances do our own Itihāsas and Purāṇas present of Ṛṣis, who in the midst of their efforts to eradicate their passions, were *a great deal more liable* to be overcome by the temptations of sights and sounds than ordinary mortals?

"To say that the metnal powers of human nature are essentially corrupt, and that the only remedy is *Apavarga,* which implies entire eradication, sounds as bad in a moralist, as it would in a physician to say that the organs of respirations are *doṣa,* because they admit malaria into the system, and cause diseases, and that the only way of guarding against the evil is suffocation, or destruction of those organs. What would you say to the doctor who, instead of prescribing the proper medicine and aliment, would advise his patient to abstain from all kind of food, and thereby to starve himself, that he might effectually escape the pains and torments of indigestion! And yet Gotama's moral treatment of the soul is no better, it must get rid, (which however it cannot,) of sensibility and activity, and exist without any characteristic signs of existence. I said you have been brought blindfolded, into the very heart of Buddhism. Is it not so in reality with reference to your doctrine of the present and future prospects of human nature? You affect to harp on the transience, instability, and vanity of the world in the very tune of Gotama Buddha, and you talk of your emancipation precisely in the same terms as he did of Nirvāṇa. If there be a difference between you, it seems to be in favour of the Buddhist leader; for his metaphysics did not technically compel him to deny the perpetual concomitance of the Soul with mind, and therefore he might have meant that Nirvāṇa was a sort of spiritual existence in which the Soul was not debarred from capacities for thought and feeling. he had also this further advantage that his theory did not preclude him from the privilege of inculcating a code of morals, to be enforced equally on the highest and the lowest of his adherents, as the direct means of attaining supreme felicity. Gotama however could not enjoin the practice of virtue so freely, for on his principles merit was hardly less an obstacle to emancipation than demerit."

Āgamika.—"I cannot certainly regret our conference of this morning—for it has opened my eyes to the defects of our philosophers, of whom I long had a sort of intuitive dread. I am now convinced that some of our leaders at least, have only been drawing us, nearer and nearer, toward the vortex of Buddhism, by broaching transcendental ideas of emancipation, unheard of in the Mantras and Brāhmaṇas. I for my part will return to the old paths, and continue to seek for admission to heaven by the performance of sacrifices. It appears to me to partake of no small irreverence to talk slightingly of the heavenly reward. All I can say is that I shall be perfectly satisfied with it—only, may I attain it!"

Satyakāma.—"I say *tathāstu* ! (So be it.) And may you be led still further to understand the True Sacrifice for sin, and may you attain, I do not say such heaven as the Purāṇas describe—but the Heaven of unspotted purity, of ever-enduring stability, and of joy without alloy,—of which our ancestors had evidently derived some idea from the primitive traditions of the human race, when they styled it *suvarga*[70] (the good society), since corrupted, perhaps both in form and idea, into *swarga*."

Āgamika's concluding sentence was articulated in a tone which for the moment produced a strong impression on us all. Even Tarkakāma, with his strong opinion of the transience and the chequered character of celestial existence, and of the vanity of earthly life and deeds, seemed for once to fear that he was perhaps, after all, himself purusing a mere *mirage*, while he was denouncing the heavenly rewards of Dharma. Satyakāma's closing reply, again, was not quite intelligible to any of us, though it received an expressive response from Āgamika, by a muscular motion on his face, which I shall not attempt to describe. I have scarcely recovered myself from the mental excitement produced by the last conference, and you must therefore excuse my inability to add any further remarks.

References

1. न जायते म्रियते वा कदाचिन्नायं भूत्वा भविता वा न भूयः। अजो नित्यः शाश्वतोऽयं पुराणो न हन्यते हन्यमाने शरीरे।
2. अथ तत्पूर्व्वकं त्रिविधमनुमानं पूर्व्ववच्छेषवत्सामान्यतोदृष्टञ्च।
3. अनृतं वै वाचा वदति। अनृतं मनसा ध्यायति। चक्षुर्वै सत्यं। अदाऽगित्याह। अदर्शमिति। तत्मृत्यं। Taittrīya Brāhmaṇa.
4. तत्र व्याप्तिविशिष्टपक्षधर्म्मताज्ञानजन्यं ज्ञानमनुमितिस्तत्करणमनुमानं तच्च लिङ्गपरामर्शः। Anumāna Khaṇḍa of Taṭtva Chintāmaṇi.
5. प्रमायाः करणं प्रमाणं। प्रमा च यथार्थानुभवः। तद्वति तदवगाहित्वं यथार्थं। Siddhānta Mañjarī.
6. अनुवादोपपत्तेश्च। II. 60. न पौनरुक्त्यं निष्प्रयोजनत्वे हि पौनरुक्त्यं दोषः उक्तस्थले त्वनुवादस्य उपपत्तेः प्रयोजनस्य सम्भवात्। Viśwanātha.
7. ननु प्रतिज्ञा न साधनाङ्गं विप्रतिपत्तेः पक्षपरिग्रहे तत्र प्रमाणाकाङ्क्षायां हेत्वभिधानस्य प्राथम्यादिति चेन्न विप्रतिपत्त्यग्रे समयवन्धानन्तरं शब्दानित्यत्वं साधयेति मध्यस्थस्य वादिनो वाकाङ्क्षायां शब्दानित्यत्वं साध्यं न च साध्यनिर्देशं विना हेतुवाक्यं निष्पूतियोगिकमन्वयं बोधयितुमीष्टे।
   Anumāna Khaṇḍa.
8. सेयं व्याप्तिर्न भूयोदर्शनगमा दर्शनानां प्रत्येकमहेतुत्वात् आशु विनाशिनां क्रमिकाणां मेलकाभावात्। * * * शतशोदर्शनेपि व्याप्त्यग्रहात्।
9. सहचारदर्शनव्यभिचारादर्शनसहकृतः स एव व्याप्तिग्राहकोस्तु आवश्यकत्वात् किं भूयोदर्शनेन न च तेन विना तर्क एव नावतरति प्रथमदर्शने व्युत्पन्नस्य तर्कसम्भवात्। Anumāna Khaṇḍa.
10. न च हेतुवचनादेव तदवगमः तस्य को हेतुरित्याकाङ्क्षायां प्रवृत्तत्वेन हेतुस्वरूपोपस्थापकस्याततपरत्वात्। Anumāna Khaṇḍa.
11. न च व्याप्तिपक्षधर्म्मतायाश्चभिरिवावयवैः प्रय्याप्तैः किं तेनेति वाच्यं अबाधितासत्प्रतिपक्षत्वयोरलाभे चतुर्णामप्यपर्य्यवसनात्। Ibid.
12. "An induction is of two kinds,[inasmuch as it may be employed] for oneself, and for another. That which is for oneself is the cause of a private conclusion [in one's own mind]. For example, having repeatedly and personally observed, in the case of culinary hearths

and the like, that where there is smoke there is fire, having gathered the invariable attendedness [of smoke by fire], having gone near a mountain, and being doubtful as to whether there is fire in it, having seen smoke on the mountain, a man recollects the invariable attendedness, viz., 'where there is smoke there is fire.' Thereupon the knowledge arises that 'this mountain has smoke, which is constantly accompanied by fire.' This is called the 'pondering of a sign' (*liṅga-parāmarśa*). Thence results the knowledge that 'the mountain is fiery,' which is the conclusion (*anumiti*). This is the process of inference for oneself."

"But, after having, for oneself, inferred fire from smoke, when one makes use of the five-membered form of exposition, with a view to the information of another, then is the process one of inference for the sake of another. For example :(1) The mountain has fire in it; (2) because it has smoke; (3) whatever has smoke has fire, as a culinary hearth; (4)and so this has; (4) therefore it is as aforesaid. By this [exposition], in consequence of the sign [or token] here rendered, the other also admits that there is fire." *Ballantyne's translation.*

13. प्रत्यक्षादीनामप्रामाण्यं त्रैकाल्यासिद्धेः Sūtra II. 8

पूर्वं हि प्रमाणसिद्धौ नेन्द्रियार्थसन्निकर्षात् प्रत्यक्षसिद्धिः 2 ।9 पश्चात् सिद्धौ न प्रमाणेभ्यः प्रमेयसिद्धिः 2 ।। 10 युगपत्सिद्धौ प्रत्यर्थनियतत्वात् क्रमवृत्तित्वाभावो बुद्धीनाम् 2 ।11 त्रैकाल्यासिद्धेः प्रतिषेधानुपपत्तिः 2 ।। 12 सर्वप्रमाणप्रतिषेधाच्च प्रतिषेधासिद्धिः 2 ।। 13 तत्प्रामाण्ये वा न सर्वप्रतिषेधः 2 ।। 14 त्रैकाल्याप्रतिषेधश्च शब्दादातोद्यसिद्धिवत् तत्सिद्धेः 2 ।। 15 प्रमेयता च तुलाप्रामाण्यवत् 2 ।। 16

14. यथोक्ताध्यवसायादेव तद्विशेषापेक्षात्संशये नासंशयो नात्यन्तसंशयो वा ।।6 ।।

15. प्रामाणतः सिद्धेः प्रमाणानां प्रमाणान्तरसिद्धिप्रसङ्गः 2 ।।17 तद्विनिवृत्तेर्वा प्रमाणसिद्धिवत् तत्सिद्धिः ।।18

16. न प्रदीपप्रकाशसिद्धिवत् तत्सिद्धेः 2 ।।19

17. आप्तः खलु साक्षात्कृतधर्मा यथादृष्टस्यार्थस्य चिख्यापयिषया प्रयुक्त उपदेष्टा साक्षात्करणमर्थस्याप्तिस्तया वर्तते इत्याप्तः ऋष्यार्य्यम्लेच्छानां समानं लक्षणं तथाच सर्वेषां व्यवहाराः प्रवर्तन्त इति एवमेभिः प्रमाणैर्देवमनुष्यतिरश्चां व्यवहाराः प्रकल्पन्ते नातोन्यथेति स द्विविधो दृष्टादृष्टार्थत्वात् यस्येह दृश्यतेऽर्थः स दृष्टार्थो यस्यामुत्र प्रतीयते सोऽदृष्टार्थ एवमृषिलौकिकवाक्यानां विभाग इति।

18. आप्तोपदेशसामर्थ्याच्छब्दार्थे सम्प्रत्ययः॥ शब्दादमुमर्थं प्रत्येमि॥

19. Aphorisms of the Nyāya Part I, printed for the Benares College.

20. प्रमाणप्रमेयसंशयप्रयोजनदृष्टान्तसिद्धान्तावयवतर्कनिर्णयवादजल्प-वितण्डाहेत्वाभासछलजातिनिग्रहस्थानानान्तत्त्वज्ञानान्निःश्रेयसाधिगमः॥

21. दुःखजन्मप्रवृत्तिदोषमिथ्याज्ञानानामुत्तरोत्तरापाये तदनन्तरापायादपवर्गः॥ विविधबाधनायोगाद्दुःखं जन्मोत्पत्तिः।

22. The learned principal of the Benares College has thus expounded Gotama's view on this point.

"The remembering of the order of the steps in 2. may be facilitated, to some "readers, by availing ones self of the distributively cumulative form of exposition "employed in the nursery tale of the house that Jack built." Thus :–

1. *Dukha.*–This is the pain that the man had.

2. *Janma.*–This is the Birth (again renewed) that gave room for the pain That the man had.

3. *Pravṛtti.*–This is 'activity' (requiring reward) that led to the birth (again renewed) that gave room for the pain that the man had.

"4. *Doṣa.*–This is the fault (of 'desire–or dislike' alike to be shunned, or stupidity) which (in the man who, if wise, had done nothing at all,) begot the activity (requiring reward) that led to the 'birth' (again renewed) that gave room for the pain that the man had.

"5. *Mithyā Jñāna.*–This means the wrong notions (of that man unversed in the truth teaching Nyāya Philosophy) which (since the man knew no better) gave rise to the 'fault' (of 'desire' or 'dislike' or stupidity,) which in the man who, if wise, had done nothing at all, begot the activity (requiring reward) that led to "the 'birth' (again renewed) that gave room for the 'pain' that the man had.

6. *Apavarga.* – This last is beatitude' promised as fruit of the truth teaching Nyāya Philosophy, which gave us right ones instead of the wrong notions, which gave rise to what Gotama styles a fault,in as much as it mischievously begot the 'activity' carefully shunned by the wise, – for 'activity'shaping itself in acts that are good or bad, and requiring reward of a like description, occasions a man to be born again, – and it was this same 'birth' that gave room for the 'pain' that the man had.

23. नास्त्यसाविह संसारे यो न दैवेन बाध्यते। Mārkaṇḍeya.

24. प्रवृत्तिर्वाग्बुद्धिशरीरारम्भः॥

25. प्रवर्त्तनालक्षणा दोषाः।

26. मिथ्याज्ञानमनेकप्रकारकं वर्त्तते। आत्मनि तावन्नास्ति इति। अनात्मन्यात्मेति, दुःखे सुखमिति, अनित्ये नित्यमिति, अत्राणे त्राणमितिसभये निर्भयमिति, जुगुप्सितेऽभिमतमिति, हातव्येऽप्रतिहातव्यमिति, प्रवृत्तौ नास्ति कर्म्म नास्ति कर्म्मफलमिति, दोषेषु नायं दोषनिमित्तः संसार इति, प्रेत्यभावे नास्ति जन्तुर्जीवोवा सत्व आत्मा वा यः प्रेयात् प्रेत्य च भवेदिति। अनिमित्तं जन्म अनिमित्तो जन्मोपरमइत्यादिमान्प्रेत्यभावोऽनन्तश्चेति नैमित्तिकः सन्नकर्म्मनिमित्तः प्रेत्यभाव इति देहेन्द्रियबुद्धिवेदनासन्तानोच्छेदप्रबन्धाभ्यां निरात्मकः प्रेत्यभाव इति। अपवर्गो भीब्म खल्वयं सर्व्वकर्म्मोपरमः सर्व्वविप्रयोगोपवर्गो वह्वत्र भद्रकं लुप्यत इति। कश्च बुद्धिमान्सर्व्वमुखोच्छेदमचैतन्यममुमपवर्गं रोचयेदिति। एतस्मान्मिथ्याज्ञानात् अनुकूलेषु रागः प्रतिकूलेषु द्वेषः रागद्देषाधिकरणाश्चासूयेर्य्यामाया-मदमानलोभादयो दोषा भवन्ति। दोषैः प्रयुक्तः शरीरेण प्रवर्तमानो हिंसास्तेयप्रतिषिद्धमैथुनमाचरति वाचानृतपरुषसूचनासंबद्धानि मनसा परद्रोहं परद्रव्याभीप्सानास्तिक्यञ्चेति। सेयं पापात्मिका प्रवृत्तिरधर्म्माय अथशुभंशरीरेण दानं परित्राणं परिचरणश्च वाचा सत्यं हितं प्रियं स्वाध्यायञ्चेति मनसा

दयामस्पृहां श्रद्धाञ्च सेयं धर्माय अथ प्रवृत्तिसाधनौ धर्म्माधर्म्मौ प्रवृत्तिशब्देनोक्तौ। यथान्नसाधनाः प्राणा अन्नं वै प्राणिनः प्राणा इति सेयं प्रवृत्तिः कुत्सितस्याभिपूजितस्य च जन्मनः कारणं। जन्म पुनः शरीरेन्द्रियबुद्धीनां निकायविशिष्टः प्रादुर्भावः अस्मिन् सति दुःखं तत्पुनः प्रतिकूलवेदनीयं बाधना षीडाताप इति त इमे मिथ्याज्ञानादयो दुःखान्ता धर्म्मा अविच्छेदेन प्रवर्त्तमानाः संसार इति। यदा तु तत्त्वज्ञानान्मिथ्याज्ञानमपैति तदा मिथ्याज्ञानापाये दोषा अपयन्ति दोषापाये प्रवृत्तिरपैति प्रवृत्त्यपाये जन्मापैति जन्मापाये दुःखमपैति दुःखापाये आत्यन्तिकोऽपवर्गो निश्रेयसमिति। तत्त्वज्ञानन्तु खलु मिथ्याज्ञानविपर्य्ययेण व्याख्यातं आत्मनि तावदस्तीति अनात्मनि अनात्मेति एवं दुःखेऽनित्येऽत्राणेसभये जुगुप्सिते हातव्ये च यथाविषयं वेदितव्यं प्रवृत्तौ अस्ति कर्म्मास्ति कर्म्मफलमिति, दोषेषु दोषनिमित्तः संसार इति, प्रेत्यभावे खल्वस्ति जन्तुर्जीवः सत्वआत्मा वा यः प्रेत्यभावो इति निमित्तत्वज्जन्म निमित्तवान् जन्मोपरम इत्यनादिः प्रेत्यभावोऽपवर्गान्त इति नैमित्तिकः सन् प्रेत्यभावः प्रवृत्तिनिमित्त इति। सात्मकः सन् देहेन्द्रियबुविदना-सन्तानोच्छेदप्रतिसन्धानाभ्यां प्रवर्तत इति अपवर्गान्ततः खल्वयं सर्व्वविप्रयोगः सर्वोपरमोऽपवर्ग इति वहूत्र कृच्छ्रं घोरं पापकं लुप्यत इति कश्च बुद्धिमान् सर्वदुःखच्छेदं सर्वदुःखासम्बिदमपवर्गं न रोचयेदिति तद्यथा मधुविषसंपृक्तान्नमनादेयमिति एवं सुखदुःखानुषक्तमनादेयमिति।

27. रक्तमांसमयस्यास्य सवाह्याभ्यान्तरं मुने।
नाशैकधर्म्मिणो व्रूहि कैव कायस्य रम्यता। Yoga-vāśiṣṭha.

28. तडित्सु शरदव्भ्रेषु गन्धर्व्वनगरेषु च।
स्थैर्य्यं येन विनिर्णीतं स विश्वसितु विग्रहे। Ibid.

29. ज़ायते मृतये लोको म्रियते जननाय च।
अस्थिराः सर्व्व एवेमे सचराचरचेष्टिताः। Yoga-vāśiṣṭha.

30. विषयाशीविषासङ्गपरिजर्ज्जरचेतसां।
अप्रौढात्मविवेकानामायुरायासकारणं। Ibid.

31. रूपमायुर्मनोबुद्धिरहङ्कारः स्थिरोहितं।
भारो भारधरस्येव सर्व्वं दुःखाय दुर्धियः। Ibid.

32. लब्ध्वापि तरलाकारे कार्य्यभावतरङ्गिणि।

संसारसागरे जन्म वाल्यं दुःखाय केवलं। Ibid.

33. वाल्यानर्थमथ त्यक्त्वा पुमानभिहिताशयः।
आरोहति निपाताय यौवनं संभ्रमेण तु। Ibid.

34. दुष्प्रेक्षं जरठं दीनं हीनं गुणपराक्रमैः।
गृध्रो वृक्षमिवादीर्घं गर्द्धोप्यम्भ्येति वार्द्धकं। Ibid.

35. पंक्तिबद्धेन्द्रियपशुं फल्गुत्तृष्णागृहाङ्गनं।
चित्तभृत्यकृतानन्दं नेष्टं देहगृहं मम। Yoga-vāśiṣṭha.

36. सर्व्वसंसारदुःखानां तृष्णौका दीर्घदुःखदा।
अन्तःपुरस्थमपि या योजयत्यपि सङ्कटे। Ibid.

37. जातास्तएव जगति जन्तवः साधुजीविताः।
ये पुनर्नेह जायन्ते शेषा जठरगर्द्दभाः। Ibid.

38. सुखस्याप्यन्तरालनिष्पत्तेः। न प्रवृत्तिः प्रतिसन्धानापहीनक्लेशस्य। Gotama iv. 56, 64.

39. Native mansucripts are generally preserved in paper saturated with yellow arsenic to guard against insects.

40. When Brāhmins hear any thing which shocks their feelings, they repeat some auspicious word, just as the Mahometans rehearse

41. मोहकलुषान्धकारं प्रज्ञाप्रदीपेन विधमथा सर्वं।
सानुशयदोषजालं विदारयत ज्ञानवज्रेण॥

* * * *

मोहादृष्टिरविद्याघातको हिरिशिरिभरितो।
त्वं वैद्य कुशलचिकित्सको ह्यमृतसुखददो

* * * *

ज्ञानिं ज्ञानकथाग्रधारका ज्ञापयसि त्रिभवे
त्रैविद्यविमोक्षदेशका त्रिमलमलनुदा। LalitaVistara.

42. Wayland's Memoir of Judson. Also in the Lalitavistara;
मोक्षं ते च लघुं सर्व्वे छित्वा वै क्लेशबन्धनम्।
यास्यन्ति निरुपादानाः फलप्राप्ति वरं शुभम्॥

दक्षिणीयाश्च ते लोके आहुतीनां प्रतिग्रहाः।
न तेषु दक्षिणा न्यूना सत्त्वानिर्वाणहेतुकी॥

43. "Painful are repeated births" (दुःखा जातिपुनः पुनः) Hardy's Manual of Buddhism. Again in Lalitavistara,
जातिजरामरणदुःखक्षयं संसारबन्धनं विमोक्षयितुं।
चरितुं विशुद्धगमान्तसमं तं शुद्धसत्त्वमनुबन्धयत॥
Compare these lines with Gotama I. 2. iv. 55.

44. कस्मिन् सति जरामरणं भवति। किं प्रत्ययं च पुनर्जरामरणम्॥
जात्यां सत्यां जरामरणं भवति। जातिप्रत्ययं हि जरामरणम्॥
कस्मिन् सति जातिर्भवति किम्प्रत्यया च पुनर्जातिः॥
भवे सति जातिर्भवति भवप्रत्यया च पुनर्जातिः॥
कस्मिन् सति भवो भवति किम्प्रत्ययश्च पुनर्भवः॥
उपादाने सति भवो भवत्युपादानप्रत्ययो हि भवः॥
कस्मिन् सत्युपादानं भवति किम्प्रत्ययश्च पुनरुपादानम्॥
तृष्णायां सत्यामुपादानं भवति तृष्णाप्रत्ययो ह्युपादानम्॥
कस्मिन् सति तृष्णा भवति किम्प्रत्यया च तृष्णा॥
वेदनायां सत्यां तृष्णा भवति वेदनाप्रत्यया च तृष्णा॥
कस्मिन् सति वेदना भवति किम्प्रत्यया पुनर्वेदना॥
स्पर्शे सति वेदना भवति स्पर्शप्रत्यया हि वेदना॥
कस्मिन् सति स्पर्शो भवति किम्प्रत्ययश्च पुनः स्पर्शः॥
षडायतने सति स्पर्शो भवति षडायतनप्रत्ययो हि स्पर्शः॥
कस्मिन् सति षडायतनं भवति किम्प्रत्ययश्च पुनः षडायतनम्॥
नामरूपे सति षडायतनं भवति नामरूपप्रत्ययं हि षडायतनम्॥
कस्मिन् सति नामरूपं भवति किम्प्रत्ययश्च पुनर्नामरूपम्॥
विज्ञाने सति नामरूपं भवति विज्ञानप्रत्ययं हि नामरूपम्॥
कस्मिन् सति विज्ञानं भवति किम्प्रत्ययश्च विज्ञानम्॥
संस्कारेषु सत्सु विज्ञानं भवति संस्कारप्रत्ययश्च विज्ञानम्॥
कस्मिन् सति संस्कारा भवन्ति किम्प्रत्ययाश्च संस्काराः॥

अविद्यायां सत्यां संस्कारा भवन्ति अविद्याप्रत्यया हि संस्काराः॥

45. कस्मिन्नसति जरामरणं न भवति कस्य वा निरोधाज्जरामरणनिरोधः॥
जात्यां असत्यां जरामरणं न भवति जातिनिरोधाज्जरामरणनिरोधः॥
कस्मिन्नसति जातिर्न भवति कस्य वा निरोधाज्जातिनिरोधः॥
भवेऽसति जातिर्न भवति भवनिरोधाज्जातिनिरोधः॥
कस्मिन्नसति विस्तरेण यावत्संस्कारा न भवन्ति। कस्य वा निरोधात्संस्कारनिरोधः॥
अविद्यायामसत्यां संस्कारा न भवन्त्यविद्यानिरोधात्संस्कारनिरोधः संस्कारनिरोधाद्विज्ञाननिरोधः॥ *LalitaVistara.*

46. Wayland's Memoir of Dr. Judson.

47. इह ते कामक्रोधा मोहप्रभवा जगत्परिनिकासाः।
साहूता इव चौरा विनाशिता ये निरवशेषाः॥
इह सा अकार्य्यकर्त्री भवतृष्णाचारिणी तथाऽविद्या।
सानुशयमूलजाला महाज्ञानाग्निना दग्धा॥
इह सा अहं ममेति च कालिपाशदुरानुगाढलितमूला।
नीवरणकठिनग्रन्थिश्छिन्ना मम ज्ञानशस्त्रेण॥
काङ्क्षा विमतिसमुदया दृष्टीजडजन्तिता अशुभमूला।
तृष्णानदीतिवेगा प्रशोषिता मे ज्ञानसूर्य्येण॥
कुहनलपनप्रहाणं मायामात्सर्य्यदोषइर्ष्याद्यं।
इह ते क्लेशरण्यं छिन्नं विनयाग्निना दग्धम्॥
सर्व्वभवबन्धनानि च मुक्तानि मयेह तानि सर्वाणि।
प्रज्ञाबलेन निखिलास्त्रिविधमिह विमोक्षमागम्य॥
इह रागमदनमकरं तृषोर्मिजलं कुदृष्टिसङ्ग्रहम्।
संसारसागरमहं सन्तीर्णो वीर्य्यबलनावा॥
इह तन्मयाऽनुबुद्धं सर्व्वपरप्रवादिभिर्यदप्राप्तम्।
अमृतं लोकहितार्थं जरामरणशोकदुःखान्तम्॥
इह तन्मयाऽनुबुद्धं यद्बुद्धं प्राक्तनैर्जिनैरपरिमाणैः।
यस्य मधुरोऽभिरम्यः शब्दो लोकेषु विख्यातः॥

48. वोधिसत्त्वस्य पूर्व्वमश्रुतेषु धर्मेषु। Lalitavistara.
49. Capt Yule's Narraive of the Mission to the court of Ava.
50. Hodgson.
51. Hardy's Manual of Buddhism, p. 472.
52. येषां त्वद्दर्शनं सोम्य एव्यसे पुरुर्षभ। न ते कल्पसहस्राणि जातु याभ्स्यन्ति दुर्गंतिं॥ LalitaVistara.
53. सुनत वचन उपजा अति क्रोधा। मायाबश न रहा मन बोधा॥ परसंपदा सकहु नहिंदेषी। तुमरे ईर्षाकपट विशेषी। मथत सिंधु रुद्रहिं वौरायेहु। सुरन प्रेरि विष पान करायेहु॥ असुरसुरा विषं शंकरहिं आपु रमा मणि चारु। स्वारथ साधक कुटिल तुम सदा कपटब्यावहार॥

Toolseedas's Rāmāyaṇa.

54. यामिमां पुष्पितां वाचं प्रवदन्त्यविपश्चितः। वेदवादरताः पार्थ नान्यदस्तीति वादिनः॥ * * त्रैगुण्यविषया वेदा निस्त्रैगुण्यो भवार्जुन।
55. Hardy's Manual, p. 446.
56. Ibid. p. 453.
57. Ibid. p. 37.
58. तदर्थं यमनियमाभ्यामात्मसंस्कारो योगाच्चात्मविध्यपायैः॥

Nyāya Sūtra iv. 111.

59. ऋणक्लेशप्रवृत्त्यनुबन्धादपवर्गाभावः॥ Nyāya iv. 59.
60. *Ballantyne's translation.*
61. प्रधानशब्दानुपपत्तेर्गुणशब्देनानुवादो निन्दाप्रशंसोपपत्तेः॥ iv. 60.
62. पात्रचयान्तानुपपत्तेश्च फलाभावः॥ iv. 62.
63. नासतो विद्यते भावो नाभावो विद्यते सतः। Bhagavad-gītā.
64. सुषुप्तस्य स्वप्नादर्शने क्लेशभाववदपवर्गः Gotama, iv. 63.
65. स्वर्गकामो यजेत।
66. ब्रह्मा विष्णुश्च रुद्रश्च सर्व्वा वा भूतजातयः नाशमेवानुधावन्ति सलिलानीव वाडवं। Yoga-vāśiṣṭha.
67. तत्र रागपक्षः काम मत्सरः स्पृहा तृष्णा लोभो माया दम्भ इति कामो रिरंसा।

68. द्वेषपक्षः क्रोध ईर्ष्याऽसूया द्रोहोऽमर्षोऽभिमान इति क्रोधोनेत्रलौहित्यादिहेतु-र्दोषविशेषः।

69. आत्मानं रथिनं विद्धि शरीरं रथमेव तु। बुद्धिन्तु सारथिं विद्धि मनः प्रग्रहमेव च॥ इन्द्रियाणि हयानाऽहुर्विषयांस्तेषु गोचरान्। आत्मेन्द्रियमनोयुक्तं भोक्तेत्याहुर्मनीषिणः॥ यस्त्वविज्ञानवान् भवत्ययुक्तेन मनसा सदा। तस्येन्द्रियाण्यवश्यानि दुष्टाश्वा इव सारथेः॥ यस्तु विज्ञानवान् भवति युक्तेन मनसा सदा। तस्येन्द्रियाणि वश्यानि सदश्वा इव सारथेः॥

Kaṭha Upaniṣad (1.3.3-6)

70. Bishop Butler.

71. तेनैवानुरूपेण यजमानः सुवर्गं लोकमेति। Taittirīya Brāhmaṇa.

DIALOGUE VI

FROM THE SAME TO THE SAME

My last letter was written in a very excited state of mind. I was wondering what Satyakāma could mean by the 'True Sacrifice for sin,' or what he could be driving at, either,by the ingenious distinction between *suvarga* and *śwarga.* I went yesterday to put these questions to him personally, but I found that Kapila and Āgamika had already come, and commenced a controversy on the Sāṅkhya system. On entering the room, I heard Satyakāma saying, "I believe Śaṅkarācārya's strictures on your system are unanswerable."

Kāpila.—"I am surprized at *your* saying so. Have you never observed the *vāk-chhala* (verbal tricks) played by that bigoted Vedāntist? When for instance he quotes against us texts implying an intellectual exercise on the part of the Creator, such as *seeing, desiring,* he reasons as if we held *prakṛti* (Nature) to be the *efficient* cause of the universe, and labours to convict us of supreme folly in supposing that unintelligent and inanimate nature can *see* or *desire.* But Śaṅkara knew, quite as well as our own selves, that *nature* is, in our system, the *material,* or substantial, not the *efficient,* cause of the world. While again he has ransacked the Vedas for every sentence or phrase that might by any stretch of criticism be turned against us, he has cautiously avoided to mention those texts which obviously teach what we inculcate. I will not be so disingenuous as to deny that there are a few passages which are apparently against us, and of these Śaṅkara has not failed to take the utmost advantage. You will perhaps not deny that the question between us and the Vedāntists is how to reconcile the two sets of conflicting texts. We hold that the texts which ascribe the creation to inanimate and unintelligent *prakṛti* as its material cause, or, in the language of our venerable Ācārya, as the *rootless root*[1], are the key whereby all others are to be interpreted.Vyāsa and Śaṅkara, on the other hand, maintain that our texts are to be overruled by those which seem to inculcate that Brahma, or the spirit, is the material of which the universe is made. I may venture to hope you will allow our argument its due weight. It is certainly more consistent than that of the Vedāntist. The universe is composed both of rational and irrational principles. We are not here discussing the origin of rational principles, because the Vedāntists and ourselves are both agreed that the Soul is uncreated and eternal. It is only the inanimate and irrational creation that we are called upon to account for. And here our much misunderstood Ācārya thought, I must add, rightly, that it would be losing sight of all moral and physical discrimination to say that an intelligent spirit could be the *substance* of inanimate matter. To say again that the universe sprang from a spirit, that the impure was a development of the pure, would be to maintain that creation was a process of deterioration. We have numerous instances of animated beings springing from inanimate matter, as vermin from filth, but we nowhere see a single instance of inanimate matter arising out of spiritual substances. I have yet to learn that he who is loth to pronounce the world, with all its grossness and impurity, to be consubstantial with the spirit, and therefore traces it to a cuase *connatural* with itself, (as the Vedas themselves phrase it,)can be guilty of the impiety which is charged upon us. You must remember that the question is not, who is the efficient cause of the Universe. *That,* the Vedāntists and ourselves are agreed, is a minor point of inquiry. Both of us, also, maintain that instrumental causality is here unnecessary, for the source from which the world was produced may have worked itself out, like mik becoming curds. We do not fear discomfiture, if we be allowed a *fair field* with the Vedāntist; if those who are to judge between us will remember that we are both speculating on the substance of which, not the agent by whom, the world was made.

"True it is," continued the advocate of the Sāṅkhya, "that Vyāsa and Śaṅkara have in some places argued for an efficient cause. But that is against the general spirit of their speculations. They ought not surely to have the benefit of their own inconsistency. After these explanations, I should be very much surprized to find you still taking the Vedāntist's part in this controversy."

Satyakāma.—"When I spoke of Śaṅkarācārya's argument against your doctrine, I did not allude to the texts which he cited from the Vedas. Nor did I mean that he, *as a Vedāntist*, had a right to say any thing to you. I cannot deny there is some force in what you say, *as the matter stands between you and the Vedāntists.* I believe that if you be bound hand and foot by dogmas of the Vedas, you may be driven to some of the conclusions which Kapila has drawn; for there is no denying the fact that the Upaniṣads do speak of an unproduced female, answering to your description of *prakṛti,* red, white, and black, (the very colours by which the three original qualities are typified,) producing many creatures like itself[2]. But I do not see any reason why you should allow the Vedas to lead you astrary. If the Vedas lay down doctrines so manifestly absurd, why should you bow to their authority? The founder of your School did not hesitate to pronounce an independent verdict about the ritual of the Vedas. Why should you allow their cosmogony to warp your judgment?

"Why should you, either, discard the notion of an efficient cause of the world? If Śaṅkarācārya is inconsistent, that does not vitiate a good argument. He may be debarred from the privilege of benefiting by it, but what is good reason in itself continues such, notwithstanding the fault of the party who adduces it. True knowledge may, according to Menu, be reverently received even from the vulgar; just as nectar is not the less acceptable when extracted from poison[3]. Now it appears to me extremely unphilosophical to speculate on the *substance* of the universe. The first thing that strikes us when we look around is the beautiful arrangement of the heavens and the earth, the uniformity of the law which regulates the planetary motions, and secures the stability of the solar system; and the adaptation of the whole to the happiness and comforts of animal life. Huge masses, far exceeding the earth in magnitude, are perpetually moving in space, not without some eccentricities in their orbits, and yet there is no collision.

"The uninterrupted succession of days and nights, of weathers and seasons; and the adaptation of the atmosphere to the properties of light and heat, whereby evaporation and condensation are so regulated that the waters on the earth are alternately drained and replenished, just in the manner suited to the wants of animal and vegetable life, precluding alike the opposite *nirītis* (plagues) of too much and too little rain; the structure again of animals and vegetables in exact conformation to the action of the elements by which they are surrounded and to the material properties of that to which their sustenance and growth are owing; all these mutual adaptations indicate design, and point, not to a plastic substance, but to an intelligent Artificer, an efficient Agent, of infinite wisdom, power, and goodness.

"I confess that Śaṅkarācārya's argument against you, *so far as it relies on the Vedas,* is singularly unsatisfactory. But his appeals to common sense, his reasoning from the beautiful structure of the world, however inconsistent with his other sayings, are irresistible. I know you may reason against *his* doctrine (the Vedānta) with equal force. But that does not embarrass *me.* My motto is truth. Let us seek out the truth, no matter what system or school is thereby falsified or stultified. Śaṅkarācārya says[4]; 'If the question is to be decided by analogy (without the authority of the Vedas) then no irrational substance, undirected by a rational essence, is seen in the world transforming itself of its own accord into something that may be useful to men. Houses and palaces with rooms for sleeping, sitting, and amusement, are seen to be erected by skilful artists, in adaptation to the seasons, for the enjoyment of pleasure and the avoiding of pain; how then can unintelligent nature form the earth and this whole universe, adapted to various works and enjoyments, organic and inorganic, containing bodies and various matter, with parts mutually and severally adapted to one another; the scene of many works and enjoyments, incomprehensible to the mind even of the most skilful artist? Such formations are never seen in clods and stones. Earth and other materials are seen to be moulded into fine shapes under the direction of potters and other manufacturers. Nature too must in like 'manner have an intelligent director. Nor is there any 'necessity, in the tracing of the original cause, to confine 'the attention to the want of a homogeneous substance, 'such as earth, overlooking the requirement of an external cause, such as the potter or other manufacturer. There could be no absurdity in the latter supposition; and it would certainly be agreeable to the Vedas, for there the cause of the universe is declared to be intelligent. Therefore because of the existence of arrangement, and of the want of conclusiveness in the reason, an unintelligent cause of the world cannot be inferred.'

"You say, learned Sir, this argument is not to the point, because you pronounce nature to be the material, not the efficient cause. But Śaṅkara justly says there is no necessity for deducing a consubstantial cause. You are not called upon to speculate on the material cause of the world. That undertaking is itself a radical defect in your system. The defect is the more glaring because you have not elsewhere provided an intelligent efficient cause.

"And here I must say the passages of the Vedas to which you look with such confidence do not bear you out. A Prakṛti, such as you assume, is no doubt spoken of, but it is nowhere asserted that it performs the creative office, *undirected by the soul.* Your Ācārya seems to glory in denying such direction.

'Nature is the real agent' says he;'the agency attributed to the soul is only apparent or illusory; the soul is no agent even in connection with nature, as it is not the iron that burns when heated, but the fire that is connected with it. Nature, though inanimate, works like the curdling of milk, or like the operation of time. Nature is the original cause. Other things are its products.The spirit, though eternal, is not the agent, because it is incompetent. The products of nature are found everywhere; hence nature is all pervading[5].'

"Now the few texts of the Upaniṣads on which you rely do indeed inculcate a duality of principle, but they do not justify the boldness with which you define one of those principles as, at the same time, both devoid of sensation, and also productive of the world. I do not find any such lesson in the three texts which you are in the habit of citing :

'Two birds inhabit the same tree as friends joined together; one tastes its fruits, the other looks on in 'abstinence.'

'Two unproduced males (there are), intelligent and unintelligent, independent and dependent; and one unproduced female joined to enjoyer and objects enjoyment; when the soul attains this three-fold Brahma, it becomes infinite, of universal form, and freed from agency.'

'One unproduced male united enjoys the unproduced female, red, black, white, and producing many creatures like herself; another unproduced male renounces her, 'the enjoyer[6].'

"Of your extreme repugnance to the idea of an intelligent creator, your Vedāntic opponents have no doubt taken ample advantage. So far indeed you have given a colour to their pantheism, and I do not doubt that many persons have been the more readily reconciled to the Vedānta by regarding it as the only refuge from the repulsive idea of a creation without an intelligent Creator.

"In this respect your theory is worse than that of the Naiyāyikas—(I mean—the modern followers of Gotama and Kaṇāda,) for though they set up atoms as eternal principles, they do not reject the agency of a supreme Intelligence. I do not deny you had some reason to argue against the Naiyāyika the other day, and to contend that Gotama or Kaṇāda was no better theist than Kapila. But if the disciples of those two Ṛṣis are determined to interpret the Nyāya and Vaiśeṣika Sūtras in a theistic sense, what right have we, outsiders, to say any thing against them? You may, if you choose, interpret the Kapila Sūtras in a similar manner, and I will not undertake to say you will not be justified in your construction, quite as much as they consider themselves to be in theirs.

"But you boldly avow that your prakṛti is the sole cause. Your Ācārya says, and you do not deny, that nature works itself up like the self-working of milk into curds. You are, so far, fully exposed to Śaṅkara's powerful battery; though his own system suffers equally by it; for he too maintains that the spirit worked up itself into the world like milk into curds!"

Kāpila.—"And he does so with a boldness which ill befits a controversalitst in a question such as this. 'For, says he, it (the creation) is accomplished like milk, through the peculiar property of the substance itself. As in the world milk or water turns of itself into curds or ice, without, requiring an external instrument, so also here. But does not milk itself when turning into curds require an external instrument, such as heat? Then how can it be said that the creation is like the operation of milk? This is no fault. Milk is only more quickly turned by heat into the state of curds, but not in a greater measure than it would itself attain. If it had not the capacity of turning into curds, it could not be forced into that state by the power of heat; for air and ether cannot be forced into that state by the power of heat[7].' And yet Śaṅkara attacks *us* for teaching the same doctrine!'

Satyakāma.—"Śaṅkara is no doubt chargeable with inconsistency, but he attacks you because you deny the existence of an intelligent Author in a creation so full of indications of design. You say that *prakṛti* is the equipoise of the three qualities of goodness, activity and darkness. The equipoise of the three qualities cannot be a substance. It is a mere relation, not an entity,—a quality, not a thing. What conception can you form of a *quality* without a *substance?* But whatever your *prakṛti* may be, you flatly deny the agency of a living and intelligent creator. Had I not read the very words of your teacher and found you maintaining the same doctrine, I should have considered it perfectly impossible for a philosopher to hold such an opinion. And here, as if to complete our perplexity, you attribute to the equipoise of the three qualities, a creative power, of which, you say, the soul is incapable, because it involves desire and activity. How can you consistently attribute to the equipoise that which implies an excess of *rajas,* or your second quality, activity? The balance must then be disturbed. It is no longer an equipoise. Śaṅkarācārya gives you a terrible hit on this point.

"Your plea that your material cause should not be argued against, as if you held it to be an efficient agent, is again nullified by your admission of an *end* in the creation. You say the *final cause*[8] of nature's agency is the emancipation of the *Puruṣa,* or soul, passively watching her proceedings. She labours for the soul's use, just as the camel carries the *kumkum* for another. With reference to those who attain knowledge, the agency of nature ceaseth, because of their aversion to the world, just as cooking ceaseth when food is prepared; but as to all others nature ceaseth not. She does not desist even when she has done with the already wise. But when the object is attained she ceaseth, like a dancing girl when dancing is over. When her fault is known she no longer approaches the soul, just as a lady of rank is ashamed to appear before her husband if she be known to have misbehaved.

"Now the idea of a final cause cannot be separated from that of design. It pre-supposes intelligence quite as much as the idea of efficient agency. That unintelligent and inanimate nature, which cannot think or feel, could have an end in view, is simply a self-contradictory assertion. That it should know when to work and when to cease is an enigma which I for my part cannot pretend to solve."

Kāpila. "Ah! but the contradiction disappears when we say that nature does so from *habit*[9], like the involuntary services of a devoted servant, – or perhaps from the attraction of works which are without beginning. Is it absurd to say that an irrational substance should perform a certain act by habit?

"Consider how forcible a principle of action habit is. Instances of it are constantly met with in the animal and even the vegetable world. The horse drags your carriage, the ox draws your plough, the elephant carries your luggage. They have drivers, it is true, but how often the drivers do nothing but *watch* the animal's motions. It is not that they whip or goad the beasts without intermission. It is habit which guides those irrational creatures. The best driver in the world will not drive those which are not influenced by habit. Witness the cases of wicked and untrained horses. There can be no absurdity in saying that *prakṛti* does for the soul what your horses are seen to do for yourselves. But you will perhaps say, that horses and oxen, though irrational, are still animated creatures, and that nature's case is not parallel with theirs. Well, what say you as to the power of steam? Have you not seen the Railway train dragged by the *iron horse,* as the locomotive is sometimes called? Is not that an instance to the purpose? Nature works similarly. Though unintelligent, she is sufficiently powerful for her purpose. As the cow's milk, itself formed from grass, though inanimate, is naturally moved for the growth of the calf[10]; as the water, though inanimate, flows naturally for the benefit of men, so inanimate nature and her products also move for the accomplishment of the soul's object."

Satyakāma.—"We are speaking of the original creation. I am astonished at your attributing such an act to habit, or the attraction of works. Habit pre-supposes past acts, which the idea of an original creation precludes. Nor could there be, *at that time,* the attraction of works, for works there could not be before the creation. Will you fall back on the old idea of an eternal succession of *adṛṣṭa,* or works, and worlds, mechanically following one another? Your Ācārya does indeed recognize *karma* (works) as the cause of differences[11] in creation, but he appears to reject the theory of an eternal succession of works and worlds like seed and plant[12].

"Again, although an irrational creature may, under the power of habit, induced by previous training under the superintendence of a rational agent, produce an *end* which that agent had in view, and an inanimate substance may, by means of an impulse it had received from a similar agent, mechanically subserve a purpose, yet such an idea is incomprehensible where no intelligent direction of any kind is admitted. Out horses, oxen, and elephants would be of no avail, if they were not trained and directed under intelligent superintendence. But your system flatly denies such direction on the part of the soul, and yet maintains that inanimate nature works for its benefit.

"If you got a wild horse from the jungles, would he spontaneously get into harness, drag your carriage, go where it is your object he should go, and stop where it ought to stop? Your Ācārya has compared Nature's operation with the camel's carrying *kumkum* for the use of men. Would the camel carry it without direction and guidance? An operation which has an *end* necessarily implies design—and though the mechanical instrument of the operation may be inanimate or irrational, the designer must be both animated and intelligent.

"You have spoken of the railway train, of the mother's milk issuing for the offspring's nourishment, of waters flowing for the benefit of men. Hear what Śaṅkarācārya says on your two last pleas :

'This is not well said for, from the fact, acknowledged by both parties, that we never see independent action in inanimate substances, such as carriages, we infer that action in the cases of milk and water must be from animated agents. The Śāstra too says : He who residing in water is different from it, is the imperishable person under whose government the other eastern rivers flow. The milk again flows because of the tender affection of the animated cow, and because of the sucking of the calf. Nor is the flowing of water spontaneous, it depending on low lands and other causes[13].'

"The *substance* of Śaṅkarācārya's reply cannot be gainsayed. He refers to a proximate and an ultimate cause. The proximate cause is the law to which things are naturally subject; the ultimate cause is that Omniscient and All-wise Governor who gave that law. The proximate cause alone, I allow, would be a mere repetition of what you say. That water flows over low grounds, or that steam acts upon every thing that presents a barrier to it, is merely enunciating the natural process. But there is an ultimate or Supreme cause, who enacted the law which steam, water, and milk all equally obey. If it were not liable to be construed in a pantheistic sense, I should have no objection to Śaṅkara's own formula as quoted from the Upaniṣad :—'He who, residing in water, is different from it,' is the governor under whose guidance steam and water exhibit the powers which prove so beneficial for men.

"The power of steam is no doubt wonderful as we see it daily in the train that passes from Rajmahal to Howrah. But can you forget the mental exercise involved in the projection of the Railway scheme—the vast preparations making for years by skilful engineers, the making of roads sand bridges, the laying of the rail, and the daily labour bestowed by intelligent workmen on the guiding of the train? The Railway is no doubt a brilliant triumph of science, but science implies intellectual exercise, not the blind force of nature.

"Do you think the locomotive moves from Rajmahal to Howrah without the intervention of intelligent engineers? Do the boiler and the hearth find water and coals for themselves as often as they are wanted, and in the exact quantities of their requirements? What would you say to a man if he showed you a book—say the Sūtras of Kapila himself with the commentary of Vijñāna Bhikṣu—and said that the words and sentences which appear in black and white were produced by a quantity of rags. Part of the rags took fire by friction, and from the smoke was produced collyrium which turned into ink. Part dissolved through damp, and became paper, which folded into pages and stuck together. The ink then traced the letters which appear on the several pages in large and small characters, distinguishing the *Sūtra* from the *Bhāṣya*—and all this, like milk turning into curds, without an author to compose Sūtra or Bhāṣya, without manufacturer to make the paper and ink, without clerk to write out the sentences, or binder to fold and stitch the papers. If a person gave you such an account of the production of the *Sāṅkhya pravachana Bhāṣya*—what would you say to him?"

Kāpila.—"That is an unfair question. We all *know* that the Sāṅkhya sūtras were composed by Kapila. How could I then believe such a story?

Satyakāma.—"Well, suppose a manuscript book were brought to you of which you *knew* nothing. Could you receive such a story of its production—especially, if you found that it was a work of great excellence as regarded philosophy and rhetoric?"

Kāpila.—"If a book contained transcendental conceptions

in regard to philosophy, it would itself be an evidence of mental effort, and of the existence of some great mind prior to its production. In a work of any value we must have (1) the conceptions of the author's mind; (2) those conceptions couched in appropriate and intelligible terms; (3) the terms correctly inflected, and put together agreeably to the rules of grammar; (4) the sentences and phrases arranged accurately and syntactically; (5) the whole again written out in the ordinary letters of the alphabet with orthographical correctness. All this could not be achieved by the fortuitous action of mere rags. A good book is universally held to betoken the prior existence of a *master mind.* Your allusion to the Sāṅkhya Sūtras, excuse me for saying so again, is unfair. It looks like a surrender of your point in this debate."

Satyakāma. – "It does not certainly appear so to *me.* You say that a good book betokens the prior existence of a *master mind.* No doubt it does. But does not the visible world the same too? Does not matter itself betoken the prior existence of mind? If matter had the power or capcaity of self-action, who endowed it with that power? Who made and fitted it with that capacity? Are not the arrangement of the universe and the structure of animal bodies superior by far to the arrangement of letters and the structure of sentences in a book? Letters could not form words, nor words signify ideas, if they were not arranged by a mind familiar with orthography and grammar. But could the sun, moon, earth, and atmosphere be placed as they are without a supreme Intelligence ordaining and regulating their poisitions, attractions, motions, and powers, so as to cause our days and months, our seasons and years, our light and heat, in exact adaptation to our wants and comforts? A book could not be produced without a master mind. The very idea appears preposterous to you. And yet you think this world could be self-produced from an inanimate and unintelligent principle, and that, with a view to the soul's emancipation! You think undirected nature sufficient to account for the beauty, symmetry, and arrangement of a universe—the combinations of which are so complex as to baffle our highest efforts to compehend them—the links and adaptations so numerous that we can never hope to live long enough to master even a small portion of them; the structure of animal organs so curiously formed that each performs a certain function, and the whole produces a certain end to which it is adapted. You think such an arrangement could be made without a Designer, a Director, a Governor. Consider once more the consequences of your theory. Think on the sort of works which you thus attribute to an inanimate, irrational principle, incapable of design or deliberation. We have a sun above us the source of light and heat. An inestimable blessing it is; but without the co-operation of just such an atmosphere as surrounds our globe, it would be impossible for us to benefit by it. Without such diffusion of its rays as is caused by the atmosphere, our houses, indeed all places in the shade, would at noon-day be as cold as ice, and as dismal as the night of an *amāvasyā,* or the last of the moon; while the open air would be a furnace of fire during day-light. When we got out of doors it would be like going suddenly from thick darkness into a blaze of light,—to the sun of a noon-day from the gloom of a midnight. I need not tell you that creatures, such as we are, could never live if the sun and the atmosphere were not so adapted to each other, as that light and heat, shot forth from the one, should, by the other, be diffused to suit our condition. Could this adaptation, far transcending any conception of Kapila's mind, proceed from a blind principle like your Nature?

"The same sun again is the centre of our system. You have no doubt heard, what I believe you are prepared to admit, that the theory of the sun's being the centre of motion in our system is a philosophic necessity, the non acknowledgement of which would lead us to the wildest schemes in order to account for the phenomena observed in the heavens. And it is the principle of attraction, of which our own Bhāskarācārya was not entirely ignorant, which regulates the motions, and prescribes the velocity with which the planets perform their revolutions. Their orbits are also fixed by the nature of that attraction.

"The advantages derived from this arrangement of the solar system are so obvious that I need scarcely mention them. To specify one instance,—the position of the earth is such that her two poles are alternately presented toward the sun during her revolution, and thus our periodical change of seasons is occasioned. Consider what the consequences would be if this change of seasons did not come round regularly. It may be all very fine in poets to extol the pleasures of an eternal spring, but fancy what the result would be of the realization of such a conception. Not only would the anticipated pleasure be annihilated by its monotonous sameness, but the effect would soon be manifest in the failure of our crops and the drying up of our ponds. After you have had abundance of rain, and passed through the cold of winter, it may be all very pleasant to have for a month or two a bland atmosphere and a mild sun. But the process of evaporation would be affected by a perpetual spring, and that, in its turn, would cause a suspension of rain. The atmosphere would itself prove hurtful to life in the absence of the elemtns of purification presented by the summer and autumn. Is it possible that inanimate nature could give a position to the earth's axis, and create a law of motion, so exactly adapted to the wants of terrestrial life?

"Consider again the wisdom manifested in the structure of animal and vegetable organs. The arrangement and mutual adaptation of the parts, harmonious as they are, are yet so complex, that they have given occasion to several sciences, each of which separately requires the study of years. Anatomy and the other departments of medical science, with Natural History, and Botany, present an accumulation of extraordinary facts, all loudly testifying to a uniformity of purpose and benevolence of design, infinitely beyond the grasp, as Śaṅkarācārya well expresses it, of 'the most skilful' of our species. The smallest insect, hardly discernible by the naked eye, presents as perfect an arrangement of organs for the sustentation of life and the reproduction of its species, as the largest animal. Who can for a moment believe that all this systematized arrangement and adaptation of parts, with a provident eye to the life and comforts of the lowest no less than the highest animal,—an arrangement and an adaptation by which crude matter turns into vegetable, and vegetable matter is assimilated with animal flesh, by which blood and milk are extracted from leaves and roots, and leaves and roots formed from gas and moisture,—could be projected and accomplished by an agent that is devoid of thought, animation, and design?

"You confess that a quantity of rags could not of themselves produce a book, and yet you say that nature, or the equipoise of the three original qualities, was able to bring such a world into existence. Is the *Sāṅkhya pravachana bhāṣya*, or any other book that may be named, a greater proof of intelligence or design, than the Universe with its complicated but harmonious arrangements? Of the one you think it preposterous that mere rags should produce it. To the other you would assign a cause more flimsy even than rags. For your *prakṛti* appears to me to be a mere name, a mere phantom. You say it is the equipoise of the three original qualities of goodness, activity, and darkness. Quality is itself no substance. Your doctrine amounts to the assertion that the external world came spontaneously into being without any cause at all. What conception can we have of *prakṛti,* as an aggregate of qualities, without a substance qualified thereby—or, to speak in the language of Naiyāyikas, without a *samavāya,* (substratum)? To such a mere theoretic nature you assign the work of creation, a work for which you say the soul was not competent. How could the soul fail to do that for which nature sufficed? Your doctrine is simply unintelligible."

Kāpila.—"I will explain what our Ācārya means, He has shown that Atoms could not be considered the first cause of all things; and, as to the soul, it is evident an intelligent principle could not be the material of which the inanimate world is composed. Besides it is *ahaṅkāra*[14] (egotism), one of the products of *prakṛti,* not the soul, that has agency. The soul can never be moved to make an effort, and without effort there could be no creation."

Satyakāma.—"But why could not the soul do every thing that was necessary without a material cause?"

Kāpila.—"Because, says the revered Ṛṣi, a *substance cannot be out of no substance.* Because also, he says elsewhere, there is necessity for a material cause."

"Can you, continued the Sāṅkhya śāstri, make a house without bricks or a box without wood?"

"I cannot," said Satyakāma, "but the Almighty can. With incomparably greater reason might I ask you to say how a mere equipoise of three qualities could supply the place of bricks?"

Kāpila appeared somewhat perplexed. Āgamika, who had all this time been listening patiently to the above conversation, interposed a remark on the etymology of the word 'Prakṛti.' "Some light," said he, "may be thrown on the subject by considering the etymology of the word. Prakṛti is derived from *kṛ* with the affix क्तिन्. Generally speaking that affix is added to express *bhāva,* or the abstract idea, sometimes the *karma,* or the object, of the action. The rule has many exceptions, but they are always obvious. I am told that the Greek language has a grammatical affix corresponding to our क्तिन्, which, released from its characteristic redundants, and inflected in the nominative, becomes तिः (*tis*) not more different from the greek. These two letters are notoriously interchanged in that language, and the affixes in the two languages may be considered similar.

"I am the more confirmed in this opinion by a passage which a friend read to me from Strabo. I suspect the Greek geographer meant by the term to represent this very *prakṛt* is of Kapila, especially as he added that it was from the same element that heaven and the stars were produced. Now what is the cosmogony of Kapila? There is the self-existent *Puruṣa,* and there is this *prakṛti,* or nature. The first product of the latter is *mind,* the immediate cause of *ahaṅkāra* or self-consciousness, from which all the rest were produced. Might not Kapila have only meant to say that the self-existent Spirit was naturally endowed, first with mind, then with self-consciousness, and so created the world."

Satyakāma.—"There would be some meaning in the theory according to the interpretation you suggest. Indeed the Matsya Purāṇa appears to identify the equipoise of the three qualities with the one-formed triad.[15] (*ekāmūrti strayodevāh,* one form and three gods) Brahmā, Viṣṇu and Maheśwara. Even the admirers of Kapila have not received his doctrine without an amendment. But he himself glories in denying creative agency to the Puruṣa or soul. *Prakṛti* worked itself up like milk in the cow's body."

"I am astonished," continued Satyakāma, turning, after a brief pause, to Kāpila, "at your Ācārya referring to the cow and her milk in support of *his* doctrine. A better example cannot easily be adduced for its refutation. Your Ācārya maintains that nature, inanimate and unintelligent, works without direction and guidance for the benefit of the soul. The instance of the cow and her milk is appealed to in illustration of this theory. That milk, it is said, comes up spontaneously for the benefit of the calf. Śaṅkarācārya replies to you that the milk does not come up spontaneously, and that its determination is owing to the tender affection of the cow and to the calf's power of suction. I admit this reply does not fairly meet your doctrine. But how does the milk come up in the cow? The animal eats the grass which goes into its stomach, where by the process of digestion food turns into *chyle,* which is carried by a curious mechanism into the reservoir of blood with which it then assimilates. The mechanism is as fine as it is curious, and by a wonderful contrivance it protects the blood vessels against any matter in the chyle which might cause inconvenience to the animal. The blood, thus replenished by food, performs a secreting function, the very conception of which strikes the mind with awe. The secretions are partly constant and partly occasional. Those that are constant are necessary for the conservation of the organs and the healthy state of the body. Those that are occasional answer certain purposes called for by the condition of the animal at a definite time. And provision is made in its physical organism for meeting such contingencies. When the animal is in a condition to bring forth young, the blood makes a new secretion, with a quality not found in any other secretion, namely, that of nutrition. This secretion we call milk. There is an organ already provided by a prospective contrivance for the reception and retention of that secretion, and there is an excretory duct annexed whereby the fluid determines to the udder at the particular juncture when it is about to be wanted. We have in all this a machinery and a contrivance, suited to an especial end and purpose, and obviously indicative of design. Now to say that an inanimate and irrational principle is capable of design is simply a contradiction in terms."

Kāpila.—"You were candid enough to admit that Śaṅkarācārya's remark on the instance of the cow and her milk is not to the point. This admission encourages me to hope that you will not lend any countenance to the popular calumny against our system. Men, incapable of nice discriminations, think they will pass muster for piety by only calling the Sāṅkhya *nirīśwara* (godless). Wiser heads have however confessed that there is no knowledge equal to that which is embodied in our system. Even the popular poet Tulasidasa[16] is compelled to speak of Kapila with religious reverence, and to acknowledge that the distinguishing characteristic of the Sāṅkhya is *tattva vicāra,* or discussion of truth. It is perfectly gratuitous to charge us with ungodliness. Any discussion may be cut short by putting on a cloak of piety after this fashion. But how stands the argument? Śaṅkarācārya has told us of houses with rooms for sleeping, sitting, and amusements, and you have just made reference to a wonderful organism in the cow's body. We never denied that. The organism in the cow's body cannot surely be more wonderful than the organism of the world itself, which we not only admit but perhaps admire even more than our adversaries. But what is the question between us? Without contravening what people call the religious intuitions of human nature, we simply declare that the physical arrangement of the universe may be sufficiently accounted for by physical causes, that nature and natural law, that is to say *prakṛti* and her prolific operations, were themselves competent to settle the positions, and give the propelling impulses which regulate the motions, and secure the stability of all things in heaven and earth. Whether you refer to the phenomena which are owing to the motions of luminaries far above, or to formations, mechanisms, and organisms near at hand on our globe, they may be all traced to the agency of the same prakṛti or natural law as their ultimate cause. The formations and organisms have been gradual, have taken time, and been developed by a slow process like milk turning into curds. And this is a conception of Kapila's mind in which, I am credibly informed, he is followed by eminent philosophers in Europe, and which is confirmed by recent discoveries in all parts of the world. I have heard from a relative, who has received a paper of commendation (Diploma) from the Doctors' College in Calcutta, that many learned Europeans have come to the conclusion that the earth has, from time immemorial, been a scene of changes, by natural development, of dead matter into organic and vegetable substances, and of vegetables into animal life. One eminent writer says, that 'in pursuing the progress of development of both plants and animals upon the globe, an advance is visible in both cases, from simple to higher forms of organization.' 'In the botanical department we have first sea, afterwards land, plants.' In the department of zoology, too, we see, first traces of the very lowest, removed by a few steps only from vegetable life, and leading by slow gradation to higher forms. The we have fishes, then land animals, commencing with reptiles, then birds, and at last the *jarāyuja,* or mammalia.

"Thus after a long series of years you see a wonderful confirmation of Kapila's grand conception. For what else is his great doctrine? He recognized onward progress in the world, and therefore protested against the fanatical doctrine of the Vedānta that the world was a product of the Supreme Spirit, as if dead matter could be a manifestation of a pure and spiritual essence. The process of creation would then be a process of deterioration—a process inconsistent with the very idea of creation. In opposition to such a fantastic notion, he taught that nature was the original of all things, and that the act of creation was one of development and progress. But as the spiritual could not proceed from the material, he added that the soul was eternal and independent. The ignorant may brand him as nirīśwara, or godless, and cover their imbecility as logicians by an affection of piety, but his doctrine is found to commend itself now to all thoughtful minds—even in Europe."

Satyakāma.—"You have given a colouring to Kapila's doctrine which I do not remember to have seen elsewhere, and you seem to think you have strengthened his cause by forming an alliance with certain philosophers of Europe. But it does not add strength to your doctrine in reality. For the eminent writer to whom you have made reference does *not* ignore an intelligent Creator, the author of nature and the giver of nature's law. His theory has reference only to proximate or secondary causes which fall within the province of science. The doctrine, however, has not, certainly, commended itself 'to *all* thoughtful minds' in Europe, for the leading men of science consider it to be based on inaccurate statements of fact and on untenable premises. But I am not going to *discuss* the theory of transmutation of species. That has been already done satisfactorily by profound investigators. All that I am concerned with at present is to say that the author to whom you have made reference does not deny a supreme Intelligence as the ultimate cause of all things,—as the initiator and ordainer of the natural law which science attempts to expound. Your medical friend who spoke to you of the development theory ought to have drawn your attention to passages like the following :

'All these considerations, when the mind is thoroughly prepared for them, tend to raise our ideas with respect to the character of physical laws, even though we do not go a simple step further in the investigation.

'But it is impossible for an intelligent mind to stop there. We advance from law to the cause of law, and ask what is that? Whence have come all these beautiful regulations? Here science leaves us, but only to conclude, from other grounds, that there is a First cause to which all others are secondary and ministrative, a primitive, Almighty will, of which these laws are merely the mandates. That great Being, who shall say where is his dwelling place, or what is his history! Man pauses breathless at the contemplation of a subject so much above his finite faculties, and only can wonder and adore! When all is seen to be the result of law, the idea of an Almighty author becomes irresistible, for the creation of a law for an endless series of phenomena, an act of intelligence above all else that we can conceive, could have no other imaginable source, and tells, moreover, as strongly for a sustaining as for an originating power[17].'

"The eminent writer to whom you have made reference does not accordingly inculcate a *nirīśwara,* (excuse me, for repeating the word,) or atheistic doctrine. How *could* there be a law without a lawgiver? or a final cause without design and purpose? or a design or purpose without a designer? It is impossible therefore for an inanimate principle, such as nature, to have worked, as you represent, without intelligent direction.

"But are you not shifting from your original ground? You contended in opposition to the Vedānta that your Prakṛti is the material or substantial cause, and now you talk of its *operation* and its *aim.* You treat it, then, as an efficient cause. Śaṅkarācārya's argument, of which you complained, recoils therefore with double force against you. How could a principle, itself inanimate and therfore incapable of thought and intelligence, produce by its operation such a vast and wonderful world with its infinite adaptations, and with such harmony in all its parts?"

Kāpila.—"Of God we can know nothing. Of physical causes we are constantly witnesses. The founder of the Sāṅkhya was only treating his subject, *scientifically,* and all that he meant to inculcate, was, that as far as pure sicence was concerned, the development of the world can be explained by natural law. The European author to whom I made reference, and from whose work you have just read a passage, confessed that the Almighty Being he spoke of was found, not in science, but out of science. Kapila did not choose to go out of science."

Satyakāma.—"But you cannot stop at what you call natural law without offering violence to a science which is higher than mere physics."

Kāpila.—"I do not quite understand your meaning. Explain yourself."

Satyakāma.—"How do you arrive at what you call the

known in science. How do you come to know what you call objects of *pratyakṣa,* or perception? A wave of light strikes your optic nerve, and hence you perceive some form before you. A vibration of the atmosphere strikes your acoustic nerve, and you perceive a sound. The particles of some substance resist your touch, and you feel its presence. Knowledge, which is itself power, is also produced by power—the force of sensation. But as you have the organs of external sensation, so you have also an organ of internal perception, the mind, which your system dignifies by the appellative *mahat* or great. Now this *great* organ has a force, no less powerful than those of external sensation, and it convinces you of the existence of certain objects quite as forcibly and constantly, as the organs of seeing and hearing do. If your organs of external sensation force on your observation the form and mechanism of the world—if your science tells you of the wonderful adaptations of means to ends on our globe—if indeed you are thereby compelled to theorize that your *prakṛti*, or nature, worked for the happiness and comforts of *Puruṣa* (Soul) in the formation of the world, (just as the king's cook aims at the king's satisfaction in his culinary office, and as an experienced servant aims at his master's convenience,)—the great organ of internal perception at once compels you to look up higher. It protests against the possibility of adaptations of means to ends without intelligent agency, and rejects the notion of such numerous harmonious mechanisms and wonderful combinations being brought into existence by mere chance. *It also repudiates your account of its oown creation from an unintelligent principle.* Mind will not admit matter to be its progenitor or superior. The fact of intelligent agency in creation becomes therefore as much a suggestion of science as any physical deduction with reference to cosmical phenomena.

"What constitutes the distinction between our ideas of matter and mind? Is it not simply this—that the one has no *pravṛtti,* no motion or action, *of itself,* and that the other has both; that the vis inertiae of matter requires to be overcome by an external impulse before matter can act, and that all impelling forces, which have an object in view, pre-suppose the existence of mind. To speak of the self-moving power of matter is to introduce a confusion of langauge calculated only to create misunderstanding and misapprehension. Design, purpose, aim are all mental operations. To speak of them as predicates of an inanimate principle is to talk like *children and madmen*[18], to adopt Kapila's own expression when administering a wholesome rebuke to the Vedāntists."

Āgamika.—"But does not Kapila virtually acknowledge a Supreme intelligence as the creator of the world? He speaks of 'an omniscient author of all things'[19]?"

Satyakāma.—"The scholiast says he thereby means the *first male*,[20] or the first agent at the commencement of a world. I would have most willingly received this Sūtra as a consoling proof of Kapila's theism, had not Kapila himself exhibited a sort of unaccountable obstinacy in arguing, not only against the existence, de facto, of a Supreme Being, but also against the possibility of a Supreme Intelligence, the author and governor of all things. The *all-knowing creator* is only a *sort of god, such a god,* says he, *is proved;* that god being, as the scholiast adds, himself a creature or a created agent[21]. In the first book it is broadly stated that the existence of God is not proved—that if there were a God he must be either bound or free, if bound, he would be incompetent for the act of creation; if free, that is to say, if unmoved by passion and desire, he could be subject to no motives, and hence would not concern himself in the act of creation; whether therefore bond or free, he could not be the creator of the universe. As to theistic passages in the Śāstra, they are, says the author of the Sāṅkhya, either mere eulogies of emancipated souls, or expressions of devotion to perfected spirits, such as (according to the scholiast) the transient or created gods Brahmā, Viṣṇu and Hara, figuratively styled eternal[22].' He defends the infallible authority of the Vedas, while thus denying the existence of an omniscient inspirer, simply by asserting that their texts are experimentally verified[23] by events, just as the teaching of medical science is established by facts.

"In the fifth book, again, Kapila resumes his atheistic argument, and commences with denying God's providence and his government of the world. 'The distribution of fruits, or rewards, is not by divine appointment, for it is regulated by works,' which, the scholiast designates *necessary*[24]. 'If, continues the author, there were any divine 'interference, then it must be for God's own purpose, and if God had a purpose in view, he would himself be a *worldly God.* If a worldly God were acknowledge, it would be using a mere technical term[25],' for, adds the scholiast, 'the theist would then be speaking like us of a created being by the technical term *God*[26]?' 'Such an act, with a purpose in view, is not possible without *rāga,* or passionate desire, for effort invariably implies such desire. 'And if he were subject to a vehement passion he could not be essentially free. Passions and affections cannot be attributed to God, for then he would be proved to be a soul with attachments. If it be said that God is creator by the very virtue of existence, then all existing souls must be gods[27], and, so adds the commentator, the doctrine of one God must be surrendered.'

"Kapila then goes on saying that the existence of God cannot be established[28] because there is no proof. There can be no evidence of sensation[29] on such a subject, nor can it be proved by Inference,[30] because you cannot exhibit an analogous instance. And as to the testimony of the Śāstra, it is decidedly for *pradhāna,* or nature[31], 'as the ultimate cuase of all things.'

"I need not follow our author further in what he says to point out certain inconsistencies in the Vedānta doctrine. But I suppose there can be no doubt of his absolute denial of a Supreme Deity."

Kāpila.—"I think my good friends you are not doing

justice to Kapila. As I said the other day, his only fault is his unflinching honesty. He will not equivocate on a serious subject such as the one under dicussion. The difficulty with all philosophers has been how to reconcile the idea of perfect freedom, suggested by the conception of a Supreme Divinity, with the bondage betokened by subjection to motives. No animated and thinking agent does any thing without a purpose, and a purpose must always betoken mental imbecillity. The followers of the Nyāya and the Vedānta feel this difficulty as keenly as ourselves, only they do not boldly avow it. The Vedāntists evade the real question by saying that God creates the world in connection with *avidyā,* (ignorance or delusion). They thus support their system by actually attributing ignorance and delusion to the creator of the universe. They virtually deny supreme intelligence to the creator. Such is the theism of our opponents before whom Kapila's teaching must dwindle into a *nirīśwara* system! I doubt whether any one can have the boldness to say that *avidyā,* or a principle of ignorance, is a more *intelligent* cause than *prakṛti* or inanimate nature. Śaṅkarācārya's wonder at the idea of inanimate nature producing such a harmonious world ill consorts with his own doctrine that the same world was created by ignorance or want of deliberation. He that can believe that a principle of ignorance could project a plan of the universe before us, need not look aghast at the idea of an unintelligent principle performing the same exploit.

"Śaṅkara is as confident that Brahma or the spirit is *nirguṇa,* or destitute of affections, as Kapila that the Puruṣa is *nissaṅga* or free from attachments. Kapila carries out his principle and maintains that the soul without attachments cannot be a creator, having no motive for any action. The Vedāntist endeavours to reconcile opposite principles by maintaining that the *nirguṇa* Spirit, also independent of motives, creates the universe in association with avidyā or ignorance.

"But the most unaccountable flight of Vedāntic imagination is in the saying that Brahma or the spirit is not really associated with delusion—that it is through avidyā or delusion that delusion is attributed to him. Kapila will have nothing to do with this tissue of inconsistencies[32]. If it is a delusion to attribute delusion to the spirit, then he is not really associated with delusion, and if without such unworthy association he could not create the universe, then it is a fallacy to call him the creator. Avidyā or ignorance must be the real creator. If the Vedāntist will only give up his addiction to party and boldly search out the truth, he must be driven to the conclusion that the world was created by a principle of ignorance, a conclusion not essentially different from ours—while ours has the further advantage of being a more intelligible and consistent theory.

"It is useless to remind us of the complex and harmonious arrangement of the world. The real question remains unchanged—how to associate a perfectly free intelligence (such as you must suppose the Creator to be) with ignorance and delusion, or with a subjection to motives and purposes."

Āgamika.—"But you do not deny, friend Kāpila,—do you?—That *puruṣa,* or the Spirit, does perform various acts in the world. Why then must you deny his creative agency?"

Kāpila.—"We do deny that *puruṣa* does any thing in reality. He is essentially free from those impulses which lead to action, and from the encumbrances of body and mind wherein consist capacities for operativeness. The soul appears operative simply because of its active accidents—just as a crystal vase appears coloured because of the red flowers placed in it, but is itself devoid of any taint or tinge. It is not affected or fettered by the operativeness of its accidents. If it appears affected, disturbed, or fettered, it is because of the mind with which it is for a time associated. The actions and passions are all of the mind not the soul.[33] Nor does this accidental and temporary association produce any permanent, or even momentary, impression on the soul, for it passes off like water on a lotus leaf without real contact, and without leaving any traces behind itself[34]. 'The soul is witness, solitary, by-stander, speculator, and passive.' 'The qualities, as agents, act; a witness neither acts nor desists from action.' 'Though the qualities be active, the stranger (soul) appears as the agent.' 'There being activity of the qualities, soul which is indifferent, or inactive, appears as if it was the agent, which it is not[35].'

"So you see we do deny the operativeness, and maintain the perfect freedom of *puruṣa.* And even if the contrary were the fact—even if we allowed that the soul was competent for certain acts, still it would not follow that he was competent for the act of creation. Supposing the soul were subject to motives and impulses, and therefore capable of ordinary agencies in the world, he would for that very reason be disqualified for the great work of creation, for which no agent, fettered by attachments, could be competent."

Āgamika.—"You have just cited a passage from the Kārikā and Gauḍapāda's commentary thereon. Those authorities seem to acknowledge the superintendence of the soul over nature. The Kārikā says 'there must be superintendence,' on which Gauḍapāda comments thus; 'As a charioteer guides a chariot drawn by horses able to curvet, to prance, to gallop, so the soul guides the body : as it is said in the Ṣaṣṭi Tantra,—Nature, 'directed by soul, proceeds.' Vācaspati also says, 'whether this (evolution) of nature be for its own purpose or that of another, it is a rational principle that acts. Nature cannot act without rationality, and therefore there must be a reason which directs nature. Embodied souls, though rational, cannot direct nature, as they are ignorant of its character; therefore there is an omniscient Being, the director of nature, which is Īśwara, or God[36].'

"Thus you see, Kāpila, that even among the upholders of your characteristic doctrine of creation by the agency of nature, men are compelled to acknowledge a Supreme Intelligence, the author and director of nature."

Kāpila.—"The Sāṅkhya is pre-eminently a system of discriminative knowledge. We are, by name and profession, guardians of the interests of truth and reason, and it would be a betrayal of those interests, if on a subject of such awe-striking solemnity as the creation, we failed to follow out our principles to their legitimate consequences. I have told you that we are not wanting in admiration of the wonderful mechanism of the universe, but we cannot persuade ourselves so far to lower our conceptions of moral and spiritual greatness as to allow the competence of a creator that is itself under the thraldom of motives and purposes. The very title of Sāṅkhya would be a misnomer if we admitted such a low standard of moral greatness in the Creator of the world."

Satyakāma.—"I feel more perplexed than ever how to understand the drift of your sayings. You have challenged our veneration by speaking of the awe-striking solemnity of the subject of Creation, and you have been raising our conception of the moral greatness of the Creator of the world. You have been raising our conceptions however only to hurl them down by a dash. You tell us of the moral greatness of the Creator, only as a prelude to your doctrine that there is no Creator of any intellectual and moral qualifications whatever; and you raise our conceptions of that greatness, only to assure us that there is no moral greatness of any standard in the world—for thought and action are affections of the mind, not the soul. They can no more touch the soul than the red roses in a vase taint the crystal of which it is composed. What is the meaning of 'awe-striking solemnity' if there be no God in the universe? Who is to strike the awe? What can be the value of knowledge at the utmost, if there be no God to be known? What can you mean by a betrayal of the interests of truth and reason, if the soul is not responsible for any acts?

"You say your difficulty in the way of acknowledging a Creator of supreme intelligence is how to reconcile subjection to motives and purposes with omnipotence. You do not deny the evidences of design which the universe displays, but you cannot allow the existence of a Designer because of the moral difficulty you have mentioned. Before this difficulty the argument from design loses its force with you.

"In the case of the Supreme Being, however, we are not called upon to say that he requires an external motive for any thing. When he does, much less are we at liberty to speculate on his motives. He has His all-wise, all-gracious plans, and he acts according to the good pleasure of His will.

"The argument from design, again, is a sheer logical argument based on the very nature of all reasoning. It cannot lose its force from any consideration whatsoever, while the moral difficulty you have raised is a creature of your own imagination. It does not consort well with the position you claim for your system, as 'pre-eminently one of discriminative knowledge,' to set aside a logical argument on a mere fanciful theory about motives and purposes. That the universe was created by a Supreme Intelligence is attested by the indications of design around us, prior to all other considerations. As to His motives and purposes, that is a point which concerns the question of His attributes, not of His existence.

"And here must we not pause to consider the nature of our inquiry before we venture a single step further? Before Him who projected the vast universe, in which our own dwelling place is but an atom, and of which our powers of sensation and reflection can reach but the smallest conceivable portion, before Him, I ask—what are we, and what are the highest flights of our imagination! Are we to venture on probing His motives and purposes? Can the human mind by any of its devices fathom the depth of His purposes—the finite grasp at the Infinite? And are we to say that His motives and purposes are abridgments of His essential freedom?

"Well does the author of the Sarva-darśana-saṅgraha say that benevolence is His purpose[37]! And that such a purpose can be no detraction from His freedom, just as a person's own body cannot be an interposing barrier to himself. His motives and purposes who shall presume to fathom? Enough for us that in all He has made we see striking adaptations to the comforts and conveniences of animal life, and thus descry signs of benevolence written in indelible characters.

"To say that an essentially free spirit is incapable of motives is to beg a moral question—and to build a moral system on a mere fanciful theory. Granted, Brāhminical philosophers have held the same theory—granted, the Vedāntists are guilty of inconsistencies;—(though I very much doubt they will protest against your version of their doctrine)—is that a reason why the divine glory should be obscured, and knowledge deprived of its highest object—the only object that can lend it dignity or importance? Do you think you have made out a great case for your system by contending that all its speculations end in this, that there is no God in the world—and that all its knowledge consists in the dogma that there is not and cannot be any intelligent and deliberate act or moral agency in the universe?

"Is not the saying that a free spirit *can* have no motive itself a gross abridgment of its freedom? The only idea we can have of a spiritual essence is that it is an existent substance endowed with mind, with will, with powers of intelligence and action, but destitute of physical organs. To deprive it of motives and emotions is to deprive it of will and of active powers. You do not deny that mind implies all this, but you will not allow that spirit is essentially and constantly connected with mind. What *can* its existence mean then? How can it differ from a nullity?

"What is the value of a freedom, either, in which there is no freedom of action? What is independence, if one is denied the choice of doing what he pleases? True freedom implies not a mental void, not a destitution of attachment and activity, not a state which can only be characterized by a negation, but a power, a power to think and to act. If it involves a negation at all, it is simply a negation of attachment to that which is evil—a negation of activity in the wrong direction."

Kāpila.—"But how can you trust to one's discriminating between that which is good and that which is evil —between a right and a wrong direction?"

Satyakāma.—"Is not that the very discrimination which your philosophy undertakes to discuss? But whether your philosophy teaches that discrimination or not, you will perhaps allow that it is no bondage to the creature to do that which his creator intended he should do. And the intention of the Creator may be inferred from the constitution of the mind itself. If desire and aversion be, as they undoubtedly are, natural to the mind, they cannot of themselves be evils. It is not a bondage to the father to love his son. It is no bondage to any—it is on the contrary true freedom to love virtue and hate vice. It is not bondage to desire or do what is good. No one has ever regretted such an impulse or act. No one has ever derived any thing but pleasure therefrom.

"There is not doubt much evil in the world. One cannot be too jealous of his affections lest they lead him astray. Care should be taken to regulate them. Human nature requires to be reformed and regenerated. But to destroy is not to reform. To renounce is not to regulate. Nay you *cannot* destroy, you cannot renounce the passions and emotions of the mind. They are natural, and, as your Ācārya admits, what is natural cannot be destroyed.[38] You will only force them to take the wrong way by refusing them a field of action in the right way."

Kāpila.—"We do not deny that passions and affections are natural to the mind. We say it is endowed both with intellectual and active powers[39]. But the mind is distinct from the soul, nor are they so associated as that the passions of the one should really affect the other. The association is temporary. The two are not essentially connected with each other."

Satyakāma.—"You mean the soul is not essentially possessed of intellectual and active powers. The freedom then which you are postulating in behalf of the soul is not the freedom which implies moral greatness. It is the freedom of which stocks and stones may boast; it is the freedom which the paralytic attains in proportion to the extent of his disease. There can be no moral greatness without moral agency, nor any moral agency without choice of action. He that is open to impulses and has the power of action, he that resists temptations to evil and deliberately chooses that which is good may assert a claim to moral greatness—not he, who is destitute of feeling and emotion, or has no power of action.

"Nor do you propound a very dignified idea of spiritual freedom when you say that the soul's tranquillity and contentedness are or ought to be like those of the harlot Piṅgalā who simply submitted to what she considered a hard necessity when it was out of her power to attain her wished-for object[40]. There is no moral virtue in such forced resignation.

"And yet on a mere moral quibble, itself militating against every moral principle, you must set at nought all the indications of benevolent design which you see in the world, and pronounce it to be a world without God. And rather than allow freedom of action to a free spirit you are content to admit the undirected agency of an inanimate and unintelligent principle. You will allow that dead matter is competent to produce the wonderfully complex mechanism of the world, but you cannot admit that an intelligent spirit, having a purpose in view, could have such competence. This is, to use a well known proverb, to strain at a gnat while swallowing a camel. And the gnat, too, is simply a creature of your own fancy; for there is no moral difficulty in the supposition of a free spirit acting freely according to the good purpose of his own will.

"I am perfectly amazed at your undertaking to rid the country of heresy and yet admitting and enforcing some of its worst tenets. The *svābhāvikas* are no doubt the most dangerous of Buddhists. And yet your theory seems to me precisely the same as theirs."

Āgamika.—"Is it possible that the doctrine of the venerable Kapila can be so bad as that!"

Satyakāma.—"The Buddhists I have named deny God's agency and attribute the creation to *svabhāva.* They speak also of the efficacy of *Karma,* or the merit of works, and reject the idea of a divine providence by asserting the necessary connection between works and their deserts. They say;—if God is the agent, then what are works for? And what is the use of *yatna* (effort) either[41]? Kapila's teaching on creation and providence appears to me to be precisely the same. He deliberately gives up the idea of an intelligent Creator by maintaining the theory of an inanimate but yet operative *prakṛti,* and he says, almost in the very words of the *svābhāvika* Buddhists, that the *distribution of rewards is not under divine direction because it is regulated by karma,* (works). I must do him the justice to add that the majority of Brāhminical philosophers have broached the same doctrines in other words. Vedāntism, as our friend Kāpila justly remarked, did not dare to assert God's creative power without associating him with *avidyā,* nor could it acknowledge his providence without at the same time teaching that God and the world were identical, and that there could be no giver or receiver of benefits or favours. Vedāntism also falls back on the old idea of *adṛṣṭa* or *karma* and its deserts, in order to account for the unequal distribution of pleasure in the world.

"Our philosophers, indeed, while professing to guard against Buddhistic teaching, have only contributed to its wider diffusion by setting forth, perhaps unconsciously, some of its characteristic tenets of a very pernicious tendency. Discontent with life and existence are taught as clearly in the Brāhminical schools as in the Buddhist sects. The merit and demerit of *karma* or works are spoken of, in some of our schools at least, not only without reference to, but also to the absolute denial of, a judicial governor of the universe. The influence of *karma* is supposed to be itself sufficiently powerful for the government of the world, and the idea of God as Creator and Supreme ruler is deliberately renounced. *Dhyāna* or meditation is inclucated as an effectual means of escape from the miseries of life and existence, but no object is presented to the mind on which *dhyāna* is to be exercised. I do not know whether Buddha himself taught all these doctrines, but there is no denying that many of his followers hold them with great tenacity—and our Kapila has evidently adopted them from the same source. He denies a Supreme Being as creator and governor of the universe, and attributes the distribution of *fruits* or rewards to the influence of *karma*. And yet, like the Buddhists, he talks of *dhyāna* and the *true knowledge* as the only means of emancipation. What importance can possibly be attached to *dhyāna* or knowledge if the world be without a God?"

Kāpila.— "I will not be so disingenuous as to deny the force of some of your observations. I must however explain our definition of *dhyāna*. Our Ācārya had said that knowledge is the only means of emancipation. But lust after the things of the world presents formidable obstructions in the way of knowledge. He accordingly tells us that *dhyāna* is the best means of suppressing lust and promoting knowledge[42]. He tells us also that *dhyāna* consists in the stoppage of intellectual exercises on other points than those which are the select objects of contemplation[43]. And this is done by controlling the breath in a proper posture and by assiduous discharge of the duties of one's[44] own stage of life, as well as by renouncement of all passions and desires."

Satyakāma.—"But what can be the 'select object' of *dhyāna* or knowledge in your system? You acknowledge no Supreme Divinity, and your great conclusion is *I am not, nor aught is mine.*"

Kāpila.—"By *dhyāna* we mean the abstraction of the mind from all objects."

Satyakāma.—"Am I to understand that *dhyāna* or meditation means that the mind does not actually meditate on any thing, and that it is in a state of entire inactivity, not dwelling on any reality whatever."

Kāpila.—"Yes—certainly you are to understand so. For though the scholiast adds, other than the select objects of contemplation,' yet that is not found in the Sūtra itself. And Kapila says elsewhere that *dhyāna implies the mind without an object*[45]."

Satyakāma.—"What can be the efficacy of such meditation, or rather such no-meditation?"

Kāpila.—"Our Ācarya, in anticipation of this very question; says that one great use of *dhyāna* is the suppression of lust[46]. When you can abstract your mind from every thing in the world, it is certain you exclude all passion and lust."

Satyakāma.—"Your *dhyāna* or meditation is then a negative idea. It does not imply the pondering of any reality in the mind, but rather dwelling on no-thing. It is natural that your knowledge should be equally negative,—for, says the Kārikā, 'through study of principles, the conclusive, incontrovertible, one only knowledge is attained, that neither I am, nor is aught mine, nor do I exist.'"

Kāpila.—"Is it not one of the most admirable features in the Sāṅkhya system that it teaches you the truth of truths—that all things are vain and transient. You may call it a negative conclusion, but are not some negative conclusions of the greatest value, and above all is it not of prime importance that men should be convinced of the vanity and nullity of vain and unreal things?"

Satyakāma.—"It is no doubt of the greatest importance to be convinced of the vanity of vain things, but why is it so? Is it not because the exposure of the vanity of vain things facilitates the knowledge of things that are real? But if, as you say, there be no God in the world, nothing pre-eminently real—if all that your discriminative knowledge has to unfold is that we *are not,* nor *is aught ours,*—I really cannot see what great value there can be in such knowledge. That knowledge is simply the information that *nothing is ours*. It might be a most valuable information, if along with the denial of things unreal, it contained an assurance of that which is real and abiding. The dispelling of error is no doubt an inestimable blessing when there is a corresponding great truth to be communicated. But in a system without God, without an active soul, with simply a passive by-stander *puruṣa,* essentially devoid of mind, and with the mere projections of an inanimate principle, themselves to be denounced as vain and transient—in an empty system such as this, what claims can be possibly set up on the score of valuable information of any kind?

"And as to the ultimate object which the system professes to have in view, the emancipation of the soul, the idea becomes preposterous when you confidently assert that the soul neither has nor is capable of any real bondage or freedom[47]. There is nothing to emancipate the soul from—for you say the soul can have no bondage. If it has any pain by reason of its connection with mind, it is merely a reflection or shadow of pain[48]. Nor could there be a possible way of emancipating it, for you say it is not so associated with mind and the senses (the only media through which it could be reached) as that sensation and reflection could affect it any more than water can affect the lotus leaf on which it drops[49]. And even if the soul could be reached, it could not be emancipated from a real bondage, because that which is essentially bound cannot on your theory be liberated.

Such is your system, and it is you say a preservative from Buddhism. But, what Buddhistic doctrine can possibly be put down thereby, appears to me an enigma incapable of solution. It cannot be its atheism, for Kapila's system is itself without God. Is it then simply its rejection of caste that you wish to remedy with the help of the Sāṅkhya? Allow me once for all to put you on your guard against the spirit that pervades your system. You care not for the honor due to God, or rather you argue against His existence; but you are particularly jealous for the honor of your own fraternity. You are not offended at Buddhists' denying the God of Heaven—on the contrary you support their doctrine in this respect, you are ready with your *prakṛti* to re-inforce their *svabhāva* in the unholy contest against God. But you cannot tolerate their denial of Brāhminincal supremacy—you cannot allow their onset against gods-of-the-earth as you delight to call yourselves."

Kāpila remained silent for some minutes. He then remarked that he had never thought of the Sāṅkhya except in connection with the Vedānta, and there could be no doubt it contrasted favourably with Śaṅkara's pantheism. He never reviewed it in its relation to Buddhism. He must confess that such a review was desirable for the purpose of investigating truth, but all he could now promise was that he would cogitate calmly on the subject.

———

References

1. मूले मूलाभावादमूलं मूलं।
2. अजामेकां लोहितकृष्णवर्णां वह्वी:प्रजा:सृजमानां सरूपां अजोह्येको जुषमाणोनुशेते जहात्येनां भुक्तभोग्यामजोऽन्य:॥ Śwetāśwatara Upa.
3. श्रद्दधानः शुभां विद्यामाददीतावरादपि। अन्त्यादपि परं धर्म्मं स्त्रीरत्नं दुष्कुलादपि। विषादप्यमृतं ग्राह्यं॥ Menu II. 238, 239.
4. यदिदृष्टान्तबलेनैवैतन्निरूप्यते नाचेतनं लोके चेतनेनानधिष्ठितं स्वतन्त्रं किञ्चिद्विशिष्टपुरुषार्थनिर्वर्त्तनसमर्थान् विकारान् विरचयत् दृष्टम्। गेहप्रासादशयनासनविहारभूम्यादयोहि लोके प्रज्ञावद्भिः शिल्पिभिर्यथाकालं सुखदुःखप्राप्तिपरिहारयोग्या रचिता दृश्यन्ते तथेदं जगदखिलं पृथिव्यादिनानाकर्म्मफलोपभोगयोग्यम् वाह्यमाध्यात्मिकञ्च शरीरादि नानाजात्यन्वितं प्रतिनियतावयवविन्यासमनेककर्म्मफलानुभवाधिष्ठानं दृश्यमानं प्रज्ञावद्भिः सम्भाविततमैः शिल्पिभिर्मनसाप्यालोचयितुमशक्यं सत् कथमचेतनं प्रधानं रचयेत्, लोष्ट्रपाषाणादिष्वदृष्टत्त्वात् मृदादिष्वपि कुमीकाराद्यधिष्ठितेषु

विशिष्टाकाररचना दृश्यते तद्वत् प्रधानस्यापि चेतनान्तराधिष्ठितत्वप्रसङ्गः न च मृदाद्युपादानस्वरूपव्यापाश्रयेणैव धर्म्मेण मूलकारणमवधारणीयं नवाह्यकुम्भकारादिव्यपाश्रयेणेति किंचिन्नियामकमस्ति। नचैवं सति किञ्चिद्विरुध्यते प्रत्युत श्रुतिरनुगृह्यते चेतनकारणत्यसमर्पणात् अतोरचनानुपपत्तेश्च हेतोर्नाचेतनं जगत् कारणमनुमातव्यं भवति॥

5. प्रकृतिवास्तवे च पुरुषस्याध्याससिद्धिः। अन्ययोगेऽपि तत्सिद्धिर्नाञ्जस्येनायोदाहवत्। अचेतनत्वेऽपि क्षीरवच्चेष्टितं प्रधानस्य। कर्म्मवदृष्टेर्वाकालादेः। प्रकृतेराद्योपादानतान्येषां कार्य्यत्वश्रुतेः। नित्यत्वेपि नात्मनो योग्यत्वाभावात्। सर्वत्र कार्य्यदर्शनात् विभुत्वं। Śāṅkhya, Sūtras, ii. 5, 8, iii. 59, 60. vi. 32, 33, 36.

6. द्वा सुपर्णा सयुजा सखाया समानं वृक्षं परिषस्वजाते।

तयोरन्यः पिप्पलं स्वाद्वात्त्यनश्नन्नन्योऽभिचाकशीति॥

ज्ञाज्ञौ द्वावजावीशनीशावजा ह्येका भोक्तृभोग्यार्थयुक्ता।

अनन्तश्चात्मा विश्वरूपो ह्यकर्त्ता त्रयं यदा विन्दते ब्रह्ममेतत्॥

अजामेकां लीहितकृष्णवर्णां वह्वीः प्रजाः सृजमानां सरूपां।

अजोह्येको जुषमाणोऽनुशेते जहात्येनां भुक्तभोग्यामजोऽन्यः॥

7. यतः क्षीरवत् द्रव्यस्वभावविशेषादुपपद्यते यथाहि लोके क्षीरं जलं वा स्वयमेव दधिहिमभावेन परिणमतेऽनपेक्ष्य वाह्यं साधनं तथेहापि भविष्यति। ननु क्षीराद्यपि दध्यादिभावेन परिणममानमपेक्षत एव वाह्यं साधनं ओष्ण्यादिकं कथमुच्यते क्षीरवद्धीति॥ नैष दोषः। स्वयमपि हि क्षीरं याञ्च यावतीञ्च परिणाममात्रामनुभवत्येव त्वार्य्यते त्वौष्ण्यादिना दधिभावाय॥ यदिच स्वयं दधिभावशीलता न स्यान्नैवौष्ण्यादिनापि वलाद्दधिभावमापद्येत। नहि वायुराकाशोवौष्णयादिना बलाद्दधिभावमापद्यते॥ *Com. Vedānt.* II. 1. 24.

8. विमुक्तमोक्षार्थं स्वार्थं वा प्रधानस्य

प्रधानसृष्टिः परार्थं स्वतोऽप्यभोक्तृत्वादुय्रकङ्कुमवहनवत्।

नर्त्तकीवत्प्रवृत्तस्यापि निवृत्तिश्चारिताथ्यात्॥ विविक्तबोधात् सृष्टिनिवृत्तिः प्रधानस्य सूदवत् पाके। अनुपभोगेपि पुमर्थं सृष्टिः प्रधानस्योष्ट्रकुङ्कुमवहनवत्। विमुक्तबोधात् न सृष्टिः प्रधानस्य लोकवत्। दोषबोधेपि नोपसर्पणं प्रधानस्य कुलबधूवत्। Sāṅ. Sūt.

9. अकार्य्यन्वेऽपि तद्योगः पारवश्यात्

स्वभावाच्चेष्टितमनभिसन्धानाद्भृत्यवत्॥ Ibid.

10. पुरुषार्थं करणोद्भवोप्यदृष्टोल्लासात्। धेनुवद्वत्साय Ibid.
वत्सविवृद्धिनिमित्तं क्षारस्य यथा प्रवृत्तिरज्ञस्य।
पुरुषविमोक्षनिमित्तं तथा प्रवृत्तिः प्रधानस्य॥57॥ सां. का॥

11. कर्मवैचित्र्यात् सृष्टिवैचिन्त्र्यम्।

12. न वीजाङ्कुरवत् सादिसंसारश्रुतेः। *Sān. Sūt.*

13. नैतत् साधूच्यते यतस्तत्रापि पयोम्बुनोश्चेतनाधिष्ठतयोरेव प्रवृत्तिरित्यनमिमीमहे उभयवादिप्रसिद्धेः रथादावचेतने केवले प्रवृत्त्यादर्शनात्। शास्त्रं च योऽप्सु तिष्ठन्नद्भ्योऽन्तरो योऽपोऽन्तरो यमयति एतस्यवा अक्षरस्य प्रशासने गार्गि प्राच्योऽन्या नद्यः स्यन्दन्ते। चेतनायाश्च धेनोः स्नेहेनेच्छया पयसः प्रवर्त्तकत्वोपपत्तेः वत्सचोषणेन च पयस आकृष्यमाणत्वात्। नचाम्वुनोऽप्यत्यन्तमपेक्षा। निम्नभूम्याद्यपेक्षत्वात् स्यन्दनस्य।

Com. Vedānt. II. 2. 3.

14. अहङ्कारः कर्त्ता न पुरुषः Sāṅ. Sūt. vi. 54.

15. सत्त्वंरजस्तमश्चैव गुणत्रयमुदाहृतं। साम्यावस्थितिरेतेषां प्रकृतिः परिकीर्तिता॥ केचित्प्रधानमित्याहुरव्यक्तमपरे जगुः। एतदेव प्रजायन्ते विख्याता वसोवोऽपिच॥ गुणेभ्यः क्षोभ्यमाणेभ्यस्त्रयोदेवा विजज्ञिरे। एका मूर्तिस्त्रयोदेवा ब्रह्मविष्णुमहेश्वराः॥ सविकारात्प्रधानात्तु महत्तत्त्वं प्रजायते। महानिति ततः ख्यातिर्लोकानां जायते सदा॥ अहंकारश्च महतो जायते मानवर्द्धनः। इन्द्रियाणि ततःपंच वक्ष्ये बुद्धिवशानि तु॥ प्रादुर्भवन्ति चान्यानि तथा कर्मवशानि तु। मन एकादशं तेषां कामबुद्धिगुणान्वितम्॥ Matsya Purāṇa.

16. श्चादि देव प्रभु दीन दयाला। जठर धरेउ जेहि कपिल कृपाला॥
साख्य शास्त्र जिन प्रगट बखाना। तत्त्व विचार निपुण भगवाना॥

17. Vestiges of the Natural history of creation.

18. वालोन्मत्तादिसमत्त्वम्।

19. सहि सर्व्ववित् सर्व्वकर्ता। iii. 56.

20. सर्व्ववित् सर्व्वकर्तेश्वर आदिपुरुषो भवति। Vijñāna Bhikṣu.

21. ईदृशेश्वरसिद्धिः सिद्धा। iii. 57.
जन्येश्वरस्य सिद्धिः। V.B.

22. मुक्तात्मनः प्रशंसा उपासा सिद्धस्य वा। i. 95.
सिद्धस्य ब्रह्मविष्णुहरादेरेवानित्येश्वरस्याभिमानादिमतोपि गौणनित्यत्वादिमत्त्वा-न्नित्यत्वाद्युपासापरा। V.B.

23. सिद्धरूपबोद्धृत्वाद्वाक्यार्थोपदेशः। i. 98.

24. नेश्वराधिष्ठिते फलनिष्पत्तिः कर्म्मणा नत्सिद्धेः। V. 1.
आवश्यकेन कर्म्मणैव फलनिष्पत्तिसम्भवात्। V.B.

25. स्वोपकारादधिष्ठानं लोकवत्। लौकिकेश्वरवदितरथा। पारिभाषिको वा।

26. संसारसत्त्वेपि चेदीश्वरस्तर्हिसर्गाद्युत्पन्नपुरुषे परिभाषामात्रमस्माकमिव भवतामपि रयात्।

27. न रागादृते तत्सिद्धिः प्रतिनियतकारणत्वात्।
तद्योगेपि न नित्युमुक्तः। v. 6, 7.
रागस्तूत्कटेच्छा। Vijñāna Bhikṣu.
प्रधानशक्तियोगाच्चेत् सङ्गापपत्तिः। सत्तामात्राच्चेत् सर्व्वैश्वर्य्यं। v. 8, 9.

28. प्रमाणाभावान्न तत्सिद्धिः। v. 10.

29. ईश्वरे तावत् प्रत्यक्षं नास्ति।

30. सम्बन्धाभावान्नानुमानं।

31. श्रुतिरपि प्रधानकार्य्यत्वस्य। v. 12.

32. नाविद्यायोगोनिःसङ्गस्य।
तद्योगे तत्सिद्धावन्योन्याश्रयत्वं॥ v. 13, 14.

33. कुसुमवच्चमणिः। तत्सन्निधानादधिष्ठातृत्वं मणिवत्। असङ्गीयं पुरुषः इति। न कर्म्मणान्यधर्म्मत्वादतिप्रसक्तेश्च। जवास्फटिकयोरिव नोपरागः किन्त्वभिमानः।

34. श्रुतिस्मृतिषु पद्मपत्रस्थलेनेव पद्मपत्रस्यासङ्गतायाः पुरुषासङ्गतायां दृष्टान्ततश्रवणाच्च।

35. Wilson's Sāṅkhya Kārikā.

36. Wilson's Sāṅkhya Kārikā.

37. करुणया प्रवृत्तिरस्त्येव * * न च स्वातन्त्र्यभङ्गः शङ्कनीयः साङ्गं स्वव्यवधायकं न भवतीति न्यायेन॥

38. स्वभावस्यानपायित्वात्॥

39. उभयात्मकं मनः। II. 26.

40. निराशः सुखी पिङ्गलावत्। IV. 11.

आशां त्यक्त्वा पुरुषः सन्तोषाख्यसुखवान् भूयात् पिङ्गलावत्। यथा पिङ्गला नाम वेश्या कान्तार्थिनी कान्तमलब्ध्वा निर्विस्मा सती विहायाशां सुखिनी वभूव तद्वत्। V. B.

41. *Sambhu Purāṇa* in Hodgson.

42. रागोपहतिध्यानं। III. 30.

ज्ञानप्रतिबन्धको यो विषयोपरागश्चित्तस्य तदुपघातहेतुर्ध्यानं।

Vijñāna Bhikṣu.

43. वृत्तिनिरोधात् तत्सिद्धिः।

ध्येयातिरिक्तवृत्तिनिरोधरूपेण सम्प्रज्ञातयोगेन तत्सिद्धिर्ध्यानस्य निष्पत्तिर्ज्ञानख्यफलोपधानरूपा भवति।

44. धारणासनस्वर्म्मणा तत्सिद्धिः। निरोधश्छर्दिविधारणाभ्यां। स्थिरसुखमासनं। स्वकर्म्म स्वाश्रमविहितकर्म्मानुष्ठानम्। वेराग्यादभ्यासाच्च।

45. ध्यानं निर्विषयं मनः।

46. उभयथाप्यविशेषश्चेन्नैवमुपरागनिरोधाद्विशेषः।

47. नैकान्ततो बन्धमोक्षौ पुरुषस्याविवेकादृते।

48. स च दुःखप्रतिविम्बरूप एव। Vijñāna Bhikṣu.

49. श्रुतिस्मृतिषु पद्मपत्रस्थजलेनेव पद्मपत्रस्यासङ्गतायाः पुरुषासङ्गतायां दृष्टान्तताश्रवणाच्च। Vijñāna Bhikṣu.

DIALOGUE VII

FROM THE SAME TO THE SAME

We have just got through the festivities of a grand marriage in our neighbourhood. The Rajah's daughter was united to a fine young man, as handsome in his person, as he is noble in his origin and graceful in his manners. You have never yet told me how you manage these social affairs in your part of the world. With us matrimonial ceremonies are generally performed at night. The bridegroom comes with a large retinue of friends, marching in procession. He is received at the door by the bride's party, and thence conducted to a spacious hall where he takes his seat as the lion of the evening. Before him are assembled, on the one hand, the party he has himself brought, and on the other the company invited by the bride's friends. Learned Brahmans often take these opportunities of making themselves known by means of literary and philosophical controversies; which commence in good humour indeed, but sometimes become sufficiently animated to require the interference of third parties for the peace of the house.

On the occasion of the wedding I have just mentioned, all pundits of any pretensions in the neighbourhood were invited to grace the assembly. Tarkakāma, Āgamika, among my new friends, as well as many old faces long familiar to me, were there. Satyakāma was not asked, for his highness, though himself of an enlarged mind, was afraid of offending the prejudices of others. The bridegroom, however, was not so timid. Young Bengal, you may have heard, does not give way to such scruples; and we had an instance the other night in the bridegroom's bringing Satyakāma in his company.

As soon as the bridegroom was conducted to his splendid velvet throne, and the numerous guests who formed the two parties for the evening had assembled, Tarkakāma came up to me and said, "Do you see, Satyakāma is here? He has, as you know, lately been carrying on hot debates on the several schools of our philosophy. I think we should have told him at the very beginning that although we assent to the teaching of the Nyāya and the Sāṅkhya in deference to the venerable Ṛṣis who propounded them, yet it is not on the Nyāya or the Sāṅkhya that our hopes of salvation are practically placed. We dare not say that Gotama or Kapila was or could be wrong, but we cerainly do not look to the system founded by either for spiritual consolation. Men may in their speculations give a preference to their analysis of the intellectual powers or their peculiar rules of reasoning; *vidyārthis* (students) may go to the school of Gotama or Kaṇāda for mental discipline, but the *mumukṣu* will not turn that way for the salvation of his soul. It is to the Vedānta that we look for such salvation. It is on the sacred teaching of this school that we rely in our efforts to escape the miseries of life. Satyakāma could not have enjoyed even a seeming triumph against us if we had taken our vantage-ground on the Vedānta, and cut short the unprofitable discussion of categories and topics. Our case has at present an unfavourable appearance because of our not having considered what would be the best tactics for us to adopt. But it is not too late to set him and ourselves right on this point. We have a good and fitting opportunity now and here."

Scarcely had Tarkakāma finished these words when our attention was arrested by a noisy debate which several puṇḍits had commenced with a view to introduce themselves to the notice of the assembled audience. It did not appear to be a regular controversy on any particular point. It was a series of desultory discussions, kept up at random, by several persons, impelled by *jigīṣā* (a desire of victory) rather than *jijñāsā* (a desire of knowledge), in which there was a greater display of learning than search after truth. It is impossible to report to you all I heard. As there was no connected argument the reasoning employed cannot be called to recollection on any principle of suggestion. I can only put down desultory passages as memory may serve them out.

One said the world was produced by the union of *prakṛti* and *puruṣa,* and that Śiva was the great God. 'I cannot, said another, allow your last saying. The Māheśwaras are all wrong. Viṣṇu is the great God. Did not Śiva confess his inferiority when he failed to protect his devotee, king Vāṇa, against the divine Kṛṣṇa[1]?' 'You are all wrong, cried a Yogi of the Sāṅkhya school, all wrong, both Māheśwaras and Bhāgavatas. The active intervention of God is not at all necessary, prakṛti is alone sufficient.' 'Prakṛti alone sufficient! (said another) I say puruṣa is alone sufficient. No necessity for a prakṛti. All this is out of nothing' 'All this is out of nothing! Then the husbandman may reap without sowing, the potter may get his vessel without working, and the lazy weaver find his cloth as successfully as his hard working associate[2]!'

One of the loudest talkers was a Vaiṣṇava of the new school of Chaitanya, and a follower of the Bhāgavata philosophy, for which he had acquired the surname of Bhāgavata. He was contending, against a follower of Śaṅkarācārya, that the Supreme Being was not and could not be *nirākāra* (formless), that he had an eternal *vigraha* or form of which no created being can have the least conception, and that those who denied this truth denied in effect the existence of God, and are to be stigmatized as those rankest of rank Buddhists who maintained that the creation and conservation of the world do not require the exercise of divine agency, the merit of *karma* being itself sufficient. 'Well has it been said that the doctrine of *māyā,* which falsifies the eternal form of God, is only disguised Buddhism[3]—a blasphemy against gods and Vedas.'

While the learned expounder of the *pañca rātra* theory was thus declaiming against the ideal Vedāntists, there came forward, from one of the hinder rows, a pundit, whose features and habiliments were somewhat different from the rest of the company, and who, I afterwards learnt, was a Buddhist śāstri attending on a Nepaulese officer (colonel, they called him) now on a visit to Bengal. The officer and the śāstri were both invited by the bride's father. "So, venerable Bhāgavata, said the Buddhist, you take us to be not only impious ourselves, but also patterns of impiety. You cannot find a more rhetorical term for rebuking your opponents than by comparing them with Buddhists. You call us revilers of gods and Vedas. Well, we shall patiently submit to your inflictions. This is not the first time when we have been called to bear them. But will you allow us to say one word in our defence?"

Bhāgavata.—"I meant no offence to you, Sir. But we shall gladly receive any explanations from you."

Buddhist.—"Well, then, I say, if we have reviled gods and Vedas, we have done nothing more than your own Bhagavān Vāsudeva has done.,"

No sooner had the Buddhist Śāstri uttered these words than a whole troop of Bhāgavatas and Vaiṣṇavas vociferated aloud—"Dont hear him! dont hear him! Oh blasphemy against the Lord! Could the Lord revile gods and Vedas? Impossible."

The assembly was now in an uproar. It was with some difficulty that a domestic Brāhmin of the Rajah restored silence and order, and told the disputants that it was unbecoming the dignity of learned and aged religionists to create such confusion and disorder. "Young men of hot blood," said he, "have been known on occasions of marriage festivities to carry literary contests to the length of smashing lights and chandeliers, but the Rajah has a right to expect better examples from venerable sāstris."

The Buddhist was now allowed to speak for himself. "If," said he, "the force of numbers and the power of eloquence are to decide between us, then I must at once retire from the contest. I am a foreigner, single-handed, and far from my country, and I do not pretend to the dialectics of your schools. But if you will listen to facts, I will point to certain sayings of your Vāsudeva in proof of my assertion that we do not revile gods and Vedas more than he has done. For how did he remonstrate with his foster father Nanda against the popular custom of tendering divine worship to Indra. 'By *karma* or the merit of works', said he, are living creatures 'born, by *karma* again they enter into dissolution. Pleasure, pain, fear, bliss, all proceed from *karma.* If there 'be a god, the distributer of the fruits of others' actions, 'he too bestows them only on workers. There is no such 'thing as a Lord of one that works not. What can Indra do to men following their respective actions? He cannot counteract what they do by virtue of svabhāva, or nature. We are subject to nature and we follow nature. Every one, whether a man, an *asura,* or a god is under the control of nature. A person receives and gives up various sorts of bodies by the instrumentality of *karma,* which is itself our friend, our foe, our stranger, our preceptor, our god. Let one therefore following his nature and doing his own work worship *karma.* That which a person is fitted to observe is in reality his god. He who, living on one principle observes another, receives no good therefrom, just as a lady of honour receives no benefit from a paramour[4].'

"I appeal to your fairness, learned Sirs, continued the Buddhist, if any precept of Śākya Siṅha can be a stronger denunciation of the divine power than the passage I have just read from the great text book of all Bhāgavatas.And as to the

Vedas, allow me to remind you how the Upaniṣad itself talks of them when it stigmatizes all four as *aparā,* or inferior, and classifies them with books which may be considered manuals for children[5]. We never intended to say any thing more severe than this. Śāṇḍilya also speaks of the four Vedas as failing to teach the way of salvation, and Śaṅkarācarya calls that saying a reviling of the Veda[6]. And your divine Vāsudeva himself condemns the florid speech of those unwise men who, 'addicted to the texts of the Veda, and bent on the enjoyment of heaven, say that there is no other way than this. The sentiments of such men are not fitted for *samādhi,* or the mental abstraction necessary for *nirvāṇa* in Brahma[7],'—terms and ideas which I very much suspect you have borrowed from our philosophy and its nomenclature."

Bhāgavata.—"Ah, but the divine Vāsudeva has elsewhere set forth the authority of the Vedas and the dignity of the gods. It is only when he was expounding the *Jñāna-Kāṇḍa,* or chapter on knowledge, that he was speaking in depreciation—not of the whole Veda, but of the *Karma-Kāṇḍa* or chapter on works."

Buddhist.—"And yet, relying on the same 'chapter on works,' he inveighed against the worship of any divinity, after the fashion of Jaimini. Well, Sirs, the only difference between us is that we hold to a consistent doctrine, whereas you make a convenience of your gods and Vedas,—sometimes defending, sometimes condemning them, just as your fancy prompts you for the moment. This only confirms me in my opinion that when our Śākya of blessed memory protested against your original system of mere rites and ceremonies, and taught the way of escaping the miseries of life and of transmigration, you would neither follow him, nor could you resist the force of his doctrines. So you borrowed some of his ideas about the bondage of works and the means of *samādhi* and *nirvāṇa.* But truth does not find its natural place in a system of error, and so you have a series of inconsistencies in your philosophy on which your best doctors are perpetually wrangling with one another. Your original Vedas say nothing of the miseries of life, decay, and transmigration, nor impress on your minds the necessity of seeking for *nirvāṇa* or *mukti*. Several of your Upaniṣads too present to your aspirations nothing higher than the sensuous enjoyment of heaven[8]; and, if some of those Vedic appendages chime in other tunes, they were evidently written after the age of Śākya, and have learnt those tunes from the lyre of our philosophy."

The debate was going on after this fashion when Tarkakāma told me there was no use sitting and listening to such incoherent discussions. He proposed that we should leave the disputants to themselves, and seek a less noisy place for ourselves. We accordingly moved to a quiet corner in one of the side wings of the hall. Āgamika, Satyakāma, Vaiyāsika, and a few other friends followed us. We formed a little group of our own. Tarkakāma, referring to our past conferences, said to Satyakāma that the Nyāya and the Sāṅkhya were intended as intellectual exercises rather than as means of escape from the troubles of a sinful world. "It was the Vedānta to which we really looked for salvation. Vyāsa and Śaṅkara are our real guides in a spiritual point of view. Gotama and Kapila may have taught us metaphysics and logic, but the author of the Brahma Sūtras and his commentator have shown us the way to life and happiness."

Vaiyāsika, not anticipating a controversy on the subject, spoke thus in support of Tarkakāma's remarks; "Do you not see, Satyakāma, the great service which our venerable Ācārya and his commentator have rendered to the cause of Theology. How nobly have they fought with men who would set up other eternal principles in rivalry with the one Supreme Spirit. Vyāsa told them, as he told the whole world, that it was perfectly needless to look for other causes than one only Brahma in order to account for the origin of the universe."

Satyakāma.—"I should be unwilling this night to enter

into a discussion with you Vaiyāsika. You and I have come in the same procession; it is not usual for friends of the bridegroom to choose such an occasion for a debate among themselves. I will simply remark that your *one* Brahma is otherwise described to have as many forms or modifications as there are things in the universe, and therefore your *one* eternal principle exceeds millions."

Tarkakāma.–"I am glad to find you enter so readily into the spirit of our social institutions. Well, I have not come in your procession; perhaps you will have no objection to discuss the question with me. How do you make out that our one Brahma is of as many forms as there are things in the universe?"

Satyakāma.–"Śaṅkarācārya, while dessenting from the Bhāgavata theory of God possessed of four modifications, Vāsudeva, Saṅkarṣaṇa, Pradyumna, and Aniruddha, acknowledges that all existing substances 'from Brahmā down to a bundle of grass' are modifications of God[9]. And he approvingly cites the text of the Upaniṣad which pronounces *all this (i.e.,* the whole universe) *to be God*[10]. The effect is declared to be identical with its cause, and that in a way which smells strongly of material pantheism."

Tarkakāma.–"Invert the predicate and you will easily understand the meaning of that text. Let 'God' be the subject, and 'all this,' the predicate. It will then read thus : 'God is all this,' that is to say, God manifests in all this. On whatever substance you may cast your eyes, you see nothing but an instance of the power of God."

Satyakāma.–"Very ingenious, friend Tarkakāma. But the 5th Sūtra of IV. 1. protests against the idea of looking on the superior as inferior, on the king as a mere coachman, on Brahma as a creature. Brahma is to be predicated of creatures, not any creature of Brahma[11]. You may say Āditya is Brahma, vital air is Brahma, lightning is Brahma, but you cannot affirm the converse. Besides you must remember I am not criticising the text itself. I spoke of the leading doctors of the Vedānta who cited it. If you refer to their writings you will find they did not cite it in the sense in which you read it. I suspect Vaiyāsika will not be thankful to you for reading that celebrated passage in a sense which will evidently stultify the authorized teaching of his school. And, Tarkakāma, you can scarcely be ignorant of the fact that the meaning you attach to that sentence, though it is suggested by some eminent critics, is not supported by the context. What are the words that follow? '*Tajjalān,*' an elliptical expression, the meaning of which no one has controverted, *(i.e.) being produced from, resolved into, and existing in Him*[12]. It would not be a natural reading to take the whole sentence in your sense; "*God is all this,* being produced from, resolved into, and existing in Him!" The sense in which Śaṅkarācārya and other eminent expositors have read the passage must be the correct signification."

Tarkakāma. – "Well, I will not press that point. But you cannot be ignorant of the fact that Vedāntists consider the universe as a mere idea, a non-entity, a no-thing. The passage cannot therefore inculcate, as you contend it does, a material pantheism, or an indefinite deification of every thing. It does not say that every *thing* is God; but that all this, which is no *thing,* is God.

Satyakāma. – "I am not sure the Vedāntists will thank you for this interpretation either, though it has the support of Benares scholarship[13]. If 'all this' means 'no *thing*', then the sentence will teach that something, which is itself no *thing,* is God, or 'the one only *thing!*' Will you tell me if the passage in question is intended to teach doctrine or enforce practice? I can understand those interpreters who say that this text, inculcating the identity of the world with God, is calculated to recommend mental tranquillity and contentment by showing that there is no room for ambition avarice and lust[14].

According to your rendering, the text pronounces the world, itself no *thing,* to be 'the one only *thing.*' Why this compliment? There is a class of Vedāntists who say the world is a non-entity, but I doubt whether their theology is at all better than that of Kapila or Kaṇāda."

Tarkakāma.—"I do not quite understand you. Explain yourself."

Satyakāma.—"Whichever view you may take of external nature, whether with the *pariṇāma-vādis,* who may be called material pantheists, you pronounce it to be a reality, or with the *vivarta-vādis,* who are a species of spiritual pantheists, you call it a non-entity, the text above cited must teach very questionable theology. It must either deify the world and inculcate the very error (which Kapila contended was necessarily involved in the Vedānt doctrine) of every thing being God, or it will nullify the creation, and declare that nothing was called into being by God. And really it is difficult to say which is the worse teaching of the two. One thing however is certain; it confirms the opinion I lately read in an English review that *pantheism is practical atheism.* He who says the world is God precludes the idea of serving that God; for where the creature itself is God, who is to be the worshipper. The Vedānt triumphantly adopts this conclusion, but we ought not therefore to be the less jealous of the impiety implied in it. It involves the very essence of Kapila's atheism. And he who says nothing was produced from him, as effectually excludes the practice of religion; for if nothing be a reality in the world, there can be no real worship of God."

Tarkakāma.—"I think, Satyakāma, you rely too much on English reviewers. If you adopt them as your masters, no wonder you will vilify the doctrine of the Vedānt as practical atheism.Like teacher like pupil. But you cannot expect me to be much influenced by the language of your English masters."

Satyakāma.—"Pardon me, Tarkakāma. I should have told

you that it was *Chirañjīva,* the author of the *Vidwān-moda-taraṅgiṇī,* that first suggested the idea which I afterwards found in the Review of which I have spoken. Listen to the words he has put into the mouth of his atheistic interlocutor; '*Atheist* (to the Vedāntist) Well, very well, you have now entered a little into my views * * * But But if the universe be in your opinion unreal, then why unnecessarily invent your 'Brahma? Without form, without agency, what can he 'be doing in the world[15]?'

"The Vedāntist, the author adds, was silenced by the question[16]. But this was not the whole extent of his humiliation. The Tārkika, or philosophical interlocutor, who seems to propound the author's own views, says afterwards to the Vedāntist; 'By pronouncing the world to 'be false, notwithstanding the evident proofs of its existence, you appear to be a master atheist, destitute alike 'of shame and fear[17].'"

Tarkakāma.—"It may be all very fine to talk in this way, but how do you know the world has 'evident proofs of its existence'? How do you know that there are external substances? The evidence of the senses is surely not to be depended upon. How can you credit the eye which has been proved to be delusive in the case of a Mirage? Will you follow the example of the irrational deer who falls a sacrifice to his thirst, thereby giving the name to the Mirage[18].

"How can you trust the ear which has practised deception on you in open day light, as, for instance, in an exhibition of ventriloquism? What confidence can the organs of smell and taste consistently call for, when they will present the same objects as sweet and savoury to some, but insipid or fetid to others? Witness the effects which assafoetida and English cheese produce on men of different tastes. Have you never walked, Satyakāma, through the China bazar of Calcutta, nor covered your nostrils before shops to which the barbarians flock for refreshment? The world, whose existence you deduce from proofs of this description, doubtless occupies a considerable space in your imagination : but I cannot conceive what right you can have to speak of it as *real,* much less to vilify those who do not follow you in your phantastic flights."

Satyakāma. – "I think I have the same right to speak of the world as a reality that any of us has to speak of any thing at all. You cannot hold an argument and at the same time deny the validity of proof. Remember the language of Gotama whom you confess to be a master of logic. 'If all evidence is to be rejected, then the refutation itself is inadmissible[19].'

"The reasons you have advanced against the validity of the evidence which our senses give, themselves demolish your argument. The facts concerning the Mirage and ventriloquism must have been communciated to you through the instrumentality of the senses; and if the senses are never to be trusted, then the facts from which you have deduced your objections fall to the ground. How do you know, but through your senses, that the Mirage and ventriloquism have deceived you?

"Kaṇāda has well said that it is only when the senses are unsound[20], or defective, or when some particular bad habit is contracted,that a person may be deceived."

"When however one sense may thus deceive you, the others may come to your relief, and disabuse your mind. If the eye is imposed upon by a *mirage,* you can soon discover the illusion by the help of the ear and the touch. If the ear is deluded by the practice of ventriloquists, the eye helps it to detect the error. You cannot I believe adduce a single instance in which all the senses were simultaneously deceived.

"But by arguing against the validiy of the senses and the doctrine of the world's reality, you are by no means doing good service to the cause of Vedāntism; for you are there by cutting away the ground on which the system rests. How does the great doctor of Vedāntism introduce his doctrine? He declares the reasonableness of desiring the knowledge of

Brahma. But who is Brahma? *He from whom is the production &c., of this*[21], says the aphorist; that is to say, as Śaṅkarācārya explains and expounds it; 'That Omniscient and Omnipotent cause, from which proceed the production, conservation, and destruction of this world, which is distinguished by names and forms, containing many agents 'and patients, and times, spaces, causes, effects, and 'fruits, adapted to one another, and the beautiful arrangement of which cannot be even imagined by the mind, is 'Brahma[22].,' The aphorism and the commentary are but expositions of the text in the Upaniṣad in which the inquirer is informed that 'He is Brahma from whom these elements are produced, by whom those which are produced are sustained, in whom departing they are resolved[23].' Now if these elements are mere phantoms, no argument based *simply* on them, can be other than phantastic. Whether the maxim (ex nihilo nihil fit,) which affirmatively is an exact rendering of our interrogatory adage[24] of the Vedas, be universally true or not, so far as the necessity of a material cause is concerned, there can be no doubt as to the logial fallacy involved in reasoning a *posteriori* from *nothing at all to something*. What sort of a *Śeṣavat anumāna* would Gotama call it, if after asserting *it has rained, because the river has risen;* you were presently to declare that *the river has not really risen.* The author of the *Vidwān-moda-taraṅgiṇī* does no injustice to the Vedāntist when he calls him a master atheist, and represents him as foiled by the unhappy man who had worked up his mind into a denial of God. Nor does Chirañjīva wrong the Vedāntist much by adding, 'If that be the case, then who are you? What do you say? And what is your Brahma? Of you, the utterer of unreality, nothing can be real[25].'

Tarkakāma. – "But does not even a shadow betoken some reality which has cast it? Does not a reflection point to its substance? Does not even the mirage prove the existence of something of which it is a distorted likeness. The world is indeed a mere shadow, but it points to Brahma as its substance."

Satyakāma. – "We must remember that a shadow is only cast by an opaque body when it intercepts the rays shot by a luminous body, and it must be cast on something from which those rays are intercepted. A shadow, if it betokens a reality at all, must prove the existence at least of *three* entities, the luminous body whose light is intercepted, the opaque body which intercepts it, and the body on which the shadow is cast. But where is the luminary before which Brahma stands as an opaque substance? Is not Brahma 'light of lights by whose refulgence all other things shine[26]?' How then can it cast a shadow like an opaque substance? Or if you prefer to use the words *reflection* and *mirage,* you must remember that a reflection, in like manner, must prove the existence at least of *two* or rather *three* substances; the luminous body, the light, and the reflecting mirror or refracting medium. The mirage too, besides pointing to the substance of which it is a distorted image, implies the existence of an *atmosphere* in which the refraction takes place. What room then can there be for your much talked of *unity of essence.* It is impossible for you to answer Kaṇāda's or Kapila's objections to your unity. You must either renounce your theory of one essence, or you must avow that you have no reasons for holding that opinion. You *can* have no reason if you deny every thing that is not Brahma, for then there can be no independent reason. What then will become of your Vedas either? If there be nothing but the Supreme Spirit, then the Vedas must be a nullity."

While Satyakāma and Tarkakāma were thus discussing the idealism of the Vedānta, I was reminded of what you so often wrote to me, learned śāstri, of the lectures which the accomplished president of your Pāṭhaśālā delivered on the subject, and specially of the analogy he pointed out between the doctrines of the Vedānta and the Philosophy of a celebrated

English Bishop. And this brings to my recollection my ingratitude in never yet thanking you for the *Reprints for the Puṇḍits* which contain the opinions of Berkeley, and propound the problem of *pressing into the ranks of progress* the generally revered system of the Vedānta. I thought it only just to Tarkakāma that he should have the benefit of the sentiments broached at Benares. We might then be able to discuss the question of assimilating the philosophy of the East with that of the West. Nothing could be more desirable than this consummation, if only it were practicable. You might then hope to see the Reverend gentlemen of Sigra and the learned alumni of your *pāṭhaśālā* allied in one great cause.

Did you, I asked Satyakāma, approvingly cite the rebuke administered to the Vedāntist in the *Vidwānmoda-taraṅgiṇī?* Do you really think that to deny the reality of the external world savours of atheism? What then would you say to Bishop Berkeley?

Tarkakāma who, it appears had read the *Reprints,* instantly took the hint, and triumphantly excalimed; "Well said! well said! the ontology of the Vedānta is the philosophy of Berkeley! How can you pronounce the one to be atheism without including the other in the same condemnation?—You seem to hesitate, friend Satyakāma, out with your usual boldness."

Satyakāma.—"I was not hesitating from fear. Indeed what can I have to fear? My object is to vindicate the truth. I care not where and in what shape that truth is found. But I was hesitating because I think you are not dealing fairly with learned Europeans by pressing them into this controversy. It is impossible for you to have read the fourth number of the *Reprints* without being convinced that Berkeley's opinions are *not* those of your Vedāntists. It was Colonel Kennedy that first suggested the idea that the opinions of Berkeley were similar to those of the Vedānta, but in the plenitude of his surprize at the *Ne plus ultra* of transcendentalism which he found in the Vedānta, he could only say that the good Bishop approached in some degree to that system. Another gentleman has since remarked that the ontology of the Vedānta is the doctrine of that prelate. But you must for your part remember that the object of those authors is to narrow as much as possible the points of difference between philosophers of Europe and India. If they have made any over-statement, it must be attributed to their charity. At any rate it is not for us to build philosophical arguments on mere compliments generously paid to the systems of our fathers. If you take unfair advantage of compliments, foreigners will be at a loss how to deal with you. Courtesy will then prove a dangerous virtue."

Vaiyāsika.—"I do not understand what you mean. But is it true that there is any resemblance between the Vedānta and Berkeley's doctrine?"

Satyakāma.—"I should like to hear what Tarkakāma says to this. A question from the bridegroom's party had better be answered by the bride's guests."

Tarkakāma.—"Not a resemblance merely, but, as it has been well said, the doctrine of Berkeley *is* the ontology of the Vedānt."

Satyakāma.—"Is it in their affirmations or negations that Berkeley and the Vedānta are consentient?"

Tarkakāma.—"Both. Berkeley acknowledges the existence of spirit, and denies that of matter. The Vedānta does the same."

Satyakāma.—"First then with reference to their affirmations:—can you tell me whether Berkeley allowed the existence of one Eternal Spirit only, or did he also assert the reality of many created spirits."

"On this point, said Tarkakāma, the Christian is of course inferior to the Brahman. Berkeley was unfortunately destitute of the light of the Vedas, and ignorant of our grand doctrine of unity. Consequently he allowed a multiplicity of real spirits."

"Such as God, angels, men, &c."

"I must say so."

"Well, said Satyakāma, how many spirits does the Vedānta allow?

Tarkakāma replied instantly, "*Ekamevādwitīyam,* one only without a second."

"And that is a cardinal doctrine of the Vedānta. Is it not?"

"Of course, or it would degenerate into a *dwaitavāda,* a system of duality."

"Is Berkeley's teaching *adwaitavāda,* a system of unity?"

"I wish, said Tarkakāma, it were, but here is his failure."

"Then in one of your cardinal points, the very point which distinguishes the Vedānta from other schools of Brāhminical philosophy, the ontology of the Vedānta is *not* the doctrine of Berkeley. The Vedānta's idea of spiritual existence is eternal and underived existence. It does not allow the possibility of a created soul really existing. It likens such souls to the reflection of the sun or the moon in the waters. It pronounces all derived existence to be a nullity. Nothing can be which has not always been. Nothing can really exist which has not always existed. But Berkeley held the real existence not only of God, but also of all created spirits. Berkeley found no difficulty in admitting that a soul could come into existence without having existed from eternity—that a spiritual substance, which once was not, could afterwards begin to be—an idea perfectly inconsistent with the ontology of the Vedānt. I am only astonished that you did not see the difference directly. Now as to the negations:—Berkeley, you say, denies identically what the Vedānta also rejects."

"No doubt about it?"

"Please to tell me, said Satyakāma, what it is that he denies."

"Matter."

"And what does the Vedānta deny."

"The same, answered Tarkakāma, even matter?"

"What is the word used in the Vedānta for *matter?*"

"It is difficult to light on a Sanskrit word that is exactly equivalent to *matter*. Haughton proposed a good many, but an ingenious writer of our own day has shown that none of them will do[27]."

"Then the objects denied in the two systems cannot be *prima facie* identical; the one sums up the things denied by a term for which the other has no equivalent. You still think their negations are the same, and that the objects denied in the one correspond to those denied in the other?"

"Yes."

"What, asked Satyakāma, are the objects denied in the Vedānta?"

"Every thing which is not Brahma. The whole universe."

"As we have seen before, much that the Vedānta denies is acknowledged by Berkeley; viz. men, angels, demons. These are spiritual essences. But you think Berkeley denies all other things; whatever is not spirit, whatever has parts or dimensions."

"Does he not?" said Tarkakāma, somewhat faltering.

Āgamika, who fancied that the Vedānta doctrine involved a sublimity which none but a Brāhmin, learned in the Veda and taught by an Ācārya in the prescribed way, could comprehend[28], was not pleased with the idea that an English Bishop, untaught of a Brāhmin, had discovered the great mysteries of philosophy. "If you find any reason for faltering, said he, the question should have been asked and considered ere you undertook to pronounce, in such a circle and on such an occasion, that the doctrine of a Mletcha dualist was identical with our divine Vedānta."

Satyakāma remarked that his friend Āgamika needs not be alarmed. If the larned disputant of the bride's party had attentively read the *Reprints for the Puṇḍits,* he might have solved that question in a way that would be quite satisfactory to the admirers of Berkeley on the one hand and the followers of the Vedānta on the other.

A member of the Rajah's family, who was listening to the discussion with great interest, produced the book in a minute from his highness's library, when Satyakāma read the following extracts from it :

'When Berkeley denied the existence of matter he 'simply denied the existence of that unknown substratum, the existence of which Locke had declared to be a necessary inference from our knowledge of qualities, but the nature of which must ever be altogether hidden from us. Philosophers had assumed the existence of substance, *i.e.,* of a noumenon lying underneath all phenomena, a substratum supporting all qualities, a something in which all accidents inhere. This unknown substance Berkeley denies. It is a mere abstraction, he says. If it is unknown, unknowable, it is a Figment : and I will none of it : for it is a Figment worse than useless : it is pernicious as the basis of all Atheism. If by matter you understand that which is seen, felt, tasted, and touched, then I say matter exists. I am as firm a believer in its existence as any one can be. Herein I agree with the vulgar. If on the contrary, you understand by matter the occult substratum, which is not seen, not felt, not tasted, and not touched, that of which the senses do not, cannot inform you, then I say I believe not in the existence of matter, and herein I differ with the philosophers and agree with the vulgar.

'I do not argue against the existence of any one thing that we can apprehend either by sensation or reflection. *That the things I see with my eyes and touch with my 'hands do exist, really exist, I make not the least question. The only thing whose existence I deny is what philosophers call matter, or corporeal substance.* And in doing this there is no damage done to the rest of mankind, who I dare say will never miss it[29].'

"It appears, said Satyakāma, from the above extracts that Berkeley only denied something which philosophers called matter, but could not explain, which no body perceived by his senses. He acknowledged the *prtayakṣasiddha-jagat* (the world proved by the senses), the denial of which savoured of atheism in the estimation of the *Vidwan-moda-taraṅgiṇī*.

"Berkeley, in short, did not deny the whole external world, nor any thing we see or touch. The only thing he denied is 'that which philosophers called matter. The Vedānta has no term for matter, and as matter, in Berkeley's use of the term, is something different from what is seen, it cannot be made out that he understood by it the identical things denied in the Vedānta. In fact it is difficult to say what Berkeley denied. It is easier to say what he did not deny. He did not deny the truthfulness of the senses, nor the facts of sensation, nor the existence of objects of sensation—all which however are denied in that school of the Vedānta which talks of 'all this as no *thing*.' *Every thing is false which is not Brahma*[30].

"You see then what a large residum Berkeley's negations leave untouched, not of spiritual essences alone, but of non-spiritual things perceptible by the corporeal senses, which the Vedānta, I mean the doctrine of the elementary treatises, nevertheless absolutely denies, by *falsifying* every thing which is not Brahma."

Tarkakāma.—"But the Vedānta's denial is not absolute. It allows a *vyāvahārika* existence to them."

Satyakāma. – "That it could not help doing. *Vyāvahārika* means what is customary, conventional, popular. If people cannot divest their minds of the reality of the world, the Vedāntist cannot help saying, it is *Vyāvahārika,* just as even Bhāskarācārya will allow it is *Vyavahārika* to say the moon is taken (by the giant) when she is in an eclipse, although he knows that the true cause of that phenomenon is the interception of the solar light by the intervention of the earth. This is not the sense in which Berkeley admits the existence of external things. *What he saw, heard, and felt, he believed to exist as really as his own being;* not in the sense in which Bhāskarācārya believed in the periodical capture of the moon.

"Whatever *vyāvahārika* existence and the Berkeleyian matter may be, it is evident that no negation in the one system is *obviously* identical with the other. If there be any *occult matter* equally denied by both, it is a hypothesis on which no theory can be built."

But how was it, I asked, that Berkeley has been so universally accused of denying the reality of the external world?

"The reason, said Satyakāma, is explained in the *Reprints.* 'True it is that owing to the ambiguities of language, Berkeley's theory does seem to run counter to the ordinary belief of mankind, because by matter men commonly understand the seen, the tasted, the touched &c. : therefore when the existence of matter is denied, people naturally suppose that the existence of the seen, the tasted, and the touched is denied, never suspecting that matter in its philosophical sense is the *not seen, not tasted, not touched.*'"

Āgamika. – "Then there does not seem to be a shadow of reason for confounding the ontology of the Vedānta with the doctrine of Berkeley, if the extracts you have read are genuine. The one denied the very thing the other allowed, viz. the seen, the tasted, the touched. How was it then that eminent men have hazarded such assertions?"

Satyakāma.—"The extracts are from the *Reprints,* and I have also verified them. There cannot be a doubt on that score. But, as it is added in the *Reprints,* 'Berkeley 'has not, it must be confessed, sufficiently guarded against 'all ambiguity. He says 'It is indeed an opinion strangely prevailing amongst men that houses, mountains, rivers, and in a word, all sensible objects have an existence, natural or real, distinct from their being perceived by the understanding.'

"I do not pretend to stand up as Berkeley's advocate, nor do I feel myself called upon to reconcile what may appear inconsistencies in him. All I contend for is that no case has been made out for asserting that the ontology of the Vedānta is the doctrine of Berkeley, and that neither in their affirmations nor in their negations are the systems characteristically consentient. The stigma of idealism which has been affixed to Berkeley's theory is no doubt owing to assertions like the following :—

'For what are the forementioned objects but the things we perceive by sense? And what do we perceive, besides our own ideas or sensations, and is it not plainly repugnant that any one of these, or any combination of them, should exist unperceived?

'In short, if there were external bodies it is impossible we should ever come to know it, and if there were not, we might have the very same reasons to think there were that we have now; suppose, what no one can deny possible, an intelligence, without the help of external bodies to be affected with the same train of sensations or ideas that you are, imprinted in the same order, and with like vividness in his mind, I ask whether that intelligence hath not all the reason to believe the existence of corporeal substances, represented by his ideas and exciting them in his mind, that you 'can possibly have for believing the same thing? Of this there can be no question; which one consideration is enough to make any reasonable person suspect the strength of whatever arguments he may think himself to have, for the existence of bodies without the mind.

'I say it is granted on all hands, and what happens in dreams, frenzies, and the like, puts it beyond dispute, that it is possible we might be affected with all the ideas we have now, though no bodies existed without, resembling them. Hence it is evident the supposition of external bodies is not necessary for the producing our ideas : since it is granted they are produced sometimes, and might possibly be produced always, in the same order we see them in at present, without their concurrence.'"

Vaiyāsika, on hearing the above extracts from Berkeley, said he was perfectly astonished at the remark that the doctrine of Berkeley was the ontology of the Vedānta. Nothing could be a greater mistake than to charge such an opinion on the founder of the Vedānta or his great commentator.

"Did you not know, he asked, that the extracts last read contain the very heresy of the Buddhists which Vyāsa and Śaṅkarācārya have taken infinite pains to refute? The learned president of the Benares pāṭhaśalā should rather have taught that the ontology of Buddhism was the doctrine of Berkeley—that its Vijñāna-vāda, demolished by our commentator, was identical with his idealism."

"Impossible! said I, "do you mean to say that the founder of he Vedānta and his celebrated commentator have denounced idealism?"

Vaiyāsika.—"I appeal to my learned friends here."

"What, said I, the very system which the atheistic interlocutor in the *Vidwan-moda-taranginī* hailed as his auxiliary, and which the author stigmatized as the teaching of a master-infidel, because it denied the visible world,—that very system contains a refutation of idealism?"

Tarkakāma and Āgamika remained silent.

Satyakāma said that the Vedānt, as taught by Vyāsa, was not idealistic, and that his fellow-companion of the bridegroom's procession was right.

"Let us have the Sūtras and commentary," he added, "you, Vaiyāsika, must have them at your finger's end: –come, give us chapter and verse."

A copy of the Vedānt Sūtras with commentary was instantly brought from the Royal library and handed to Vaiyāsika, who, on opening the book, said, "The 28th Sūtra of the 2nd Section of the second Chapter reads : 'Not unreality, because of perception[31],' or perhaps apprehension would be a better rendering of *upalabdhi*. This Sūtra was intended for the refutation of Buddhistic idealism which denied the reality of the world, and which Śaṅkara thus epitomized[32] :

'In that theory of *Vijñāna* (cognitions or ideas,) all dealing with proof and the provable is an internal process by 'means of images existing in the understanding. Even 'if there were external objects, their proof could not 'be had except by its existing in the understanding. 'If it be asked, how is it known that all operations are internal, and that external objects have no existence apart from cognitions? The reply is–from sheer impossibility. 'External objects must be comprehended either as atoms, or as their aggregates, pillars &c. But there cannot 'be atoms distinct from pillars &c., for it is impossible 'there should be cognition of atomic appearances. Nor can they be the pillars, their aggregates, for it is impossible to regard them as at the same time both different from and identical with atoms. * * * Again; of the general apprehensions produced by perception, that which becomes especial with reference to individual objects, such as the notion of pillar, the notion of wall, the notion of pot, the notion of cloth, is not produced but by peculiarities in the notion itself. Hence it must be acknowledged that objects are similar to cognitions. And this being acknowledged, the theory of real objects is rendered nugatory, because it is contradicted by the cognition of their forms. * * * This is also to be regarded in the light of dreams, &c. As dreams, jugglery, mirage, fairy towns, become, without the presence of external objects, forms of apprehensions and apprehenders; in the same manner may the notions of pillars &c. come in when one is awake, for in either case the notion is the same. If it be asked, how a variety of notions is occasioned if there be no external objects; the answer is, from a variety of fancies. There can be no dificulty in supposing that in this world without a beginning fancies and cognitions may have mutually caused each other's varieties like seed and sprout. That the variety in notions is owing to a variety of fancy is evident from positive as well as negative proof. We are both agreed that in dreams and other visions there is a variety of 'notions occasioned by fancy even in the absence of external objects. Only [we Buddhists maintain the same is also the case in the presence of objects] we do not allow a variety of notions occasioned by objects in the absence of fancy. Hence there is no real extenal object.'

"This, learned Sirs, continued Vaiyāsika, was a theory of the Buddhists who pronounced the world to be a mere phantom. Śaṅkara has by no means made an over-statement of their doctrine. Their popular books liken the universe to a *māyā, a mirage,* a flash of lightning, a froth[33]. They no doubt carried the ideal theory further than Berkeley, but substitute the word *idea* for *vijñāna,* and you put the very words of the Christian Bishop into the mouths of those Buddhists. And now listen to the masterly way in which our accomplished leader demolished the whole of that phantastic argument[34].

'Not unreality, because of perception. It is impossible to maintain that there is no external object. Why? Because of perception. External objects are severally perceived such as a pillar, a wall, a pot, a cloth. It is impossible there can be unreality in that which is perceived. As if a man, while enjoying a good dinner, were to say, I am not eating, nor am I enjoying it, the saying would not be handsome; so if, while himself apprehending an object by sensation, a person were to say, I am not apprehending it, nor is there any external substance, how could his disclaimer be acceptable? If it be objected, I do not say, I do not *perceive* any object, but that I do not perceive *anything besides the perception.* Well, you say this because your mouth is ungoaded, but you do not speak reasonably; for from the very act of perception, something distinct from perceptions must also be apprehended by the force of objects. No one indeed perceives that a pillar or a wall is a *mere perception,* but every one perceives it as an *object of perception.* Thus do (idealistic) men, too, perceive things; for, even while denying external objects, they virtually acknowledge them by avowing that the forms, internally apprehended, are *like* the externals. Partaking of the knowledge of externals, universally prevalent among men, and yet desirous of denying external objects, they turn them into a simile by using the phrase *like the externals.* Otherwise [*i.e.,* if they did not perceive external objects] why should they use the phrase *like the externals.* No one can say Viṣṇu Mitra appears like a barren woman's son. Those therefore who perceive things as they are, should say that the externals themselves appear, not that appearances like externals are seen. Perhaps it will be urged that because of the [antecedent] impossibility of external objects you talk of appearances like externals. This is not a right saying at all, for possibility or impossibility is determined by the impulse or non-impulse of proof, not the impulse or non-impulse of proof by possibility or impossibility. That which is establihsed by perception or any other proof is possible : that which cannot be established by any proof is impossible. Now external objects being established, like the spirit itself, by all descriptions of proof, why should exceptions be taken to the one, when they are not taken to the other, and the former be pronounced impossible? Nor, again, because cognitions may resemble objects, therefore objects must be negatived; for there could not be such resemblance with objects if there were no objects, and because those objects are externally apprehended.'

"Śaṅkarācārya, you will observe, contends that there is the same proof for the reality of the external world as there is for that of the internal spirit. It is impossible to conceive how learned men could persuade themselves, merely on the authority of a few pages of elementary manuals, that the ontology of the Vedānt was the doctrine of European idealism. Our commentator goes on smashing to fragments all the idealistic arguments of the Buddhists. He denounces the theory that there could be cognition, or any intellectual process, without objects to act upon. 'If you say, he continues, 'that cognitions, being of the nature of light, are self-produced, like a self-shining lamp, without the force of external objects, you utter a most unreasonable doctrine that the spirit acts on itself; as if one could say fire burns its own self. But that which every body calls reasonable, the perception of external objects by cognitions distinct from themselves, you do not allow. Oh, what great wisdom you show[35]!'

"The 29th Sūtra denies that external objects are like dreams and visions because the characteristics of the two are different[36]. And Śaṅkara thus expounds it : 'As to 'what has been said by the denier of exrternal objects 'that waking sensations of pillars &c. may be caused like the visions of dreams without the prsence of external objects, the sensations being alike in both cases, we thus reply to it. Waking sensations cannot be like visions of dreams, because the two are different. There is a difference between dreaming and waking. What now is the difference? We reply, Contradiction and Non-contradiction. What is perceived in a dream is contradicted by the waking conviction, my interview with a great man is untrue, there has been no interview with a great man, my mind was deceived in sleep, hence it is a misapprehension. Jugglery and similar appearances are also contradicted in that manner. But waking sensations are never contradicted in any state[37].

The Nepaulese Buddhist, worried by the Bhāgavatas, had sought refuge in our little circle while the extracts from Śaṅkara were yet being read; and he was now going to speak in defence of his doctrine, when the military musicians commenced beating their drums and blowing their trumpets, and the European guests, ladies as well as gentlemen, began to dance in front of the bride-groom. The attention of all present was thereby concentrated in the middle hall, and our philosophical discussion was at once interrrupted. Āgamika's simplicity amused us not a little, when, mistaking the company for professional dancers, he expressed his indignation at the station-doctor, the only European face he could recognize, engaging in such a questionable occupation from mere pecuniary motives. I told him that the company was not one of professional dancers, but of respectable ladies and gentlemen, who were expressing their joy on the happy event they had come to celebrate, by joining in a dance for the amusement of all present. "Then, said Āgamika, even Indra's court could not exhibit a scene, so beautiful, and this was not an occasion when any argument for Buddhistic idealism can prevail against the reasoning of Śaṅkarācārya. It would certainly be most unhandsome at this moment to say we are not perceiving any objects by our eyes and ears."

References

1. श्रीरुद्र उवाच। * * * अहं ब्रह्माथ विबुधा मुनयश्चामलाशयाः। सर्व्वात्मनाप्रपन्नास्वामात्मानं प्रेष्ठमीश्वरं। Srī Bhagāvata, X. 63.

2. कृषीबलस्य क्षेत्रकर्म्मण्यप्रयतमानस्यापि सस्यनिष्पत्तिः स्यात् कुलालस्य मृत् संस्क्रियायामप्रयतनमानस्यापि अमत्रोत्पत्तिश्च तन्तुवायस्यापि तन्तूनतन्वानस्यापि तन्वानस्येव वस्त्रलाभः। Śaṅkara Com. Vedānt, II. 2.27.

3. मायावादमसच्छास्त्रं प्रच्छन्नं बौद्धमेव च। Padma Purāṇa.

4. कर्म्मणा जायते जन्तुः कर्म्मणैव प्रलीयते। सुखं दुःखं भयं क्षेमं कर्म्भणैवाभिपद्यते॥ अस्ति चेदीश्वरः कश्चित् फलरूप्यन्यकर्म्मणां। कर्त्तारं भजते सोपि नह्यकर्तुः प्रभुर्हि सः॥ किमिन्द्रेणेह भूतानां स्वं स्वं कर्म्मानुवर्तिनां। अनीशेनान्यथा कर्तुं स्वभावविहितं नृणां॥ स्वभावतन्त्रो हि जनः स्वभावमनुवर्तते। स्वभावस्थमिदं सर्व्वं सदेवासुरमानुषं॥ देहानुच्चावचान्

जन्तुः प्राप्योत्सृजति कर्म्मणा। शत्रुर्मित्रमुदासीनः कर्म्मैव गुरुरीश्वरः॥ तस्मात् संपूजयेत् कर्म्म स्वभावस्थः स्वकर्म्मकृत्। अञ्जसा येन वर्तेत तदेवास्य हि दैवतं॥ आजीव्यैकतरं भावं यस्त्वन्यमुपजीवति। न तस्माद्विन्दते क्षेमं जारान्नार्य्यसती यथा॥ Bhagāvata, x. 24. 13-20.

5. तत्रापरा ऋग्वेदो यजुर्वेदः सामवेदोऽथर्ववेदः शिक्षा कल्पो व्याकरणं निरुक्तं छन्दो ज्योतिषमिति। अथ परा यया तदक्षरमधिगम्यते।

Muṇḍaka.

6. चतुर्षु वेदेषु परं श्रेयोऽलब्ध्वा शाण्डिल्य इदं शास्त्रमधिगतवानित्यादिवेदनिन्दा-दर्शनात्। Vedānt Com. II. 2. 45.

7. Bhagavad-Gītā. II.

8. य एवमेता महासंहिता व्याख्याता वेद। सन्धीयते प्रजया पशुभिर्ब्रह्मवर्चसेनान्नाद्येन सुवर्गेण लोकेन॥ Taittiriya.

अतोऽत्रापि य एवं वेद सन्धीयते प्रजादिभिः स्वर्गान्तैः प्रजादिफलमाप्नोतीत्यर्थः॥ Śaṅkara on ditto.

स एव विद्वानस्माच्छरीरभेदादूर्द्ध उत्क्रम्यामुष्मिन् स्वर्गे लोके सर्व्वान् कामानात्प्वाऽमृतः समभवत् समभवत्॥ Aitareya.

यो वा एतामेवं वेदापहत्य पाप्मानमनन्ते स्वर्गे लोके ज्येये प्रतितिष्ठति प्रतितिष्ठति॥ Kena.

9. न चैते भगवद्व्यूहाश्चतुः संख्यायामेव व्यवतिष्ठेरन् ब्रह्मादिस्तम्बपर्य्यन्तम्य समस्तम्य जगतो भगवद्व्यूहत्वावगमात्। Ved. Com. II. 2, 44.

10. सर्वं खल्विदं ब्रह्म तज्जलान्।

11. ब्रह्मदृष्टिरादित्यादिषु स्यादिति। कस्मात् उत्कर्षात् एवमुत्कर्षेणादित्यादयोदृष्टा भवन्ति उत्कृष्टदृष्टेस्तेष्वध्यासात्। तथा च लोकिकोन्यायोनुमतो भवति। उत्कृष्टदृष्टिर्हि निकृष्टेध्यसितव्येति लौकिको न्यायः यथा राजदृष्टिः क्षत्तरि सचानुगन्तव्यः विपर्य्ययेप्रत्यवायप्रसङ्गात्। नहि क्षत्तृदृष्टिपरिगृहीतो राजा निकर्षं नीयमानः श्रेयसे स्यात्।

Śaṅkarācārya.

12. यस्मात् सर्व्वमिदं विकारजातं ब्रह्मैव तज्जत्वात् तल्लत्वात् तदनत्वाच्च। Ibid. I. 2. 1.

13. "*All, that is, no thing : Brahma being the one only thing.*" Benares Magazine vol. V. p. 421.

14. न च सर्व्वस्यैकात्मत्वे सति रागादयः सम्भवन्ति तस्माच्छान्त उपासीत। Śaṅkara. Com. Vedānt, I. 2. 1.

15. नास्तिकः। साधु रे साधु किंचिन्मन्मते प्रविष्टोऽसि॥
जगन्मृषैवेति भवन्मतं चेत् किं कल्प्यते ब्रह्म निरर्थकं तत्।
आकारशून्येन गतक्रियेण कर्त्तव्यमेतेन किमस्तिलोके॥

16. इत्याकर्ण्य चकिते तूर्ष्णीभूते वेदान्तिनि सस्मितं सर्व्वे तार्किकमवलोकयन्ति॥

17. प्रत्यक्षसिद्धमप्येतज्जगन्मिथ्येति कीर्त्तयन्। लज्जाभयोभयत्यागान्नास्तिकस्य प्रभुर्भवान्॥

18. मृगतृष्णा मरीचिका॥

19. सर्व्वप्रमाणप्रतिषेधाच्च प्रतिषेधासिद्धिः। Nyāya Sūtra, II. 3.

20. इन्द्रियदोषसंस्कारदोषाच्चाविद्या।

21. जन्माद्यस्य यतः। Vedānt Sūtra, I. i. 2.

22. अस्य जगतो नामरूपाभ्यां व्याकृतस्यानेककर्त्तृभोक्तृसंयुक्तस्य प्रतिनियतदेशकालनिमित्तक्रियाफलाश्रयस्य मनसाप्यचिन्त्यरचनारूपस्य जन्मस्थितिभङ्गं यतः सर्व्वज्ञात् सर्व्वशक्तेः कारणाद्भवति तद्ब्रह्मेति वाक्यशेषः।

23. यतो वा इमानि भूतानि जायन्ते येन जातानि जीवन्ति यत्प्रन्त्यभिसंविशन्ति तद्विजिज्ञासस्व तद्ब्रह्म॥

24. कथमसतः सज्जायेत। Chāndogya.

25. तार्किकः सहासं। एवं सति त्वमपि कः किं ब्रवीषि किंवा त्वद्ब्रह्म सकलमपि मिथ्येव मिथ्यावादिनस्ते॥

26. तच्छुभ्रंज्योतिषांज्योतिः तमेव भान्तमनुभाति सर्व्वं तस्य भासा सर्व्वमिदं विभाति। Muṇḍaka.

27. There is no Sanskrit word of "Matter." Ballantyne's prize Essay p. 123.

28. आचार्याद्धैव विद्या विदिता साधिष्ठं प्रापयति। Chāndogya.

29. Reprints for the Puṇḍits No. 4,

30. ब्रह्मभिन्नं सर्व्वं मिथ्या। Vedānta Praribhāṣā.

31. नाभाव उपलब्धेः।

32. तस्मिंश्च विज्ञानवादे बुद्धयारूपेण रूपेणान्तःस्थ एव प्रमाणप्रमेयफलव्यवहारः सर्व उपपद्यते सत्यपि वाह्येर्थे बुद्धयारोहमन्तरेण प्रमाणादिव्यवहारानवतारात्। कथं पुनरवगम्यते अन्तःस्थ एवायं सर्वो व्यवहारो न विज्ञानव्यतिरिक्तो वाह्योऽर्थोस्तीति। तदसम्भवादित्याह। स हि वाह्योऽर्थोऽभ्युपगम्यमानः परमाणवो वास्यु। तत्समूहोवा स्तम्भादयः स्युः। तत्र न तावत् परमाणवः स्तम्भादिप्रत्ययपरिच्छेद्या भवितुमर्हन्ति परमाण्वाभासज्ञानानुपपत्तेः। नापि तत्समूहास्तम्भादयः तेषां परमाणुभ्योऽन्यत्वानन्यत्वाभ्यां निरूपयितुमशक्यत्वात्। अपिचानुभवमात्रेण साधारणात्मनो ज्ञानस्य जायमानस्य योऽयं प्रतिविषयपक्षपातः स्तम्भज्ञानं कुडयज्ञानं घटज्ञानं पटज्ञानमिति नासौ ज्ञानगतं विशेषमन्तरेणोपपद्यत इत्यवश्यं विषयसारूप्यं ज्ञानस्याङ्गीकर्तव्यम्। अङ्गीकृते च तस्मिन् विषयाकारस्य ज्ञानेनैवावरुद्धत्वादपार्थिकार्थसद्भावकल्पना। स्वप्नादिवच्चेदं द्रष्टव्यं। यथा हि स्वप्नमायामरीच्युदकगन्धर्वनगरादिप्रत्ययाः विनैव वाह्येनार्थेन ग्राह्यग्राहकाकारा भवन्ति। एवं जागरितगोचरा अपि स्तम्भादिप्रत्यया भवितुमर्हन्तीत्यवगम्यते। प्रत्ययत्वाविशेषात्। कथं पुनरसति वाह्यार्थे प्रत्ययवैचित्र्यमुपपद्यते वासनावैचित्र्यादित्याह अनादौ संसारे वीजाङ्कुरवद्विज्ञानानां वासनानाञ्चान्योन्यनिमित्तनैमित्तिकभावेन वैचित्र्यं न प्रतिषिध्यतेअपिचान्वयव्यतिरेकाभ्यां वासनानिमित्तमेव ज्ञानवैचित्र्यमित्यवगम्यते स्वप्नादिष्वन्तरेणाप्यर्थं वासनानिमित्तस्य ज्ञानवैचित्र्यस्योभाभ्यामावाभ्यामप्यभ्युपगम्यमानत्वात् अन्तरेण तु वासनामर्थनिमित्तस्य ज्ञानवैचित्र्यस्य मयानभ्युपगम्यमानत्वात् तस्मादप्यभावो वाह्यस्यार्थस्येत्येवम् प्राप्ते व्रूमः॥

33. सर्व्व अनित्या अकामा अध्रुवा न च शाश्वतापि न कल्पाः। माया मरीचिसदृशा विद्युत् फेणोपमाश्चपलाः। Lalita-vistara.

34. नाभाव उपलब्धेरिति न खलु अभावो वाह्यस्यार्थस्थायाध्यावसातुम् शक्यते कस्मात् उपलब्धेः उपलभ्यते हि प्रतिप्रत्ययं वाह्योर्थः स्तम्भः कुड्यम् घटः पट इति नचोपलभ्यमानस्यैवाभावो भवितुमर्हति। यथाहि कश्चिद्भुञ्जानो भुजिसाध्यायां तृप्तौ स्वयमनुभूयमानायामेवं ब्रूयात् नाहं भुञ्जे नच तृप्यामीति तद्वदिन्द्रियसन्निकर्षेण स्वयमुपलभमान एव वाह्यमर्थं नाहं उपलभे, न च सोस्तीति ब्रुवन् कथमुपादेयवचनः स्यात्। ननु नाहमेवं ब्रवीमि नकञ्चिदर्थमुपलभ इति किन्तूपलब्धिव्यतिरिक्तं नोपलभ इति ब्रवीमि वाढमेवं

ब्रवीषि निरङ्कुशात्वात्ते तुण्डस्य नतु युक्त्योपेतं ब्रवीषि यत उपलब्धिव्यतिरेकोपि बलादर्थस्याभ्युपगन्तव्यः उपलब्धेरेव नहि कश्चिदुपलब्धिमेव स्तम्भकुड्यञ्चेत्युपलभते उपलब्धिविषयत्वेनैवतु स्तम्भ-कुड्यादीन् सर्वे लौकिका उपलभन्ते अतश्चैवमेव सर्वे लौकिका उपलभन्ते यत् प्रत्याचक्षाणा अपि वाह्यमर्थमेवमाचक्षते यदन्तर्ज्ञेयरूपं तद्वहिर्वदवभासत इति तेपि हि सर्व लोके प्रसिद्धां वहिरवभासां सम्बिदं प्रतिलभमानाः प्रत्याख्यातुकामाश्च वाह्यमर्थं वहिर्वदितिवत्करणं कुर्व्वन्ति इतरथाहि कस्माद्वहिर्वदिति ब्रूयुः। न हि विष्णुमित्रो बन्ध्यापुत्रवदवभासत इति कश्चिदाचक्षीत तस्माद्यथानुभवं तत्त्वमभ्युपगच्छद्भिर्वहिरेवावभासत इति युक्तमभ्युपगन्तुं नतु वहिर्वदवभासत इति। ननु वाह्यस्यार्थस्यासम्भवात् वहिर्वदवभासत इत्यध्यवसितं नायं साधुरध्यवसायः यतः प्रमाणप्रवृत्त्य-प्रवृत्तिपूर्वकौ सम्भवासम्भवाववधार्य्येते न पुनः सम्भवासम्भवपूर्विके प्रमाणप्रवृत्त्यप्रवृत्ती यद्धि प्रत्यक्षादीनामन्यतमेनापि प्रमाणेनोपलभ्यते तत्सम्भवति यत्तु न केनचिदपि प्रमाणेनोपलभ्यते तन्नसम्भवति इह तु यथास्वं सर्वैरेव प्रमाणैर्वाह्योर्थ उपलभ्यमानः कथं व्यतिरेकाव्यतिरेकादिविकल्पैर्न सम्भवती-त्युच्येत उपलब्धेरेव न च ज्ञानस्य विषयसारूप्याद्विषयनाशो भवति। असति विषये विषयसारूप्यानुपपत्तेः बहिरूपलब्धेश्च विषयस्य।

35. अथ विज्ञानं प्रकाशात्मकत्वात् प्रदीपवत् स्वयमेवानुभूयते न तथा वाह्योर्थ इति चेत् अत्यन्तविरुद्धां स्वात्मनि क्रियामभ्युपगच्छसि अग्निरात्मानं दहतीतिवत् अविरुद्धन्तु लोके प्रसिद्धं स्वात्मव्यतिरिक्तेन विज्ञानेन वाह्योर्थोनुभूयत इति नेच्छसि अहो पाण्डित्यं महद्दर्शितं।

36. वैधर्म्याच्च न स्वप्नादिवत्।

37. यदुक्तं वाह्यार्थपलापिना स्वप्नादिप्रत्ययवज्जागरितगोचरा अपि स्तम्भादिप्रत्यया विनैव वाह्येनार्थेन भवेयुः प्रत्ययत्वाविशेषादिति। तत्प्रतिवक्तव्यं अत्रोच्यते। न स्वप्नादिप्रत्ययवज्जाग्रत्प्रत्यया भवितुमर्हन्ति। कस्मात् वैधर्म्यात्। वैधर्म्यं हि भवतिस्वप्नजागरितयोः किं पुनर्वैधर्म्यं बाधाबाधावितिब्रूमः। बाध्यते हि स्वप्नोपलब्धं वस्तु प्रवुद्धस्य मिथ्यामयोपलब्धो महाजनसमागम इति। न ह्यस्ति महाजनसमागमो निद्राग्लानन्तु मे मनोवभूव तेनैषा भ्रान्तिरुद्वभुवेति। एवं मायादिष्वपि भवति यथायथं बाधः। नैवं जागरितोपलब्धं वस्तु स्तम्भादिकं कस्याञ्चिदप्यवस्थायां बाध्यते।

DIALOGUE VIII

FROM THE SAME TO THE SAME

The conference we held at the marriage assembly in a corner of the Hall was reported to the Rajah by his nephew, who was listening with great attention to the arguments adduced on both sides. The following day his highness gave a private audience to Vaiyāsika, Āgamika, Satyakāma, and myself. He thanked us all for the interest we took in the happy event of his daughter's marriage. He felt proud, he said, that his assembly was graced by such learned men, and that his house was the scene of a discussion, in which certain ideas were elicited, which he for his part had not met with elsewhere, and which might possibly throw new light on the history of Indian philosophy. "It is a great pity that the Brahma Sūtras and Śaṅkara's commentary are so little known. I have not met with a single puṇḍit, with the exception of the venerated Vaiyāsika, who was familiar with the whole of the *Śarīrika mīmāṅsā bhāṣya.* Vedāntic scholars in my circle profess to have read only such manuals as the *Vedānta sāra* and the *Paribhāṣā.* Their acquaintance with the Sūtras and commentary never extended beyond the opening section of the opening chapter. When therefore I first read in a native newspaper at Bombay, now more than a quarter of a century ago, that Colonel Kennedy had discovered some resemblance between the theory of Bishop Berkeley and the Vedāntic doctrine, I sought for further information from my father's puṇḍits, but in vain. Colonel Kennedy's idea was lately adopted and enforced by the authorities of the government College at Benares. I then thought it must be substantially correct. You have however now successfully disproved it, as far as Vyāsa's Vedānt is concerned. But, Satyakāma, what have you gained by it? The disproof of that idea does not necessarily throw discredit on the Vedānt, for my friend Vaiyāsika was no less impatient than yourself of the statement, which has of late been so widely circulated, that the ontology of the Vedānt is the doctrine of Berkeley."

Satyakāma.—"Please your highness, I cannot say what I have gained, or whether I have gained any thing, nor do I know that I came with the expectation of gaining any thing besides the pleasure of congratulating you on the happy occasion which brought us together. With reference to our conference, the right way to look at it is to consider—not if a particular system is necessarily overthrown thereby, but if in the course of fair discussion truth of any kind is elicited. If a wrong idea, which had been much in vogue of late, has been disproved, it must so far be a service to truth. Your highness will now know how to deal with persons that may say in your presence that the ontology of the Vedānt is the doctrine of Berkeley."

Rājāh.—"But will you accept my friend Vaiyāsika's suggestion that the ontology of Buddhism is the doctrine of Berkeley? Are you gratified at the idea that Berkeley is proved a Buddhist?"

Satyakāma.—"Certainly not, please your highness. I always protested against making free with Berkeley's name in an Indian discussion. What he wrote had reference to philosophers that lived far away from us. Even Europeans find it difficult to say what Berkeley's opinions were. We cannot expect so to understand them in a hurry as to find analogies between them and Indian theories. I did not think it necessary last night to undertake the defence of Berkeley, because I thought his reputation for piety and theological orthodoxy was far too well established to require any advocacy from myself."

Rājāh. — "Do you think, Vaiyāsika, you have gained anything for the Vedānt by last night's conference?"

Vaiyāsika. — "Blessings on your highness! I agree with Satyakāma that if a popular error has been disproved the result itself must be a gain to truth, and I must rejoice over it. I think also that the Vedānt, as inculcated in the Sūtras, does not involve the doctrine of *Māyā,* which some of our Śāstras condemn as Buddhism in disguise. The erroneous notion, disproved last night, virtually connected the Vedānt with the doctrine of *Māyā.* It is only just to our system that people should know it was not originally allied to that theory, and that it contended strenuously, against the Buddhists, for the reality of external objects. Whether later writers have mixed it up with the doctrine of *Māyā,* or not, is quite a different question."

The Chobdar now came in, and, with hands joined, announced that the Nepaulese colonel and the Buddhist Śāstri had come to bid farewell before leaving the station for Calcutta. "Show them, said his highness, into this private-audience chamber. You will not mind their presence, my learned friends. I am sure the Colonel will be pleased to see you. He takes great interest in philosophical discussions. He has adopted the Buddhist faith, though by birth a Kṣatriya, and a Hindu. The Śāstri, you saw last night, is his domestic priest."

The Colonel entered the room with his Śāstri, and was courteously received. The Rajah apologized to the Śāstri for the annoyance he had received the night before from the turbulent Vaiṣṇavas, and told him what the nature of *our* conference was—that some of us were anxious to disclaim the doctrine of Māyā, and that therefore Vaiyāsika was reading Śaṅkarācārya's arugment against the idealism of Buddhists.

"You have every right, said the Buddhist, to disclaim what you do not hold. I will not deny that Śaṅkara in his commentary on the Vedānt contends against, what you call, our idealism, but his argument is virtually shown to be untenable—not only by his own admissions in his commentaries on the Upaniṣads, but also by the general reception of our doctrine by all recent writers on the Vedānt."

Rajah.—"I do not quite understand you. Do you mean that Vedāntic writers have generally adopted any of your doctrines."

Buddhist.—"I have no doubt they have. In fact all your schools of philosophy have taken lessons from us."

Rajah.—"What lessons? Speak more definitely."

Buddhist.—"Blessings without number on your highness! The doctrine of *Māyā* and all your ideas of *Mukti* and *nirvāṇa* are borrowed from us. We first taught you to reflect on the miseries of life and transmigration, and to seek for perfect release from the bondage of works. Your highness will allow that our system is older than that of Vyāsa or Gotama."

Rajah.—"Of course I must allow that, for the Ṛṣis who founded our schools aimed at the refutation of Buddhism as one of their principal objects."

Buddhist.—"I do not know whether they *aimed* at the refutation of Buddhism. They have certainly done much for the *reproduction* of Buddhism, for which we must ever be thankful to them."

Rajah.—"How so? You astonish me. Speak more plainly. Name the doctrines one by one which you think we have learnt from you."

Buddhist.—"The very doctrine of *Māyā,* of which you were speaking before we came."

Rajah.—"How do you know we learnt it from you?"

Buddhist.—"Because before the rise of our Śākya Muni (blessings on him!) you knew nothing but rites and ceremonies, and your sole business was how to fulfil them agreeably to the formula of your Vedas. The great objects of your ambition were the good things of earth and heaven. For them you worked, for them you sacrificed, for them you prayed. Śākya was the first to teach you that the good things of earth and heaven were transient and illusory—that the external world by which you were so fascinated was a phantom, a māyā, a mirage, a mere flash of lightning. You cannot point to a single sage of your school who taught that idea before the age of Buddha."

Rajah.—"What! not Vaśiṣṭa, Vālmīki, or Viśwāmitra?"

Buddhist.—"It is not for me to say when those Ṛṣis lived, or what they taught; but I think I may affirm that none of you Ṛṣis can, like our Śākya, be singled out, even in your own traditions, as the original teacher of a novel doctrine in depreciation of the sensuous and carnal enjoyments promised in your older Vedas, and certainly no work, written decidedly before the age of Buddha, contains any description of the world as a mere phantom or mirage."

Rajah.—"What do you mean by writings before the age of Buddha?"

Buddhist.—"The Vedas certainly,—by which I mean, what your own writers themselves generally understand by the term, the Mantras and Brāhmaṇas. These do not represent the world as an illusion, nor direct the mind to any higher aspirations than sensuous enjoyments, whether of heaven or of earth."

Rajah.—"What say you of the Upaniṣads?"

Buddhist.—"The term Upaniṣad, please your highness, itself a vague designation, cannot mark out a separate division of the Vedas. It is applied to certain parts from doctrinal considerations. Any thing is called an Upaniṣad which sets forth a certain favourite doctrine—the doctrine of Brahma. Hence even the Bhagavad-gītā is called an Upaniṣad. I think therefore the authority of the Upaniṣads, as historical guides, cannot be very weighty. A small section might at any time have been added to a Veda with a view to set up a claim for antiquity in behalf of a favourite doctrine. Such claims ought to be received with great suspicion—especially when you consider that, in order to recommend their own novel doctrines, some of those spurious additions have gone the length of slighting the original Vedas themselves, and treating them with quite as much contempt as Śākya could ever have poured on them, calling them the repositaries of inferior doctrines, and classing them with mere children's books. And if any of the Upaniṣads bear marks of decided antiquity, they do not inculcate the doctrine of *māyā*.

"That the doctrine of the Brāhmins was not originally a *māyā-vāda* is evident from the Vedas themselves—*i.e.,* the Mantras and Brāhmaṇas. When, then, was it first taught? Who introduced it, where, and how? What is the history of this great innovation,—this transition from doctrines purely carnal to a denial of the material world? How came you into possession of that which you must acknowledge you did not possess originally, and which is decidedly not a natural development of your primitive doctrine of sacrifices and heavenly enjoyments? You cannot answer these questions. You cannot account for your possession of the doctrine of Māyā. We can. We tell you that Śākya taught it first—that, reflecting on the vanity of the world, he condemned the whole as a shadow without substance, a *māyā,* a *mirage.* His life is the best history of the doctrine. While you were scrambling and fighting for the pleasures of life, he renounced them all as vain and illusory. Myriads were convinced by his precepts and his example. But his party could not ultimately hold their place in Hindoostan. They were turned out, but their teaching was left as a legacy to their country. You banished them under the influence of party-spirit, but nevertheless the watchword of your philosophy has since continued to be *māyā.*"

Rajah.—"Well, my Buddhist friend—what other stolen goods do you find amongst us?

Buddhist.—"Our doctrine of *Nirvāṇa* and *mukti*. It is well known that your original Vedas propound to your aspirations nothing but the sensuous enjoyments of life, whether in heaven or earth,—houses, lands, cattle, and similar things. It is equally well known that Śākya Muni taught his disciples to regard those very enjoyments as vain, illusory, and fleeting, and to look forward to nirvāṇa, or complete release from life and transmigration. Teaching this transcendental doctrine, he exemplified it in his life—renouncing his home which was a palace, his dignity which was that of a throne, his enjoyments which were those of empire and sovereignty. These are facts patent to all the world, and you dare not dispute them. They are interwoven with the rise and progress of our society—a society which now overspreads the greater part of the vast continent of Asia. Even children are catechized on the vanity of this passing world from the great wall of China to the utmost boundary of Ceylon. If now you say you knew the same doctrine before the birth of Śākya, the burden of proof is decidedly on you. You are bound to account for the way you got possession of what we assert, and you cannot deny, to be a characteristic tenet of our great corporation. And you failing to prove your acquisition of it from a Brāhminical source, we hold ourselves justified in charging you with borrowing it from us.

"I repeat, your original Vedas say nothing of the miseries of life and transmigration, or of the necessity of complete escape from the bondage of works. Apavarga, nirvāṇa, and mukti are words unknown to your Vedas. You will refer me to your Upaniṣads. As the burden of proof is on you, because the doctrine of *mukti* involves an impatience of life, not only unknown to your earlier system, but at variance with its essential doctrines, you must adduce some stronger evidence than the Upaniṣads, and give a better account of its introduction than is furnished in those writings, before you can justly claim the merit of originating a doctrine so foreign to your ancient philosophy. I repeat the testimony of the Upaniṣads cannot be held satisfactory in a historical research. The name Upaniṣad is arbitrarily applied to works, or rather tracts, setting forth a favourite doctrine—that of Brahma. Such of the Upaniṣads, again, as chime, in our tunes and in our very words, on the miseries of life, both earthly and heavenly, and on the necessity of emancipation, contain references to doctrines and ideas so manifestly modern, that they cannot, consistently with historical criticism, be classed with the original Veda in point of antiquity.

"Some of them stand, also, in open rivalry with the four Vedas which they stigmatize as inferior. This shows that they are compositions of a much later date, when the Vedas had partially lost credit with the learned, probably owing to our own forcible denunciations of mere rites and ceremonies.

"Please your highness, I must crave your indulgent consideration of the points I have had the good fortune to advance in your presence. I think we may fairly claim the honor of having, at the cost of expatriation, somewhat diverted the Brāhminical mind from an empty ritual, stained with the blood of helpless animals, and of having taught it the elements of a philosophy to which it betakes itself to this day for rest and consolation. Śaṅkara may have argued strongly against our denial of the reality of external objects, but it is that very denial—it is the idea of a *māyā* and the prospect of *mukti* and *nirvāṇa,* which at the present moment constitute the hopes, and regulate the aspirations of all minds, capable of rising above the world and its fascinations."

The Nepaulese colonel apprehending that the hortatory strain, which the Buddhist had adopted, might be disrespectful to the Rajah, here stoppd his spiritual guide. "Enough, said he, enough!—a word to the wise.—You have stated our argument, and the Rajah will no doubt give it a fair consideration."

The colonel, then, after a few minutes of social conversation with the Rajah, took leave agreeably to the mode prevalent among men of distinction and dignity.

When the Nepaulese officer had left the room the Rajah asked Vaiyāsika what he thought of the Buddhist's charges against our philosophy.

"As far, said Vaiyāsika, as the doctrine of Māyā is concerned, I cannot say that the Buddhist's charge is entirely without foundation. Vyāsa does not inculcate that doctrine, nor do the Upaniṣads *Taittirīya, Aitareya* and *Kena*. Vijñāna Bhikṣu, in his commentary on the Sāṅkhya sūtra (1.22), only does us justice when he draws a marked distinction between the Brahma Sūtras and the theory of *māyā*. 'There is not a single Brahma Sūtra, says he, in which our bondage is declared to be a mere deception. As to the novel theory of māyā, propounded by persons calling themselves Vedāntists, it is only a species of the Vijñāna-vāda (of Buddhists).' The commentator then quotes the well known passage in the Padma-purāṇa in which that theory is called *disguised Buddhism.* He proceeds to say, 'that theory is not a tenet of the Vedānta, and it must be understood that the doctrine of the newfangled disguised Buddhists, who assert the theory of māyā, and reduce our bondage to a mere delusion, is in this way refuted[1].'"

Rajah.—"But is it not singular that learned Europeans, who have written on our philosophy in a friendly spirit, should not have discovered that the theory of Māyā is not inculcated in the Brahma sūtras, and that they should in reality be complimenting Buddhism by seeking analogies between their Bishop Berkeley and our Vedānta."

Satyakāma.—"Please your highness, there were at least two Europeans who knew how to distinguish between the original Vedānt and the theory of Māyā. Your highness has no doubt heard that an eminent scholar, Colebrooke by name, wrote digests of the sūtras of our several schools for the information of his countrymen. In his digest of the Vedānta, he translated many of Vyāsa's aphorisms, inculcating that God is the material cause of the universe, and remarked in conclusion that the notion that the versatile world is an illusion (Māyā); that all which passes to the apprehension of the waking individual is but a phantasy, presented to his imagination, and that every sensible thing is unreal and all is visionary, does not appear to be the doctrine of the text of the *Vedānt*. I have remarked nothing, he added, that countenances it in the Sūtras of *Vyāsa,* nor in the gloss of *Śaṅkara,* but much concerning it in the minor commentaries and elementary treatises.'

"This conclusion of Colebrooke proved unsatisfactory to Colonel Kennedy, the Bombay Officer you have already mentioned, who, in a letter to the Royal Asiatic Society, remarked : I am therefore at a loss to understand the grounds on which Mr. Colebrooke, in his essay on this system, has thus stated : 'The succeeding section affirms the important tenet of the Vedānta, that the Supreme Being is the material as well as the efficient cause of the universe; it is a proposition directly resulting from the tenor of the passages of the Vedas, and illustrations and examples adduced.' For the copy of the Sūtras now before me is divided in a different manner from the one referred to by Mr. Colebrooke, and I have not been able to find in them a single Sūtra which, in my opinion, would bear such a meaning. In fact, 'the Sanskrit language does not contain any term equivalent to the word matter; and even the four principal schools of Hindu philosophy concur in rejecting the notion of matter which has invariably prevailed in Europe[2].

Rajah.—"But who was the other European, who, you say, did not fall into the popular error about the Vedānta?"

Satyakāma.—"Sir G.C. Haughton; who defended Colebrooke and to whom Colonel Kennedy replied saying : 'If therefore, Māyā, or illusion, is not the doctrine of the Vedāntikas, as Sir G. C. Haughton maintains, and their belief is that the Creator and nature are one, and that he is the efficent and material cause of the universe, it must necessarily follow that their tenets are precisely the same as those which have been held to constitute material pantheism by every writer on philosophy. But, so far are the *Vedāntikas* from identifying God with matter, that they have always denied the existence of matter, and maintained that one sole undivided spiritual essence alone exists. * * * For otherwise, he (Sir G. Haughton) must have perceived that, if the creation is held to be material, the identifying the Creator with the creation necessarily turns the *Vedānta* system into one of pure materialism[3]."

Rajah.—"Well, Vaiyāsika, if you maintain that the doctrine of māyā is not an original tenet of the Vedānt, then you do pronounce us guilty of possessing stolen goods."

Satyakāma.—"Not exactly so, please your highness, if I may interpose a remark by way of qualifying the verdict. You may have, in your possession, goods claimable by Buddhists, but you may also on your part ask, whence did they themselves get them? We have heard of Śākya's teaching certain doctrines, but whence did Śākya himself learn them? He was brought up under the influence of Brāhminism, and if Brāhminism has taken lessons from his school, it is simply the tutor learning in his turn from a smart pupil."

Rajah.—"Speak more plainly, Satyakāma. Have we learnt from Buddhism any thing which our Vedas and Upaniṣads do not inculcate?"

Satyakāma.—"You have just heard Vaiyāsika repudiate the doctrine of Māyā, and refer to certain authorities which condemned it as Buddhism in disguise. That is certainly a lesson which Brāhminical philosophers have taken from Śākya Muni. The Upaniṣads, with perhaps one or two exceptions, (of which I shall speak presently), taught no such lesson. They do not maintain that the world is a mere phantom or shadow, a no *thing*. Most of them on the contrary promise sensuous enjoyments both here and hereafter as the rewards of knowledge. The *Taittirīya* says repeatedly, He who knows these great summaries of doctrine, thus explained, will obtain offspirng, cattle, holiness, food, and heaven[4].' These words form a sort of chorus, which is repeated five or six times in the short compass of the tract. The *Aitireya* too contains a similar chorus which it repeats at the end of two out of its three sections called the Upaniṣad part. He, knowing this, went upward on the dissolution of body, and, attaining all desires in that heavenly world, became immortal[5].' The *Kena* promises the same 'heavenly world' to those who attain knowledge[6]. The *Kaṭha,* also, to which a discerning translator has assigned a date posterior to the Sāṅkhya[7], is quite ignorant, notwithstanding its transcendentalism in other respects, of the idea that the world is a phantom and a shadow. The *Praśna* says, 'he who, thus knowing, knows the vital air, will not be wanting in offspring, and will be immortal[8].' It certainly does not inculcate the doctrine of Māyā. The word māyā does indeed occur in this Upaniṣad, but it is in the sense of a moral turpitude, akin to deceit and falsehood[9], disqualifying men from entering the world of Brahma, not in the philosophical sense of an illusion. The same Upaniṣad says, also, 'all this and whatever is of repute in heaven is subject of life. Do thou protect us, as a mother protects her sons; give us also prosperity and knowledge[10].' The *Iśa* says, 'performing duty in this world, one is to desire a life of a hundred years[11],' and adds nothing as to the unreality of the world. Nor has the Māṇḍukya, notwithstanding the grand *Kārikā* which Gauḍapāda has made on it, any thing to say against the reality of the external. It promises the *attainment of all desires,* and *of pre-eminence,* with a *learned progeny,* as the rewards of knowledge[12]. The *Bṛhadāraṇyaka* and *Chāndogya,* both a good deal larger than the tracts already named, are also silent on the subject of Māyā, or illusion. They say nothing about the unreality of the world.

"The *Bṛhadāraṇyaka* says, he who knows thus, *becomes a god,* and *attains heaven.* The ignorant, departing from this world, become slaves, the knowers, Brāhmins[13]. The *Chāndogya* assures to those who understand its mysteries, a heroic progeny, and heavenly enjoyments, as well as a life of *sixteen hundred years,* together with the free choice of *any pleasures* for which they may have a taste, whether it be for those of *food and drink,* or of *perfumery,* or of *music,* or whether it be for objects of filial, fraternal, or conjugal affection[14]. The *Muṇḍaka* is more sparing in its promises of sensuous enjoyments, but it does not decidedly countenance the theory of Māyā, and as this is the Upaniṣad which passes a sweeping censure on the Vedas, calling all four (to use the Buddhist Śāstri's words) the repositaries of inferior doctrines, and placing them in the same category with grammars and children's manuals,—it would hardly be correct chronologically to class it among books whose shortcomings it professes to supply. It would almost be a contradiction in terms to say that the *Muṇḍaka* is a section of the Atharva-veda, which it condemns, along with the others, as inferior science. And if it must be referred to a post Vedic age, it would be difficult to affirm that it was composed before the age of Buddha. But even the Muṇḍaka says nothing directly of Māyā, though it marks a period, still riper than that of any other Upaniṣd above named, and still further removed from the date of the original Vedas. It boldly condemns sacrifical rites with their eighteen members as vain and futile, and affixes the stigma of folly to those who perform or rely on them[15]. But it does not plainly say that the world is a phantom, or a shadow without substance."

Rajah.—"But the Buddhist Śāstrī seemed to admit that

some of the Upaniṣads did affirm the doctrine of māyā—only he would not allow their existence in the Vedic period. He likewise claimed the doctrine of Nirvāṇa or mukti as Buddhistic property."

Satyakāma.—"I cannot say that he has a right to claim the doctrine of *mukti* as the peculiar property of his sect, though the formation of a distinct school, fearlessly inculcating the ncessity of Nirvāṇa and Mukti, in open opposition to sacrificial rites and ceremonies, was perhaps an unprompted act of Śākya. The Brāhmins had long been panting for some reward more permanent than the terminable enjoyment of heaven. In some of the Upaniṣads, the Bṛhadāraṇyaka and the Chāndogya for instance, we see the commencement of a notion, that those who attain to the knowledge of their mysterious teaching *do not revolve again*[6], which Śaṅkara understands to imply a release from the necessity of transmigration. I do not see any trace of this notion in the *Taittirtīya, Aitareya, Māṇḍukya, Praśna, or Kena.* These were probably the productions of an anterior age, when the Brāhmins had only begun to identify the Creator with the creation, and when their pantheism had not yet got to its maturity. The notion of a release from life and birth had not attained any thing like the vigour of age in the *Bṛhadāraṇyaka* and *Chāndogya* either, for while the conception of sensuous enjoyments, as the rewards of knowledge, is constantly met with, that of a freedom from transmigration is but rarely found. Nor can the latter be said to occupy its natural place in the midst of boons, not only described in the language of voluptuaries, but also sometimes opposed to all ideas of decency[7]. One of the Upaniṣads, again, in which this crude notion of release from the necessity of transmigration is found, speaks of 'Kṛṣṇa, son of Devaki,' receiving a certain lesson from Ghora, son of Aṅgiras. The name, Kṛṣṇa, was not itself unknown in the Vedic period, but the 'son of Devaki' was a character of a later date. If then the passage be accepted as genuine, it must militate very much against the antiquity of the Chāndogya. If, on the other hand, the idea of an interpolation be admitted, I do not see any reason for not extending it to a few more isolated passages, promising freedom from sensuous existence, —a notion not less at variance with other Vedic promises than is the appellative *Devakiputra* with the ordinary rule of Vedic patronymics.

"The transcendental idea of emancipation has a more definite form in the *Muṇḍaka* and the *Kaṭha,* but these are Upaniṣads which, for reasons already mentioned, we may fairly assign to a much later, probably a post Buddhistic age. And it is only in the *Śwetāśwatara* that we see the notion in its full grown shape, and it was perhaps this very Upaniṣad which the Buddhist had in his mind, when he made the admission to which your highness refers. There we have the theory of māyā, and we hear of God as its projector in the sense of a juggler[8]. There, too, we have the doctrine of mukti, or release from transmigration and bondage. But, as the Buddhist contended not unreasonably, there we also see evident marks of a still more advanced era in the history of Brāhminical philosophy, and it would only harmonize the better with ascertained facts to ascribe its origin, or at least its recasting, to a period after the rise of Buddha."

Rajah. — "But what evident marks of a still more advanced age do you detect in it? The simple doctrine of Māyā cannot be held as such, for we have not conceded the Buddhist's claim that his sect originated it, albeit some of our own writers have called it Buddhism in disguise."

Satyakāma. — "As we are considering the Buddhist's charges against Brāhminism, it would certainly be unfair to call the *Śwetāśwatara* a post-Buddhistic work, merely because it inculcates the doctrine of māyā. But I think I can adduce at least two or three independent reasons for assigning it to an age much riper than the Vedic period. It appears to be a sort of *Śaiva* Upaniṣad. It sets forth the glory of Śiva. It speaks of Maheśwara, 'the surpreme among gods,' as the 'adorable Lord of the world[9].' The words Rudra, Iśāna, Hara, Bhava, which are all proper names of Śiva, are interspersed in the tract as designations of the Supreme Being. When five or six of the characteristic names of Śiva are repeatedly found, in a small tract of a hundred and twelve ślokas, as appellatives of the Creator, the fact may be considered conclusive proof of its fabrication by a modern Śaiva hand. The supreme being, Rudra, is again accosted as *Giriśanta* and *Giritra, or protector of the mountain,* holding an arrow in his hand. He has a *Śivā* or *Aghorā*—as his *body personified,* in the sense of a female emanation. These are descriptions which can only become intelligible by a reference to the legendary acts of Śiva, recounted in the Itihāses and Purāṇas. There we have Śiva, the lord of Kailāsa and Himālaya, armed with the bow Pināka, and having, as a wife, Pārvatī, otherwise called Śivā, originally an emanation from himself. The conception of Śiva and Śivā in later mythology is the very conception of the Supreme Being and Śivā, of Maheśwara and Prakṛti or Māyā[10], contained in the *Śwetāśwatara.*

"My next reason is that Kapila, the author of the Sāṅkhya, and his system the Sāṅkhya Yoga, are mentioned and lauded, and several terms are used which are peculiar to that system, such as *pradhāna, prakṛti, sākṣī,* together with something like a description of two eternal principles, which the modern followers of the Sāṅkhya are fond of quoting to this day in defence of their theory. This may be considered indisputable proof of the tract being a post-Sāṅkhya, and therefore a post Buddhist, Upaniṣad. And I may add in further confirmation of this view that the Śwetaśwatara speaks of the creation of Brahmā, and the production of the Veda through him under the agency of the Supreme Being[11], a legend of which no other Upaniṣad makes any mention, and which decidedly belongs to the later mythological period of the Purāṇas.

"Again atheistic speculations, deliberately attributing the

production of the universe to other causes than the Supreme Being, were unknown in the Vedic period, and are clearly *post* Buddhistic in point of date. The Śwetaświatara, however, addresses itself to a community in which such infidel speculations had already gained currency. It starts with the questions, 'Is Brahma the cause? Whence are we produced? Is time, nature (swabhāva), or succession of works, or chance, or the elements, or Puruṣa, the causes[12]." Now most of these hypothetical causes of the universe were originally inculcated in Buddhistic schools, though they may have been afterwards countenanced by Brāhminical atheists. Several Buddhistic schools were in fact designated by terms which were derived from some of those very theories. We have the *Swābhāvikas* from *Swabhāva,* or nature, to which they attributed the origin of all things. We have the *Kārmikas* from *Karma,* or works, which they considered as one of the causes, at least, of the universe. We have also those who contended that the conjunction of the material elements is sufficient of itself to produce intelligence, just as the intermixture of fermenting drugs begets the power of intoxication.[13] The *Śwetāświatara* must be glancing at those infidels when it proposes to refute the throries just mentioned, and especially when it adds afterwards, 'Some wise men talk of Nature (*Swabhāva*), others of time[14].' We have heard of no infidels in the Pre-buddhistic period attributing the creation of the universe to the sole operation of Nature or time, or the conjunction of the material elements, although we find some such doctrine reproduced in the Sāṅkhya. It would certainly be the very extreme of *sāhasa* (boldness) to deny under these circumstances that the Śwetāśwatara was written after the rise of Buddha.

"Your highness will observe that the doctrine of Māyā is definitely inculcated only in the *Śwetāśwatara* Upaniṣad, and that appears to be a *post* Buddhistic work. There can be no absurdity in attributing the eventual reception of that theory by the Brāhmins to the influence of Śākya's teaching. As to the idea of mukti or emancipation, the Brāhmins had certainly been pondering it for some time before the rise of Buddhism. It was probably they themselves who instilled it into the mind of Śākya. It was perhaps their own aspirations after something better than the degrading pleasures of Indra's territories, that first suggested the futility of rites and ceremonies to the fertile imagination of the young prince of Kapilāvastu. But it was the prince himself who appears to have imparted a coherent shape to the doctrine, which in some of the Pre-buddhistic Upaniṣads appears in a chaotic state of disconnected fragments, not unfrequently by the side of the very contrary idea of sensuous enjoyments. Śākya appears to have first separated the two by contending that rites and ceremonies do not contribute to our highest good, and that it was nirvāṇa alone which could secure our final escape from the miseries of sensuous life. In Post-buddhistic writings the notion of emancipation which pervades the philosophy of the Nyāya, the Sāṅkhya, and the Vedānt, appears in a consistent form as distinct from that of heavenly enjoyment. *Swarga* and *apavarga* are always constrasted. The Buddhists therefore have some right to say you have received lessons from them, though their own leader was originally your own pupil, indoctrinated in early life by your predecessors in the faith."

Rajah.—"But does not the disproof of the Māyā-vāda acquit the Vedāntist of the charge *master-atheist?*"

Satyakāma.—"If it acquit the Vedāntist of that charge, it arraigns him at once on another. Reverting to the text, *all this is God*, how can we acquit him of the charge of *deifying every material thing,* that is to say of teaching a system of gross pantheism? Since the theory of Māyā, which was his only defence against this latter charge, must as a plain matter of fact be separated from the Vedānta, I do not see how Colonel Kennedy's hypothetical inference can be denied."

Rajah.—"Whatever Colonel Kennedy's view of the discussion might have been, a single text, approvingly cited by the commentator, cannot decide such a weighty question. All that you may be allowed to say is, what Vaiyāsika himself contends for, that Vyāsa and Śaṅkara were not idealists. But you have not proved that they really taught material pantheism."

Satyakāma.—"Your highness is quite right in saying that this is a question which cannot be decided by a single text, however pointed; I mean, if you concede that the Vedas and the Sūtras are, in some respects at least, human compositions. For if you ahdere unflinchingly to the story of Brahma's breathing the Vedas out, whole and entire, then even a single text ought to decide the question however weighty. Still I will not press that point for the present, but, treating the Vedas and the Sūtras as human compositions, will make such allowances as the rules of liberal criticism may call for. A single isolated passage may be explained away in such a case. The general tenor of the work must afford the key to the interpretation of detached texts.

"May we then, with your highness's permission, review the general tenor of the sūtras of Vyāsa with reference to the relation which Brahma bears to the world? [The Rajah nodded, and Satyakāma continued.] Professing to deduce his system from a critical examination of the texts of the Vedas, Vyāsa commences his work by assailing the Sāṅkhya, and denounces Kapila's theory on the origin of the Universe. He prosecutes this aggressive war against Kapila, by appeals to the Vedas, almost throughout the whole of the first chapter. He labours to show that the dogmas of his antagonists are contradicted by express passages of the Upaniṣads, and that the texts on which they rely may be otherwise explained. In the course of this war on the Sāṅkhya, he takes occasion to declare that wherever the Vedas speak of any substance, as a cause of the universe, they can mean no other than the one Supreme Intelligence which prevades all space, and which will eventually be the receptacle of all things. He says the *puruṣa* (soul) *in the sun, the puruṣa in the eye, the little puruṣa no bigger than a thumb, the puruṣa of the measure of a span, the ether in the heart, all* these personifications, set forth in the Upaniṣads, are no other than the supreme Brahma who is without a second. So likewise the passages which speak of certain inanimate things as the primary element, *e.g.*, food, air, breath of life, light, ether, are referred to Brahma. If it be asked what right the author had to identify those descriptions with Brahma, the commentator reminds you of the great charter of Pantheism, the text, *All this is Brahma.* Vyāsa does not however say, except by implication, that the world is identical with Brahma, or that Brahma is *Prakṛti,* nature, or *substance* of the universe, before the 23rd sūtra of the 4th Pāda of the 1st chapter."

Rajah.—"But does he, in the earlier portion of his work, say by implication that the world is identical with Brahma?"

"The idea is undoubtedly found, said Satyakāma, in the following sūtras : 'Because of resolution of absorption into the spirit.' (I. i. 9.) 'It (the Veda) declares its (the world's) assimilation into Him. (I. i. 19.) 'He is the Eater, because he takes into Himself moveables and immoveables.' (I. ii. 9.) 'Because it is distinguished as the place to be approached by the emancipated.' (I. iii. 2.) 'It (the Sāṅkhya) is not true, it is disproved, because of observation.' (I. i. 5.) 'From desires, too, there is no room for the Sāṅkhya inference[25].' (I. i. 18.) The two Sūtras, last mentioned, evidently refer to texts in which the Supreme Being is represented as desirous of *multiplying himself* by the process of creation.

"I, of course, continued Satyakāma, make use of Śaṅkara's authorized gloss in interpreting the above sūtras, but I am not confounding the commentator's *deductions* with the author's language. The light which the commentator throws on the Sūtras must be accepted, but it would be quite unphilosophical to attribute to the author of the Sūtras all that the fertile mind of his commentator has imagined. Were I to consider every sentence of Śaṅkara to be an exact index of Vyāsa's mind, I could recognize many more decided instances of his pantheism before coming to the 23rd sūtra I. iv. But it is at that sūtra that the author commences a series of aphorisms, unhesitatingly pronouncing God to be the material cause of the world."

Rajah.—"Do you mean to say that Śaṅkara's commentary contains any misconception of Vyāsa's teaching?"

Satyakāma.—"I do not exactly mean that, but I do not wish to lose sight of the distinction between the author and his commentator."

Rajah.—"What do you say, Vaiyāsika, to this?"

Vaiyāsika.—"As Satyakāma has not charged the commentator with *misrepresenting* the author's views, I do not wish to say anything."

Rajah.—"What authority then do you attach to Śaṅkara's commentary?"

Vaiyāsika.—"Śaṅkara deserves all credit for learning, honesty, and clearness of mind. He at once gets at the mind of his author, and expounds the meaning plainly and fully. I cannot conceive the possibility of his misapprehending a single expression of Vyāsa,—nor can I imagine it to be within the range of a mortal's capacity to add to or subtract from what Śaṅkara has said. To say less would involve a sacrifice of fulness. To say more would be incurring prolixity. There is nothing redundant in his commentary, nor any thing defective. You cannot improve it by adding or curtailing. Still Śaṅkara was not a Ṛṣi. The author of the *Śaṅkaradigvijaya* has indeed represented him as an incarnation of Śiva[16], but we have not received that story in any other light than that of a complimentary tribute for his successful refutation of Buddhism. We cannot say he was essentially infallible. Vyāsa was a Ṛṣi. He was essentially infallible, for Ṛṣis cannot err."

Satyakāma.—"Have not different Ṛṣis,—Gotama, Kapila, Vyāsa,—taught mutually conflicting doctrines? Are we then still to suppose them all to be infallible?"

Raja.—"But a learned writer has suggested that their differences are capable of being reconciled[17]."

Vaiyāsika.—"Without waiting for Satyakāma's reply, I shall at once admit that the differences are not capable of being reconciled. At least Śaṅkarācārya did not think they were. He not only condemns the opinions of the Nyāya and the Sāṅkhya on the origin of the universe, but he brands their authors as discordant heretics[18]. There is certainly no reason for saying that Gotama lays greater stress on *sensation* than Kapila, or that Kapila speaks more of *emotions* than Gotama. Nor can it be urged that the authors of the Nyāya and the Sāṅkhya undertook to teach their systems on *the foundation of the Vedas.* The fact of their differences is certainly a difficulty with us, but still we hold that Ṛṣis are infallible. We are not bound to receive their teaching if it be opposed to the Veda, but we must not be wanting in reverence to their memory. But why do you press on our attention a point which we confess is attended with some difficulty, and which is irrelevant to our present discussion? Go on with your review of the Vedānt teaching."

Satyakāma—"Well then, with reference to Sūtra 23. iv. I., it runs thus[29],—'He is also *prakṛti* (the substance 'of the world) because the Question and Example require 'it.' Śaṅkara expounds the aphorism thus. 'It has already been said that as inquiry into duty is necessary for propserity, so inquiry into Brahma is also necessary for emancipation. Brahma again has been defined as 'He' from whom are the prdouction &c., of this.' But that definition is equally applicable [both to material and 'efficient causes] to the substance, such as the clay and gold are in the case of the jar and necklace, and to the agent such as the potter and the goldsmith. Hence the 'doubt, *of what kind is the causality of Brahma?* Here it might appear that He is only the efficient cause. Why? 'Because we hear of observation preceding the agency. The agency of Brahma is indeed found preceded by observation, in the following texts. 'He observed. He created the vital air.' Now agency with observation is seen only in efficient causes such as potters and others. Therefore it is proper to understand the causality of God as simply that of an agent. The universe, again, as a work, is composed of parts, inanimate, impure. Its cause must likewise be of the same kind, for cause and effect are homogeneous. But Brahma does not answer to this description; witness the texts, 'without parts, without work, quiet, unblemished, unstained.' 'In fine, a material cause, different from Brahma, and 'possessed of impurity and similar qualities,—such a cause as is set forth in the *smṛti,*—should be looked for; and as to the text declaring the causality of Brahma, it would be quite sufficient to consider Him as the efficient agent (alone). To this argument, (continues Śaṅkara) we reply : Brahma is to be understood 'as the *Prakṛti,* the substance or material, and also the the efficient cause. Not simply the efficient cause. Why? Because the congruity of the question and example rquires it. This is the question, 'Did you ask him for the doctrine by which that which is unheard becomes heard, that which is unthought of becomes thought of, that which is unknown becomes known?' 'Herein it was understood that by the knowledge of one, 'all others, though unknown, become known. Now it is by the knowledge of the material cause, that every thing else is known, because the material cause is inseparable from the effect. But the efficient cause is not inseparable from the effect, because a difference between the architect and the edifice is seen in the world. This, again, is the example, —'As O beloved! by means of one clod of earth every earthy form is known, it being in truth only earth, though called, in words, a modification.' Thus is the material cause set forth in the Vedas. Also, as by means of one magnet, every [magnetized] iron becomes known, and as by means of one nail-clipper, every black iron is known.' So also elsewhere, 'What is that, Sir, which being known, all this becomes known?' on this question the 'example is; as in the earth herbs are produced.' 'The Spirit being seen, heard, thought of, known, all this is known,'—on this question the example is, 'as one cannot take hold of the external sound of a drum that is beaten, but by taking up the beaten drum itself, the sound of the stroke is also taken up.' Thus in every Vedānt 'text bearing on the point, the question and example are 'to be known as proving material causality. Again, in the sentence, 'From whom all these creatures proceed, '—*from whom* is in the ablative case; hence since it refers especially to the maker's material, it must be expressive of the material cause. His efficient causality is to be deduced from the want of any other agent. As in the world, the material causes, such as earth and gold, need the working of potters, goldsmiths, and other agents, not so does the material cause Brahma need another agent, for before the creation we learn there was one only without a second. The want of another agent is also deducible form the congruity of the question and example, for if there were another agent, separable from the material, then by means of one thing every thing else could not be known, and the question and example would become incongruous. Hence from the want of another agent, is deduced the spirit's agency, and from the want of another substance his material causality.'

"The next Sūtra (24th) confirms the above view. 'From the doctrine of his desire too.' Śaṅkara thus expounds it. 'The doctrine of desire, too, demonstrates the spirit's efficiency and material causality. He desired, 'let me become many, let me be born.' Also 'He saw '&c.' 'Here from the independent action preceded by deire he is inferred as the actor; from the words 'let me become many,' because of individual souls being the objects of the thought or intention of multiplication, he is inferred to be the substance or material cause also[20].' The founder of the Vedānta School goes on urging the same doctrine. 'Because the two processes [of springing from and being resolved into] are both manifestly spoken of in the Vedas[21].' Śaṅkara explains it thus : 'This is the exposition of the state of *prakṛti*. Hence too is 'Brahma the material cause, for the Vedas, manifestly taking Brahma to be the only cause, speak of production and absorption. All these elements proceed from ether and are resolved into ether.' That from which any thing proceeds and into which it is resolved is called the material cause—as the earth is of rice and wheat. 'By the use of the word 'manifest,' too, he shows that 'the words from ether exclude the supposition of any other material. Nor is the resolution of an effect ever seen to be into any other than the material cause.' Again, says Vyāsa, 'Because of his creating himself—by mutation.' Śaṅkara thus expounds it : 'Hence too is Brahma the material cause—for with reference to his operation, it is said 'He himself created himself' thereby indicating that he was both the agent and the object of the creation—'himself' signifying the object—he himself 'created' signifying the agent. But now how can one, 'already held to be the Maker, be again represented as an object, *being made?* We reply, by mutation. The spirit, before proved to be existent, altered himself, by a particular modification. It is by particular modifications that the mutation of materials like earth and other things is found. The specification, too, of 'He himself' excludes the supposition of another agent[22].' Vyāsa continues: 'He is also sung as the womb[23].' Śaṅkara 'explains it thus—'Hence also is Brahma the material cause, for the expression 'Brahma is the womb' is read in the Vedānt, thus 'the Lord, the creative soul, Brahma, is the womb,' also, 'the self-restrained see the womb of the creation.' The womb is popularly understood to be the material cuase—thus the earth is the womb of herbs and trees. The fourth section, and consequently the first chapter, concludes with the aphorism, 'Hereby all (hostile tenets) are refuted[24].'

"The above extracts, continued Satyakāma, prove that according to the teaching of Vyāsa and Śaṅkara the substance or material of the universe is God, and that the world is only a development of Him. Such a view of Brahma's relation to the world could not but be startling. Many were the objections preferred by the followers of the Sāṅkhya and Nyāya, which Śaṅkarācārya cited and answered. I cannot say he has fairly met them,—but let us now review that discussion.

Objection[25].—'Brahma is not the material cause for this has a characteristic difference, and so also the 'Veda says.' This is Vyāsa's epitome of his adversaries' sayings. Śaṅkara thus expounds it. 'The objection, raised on the authority of the Smṛti against Brahma's substantial and efficient causality has been refuted; that founded on argumentation is now being disposed of. It may be asked how could there be room for argumentation on a point settled by the Śāstra? May not the Śāstra be an independent authority in the case of Brahma, as it is in the case of Dharma? But then it would be a question of practice, whereas Brahma is a demonstrable substance. Hence further evidence is admissible. And so he anticipates the logical objection, 'This has a characteristic difference &c.' You say that the sentient Brahma, the cause of the world, is also its *prakṛti*. This is not congruous. Why? Because of the characteristic difference between this, the fabric, and its substance. This world, which you would describe as a production of Brahma, is of a different character from Him, being perceived to be non-sentient, impure. And Brahma is declared to be of a different character from the world, *i.e.*, sentient and pure. The releation of material and fabric is never seen where there is characteristic difference; for neckchains and other golden fabrics cannot have earth for their material, nor earthen pots, gold.Earthen fabrics are made only of earth, and golden of gold. So this world, too, being connected with pleasure, pain, and delusion, must be the 'production of a non-sentient cause, also connected with pleasure, pain, and delusion, and not of Brahma, which is of a different character. That Brahma has a characteristic difference is evident from our observation of the world's being non-sentient and impure. This world is indeed impure, because, being a compound of pleasure, pain, and delusion, it is a cause of delight, sorrow, and grief, and because it consists of the opposite varieties of heaven and hell. And it is non-sentient, for we see that it serves the sentient as an object or an instrument. But there cannot be the relation of server and served where there is equality. Nor can two lamps serve each other. But cannot the sentient too serve as the object and instrument of the enjoyer, after the manner of master and servant? No! for even as regards master and servant, it is the non-sentient part that serves the sentient. That which is the attribute of one that is sentient, such as the understanding, itself non-sentient, does service to another that is sentient, but the sentient himself does neither service nor damage to another sentient. Sentient actors have no superior. Thus do the followers of the Sāṅkhya believe. Therefore object and instrument are non-sentient. Nor is there any sign of sentiency in wood and earth, and this distinction between the sentient and non-sentient is notorious in the world. Therefore because of its characteristic difference from Brahma, this world cannot have him for its material. Perhaps some one will say, "since the Vedas declare that the world has a sentient being for its material, I shall for that very reason hold the world to be sentient, because the quality of the material follows in the fabric. Its sentiency may be latent owing to some especial modification. As in souls, obviously sentient, sentiency does not properly appear in the state of sleep or trance, so the sentiency of wood and earth may also be only latent. Because also of this difference of manifestation and non-manifestation, and of colour and no colour, notwithstanding that sentiency is common to objects and instruments and to spirits, the predominant quality is not affected. As also flesh, sauce, and rice, though all of one common element, earth, are still subservient to each other, because of their several distinctions, so also here. Therefore the known distinction is not affected.' 'It is with difficulty that this person explains away the characteristic difference between sentiency and nonsentiency, but he cannot explain away the characteristic difference between purity and impurity. Nor can he really explain away the other either, and therefore it is added [by Vyāsa in his summary of the Sāṅkhya objection,] 'And so also the Veda.' This sentiency of all things, which is not held among men, is a mere hypothetical deduction from the Vedic teaching of a sentient material cause, depending solely on tht teaching. But it is negatived by Vedic teaching itself, for the Veda also inculcates that (chracteristic difference). 'And so' the Veda itself expresses the characteristic difference—thus, 'Knowledge and ignorance'—teaching thereby that some part being non-sentient, the nonsentient world is characteristically different from the sentient Brahma. But do not some texts inculcate the sentiency of the elements and organs, (otherwise) considered non-sentient? Thus, 'the earth spake, the waters 'spake,' and, 'that light saw, those waters saw.' These texts teach that the elements are sentient. So do others about the organs, thus, 'these my vital airs debating on 'what is good went to Brahmā'—also, 'they said, do thou 'sing us.' To this the objector replies, (as Vyāsa represents 'him in the next Sūtra II. i. 5.) 'But that is proved to be a mere personification, both by the distinction and the usage. Śaṅkara again thus expounds Vyāsa's curt representation of his adversary's rejoinder : 'The word *but* contradicts the previous supposition. From texts such as 'the earth spake,' one cannot suppose that the elements and organs are sentient, because it is a mere personification. Sentient gods, imagined as personifications of earth and other elements, and of speech and other organs, are described as speaking and discoursing, which are acts of sentient beings; not that elements and organs speak. Why? Because there is the distinction and the usage. A distinction has been before established between enjoyers and elements and organs, marking the division between sentient and non-sentient. That would not consort with the notion of every thing being sentient. Moreover in the *Kauṣitakī,* the vital airs are distinguished by the word *gods,* in order to show that the sentient divinities which direct them, are meant, and not the mere organs themselves, thus these my gods debating what is good, and, these 'gods know the supreme felicity to be in the vital air.' And in the figurative language of the Mantras, as well as in the Itihāsas and Purāṇas, there are every where personifications of sentient gods introduced. Again, texts, such as Agni becoming speech, entered the mouth,' exhibit gods personifying the organs. In the context of the passage about vital airs, also, we have, they, the vital airs, went and spoke to Prajāpati the father.' The going to Prajāpati was for the ascertainment of excellency, and the speech, directly and indirectly, sets forth the excellence of the vital airs. So also the taking of offerings to him. Such following of acts like ours confirms the personification. In the passage, 'that light saw,' we are also to observe that the seeing is predicated of the presiding Supreme Divinity, personifying his own modification. The world is therefore characteristically different from Brahma, and because of the difference he cannot be its material.'

"I have no great respect, continued Satyakāma, for the Sāṅkhya philosophy, but the above argument, enforced by its adherents, appears irresistibly powerful. I do not acquiesce in every thing continued in the objection, so candidly and elaborately represented by Śaṅkara, but there is no denying that the external universe *is* characteristically different from Brahma, and that it cannot have the spirit for its *subject matter,* which indeed is a contradiction in terms."

Rajah.—"But has not Śaṅkarācārya given a sufficient reply to that argument?"

Satyakāma.—"His reply is singularly unsatisfactory. Let us consider it in detail. The next Sūtra (II. i. 6,) reads, But it is seen[26],' which Śaṅkara thus expounds. That which you urge, that the universe cannot, because of its characteristic difference, have Brahma for its substance, is not conclusive;

for from men and other animals, well known to be sentient, the production of hair, nails, and other things, different in character, is witnessed in the world; and that of scorpions and other insects from cowdung and other things, well known to be nonsentient. If you object that the causes of hair and nails, which are non-sentient, are only the bodies of men and other animals which are no other than non-sentient, and the productions of cowdung and other matter, which are non-sentient, are the bodies of scorpions and other inscects which are no other than non-sentient; my reply is, here too there is a difference in the characters; something non-sentient becomes the receptacle of the sentient and something does not. Hence there is a difference. Great, again, is this natural mutation, because of the difference in colour between the human and other bodies (on the one hand,) and hair, nails, &c. (on the other); so also between cowdung and other matter and scorpions and other insects. Nor could there be the relation of material and fabric if there were too much similarity [and no difference at all in the characters]. Again if you say that there is a certain earthiness, or other natural character, in the human and other bodies, which is also found in hair, nails, and other things, and a similar one in cowdung and other matter, which is also found in scorpions &c. I reply, so is there a natural character in Brahma, even his entity, which is also found in ether and other things. By finding fault with the notion of the universe having Brahma for its material, because of a difference of characters, tell me, do you refer to the absence of the whole of Brahma's nature in the effect, or of any part of it, or merely of His Intelligence? In the first case your argument would destroy the very possibility of the relation of material and fabric, for there cannot be such things, if the one is to have no excess above the other. In the second case the argument is not founded in fact, for, as I have already said, one natural character of Brahma, *i.e.,* his entity, exists in ether and other things. As to the third case, it has no example. Against them who assert that Brahma is the cause, what example can be adduced of a thing which is not endowed with sentiency *having other material than* Brahma,—when we declare that all this, which has sprung from a substance, has Brahma for its material?'

"I submit, continued Satyakāma, the reply is not satisfactory. The example of hair and nails, as products of the animal body, gives no countenance to the relation which Śaṅkara would establish between the world and Brahma. Hair and nails, themselves material, (or earthy as he himself calls them), are produced from the animal body, also material, or earthy. The example would be analogous if hair and nails were products of the *immaterial* and *unearthy soul.* The Sāṅkhya would not however admit such a premiss, nor does Śaṅkara, though commencing the argument with such a suggestion, insist on it in the end. But then he tells us that as the relation of cause and effect between the animal body and hair and nails is verified by the property of earthiness, common to both, so may the relation of cause and effect, or rather material and fabric, between Brahma and the universe, be verified by the common property of entity. We shall see afterwards, when we review his theory of *avidyā,* or ignorance, whether this common property is compatible with that theory. Meanwhile I must remark that this part of his argument involves an *ati-vyāpti*. It proves too much. To say that mere entity is a character on which the relation of cause and effect, or rather of material and fabric, may be founded, is simply to assert that merely because two things exist, the one may be a material of the other. Then any thing may be proved to be a material of every fabric. When you are called upon to show in what respect can this fabric, the universe, exhibit a sameness of quality with its material Brahma, you say it is in repsect of entity. But entity is a universal attribute of every thing that exists. It cannot be a characteristic attribute of a particular cause or effect. The argument involves the fallacy which Kaṇāda has expressed by the formula, *because it has horns, therefore it is a cow.* The general attribute of all horned animals cannot be an especial attribute of the individual cow.

"Then, again, the Sāṅkhya comes forward with a counter assertion, directly negativing the Vedāntist's proposition. He says the non-sentient *cannot* be a product of the sentient. An assertion, such as this, might be at once disproved by a single example, if one could be adduced, and it is therefore for the opponent of the Sāṅkhya to dispose of it in that way if he can. Sāṅkara however challenges an example in support of the Sāṅkhya's negative proposition, and asks for a parallel instance of an inanimate fabric being produced from a material other than Brahma. It would be easier for him to disprove the Sāṅkhya's negative, than for the Sāṅkhya to adduce an instance in its support. Still it might not be unjust in itself to demand such an example. But Śaṅkara, when he demands the example, demands it in such a way as would make it absolutely impossible for the Sāṅkhya to satisfy him. He assumes that whatever exists has Brahma for its material! This is to ask for a thing you have antecedently resolved not to accept. It is in fact a mockery, and is in other words an evasion of the argument. No man can undertake to argue a case where his adversary plainly tells him he will admit no counter evidence. When you allowed room for the Sāṅkhya's argument—when you boasted that if *Veda alone were proof* and arguments disallowed, then the question of Brahma would be degraded into one of mere practice—nay, when you confidently added, that, as, when there are conflicting texts one may be overruled by another, so, in the conflict of arguments, Veda itself may be overruled by the force of proof[27]—you virtually staked the correctness of your inference on the result of a logical discussion. But directly you enter into the argument, you endeavour to stop your adversary's mouth by a *sādhya-sama,* or an assumption, which not only amounts to, but is rather identical with the very proposition under examination. If such was your intention, why did you not say so to the Sāṅkhya at the first onset? Why did you meet him in the field of argumentation? Why did you not say plainly that since you cannot agree with the Sāṅkhya on first principles, you are mutually *nigrahasthāna* to each other, or not in a position to carry on a discussion."

Rajah. – "Well, go on with your review of the Vedānta Sūtras, we shall have plenty of time for discussion afterwards."

Satyakāma. – "I cheerfully acquiesce. Here then is another objection preferred by the followers of the Sāṅkhya.[28] Because of contact with in dissolution, there is incongruity. They say if a gross, material, inanimate, divisible, and impure effect have Brahma for its cause, then at the dissolution, when the effect resolves into, and becomes inseparable from, the cause, it will defile the cause by association with its own qualities. Therefore since at the dissolution the cause Brahma must become impure like its effect, the doctrine of the Upaniṣad, that the cause of the universe is omniscient Brahma, becomes incongruous. Moreover, because of all distinctions being then dissolved (by absorption in Brahma) there cannot, at the reproduction, be a production of the distinction of enjoyer and enjoyment owing to want of direction. This is another incongruity, Again, enjoyers being at that time inseparable from the supreme Brahma, and a re-production being inevitable even at the dissolution occasioned by works, the emancipated also are liable to that reproduction. This is another incongruity still. If you say the universe may, even in dissolution, remain distinct from the Supreme Brahma, then there cannot be a dissolution at all, nor can the effect be inseparable from the cause. This is likewise an incongruity.'

The Vedāntist replies[29] : Not so, there being example.' Śaṅkarācārya expounds the aphorism in the following manner. 'There is no incongruity in our doctrine. That which is said as to the effect defiling the cause by contact with its own qualities on being resolved thereinto; it is not a valid objection. Why? Because we have instances on our side. There are instances of effects not defiling the cause by contact with their own qualities on being resolved thereinto; *e.g.*, earthen saucers and other manufactures, having mud for their material, and being in their separate states distinguished as large, small, middling, do not, when resolved into their material, affect it with their own qualities. Neckchains, having gold for their material, do not, when dissolved, affect their material with their own qualities. The fourfold organic modifications, too, of earth (viviparous, oviparous &c.) do not in dissolution affect it with their own qualities. But on your side there is no example. Nor would it be a dissolution at all, if the effect, when resolved into the cause, could continue with its own qualities. And though we say that the cause and effect are inseparable, we mean by such words as *mere names,* that the effect is of the same nature as the cause, not the cause as the effect. The objector, again, far understates his own argument, when he says that the effect may, in dissolution, affect the cause with its own qualities. For the same contact remains in the state of existence too, because cause and effect are held inseparable. All this is the same as this spirit. All this is Spirit.' This is immortal in its front, even Brahma.' All this is indeed Brahma.' These texts teach that the cause and effect are inseparable in all the three states. Now the argument by which this difficulty is removed holds equally good in regard to dsissolution also, viz. that the effect and its qualities, being fictions of Ignorance, cannot affect the cause. There is also this other example. As a juggler is not himself touched in any of the three states by the projected illusion, because of its not being a substance, so the Supreme Spirit is untouched by the illusion of the world. As also a seer of dreams is not touched by the illusion, seen in dreams, because the pleasing vision does not follow the waking state so the one invariable observer of the three-fold states [of production, continuance, and dissolution] is not touched by the variable three-fold state. For the appearanace of the Supreme Spirit, as in the form of the three-fold states, is but an illusion, like that of a rope in the form of a snake.

Thus has it been said by scholars versed in the Vedānt doctrine: when the animal soul, sleeping under an eternal delusion, awakes, then it understands itself to be uncreated, unsleeping, undreaming, without a second.' Thus that which has been said that in dissolution the cause may be defiled by the grossness of the effect, is absurd. This, again, which has been said that all distinctions being then merged in a state of no distinction, there cannot be a directing cause for the reproduction of the distinctions, is also no objection, for there are examples, on our side. As in sleep and *samādhi* (or fixed meditation), notwithstanding the natural attainment of a state of no distinction, the distinctions come to pass again in the waking state, as before, because of ignorance not being destroyed,—so may it be here too. There is the Veda here also; All these creatures, having attained to the [eternally] existent, did not know that they had attained to the [eternally] existent.' Whatever they be in this state, whether it be a tiger, or a lion, or a wolf, or a boar, or an insect, or a fly, or a gnat, or a musquito, they become the same [in the reproduction]. As in the state of existence [in life], notwithstanding that there is no distinction from the Supreme being, still the practice of distinction after the manner of a dream is, owing to ignorance, not precluded, so may the capacity of distinction be inferred also in dssoultion owing to ignorance. By this the idea of the reproduction of the emancipated is also refuted, because their ignorance is dispelled by full knowledge. With reference to the other supposed alternative, that the world may, then, in dissolution remain distinct from the Supreme Brahma, that is also refuted, simply by its not following necessarily from the premises. Hence this doctrine of the Upaniṣad is consistent.'

Rajah.—"I do not wish to interrupt you, Satyakāma, but is not this a Sūtra in which Vyāsa and Śaṅkarācārya inculcate the theory of Māyā? What do you say Vaiyāsika to this?"

Vaiyāsika.—"Please your highness, there is nothing in

the language of Vyāsa that countenances such a theory. He only relies on examples seen in the world, which Śaṅkara correctly expounds notwithstanding that he adds something about Ignorance."

Satyakāma.—"And I may add with reference to Śaṅkara himself that he seems to make use of a convenient theory, inculcated by certain scholars versed in the Vedānt doctrine,' rather than inculcate it himself. He certainly takes advantage of it in self-defence, and so far acquiesces in that doctrine, but he does not enforce of argue for it. His primary argument, suggested by the words in the Sūtra, has reference to examples.' Earthen saucers do not, when in dissolution, affect their material with their specific qualities, nor neck-chains their gold."

Rajah.—"Well go on, Satyakāma, but we must consider afterwards to what extent Śaṅkara has adopted the theory of Māyā after having so forcibly written against the idealism of Buddhists."

Satyakāma.—"A third Sāṅkhya objection is thus represented[30]. It may be said this distinction between enjoyer and enjoyment is well known in the world. The sentient soul is the enjoyer. Objects, such as sound, are enjoyments. For instance Devadatta is enjoyer. Food is enjoyment. The distinction would be destroyed if the enjoyer were to become the enjoyment, or the enjoyment the enjoyer. Such interchange of conditions between the two would be inevitable, if they are identical with their supreme cause Brahma. This confounding of the distinction is not reasonable. As the distinction between enjoyer and enjoyment is visible at the present moment, so must it be supposed as to the past and future. Therefore because of the confounding of the well known distinction between enjoyer and enjoyment, this theory of Brahma as the cause is absurd. If any one bring forward this objection, the author (Vyāsa) would reply, 'it is as in the world.'

Such a difference is proved even on our theory, because it is seen in the world. For it is usual to consider, at the same time, as different from one another, and also characteristically alike, waves, froths, and bubbles which are various modifications of the sea, though essentially water, and therefore identical with it. Nor can froths and waves which, though of the same substance as water, are various modifications of the sea, lose their separate individualities; neither are they different in substance from the sea because they are individually separate. So here too there is no *confusion* of enjoyer and enjoyment, nor is any thing different from the supreme Brahma."

A fourth objection is thus noticed[31]. Because of one being styled the other, there is the objection of doing injury.' Śaṅkara thus expounds it. The theory of a sentient cause is again objected to. If the production of the universe be from a sentient cause, then objections present themselves on the score of doing injury. Why? Because of one being styled the other. The Veda styles another, that is the embodied soul, Brahma; thus in the assurance [given to Śwetaketu as follows.] He is the Spirit, thou art He, O Śwetaketu.' Or [as it may be otherwise construed] another, that is Brahma, is styled the embodied soul : thus, Having created it, he entered into itself,' representing God, the unchanged creator, to be the embodied soul by his entrance into his own production. The same also appears from the text, by entering as this animal spirit I will make names and forms.' The supreme divinity, describing the animal soul by the word spirit, shows that the embodied soul is not different from Brahma. Therefore that which is the agency of Brahma is in truth the agency of the embodied soul. Hence, being an independent actor, he would do that which was for his own benefit, and pleasing to himself,—not that which was injurious to himself, namely, the assemblage of vanities, such as birth, death, decay, and disease. No one indeed makes of his own accord a prison for himself, and enters it; nor, being himself perfectly unstained, would he betake himself to a body that is extremely foul. And even if he had created a world some how or other, he would willingly renounce that which was a cause of pain, and take to that which was a cause of pleasure. And he would remember that this variegated and diversified world was created by himself. For every person, when he has distinctly performed an act, remembers, this was done by myself.' Again, as a conjurer can, at pleasure, easily dissolve an illusion, [or charm], projected [or set up] by himself, so would the embodied soul dissolve this his own creation. But the embodied soul cannot, at pleasure, easily dissolve the body, though his own. Thus from non-observation of beneficial acts, it may be inferred that the world is produced from an irrational and inanimate cause.'

It is thus answered 'But it is the superior, because a difference is inculcated.' Śaṅkara thus expounds it. The word *but* contrdicts the foregoing objection. We call that the world's creator which is omniscient, all powerful, Brahma, eternal, pure, intelligent, free, true in his nature, superior to and different from the embodied soul. There cannot against him be objections on the score of doing injury. He has no benefit to bring about, nor injury to avert, being eternally free. Nor can there ever be in him any lack of knowledge, or of power, being omniscient and all powerful. The embodied soul however is not so. Against him such objections may be taken on the score of doing injury. But we do not call him the creator of the world. Why so? Because a difference is inculcated. The spirit is to be seen, heard, thought of, meditated on, sought, enquired after. The embodied soul is then endued with the existent. The spirit followed by the knowing spirit.' Such inculcation of distinction between agent and object shows that Brahma is superior to the embodied soul. But is not identity also inculcated? Thus, thou art He! How then can the two contradictory ideas, identity and distinction, stand? This is no fault. Both are possible in their respective places after the manner of the ether and the ether-in-a-pot. Moreover, when identity is inculcated after the fashion of the identification, 'thou art He,' then the worldliness of the animal soul and the creativeness of Brahma are both passed away. Since the practice of all distinctions, set up by Ignorance, is contradicted by full knowledge, where then is the creation, and where the objection on the score of doing injury? The total exhibition of name, form, act, object, instrument, being set up by ignorance is an error, a creature of thoughtlessness. I have repeatedly told you that the world, characterized by good or evil acts, does not in reality exist, it being like the fancies of birth, death, separation, and division. But if the practice of distinctions be not disallowed, then such texts, as 'He is to be sought after,' inculcating a distinction, establish the superiority of Brahma, and preclude the ascription of fault because of doing injury[32].'

The same objection is again answered. It [the objection] is refuted, after the manner of stones &c. Śaṅkara says, Moreover, as in the world, of stones, though endowed with the common property of earthiness, a great variety is seen, some being gems of great value, e.g. diamonds and *vaidurya,* others of middling worth, e.g. *sūryakānta,* others, again, of low estimate, fit for casting at dogs and birds; as also of seeds, though all partaking of the same earthiness, a great variety [of developments] is found, of leaves, flowers, fruits, perfumes, and flavours, e.g. in the sandal and champā plants; as also, in fine, of the same substance of food, various effects are produced, e.g. blood, wool, so may there be a variety of productions from the same Brahma, in the distinction between the animal and the knowing souls. Hence 'it is refuted'—meaning, the objection adduced by the adverse party is refuted. It may also be said that the product, being agreeably to the Veda, a mere nominal one, appears various like visions seen in dreams[33].'

Another objection is thus met. If you say, No! because an elaborate process is seen, I reply, No! it is like milk.'

Śaṅkara says : The saying that one sentient Brahma is the only cause of the world is not demonstrable, because an elaborate process is seen. In this world, potters and other workmen, as manufacturers of jars, clothes, and other things, are found to accomplish their works, by succesfully using the instrumentality of many agencies, earth, staff, wheel, string. You say Brahma had no helper. If he had no other instruments to assist him, how could he be the Creator? Hence Brahma is not the cause of the world. If this be said, it is no fault. For it is accomplished like milk, through the peculiar property of the substance itself. As in the world milk or water turns of itself into curds or ice, without requiring an external instrument, so also here. But does not milk itself when turning into curds require an external instrument, such as heat? Then how can it be said that the creation is like the operation of milk? This is no fault. Milk is only more quickly turned by heat into the state of curds, but not in a greater measure than it would itself attain. If it had not the capacity of turning into curds, it could not be forced into that state by the power of heat; for air and ether cannot be forced into that state by the power of heat. By the fullness of the instrument, also, is its fullness accomplished. But Brahma has fullness of power. His fullness cannot be accomplished by any thing else. There is the Veda too, saying, He has no work or instrument. He has no equal or superior. His power is heard to be supreme and diversified, and the exercise of his knowledge and strength, natural. Therefore, because of his diversified power, though but one Brahma, his diversified change, like milk, is proved[34]?

The objection is further answered[35], Like gods and other beings, in the world.' Śaṅkara's gloss is as follows : 'Be it so. Milk and other non-sentient things are proved by observation to change into curds &c. without requiring external instruments. But sentient agents, such as potters, are found to engage in their occupations only by applying their tools and instruments to their respective works. Why then should sentient Brahma engage without help? We reply, Like gods and other beings. As in the world, Ṛṣis, and other beings of superior power, though sentient, are, without requiring any external instruments, found, on the authority of the illustrative language of Mantras, and of Itihāsas and Purāṇas, to create bodies, houses, chariots and many other things of various descriptions by the simple exercise of volition, by virtue of their especial dignities,– and as spiders weave their nets of themselves–as also cranes conceive without the assistance of their males– as again assemblages of the lotus move, without requiring any external help, from pool to pool, so may Brahma, though sentient, himself create the universe without any external instrument.'

Another objection is thus anticipated[36] : 'The whole would be affected, or violence done to the Veda that he is without parts.' Śaṅkara says, It is proved that the one sentient Brahma, changing himself without a second, and without requiring external helps, becomes the causes of the world. But with a view to clear the sense of the Śāstra, he again anticipates an objection : 'The whole would be affected.' Brahma, as a whole, would be changed into the form of his product, because he has no parts. If Brahma were, like earth and other materials, composed of parts, then one portion might be lost, and one portion might stand. But texts, like the following, preclude the possibility of any qualifications, and describe him as without parts. Without parts, without work, quiet, unstained, without blemish. The heavenly soul is without form, uncreated within and without' This great substance is without bounds, without end. He is a mass of knowledge. This is a spirit, not such, not such. Not stout, not thin. The alteration of a part being thus impossible, if the whole be supposed to be altered, then there will be a destruction of the root itself, and the exhortation to *observe him* prove futile. Besides, from the want of a Brahma, separate from his production, there would be violence done to the texts which describe him as uncreated. If to obviate this difficulty he were held to be composed of parts, then the texts, already cited, which inculcate he is without parts, would be outraged. If, again, he were supposed to have parts, he would be proved uneternal. On all accounts therefore this theory appears impracticable.

Answer to the objection. 'But because of the Veda, because of its being founded on texts.' Śaṅkara thus expounds it. The word *but* refutes the objection. There is indeed no fault on our side. There is no affection of the whole. Why? Because of the Veda. For as the production of the world from Brahma is heard, so is also his continuance, separate from the production, heard from the description of the substance and modification as distinct. That divinity observed, I am these three gods. By entering as animal soul I will make names and forms.' So much is his dignity. The soul is greater than he. The world is a quarter of Him. Immortality is three quarters of Him in heaven.' His existence, as separate from his production, is also evident from the declaration of his dwelling in the heart, and from that of being endowed with [eternal] entity. If Brahma were, in his totality, to be held as a production, then the following text, 'one is endowed with [eternal] enity,' describing the state of sleep, would be futile, because the altered Brahma must be held to be transient, and because of the non-existence of unaltered Brahma. Also because of Brahma not being subject to sensuous perception, and the mutation, or product, being subject to it. Therefore Brahma is unaltered. Nor can there be any violence done to texts which inculcate that He is without parts, for that very description is inculcated in the Veda, and received. 'It is founded on texts.' Brahma is dependent on Vedic testimony, not on that of the senses &c. He is to be received as inculcated in the Veda. The Veda describes Brahma both as unaffected in his totality, and also as being without parts. In worldly things, too such as stones, Mantras, medicines, owing to varieties of place, time, and occasion, powers are seen, productive of contradictory effects. They can, neither, be understood by mere argumentation without the indoctrination, that of such a substance, such are the powers, with such helps, such objects, and for such uses. What wonder then that the form of Brahma, who is of inconceivable power, cannot be established but by Vedic teaching? And the Paurāṇikas say, 'one is not to apply argumentation to topics that are inconceivable; that which is above nature is a sign of the inconceivable.' There the truth of matters that transcend the senses is based on the Veda alone. But may it not be said that contradictions cannot be established even by the Veda, such as the tenet that Brahma, though without parts, alters, but not in his totality? If Brahma be without parts, then, either he would not alter at all, or would alter in his totality. To say that he alters in one form, and remains in another, is, by introducting a distinction of forms, to say he has parts. With reference to practice, contradictory injunctions may be both alternately performed, and so there be no contradiction, the performance being dependent on the soul itself. But contradictions [in ontology] cannot be reconciled by means of alternation, for a substance is not dependent on the soul; therefore this doctrine is impracticable. This is no objection—because the distinction of forms is held to be a creation of ignorance. A substance is proved to be composed of parts by distinction of forms created by ignorance. For the moon, observed as many by the diseased eye, does not therefore really become numerous. By a distinction of forms, created by ignorance, signifying names and figures, modified and unmodified, and not describable either as *that* or *another,* Brahma is held to be subject to alteration, and other conventional ideas, but he remains unaltered, in his essential form, superior to all conventional notions. The expression, that distinctions of names and forms, created by ignorance, are merely in words, protects the text about Brahma's being without parts, from being outraged. Nor is this text about alteration intended to set forth alteration, for there could be no [practical] fruit resulting from such doctrine, but the following aims at setting forth Brahma's spiritual essence, freed from all conventional notions, for there is a [practical] fruit resulting from that teaching, viz. (commencing with the words 'he is a spirit, not such, not such'.) O Janaka thou hast attained fearlessness.' Therefore there is no fault on our side[37].'

Another objection is again brought forward : Not so, for there must be an object.' Śaṅkara says, 'He again anticipates an objection to the universe being a production of a sentient being. The sentient supreme could not have fabricated this spectre of a world, for efforts must have objects. In the world a sentient person, acting on previous deliberation, is seen to engage, even in small efforts, to say nothing of great efforts, moved by some objects of his own. There is also the text concurring with this popular idea, – 'Every thing is not agreeable to every one's desire, but every thing is agreeable to the Spirit's desire.' The effort is indeed a great undertaking, that the world, with its varieties of high and low, should be fabricated. But if this effort on the part of the sentient Supreme Spirit be supposed to have an object of his own, then the all-contentedness of the Supreme Spirit, taught in the Veda, would be contradicted. And if such an object be not supposed, there could not be the effort. Perhaps it may be said that a maniac, though sentient, is sometimes seen to engage in efforts, by a default of his understanding, without an object of his own. The Supreme Spirit may have engaged in a similar manner. But in that case violence would be done to the Vedic doctrine of his omniscience. Therefore creation from a sentient cause is impossible[38].'

The objection is thus answered. 'But it is only a sport, as in the world.' Śaṅkaṛa expounds it thus : By the word *but* he repels the objection. As in the world a king or courtier, having attained all his wishes, may be seen, in games and amusements, to engage in efforts, merely as sports, without aiming at any objects, –and as acts of respiration also take place naturally without aiming at any other external objects, –so does God's effort naturally take place, after the manner of a sport, without looking for any other objects. The assignment of an ulterior object to God is not consistent with reason or Veda. Nor can nature oppose an argument. Although the fabrication of this spectre of a world appears to us like a great undertaking, yet to God it is a mere sport, because his power is unbounded. Although again with reference to worldly sprots, some subtle object may be imagined, still no object can be imagined here, for the Veda says, He is one that has attained his wishes. Nor can the want of an effort, or a mad effort, be supposed, because of the texts inclucating creation and all power[49].'

"Please your highness, continued Satyakāma, I must submit that Śaṅkara's replies to the Sāṅkhya are not at all conclusive. He commences with logic, but falls back on the Veda, and then, at last, when neither logic nor Veda is of any avail, he has recourse to the traditional doctrine of his school that the world is a fiction of ignorance, that there is no real universe, that it is Brahma himself that appears to you in the form of the world, just as a rope may do in that of a snake, and that there is no creation in reality! Without going into the question of Māyā, at present, I shall only say that Śaṅkara has himself argued for the reality of the external world, which in most of his answers here he also takes for granted, and his arguments lead to the theory that so far as the world is a reality, it is itself God. He quotes texts which declare that the world is the same as this spirit or God. That the world is a reality is a doctrine, he himself inculcates elsewhere, and it is only by self-contradiction that he can maintain his position against the Sāṅkhya."

Rajah. – "What self-contradiction?"

Satyakāma. – "He says in his reply to the Sāṅkhya, 'The appearance of the Supreme Spirit, as in the form of the three-fold states, is but an illusion, like that of a rope in the form of a snake.' He says, elsewhere, in his reply to the Buddhists, 'Desirous of denying external objects, they turn them into a simile by using the phrase *like the externals.*' He rebukes the Buddhists for denying the reality of the external world, and yet saying that the forms internally perceived, are *like the externals*. The rebuke is certainly well deserved, for, as he justly adds, no one can say Viṣṇu Mitra is 'like a barren woman's son.' But the same rebuke may with equal propriety be administered to himself for denying the reality of the 'three-fold states,' and yet maintaining that the Supreme Spirit appears *in those forms*. To use his own words, again, 'no one can say that Viṣṇu Mitra is like a barren woman's son.' If the 'spectre of a world' be an unreality, 'like a barren woman's son,' then it is absurd to say God *appears in that form*. If the 'spectre' be not altogether 'like a barren woman's son,' whatever minimum of reality may be ascribed to it, as an object of sensuous perception, must so far be material, and if that minimum of material reality be solemnly styled God, it must be material pantheism to the same extent."

"But, answered Vaiyāsika, neither Vyāsa nor Śaṅkarācārya has said that God is a gross material substance."

"It is true he has never said that. It is also true that he desired that the world should be looked upon as God, not God as the world[50]; but the conversion cannot be altogether precluded if Brahma be an undivided and indivisible essence. Indeed when the Vedāntic doctor brings in his caveat against the assimilation of God with the world, he does so as a matter of ethical policy. It will only be enhancing the coachman's dignity to give him a royal title. No one in our country takes offence on being addressed a king. In truth the word Mahārāja has become a mere term of compliment like the English *Sir.* But you will not do well to address the King as a subject. That will be a degradation of the royal dignity. This is a way of reasoning which ill suits the solemnity of the subject. It is only by way of compliment that a subject can ever be addressed with royal appellatives, and the appellatives themselves have in such a case a *gauṅa,* or figurative, signification. But if you were seriously and solemnly to call an ordinary person your King, as verily and indisputably the Vedānt does every creature, it would involve the guilt of high treason against your rightful sovereign. Even though you did not dishonor your King by calling him a subject, still if you render royal honors to all his subjects, you virtually degrade him by elevating every body else to the level of his dignity. Levelling may be brought about in two ways. You may either bring down your high places to the level of the low, or you may raise your low grounds to the height of your eminences. In either case there will be a levelling. And so you may destroy the royal dignity either by degrading the king, or by unduly exalting the subject. You may not say in so many words that God is an impure material substance; it is impossible for a cultivated mind so barefacedly to belie our moral persuasions as to affirm that God is an impure material substance. And yet when the world is pronounced to be identical with Him, that revolting doctrine is involved in the declaration. Men have, since the days of Vyāsa, endeavoured to refine the grossness of the theory by inculcating that the world is an illusion, not a reality. Vyāsa however has himself never said so, and you, Vaiyāsika, yourself read out, at the marraige assembly, Śaṅkarācārya's strictures on Buddhistic idealism. Whether Śaṅkara is consistent or not is a different question. The case is worse for the Vedānt if he has not been able to maintain his consistency, if its great champion, while inculcating that the external universe has the same evidence for its reality as the internal spirit, is driven, in his encounter with antagonistic objections, to self contradictions. We may examine more fully by and by his tenets as to the illusory character of the world. I shall simply remark now that even if author and commentator had both declared the world to be an illusion that would not save their doctrine; for what would then become of Śaṅkara's assertion that there is the chracteristic attribute of entity as a common qualification between Brahma and the world. His argument would be destroyed by his own pen, if he wrote that the world was not a real entity, after having argued that the quality of entity in the cause, Brahma, is found in the effect, the world,—the only common attribute which he could cite in defence of his theory against the Sāṅkhya."

Āgamika.—"But what inconsistency could there be in the saying that God projected this spectre of a world, which has an illusory entity, but is himself a real entity and no illusion?"

Satyakāma.—"Śaṅkara himself has told us that there is no medium between entity and non-entity[41]. If an illusion means no *thing,* then it is a mere play on words to speak of illusory entity. In case you pronounce the world to be a mere illusion, it cannot have the quality of entity as a common characteristic attribute with Brahma. Besides what is the doctrine under discussion? Is it not this, Brahma is not only the author or efficient cause, but also the *prakṛti,* or substance, the subject matter of the world? If the world be an illusion projected by himself, he cannot be its substance or subject matter. The Māyī, or conjurer, may be the author, he cannot be the *substance* of the illusion by means of which he beguiles or deceives you. If it be a *sensible* illusion, its substance or basis, however subtle, must also be an object of sensuous perception, and therefore material. And if the Māyī is himself both the substantial and efficient cause of his illusion—if the illusion be himself,—and it is at the same time an object of sensuous perception, then the projector must also be an object of sensuous perception, or in other words material."

The Chobdar now came in and said that puṇḍit Tarkakāma was waiting in the public hall, desiring to confer his benediction on the Rajah.

"Show him into this room," said the Rajah. Tarkakāma entered the room and pronounced his benediction. As soon as he was comfortably seated, his highness said, "we are discussing the Vedānt doctrine. Satyakāma contends that it inculcates material pantheism."

Tarkakāma.—"Material pantheism! There is no word for matter in the whole Vedānt, nor in the Sanskrit language."

Satyakāma.—"That may be true, but the idea conveyed by the word matter exists both in the Vedānt and in Sanskrit. The external world, as the object of sensuous perception, corresponds to that idea, and the external world is declared to be God. This is material pantheism. What again can the word *prakṛti* mean but matter? And God is, in so many words, called the *prakṛti* of the world."

Tarkakāma.—"But what objections can you have to the opinion that all this, the whole universe, is God?"

Satyakāma.—"If you say the external world is identical with God, then there cannot be a God over it, and the assertion involves the Sāṅkhya theory of there being no God besides or above the universe, which is described as a spontaneous production from nature. The assertion would amount to atheism, for if there be no God besides the world itself, there can be no God over and above it. Or if you say the world is God in the same sense in which froth is water, you affirm that it is consubstantial with God, which is saying, in other words, that the material is consubstantial with the spiritual,—that matter and spirit are the same substance. This is a clear contradiction in terms, and involves the very confusion of ideas, which all our philosophers call a false notion. If again you say that the world is God because it is an emanation from Him, then in case you call that emanation a substance or thing, it must so far be a part or particle of the divinity. The divinity cannot then be an integral substance, devoid of parts, or incapable of increase of diminution, for the smallest particle must still be a part, the separation of which, as at the creation, must be a diminution of the Deity, and its reunion at the dissolution an increase of the same. But you declare rightly that God is devoid of parts, member, or body. Or if you say that the world, as an emanation from Deity is absolutely nothing, a mere charm, so that its separation involves no decrease, nor its restoration any increase of the divine substance, then you not only contradict Vyāsa's and Śaṅkara's own arguments for the reality of the world, but you maintain that which is falsified by every branch of evidence to which appeal can possibly be made in a discussion between man and man. If, finally, you declare in a *gauṇa,* or figurative, sense that the world is God, only meaning thereby that it bears witness to, and is dependent on, the power and wisdom of God, you ought, in order to avoid the possibility of mistake on such a solemn subject, clearly and unequivocally to confess, at the same time, that the world is not and can never be really and essentially God–that the formula 'thou art He,' is not only not *mahāvākya* or a great mysterious saying, but that it is only a complimentary *atyukti* or hyperbole,–that the knower of God is not and cannot be God,–and that God and the universe are distinct substances as Creator and creature.

"But Śaṅkarācārya insists on the identity of the soul with God in a literal sense of the term. He says that identity is not founded on a mere community of attribute or quality, whereby a small thing may be classed as one with a greater; nor is it a mistaking of one thing for another, as when it is said, Mind is Brahma, Āditya is Brahma. Neither is the identity founded on any occasional acts of assimilation, or absorption, such as the resolution of things into the atmosphere, or the vital air, as it is heard in the *Saṅvarga vidyā* : The atmosphere is the great receptacle. When fire blazes up, or is extinguished, it is resolved into the atmosphere, when the sun sets, it is resolved into the atmosphere, when the moon sets, it is resolved into the atmosphere. Whatever dries up resolves itself into the atmosphere. The atmosphere receives them all.' Nor again is that identity after the fashion of vicariously taking the consecrated butter for the woman, as in the New and Full moon sacrifices. If the unity of the soul with Brahma were taken in these factitious senses, violence would be done to texts teaching the substantial unity of the soul with God, such as, 'Thou art He,' 'I am Brahma' 'This soul is Brahma[42].'

"The Vedāntic theory, continued Satyakāma, is simply a delusion. It is itself *avidyā,* conflicting with what logicians call accurate knowledge. A writer of no mean authority says; 'Thou art verily rifled, O thou animal soul, of thy understanding, by this dark theory of Māyā, because like a maniac, thou constantly ravest, 'I am Brahma.' Where is thy divinity, thy sovereignty, thy omniscience? O thou animal soul! Thou art as different from Brahma as is a mustard seed from Mount Meru[53].' Certainly the idea we have of God, and the experience we have of the visible universe, are widely different. God, you rightly say, is without body, and without parts. The universe has both. God is not an object of external perception. The universe is. You cannot see, hear, or touch God. You may the world. God is immutable. The world is changeable. God is not subject to decay. The universe is. The two therefore can neither be identical nor consubstantial. They do not bear the relation which earth and jar, gold and neckchain, yarn and cloth, sea and froth, bear to one another. I thought the simple citation of passages which contain such extravagant sentiments would be a sufficient refutation of the theory. That was the reason of my not adding many remarks of my own. If all this be God, then matter and spirit are one. What a confusion of ideas this must be! What criteria for the distinguishing of truth and falsehood will then remain?"

Tarkakāma.—"If you mean that the Vedānt destroys differences and distinctions, you confess to a fact which is the glory of the system. It does obliterate distinctions and differences."

Satyakāma.—" I cannot conceive what glory there can be in obliterating distinctions that exist essentially, or in identifying things naturally different. The writer I have just cited, adds on this point : 'Thou art a finite soul, He is infinite. Thou canst occupy but one space at a time, 'He is always every where. Thou are momentarily happy or miserable, He is happy at all times. How then canst thou say,

'I am He?' 'Hast thou no shame[54]?' The self-denying devotee, the sensual voluptuary, and the blood-thirsty tyrant must be the same according to your theory, because each is God."

Tarkakāma. – "The Vedānta never encourages a voluptuary to say, I am God. It only teaches that the knower of God becomes Brahma."

"No one can *become,* said Satyakāma, what essentially he is not. You must alloow me to quote another passage yet from *Gauḍa-pūrṇānanda.* 'Glass is glass, stone is stone, shell is shell, silver is silver. There can never be a cessation of their distinctive notions. Never does a Śūdra, although devotedly worshipping Brāhmins, without intermission, become himself a Brāhmin. He may obtain a little merit, but the Śūdra race cannot attain to Brāhminhood[55].' There is no such thing as a transmutation of individuality. If the Vedānta teaches that certain men may each become God by the knowledge of Brahma, but that every man is not God, it teaches what is simply an impossibility.

"Again Śwetaketu was assured, 'Thou art He,' before he was perfected in knowledge. Hence it is acknowledged by implication that he was essentially God. Śaṅkara distinctly taught this by repudiating any other sense of the soul's unity with God.

"All men must thus be identical, because each soul is essentially God, whether it be aware of it or not. This is an inference which, as I have just shown, I am not gratuitously deducing from your principles. Those who think with you have drawn it themselves. But that all are identical is disproved by the very fact of this conference. On no trustworthy evidence can you or I say that we are the same individual. We have every possible kind of proof to believe that we are separate persons. The difficulty we feel in agreeing on vital points is itself no small evidence of what I say. But even if we could agree in all things – if we were of one heart and one mind, we would still continue separate personalities. If you were pinched, I should not feel it. If you saw a fine sight, I should not participate in your sensation. Our hearts might be so knit that we should perfectly sympathize with each other; and so when you communicate your joy or your sorrow I may be a partaker of it. But it would be a gross error to say we are identical. That error is involved in the theory that every person is God.

"Kaṇāda says rightly, that souls are manifold, because of varieties in condition. The scholiast Śaṅkara Miśra says on that aphorism : 'Souls are manifold. 'Why? Because of varieties. One is respectable, another poor. One is happy, another miserable. One is high, another is low. One is a scholar, another a clown. These varieties, which cannot be reconciled with the unity of the Spirit, prove the distinction of souls[56].'

"Consider the moral consequences of the pantheistic doctrine. The founder of the system himself is anxious that his followers should still continue in the performance of the duties they owe to God and man. But if God and man be identical, then there can be no relation in life to give rise to the notion of duty. If there be only one essence in the world, then, 'who will regard, or honour, and whom?'—says the Upaniṣad. Where there is a difference of personality, one can perform certain offices to another. Such an interchange of offices is impossible where all are one[57]. It would be absurd to say that one can adore or worship himself. In truth Vedāntic authors have boldly asserted that they are subject to no law, no rule, and that there is no such thing as virtue or vice, injunction or prohibition.

"Ponder now the drift of your theory. To give up all distinctions between right and wrong—all morals, all religion, all science, all philosophy—would be to reduce human nature to a chaotic state—to destroy the bands of society, and outrage the sanctity and decency of domestic life. Once more I remind you of what the pious author, already cited, says : 'If I and the whole universe be God, then you and I are one. Then my wealth, my children, my wife, must be our common property, without any distinction. If, again, there be such unity, how can there be injunction or prohibition? If you are decided that there is no difference, then what faults have the Buddhists committed[48]? What barrier can you oppose to the encroachments of bad passions, if men are to be persuaded that there can be in reality no law binding on any individual; that virtue and vice, right and wrong, are mere *vyāvahārika,* or conventional ideas, founded on misapprehension; that no one can do good or evil to his neighbour, there being no such thing as a neighbour, for all are one."

Rajah.—"Is it fair, Satyakāma, to deduce far-fetched inferences of an immoral tendency from a system which repudiates such tendency? Can you show on any respectable authority that principles of an immoral tendency have been practically deduced from the doctrine of the soul's unity with God?"

Satyakāma.—"Without making any remarks on your highness's first question, I shall only say, in reply to the second, that I think I can show that inferences of an immoral tendency have been deduced from the Vedānt doctrine of the identity of the creature with the Creator. The Upaniṣads do not allow the possibility of any offices being done by one person to another. This is in itself a denial of all kinds of duty or obligation. And it is Śaṅkarachārya's own argument when he justifies the inequalities found in the world by the plea that God and the world being essentially one, there can be no such thing as injustice!

Śaṅkara's argument has again been enforced in another way in the *Śrī-Bhāgavata,* second only perhaps, to the *Pañca-rātra,* in point of authority as a text-book of *Bhāgavatas.* These theosophists receive the panthesitc element of the Vedānt, notwithstanding their peculiarities in other respects.

The character which they set up as the incarnation of the Supreme Being was a foul pattern of sensuality and lust. No community can encourage such sensuality without bringing instant ruin on itself. Now the Bhāgavatas do not say that sensuality and lust are themselves innocent. How then do they justify the irregularities of the youthful Kṛṣṇa? Chiefly by relying on the theory of pantheism. King Parīkṣit asks Śuka, 'The Lord of the world became incarnate with a view to establish virtue and put down vice. How could he, then, the preacher, the author, and the keeper of the bridges of virtue, behave so inconsistently, and dally with other men's wives?' Śukadeva says in reply, 'He who lives within the cowherdesses, their husbands, and indeed all embodied souls, is the rightful owner and possessor of the sporting body[59].' This is a practical application of the pantheistic dogma of the Upaniṣads and the Brahma-sūtras, at which one cannot help looking aghast, and your highness will allow it is a serious warning against the reception of that dogma."

Tarkakāma.—"But Śuka does not say that the example of Vāsudeva can be safely followed by a mortal. 'He who is not himself divine should not commit such acts even in his mind. If a mortal were foolish enough to do so, he would perish as inevitably as if one, not being Rudra, took the sea-produced poison. The words of the gods are true, their acts only occasionally right. What is agreeable to their words, the wise are to observe in their conduct[50].'"

Satyakāma.—"It will be practically hard to persuade men to observe the precepts of those whose examples they are instructed to avoid. But the gods (*Iśwarāṇām*), spoken of in the plural, necessarily include other persons than Vāsudeva, and they represent a dignity, certainly within the reach of mortal ambition, according to the transcendental system of Bhāgavata pantheism. 'Every thing is Kṛṣṇa from Brahmā to a bundle of grass[51].' So that every person can consider himself Bhagavān, and, as such, claim the same liberty of action as Vāsudeva. Especial mention is made of the dignity of the Guru, or spiritual preceptor, who is entitled to equal honour with Kṛṣṇa himself[52]. The Gurus and other men of note in the Vaiṣṇava community, eagerly accept the honor thus conferred on them, and do not scruple to avail themselves of the privilege, therewith joined, of following Kṛṣṇa's example. I do not wish to pry into the secrets of society, but it is no breach of charity, or departure from decorum, to notice what appears on the surface. Men there are who profess to have abandoned the world for the sake of their Bhagavān, and who are sometimes regarded as having, even in life, earned a sort of equality with him. They are then considered as Prabhus, or Lords, and females are never wanting who glory in the title of *sevā-dāsī,* or ministering slaves, and who take as much pride and delight in placing their *tan, man,* and *dhan,* (body, mind, and wealth) at the service of· those *prabhus,* as the cowherdesses of Vṛndāvan had ever done in devoting their *whole selves* to Kṛṣṇa.

"Śuka himself adds in justification of Kṛṣṇa, that if sages, who emancipated from the bondage of works by contact with the dust of his own lotus feet, and by the peculiar power of *yoga,* or contemplation of personal unity with him, are at liberty to act as they please, then what restraints could be imposed on the body voluntarily adopted by the god[63]."

Rajah. – "But I am not yet satisfied that Vyāsa did not elsewhere say something in modification of this apparent assimilation of God with the material world."

Tarkakāma. – "Śaṅkarācārya says plainly that the Universe is an illusion. How could he materialize the Detiy by his doctrine?"

Satyakāma. – "He falls back on that traditional teaching only with a veiw of answer objections. He does not assert it as a primary doctrine of his school. It is only when logic and Veda both fail, that he betakes himself to that theory. In order to arrive at right conclusions on this point, we must discriminate between Vyāsa the founder, Śaṅkara the commentator, and the minor commentaries and elementary treatises, of the system. That the Vedānta doctrine was very much modified by the successors of Vyāsa, no one in his senses can deny : and therefore it is a great historical inaccuracy to attribute to the founder the doctrines contained in the Pañcadaśī, and little manuals such as the Vedānta Sāra and the Paribhāṣā. Vyāsa repeatedly identified the world with God, and contended strenuosly for the reality of the external Universe.

"The characteristic doctrine of the Vaiyāsika Vedānta is that God being himself the efficient and substantial cause of all things, the universe is necessarily consubstantial with Him. The characteristic doctrine of later Vedāntists, (the *vedāntibruvas,* or the so-called Vedāntists, to use Vijnāna Bhikṣu's term[54],) is that the Universe is but an illusion, projected by God, and is itself God. It is no doubt in reference to Vyāsa himself that the master spiritualizer, Gauaḍapāda, says, in his Kārikā on the Māṇḍukya Upaniṣad, that 'it is contemplators of the creation who consider this to be an expansion of God[55].'

"I confess I cannot speak of the commentator's teaching with the same confidence as the founder's. Śaṅkarācārya lived at a time when the pantheism of the original Vedānta had been much modified by the general reception of the Buddhistic doctrine of Māyā. In expounding the Sūtras, Śaṅkara, while stoutly contending for the doctrine delivered by Vyāsa, and opposing the idealism of the Buddhists, could not maintain his consistency in his conflict with the Sāṅkhya, and so allowed himself, in some respects, to diverge from the old doctrine. He spoke of the world as the creation of *Avidyā,* or ignorance, thereby giving some reason to the followers of the Sāṅkhya to charge him with inconsistency, and although he has generally avoided calling the universe itself an illusion, he has in one or two places, at least, described it as such. But by speaking of the world as the creation of *Avidyā,* he did not necessarily deny its reality. The Brāhminical mind had from times immemorial found it difficult to believe that great exploits could ever be performed without some impulse, contra-distinguished from reason and deliberation, and akin to

Avidyā. The passions and emotions were supposed to be the very opposites of reason and discrimination;l and, long before the rise of philosophical schools, Indra, fabled as the lord of heaven, was supposed to have been equal to his great efforts, (one of which as least involved the act of creation) only because he had been under intoxication[66]!

"Śaṅkara however, does not use the favourite phraseology of later spiritualizers, that the illusion is neither existent nor non-existent. His own ideas of substantial reality are marked by an exactitude, utterly at variance with such a loose proposition, – a mode of talking which, as Kapila rightly says, becomes none but idiots and children[67].'

"Śaṅkara's view of substantial existence is very different from that of spiritualizers who distinguish *vyāvahārika,* or conventional, from *pāramārthika,* or real, existence. The terms are indeed found in his writings, but he has not technicalized them after the fashion of the Paribhāṣā and the Vedānta Sāra. To prevent mistakes, however, I must add that great as my admiration is of Śaṅkarācārya's talents, I cannot repose much confidence in his opinions, he has so often contradicted himself on points of vital importance. You know how he has reasoned, against the Buddhits, that waking sensations are essentially different from dreams, and yet, in his commentary on Gauḍapāda's Kārikā on the *Māṇḍukya* Upaniṣad, he follows that writer in comparing our waking sensations of the world with dreams, and joins him in placing 'contemplators of the creation' in opposition to 'contemplators of the chief good, who take no interest in the creation'![68]"

Rajah. – "But you say Vyāsa does not inculcate the doctrine of Māyā in his sūtras. I have read of an English scholar's citing one in proof of that doctrine."

Satyakāma. – "The 3rd of III. ii. was cited by Colonel Kennedy, but under a great mistake. It reads thus : 'But it is a mere illusion, because its reality does not appear by the whole of the properties of real substances[59]. The latter part is of course elliptical. As the Colonel was not satisfied with

Śaṅkara's explanation, let us consider the Sūtra in detail. The 2nd Pāda of the 3rd chapter commences with dicussing the question whether the ideas which arise in the mind in dreams are real, as are those which arise in the waking state. 'In the intermediate state [between sound sleep and waking, *i.e.,* in dreams] is there a real creation? for it is so said[60]. Śaṅkara proves by citing a Vedic text that the 'intermediate state' means a dream. He thus expounds the question contained in the Sūtra : 'There is the doubt, Is the creation (or imagination in dreams) real, as is the case in the waking state? * * * for the Veda says so[61].' The question is repeated in the 2nd Sūtra where reference is made to other Vedic passages, seemingly inculcating that dreams are real. In the 3rd Sūtra (that which the Colonel quoted) the author decides the question by declaring that a dream is a mere 'Māyā,' or delusion, for its reality is not established by the collection of proofs by which real substances are distinguished.

"The late Rajah Ram Mohun Roy interpreted the last mentioned Sūtra after the manner of Śaṅkara, in his Bengalee edition. He thus translates the question contained in the 1st Aphorism : 'Since the creations in a state of dreaming are like God's works, let them also be true, like His other creations. This question he determines in the following Sūtra. Those things which are presented in a dream are mere illusions; for, of those which are seen in dreams, the reality is not sufficiently manifest[62].' Thus the very Sūtra, which the learned Colonel had cited to prove his theory, proves precisely the contrary by implication. The author of the Vedānta calls dreams *māyā,* or illusions, because they are unlike the realities perceived in the waking state.

"To me, however, spiritualistic pantheism, as it is called, I mean that which Col. Kennedy attributes to the Vedānta, appears scarcely better than material, or that which the 'so-called Vedāntists' are anxious to disown. For it is as great a departure from truth, and as dangerous an error, to spiritualize matter, as it can be to materialize the spirit. You shrink from the idea of identifying the visible world with God, because the material world is not, and cannot be, a spiritual substance, much less, God, and because such an idea is subversive of the very first principles of religion. But is it not equally erroneous to say that the world is false, that all our senses are under a deception, and that God has deliberately projected certain appearances for the very purpose of practising that deception? I am quite sure it is equally subversive of the interest of religion and morals. And I may add it is more dangerous, because more insidious in its plausibility. For there can be no religion, there can be no devotion, without a subject and an object. There must be the devotee, and there must be the object of devotion. If however the world is a nullity, if the human soul itself is a mere reflection, then I ask in the words of the Upaniṣad, *who will worship, whom, and how?*"

"The successors of Vyāsa, who were unwilling to identify matter with God, and therefore pronounced the world to be an illusion, were aware of the difficulties connected with their new position. The denial of a world, which was evident to all our sense, was itself so much opposed to nature and common sense, that they taxed their ingenuity, as far as they could, to qualify that denial. They introduced the terms *vyāvahārika* and *pāramārthika,* or *conventional* and *real* existences, in order to save their doctrine. The former they attributed, the latter they denied, to the world. If asked, *how all this can be God,* –they would tell you the material world was a *Māyā,* an illusion, and that by not recognizing any visible entity, they virtually inculcated nothing but monotheism. But the true inference from their position was–not unity of Deity, but unity of being.

"If however charged, on the other hand, with the absurdities, so well set forth in the *Vidwan moda taraṅgiṇī,* they instantly shift from their position, and tell you they did not entirely deny the visible world. It had an existence in *vyavahāra,* though it was, *paramārhataḥ,* no reality.

But the soul of man itself has no other than *vyāvaharika* existence. Do you think you are an entity?–You may be one in popular parlance—you are not so *paramārthataḥ,* in reality. 'This one, says the Vedānta Sāra, which, fancies itself to be agent and patient, and passes to and fro between this and the other world, is called the 'vyāvahārika jīva, or conventional soul[73].'

"The inference from the principles of this spiritualistic pantheism is inevitable, that in the sense in which the material world is existent, it is identical with God; and since it is existent in the same sense, and quite to the same extent, as the human soul is existent; it must be God in the same sense in which a human being is not a non-entity. The Vedāntist may solemnly swear *by his life* that the universe is God! The profound thinker, I have already cited several times, suggests, that the asserter of *māyā,* if called on to declare, after the manner of jury-men, whether such and such persons, being guilty of theft, are to be punished by the King, will affirm on his oath that the whole is a tissue of falsehood[74].

"Vyāsa's Vedānta was an unsuccessful attempt to reason from nature up to nature's God. The aphorist was certainly a contemplator of the creation and its wonders. He eyed the world—was struck by its reality and beauty, and fancied that it proceeded from God, as a spark proceeds from fire, or froth from the sea."

Tarkakāma.—"But how can you avoid the train of thought which passed in Vyāsa's mind? How can you deny that the universe is to God what the spark is to fire, and froth to the sea? It must have a substantial cause, and if you deny that God is its cause, will you prefer to be an atheist?"

Satyakāma.—"I do not think one needs be in such a dilemma. It is not necessary to be an atheist in order to meet the Vedāntic conclusion with a negative. It is quite sufficient for all purposes of theism to consider God as the *efficient* cause and author of the world, without going the length of pronouncing it to be consubstantial with Him."

Tarkakāma.—"How could God make a substantial world of *no substance.*"

Satyakāma. – "I will simply refer to Vyāsa's own aphorism, 'Like the gods and others.' He maintains that it is possible for gods, Ṛṣis, and others of great power to produce effects by their own volition. Why could not the Supreme Being likewise create, by the exercise of His own will, the Universe before us, as a real substance – dependent indeed on Himself, and differing from Him *infinitely,* (for who, save God Himself, can fathom the gulf that separates the SELF-EXISTENT from the created?) and yet real, not deceptive, or fallacious? No other conception of creative power is worthy of the Almighty. All other theories of creation are, not only unnecessary, but liable to insuperable objections and difficulties. It was only to escape from those difficulties that the successors of Vyāsa had recourse to the *māyā-vāda* of Buddhism. But if they escaped one error, they ran headlong into an opposite one. In order to preserve the spiritual purity of the God whom their founder had identified with the visible world, they denied the reality of His productions; not remembering that unless the world were originally received as a real effect, its cause could never have been deduced by human reasoning. Nor could there be any pious intuitions in a soul, that, in the plenitude of Vedāntic knowledge, would deny its own existence. Howsoever deduced, whether aetiologically or morally, the truth of God's existence would, as an article of human belief, be affected in the same proportion in which the reality of the visible world and of the human soul was denied. The Vedāntist forgot that the moment the effect was denied, the ground on which the deduction of the cause rested was cut away; the instant the deducer's existence was doubted, his moral persuasions lost all their value.

"If the Vedāntism of Vyāsa, who was a 'contemplator of the creation,' materialized, and thereby degraded, the Divinity, the pantheism of Gauḍapāda, who 'took no interest in the creation,' deified humanity. I for one will not undertake to say which of the two is, physically, the grosser error, – morally, the more pernicious delusion, – or, theologically, the more dangerous dcotrine."

Tarkakāma.—"Excuse my repeating a question which I put last night, but to which you gave no distinct reply. Does not even a shadow betoken some reality which has cast it, or a reflection point to its substance? The world, though itself a mere shadow, may prove the existence of God as its substance."

Satyakāma.—"If you mean by the word reflection, or shadow a reflection, or shadow, of God, as Śaṅkara suggests[65], I shall only remind you of the learned commentator's own admission in his scholia on the *Taittirīya*[66]. He allows that God, being Himself infinite and without form, cannot have a reflection, or cast a shadow—especially as there cannot be a medium or receptacle for such a reflection or shadow. If, again, there could be such a receptacle, would it not be material, and if it were identified with God, would that not be a material pantheism?

"Now there can be no such thing as a substance existing *conventionally,* but not *really.* Things there may be, existing in the opinions of men, or implied in their conduct, but if we deny their reality, we can only mean that they are mere fancies, and therefore not actually existing substances. Śaṅkarācārya has said, what it is impossible to gainsay, 'that the question of the reality of a substance is not dependent on human notions. It depends on the substance itself. To say of a post that it is either a post, or a man, or something else, is not to enunciate the turth. That it is a man, or something else, is a false notion. That it is a post is alone the truth, since it is dependent on the substance itself. Thus the determination of an existing substance depends on the substance itself[77].' It must either exist, or not exist, whatever men may say or think. In fact conventional, as opposed to real, can only mean imaginary, in other words, false. It is conventional, even with the followers of Bhāskarācārya, to say that the sun mounts the *udayācala* (or the eastern mountains) in the morning, it is a *vyavahāra,* or custom, to say so, though they know very well that it is a mythological fable. There are no such eastern mountains, notwithstanding their *vyāvahārika* existence. So also with reference to eclipses, it is a *vyavahāra,* or popular custom, to believe that the solar or lunar orb is in the giant's grasp, and, on that belief, to perform certain ceremonies. But here what is a *vyāvahārika* truth is, in essence, a gross error."

Tarkakāma.—"But the cases are not parallel. When the Vedānta tells a person that while he is in society he ought not to slight what is *vyāvahārika,* it merely means that conventional rules ought not to be set aside. Will you not acknowledge that a man's duty may vary with his position? A man in a state of ignorance must perform the duties attached to that state, and he must not aspire after the rights of the truly wise."

Satyakāma.—"You mean you will not allow the astronomer to evade the performance of *pursaścharaṇa* ! But the question at present is not respecting a man's duty, but the truth of substances. Whether duties may vary, as Śaṅkara admits, we shall consider bye and bye—but, as that eminent commentator says, it is impossible for physical realities to change with the notions of society. Objective truth is independent of the subjective man.

"The moment you deviate from this unalterable rule of truth, you can have no confidence in any reality. What evidence can you have even of spiritual reality, but from traces of spiritual agency visible in the world, or from moral convictions in the mind itself? If you falter in your admission of those traces, and of the real existence of that mind, how can you be sure of any truth?"

Tarkakāma.—"When the Vedāntist says that every thing is false which is not Brahma, or when he says the visible world, and even the human soul, have *vyāvahārika,* not *pāramārthika,* existence, he merely means that nothing can have the kind of reality which God has."

Satyakāma.—"When you say that the human soul and the visible world have a different kind of reality from the reality of God, and then add that both are God, you talk simply in unintelligible language. If the two classes of reality are different, then what do you mean by identifying them?

"No fallacy is more insidious than that of ambiguity, in ascribing two different meanings to the same word, and in the same argument. If you say the universe is of the same substance with God, and that the soul is identical with the Supreme Being in the strict sense of the term, (excluding the figurative senses of *sampat* &c.,) then you must either unduly exalt the world, or grossly degrade the divinity. In either case you strike at the root of *Dharma,* or duty. You cannot, with any fairness or consistency, impose upon persons duties which on your own theory are impossibilities. Whether you acknowledge the universe to be God, or deny the existence of every thing that is not Brahma, you can have no law, no ethics, no discipline."

Tarkakāma.—"We allow that a man in a state of ignorance is bound by laws, rules, and duties."

Satyakāma.—"You allow that which your better sense contradicts. You hold that in truth there can be neither law nor lawgiver. The bolder spirits among you glory in denying injunctions or prohibitions."

Tarkakāma.—"When a man arrives at such a state of knowledge he needs no law."

Satyakāma.—"How can you prevent a sensualist from being encouraged in his evil course by your doctrine?"

Tarkakāma.—"He has no right to deviate from the path of his duties."

Satyakāma.—"If you tell him so, he will only wonder you can keep your countenance, while you lecture him to do that which your better sense pronounces to be an illusion, a fabrication of ignorance. May he not say that since whatever he does must be an illusion, he had better remain satisfied with that which suits his pleasures best? What can you with any consistency say in order to exhort him to holiness of life?"

Tarkakāma.—"I will tell him that if he goes on at that rate, he will never enjoy Brahma."

Satyakāma.—"Do not say, 'Never', for you hold that at

general dissolutions, every thing is swallowed up by Brahma. Whether a man be good or bad, he cannot help enjoying Him on those occasions. The stream, whether turbid or limpid, must flow into the ocean."

Tarkakāma.—"I will remind him of what Vyāsa says that if he attended to his duties, he might be much more quickly emancipated from the bondage of the world."

Satyakāma.—"Which in itself is nothing. The soul is no more in bondage than the crystal in the vicinity of blue cloth in tinged[78]. If there be no world, there can be no bondage. Your spiritual pantheism again is a libel on God. You say the world is a māyā, an illusion, and that God is the *mayī,* the conjurer who thus deceives you. Is it not grossly revolting to our moral feelings to say that God has deliberately projected a false appearance with a view to beguile rational minds of His own creation? And if the world be a mere spectacle—a mere charm—why again dignify it by the appellation of God?"

The sun had, by this time, got very near to the western hills, and was about to give rest to Aruṇa and his horses by betaking himself to the mountain summit. The Rajah desired us to lodge for the night in his gardens, where the requisite utensils would be provided for our evening prayers, and where a Koolin Brāhmin had charge of the culinary department—"so competent for the office," said his highness, "and—so competent for the office," said his highness, "and—without the least injury to animal life, that if the Mlechas could have but made sure of such dishes every day, the world would at once have got rid of the butcher's profession."

Leaving the Rajah in his palace, we came to the gardens, and attended first to our evening duties, and then proceeded to consider our physical wants for the night. But here a difficulty presented itself. The ingenious member of our sacred fraternity, at the head of the culinary office, was of the Vaidic Śreṇi. Vaiyāsika, who was a *Rāḍi*, and Āgamika, who was a Vārendra, were, as matters of course, obliged to deny themselves the dainties of the royal kitchen. Tarkakāma said that although he was of the same *śreṇi* as the provisioner royal, yet he could not persuade himself to taste food prepared by one who was a Śūdra's hireling cook. As for myself, I had been so long in the habit of observing your close practice of absolutely refusing to partake of food, dressed by strangers, that I excused myself by telling the Koolin president of cookery, I had been accustomed to Hindoostani dishes, and had lost all relish for those of Bengal. Satyakāma accordingly engrossed to himself all the good things which, the Rajah said, required only to be tasted, in order to put a stop to the slaughter of dumb creatures for the table. We had to cook each for himself. All being of different *śreṇis,* no one could perform that accommodating office for another. Utensils and raw materials were liberally and richly supplied, and we soon prepared every thing we could possibly require, and passed the night merrily and joyously.

References

1. ब्रह्ममीमांसायां केनापि सूत्रेणाविद्यामात्रतो बन्धस्यानुक्तत्वात्। यत् तु वेदान्तिब्रुवाणामाधुनिकस्य मायावादस्यात्र लिङ्गं दृश्यते तत् तेषामपि विज्ञानवाद्येकदेशितया युक्तमेव। नतु तद्वेदान्तमतम्। अनयैव रीत्या नवीनानामपि प्रच्छन्नबौद्धानां मायावादिनामविद्यामात्रस्य तुच्छस्य बन्धहेतुत्वं निराकृतं वेदितव्यम्।
2. Transactions of the Royal Asiatic Society Vol. III.
3. Col.Kennedy in Asiatic Journal.
4. See note 8 of Dialogue VII.
5. See the same.
6. See the same.
7. "In the order of manifestations or emanations from the absolute spirit, it deviates, however, from that adopted by other Upaniṣads and by the later Vedānta, and is evidently more closely allied to the Sāṅkhya. The order is here:—The unmanifested (avyakta), the great soul,

(mahātma or mahat), intellect,(buddhi), mind, the objects of the senses and the senses. The same order is followed by the Sāṅkhya, with the exception, that they have not between the unmanifested and intellect the intervening "mahat," which with them is eqivalent to intellect. The "manas" (mind) has here also the same function as in the Sāṅkhya the ahaṁkāra (self-consciousness). Hence it is probable, that this Upaniṣad was written at a time, when the Sāṅkhya had already been founded." *Dr. Röer, in Bibliotheca Indica.*

8. य एवं विद्वान् प्राणं वेद न ह्यस्य प्रजा हीयतेऽमृतो भवति॥

9. न येषु जिह्ममनृतं न माया चेति॥

10. प्राणस्येदं वशे सर्व्वं त्रिदिवे यत्प्रतिष्ठितं। मातेव पुत्रान् रक्षस्व श्रीश्च प्रज्ञाञ्च विधेहि नः।

11. कुर्वन्नेवेह कर्म्माणि जिजीविषेच्छतं समाः॥

12. आप्नोति ह वै सर्वान् कामानादिश्च भवति य एवं वेद। * * उत्कर्षति ह वै ज्ञानसन्ततिं समानश्च भवति नास्याब्रह्मवित् कुले भवति य एवं वेद॥

13. देवो भूत्वा देवानप्येति य एवं विद्वानेतदुपास्ते। This is repeated several times in the form of a chorus. एति स्वर्गं लोकं य एवं वेद॥

यो वा एतदक्षरं गार्ग्यविदित्वाऽस्माल्लोकात् प्रैति स कृपणोऽथ य एतदक्षरं गार्गि विदित्वाऽस्माल्लोकात् प्रैति स ब्राह्मणः॥

14. स य एतानेव पञ्च ब्रह्मपुरुषान् स्वर्गस्थलोकस्य द्वारपान् वेदास्य कुले वीरो जायते प्रतिपद्यते स्वर्गं लोकं य एतानेवं पञ्च ब्रह्मपुरुषान् स्वर्गस्य लोकस्य द्वारपान् वेद। * * षोडशं वर्षशतं जीवति य एवं वेद। * * स यदि पितृलोककामो भवति सङ्कल्पादेवास्य पितरः समुत्तिष्ठन्ति तेन पितृलोकेन सम्पन्नो महीयते। अथ यदि मातृलोककामो भवति सङ्कल्पादेवास्य मातरः समुत्तिष्ठन्ति तेन मातृलोकेन सम्पन्नो महीयते। अथ यदि भ्रातृलोककामो भवति सङ्कल्पादेवास्य भ्रातरः समुत्तिष्ठन्ति। तेन भ्रातृलोकेन सम्पन्नो महीयते। अथ यदि स्वसृलोककामो भवति सङ्कल्पादेवाप्य स्वसारः समुत्तिष्ठन्ति तेन स्वसृलोकेन सम्पन्नो महीयते। अथ यदि सखिलोककामो भवति सङ्कल्पादेवास्य सखायः समुत्तिष्ठन्ति तेन सखिलोकेन सम्पन्नो महीयते। अथ यदि गन्धमाल्यलोककामो भवति सङ्कल्पादेवास्य गन्धमाल्ये

समुत्तिष्ठतस्तेन गधमाल्यलोकेन सम्पन्नो महीयते। अथ यद्यन्नपानलोककामो भवति सङ्कल्पादेवास्यान्नपाने समत्तिष्ठस्तेनान्नपानलोकेन सम्पन्नो महीयते। अथ यदि गीतवादित्रलोककामो भवति सङ्कल्पादेवास्य गीतवादित्रे समुत्तिष्ठतस्तेन गीतवादित्रलोकेन सम्पन्नो महीयते। अथ यदि स्त्रीलोककामो भवति सङ्कल्पादेवास्य स्त्रियः समुत्तिष्ठन्ति तेन स्त्रीलोकेन सम्पन्नो महीयते। यं यमन्तमभिकामो भवति यं कामयते सोऽस्य सङ्कल्पादेव समुत्तिष्ठति तेन सम्पन्नो महीयते॥

15. प्लवा ह्येते अदृढा यज्ञरूपा अष्टादशोक्तमवरं येषु कर्म्म। एतच्छ्रेयो येभिनन्दन्ति मूढा जरामृत्युं ते पुनरेवापि यन्ति॥

16. तेषां न पुनरावृत्तिः। न च पुनरावर्त्तते। इमं मानवमावत्ते नावर्त्तन्ते॥

17. Dr. Röer was obliged to translate nearly the whole of the concluding chapter of the Bṛhadāraṇyaka into Latin because of its gross indecencies. "It would not bear an English rendering." See not page 273. *Bibliotheca India* No. 135.

18. य एक जालवान् ईशित ईशनीभिः। यस्मान् मायी सृजते विश्वमेतत्॥

19. तमीश्वराणां परमं महेश्वरं * * विदाम देव भुवनेशमीड्यं॥

20. या ते रुद्र शिवा तनूरघोराऽपापकाशिनी। तया नस्तनुवा शन्तमया गिरिशन्ताभिचाकशीहि॥ यामिषुं गिरिशन्त हस्ते विभर्ष्यस्तवे। शिवां गिवित्र तां करु मा हिंसीः पुरुषं जगत्॥

मायान्तु प्रकृतिं विद्वान् मायिनन्तु महेश्वरं॥

21. यो ब्रह्माणं विदधाति पूर्वं यो वै वेदांश्च प्रहिणोति तस्मै। The idea contained in last sentence is almost identical with that in the *Śrī Bhāgavata.*

तेन ब्रह्म हृदा य आदि कवये॥

22. किं कारणं ब्रह्म कुतः स्म जाता * * कालस्वभावो नियतिर्यदृच्छा भूतानि योनिः पुरुष इति चिन्त्या॥

नियतिरविषमपुण्यपापलक्षणं कर्म्म॥ Śaṅkara.

23. अत्र चत्वारि भूतानि भूमिवार्यनलानिलाः। चतुर्भ्यः खलु भूतेभ्यश्चैतन्यमुपजायते। किण्वादिभ्यः समेतेभ्यो द्रव्येभ्यो मदशक्तिवत्॥ Sarva Darśana Saṅgraha.

24. स्वभावमेके कवयो वदन्ति। कालं तथान्ये परिमुह्यमानाः॥

25. स्वाप्ययात्। अस्मिन्नस्यच तद्योगं शास्ति। अत्ता चराचरग्रहणात् मुक्तोपसृप्यव्यपदेशात्। ईक्षते र्नाशब्दं। कामाच्च नानुमानापेक्षा॥

26. यतीन्द्रः शङ्करो नाम्ना भविष्यामि महीतले॥

27. "Assuming, each of them implictly, the truth of the Vedas, and proceeding to give, on that foundation, a comprehensive view of the totality of things, the three systems differ in their *point of view.* To illustrate this, suppose that three men in succession take up a cylindrical ruler : the one, viewing it with its end towards his eye, sees a circle; the second, viewing it upright before his eye, sees a parallelogram; the third,viewing it in a direction slanting away in front of his eye, sees a frustum of a cone. These three views are different, but no wise irreconcileable. So far are they from being irreconcileable, that it might be argued that *all* of them must be accepted in succession, before any adequate conception of the form of the ruler can be arrived at. Now, in somewhat such a way, the three Hindu systems differ mainly in their severally regarding the universe from different points of view, –viz.,as it stands in relation severally to *sensation, emotion,* and *intellection.* –The *Naiyāyika,* founding on the fact that we have various *sensations,* enquires what and how many are the channels through which such varied knowledge flows in. The *Sāṅkhya,* struck with the fact that we have *emotions,* –with an eye to the question *whence* our impressions come, –enquires their *quality.* The *Vedāntin,* rising above the question as to what is pleasing, displeasing, or indifferent, asks simply, what is,and what is *not.*" –*Ballantyn'e prize Essay pp. xvi, xvii.*

28. तीर्थकराणां कपिलकणभुक्प्रभृतीनां परस्परविप्रतिपत्तिदर्शनात्। Com. Vedānt, II. i. 4.

29. प्रकृतिश्च प्रतिज्ञादृष्टान्तानुपरोधात्। यथाभ्युदयहेतुत्वाद्धमर्मो जिज्ञास्य एवं निःश्रेयसहेतुत्वाद् ब्रह्मापि जिज्ञास्यमित्युक्तं। ब्रह्म च जन्माद्यस्य यत इति

लक्षितं। तच्च लक्षणं घटरुचकादीनां मृत्सुवर्णादिवत् प्रकृतित्वे कुलालसुवर्णकारादिवन्निमित्तत्वे च समानमित्यतो भवति विमर्शः किमात्मकं पुनर्ब्रह्मणः कारणत्वं स्यादिति। तत्र निमित्तकारणमेव तावत् स्यादिति प्रतिभाति। कस्मात्, ईक्षापूर्व्वककर्त्तृत्वश्रवणात्। ईक्षापूर्व्वकं हि ब्रह्मणः कर्तृत्वमवगम्यते स ईक्षाञ्चक्रे स प्राणमसृजतेत्यादिश्रुतिभ्यः ईक्षापूर्व्वकञ्च कर्तृत्वं निमित्तकारणेष्वेवकुलालादिषु दृष्टंतद्वत् परमेश्वरस्यापि निमित्तकारणत्वमेव युक्तं प्रतिपत्तुं। कार्य्यं चेदं जगत् सावयवमचेतनमशुद्धं च दृश्यते। कारणेनापि तस्य तादृशेनैव भवितव्यं। कार्य्यकारणयोः सारूप्यदर्शनात्। ब्रह्म च नैवं लक्षणमवगम्यते निष्कलं निष्क्रियं शान्तं निरवद्यं निरञ्जनमित्यादिश्रुतिभ्यः। पारिशेष्याद्ब्रह्मणोऽन्यदुपादान-कारणमशुद्धादिगुणकं स्मृतिप्रसिद्धमभ्युपगन्तव्यं ब्रह्मकारणत्वश्रुतेर्निमित्तमात्रे पर्य्यवसानादित्येवं प्राप्ते ब्रूमः। प्रकृतिश्चोपादानकारणं च ब्रह्माभ्युपगन्तव्यं निमित्तकारणं च। न केवलं निमित्तकारणमेव कस्मात् प्रतिज्ञादृष्टान्तानुपरोधात्। एवं प्रतिज्ञादृष्टान्तौ श्रुतौ नोपरुध्येते। प्रतिज्ञा तावत् उत तमादेशमप्राक्ष्यो येनाश्रुतं श्रुतं भवति अमतं मतमविज्ञातं विज्ञातमिति तत्र चैकविज्ञानेन सर्व्वमन्यदविज्ञातमपि विज्ञातम्भवति इति प्रतीयते। तच्चोपादानकारणविज्ञाने सर्वविज्ञानं सम्भवति उपादानकारणाव्यतिरेकात् कार्य्यस्य निमित्तकारणादव्यतिरेकस्तु कार्य्यस्य नास्ति लोके तक्षप्रासादव्यतिरेकदर्शनात्। दृष्टान्तोऽपि यथा सौम्यैकेन मृत्पिण्डेन सर्व्वं मृण्मयं विज्ञातं स्याद्वाचारम्भणं विकारो नामधेयं मृत्तिकेत्येव सत्यं इत्युपादानकारणगोचर एवाम्नायते। यथैकेन लोहमणिना सर्व्वं लोहमयं विज्ञातं स्यात् एकेन नखनिकृन्तनेन सर्व्वं कार्ष्णायसं विज्ञातं स्यादिति च। तथान्यत्रापि कस्मिन्नु भगवो विज्ञाते सर्व्वमिदं विज्ञातं भवतीति प्रतिज्ञाय यथा पृथिव्यामोषधयः सम्भवन्तीति दृष्टान्तः। आत्मनि खल्वरे दृष्टे श्रुते मते विज्ञाते इदं सर्व्वं विदितमिति प्रतिज्ञाय स यथा दुन्दुभेर्हन्यमानस्य न वाह्याञ्छब्दाञ्छक्नुयाद्ग्रहणाय दुन्दुभेस्तु ग्रहणेन दुन्दुभ्याघातस्य वा शब्दो गृहीत इति दृष्टान्तः एवं यथासम्भवं प्रतिवेदान्तं प्रतिज्ञादृष्टान्तौ प्रकृतित्वसाधनौ प्रत्येतव्यौ। यत इतीयमपिपञ्चमी। यतो वा इमानि भूतानि जायन्ते इत्यत्र जनिकर्त्तुः प्रकृतिरिति विशेषस्मरणात् प्रकृतिलक्षण एवोपादाने द्रष्टव्या। निमित्तत्वन्तु अधिष्ठात्रन्तराभावादवगन्तव्यं। यथा हि लोके मृत्सुवर्णादिकमुपादानकारणं कुलालसुवर्णकारादीन-धिष्ठातृनपेक्ष्य प्रवर्त्तते नैवं ब्रह्मण उपादानकारणस्य सतोऽन्योऽधिष्ठा-तापेक्ष्योऽस्ति।- प्रागुत्पत्तेरेकमेवाद्वितीयमित्यवधारणात् अधिष्ठात्रन्तराभावोऽपि

प्रतिज्ञादृष्टान्तानुपरोधादेव चोदितो वेदितव्यः। अधिष्ठातरि ह्युपादानादन्यस्मिन्नभ्युपगम्यमाने पुनरप्येकविज्ञानेन सर्व्वविज्ञानस्यासम्भवात् प्रतिज्ञादृष्टान्तोपरोध एव स्यात्। तस्मादधिष्ठात्रन्तराभावादात्मनः कर्त्तृत्वं उपादानान्तराभावाच्च प्रकृतित्वं॥

30. अभिध्योपदेशाच्च। अभिध्योपदेशश्चात्मनः कर्त्तृत्वप्रकृतित्वे गमयति सोऽकामयत वहु स्यां प्रजायेयेति तदैक्षतेति च तत्राभिध्यानपूर्विकायाः स्वातन्त्र्यप्रवृत्तेः कर्त्तेति गम्यते वहु स्यामिति प्रत्यगात्मविषयत्वात् बद्ध भवनाभिध्यानस्य प्रकृतिरित्यपि गम्यते॥

31. साक्षाच्चोभयाम्नानात्। प्रकृतित्वस्यायमभ्युच्चयः इतश्च प्रकृतिर्ब्रह्म यत्कारणं साक्षाद्ब्रह्मैव कारणमुपादायोभौ प्रभवप्रलयावाम्नायेते सर्व्वाणि ह वा इमानि भूतान्याकाशादेव समुत्पद्यन्ते आकाशं प्रत्यस्तं यन्तीति यद्धि यस्मात् प्रभवति यस्मिंश्च प्रलीयते तत्तस्योपादानं प्रसिद्धं यथा व्रीहियवादीनां पृथिवी साक्षादितिचोपादानान्तरानुपादानं सूचयति आकाशादेवेति प्रत्यस्तमयश्चनोपादानादन्यत्र कार्य्यस्य दृष्टः॥

32. आत्मकृतेः परिणामात्। इतश्च प्रकृतिर्ब्रह्म यत्कारणं ब्रह्मप्रक्रियायां तदात्मानं स्वयमकुरुतेति आत्मनः कर्म्मत्वं कर्त्तृत्वञ्च दर्शयति आत्मानमिति कर्म्मत्वं स्वयमकुरुतेति कत्तृत्वं कथं पुनः पूर्व्वसिद्धस्य सतः कर्तृत्वेन व्यवस्थितस्य क्रियमानत्वं शक्यं सम्पादयितुं परिणामादिति ब्रूमः पूर्वसिद्धा हि सन्नात्मा विशेषेण विकारात्मना परिणमयामासात्मानमिति। विकारात्मनाच परिनामो मृदाद्यासु प्रकृतिषूपलब्धः स्वयमिति च विशेषेणान्निमित्तान्तरानपेक्षत्वमपि प्रतीयते॥

33. योनिश्च हि गीयते। इतश्च प्रकृतिर्ब्रह्म यत्कारणं ब्रह्मयोनिरित्यपि पठ्यते वेदान्तेषु कर्त्तारमीशं पुरुषं ब्रह्म योनिमिति यद्भूतयोनिं परिपश्यन्ति धीरा इति च। योनिशब्दश्च प्रकृतिवचनः समधिगतो लोके पृथिवी योनिरोषधिवनस्पतीनामिति॥

34. एतेन सर्व्वे व्याख्याता व्याख्याताः।

35. न विलक्षणत्वादस्य तथात्वञ्च शब्दात्। ब्रह्मास्य जगतोनिमित्तं कारणं प्रकृतिश्चेत्यस्य पक्षस्याक्षेपः स्मृतिनिमित्तः परिहृतः तर्क्कनिमित्त इदानीमाक्षेपः परिह्रियते। कुतः पुनरस्मिन्नवधारिते आगमार्थे। तर्कनिमित्तस्याक्षेपस्यावकाशः ननु धर्म्म इव ब्रह्मण्यप्यनपेक्षं आगमो भवितुमर्हति भवेदयमवष्टम्भो यदि प्रमाणान्तरानवगाह्यः आगममात्रप्रमेयोऽयमर्थः स्यादनुष्ठेयइवधर्म्मःपरिनिष्पन्नरूपन्तु ब्रह्मावगम्यते परिनिष्पन्ने च वस्तुनि प्रमाणान्तराणामस्त्यवकाशो

अतस्तर्कनिमित्तः पुनराक्षेपः क्रियते न विलक्षणत्वादस्येति। यदुक्तं चेतनं ब्रह्म जगतःकारणं प्रकृतिरिति तन्नोपपद्यते कस्मात् विलक्षणत्वादस्य विकारस्य प्रकृत्याः। इदं हि ब्रह्मकार्य्यत्वेनाभिप्रेमयमाणं जगत् ब्रह्मविलक्षणमचेतनम-शुद्धञ्च दृश्यते ब्रह्म च जगद्विलक्षणं चेतनं शुद्धश्च श्रूयते न च विलक्षणत्वे प्रकृतिविकारभावोदृष्टः। नहि रुचकादयो विकारा मृत्प्रकृतिका भवन्ति शरावादयो वा सुवर्णप्रकृतिकाः मृदैवतु मृदन्विता विकाराः प्रक्रियन्ते, सुवर्णेन च सुवर्णान्विताः तथेदमपि जगदचेतनं सुखदुःखमोहान्वितं सदचेतनस्यैव सुखदुःखमोहात्मकस्य कारणस्य कार्य्यं भवितुमर्हति। न विलक्षणस्य ब्रह्मणः ब्रह्मविलक्षणत्वञ्चास्य जगतोऽशुद्धचेतनत्वदर्शनादवगन्तव्यं अशुद्धं हीदं जगत् सुखदुःखमोहात्मकतया प्रीतिपरितापविषादादिहेतुत्वात् स्वर्गनरकाद्युच्चावचप्रपञ्चत्वाच्च। अचेतनञ्चेदं जगत् चेतनं प्रतिकार्य्यकरण-भावेनोपकरणभावोपगमात् नहि साम्ये सत्युपकार्य्योपकारकभावो भवति। नहि प्रदीपौ परस्परस्योपकुरुतः। ननु चेतनमपि कार्य्यकरणं स्वामिभृत्यन्यायेनभोक्तुरूपकरिष्यति न स्वामिभृत्ययोरप्यचेतनांशस्यैव चेतनं प्रत्युपकारकत्वात् योह्येकस्य चेतनस्य परिग्रहो बुद्ध्यादिरचेतनभागः सएवान्यस्य चेतनस्योपकरोति। न तु स्वयमेव चेतनञ्चेनान्तरस्योपकरोत्यपकरोति वा निरतिशयाह्यकर्त्तारश्चेतना इति साङ्ख्या मन्यन्ते। तस्मादचेतनं कार्य्यकरणं। न च काष्ठलोष्टादीनां चेतनत्वे किञ्चित् प्रमाणमस्ति। प्रसिद्धश्चायं चेतनाचेतनप्रविभागोलोके। तस्माद् ब्रह्मविलक्षणत्वान्नेदं जगत्तत्प्रकृतिकं। योपि कश्चिदाचक्षीत श्रुत्वा जगतश्चेतनप्रकृतिकतां तद्बलेनैव समस्तं जगच्चेतनमवगमिष्यामि प्रकृतिरूपस्य विकारेऽन्वयदर्शनात् अविभावनन्तु चैतन्यस्य परिणामविशेषाद्भविष्यति यथा स्पष्टचैतन्यानामप्यात्मनां स्वापमूर्च्छाद्यवस्थासु चैतन्यं न विभाव्यते। एवं काष्ठलोष्टाहीनामपि चैतन्यं न विभावयिष्यते। एतस्मादेव च विभावितत्वाविभावितत्वकृता-द्विशेषाद्रूपादिभावाभावाभ्याञ्च कार्य्यकरणा- नामात्मनाञ्च चेतनत्वाविशेषेपि गुणप्रधानभावो न विरोत्स्यते यथाच पार्थिवत्वाविशेषेपि मांससूपौदनादीनां प्रत्यात्मवर्त्तिनोविशेषात् परस्परोपकारित्वं भवति एवमिहापि भविष्यति प्रविभागप्रसिद्धिरप्यत एव न विरोत्स्यत इति तेनापि कथञ्चिच्चेतनत्वाचेतनत्व-विलक्षणत्वं परिह्रियेत शुद्धशुद्धिलक्षणन्तु विलक्षणत्वं नैव परिह्रियते नवेतरदपि विलक्षणत्वं परिहर्तुं शक्यत इत्याह तथात्वञ्च शब्दादिति। अनवगम्यमानमेवहीदं लोके समस्तस्य वस्तुनश्चेनत्वं चेतनप्रकृतिकत्वश्रवणात् शब्दशरणतया केवलयोत्प्रेक्षते, तच्चशब्देनैव विरुध्यते। यतः शब्दादपि तथात्वमवगम्यते।

तथात्वमिति प्रकृतं विलक्षणत्वं कथयति शब्द एव विज्ञानञ्चाविज्ञानञ्चेति कस्यचिद्भागस्याचेतनतां श्रावयन् चेतनाद्ब्रह्मणो विलक्षणमचेतनं जगत् श्रावयति। ननु चेतनत्वमपि क्वचिदचेतनत्वाभिमतानां भूतेन्द्रियाणां श्रूयते, यथा मृदब्रवीदापोऽब्रुवन्निति तत्तेज ऐक्षत ता आप ऐक्षन्तेतिचैवमाद्या भूतविषयाचेतनत्वश्रुतिः इन्द्रियविषयापि तेहेमे प्राणा अहंश्रेयसेविवदमाना ब्रह्माणं जग्मुरिति तेहवाचमूचुस्त्वं न उद्गायेतिचैवमाद्येन्द्रियविषयेति अत उत्तरं पचति। ⋆ अभिमानिव्यपदेशस्तु विशेषानुगतिभ्यां। ⋆ तु शब्द आशङ्कामयनुदति। न खलु मृदब्रवीदित्येवं जातीयकया श्रुत्या भूतेन्द्रियाणां चेतनत्वमाशङ्कनीयं यतोभिमानिव्यपदेश एषः मृदाद्यभिमानिन्यो वागाद्यभिमानि-न्यश्च चेतना देवतावदनसंवदनादिषु चेतनोचितेषु व्यवहारेषु व्यपदिश्यन्ते। न भूतेन्द्रियमात्रं कस्मात् विशेषानुगतिभ्यां विशेषो हि भोक्तृणां भूतेन्द्रियाणाञ्च चेतनाचेतनप्रविभागलक्षणः प्रागभिहितः सर्व्वचेतनतायां चासौनोपपद्येत। अपि च कौषीतकिनः प्राणसंवादे करणमात्राशङ्काविनिवृत्तयेऽधिष्ठातृचेतनपरिग्रहाय देवता शब्देन विशिषन्ति एताहवै देवता अहंश्रेयसे विवदमाना इति तावाएताः सर्व्वा देवताः प्राणेनिः श्रेयसं विदित्वेति च। अनुगताश्च सर्व्वत्राभिमामिन्यश्चेतना देवता मन्त्रार्थवादेतिहासपुराणादिभ्योवगम्यन्ते। किञ्च अग्निर्व्वाग्भूत्वा मुखं प्राविशदित्येवमादिका च श्रुतिः करणेष्वनुग्राहिकां देवतामनुगतां दर्शयति प्राणसंवादवाक्यशेषे च तेहप्राणाः प्रजापतिं पितरमेत्योचुरिति श्रैष्ठनिर्द्धरणाय प्रजापतिगमनं तद्वचनाच्चैकैकोत् क्रमणेान्वयव्यतिरेकाभ्यां प्राणश्रेष्ठयप्रतिपत्तिः तस्मै वलिहरणमिति चैवं जातीयकोऽस्मदादिष्विव व्यवहारोनुगम्यमानोभिमानि व्यपदेशं द्रढयति। तत्तेज ऐक्षतेत्यपि परस्या एव देवताया अधिष्ठात्र्याः स्वीकारेष्वनुगताया इयमीक्षा व्यपदिश्यत इति द्रष्टव्यं। तस्माद्विलक्षणमेवेदं ब्रह्मणो जगत् विलक्षणत्वाच्च न ब्रह्मप्रकृतिकमित्याक्षिप्ते प्रतिविधत्ते।

36. दृश्यतेतु। तु शब्दः पूर्वपक्षं व्यावर्त्तयति। यदुक्तं विलक्षणत्वान्नेदं जगद्ब्रह्मप्रकृतिकमिति नायमेकान्तः दृश्यते हि लोके चेतनत्वेन प्रसिद्धेभ्यः पुरुषादिभ्यो विलक्षणानां केशनखादीनामुत्पत्तिरचेतनत्वेन च प्रसिद्धेभ्यो गोमयादिभ्यो वृश्चिकादीनां। नन्वचेतनान्येव पुरुषादिशरीराण्यचेतनानां केशनखादीनां कारणानि अचेतनान्येव वृश्चिकादिशरीराण्यचेतनानां गोमयादीनां कार्य्याणीत्युच्यते। एवमपि किंचिदचेतनं चेतनस्यायतनभावमुपगच्छति किंचिन्नेत्यस्त्येव वेलक्षण्यं। महांश्चायं पारिणामिकः स्वभाव- विप्रकर्षः पुरुषादीनां केशनखादीनाञ्च रूपादिभेदात् तथा गोमयादीनां वृश्चिकादीनाञ्च अत्यन्तसारूप्ये च प्रकृतिविकारभाव एव प्रलीयेत। अथोच्येत अस्ति

कश्चित् पार्थिवत्वादिस्वभावः पुरुषादीनां केशनखादिष्वनुवर्त्तमानः गोमयादीनाञ्च वृश्चिकादिष्विति ब्रह्मणोऽपि तर्हि सत्तालक्षणः स्वभाव आकाशादिष्वनुवर्त्तमानो दृश्यते। विलक्षणत्वेन च कारणेन ब्रह्मप्रकृतिकत्वं जगतो दूषयता किमशेषस्य ब्रह्मस्वभावस्याननुवर्त्तनं विलक्षणत्वमभिप्रेयते उत यस्य कस्यचित् अथ चैतन्यस्येति वक्तव्यं प्रथमे विकल्पे समस्तप्रकृतिविकारोच्छेदप्रसङ्गः। नहि असत्यतिशये प्रकृतिविकारभाव इति भवति। द्वितीये चाप्रसिद्धत्वं। दृश्यते हि सत्तालक्षणोब्रह्मस्वभाव आकाशादिष्वनुवर्त्तमान इत्युक्तं। तृतीये तु दृष्टान्ताभावः किं हि यच्चैतन्येनानन्वितं तदब्रह्मप्रकृतिकं दृष्टमिति ब्रह्मकारणवादिनं प्रत्युदाह्रियेत समस्तस्यास्य वस्तुजातस्य ब्रह्मप्रकृतिकत्वाभ्युपगमात्॥

Ibid, II. i. 7.

37. यदि प्रमाणान्तरानवगाह्यः आगममात्रप्रमेयोयमर्थः स्यादनुष्ठेय इव धर्म्मे। * * * यथा च श्रुतीनां परस्परविरोधे सत्येकवशेनेतरा नीयन्ते एवं प्रमाणान्तरविरोधेपि तद्वशेनैव श्रुतिर्नीयते।

Com. Vedānt, II. i. 4.

38. अपीतौ तद्वत्प्रसङ्गादसमञ्जसं॥ अत्राह यदि स्थौल्यसावयवत्वाचेतन-त्वपरिछिन्नत्वाशुद्धादिधर्म्मकं कार्य्यं ब्रह्मकारणकमभ्युपगम्येत तदाऽपोतौ प्रलये प्रतिसंमृज्यमानं कार्य्यं कारणेऽविभागमापद्यमानं कारणमात्मीयेन धर्म्मेण दूषयेदित्यपीतौ कारणस्यापि ब्रह्मणः कार्य्यस्येवाशुद्धादिरूपताप्रसङ्गात् सर्व्वज्ञं ब्रह्म जगतः कारणमित्यसमञ्जसमिदमौपनिषदं दर्शनं। अपिच समस्तस्य विभागस्याविभागप्राप्तेः पुनरुत्पत्तौ नियमकारणाभावाद्भोक्तृभोग्यादि-विभागेनोत्पत्तिर्न प्राप्नोति इत्यसमञ्जसं। अपिच भोक्तृणां परेण ब्रह्मणाऽविभागं गतानां कर्म्मादिनिमित्तप्रलयेपि पुनरुत्पत्तावभ्युपगम्यमानायां मुक्तानामपि पुनरुत्पत्तिप्रसङ्गादसमञ्जसं। अथेदं जगदपीतावपि विभक्तमेवपरेण ब्रह्मण-वतिष्ठेत एवमप्यपीतिरेव न सम्भवति कारणाव्यतिरिक्तञ्च कार्यं न सम्भवतीत्यसमञ्जसमेवेति॥

Ibid. II. i. 8.

39. अत्रोच्यते॥ नतु दृष्टान्तभावात्॥ नैवास्मदीये दर्शने किञ्चिदसामञ्जस्यमस्ति, यत्तावदभिहितं कारणमपि गच्छत् कार्य्यं कारणमात्मीयेन धर्मेण दूषयेदिति तददूषणं, कस्मात्, दृष्टान्तभावात् सन्ति हि दृष्टान्ताः यथा कारणमपि गच्छत् कार्य्यं कारणमात्मीयेन धर्म्मेण नदूषयति। तद्यथा शरावादयो मृत्प्रकृतिका विकारा विभागावस्थायामुच्चावचमध्यमप्रभेदाः सन्तः पुनः

प्रकृतिमपि गच्छन्तो न तामात्मीयेन धर्म्मेण संसृजन्ति रूचकादयश्च सुवर्णविकारा अपीतौ न सुवर्णमात्मीयेन धर्म्मेण संसृजन्ति पृथिवीविकारश्च चतुर्व्विधो भूतग्रामो न पृथिवीमपीतावात्मीयेन धर्म्मेण संसृजति। त्वत्पक्षस्यतु न कश्चिद्दृष्टान्तोस्ति अपितिरेव हि नसम्भणेत् यदि कारणे कार्यं स्वधर्म्मेणैवावतिष्टेत अनन्यत्वेपि कार्यकारणयोः कार्यस्य कारणात्मत्वं नतु कारणस्य कार्यात्मत्वं आरम्भणशब्दादिभ्यः इति वक्ष्यामः। अत्यल्पञ्चेदमुच्यतेकार्यमपीतावात्मीयेन धर्म्मेण कारणं संसृजेदिति स्थितावपिहि समानोयं प्रसङ्गः कार्यकारणयोरनन्यत्वाभ्युपगमात् इदं सर्व्वं यदयमात्मा आत्मैवेदं सर्व्वं ब्रह्मैवेदमृतं पुरस्तात् सर्वं खल्विदंब्रह्मेथेवमादिभिर्हि श्रुतिभिरविशेषेण त्रिष्वपिकालेषु कार्यस्य कारणादनन्यत्वं श्राव्यते। तत्र यः परिहारः कार्यस्य तद्धर्म्भाणाञ्चाविद्याध्यारोपितत्वान्नतैः कारणं संसृज्यत इति अपितावपि ससमानः। अस्ति चायमपरो दृष्टान्तः यथास्वयं प्रसारितय मायया मायावी त्रिष्वपि कालेषु न संस्पृश्यते अवस्तुत्वात् एवं परमात्मापि संसारमायया नसंस्पृश्यतइति। यथाच स्वप्नदर्शकः स्वप्नदर्शनमायया न संस्पृश्यते प्रबोधसं प्रसादयोरनन्वागतत्वात्। एवमवस्थात्रयसाक्ष्येकोऽव्य-भिचार्यवस्थात्रयेण व्यभिचारिणा न संस्पृश्यते। मायामात्रं ह्येतत् यत् परमात्नोवस्थात्रयात्मनाऽवभासनं रज्जाइव सर्पादिभावेनेति। अत्रोक्तं वेदान्तार्थसंप्रदायविद्भिराचार्य्यैः अनादिमायया सुप्तो यदा जीवः प्रबुध्यते। अजमनिद्रमखप्नमद्वैतं बुध्यतेतदेति। तत्र यदुक्तमपीतौ कारणस्यापि कार्य्यस्येव स्थौल्यादिदोष प्रसङ्ग इति एतदयुक्तं यत्पुनरेतदुक्तं समस्तस्याविभागप्राप्तेः पुनर्विभागेनोत्पत्तौ नियमकारणं नोपपद्यत इति अयमप्यदोषः दृष्टान्तभावादेव यथाहि सुषुप्तिसमाध्यादावपि सत्यां स्वाभाविक्यामविभागप्राप्तौ मिथ्या ज्ञानस्यानपोदितत्वात् पुर्व्ववत् पुनः प्रबोधे विभागो भवति एवमिहापि भविष्यति। श्रुतिश्चात्र भवति इमाः सर्व्वाः प्रजाः सति संपद्य नविदुः सति सम्म्पद्यामहइति तहह व्याघ्रो वा सिंहो वा वृको वा वराहो वा कीटो वा पतङ्गो वा दंशो वा मशको वा यद्यद्भवन्ति तत्तदा भवन्तीति। यथाह्यसंविभागेपि परमात्मनि मिथ्याज्ञानप्रतिवद्धो विभागव्यवहारः स्वप्नवदव्याहतः स्थितौ दृश्यते एवमपोतावपि मिथ्याज्ञानप्रतिबद्धैव विभागशक्तिरनुमास्यते। एतेन मुक्तानां पुनरुत्पत्तिप्रसङ्गः प्रयुक्तः सम्यग्ज्ञानेन मिथ्याज्ञानस्यापोदितत्वात्। यः पुनरमयमन्तेऽपरोविकल्प उत्प्रेक्षितोऽथेदं जगदपीतावपि विभक्तमेव परेण ब्रह्मणावतिष्ठेतेति सोप्यनभ्युपगमादेव प्रतिषिद्धः तस्मात् समञ्जसमिदमौपनिषदं दर्शनं॥

Ibid. II. i. 9.

40. प्रसिद्धोह्ययं भोक्तुभोग्यविभागो लोके भोक्ताच चेतनः शरीरो भोग्याः शब्दादयोविषया इति यथा भोक्ता देवदत्तो भोग्य ओदन इति, तस्य च विभागस्याभावः प्रसज्येत यदि भोक्ता भोग्यभावमापद्येत भोग्यं वा भोक्तृभावमापद्येत। तयोश्चेतरेतरभावापत्तिः परमकारणाद् ब्रह्मणोऽनन्यत्वात् प्रसज्येत। न चास्य प्रसिद्धस्य विभागस्य बाधनं युक्तं यथात्वद्यत्वे भोक्तृभोग्ययोर्विभागो दृष्टस्तथातीतानागतयोरपि कल्पयितव्यः तस्मात् प्रसिद्धस्य भोक्तृभोग्यविभागस्याभावप्रसङ्गादयुक्तमिदं ब्रह्मकारणतावधारणमिति चेत् कश्चिच्चोदयेत्तं प्रतिब्रूयात् स्याल्लोकवदिति। उपपद्यत एवायमस्मत्पक्षेपि विभागः एवं लोके दृष्टत्वात्। तथाहि समुद्रादुदकात्मनोऽनन्यत्वेऽपि तद्विकाराणां फेणवीचीतरङ्गबुहुदादीनामितरेतर विभाग इतरेतरसंश्लेषादिलक्षणश्च व्यवहार उपलभ्यते नच, समुद्रादुदकात्मनोऽनन्यत्वेऽपि तद्विकाराणां फेणतरङ्गादीनामितरेतरभावापत्तिर्भवति। नचैतेषामितरेतरभावानुपपत्तावपि समुद्रात्मनोऽन्यत्वं भवति एवमिहापि नच भोक्तृभोग्ययोरितरेतरभावापत्तिर्नच परस्माद्ब्रह्मणोऽन्यत्वमिति भविष्यति॥ Ibid. II. i. 13.

41. इतरव्यपदेशाद्धिताकरणादिदोषप्रसक्तिः। अन्यथा पुनश्चेतनकारणवाद आक्षिप्यते। चेतनाद्धि जगत्प्रक्रियायामाश्रीयमाणायां हिताकरणादयो दोषाः प्रसज्यन्ते कुतः इतरव्यपदेशत् इतरस्य शारीरस्य ब्रह्मात्मत्वं व्यपदिशति श्रुतिः, स आत्मा तत्त्वमसि श्वेतकेतोइतिप्रतिबोधनात् यद्वा इतरस्य च ब्रह्मणः शरीरात्मत्वं व्यपदिशति तत् सृष्ट्वा तदेवानुप्रवाविशदिति सष्टुरेवाविकृतस्य ब्रह्मणः कार्य्यानुप्रवेशेन शारीरात्मत्वप्रदर्शनात्। अनेन जीवेनात्मनानुप्रविश्य नामरूपे व्याकरणवाणीतिच परादेवता जीवमात्मशब्देन व्यपदिशन्ती न ब्रह्मणोभिन्नः शारीर इति दर्शयति। तस्माद्यहूणः स्रष्टृत्वं तच्छरीरस्यैवेत्यतः स्वतन्त्रः कर्त्ता सन् हितमेवात्मनः सौमनस्यकरं कुर्य्यात् नाहितं जन्ममरणजरारोगाद्येकानर्थजालं। नहि कश्चिदपरतन्त्रो बन्धनागारमात्मनः कृत्वानुप्रविशति नच स्वयमत्यन्तनिर्मलः सन्नत्यन्तं मलिनं देहमात्मत्वेनोपेयात् कृतमपिकथञ्चिद्यत् दुःखकरं तदिच्छया जह्यात् सुखकरं चोपाददीत स्मरेच्च मयेदं जगद्विविधं विचित्रं विरचितमिति सर्व्वो हि लोकः स्पष्टं कार्य्यं कृत्वा स्मरति मयेदं कृतमिति। यथा च मायावी स्वयं प्रसारितां मायामिच्छया आयासेनोपसंहरति एवं शारीरोपीमां सृष्टिमुपसंहरेत् स्वकीयमपि तावच्छरीरं शारीरोनशक्नोति अनायासेनोपसंहर्त्तुं। एवं हितक्रियाद्यदर्शनादन्याय्या चेतनाज्जगत्प्रक्रियेति मन्यते॥

42. अधिकन्तु भेदनिर्देशात्॥ तुशब्दः पुर्व्वपक्षं व्यावर्त्तयति। यत् सर्व्वज्ञं सर्व्वशक्ति ब्रह्म नित्यशुद्धबुद्धमुक्तसत्यस्वभावं शारीरादधिकमन्यत् तद्वयं जगतः स्रष्टृ ब्रुमः न तस्मिन् हिताकरणादयोदोषाः प्रसज्यन्ते। नहि तस्य हितं किञ्चित् कर्त्तव्यमस्ति अहितं वा परिहर्त्तव्यं नित्यमुक्तत्वात्। नच तस्य ज्ञानप्रतिबन्धः शक्तिप्रतिबन्धो वा क्वचिदप्यस्ति सर्व्वज्ञत्वात् सर्व्वशक्तित्वाच्च। शारीरस्त्वनेवंविधस्तस्मिन् प्रसज्यन्ते हिताकरणादयो दोषाः नतु तं वयं जगतः स्रष्टारं ब्रुमः। कुत एतत् भेदनिर्देशात् आत्मा वा अरे द्रष्टव्यः श्रोतव्यो मन्तव्यो निदिध्यासितव्यः सोन्वेष्टव्यः सविजिज्ञासितव्यः सता सौम्य तदा संपन्नो भवति शारीर आत्मा प्राज्ञेनात्मना अन्वारुढ इत्येवं जातीयकः कर्तृकर्म्मादिभेदनिर्देशोजीवादधिकं ब्रह्म दर्शयति। नन्वभेदनिर्देशोपि दर्शितः तत्त्वमसीत्येवञ्जातीयकः कथं भेदाभेदौविरुद्धौ सम्भवेयातां। नैषदोषः। आकाशघटाकाशन्यायेनोभयसम्भवस्य तत्र तत्र प्रतिष्ठापितत्वात्। अपिच यदा तत्त्वमसीत्येवञ्जातीयकेनाभेदनिर्देशेनाभेदः प्रतिबोधितो भवति अपगतम्भवति तदा जीवस्य संसारित्वं ब्रह्मणश्च स्रष्टृत्वं समस्तस्य मिथ्याज्ञानविजृम्भितस्य भेदव्यवहारस्य सम्यग्ज्ञानेन बाधितत्वात् तत्र कुत एव सृष्टिः कुतोवा हिताकरणादयो दोषाः। अविद्याप्रत्युपस्थापिता मरूपकृतकार्य्यकरणसंघातोपाध्यविवेककृताहि भान्तिर्हिताहितकरणादिलक्षणः संसारो नतुपरमार्थतोस्तीत्यसकृदवोपामजनममरणच्छेदनभेदनाद्यभिमानवत्। अबाधिते तु भेदव्यवहारे सोन्वेष्टव्य इत्येवञ्जातीयकेन भेदनिर्देशेनावगम्यमानं ब्रह्मणोधिकत्वहिताकरणादिदोषप्रसक्तिं निरुणद्धि॥

43. अश्मादिवच्च तदनुपपत्तिः॥ यथा च लोके पृथिवीत्वसामान्यात्मतानामप्यश्मनां केचिन्महार्हा मणयोवज्रवैदूर्य्यादयोऽन्ये मध्यमवीर्य्याः सूर्य्यकान्तादयोऽन्ये प्रहीणाः श्वावायसक्षेपणार्हाः पाषाणा इत्यनेकविधं वैचित्र्यं दृश्यते ययाचैकपृथिवीव्यपाश्रयाणामपि वीजानां बहुविधं पत्रपुष्पफलगन्धरसादिवैचित्र्यं चन्दनचम्पकादिषूपलभ्यते यथाचैकस्याप्यन्नरसस्य लोहितादीनि केशलोमादीनि च कार्य्याणि विचित्राणि भवन्ति एवमेकस्यापि ब्रह्मणो जीवप्राज्ञपृथक्तवकार्य्यवैचित्र्यं चोपपद्यत इत्यतस्तदनुपपत्तिः परपरिकल्पितदोषानुपपत्तिरित्यर्थः। श्रुतेश्च प्रामाण्याद्विकारस्य वाचारम्भणमात्रत्वात् स्वप्नदृश्यभाववैचित्र्यवच्चेत्यभ्युच्चयः॥

44. उपसंहारदर्शनान्नेतिचेन्नक्षीरवद्धि। चेतनं ब्रह्मैकमद्वितीयं जगतः कारणमिति यदुक्तं तन्नोपपद्यते कस्मात् उपसंहारदर्शनात्। इह हि लोके कुलालादयोघटपटादीनां कर्त्तारोमृद्दण्डचक्रसूत्राद्यनेककारकोपसंहारेण

संगृहीतसाधना: सन्तस्तत्तत् कार्य्यं कुर्व्वाणा दृश्यन्ते ब्रह्मचासहायं तवाभिप्रेतं तस्य साधनान्तरानुपसंग्रहे सति कथं स्रष्टृत्वमुपपद्येत तस्मान्न ब्रह्म जगत्कारणमिति चेन्नैष दोषः। यतः क्षीरवत् द्रव्यस्वभावविशेषादुपपद्यते यथाहि लोके क्षीरं जलं वा स्वयमेव दधिहिमभावेन परिणमतेऽनपेक्ष्य वाह्यं साधनं तथेहापि भविष्यति। ननु क्षीराद्यपि दध्यादिभावेन परिणममानमपेक्षत एव वाह्यं साधनं औष्ण्यादिकं कथमुच्यते क्षीरवद्धीति। नैष दोषः। स्वयमपि हि क्षीरं याञ्च यावतीञ्च परिणाममात्रामनुभवत्येव त्वार्य्यते त्वौष्णयादिना दधिभावाय। यदिच स्वयं दधिभावशीलता न स्यान्नैवौष्ण्यादिनापि बलाद्दधिभावमापद्येत। नहि वायुर्वाकाशोवौष्ण्यादिना बलाद्दधिभावमापद्यते। साधनसम्पत्त्या च तस्य संपूर्णता सम्पाद्यते। परिपूर्णशक्तिकन्तु ब्रह्म न तस्यान्येन केनचित् पुर्णता सम्पादयितव्या। श्रुतिश्च तत्र भवति न तस्य कार्य्यं करणञ्च विद्यते न तत् समञ्चाभ्यधिकश्च दृश्यते। परास्य शक्तिर्विविधैव श्रूयते स्वाभाविकी ज्ञानबलक्रियाचेति। तस्मादेकस्यापि ब्रह्मणो विचित्रशक्तियोगात् क्षीरादिवद्विचित्रः परिणामश्चोपपद्यते।

45. देवादिवदपि लोके। स्यादेतत् उपपद्यते क्षीरादीनामचेतनानामनपेक्ष्यापि वाह्यं साधनं दध्यादिभावो दृष्टत्वात् चेतनाः पुनः कुलालादयश्च साधनसामग्रीमपेक्ष्यैव तस्मै तस्मै कार्य्याय प्रवर्त्तमाना दृश्यन्ते कथं ब्रह्मचेतनं सदसहायं प्रवर्त्तेतेति। देवादिवदितिब्रुमः। यथा लोके देवाः पितर ऋषय इत्येवमादयो महाप्रभावाश्चेतना अपि सन्तोऽनपेक्ष्य किञ्चिद्वाह्यं साधनमैश्वर्य्यविशेषयोगादभि-ध्यानमात्रेण खत एव वहूनि नानासंस्थानानि शरीराणि प्रासादादीनि रथादीनि च निर्मिमाणा उपलभ्यन्ते मन्त्रार्थवादेतिहासपुराणप्रामाण्यात्। तन्तुना भश्च स्व एव तन्तून् सृजति वलाकाचान्तरेणैव शुक्रं गर्भं धत्ते पद्मिनी चानपेक्ष्य किञ्चित् प्रस्थानसाधनं सरोन्तरात् सरोन्तरं प्रतिष्ठते एवं चेतनमपि ब्रह्मानपेक्ष्यं वाह्यं साधनं स्वत एत जगत् स्रक्ष्यति॥

46. कृत्स्नप्रसक्तिर्निरवयवत्वशब्दकोपोवा। चेतनमेकाद्वितीयं ब्रह्मक्षीरादिवद्देवता-दिवच्चानपेक्षितवाह्यसाधनं स्वयम्परिणममानं जगतः कारणमिति स्थितं। शास्त्रार्थपरिशुद्धयेतु पुनराक्षिपति कृत्स्नप्रसक्तिः कृत्स्नस्य ब्रह्मणः कार्य्यरूपेण परिणामः प्राप्नोति निरवयवत्वात्। यदि ब्रह्म पृथिव्यादिवत् सावयवमभविष्य-त्ततोऽस्यैकदेशः पर्य्यणंस्यत एकदेशश्चावास्थास्यत निरवयवन्तु ब्रह्मश्रुतिभ्याव-गम्यते निष्कलं निष्क्रियं शान्तं निरवद्यं निरञ्जनं दिव्योह्यमूर्त्तः पुरुषः सवाह्याभ्यन्तरोह्यजः इदं महद्भुतमनन्तरमपारं विज्ञानघनएव सएष नेति नेति

नेत्यात्माऽस्थूलमनणिवत्याद्याभ्यः सर्व्वविशेषप्रतिषेधयित्रीभ्यः। ततश्चैकदेश-परिणामासम्भवात् कृत्स्न प्रसक्तौ सत्यां मूलोच्छेदः प्रसज्येत द्रष्टव्यत्वोपदेशानर्थक्यञ्चापन्नं प्रयत्नदृष्टत्वात् कार्य्यस्य। तहतिरिक्तस्य च ब्रह्मणोऽभावादजत्वादिशब्दव्याकोपश्च। अथैतद्दोषपरिजिहीर्षया सावयवमेव ब्रह्माभ्युपम्येत तथापि ये निरवयवत्वस्य प्रतिपादकाः शब्दाः उदाहृतास्ते प्रकुप्येयुः। सावयवत्वे चानित्यत्वप्रसङ्ग इति सर्व्वथाऽयं पक्षोन घटयितुं शक्यत इत्याक्षिपति॥

47. श्रुतेस्तु शब्दमूलत्वात्॥ तु शब्देनाक्षेपं परिहरति नखल्वस्मत् पक्षे कश्चिदपि दोषोस्ति न तावत् कृत्स्नप्रसक्तिरस्ति कुतः श्रुतेः यथैवहि ब्रह्मणो जगदुत्पत्तिः श्रूयते एवं विकारव्यतिरेकेणापि ब्रह्मणोवस्थान श्रूयते प्रकृतिविकारयोर्भेदेन व्यपदेशात् सेयन्देवतैक्षत हन्ताहमिमास्तिस्रो देवता अनेन जीवेनात्मनानुप्रविश्य नामरूपेव्याकरवाणीति तावानस्य महिमा ततोज्यायांश्च पुरुषः पादोस्य विश्वाभूतानि त्रिपादस्यामृतं दिवीतिचैवंजातीयकात् तथा हृदयायतनत्ववचनात् ससम्पत्तिवचनाच्च। यदिच कृत्स्नं ब्रह्म कार्य्यभावेनोपयुक्तं स्यात् सता सौम्य तदा सम्पन्नोभवतीति सुषुप्तिगतं विशेषणमनुपपन्नं स्यात् विकृतेन ब्रह्मणानित्यं सम्पन्नत्वात् अविकृतस्य च ब्रह्मणोऽभावात् तथेन्द्रियगोचरत्वप्रतिषेधाद्ब्रह्मणो विकारस्य चेन्द्रियगोचरत्वोपपत्तेः। तस्मादस्ति अविकृतं ब्रह्म। नच निरवयवत्वशब्दव्याकोपोस्ति श्रूयमाणत्वादेव निरवयवत्वस्याप्यभ्युपगभ्यमानत्वात्। शब्दमूलञ्च ब्रह्म शब्दप्रमाणाकं नेन्द्रियादिप्रमाणकं तद्यथाशब्दमभ्युपगन्तव्यम्। शब्दश्चोभयमपि ब्रह्मणः प्रतिपादयति अकृत्स्नप्रसक्तिं निरवयवताञ्च। लौकिकानामपि मणिमन्त्रौषधीप्रभृतीनां देशकालनिमित्तवैचित्र्यवशात् शक्तयो विरुद्धानेककार्य्यविषया दृश्यन्ते ता अपि तावन्नोपदेशमन्तरेण केवलेन तर्केणावगन्तुं शक्यन्ते अस्य वस्तुन एतावत्य एतत् सहाया एतद्विषया एतत् प्रयोजनाश्च शक्तय इति किमुताचिन्त्यप्रभावस्य ब्रह्मणोरूपं विनाशब्देन न निरूप्येत। तथाचाहुः पौराणिकाः अचिन्त्याः खलु ये भावा नतांस्तर्केण योजयेत्। प्रकृतिभ्यः परयच्च तदचिन्त्यस्य लक्षणमिति। तस्माच्छब्दमूल एवातीन्द्रियार्थयाथात्म्याधिगमः। ननु शब्देनापि न शक्यते विरुद्धार्थः प्रत्याययितुं निरवयवञ्च ब्रह्म परिणमते च नकृत्स्नमिति यदि निरवयवं ब्रच स्यान्नैव परिणमेत कृत्स्न मेव वा परिणमेत। अथ केनचिद्रूपेण परिणमेत केनचिद्रूपेणावतिष्ठेतेति रूपभेदकल्पनात् सावयवमेव प्रसज्येत। क्रियाविषये ह्यतिरात्रे षोडशिनं गृह्णाति नातिरात्रे षोडशिनं गृह्णातीत्येवं जातीयकायां

विरुद्धप्रतीतावपि विकल्पाश्रयणं विरोधपरिहारकारणं भवति पुरुषतन्त्रत्वादनुष्ठानस्य। इह तु विकल्पाश्रयणेनापि न विरोधपरिहारः सम्भवति अपुरुषतन्त्रवाद्वस्तुनः तस्माद्दुर्घटमेतदिति। नैषदोषः अविद्याकल्पितरूपभेदाभ्युपगमात् नह्यविद्याकल्पितेन रूपभेदेन सावयवं वस्तु सम्पद्यते। नहि तिमिरोपहतनयनेनानेकइव चन्द्रमा दृश्यमानोऽनेक एव भवति। अविद्याकल्पितेन च नामरूपलक्षणेन रूपेभेदेन व्याकृताव्याकृतात्मकेन तत्त्वान्यत्वाभ्यामनिर्वाच्येन ब्रह्म परिणामादि सर्व्वव्यवहारास्पदत्वं प्रतिपद्यते पारमार्थिकेन च रूपेण सर्व्वव्यवहारातीतमपरिणतमवतिष्ठते। वाचारम्भणमात्र-त्वाच्चाविद्याकल्पितस्य नामरूपभेदस्य न निरवयवत्वं ब्रह्मणः कुप्यति। नचेयं परिणामश्रुतिः परिणामप्रतिपादानार्था तत्प्रतिपत्तौ फलानवगमात्। सर्व्वव्यवहारहीनब्रह्मात्मभावप्रतिपादनार्था त्वेषा तत्प्रतिपत्तौ फलावगमात् स एष नेतिनेत्यात्मेत्युपक्रम्याह अभयं वैजनक प्राप्तोसीति। तस्मादस्मत्पक्षे न कश्चिदपिदोषप्रसङ्गोस्ति॥

48. न प्रयोजनवत्त्वात्। अन्यथा पुनश्चेतनकर्तृकत्वं जगतः आक्षिपति न खलु चेतनः परमात्मेदं जगद्विम्बं विरचयितुमर्हति कुतः। प्रयोजनवत्त्वात् प्रवृत्तीनां। चेतनोहि लोके बुद्धिपूर्व्वकारी पुरुषः प्रवर्त्तमानो न मन्दोपक्रमामपि तावत् प्रवृत्तिमात्मप्रयोजनानुपयोगिनीमारभमाणो दृष्टः, किमुत गुरुतरसंरम्भां? भवति च लोकप्रसिद्धानुवादिनी श्रुतिः। न वा अरे सर्व्वस्य कामाय सर्व्वं प्रियम्भवत्यात्मनस्तु कामाय सर्व्वं प्रियम्भवतीति। गुरुतरसंरम्भा चेयं प्रवृत्तिर्यदुच्चावचप्रपञ्चं विरचयितव्यं। यदीयमपि प्रवृत्तिश्चेतनस्य परमात्मन आत्मप्रयोजनोपयोगिनी परिकल्प्येत, परितृप्तत्वं परमात्मनःश्रूयमाणं बाध्येत। प्रयोजनाभावे वा प्रवृत्त्यभावोपि स्यात्। अथ चेतनोपि सन्नुन्मत्तो बुद्धयपराधादन्तरेणैवात्मप्रयोजनं प्रवर्त्तमानो दृष्टस्तथा परमात्मापि प्रवर्त्तिष्यत इत्युच्येत, तथा सति सर्व्वज्ञत्वं परमात्मनः श्रूयमाणं वाध्येत, तस्मादश्लिष्टा चेतनात् सृष्टिरिति। II. i. 32.

49. लोकवत्तु लीलाकैवल्यं। तु शब्देनाक्षेपं परिहरति। यथा लोके कस्यचिदाप्तैषणस्य राज्ञो राजामात्यस्य वा व्यतिरिक्तं किञ्चित् प्रयोजन-मनभिसन्धाय केवलं लीलारूपाः प्रवृत्तयः क्रीडाविहारेषु भवन्ति। यथा चोच्छ्वासप्रश्वासादयोऽनभिसन्धाय वाह्यं किञ्चित् स्वभावादेव भवन्ति त्वमीश्वरस्याप्यनपेक्ष्य किञ्चित् प्रयोजनान्तरं स्वभावादेव केवलं लीलारूपा प्रवृत्तिर्भविष्यति। नहीश्वरस्य प्रयोजनान्तरं निरूप्यमाणा न्यायतः श्रुतितो वा सम्भवति। न च स्वभावः पर्य्यनुयोक्तुं शक्यते। यद्यप्यस्माकमियं

जगद्विम्बविरचना गुरुतरसंरम्भेवाभाति तथापि परमेश्वरस्य लीलैवकेवलेयं अपरिमितशक्तित्वात्। यदि नाम लोके लीलीस्वपि किञ्चित् सूक्ष्मं प्रयोजनमुत्प्रेक्षेत तथापि नैवात्र किञ्चित् प्रयोजनमुत्प्रेक्षितुं शक्यते, आप्तकामश्रुतेः। नाप्यप्रवृत्तिरुत्मत्तप्रवृत्तिर्व्वा, सृष्टिश्रुतेः सर्व्वज्ञत्वश्रुतेश्च। II. 8.33.

50. ब्रह्मदृष्टिरुत्कर्षात्॥ Vedānta, IV. i. 5.

तथाच लौकिको न्यायोनुमतो भवति उत्कृष्टदृष्टिर्हि निकृष्टेध्यसितव्येति लौकिकोन्यायः यथाराजदृष्टिः क्षत्तरि सचानुगन्तव्यः विपर्य्यये प्रत्यवायप्रसङ्गात् नहि क्षत्तृदृष्टिपरिगृहीतो राजा निकर्षं नीयमानः श्रेयसे स्यात्॥

51. न तु वस्त्वेवं नैवं अस्ति नास्तीति वा विकल्प्यते I. 1. 2.

52. न चेदं ब्रह्मात्मेकत्वविज्ञानं संपद्रूपं। यथा अनन्तं वैमनोऽनन्ता वैविश्वेदेवा अनन्तमेव सतेन लोकं जयतीति। नचाध्यासरूपं यथा मनोब्रह्मेयुपासीत। आदित्यो ब्रह्मेत्यादेश इति मन आदित्यादिषु ब्रह्मदृष्ट्यध्यासः। नापि विशिष्टक्रियायोगनिमित्तं। वायुर्वाव संवर्गः प्राणोवाव संवर्ग इत्यादिवत्। नाप्याज्यावेक्षणात् कर्माङ्गसंस्काररूपं। सम्पदादि रूपेहि ब्रह्मात्मैकत्वविज्ञानेऽभ्युपगम्यमाने तत्त्वमस्यह ब्रह्मास्ययमात्मा ब्रह्मेत्येवमादीनां वाक्यानां ब्रह्मात्मैकत्ववस्तुप्रतिपादनपरः पदसमन्वयः पीड्येत। I. 1. 4.

The technical words here used are thus explained.

सम्पन्नामाल्पे वस्तुन्यालम्वने सामान्येन केनचित् महतो वस्तुनः सम्पादनं। अध्यासः शास्त्रतोऽतस्मिंस्तद्धीः। संवर्गविद्यायां श्रुतं वायुर्वाव संवर्गो यदा वा अग्निरुद्वापयति उपशाम्यति वायुमेवाप्येति विलीयते यदा सूर्य्योस्तमेति वायुमेवाप्येति यदा चन्द्रोस्तमेति वायुमेवाप्येति यदा य उच्छुष्यन्ति वायुमेवापयन्ति वायुर्ह्येतान् सर्वान् संवृङ्क्ते॥ Ratnaprabhā.

53. मायावादमतान्धकारमुषितप्रज्ञोसि यस्मादहं ब्रह्मास्मीति वचो मुहर्मुहर्वदसि रे जीव त्वमुन्मुत्तवत्। ऐश्वर्य्यं तव कुत्र कुत्र विभुता सर्वज्ञता कुत्र ते तन्मेरोरिदं सर्षणेण हि भिदा जीव त्वया ब्रह्मणः॥

Tattva-muktāvalī by Gauḍapurṇānanda.

54. परिछिन्नोजोवस्त्वमसि खलु स व्यापकतमस्त्वमेकत्रस्थाता भवसि सहि सर्व्वत्र सततं। सुखी दुःखी त्वं रे क्षणिकः स सुखी सर्व्वसमये कथं सोहं वाक्यं वदसि वत लज्जां न कुरुषे॥

55. काचःकाचो मणिरपि मणिः शुक्तिरेवास्ति शुक्तिः रूप्यं रूप्यं न भवति

कदाप्यत्ययं ज्ञानमेघां। ★ ★ भक्त्या सदा ब्राह्मणपूजनेन शूद्रोपि ब्राह्मणतामुपैति। किञ्चिद्गुणस्यैव भवेत् प्रवेशो न ब्राह्मणः स्यात् खलु शूद्रजातिः॥

56. व्यवस्थातो नाना। III. ii. 20.

नाना आत्मानः कुतः व्यवस्थातः व्यवस्था प्रतिनियमः यथा कश्चिदाष्ढ्यः कश्चिद्रङ्कः कश्चित् सुखी कश्चिद्दुःखी कश्चिदुच्चाभिजनः कश्चिन्नीचाभिजनः कश्चिद्विद्वान् कश्चिज्जाल्म इतीयं व्यवस्था आत्मभेदमन्तरेणानुपपद्यमाना साधयत्यात्मनां भेदं॥

57. यत्र हि द्वैतमेव भवति तदितर इतरं पश्यति तदितर इतरं जिघ्रति तदितर इतरं शृणोति तदितर इतरमभिवदति तदितर इतरं मनुते तदितर इतरं विजानाति यत्र वा अस्य सर्व्वमात्मैवाभूत्तत्केन कं जिघ्रेत्तत्केन कं पश्येत्तत्केन कथं शृणुयात्तत्केन कमभिवदेत्तत्केन कं मन्वीत तत्केनकं विजानीयात्। Bṛhad.

58. सकलमिदमहञ्च ब्रह्मभूतं यदि स्यात् त्वमहं खलु तदास्यादावयोरैक्यमेव। धनुसुतदारामामकीनास्तदास्युर्मम तवच भवेयुर्नावयोरस्ति भेदः॥ विधिनिषेधश्च कदा कथं स्यादैक्यं यतो नास्ति च सर्व्वभेदः। निर्णीतमद्वैतमतं त्वया चेत् बौद्धैस्तदा कोविहितोपराधः॥

59. श्री परीक्षिदुवाच। संस्थापनाय धर्मस्य प्रशमायेतरस्यच अवतीर्णोहि भगवानंशेन जगदीश्वरः। स कथं धर्मसेतूनां वक्ता कर्ताभिरक्षिता। प्रतीपमारचद्ब्रह्मन् परदाराभिमर्षणं॥ श्री शुक उवाच। गोपीनां तत्पतीनाञ्च सर्वेषाञ्चैव देहिनां। योन्तश्चरति सोध्यक्ष एष क्रीडनदेहभाक्। Śrī-Bhāgavata.

60. नैतत् समाचरेज्जातु मनसापि ह्यनीश्वरः। विनश्यत्याचरन्मौढ्याद्यथाऽरुद्राब्धिजं विषं। ईश्वराणां वचः सत्ये तथैवाचरितं क्वचित् तेषां यत्स्ववचोयुक्तं बुद्धिमांस्तत् समाचारेत्। Śrī-Bhāgavata.

61. आब्रह्मस्तम्बपर्य्यन्तं सर्वं कृष्णाश्चराचरं। Nārada pañcrātra.

62. सद्वंशजातः शिष्यश्च शुद्धः सुब्राह्मणः सुधीः।
मन्यते कृष्णतुल्यञ्च गुरुं परमधार्मिकः॥
गुणरूपी स्वयं कृष्णः शिष्याणां हितकाम्यया।
गुरौ तुष्टे हरिस्तुष्टो हरौ तुष्टे जगत्रयं॥
गुरुर्ब्रह्मागुरुर्विष्णुः गुरुदेवो महेश्वरः।
गुरुदेवपरं ब्रह्म गुरुः पूज्यः परात्परः॥ Ibid.

63. यत्पादपङ्कजपरागनिषेवतृप्ता योगप्रभावविधुताखिलकर्मबन्धाः। खैरं चरन्ति

मुनयोपि न नह्यमानास्तस्येच्छयातवपुषः कुत एव बन्धः॥

Śrī-Bhāgavata.

64. See Vijñāna Bhikṣu.
65. विभूतिं प्रसवन्त्वन्ये मन्यन्ते सृष्टिचित्तकाः॥
66. अवशे द्यामस्तभायद्बृहन्तमा रोदसी अष्पृणदन्तरिक्षं।
स धारयत् पृथिवीं पप्रथच्छ सोमस्य ता मद इन्द्रश्चकार॥
Max Muller's Ṛg Veda, Vol. II. p. 488.
67. अनियतत्वेऽपि नायौक्तिकस्य संग्रहोऽन्यथा वालोन्मत्तादिसमत्त्वं॥
Sāṅkhya Sūtra, I. 29
68. स्वप्नस्वरूपा मायास्वरूपा च। सृष्टिचिन्तका मन्यन्ते नतु परमार्थचिन्तकानां सृष्टावादरः॥
69. मायामात्रन्तु कात्स्र्न्येनानभिव्यक्तस्वरूपत्वात्॥
70. सान्ध्येसृष्टिराहहि III.ii. 1.
71. तत्रसंशयः किं प्रबोध ईव स्वप्नेपि पारमार्थिकी सृष्टिराहो स्विन्मायामयीति Com, on Do.
72. अयङ्कर्तृत्वभोक्तृत्वाभिमानित्वेन इहलोकपरलोकगामी व्यावहारिको जीव इत्युव्यते॥
73. एते चोराः किमिति धरणीनायकेनापि दण्ड्याः मायावादी सशपथमिदंवक्ति सर्वन्तु मिथ्या॥ Tattva-muktāvalī by Gauḍapūrṇānanda.
74. Śaṅkara in some places of his commentaries.
75. न त्वात्मनोऽमूर्त्तत्वादाकारादिकारणस्यात्मनो व्यापकत्वात्। तद्विप्रकृष्टदेश-प्रतिविम्बाधारवस्त्वभावाच्च प्रतिविम्बवत् प्रबेशान् युक्तः॥
76. न वस्तुयाथात्म्यज्ञानं पुरुषवुद्ध्यपेक्षं किं तर्हि वस्तुतन्त्रमेव तत्। नहि स्थाणावेकस्मिन् स्थाणुर्वा पुरुषोवान्योवेति तत्त्वज्ञानम्भवति। तत्र पुरुषोवान्योवेति मिथ्याज्ञानं स्थाणुरेवेति तत्त्वज्ञानं वस्तुतन्त्रत्वात्। एवं भूतवस्तुविषयाणां प्रामाण्यं वस्तुतन्त्रं। I.i. 2.
79. शुद्धात्मा नीलवस्त्रादियोगेन स्फटिको यथा। Ātmabodha.

DIALOGUE IX

FROM THE SAME TO THE SAME

My last letter informed you of our doings on the day we spent at the Rajah's house. I shall now report to you what passed on the morrow. We had scarcely done our prescribed duties of the first *prahara,* (or, quarter of day,) when the *adhikārī,* in charge of the garden, came, and said, that the Rajah had sent a Jemadar to communicate his remembrance of us in the private-audience chamber. We responded to the summons, and repaired to that chamber. His highness was engaged in conversation with a *Daṇḍi,* who had taken to his staff the year before, and, giving up his home, had ever since been performing the exercises of a Yogi in the hope of attaining to *Samādhi* and *Nirvāṇa.* On our reaching the audience-chamber, and taking our seats, the Daṇḍi turned to Satyakāma, and spoke as follows : "The Rajah has told me of the discussion you had yesterday. I will not deny that your arguments have some force, but I still feel, that on several important points, you have totally misapprehended our views. You say there is no medium between reality and unreality, and that, if we call the world an illusion, we cannot argue from it as a reality. You say we cannot be sure of any truth if we consider the world an illusion, and the human soul a mere *Vyāvahārika jīva.* You also argue that on our theory no one can have a motive for virtue, nor can there be such a thing as law or duty. You accuse us too, of gross inconsistency in talking of emancipation from a bondage which in reality has no existence, because the world is itself an illusion.

"Now, whatever Vyāsa or Śaṅkarācārya may have said on the nature of substantial existence, I can point out a palpable middle term between reality and unreality. There is such a thing as a self-subsisting independent existence, and there is such a thing as dependent existence. The former we attribute to the Deity, the latter to the world. We accordingly say, emphatically, that He alone is *sat,* or really existent. He lives *paramārthataḥ*. We add that the world is *asat,* that is not real in this absolute sense, because it is not self-subsisting, and therefore transient. And yet we do not pronounce it to be such an unreality as that we could not argue for any truths founded on its existence. It is certainly real, in some sort; for it is producing actual impressions on the senses, and surely we may with logical propriety deduce the existence of a first cause from an illusion; for how could the illusion be produced without the agency of a cause? It requires to be accounted for as much as any phenomena on *your* hypothesis. Then again as to the human soul, the recipient of the impressions occasioned by the illusion, whatever the Vedānta Sāra may say, we do not attribute to it a mere *vyāvahārika* existence; nor do we consider it as part of the Universe, for the human soul is consubstantial with God. With reference to practical duties, our theory cannot disturb them, for howsoever the ignorant voluptuary may argue to the contary, we say, what every thinking man will readily understand, that in the state of *avidyā,* the observance of duty is the safest, and, when *avidyā* is removed, and the soul gets the fulness of divine illumination, the violation of duty will be as impossible as its observance unnecessary. Nor can you justly say that we toil to no purpose in seeking for emancipation from a bondage, which, notwithstanding its illusory character, produces real apprehensions and fears in the mind. We are actually in terror under its influence, and therefore it is said, 'O Janaka, thou has attained fearlessness!'"

Satyakāma.—"I think, revered and learned Sir, the new explanations you have introduced into the Vedānt philosophy fail to impart to it any additional strength. Your view of the Vedānta appears to be derived from foreign sources, and is therefore somewhat different, not only from Vyāsa's and Śaṅkara's, but also from the minor treatises, such as the Paribhāṣā and the Vedānta Sāra. It is impossible in a general refutation of a system to anticipate every thing that an individual follower of the doctrine, especially one who is acquainted with other systems of philosophy, may conceive in his mind, apart from the positions laid down by leading expositors. Your philosophical principle seems to be that which Kapila recommends in Sāṅkhya Sūtra iv. 13. 'Notwithstanding much reading to Śāstra, and much instruction from tutors, one is to take the substantial part only, like the bee[1].' The bee flies from flower to flower and takes only the meliferous matter. You seem to be collecting ideas in the same eclectic way. Now it would be a great historical inaccuracy to give to such a collection the name of Vedāntism. But as you have unbosomed yourself so frankly, I am bound to tell you what I think on the subject.

"That God's existence is independent and self-subsisting, is a doctrine which you cannot hold more firmly than myself. If by adding that the world has a dependent existence, you only mean that the world is a created, and, therefore, not a self-existent, substance, it is impossible for us to differ on that point either. You cannot then call it an illusion, for surely God is able to create a real substance by the power of his will. Why must you compare Him with a conjurer, that calls up an appearance, having no existence except in a deceived imagination? Why should you limit His power by such an unworthy comparison? If your meaning be that the world has no existence but in human ideas, cognitions, or impressions, then that is the very theory of the Buddhists which has been so successfully refuted by Śaṅkarācārya. I can only repeat that eminent philosophers language, that the world has an existence, independent of human notions.

"Assuming, however, that the only difference in point of real existence that you desire to establish between God and the Universe is the necessary one of Creator and creature, my objection to the Vedāntic tenet, that the Universe is identical with God, does not lose its force at all. That identification would, on the theory now before us, clearly amount to material pantheism. It must either be a degradation of the Creator, or a deification of the creature.

"Since, again, you call the world an illusion, I do not understand how you can reconcile such language with the notion of its existence (however dependent) as a creature. For I still contend that an existent creature cannot be an illusion. An illusion may, as an effect, prove the agency of a cuase. That I do not deny. But the phantom, as Śaṅkarācārya himself admits, must have a medium, a really existing medium, separate from its projector. The medium then must be a second substance, and so contradict your theory of one essence without a second. The medium, again, must be something material, for the illusion is an object of sensuous perception, and, if '*all this*' be God, the material medium must be deified too. Supposing, however, the world to be an illusion and no-thing, what do you mean by saying, All this is God? What can be the drift, what the motive of such an assertion? What truth can you explain, what knowledge can you impart, what object can you attain by calling that to be God which you are convinced is a no-thing? What can you be possibly aiming at by saying, almost in the same breath, 'every thing from Brahmā to a bundle of grass is false,' AND AGAIN, 'every thing, animate or inanimate, from Brahmā to a bundle of grass is Kṛṣṇa, *i.e.,* God?'[2]

"When, moreover, calling the world an illusion, you still contend that it has perils which require to be remedied by a laborious process of philosophy, your argument is simply unintelligible."

Yogi.—"Even an illusory peril may produce real fears in

the mind. So long as a man is subject to such fears, the peril must be considered *real,* and remedied accordingly."

Satyakāma.—"Well how do you propose remedying the illusory peril?"

Yogi—"By teaching that nothing is existent but the Supreme Being. All else being a vanity, as the Javans say. *Allah bas, baki haus* (God is sufficient, the rest is vanity)."

Satyakāma.—"But the Javans do not say that the world is an illusion. They call it a vanity, because it has nothing solid, nothing abiding, nothing worthy of love or attachment. You again contend that the vanity is God. The Javan theory may have a tendency to lead men to look up to God as their only refuge from evil, but your theory teaches there is no real evil, or the evil is God himself, and, there being one essence alone, no possibility of law or duty."

Yogi.—"But we do admit both law and duty. We tell men that, so long as they are in a state of *Avidyā,* or ignorance, it is safe for them to conform to the duties of their respective classes."

Satyakāma—"People look for what is practically safe when they are in a dilemma. The deluded subject of *Māyā,* whom you wish to reclaim, will naturally ask, why you speculate on what is merely safe, or expedient, if you are sure the world is an illusion, and there is no real evil? To tell a man that he must do his duty, merely, because it is safe to do so, is in fact to tell him that he is not bound by duty. It is to lose sight altogether of the definition of duty. Duty is what *ought* to be done. Such a duty, that is to say strict duty, cannot however exist where all is illusion, but Brahma. Duty presupposes the existence of two parties, the person bound by the duty, and the party to whom he is bound. The question of the Upaniṣad, however, bold in setting duty as defiance, is, on its own principles, unanswerable, *Who will regard, whom and how?* Do you think you will produce any impression on your neighbour by playing fast and loose with him on points of duty?"

Yogi.—"If my neighbour is determined to act like a depraved person I cannot help it. If he be a mass of corruption, nothing will save him."

Satyakāma.—"But how can you expect better things from Māyā? How can there be a real mass of corruption, either, if all is illusion but Brahma? I of course believe that not your neighbour only, but all men are naturally depraved, though capable of the highest improvement. And it may be expected of a scheme propounded for the amelioration of the human race, that it will meet the disease with which our race is afflicted, and work on the affections of our nature, so as to promote virtuous and restrain vicious inclinations. But this service can never be performed by a system which confounds all distinctions of right and wrong, by pronouncing every thing to be an illusion but Brahma.

"What again is the precise meaning of your theory of māyā? What is māyā? Is it a deceptive power, or is it the deception itself? Is it the illusion by which you are deceived, or is it the delusive influence through which God presents the illusion to your senses? Śaṅkarācārya appears to take it in the sense of a delusive influence, the instrumental cause of the illusion—for he talks of the world as a creation of ignorance. This is something like the old story of Indra's propping up the heavens in a state of intoxication, but, in this sense, the creation itself may be a substance. A real and abiding effect may be produced under intoxication."

Yogi.—"We say it is either no-thing, or a distorted reflection of the only one thing existent, that is God."

Satyakāma.—"Is it not an extremely low view of the Divinity to say that He appears to us in the form of the world, that He has projected a distorted reflection of Himself with a view to delude His rational creatures? We are all agreed that religious errors are the most serious of all errors, and of all religious errors, the greatest must be that which consists in a false notion of the Divine attributes. Is it possible to believe that God would deliberately produce such an error in his creatures by projecting a distorted likeness of Himself?

"And here allow me to direct your attention to the opinions which Rāmānuja expressed on this point. He, like yourself, had abandoned the pleasures of the world, and looked for a higher spiritual position than most men think of. It is not for me to say anything as to his success, but his remarks on the subject of our present discussion, as recorded by one of his followers, will perhaps have some weight in your estimation[3]. In the recesses of all śāstras we are told of both knowledge and ignorance, of virtue and vice, or right and wrong sciences. Thus we see [opposites in] pairs everywhere, and God and the soul are also notoriously so. How then can they have unity? Let holy men answer this with a candid mind. The word *tat* (it) stands for the ocean of immortality, full of supreme felicity. The word *twam* (thou) stands for a miserable person, distracted in mind, through fear of the world. The two cannot therefore be one. They are substantially different. He is to be worshipped by the whole world. Thou art but His slave. There can be no designation, nor substantial existence, nor definition, where there is no foundation or reason. How can Brahma be understood or inferred on the theory of Māyā? His existence we deduce as the author of the universe, for all this appears, on the evidence of inference, to have a cause. This earth must surely have an author, for, like pots and other things, it is but a production. Mark the great difference between the Lord, and men, working with axes, choppers, and ploughshares. These are sore troubled by the six waves of their passions. They toil, and labour, and are exhausted. He effects every thing by a mere turn of his brow. How could there be an image or reflection of the Infinite and spotless one? How could the Veda, either, declare the merit and demerit of a non-sentient (reflection), or the reflection itself be a subject of pain or pleasure? There may be a reflection of a finite substance; how could there be such a thing of the Infinite. Rāmānuja, the first among great men, condemned this theory of an image and reflection. That his opinions were not received by great men makes them only still dearer. I am sometimes happy, sometimes miserable. He, the [Supreme] Spirit, is always happy. Such is the discrimination. How then can two distinct substances be identical? He is an eternal Light, without anything to obscure it—pure, the one superintendent of the world. But the animal soul is not so. Thus a thunder-bolt falls on the tree of no-distinction. How canst thou, oh slow of thought! say, I am He, who has set up this immense sphere of the universe in its fulness? Consider thine own capacities with a pure mind. Can a collection of infuriated elephants enter into the stomach of a musquito? Whose art thou? Whence art thou come? What is the connection of this bondage of the world? Ponder these questions in thy mind, give up the way of the erring. By the mercy of the Most High a little understanding has been committed to thee, it is not for thee, oh perverse one, to say, therefore I am God. That would be, as if some wicked person, having received [from a king], elephants, horses, and infantry, were to form the intention of usurping the royal dignity. Some sophists, sunk in a sea of false logic, addicted to evil ways, labouring to bring about the destruction of the world by false statements, themselves deceived and deceiving the world, say I am God, and all this universe is God. Their wicked device is now abundantly exposed. To speak of a void of qualities in the ocean of qualities! Oh theirs is like the stream of a flock of sheep. Having made a separate paraphrase of the sūtras, they are deceiving the followers of their own doctrine. All the qualities of sovereignty and activity are eternally God's. He is therefore one endowed with qualities (*guṇi*), how can He be *nirguṇa,* or devoid of qualities? The assertion of the void of qualities is mere disputation. A substance without attributes, like the sky-flower, is never admitted either in the Veda, or in the world. If the Vedas were to set forth such an object, they would no longer be any authority. As the stone, or utensils, and the sacrificer are instruments of a sacrifice, so is this theory of no-attribute or no-duty an instrument for the obstruction of Dharma or virtue.'

"To these extracts I shall only add a few passages from Rāmānuja's own philosophical work. With reference to the pantheistic dogma, that individual animal souls are but reflections of the Supreme Spirit, he says; Some persons[4], betaking themselves to the doctrine of God's being the only entity, have come to the conclusion that animal souls are but reflections of the one Supreme Being. Their happiness, misery, and other conditions are owing to their different receptacles, just as the same face may appear, variously, small, large, obscure, and clear, when reflected from various gems, swords, and looking-glasses. * * This difference in condition is [they say] owing to a fabricated distinction. Now, it may be asked, whose fabrication is it? Not surely God's, for He is incapable of such fabrication, being Himself pure knowledge. Nor can it be the animal soul's, for then there would be reciprocal supprot [i.e., a vicious circle]; thus, the soul itself is dependent [for its existence] on the fabrication, and the fabrication is owing to the soul.'

"Rāmānuja asks again, Of the soul, fabricated by ignorance, who is the fabricator? This ought to be determined. Not surely the ignorance itself, for it is inanimate. Nor the soul, for then it would be a case of self-fabrication, because [you say] the soul is the object of the fabrication by Ignorance, after the manner shell and silver. If you say God is himself the fabricator of the notion of soul, then you introduce ignorance into the Deity. And, if you do not introduce ignorance into the Divinity, [may I ask] whether God looks on souls or not? If he does not look, then [the Vedic description of] the creation of varieities of names and forms after observation, is falsified. If you say he looks [on the fabricated souls] then, since the one integral Brahma cannot look on souls without the intervention of ignorance, you necessarily talk of his ignorance. Therefore the theory of distinction founded on māyā and ignorance is refuted. For even the conjurer (mayī), Brahma, cannot look on souls without the intervention of Ignorance. Nor can the conjurer delude others without seeing them. Nor can a māyā itself be the means of observation on the part of the mayī, or conjurer. The instrument of its delusiveness is observation of others. But you will say that the māyā of Brahma, bringing about his observation of souls, is the cause of the soul's delusion. Then the māyā, bringing about the observation of others on the part of the one integral self-apparent Brahma, is, in other words, his ignorance. You may say that ignorance is the cause of a wrong observation, but māyā, which only brings about an observation, on the part of Brahma, of all besides him being false, is not the cause of a wrong observation, and therefore there is no ignorance in him. But you cannot say that when the moon is seen as one, it is seen as two, even if there be ignorance in the cause. If Brahma saw every thing to be false besides himself, he would not think of deluding it again. For none but a mad man would study to delude that which he knew to be false.'

Why again,' asks Rāmānuja, should this useless idle delusion be exercised [by God]? If you say, as a sport, [I ask again] why should a being of unbounded joy engage in sport? If you retort that sports are found in the world to be engaged in, only by men whose enjoyments are full, [I reply] this does not hold good here, for none but mad men would entertain the sportful sentiment in a case where the objects of sport are admitted to be unreal and illusory, and the sporter to be real, and himself the projecter of the illsuions.'

"Beware then, my dear Sir, of the consequences of playing fast and loose on such questions as these. To say that God has projected an illusion for deluding his creatures, or that, being essentially *nirguṇa,* or devoid of qualities, He becomes active under the influnece of māyā, is equally opposed to godliness. You cannot, if you believe Him to be all Truth, allow the possibility of His projecting a deceptive spectacle; nor can you, if you believe Him to be all knowledge and all power, assent to the theory of his making anything under the influence of *avidyā,* or ignorance, which cannot but the be akin to the *mad effort* which Śaṅkara repudiates[5], and which cannot differ essentially from the intoxication attributed to Indra."

Yogi.—"The right way to look on our doctrine is to contemplate its drift. We say that God alone exists, because He is the only independent reality. We say again that the world is an illusion, because it is transient, impure, and corrupt. We say also, each, He is myself and I am He[6], because, by becoming one with God, we desire to escape the perils of the world, and the lusts of the flesh."

Satyakāma.—"I can have no objection to your use of the most exclusive terms that human language can supply, to express the self-dependent existence of God, as the only eternal essence. You may also adopt the strongest words you can find, to express the vanity of the world, because of its transiency, impurity, and corruptibility. All I contend for is, that you must hold both those ideas with their proper limitations. God is self-existent and eternal. You may emphatically call Him the *sat,* you may say He is *sat* in a sense in which nothing else is *sat.* He is an entity in a sense in which nothing else is an entity—for he is eternal and self-existent. But you must remember the proper limitation of the doctrine. God is the eternal *sat,* but if *sat* be taken in its grammatical sense, as the present participle of the verb *as* (to be), then the world is also *sat,* or existent, as a creature, though not eternal, and so, strictly speaking, God is not the only *sat.*

"Nor must you forget when you call the world a vanity, an empty vanity, because of its transience, impurity, and corruptibility, that there is a limitation here too, beyond which you cannot advance a single step without falling into serious errors. Use the strongest words you please, to indicate its transience and impurity, but remember that though transient, it is still existent, and though corrupt, it is capable of purification, and that it is only with a view to that purification that one is bound to study and meditate what is right and true. You must not forget that our notion of divinity, however intuitive, is educed and fashioned from the exhibition of God's power in the world before us. To deny that world is to deny the premises on which that notion is founded. Our ideas of omnipotence and omniscience likewise pre-suppose the existence of many things as products, in esse or in posse, of an efficient power, and as objects of a searching knowledge. Would it not be absurd to talk of all power and all knowledge, if nothing existed, or was to be done or known? To deny the world is therefore to deny the power and wisdom of God.

"And while you may entertain the highest possible notions of the divine existence, and the lowest possible views of the world's entity, you must avoid the strange inconsistency of identifying the two opposite ideas, and teaching that all this, which is no-thing, is the only thing existent. Such opposites, as Rāmānuja very properly says, can never be unified, and, if they could be unified, then Brahma might, alternately, be pronounced to be false, and the universe, to be true[7]! Nor must you encourage frail and corrupt humanity to say, I am God."

Yogi. – "The frail and corrupt humanity says, He is myself and I am He,' because it thereby endeavours to detach itself from the Universe. We say to a person thou art He,' because we wish him to meditate on his heaven-born prerogative as an immortal spirit, and to rise above the world. The more he rises above the world, the more is he assimilated to the divine nature."

Satyakāma. – "It is no doubt a grand truth that the more

a person rises above the world, the more he approaches the divine essence. But here too there is a limitation beyond which one may fall into the greatest impiety under a semblance of godliness. The human soul, though immortal, is still a creature. It may, by rising above the world, approach, but it can never attain, the divinity. The creature can never rise to be the Creator. The highest aspiration may be entertained, and piously entertained; only they must be short of aspiring after the divinity itself.

"You, Sir, who have left your home, and cut asunder all earthly ties,—you have no doubt taken a step which, under further light from heaven, and with the divine blessing, may guide you unto all truth, and lead you to God. You may thus attain a position hereafter which angels may covet for themselves, and I heartily wish you all spiritual success. But pherhaps you will allow me.to remark that certain ties are bound up with *duties* to society and to those whom God has placed under our protection. Such ties cannot be cut asunder with impunity. And I cannot, under any circumstances, say to you, thou art He—without being guilty of treason against God, nor can you accept such assurance without impiety, and without the greatest self-deception, for you are not, and can never become,—though you may attain the highest state which a creature can attain, yet, I repeat, you can never become—GOD."

Yogi.—"But what state short of the divinity can be free from transience and impurity? If a high place in heaven be all that we are permitted to aspire after, the reward of knowledge can be little better than that of ignorance. Earth with all its faults is not essentially worse than Indra's palace, one of the highest seats in Heaven."

Satyakāma.—"Heaven, my dear Sir, such as the Purāṇas describe, with the corrupt attendants of Indra, is certainly not a place to be desired. But why shall we accept that corrupt description of the Purāṇas? Why may we not look forward to a heaven, which, as the direct manifestation of God's presence, is itself stable and enduring,—the residence of myriads of immortal souls that have obtained deliverance from earthly troubles, and that are now unceasingly contemplating, admiring, and lauding the divine perfections? Our ancestors used the word *suvarga* for heaven, which meant good company. *Swarga* may have been derived from *suvarga,* as *swarṇa* (gold) is from *suvarṇa.* At any rate why may we not believe that there is a heaven answering to the literal meaning of that word—a good company, a holy company, neither transient nor impure—such as shall endure for eternity?"

The Yogi turned toward the Rajah and said, "Your highness will excuse me, if I leave the discussion of these questions in the hands of your Puṇḍits. Satyakāma's words, and Rāmānuja's sentiments, suggest certain considerations on which I would rather exercise my mind in retirement, than carry on a debate in this assembly. Blessings on the Rajah and his household! Salutation to the Brāhmins!" So saying he bowed, and left the room.

A few minutes after the Yogi had thus abruptly left the room, the Rajah said, "The Daṇḍī, you must remember, is a practical pantheist. He seeks to carry out in his life, what Śaṅkara discusses in his book. Our philosophical works are written chiefly by controversialists. They give us no insight into the practical man. Such an insight can only be found in the life and conversation of men like this Yogi."

Satyakāma.—"Please your highness, pantheism appears to be the very antagonist of the practical man. It is a sheer impracticability. It is incapable of being carried out in life. I can only wonder, when I hear of a person exhorting his neighbour to follow the discipline of pantheism. Every teacher that addresses his pupil, *Saumya,* (O gentle youth!), every pupil that addresses his master, *Bho Bhagavan* (O Sir), every author that writes, *iti chen-na* (if this be said, I deny it), every commentator that pleads for his author's texts, every argument in reply to a hostile opinion, every warning and every assurance, is a testimony against pantheism, is a practical protest against the dogma that the universe is God, or that whatever is not Brahma is a phantom—against the theory of *adwaita,* (unity). There could be no teaching, no commentary, no controversy, no lecture, no warning, no assurance, if one only being existed in the universe, and nothing else. The very terms *vyāvahārika* and *pāramārthika,* which were invented in defence of the system, bears testimony against it, by testifying to the existence of the community in which the vyavahāra is found. Here then we see that every thing, in which human knowledge consists, is opposed to the Vedānt, and this means that the Vedānt is falsified by every description of proof, admissible in human argument. It is opposed to those things which (Śaṅkara himself being judge[8]) are established by all manner of evidence. The Vedānt, in fine, is in conflict with fact and argument. The very texts which set forth the spirituality of God by means of negations, which say he is *without parts, without works, without faults, without spot*[9], prove, by implication, the existence of a world in which there are parts, agencies, faults, and spots. Why otherwise the protest against such things being attributed to the Deity? No one makes a protest against Viṣṇu Mitra being taken for a barren woman's son.

"The threefold means which Śaṅkara himself dogmatically sets forth in his *Ātmopadeśa* are all conclusive evidences against his own doctrine. Pondering the Guru's words, thou art the Supreme Being, endowed with such and other attributes,' and receiving the text of the Vedas, 'I am God,' having thus in three several ways, *i.e.,* by the precept of the guru, by the word of God, and by his own contemplation, persuaded himself I am God,' he became liberated[10].' If there be the least reality in this esoteric description, it militates against the doctrine of one being, for here three parties are mentioned, the Guru, the pupil, and God. If as all our philosophers are agreed, and, as Śaṅkara says also in the catechetical tract I have just named, that ignorance, or bondage, consists in thinking that to be the spirit which is not spirit[11], then that very delusion pervades the text, (this whole world is a spirit,') which that great Vedāntist quotes, and on the strength of which he counsels all who have brought themselves under that delusion, *to act as they please,* and assures them that *no one could impose any prohibitory law on them*[12].

"Your highness may have heard of a vulgar notion among the lower orders of our countrymen, that certain princes (yourself among others) are endowed with the privilege of annually committing one or more homicides (the number being supposed to be specified in your patents from the foreign office) without being called to account. Śaṅkarācārya, however, gives, in his charter of Vedāntism, unlimited liberty of action, without reckoning. There it appers a far more terrible privilege than what the peasantry think you to be invested with. But we find it is naturally limited by the restrictive rules of admission to the privileged class. And certainly the standard of qualification for matriculating in the Vedāntic College is high enough. The first rule of initiation is renouncement of all desire of enjoyment, here or hereafter. In the catechetical lecture, already cited, Śaṅkara tells us how this qualification is obtained. By a lucky chance, or by some peculiar merit, a man gets through the ceremonial acts enjoined in the Vedas, and thereby his mind is freed from desires.'[13] Another qualitification is *faith* or *confidence* in the words of the guru and the Vedas. Now, I contend, if these rules of initiation be truthful, then the doctrine of one being is necessarily falsified, for they pre-suppose the existence of the guru and of all things which are necessary for the performance of the Vedic ritual; and if the rules are themselves illusory, the Vedāntic initiation must itself be an illusion, and if the initiation be false, the indoctrination must be false too—for *he only gets knowledge who has got an ācārya* (tutor)[14]. The Vedānt will not allow that its grand consummation can be brought about without a qualified tutor. If there be no ācārya, there can be no teaching, and if the indoctrination is a delusion, the conclusion of this spiritual exercise, *i.e.*, *mukti,* must be the grandest of delusions, and the whole system of Vedāntism, all its texts and sayings, its precepts and promises, its ācārya and adhikārī (qualified pupil) are therefore built, like a house (as Rāmānuja suggests[15]) upon an imaginary mathematical line! But is there such a creature as a real Vedāntist to be found anywhere?' Is there any man, *can* there be any person, who seriously thinks he is God, and that all else is false? What does he do with his eyes and ears? Does he see any thing? Does he hear anything? Does he feel anything? A Vedāntist, if he cannot answer these questions, has no right to say anything to any body."

Rajah.—"But to put a historical question,—I did not understand before that the Bhāgavatas rejected pantheism, as Satyakāma has just shown from Rāmānuja, and Gauḍa-purṇānanda."

Satyakāma.—"Please your highness, I did not mean that all the Bhāgavatas rejected pantheism. Rāmānuja and his followers alone rejected it, but others, e.g., the Rāmānadis, accepted its dogmas. Rāmānuja himself held some of the tenets connected with pantheism. Only he would not allow that the universe, or the human soul, was God."

Rajah.—"What pantheistic doctrine then *could* he hold!"

Tarkakāma.—"He allowed that at general dissolutions the world was absorbed in the Divinity, but denied that it could be unified with it. Thus, Many flavours of trees, there are in honey, but separable from it. How otherwise could it remove the three-fold disorders? Souls, in like manner, are absorbed in the Lord at the dissolution, but are not unified with Him, for they are again separated at the creation. As there is a difference between rivers and the sea, between sweet and salt waters, so is there a difference between God and souls, because of their characteristic distinctions. Rivers, when joined with the sea, are not altogether unified with it, though they do appear inseparable. There is a real difference between salt and sweet waters. Men cannot discriminate between milk and water, when the two are mixed up, but the swan at once makes out the separation between milk and water[16]. In the same manner when souls are absorbed in the Supreme Lord, Brahma, at the dissolution, the devout, contemplating the Guru's words, can make out the difference. Even milk, when mixed with milk, and water with water, do not obtain unification, merely because they are supposed to be unified. Neither do souls, when absorbed in the Supreme Being by virtue of meditation, obtain identity with Him. So say all pure-minded saints[17].'"

Satyakāma.—"Another objection of Rāmānuja was to the following effect. It apparently militated, however, as much against the idea of an eternal succession of worlds, or ages, and against the eternity of individual souls, as against pantheism. 'It is inconsitsent,' says he, in the asserters of unity to speak of tutor and pupil, and to say that some are emancipated, others in bondage, for since the succession of ages past is infinite, even if you allowed a single case of emancipation in each age, all souls must have been already emancipated, and none left in bondage. If it be said that souls are also infinite, hence there are some still in bondage,—what is meant by this infinite? Innumerable, will you say? That cannot be. For although because of its multiplicity, it appears innumerable to persons of little knowledge, it is capable of being numbered by God who is omniscient. To say He cannot number it, would be to say He is not Omniscient. If you say that souls being themselves innumerable, it is no denial of God's Omniscience to say He does not know a number which does not actually exist, I reply that there cannot be a want of number where things are separable. Souls must have a number, since they are separable like grain, mustard, pots, and cloths[18].'

"Rāmānuja contends strenuously against the doctrine of unity, and the arbitrary manner in which its advocates alternately pronounce the universe to be no reality and God. He accordingly exhorted men to renounce the theory of Adwaita, or unity of being, and acknowledge that of *Dwaita*[19]."

Tarkakāma.—"And also to devote themselves to the worship of Hari[20]."

Rajah.—"What then is the point of difference between the Rāmānandis and the Rāmānujas? I thought they both united in some common point in opposition to the Vedānt."

Tarkakāma.—"Your highness is right. All Bhāgvatas, Rāmānandis as well as Rāmānujas, maintain that God subsists in an eternal body which is His essential form. 'It is heard,' say they, 'in the Purāṇas, that all this proceeded from the lotus-navel of God. Hence is his body proved, for how could there be a navel without a body[21].' Rāmānuja thus writes in defence of the doctrine of God's having an eternal corporeal form. He answers the objections brought forward by those, who contended that God could not have a corporeal frame without being subject to growth and decay, pleasure and pain, like animal souls. The corporeal frame[22] of the animal soul, says he, is not the real cause of the sound or unsound state of its physical system, nor of its liability to pleasure or pain. The real cause is the virtuous or vicious acts committed by itself. That which is said in the Veda, the corporeal is not free from pleasure and pain, has reference to the body, received in consequence of previous acts. But the Veda also speaks, elsewhere, of the essential corporeal form of the emancipated soul, free from the bondage of works. He becomes of one form, or of three forms. If he desires the world of the *fathers,* he wanders there, eating, sporting, indulging. Here there is no smell of evil, or vanity. And as to the Supreme Being, free from sins, although in his gross and subtle forms, the whole universe be His body, still there can be no smell of the bondage of works in Him, nor again of any evil or vanity. It is as in the world, —the liability to pleasure pain is not owing merely to corporealness on the part of subjects, who (the king being himself the ruler,) enjoy or suffer from his kindness or severity, according as they submit or not to his government. Thus says the Drāviḍa commentator. As in the world, when there is a terrific plague of gnats in the country, the king's body, unceasingly fanned by punkhas, is not affected by the evils, and he can govern his people at pleasure, and enjoy perfumes and other good things which his subjects cannot procure, so also the Lord of the universe (God), with the *chāmara* of his own power in motion, is not affected by evils, but can protect the various worlds, and command enjoyments, not within the reach of any others." Here the Rāmānandis and Rāmānujas stand on common ground. But they soon part company. The Rāmānandis assert that God is both *saguṇa* and *nirguṇa.* Tulasīdāsa, one of their own popular poets, strongly inveighs against those, who, like the Rāmānujas, reject the theory of *nirguṇa,* or void of qualities[23]. And he thus explains how *saguṇa* and *aguṇa* are reconcilable. There is no difference between the *saguṇa* and *aguṇa.* Thus do the Munis, Purāṇas, sages, and Vedas say. He who is void of quality and shape, who is invisible and uncreated, the same becomes joined with qualities out of love for His devotees. But how can one who is without qualities become joined with qualities? Even as water and ice and hailstones are not different substances[24]."

The orderly now came and said that the Kumar (the Raja's son) was coming with two new friends whom he was desirous of presenting to his highness. The prince entered the room, in a minute or two, prostrated himself before his father, introduced his friends, and then remained standing for several minutes. On the Rajah giving the order, he took a seat with the young Baboos that accompanied him. His highness told them that we had been debating on the doctrines of the Vedānt, and gave a summary of what had been advanced on both sides of the question. On hearing the summary, one of the Baboos, Ādhunika by name, made the following remark: "I will not allow that the Vedānta is pantheistic in any sense of the term. I will not undertake to decide whether pantheism is right or wong. If I do so, I may possibly be pronouncing judgment against some of the brightest intellects of the age. But I can boldly say that the Vedānta does not necessarily partake of either material or spiritual pantheism."

Vaiyāsika. – "Do you mean to say that Vyāsa and Śaṅkara do not inculcate the identity of the world with God."

Ādhunika. – "I do not deny that is the teaching of Vyāsa and Śāṅkārācārya. How could you suppose for a moment I was ignorant of it. But the Vedānta Darśana of Vyāsa is of no higher authority than the Nyāya, Sāṅkhya, or any other Darśana, or school of Hindu philosophy. The Vedāntic schools of Vyāsa maintain the doctrine of the consubstantiality of the human soul with God, and support their opinion by several citations from the Vedas. The Nyāya school admits the distinct nature of the soul and maintains its position by citations from the same Vedas; to jumble up together the Upaniṣads, which are parts of the revealed Vedas, and the Vedānta Darśana of Vyāsa, the creation of man, as things of equal authority, is not proper[25].' I am not an advocate of the Vedānta founded by Vyāsa. I am for the system contained in the Upaniṣads, the pure Vedānt. Ours is the old system of the Vedas. Vyāsa's is of yesterday. We wish to reutrn to the old paths, from which Vyāsa and Śaṅkarācārya had diverged so much. Why do you stare? Has not your highness heard of the German reformer Luther'[26]? He maintained that the adherents of the Pope had corrupted the simplicity of the Bible, and he sought to return to the primitive religion. Our aim is similar. We wish to revert to the original system of the Vedas."

"Is it then your aim, asked Satyakāma, to restore the worship of fire, air, and the heavenly bodies?"

"No, that is contained in the Mantras, and other ceremonial parts of our Śāstra. Our system is in the Upaniṣads."

Satyakāma.—"Are the Upaniṣads then older compositions than the Mantras?"

"People are accustomed, said Ādhunika, to call the Vedas eternal. I cannot undertake to say the Upaniṣads are older than the Mantras."

"The Mantras are written in a language which appears older than that of the Upaniṣads, are they not?" asked Satyakāma.

Ā.—"As far as the structure of sentences is concerned, I should say so. But this is not a quite conclusive reason against the popular tradition."

"It would be a conclusive reason, said Satyakāma, in the absence of any evidence to the contrary. But I am not particularly desirous of discussing that point with you. You must at any rate acknowledge that the Upaniṣads are not older than the Mantras."

Ā.—"I never pretended they were."

S.—"What mean you then by the *old* paths, if the Upaniṣads be not older than the Mantras."

Ā.—"I mean that our system is that excellent science which includes all knowledge, even the science of Brahma[27], taught by the first of the gods to his son Atharvan, the science that is distinguished by the appellation of *parā,* the eminent."

S.—"Then you acknowledge the mythological pantheon. You say, the first of the gods."

Ā.—"We acknowledge it so far as to believe that the worship of the sun and fire and other gods, together with the whole allegorical system, was only inculcated for the sake of those whose limited understandings rendered them incapable of comprehending and adoring the Invisible Supreme Being, so that such persons might not remain in a brutified state, destitute of all religious principles.[28]"

S.—"Allegorical instruction, I thought, was intended for the wise. Illiterate people of little judgement require plain teaching. But you seem to think that the vulgar would benefit by idolatrous doctrine. I cannot conceive how idolatrous doctrine or practice can lead to good results. You would not cure high treason by teaching men to render allegiance to a pretender. But to return to our subject. The same Upaniṣad speaks of an *apara,* or inferior science too, does it not?"

Ā.—"Yes, the Ṛg, Yajus, Sāman and Atharvan, with grammar, versification, astronomy, are the inferior science[29].

S.—"The two must have been simultaneously communicated at the creation, for the Vedas, they say, are eternal."

Ā.—"God provided two kinds of doctrine for the wise and the unwise."

S.—"Which classes did not exist at the time, for there was only one spirit and nothing else in the beginning."

Ā.—"But God foreseeing that there would be wise and unwise in the world, might have made provision for the mental improvement of both."

S.—"That is to say, breathed out the Upaniṣads for the one, and the other Vedas for the other."

"It might be so," said Ādhunika."

Satyakāma.—"Was it as a punishment for folly and a reward for wisdom that He gave the two different sorts of books? or was it that the unwise could not comprehend the sublimity of the Upaniṣads, and therefore were left to grope their way through the other Vedas?"

Ā.—"They were not fit for the lessons contained in the Upaniṣads. They could not appreciate the purity of our doctrine, and rather than that they should remain without any guide at all, the Vedas were given to them out of compassion for their weakness. They were allowed to indulge in carnal observances and *mantras* unitl they should be wiser."

S.—"But the Upaniṣads, too, contain descriptions, not only of carnal observances, but also of obscenities, still worse than Jayadeva's *battles of love.*"

Ā.—"There are a few such passages, but we pass them over."

S.—"Not a few passages, but rather a large sprinkling of obscentities in some of them. But waiving the questions which your remark suggests, I will simply ask, is not the following a portion of the excellent knowledge revealed at the beginning, as your Upaniṣads will have it? 'As a spider projects and receives back (his web), as herbs grow in the earth, as from a living person the hairs of the head and body, so from the Imperishable is the universe produced[30].'"

Ādhunika.—"Yes, the Muṇḍaka Upaniṣad says so, and a sublime conception it is."

Satyakāma.—"It may be a sublime conception, but the transition is easy from the sublime to something very different. Does not the passage savour of the gross pantheism which you said was a corruption of the Vaiyāsika Vedānt?"

Ā.—"It does not necessarily involve pantheism."

S.—"No! I do not see how I can derive any sound doctrine from that passage. But what do you think of the celebrated text, 'All this is God.'"

"That, said Ādhunika, should be understood as an 'effusion of fervid devotion, when contemplating the omnipresence of the Deity'[31]."

S. – "Whose fervid devotion? I thought you held that the Upaniṣads, in common with the other Vedas, were revealed by God himself at the creation. It is impossible to conceive that God would make an overstatement of the fact, from any feeling, which, however natural to mean, would in Him be unaccountable.

"But, continued Satyakāma, that one passage is not all. The Upaniṣads abound with texts declaring that God is the one spirit, the substance of which the universe is composed, that the creation is but a multiplication and development of Himself. That the world is to Him what froth is to the sea, the butter to the milk, the web to the spider, the cloth to the yarn. This is systematically taught from beginning to end. The air is God. The food is God. The mind is God. The vital air is God[32]."

Rajah. – "Is it fair to cull such detached texts to serve a particular purpose? You do not surely mean that the Upaniṣads set up the air or food as God."

Satyakāma. – "The Upaniṣads, please your highness, cannot be taken as the works of the same author, or even as productions of the same age. With this single exception that each inculcates pantheism of one sort or another, the scope of no two of them can be considered precisely the same. Some of them appear to speculate, much after the fashion of development philosophers, on the physical primeval element of the universe, and whatever is for the moment taken as a first principle, is declared to be Brahman or God. The *Taittirirya,* for instance, gives the following definition of Brahma or God : 'That from which these elements are produced, by which, being produced, they exist, and into which, at dissolution, they are resolved, is Brahma or God.' Giving this definition of Divinity, the Upaniṣad goes on to show that it is applicable to food, to the vital air, to the mind, to *vijñāna* (knowldge), and to *ānanda* (joy), and repeats in turns, that the production and final resolution of the universe may be traced to all those five principles.[33] The same Upaniṣad speaks, elsewhere, of the production of ether 'from that or this Spirit', and from ether air, from air fire, from fire water, from water earth, from earth herbs, from herbs food, from food *retas,* from *retas* the *puruṣa* (personal soul), which is pronounced to be *annarasamaya* (all food.) It is then added 'those who worship food as God, obtain all food,' and that 'all creatures are produced from food.' The Upaniṣad proceeds to say that from the soul which is all food, another, the inner spirit, is produced, which is *prāṇamaya* (all vital air), thence again *manomaya* (all mind), thence *vijñāna-maya* (all knowldge), thence *ānanda-maya* (all joy)[34]. Vyāsa and Śaṅkara thought that passages such as these could not be explained except on the pantheistic theory."

"All seemingly pantheistic passages, said Ādhunika, must be so interpreted as to be consistent with other texts expressly declaring the unity of God, and His distinction from the world."

S.—"It was in trying to reconcile the texts in question with the unity of God, that Vyāsa was led to Pantheism. The other idea of His distinction from the world forced Vyāsa's successors to the necessity of denying the reality of that world. If you can interpret the texts to which I have referred, without either identifying the world with God, or denying its reality, you will achieve an exploit which no Vedāntist, from Vyāsa to Sadānanda downwards, had been able to accomplish. But what are the texts, pray, which expressly declare the unity of God, and His distinction from the world?"

Ā.—"As to the unity of God, you have our celebrated formula, which we inscribe on our solemn documents, and with which we conclude our devotions : *Ekamevādwītiyam*—'God is one only without a second.'"

S.—"The word 'God' does not occur in the passage."

Ā.—"No, but it is understood; you must supply the ellipsis."

"We shall see, said Satyakāma, how the ellipsis is to be supplied; but you, who are so jealous of corrupt criticisms of the Upaniṣads, ought to be careful how *you* construe your sacred books. Give us the whole passage, where the formula occurs, and we shall then be able intelligently to consider what the ellipsis is."

Ā.—"This, O gentle (pupil), was even an entity at the beginning, one without a second.[35]"

"How then, asked Satyakāma, can you, as a matter of course, interpolate the word 'God' here. The subject is 'this' (idam); is it not?"

Ā.—"Of course."

S.—"Well; to what does the word *this,* in the neuter gender, generally refer in the language of the Upaniṣads? Is it not to the visible universe?"

"I cannot say readily, answered Ādhunika, to what it generally refers, but I should say there can be no doubt it refers to God *here.*"

"Is not the passage you quoted the solution of a question which had been disputed? Give us the whole paragraph."

A.—"'This, O gentle (pupil), was even existent at the beginning, one only without a second. Some say, indeed, this was even non-existent at the beginning, one only without a second : hence out of a non-existent an existent may be begotten. But how, O gentle (pupil), can this be? He said, how out of a non-existent can an existent be begotten? This, O gentle (pupil), was even an entity at the beginning, one without a second'".[36]

"You will find it difficult, said Satyakāma, to maintain that the word *this* refers to God, throughout the passage without involving pantheism. No one that acknowledged a God would doubt His existence at the beginning. Śaṅkara's commentary is perfectly intelligible. He understands 'this' to refer to the visible world, and the question to be whether the world was existent or non-existent at the beginning, *i.e.,* before the creation. The Upaniṣad decides that the Universe was existent in its material cause (God), and was thus one without a second at the beginning, – it being, as the commentator adds, a protest against the Sāṅkhya, which inculcated two eternal principles, Nature and Soul, and against the Vaiśeṣika, which assumed the eternity of innumerable Atoms. And thus the very text in which your community reposes so much confidence, which is exalted into a formula to express its characteristic doctrine, is inexplicable except in a pantheistic sense. I do not think you will contend for the possibility of considering God as the material cause of the world without countenancing pantheism."

Ādhunika. – "But there is a passage, the very first verse in the Aitareya Upaniṣad, in which the Spirit Himself is called *one.*"

Satyakāma. – "I fear that passage will give you no better help. It reads thus; 'This was a spirit, even one, at the beginning[37].' You must remember that *idam* (this) is in the neuter gender, and therefore cannot as an adjective pronoun, belong to *ātma* (spirit) in the masculine. *Idam* must be the subject, *ātma* the predicate. I am afraid you will find this passage even more pantheistic than the one from the Chāndogya. It directly pronounces the external world to have been, at the beginning, one only spirit, from which it was afterwards evovled in its present form."

Ā. – "But what say you to the following beautiful passage from the Muṇḍaka; 'Know him, the spirit, to be one. Give up all words contrary to this. This is the bridge of immortality'[38]."

S. – "It is in itself, and as you have translated it, certainly a beautiful passage. But take it in connection with what precedes and what follows, and the beauty will very soon disappear. The preceding clause is, 'In Him are placed the heaven, the earth, the sky, the mind, with all the vital airs[39]' And that which follows your quotation is; 'In whom the arteries are collected like spokes at the nave of a carriage-wheel. He moves inside, becoming variously affected'[40] That *one spirit* of yours is thus identified with the human soul, for that which is variously affected within a person can be nothing else than his soul."

Ādhunika. — "You cannot explain away every passage expressive of the unity of God. There are scores of texts in the Śwetaśwatara Upaniṣad which cannot be interpreted in a pantheistic sense."

Satyakāma. — "I doubt very much whether the Swetāśwatara will give you any substantial help. It contains passages as decidedly pantheistic as any other Upaniṣads, and if you can light on detached stray passages, declaratory of the unity of God, it will not in any way decide the question between us. Unity is not only not opposed, but is actually necessary, to the idea of pantheism. It is the one God with whom all things visible and invisible are identical, that forms the essence of Pantheism.

"If however the Śwetāśwatara bears any testimony against Pantheism, it is in those two celebrated texts which the followers of the Sāṅkhya philosophy are so fond of citing, and in which a duality of principle appears to be inculcated. You cannot derive from it any sound lesson on divinity, not only because two or three texts must in ordinary justice be made to yield to the majority of passages which are indisputably for pantheism, but also because the acknowledgement of two eternal principles will be no less subverisve of a pure monotheism than the identification of the world with God could be.

"If your opinions do not preclude a critical examination of the Upaniṣads, I should say that the Swetāśwatara appears, prima facie, to be of a much later date than the others. It is, I may say, in some respects, a Sāṅkhya Upaniṣad, either composed, or corrupted, at a more recent period by the followers of that school. It not only speaks of an uncreated female principle, red, white, and black, producing many creatures connatural with iself, and thus presenting the very picture of the *prakṛti* of the Sāṅkhya; but it also makes highly honourable mention of Kapila, and sets forth the excellence of the Sāṅkhya Yoga.[41] 'He who being one resides from generation to 'generation in various forms and in all productions, first filled the Ṛṣi Kapila His son with knowledge and beheld him born'.[42]

"Another proof of the Śwetāśwatara being a more recent Upaniṣad than the others is found in its constant repetition of the names which the followers of Śiva have set apart for their favourite god. Iśana, Rudra, Śiva, Giriśanta, Giritra Maheśwara, Bhava may, most of them, it is true, be construed as appellatives, and may not necessarily be proper names; but the coincidence of so many epithets, popularly expressive of the god Śiva, in the same Upaniṣad, leads to the suspicion that the Śaiva sect had something to do with its composition. The mystic union of Prakṛti and Puruṣa, inculcated in the Sāṅkhya philosophy, is the foundation of the mythological legends of Śiva, whose characteristic is the lingam, and of Pārvatī, the personification of female energy., And this union of Śiva and Pārvatī is also hinted at in the Śwetāśwatara.

"But whatever be your opinion of the origin of that upaniṣad, certain it is, it will afford no harbour for any thing like sound theology. It is a compound of Vedānt pantheism and of the Sāṅkhya duality. It is difficult to say which ingredient is the worse of the two. The one identifies the world with God. The other sets up up an eternal female principle producing the world in connection with the soul (*Puruṣa*) or the male principle. You cannot get a good monotheistic passage, free, on the one hand from pantheism, and, on the other, from the idea of duality, just mentioned.

"Nor can a few monotheistic passages explain away the vast number that are pantheistic. God may have been, in a few solitary texts, declared to be distinct from the world, and free from the impurity attached to matter, and yet those texts may be perfectly consistent with others in which the world is pronounced to be consubstantial with Him. In order to enunciate Pantheism, one must have a subject, which may exist in mental analysis distinct from that which is its predicate. Two ideas may, at first, be separately conceived, and then pronounced to be identical. When the Upaniṣad says, 'all this is God,' the subject 'all this' may have been originally presented to the writer's mind as distinct from the predicate 'God,' and then he may have determined that *all this,* which was before and around him, was *God.* Unless you can make out that there is no real identification of the subject and predicate, no real declaration that Brahma is himself the *Prakṛti,* passages merely expressive of their distinctness can have no force in overruling texts decidedly pantheistic. Then again you must not argue on the supposition that we are agreed as to the divine authority of the Vedas. I am not bound to interpret them in an unnatural way, merely that I may maintain their consistency. You may feel yourself under such a necessity, but until you can demonstrate their divine inspiration by satisfactory evidence, no such necessity can be laid upon *me.* Fair criticism, which is due to all ancient writings, is due to the Vedas and Upaniṣads too. It is of course opposed to the rules of fair criticism not to consider the end and scope of a writer, or any peculiar idiom which may be observable in his works.It would be unjust and improper hastily to conclude that the works are self-contradictory, or recklessly to interpret texts without taking into account how far they may be consistent with one another. But you can not call upon me to submit to unnatural rules of interpretation with the sole object of proving the doctrine of one Upaniṣad to be consistent with that of any other, so that there may be no theory in the Muṇḍaka contradictory to the lessons of the Śwetāśwatara; for you have not yet shown that the Upaniṣads have all the same paternity. Nor can you require me to surrender my private jdgement before you have proved that the Vedas are of divine authority. I conceive I may undertake to say that you have no external proof to bring forward in behalf of such authority."

Ādhunika.—"We do not pretend to bring forward such proofs[43]. There are no historical records in our country. You cannot expect such proofs. But the internal evidence which the *real* doctrines of the Vedas afford ought to satisfy a reasonable inquirer of their divine authority."

Satyakāma.—"That evidence cannot be admitted at least before the Vedas are acquitted of the charge of pantheism, now under consideration. Passages really pantheistic cannot, I say, be overruled by texts, merely setting forth a distinction between God and the world. The pantheism I am charging on the Upaniṣads does not imply that God and the universe are one in such a sense as that it would be a truism to say, 'All this is God.' That pantheism is inculcated in three different ways: *first,* by teaching that God is material cause of the world: *Secondly,* by maintaining that the soul and the universe are consubstantial with God; *thirdly* by asserting that he who knows God is absorbed in, and identified with, Him.

"The Upaniṣads clearly inculcate that God is the material cause (call it substantial, if your prefer it) of the world. That form which a thing is produced and into which it is resolved is called its material cause. The following texts will prove the teaching of your Vedas on this point :

"Brahma is he from whom all these elements are produced, and into which they are resolved[44].'

'As the spider projects its web, as small sparks proceed from fire, so from this Spirit are produced all animals, all worlds, all gods, all creatures[45].'

'As a water bubble, when cast into the water, is resolved

into water, so that no one can restore it;l whencesoever it be taken, it will be saline; so this great being (in yourself), which has neither end nor limit, will be resolved into the solid aggregate of knowledge (God)[46]."

'This God of all, this omniscient, this in-goer, this origin or womb of all, is the source and resolution of creatures[47].'

'This was in the beginning one, even Brahma[48].'

'This was in the beginning a spirit, even one[49].'

'This was in the beginning a spirit like a male person[50].'

'This is the truth, as from a blazing fire consubstantial sparks proceed thousand-fold, so from the Imperishable, O gentle pupil, diverse entities are produced, and they return into him too[51].'

'He desired, Let me become many—let me be produced. He conceiving knowledge created all this. Having created it, He got into it[52].'

'He observed, Let me become many, let me be produced[53].'"

Ādunika.—"The text, 'Let me become many, let me be produced,' is only in accommodation to our ancient conventional *idea* that the father is begotten in the son[54]."

Satyakāma.—"I thought your opinion was that the *Upaniṣads were given by God at the creation,* before conventional idioms could be formed. It seems your mind is far from being *saturated* with that belief. I see you involuntarily treat it as an ordinary work, and reason from its style as a 'creation of man.'"

Ādhunika.—"May not an inspired work be characterized by particular idioms?"

Satyakāma.—"If composed by a mortal under divine direction, it may still bear traces of the writer's idiom and style: but if it were revealed at the creation, before idiom and style could be formed, it must be independent of such human peculiarities."

"We do not receive, said Ādhunika, nor do we literally interpret the fable respecting the revelation of the Vedas at the time of the creation."

Satyakāma. – "But the fable is contained in the Vedas themselves. The Śwetāśwatara says, that God revealed the Vedas at the creation. How can you receive the Vedas as the word of God if you reject that fable? But as regards the passage under consideration, you cannot prove that the conventional idea you speak of really existed at any time. The father is indeed said to be born in the son; that is because the latter is of the substance of the former. But no writer ever said that the potter was begotten in the jar. On your own confession, then, the text teaches that the world is *consubstantial* with God, – which is the second charactersitic of pantheism taught in the Upaniṣads. That this characteristic is prominently inculcated will be apparent from the following passages :

'This was nonentity in the beginning; then was entity produced. It made itself[55].'

"If the Upaniṣad is not inculcating the atheistic dogma of Kapila, that nature made itself into the form of the universe, the obvious meaning is that the world is a formation of Brahma, and is consubstantial with Him.

'As the one fire having entered into the world became diversified in form, so the one spirit pervading all creatures, inside and outside, becomes many forms. As the one air having entered into the world became diversified in form, so the one spirit pervading all creatures, inside and outside, becomes various forms[56].'

"The Chāndogya teaches the relation, in which the world stands to God, thus : 'As, O gentle pupil, by means of one clod of earth, every earthy form is known, being in truth only earth, though called in words a modification, and as, O gentle pupil, by means of one magnet every magnetized iron becomes known, being in truth only iron, though called in words a modification, and 'as by one nail-parer every black iron, is known, being in truth only black iron, though called in words a modification; so is the doctrine I delivered[57].' Then follows the assertion of one original principle which was multiplied into many. Connect the above passages with the text, 'All this is God,' and the meaning of the Upaniṣad can no longer admit of doubt. Again,

'Here all these become one[58].'

'This universe is even Puruṣa (or a male person)[59].'

'All this is Brahma. This spirit is Brahma. This spirit is four-footed, [has four quarters[60].]'

"Equally decisive of Pantheism are those passages which declare that the student is unified with God on attaining to the knowledge of Brahma. Nay sometimes he is identified with God even before fullness of knowledge. 'He that knows God becomes God.' 'He is a spirit. Thou art he, O Śwetaketu[61].' This is given as a sort of refrain, and is repeated nine times in the Chāndogya.

"I am Brahma'.[62] 'Whoever knows this, I am Brahma, he knows this all. Even the gods are unable prevent his becoming Brahma[63].'

'As flowing rivers are resolved into the sea, losing their names and forms, so the learned, freed from name and form, get into the heavenly and super-excellent Spirit. He who knows that supreme Brahma becomes Brahma[64].'

'The knowers of Brahma, understanding the difference here, are resolved into Brahma, being bent on Him and freed from birth. He who sees this by true devotion is received into the Spirit, even as oil is in sesamum seed, butter in curds, water in streams, and fire in the flint[65].'

'Where there is something like duality, there one may see the other, one may smell the other, one may hear the other, one may honour the other, one may regard the other, one may know the other; but where the whole of this is one spirit, there whom and by what can one smell? Whom and by what can one see? Whom and by what can one hear? Whom and by what can one honour? whom and by what can one regard? whom and by what can one know[66]? 'That is his excellent state in which he thinks, I am all[67].'

"The Bṛhadāraṇyaka again contains the following catechetical lecture :

'Ushasta aksed Yājñavalkya, Declare to me the all-pervading spirit, 'who is manifestly and perceptibly, Brahma.'

'Yājñavalkya answered, This thy spirit is all-pervading.'

U. Which is that all-pervader, Yājñavalkya?'

Y. The same who performs the physical functions of the five vital airs. This thy spirit is the all-pervader.

U. This is like an evasive description of the cow or the horse. Tell me which is the all-pervading spirit, manifestly and perceptibly, Brahma.'

Y. Your spirit is the all-pervader.

U. Which is that all-pervader, Yājñavalkya?'

Y. Look not at him who sees through sight, hear not him who hears through the hearing, think not of him who thinks through thinking, know not him who knoweth through knowning. This thy spirit is all-pervader. The rest is subject to decay[68].'

"I need not stop to remark on the meaning of some of these antitheses, on which even eminent commentators are not agreed; but no one dissents from the obvious construction of the identity of the querist with the Supreme Being. Another inquirer is introduced, Kahola, by name, asking precisely the same questions, and he is answered in a similar manner, that his spirit was the all-pervader, 'that is above hunger and thirst, grief, anxiety and death[69].' Eventually Yājñavalkya says to the querist Uddālaka :

'This thy spirit which, remaining in earth, is different from the earth, which the earth itself does not know, whose body is the earth, which, being within, directs the earth, is the immortal In-goer. This thy spirit which, remaining in water, is different from water, which the water itself does not know, whose body is the water, which, being within, directs the water, is the immortal In-goer. This thy spirit which, remaining in fire, is different from fire, which the fire itself does not know, whose body is the fire, which being within, directs the fire, is the immortal In-goer. This thy spirit which, remaining in ether, is different from ether, which the ether itself does not know, whose body is the ether, which, being within, directs the ether, is the immortal In-goer. This thy spirit which, remaining in air, is different from the air, which the air itself does not know, whose body is the air, which, being within, directs the air, is the immortal In-goer. This thy spirit which, remaining in heaven, is different from heaven, which the heaven itself does not know, whose body is heaven, which, being within, directs the heaven, is the immortal in-goer[70].'

"It is not necessary to quote the whole of this long passage in which the querist's spirit (in common, adds the commentator, with that of every other man) is declared to be the immortal In-goer, pervading all things, the sun, the cardinal points, the moon and the stars, the firmament, darkness, light, the vital air, speech, the eye, the ear, the mind, the skin, knowledge, the *retas* itself being expressly included in the list.—The same spirit of the querist is, in conclusion, pronounced to be 'the seer, though unseen, the hearer, though unheard, the thinker, though unthought of, the knower, though unknown, there being 'no other seer, no other hearer, no other thinker, no other knower[71].'

"The preceding passages are so significant that I cannot conceive how any one can doubt their meaning. They indisputably inculcate a compound of material and mystical panthewism. Had there been the least ambiguity in them. I might have understood your anxiety to give them the benefit of the doubt. The texts I have cited are however so pointed, that I am unable to enter into your feelings."

Ādhunika. – "Will you not accord to us the same liberty of interpretation that you claim for yourself. We choose to construe them consistently with pure monotheism. What is the use of telling us we are bad interpreters? What is your object? Is it to convert us to pantheism, or to read us lectures on philology"?

Satyakāma. – "Neither. My object is to enter a protest against assumptions calculated, on the one hand, to pervert historical truths, and, on the other hand, to circulate wrong ideas on the teaching of the Vedas. If you abjure pantheism, while accepting the Upaniṣads, your renouncement of a gross error must be a subject of congratulation, but your adherence to books, which teach that error and do not contain the true word of God, cannot but be a cause of anxiety."

Here Ādhunika paused for a moment, when the Kumāra, finidng he could speak without interrupting any party, said to his father, that he had come to ask permission for amusing himself with the *khas* billiard table for half an hour. "You need not," said his highness, "have waited for permission, my only liquidator of debts to ancestors! You may go into that amusement-room, whenever and with whomsoever you please. I am only too glad to find you have a taste for such manly exercises. But stop for one moment. I wish you to write down what presents are to be made to my learned friends, who attended your sister's wedding-party, and have since been with me from yesterday."

The Kumāra pulled out a golden pencil from his pocket

and wrote out an order on the Dewan of the Household. The Rajah, without stopping to read the list, ordered it to be taken to the Dewan.

While the Kumāra's autograph was on its way to the royal Wardrobe (*Toshakhana*) and the Treasury, we were in pleasant expectation of what was coming, (I may at least confess for myself). Āgamika, however, could not, when the Kumāra had left the room with his young friends, suppress his astonishment at the view which Ādhunika had taken of the Vedānt. Vaiyāsika said, "The Baboo belongs to the new school initiated by Rammohun Roy. But Ādhunika has evidently been absent from the Head-quarters of his own school longer than myself, for, when I was there last, I noticed that the divine authority of the Vedas and Upaniṣads had been given up as a false idea! The Brāhma-dharma was now inculcated as *sahaja-jñāna,* or simple natural theology."

Rajah.—"Is it possible they have changed again? The school commenced with the acknowledgement of all the śāstras,—Purāṇas, Smṛtis, as well as Vedas. At least Rammohun Roy did not avowedly reject any of them, though he did not follow the orthodox interpretation. In his preface to the Iśopaniṣad he admitted the authority of the whole body of our śāstras. His successors set aside the Smṛti and the Purāṇas, and adhered to the Vedas alone. And now they have given up the Upaniṣads too! Why a learned writer claimed consideration for those writings on the very ground of their finding acceptance in Bengal[72]."

Scarcely had his highness finished these words when a number of servants, dressed in diverse colours, entered the room with silver trays, shawls, silks, and gold coins. Each of us received a tray with a pair of costly Cashmere shawls, silk dhooties, and twenty pieces gold coin. Laden with these gifts we took leave of the Rajah, wishing him a long life of health and prosperity.

References

1. वहुशास्त्रगुरूपासनेपि सारादानं षट्पदवत्॥

   तदुक्तं। अणुभ्यश्च महद्भ्यश्च शास्त्रेभ्य: कुशलो नर:। सर्वत: सारमादद्यात् पुष्पेभ्य दव षट्पद:॥

2. ब्रह्मादितृणपर्य्यन्तं सर्वं मिथ्यैव स्वप्नवत्। आब्रह्मस्तम्बपर्य्यन्तं सर्वं कृष्णश्चराचरं॥ Nārada-pañca-rātra.

3. ज्ञानञ्चाज्ञानमेव द्वयमपि विदितं सर्वशात्रान्तराले धर्म्माधर्म्मौ च विद्या तदनुतदितरा पृष्ठलग्ना विभाति। एवं सर्वत्र युग्मं भवति खलु तथा ब्रह्मजीवौ प्रसिद्धौ कस्मादैक्यं तयो: स्यादकपटमनसा हन्त सन्तो वदन्तु॥

   तच्छब्दार्थ: प्रघटपरमानन्दपूर्णामृताब्धिस्त्वंशब्दार्थो भवभय-भरव्याग्रचित्तोतिदु:खी। तस्मादैक्यं न भवति तयोर्भिन्नयोर्वस्तुगत्या भेद:सेव्य: स खलु जगतां त्वंहि दासस्तदीय:॥

   नाभिधा समवायो वा हेत्वाभावाच्च लक्षणा। मायावादिमते ब्रह्म बोध्यते केन हेतुना। तं हेतुं मुख्यया वृत्या जगत्कर्त्तेति कथ्यते सकर्तृकत्वमेतेषामनुमानाच्च सिद्धयति। इयं सकर्तृका नूनं क्षितिर्भवितुमर्हति। कार्य्यत्वं तत्र हेतु: स्यात् घटादौ दृश्यते यथा॥

   तत्कथ्यते भगवतो महदन्तरं यत् कुद्दालदात्रहलपाणिभृतां जनानां। एते षडूतिविवशा: श्रमभारखिन्ना भ्रूभङ्गमात्रविषये स करोति सर्व्वं॥

   तथाहि कस्मात् प्रतिविम्बमासीत्तस्यापरिच्छिन्ननिरञ्जनस्य। जडस्य कस्मान्निगमोक्तधर्म्माधर्म्मौ च तत्तत्सुखदु:खभोगम्। प्रतिविम्बं भवेन्नूनं परिच्छिन्नस्य वस्तुन:। अपरिच्छिन्नता पूर्णा तस्य तद्भविता कथं। रामानुज: शिष्टगणाग्रगण्यो निनिन्द विम्बप्रतिविम्बवादं। शिष्टैर्गृहीतं न यतोमतं तत् तस्माद्भवेच्चारुतरं न नूनं॥

   अहं सुखी क्वापि भवामि दु:खी सुखस्वरूपी सततं स आत्मा। एवं हि भेद: कथमैक्यमेव तयोर्द्वयोर्भिन्नपदार्थयो: स्यात्। नित्यं स्वयं ज्योतिरनावृतो सावतीवशुद्धोजगदेकसाक्षी। जीवस्तु नैवंविध एव तस्मादभेदवृक्षोपरि वज्रपात:॥

   येन व्याप्तमखण्डमण्डलमिदं ब्रह्माण्डभाण्डादिकं रे रे मन्दमते त्वया कथमहो सोहं वच: कथ्यसे। पश्य त्वं निजवैभवं स्वहृदये कृत्वा मतिं

निर्म्मलां व्यूहः किं मशकोदरे प्रविशति प्रोद्दामदिग्दन्तिनां। कस्य त्वं कुत आगतः कथमरे संसारबन्धक्रमस्तत्त्वं तत् परिचिन्तय स्वहृदये भ्रान्तस्य मार्गं त्यज॥

न्यस्तः श्रीपरमेश्वरस्य कृपया चैतन्यलेशस्त्वयि त्वं तस्मात् परमेश्वरः स्वयमहो नायाति वक्तुं शठ। लब्ध्वा कश्चन दुर्जनः खलु यथा हस्त्यश्वपादातकं भूयादेव तदीशराजपदर्वी चक्रे ग्रहीतुं मनः॥

केचिद्वादबलाः कुतर्कजलधौ मग्नाः कुमार्गे रता मिथ्याजल्पनकल्पनाशनयुता भ्रान्ता जगद्भ्रामकाः। ब्रह्मैवाहमिदं चराचरमपि ब्रह्मैव दृश्याखिलं प्राहुर्यत्तदसन्मोरथ इति व्याख्यातमन्तःस्फुटं।

नैर्गुण्यवादो गुणसागरेपि तेषामहो गड्डरिकाप्रवाहः। सूत्रस्य भाष्यं पृथगेव कृत्वा प्रतारयन्ति स्वमतप्रपन्ना। ऐश्वर्य्यकर्त्तृत्वमुखाः समग्रा नित्या गुणास्ते परमेश्वरस्य। अतो गुणी निर्गुण एव कस्मान्नैर्गुण्यवादस्तु विवाद एव॥

प्रतीयते क्वापि न वेदलोके निर्धर्म्मकं वस्तु खपुष्पतुल्यं। प्रतीतिरास्ते यदि तस्य वेदे वेदाः प्रमाणं खलु नो तदा स्यात्। प्रस्तरो यजमानो वै यथात्र यज्ञसाधनं। धर्म्मवाधं तथात्रापि निर्धर्म्मस्तु प्रतीयते॥

4. अत्र केचिदद्वितीयत्वं ब्रह्मण उपयन्त एवैवं समादधते एकस्यैव ब्रह्मणः प्रतिविम्बभूतानां जीवानां सुखित्वदुखित्वादय एकस्यैव मुखस्य प्रतिविम्बानां मणिकृपाणदर्पणादिषूपलभ्यमानानामल्पत्वमहत्त्वमलिनत्वविमलत्वादिवत्तत्तदुपाधिवशाद्यवस्थाप्यन्ते। * * * काल्पनिकन्तु भेदमाश्रित्येयं व्यवस्थोच्यते कस्य पुनः कल्पना न तावद्ब्रह्मणस्तस्य परिशुद्धज्ञानात्मनः कल्पनाशून्यत्वात्। नापि जवीनामितरेतराश्रयप्रसङ्गात्। कल्पनाधीनो हि जीवो जीवाश्रया च कल्पनेति॥

किञ्च अविद्या कल्प्यस्य जीवस्य कल्पकः क इति निरूपणीयं न तावदविद्या अचेतनत्वात् नापि जीव आत्माश्रयदोषप्रसङ्गात् शुक्तिकारजतादिवदविद्याकल्प्यत्वाच्च जीवभावस्य ब्रह्मैव कल्पकमिति चेत् ब्रह्माज्ञानमेवायातं किञ्च ब्रह्माज्ञानानभ्युपगमे किं ब्रह्म जीवान् पश्यति वा नवा न पश्यति चेत् ईक्षापूर्विका विचित्रसृष्टिर्नामरूपव्याकरणमित्यादि ब्रह्मणो न स्यात् अथ पश्यति अखण्डैकरसं ब्रह्म नाविद्यामन्तरेण जीवान् पश्यतीति ब्रह्माज्ञानप्रसङ्गः। अतएव मायाविद्याविभागवादोपि निरस्तः, अज्ञानमन्तरेण हि मायिनोपि ब्रह्मणो जीवदर्शित्वं न स्यात् न च मायावी परानदृष्ट्वा मोहयितुमलं नापि माया मायाविनो दर्शनसाधनं दृष्टिषु परेषु तन्मोहसाधनमात्रत्वात्तस्याः अथ

ब्रह्मणो माया तस्य जीवदर्शित्वं कुर्वती जीवमोहनस्य हेतुरिति मन्यसे तर्हि परिशुद्धस्याखण्डैकर सस्वप्रकाशस्य ब्रह्मणः परदर्शनं कुव्रती माया परपर्याया अविद्यैव स्यात्। अथ मतं विपरीतदर्शनहेतुरविद्या माया तु मिथ्याभूतं ब्रह्मव्यतिरिक्तं मिथ्यात्वेन दर्शयन्ती न ब्रह्मणो विपरीतदर्शनहेतुः अतस्तस्य नाविद्यात्वमिति नैवं चन्द्रैकत्वे ज्ञायमाने द्विचन्द्रदर्शनं हेतोरप्यविद्यात्वात्। यदि च ब्रह्म मिथ्यात्वेनैव स्वव्यतिरिक्तं जानाति न तर्हि तन्मोहयति न ह्यनुन्मत्तो मिथ्यात्वेन ज्ञातान् मोहयितुमीहते॥ * * * अपुरुषार्थेन मोहनेन किं प्रयोजनं क्रीडेति चेत्। अपरिच्छिन्नानन्दस्य किं क्रीडया। परिपूर्णभूगानामेव क्रीडा पुरुषार्थत्वेन लोके दृष्टा इति चेत् नैवमिहोपपद्यते, नह्यपरमार्थतया प्रतिभासमानैर्निष्पन्नया परमार्थभूतेन च तत्प्रतिभासिनानुन्मत्तानां क्रीडारसो निष्पद्यते॥

Rāmānuja's Śārīraka Bhāṣya.

5. See page 370.

6. सकारेण वहिर्याति हकारेण विशेत् पुनः। प्राणस्तत्र स एवाहमहंस इति चिन्तयेत्। Yoga Śāstra in Śrīdhara swāmi's Com. Bhag. Gīta.

7. ये तु कार्य्यकारणयोरनन्यत्वं कार्य्यस्य मिथ्यात्वाश्रयेण वर्णयन्ति न तेषां कार्य्यकारणयोरनन्यत्वं सिध्यति सत्यमिथ्यार्थयोरैक्यानुपपत्तेः। तथा सति ब्रह्मणो मिथ्यात्वं जगतः सत्यत्वं वा स्यात्॥ Rāmānuja's Śār.Bhāś.

8. See page 300.

9. निष्कलं निष्क्रियं शान्तं निरवद्यं निरञ्जनं।

10. एतैरन्यैश्च विशेषणैर्विशेषितं परं ब्रह्म त्वमसि इति गुरुवाक्यं स्वानुभवन् ब्रह्माहमस्मीति श्रुतिं गृहीत्वा एवं गुरोराज्ञया एवं देववाक्यतः गुरुतः स्वतः त्रिप्रकारेण ब्रह्माहमस्मीति ज्ञात्वा स मुक्तः॥

11. अनात्मन्यात्मधीर्बन्धः॥ A'tmopadeśa.

12. त्वमभयं प्राप्तः संसारदुःखान्मुक्तोसीति एतत् सर्वं विमृष्य यथेच्छं कुरु * * आत्मैवेदं जगत् सर्वं ज्ञातं येन महात्मना। यदृच्छया वर्तमानं तं निषेद्धुं क्षमेत कः॥ A'tmopadeśa.

13. अकस्मात् कथञ्चित् पुण्यवशाद्वा वेदोदितेनेश्वरार्थं कर्मानुष्ठानेनापगत-रागादिमनः॥ Ibid.

14. आचार्य्यवान् पुरुषो वेद ॥
आचार्य्याद्ध्यैव विद्या विदिता साधिष्ठं गमयति। Chāndogya.

15. प्रासादनिर्माणादिवदनुपपन्नतैकरेखायामवस्तुभूतायां।
Rāmānuja Śār. Bhāṣ.

16. There is a common saying among the Hindus that if a cup of milk be presented to a swan (haṅsa), it will take the milky substance alone, leaving out the watery.

17. नानारसा मधुनि भिन्नतया तरूणां सन्ति त्रिदोषहरणं कथमन्यथा स्यात्। जीवास्तथा भगवति प्रलये विलीना नैक्यं गताः खलु यतः पृथगेव सृष्टौ। नदीसमुद्रयोर्भेदः शुद्धोदलवणादयोः। तथा जीवेश्वरौ भिन्नौ विलक्षणगुणान्वितौ॥ नद्यः समुद्रे मिलिताः समन्तान्नैक्यं गता विभिन्नतया न भान्ति क्षारोदशुद्धोदकयोर्विभेदाद्यास्ते तयोर्वास्तव एव भेदः। दुग्धे तोयं मिलितमपरे नैव पश्यन्ति भेदं हंसस्तावत् सपदि कुरुते क्षीरनीरस्य भेदं। एवं जीवा लयमधि परे ब्रह्मणीशे विलीना भक्ता भेदं विदधति गुरोर्वाक्यमासाद्य सद्यः। दुग्धं दुग्धे जलमपिजले मिश्रितं सर्व्वथा तन्नैकीभूतं नियतमुभयोर्मानसस्यैव यस्मात्। एवं जीवाः परमपुरुषे ध्यानयोगाद्विलीना नैक्यं प्राप्ता विमलमतयः सन्त एवं वदन्ति॥ *Tattwa Muk.*

18. अतःस्वपरभागो बद्धमुक्तशिष्याचार्य्यादिव्यवस्थाश्चैकस्याविद्या- कल्पिता- द्वैतवादिनापि बद्धमुक्त्याव्वस्था दुरुपवादां अतीतानां कल्पाना- मानन्त्यादेकै- कस्मिन् कल्प एकैकमुक्तावपि सर्वेषां मोक्षसंभवादमुक्तानुपपत्तेः। अनन्तत्वादात्मनाममुक्ताश्च सन्तीति चेत् किमिदमन्तत्वं असंखेयत्वमिति चेत्। न। भूयस्त्वादल्पज्ञैरसंख्येयत्वेपीश्वरस्य सर्वज्ञस्य सांख्येया एव तस्याशक्यत्वे सर्वज्ञत्वं न स्यात्। आत्मनां निःसंख्यत्वादीश्वरस्य अविद्यमानसंख्यावेदनाभोवो नासार्वज्ञमावहतीति चेत् भिन्नत्वे संख्याविधुरत्वं नोपपद्यते आत्मानः संख्यावन्तो भिन्नत्वात् माषसर्षपघटपटादिवत्। Rāmānuja Śār. Bhāṣ.

19. अद्वैताख्यं मतं विहाय झटिति द्वैते प्रवृत्तो भव। Tattwa Muk.

20. सोहं ज्ञानमिदं भ्रमस्तव भज त्वं पादपद्मं हरेः। Ibid.

21. श्रुतं पुराणे जगदीश्वरस्य नाभ्यम्बुजात् सर्वमिदं वभूव। शरीरसिद्धिस्तत एव यातो नाभिः कथं हन्त विना शरीरं। Tattwa Muktāvalī.

22. नहि जीवस्य शरीरधातुसाम्यवैषम्यनिमित्तं सुखदुःखयोर्भोक्तृत्वं सशरीरत्वकृतं

अपितु पुण्यपापरूपकर्मकृतं न हवै सशरीरस्येत्यपि कर्मारब्धदेहविषयं स एकधा भवति त्रिधा भवति स यदि पितृलोककामो भवति स तत्र पयति जक्षत् क्रीड्न् रममाण इति कर्मबन्धविनिर्मुक्तस्याविर्भूतस्वरूपस्य सशरीर स्यैवा- पुरुषार्थगन्धाभावात् अपहतपाप्मनस्तु परमात्मनः स्थूलसूक्ष्मरूपकृत्स्न-जगच्छरीरत्वेपि कर्मबन्धगन्धो नास्तीति। ननु नामापुरुषार्थगन्धप्रसङ्गः लोकवत्, यथा लोके राजशासनानुवर्तिनां च राजानुग्रहनिग्रहकृतसुखदुःखयोगेपि न सशरीरत्वमात्रेण शासके राज्ञयपि शासनानुवृत्त्यतिवृत्तिनिमित्तसुखदुःखयो-र्भोक्तृत्वप्रसङ्गः। यथाह द्राविडभाष्यकारः, यथा लोके राजाप्रचुरदन्दशूकघोरे नर्थसङ्कटेपिप्रदेशे वर्तमानो व्यजनाद्यवघूतदेहोदोषैर्न स्पृश्यते अभिप्रेतांश्च लोकान् परिपिपालयिषति भोगांश्च गन्धादीन् नविश्वजनोपभोग्यान् धारयते, तथासौ लोकेश्वरोभ्रमत्स्वसामर्थ्यचामरोदोषैर्नस्पृश्यते रक्षते च लोकान् ब्रह्मलोकादीन् भोगांश्चाविश्वनोपभोग्यान् धारयति। Śār. Bhāṣ.

23. जिनके अगुणनसगुणबिवेका जल्पहिं कल्पितवचन अनेका॥ Rāmāyaṇa.

24. सगुणहिं अगुणहिं नहिं कछु भेदा। गावहिं मुनिपुराण वुधवेदा॥ अगुण अरूप अलख अज जोई। भक्त पेमबश सगुण सो होई॥ जो गुणरहित सगुण सो कैसें। जलहिम उपल बिलग नहिं जैसें॥

Rāmāyaṇa.

25. "Remarks" on a Lecture on Vedāntism by Rev. K. M. Banerjee.

26. The Reformer Newspaper. It was established more than thirty years ago in Calcutta and professed to be based on the principles of True Vedāntism.

27. ब्रह्मा देवानां प्रथमः सम्बभूव विश्वस्य कर्त्ता भुवनस्य गोप्ता। स ब्रह्मविद्या सर्वविद्याप्रतिष्ठामथर्व्वाय ज्येष्ठपुत्राय प्राह॥ Muṇḍaka.

28. "Vedāntic doctrines vindicated."

29. See End Note 5 of Dialogue VII.

30. यथोर्णनाभिः सृजते गृह्णते च यथा पृथिव्यामोषधयः सम्भवन्ति यथा सतः पुरुषात् केशलोमानि तथाक्षरात् सम्भवतीह विश्वम्॥ Muṇḍaka.

31. "Remarks &c."

32. नमस्ते वायो त्वमेव प्रत्यक्षं ब्रह्म। अन्नं ब्रह्म। प्राणो ब्रह्म। मनो ब्रह्म॥

33. अन्नाद्ध्येव खल्विमानि भूतानि जायन्ते। अन्नेन जातानि जीवन्ति। अन्नं

प्रयन्त्यभिसंविशन्तीति। ⋆ ⋆ प्राणाद्ध्येव खल्विमानि भूतानि जायन्ते। प्राणेन जातानि जीवन्ति। प्राणं प्रयन्त्यभिसंविशन्तीति। ⋆ ⋆ मनसो ह्येव खल्विमानि भूतानि जायन्ते। मनसा जातानि जीवन्ति। मनः प्रयन्त्यभिसंविशन्तीति। ⋆ ⋆ विज्ञानाद्ध्येव खल्विमानि भूतानि जायन्ते। विज्ञानेन जातानि जीवन्ति। विज्ञानं प्रयन्त्यभिसंविशन्तीति। ⋆ ⋆ आनन्दाद्ध्येव खल्विमानि भूतानि जायन्ते। आनन्देन जातानि जीवन्ति। आनन्दं प्रयन्त्यभिसंविशन्तीति॥

34. तस्माद्वा एतस्मादात्मन आकाशः सम्भूतः। आकाशद्वायुः। वायोरग्निः। अग्नेरापः। अदभ्यः पृथिवी। पृथिव्या ओषधयः। ओषधीभ्योऽन्नं। अन्नाद्रेतः। रेतसः पुरुषः। स वा एष पुरुषोऽन्नरसमयः। ⋆ ⋆ सर्वं वैतेऽन्नमाप्नुवन्ति। येऽन्नं ब्रह्मोपासते। ⋆ ⋆ तस्माद्वा एतस्मादन्नरसमयात्। अन्योऽन्तरात्मा प्राणमयः। तस्माद्वा एतस्मात्प्राणमयात्। अन्योऽन्तर आत्मा मनोमयः तस्माद्वा एतस्मान्मनोमयात्। अन्योऽन्तर आत्मा विज्ञानमयः। तस्माद्वा एतस्माद्विज्ञानमयात्। अन्योऽन्तर आत्मानन्दमयः॥

35. सत्तैव सौम्येदमग्र आसीत् एकमेवाद्वितीयम्। Chāndogya.

36. सदेव सौम्येदमग्र आसीदेकमेवाऽद्वितीयं तद्वैक आहुरसदेवेदमग्र आसीदेकमेवाद्वितीयं तस्मादसतः सज्जायेत कुतस्तु खलु सौम्येवं स्यादिति होवाच कथमसतः सज्जायेतेति सत्त्वेव सौम्येदमग्र आसीत् एकमेवाद्वितीयं। Chāndogya.

37. आत्मा वा इदमेक एकाग्र आसीत्। Aitareya.

38. तमेवैकं जानथ आत्मानमन्या वाचो विमुञ्चथ अमृतस्यैष सेतुः॥

Muṇḍaka.

39. अस्मिन् द्यौः पृथिवी चान्तरिक्षमोतं मनः सहप्राणैश्च सर्वैः॥

40. अराइव रथनाभौ संहता यत्र नाड्यः स एषोऽन्तश्चरते वहुधा जायमानः।

Muṇḍaka.

41. तत्कारणं साङ्ख्ययोगाधिगम्यं ज्ञात्वा देवं मुच्यते सर्वपाशैः॥

42. ऋषिं प्रसूतं कपिलं यस्तमग्रे ज्ञानेर्विभर्त्ति जायमानश्च पश्येत्॥

43. "The Vaidas having existed from a time when Indian literature and indeed all literature, was only (as it were) in a state of germination, it is impossible to prove the divine origin of these sacred books by any historical

testimonies, the value of which was not understood at the time." *Vaidāntic doctrines vindicated.*

44. यतो वा इमानि भूतानि जायन्ते ⋆ ⋆ यत् प्रयन्त्यभिसंविशन्ति तद्ब्रह्म॥ Taittirīya.

45. स यथोर्णनाभिस्तन्तुनोच्चरेद्यथाग्नेः क्षुद्रा विस्फुलिङ्गा व्युच्चरन्त्येवमेवात्मनः सर्वे प्राणाः सर्वे लोकाः सर्वे देवाः सर्वाणि भूतानि व्युच्चरन्ति॥ Bṛhad.

46. स यथा सैन्धवखिल्य उदके प्राप्त उदकमेवानुविलीयते नहास्योद्ग्रहणायेव स्यात् यतो यतस्त्वाददीत लवणमेवैवं वा अर इदं महद्भूतमनन्तमपारं विज्ञानघन एव। Bṛhad.

47. एष सर्वेश्वर एष सर्वज्ञ एषोन्तर्याम्येष योनिः सर्वस्य प्रभवाप्ययौहि भूतानां Māṇḍukya.

48. ब्रह्म वा इदमग्र आसीदेकमेव॥

49. आत्मैवेदमग्र आसीदेक एव Bṛhad.

50. आत्मवेदमग्र आसीत् पुरुषविधः॥ Ibid.

51. तदेतत्सत्यं यथा सुदीप्तात् पावकाद्विस्फुलिङ्गाः सहस्त्रशः प्रभवन्ते सा रूपाः तथाक्षराद्विविधाः सोम्य भावाः प्रजायन्ते तत्र चैवापि यन्ति॥ Muṇḍaka.

52. सोऽकामयत वहुस्यां प्रजायेयातः स तपोऽतप्यत स तपस्तप्त्वा इदं विश्वमसृजत यदिदं किञ्च तत्सृष्ट्वा तदेवानुप्राविशत्। Tait.

53. तदैक्षत वहुस्यां प्रजायेयेति। Chāndogya.

54. This is the way in which the Neo-Vedāntists endeavour to explain away the passage "The text वहुस्यां प्रजायेय does not mean, as the Revd. gentleman asserts, that God has been many, and that the objects of the universe are of the same substance with God. It is a conventional thought peculiar to ancient Sanskrit writings to consider the Creator himself as born in his creation, as for example आत्मा वा जायते पुत्रः *Veda.* As a man's self is born in his son, yet remains distinct from him, so God, having created man and the world, remains distinct from them." *Remarks &c.*

55. असद्वै इदमग्र आसीत् ततो वै सदजायत तदात्मानं स्वयमकुरुत॥ Tait.

56. अग्निर्यथैको भुवनं प्रविष्टो रूपं रूपं प्रतिरूपो वभुव एकस्तथा सर्वभूतान्तरात्मा रूपं रूपं प्रतिरूपो वहिश्च वायुर्यथैको भुवनं प्रविष्टो रूपं रूपं प्रतिरूपो वभूव एकस्तथा सर्वभूतान्तरात्मा रूपं रूपं प्रतिरूपो वहिश्च। Kaṭha.

57. यथा सोम्यैकेन मृत्पिण्डेन सर्वं मृन्मयं विज्ञातं स्याद्वाचारम्भणं विकारो नामधेयं मृत्तिकेत्येव सत्यं यथा सोम्यैकेन लोहमणिना सर्व्वं लोहमयं विज्ञातं स्याद्वाचारम्भणं विकारो नामधेयं लोहमित्येव सत्यं यथा सोम्मैकेन नखनिकृन्तनेन सर्वं कार्ष्णायसं विज्ञातं स्याद्वाचारम्भणं विकारो नामधेयं कृष्णायसमित्येव सत्यं एवं सोम्य स आदेशो भवतीति। Chāndogya.

58. अत्र ह्येते सर्व्व एकं भवन्ति। Bṛhad.

59. पुरुष एवेदं विश्वं Muṇḍaka.

60. सर्वं ह्येतद् ब्रह्मायामात्मा ब्रह्म सोयमात्मा चतुष्पात्। Muṇḍaka.

61. एतदात्म्यमिदं सर्व्वं तत्सत्यं स आत्मा तत्त्वमसि श्वेतकेतो। Chāndogya.

62. अहं ब्रह्मास्मीति। Bṛhad.

63. य एवं वेदाऽहं ब्रह्मास्मीति स इदं सर्व्व भवति तस्य ह न देवाश्च नाभूत्या ईशते। Bṛhad.

64. यथा नद्यः स्यन्दमानाः समुद्रेऽस्तं गच्छन्ति नामरूपे विहाय तथा विद्वान्नामरूपाद्विमुक्तः परात्परं पुरुषमुपैति दिव्यं। स योहवै तत्परमं ब्रह्म वेद ब्रह्मैव भवति। Muṇḍaka.

65. अत्रान्तरं ब्रह्मविदो विदित्वा लीना ब्रह्मणि तत्परा योनिमुक्ताः। तिलेषु तैलं दधिनीव सर्पिरापः स्रोतःस्वरणीषु चाग्निः एवमात्मनि गृह्यतेऽसौ सत्येनेनं तपसा योऽनुपश्यति। Śwetāśwatara.

66. See End note No. 57 of Dialogue VIII

67. सर्वोऽस्मीति मन्यते सोऽस्य परमो लोकः। Bṛhad.

68. अथ हैनमुषस्तश्चाक्रायणः पप्रच्छ याज्ञवल्क्येति होवाच यत्साक्षादपरोक्षाद् ब्रह्म य आत्मा सर्व्वान्तरस्ते मे व्याचक्ष्व इत्येष त आत्मा सर्व्वान्तरः कतमो याज्ञवल्क्य सर्व्वान्तरो यः प्राणेण प्राणिति स त आत्मा सर्व्वान्तरो योऽपानेनापानिति स त आत्मा सर्व्वान्तरो यो व्यानेन व्यानिति स त आत्मा सर्व्वान्तरो य उदानेनोदानिति स त आत्मा सर्व्वान्तर एष त आत्मा सर्व्वान्तरः॥

स होवाचोषस्तश्चाक्रायणो यथा विब्रूयादसौ गौरसावश्च इत्येवमेवैतद्व्यपदिष्टं

भवति यदेव साक्षादपरोक्षाद्ब्रह्म य आत्मा सर्व्वान्तरस्तं मे व्याचक्ष्वेत्येष त आत्मा सर्व्वान्तरः कतमो याज्ञवल्क्य सर्व्वान्तरः।

नदृष्टेर्द्रष्टारं पश्येर्न श्रुतेः श्रोतारं शृणुयार्न मतेर्मन्तारं मन्वीथा न विज्ञातेर्विज्ञातारं विजानीयाः।

एष त आत्मा सर्व्वान्तरोऽतोऽन्यदार्त्तं॥

69. योऽशनायापिपासे शोकं मोहं जरां मृत्युमत्येति॥

70. यः पृथिव्यां तिष्ठन् पृथिव्या अन्तरो यं पृथिवी न वेद यस्य पृथिवी शरीरं यः पृथिवीमन्तरो यमयत्येष त आत्मान्तर्याम्यमृतः॥3॥

योऽप्सु तिष्ठन्नद्भ्योऽन्तरो यमापो न विदुर्यस्यापः शरीरं योऽपोऽन्तरो यमयत्येष त आत्मान्तर्य्याम्यमृतः॥4॥ योऽग्नौ तिष्ठन्नग्नेरन्तरो यमग्निर्न वेद यस्याग्निः शरीरं योऽग्निमन्तरो यमयत्येष त आत्मान्तर्याम्यमृतः॥5॥ योऽन्तरिक्षे तिष्ठन्नन्तरिक्षादन्तरो यमन्तरिक्षं न वेद यस्यान्तरिक्षं शरीरं योन्तरिक्षमन्तरो यमयत्येष त आत्मान्तर्य्याम्यमृतः॥6॥ यो वायौ तिष्ठन्वायोरन्तरो यं वायुर्न वेद यस्य वायुः शरीरं यो वायुमन्तरो यमयत्येष त आत्मान्तर्य्याम्यमृतः॥7॥ यो दिवि तिष्ठन्दिन्वोऽन्तरो यं द्यौर्न वेद यस्य द्यौः शरीरं यो दिवमन्तरो यमयत्येष त आत्मान्तर्य्याम्यमृतः॥

71. अदृष्टो द्रष्टाऽश्रुतः श्रोताऽमतोमन्ताऽविज्ञातो विज्ञाता नान्योऽतोऽस्ति द्रष्टा नान्योतोऽस्ति श्रोता नान्योतोऽस्ति मन्ता नान्योतोऽस्ति विज्ञातैष त आत्मान्तर्याम्यमृतोऽन्यदार्त्तं॥

72. 'But the challenger cannot claim the choosing of the ground, and the Missionary who heartily seeks the conversion of these men will seek it vainly if he shirk the task, however irksome, of exploring the field where alone the Vedāntists of modern Bengal will consent to be found. He must try to take accurate account of the Upaniṣads; that is to say, he must not content himself with picking out a few of the passages which are most open to ridicule, but he must endeavour candidly to understand what it is, in these treatises, that *satisfies* the modern thinkers of Bengal, *Ballantyne's Christianity contrasted with Hindu philosophy, p.* 51.

DIALOGUE X

FROM THE SAME TO THE SAME

I told you in my last how we returned home from the Rajah's, laden with presents. We were all happy and cheerful with the single exception of Āgamika, who appeared to be labouring under some inward perturbation. None asked him any questions at the time, but I called the day after, to inquire after his health. "I am quite well," said he, – "physically, but feel rather unhappy at the progress of sceptical sentiments. Even the new class of Vedāntists have given up the divine authority of the Upaniṣads. What is all this leading to? Is it possible for human society to keep together for a single century without the discipline and direction of God's word?"

The good Brāhmin was talking after this fashion when Satyakāma came in, also to make friendly enquiries. Āgamika turned to him, and, after some desultory observations on the Vedānt controversy, said : "I cannot help complaining, Satyakāma, that you have not been dealing fairly with Vyāsa and Śaṅkarācārya. You have been forcing them to submit to an ordeal against which they have often protested. They do not pretend to base their doctrine on the suggestions of reason. If they had done so, perhpas I might have joined you to a certain extent in finding fault with their deductions. But their appeal is to the Vedas, the eternal and infallible Vedas, which were co-eval with the creation. As the productions of Brahma's wisdom, they contain truths which it would be an act of profaneness to gainsay. For every doctrine contained in the

Uttara Mīmāṅsā, Śaṅkarācārya has adduced ample proof from the Vedas. There is, I think, not a single Sūtra which is not supported by the unerring texts of the Upaniṣads. Nay, he has in more than one place plainly expressed his jealousy of argumentations not founded on those records of eternal truth. He has never hesitated to avow that his teaching is regulated by passages breathed out by the Creator. It is only when reason is subservient to the Vedas, and, as a faithful handmaid, assists in enforcing their doctrine, that he allows her room. 'The knowledge of Brahma, says he, proceeds from a critical consideration of the sense of Vedic texts, not from inference and other proofs; and the Vedānta texts being recognized as setters forth of the cause of the world's production, inference, when it is a proof not opposed to those texts, is not excluded from confirming their meaning[1].'

"You do not, continued Āgamika, really meet Śaṅkarācārya, when you use against his system arguments quite irrelevant to his position. How can I, or any body else, submit to your wisdom, when we believe it to be opposed to that of the Omniscient?"

Satyakāma.—"But *does* the Veda contain the wisdom of the Omniscient? This question has never yet been discussed. You assume it as already decided in your favour. I do not deny that Śaṅkarācārya is generally borne out by texts of the Vedas. I say *generally*, because I do not wish absolutely to pronounce judgement, as between him and the leaders of other schools. But you must prove that the Vedas are records of eternal truth, before their texts can be allowed to drown the voice of reason, and stifle the dictates of conscience."

Āgamika.—"Has not Śaṅkarācārya himself proved that point? 'Nor could such Śāstras, says he, as the Ṛk and other Vedas, endowed with the characteristics of omniscience, proceed from any other than the Omniscient'[2]."

Satyakāma.—"Do you call that proof? In Gotama's vocabulary, the reason adduced would be called *Sādhyasama,* a mere petitio principii. Śaṅkara assumes that the Vedas contain characteristic marks of omniscience, and thence argues that they proceeded from the Omniscient. The hypothesis is almost identical with the inference. The argument is not a process of logic. It is a mere assertion. Nor must it be forgotten that Śaṅkara is not, in the above passage, proving the authority of the Vedas. His object is to demonstrate the omniscience of God by asserting that of the Vedas which proceeded from Him. He assumes but does not prove that point."

Āgamika.—"But does not the Veda itself decide the question. 'Being desirous of liberation, I seek Him, the 'manifestation of spiritual understanding, who in the beginning created Brahmā and revealed to him the Vedas[3]. 'That which all the Vedas set forth—I declare[4].' 'This Ṛg-Veda was breathed out by that great Being'[5]."

Satyakāma.—"Why do you commence and stop just where Śaṅkara commenced and stopped when citing those passages? Why do you give the text second-hand? Read out the passages whole and entire from the Upaniṣads themselves?"

Āgamika.—"As from the fire contained in damp-fuel, smoke comes out separate, so, (O Maitreyi) was breathed out of the great Being this, namely, the Ṛg-veda, the Yajur-veda, the Sāma-veda, the Atharva, Aṅgirasa, the Itihāsa, Purāṇa, Sciences, Upaniṣads, Ślokas, Sūtras, After-expositions. All these were breathed out of Him'[6]."

Satyakāma.—"Does not this prove too much for you?"

Āgamika.—"Śaṅkara has shown that all these stand simply for the Vedas, for in his commentary on the passage he remarks : 'The Veda is not like any other work; having issued like a man's breath, without any personal exertion'[7]."

"I thought, rejoined Satyakāma, you said a little while ago that the Vedas were productions of the wisdom of Brahma. But it appears now that they issued from the Omniscient like human breath without any other effort on his part. We cannot then say that they contain his deliberate teaching. He did not intelligently utter them; they escaped Him like somke from fire. You have no right to say that an involuntary emanation of that kind is the production of his intellect."

Āgamika.—"He is called *prajnāna-ghana,* a mass of intelligence. Whatever issues from Him must also partake of the Omniscient."

Satyakāma.—"But the Vedas say that every thing issues from Him. He is not a mass of intelligence only, but 'this spirit, Brahma, is all mind, all vital air, all eye, all ear, all earth, all water, all air, all ether, all light, all no-light [or darkness,] all desire, all no-desire, all anger, all no-anger, all virtue, all vice, all everything'[8]. Is not this the language of the Upaniṣad? How can you then trust the Veda to be all knowledge, merely because it escaped him?"

"You are so fond of vilifying the Vedas," said Āgamika, somewhat irritated. "That is your besetting sin. You are such a contemner of the Veda."

"I thought, said Satyakāma, I was speaking guardedly enough by making no observation of my own, and confining myself to the very language of the Veda."

Āgamika.—"You will draw us again into the whole question of the Vedānta. We have had that to our heart's content."

Satyakāma.—"My impression is, you conceded that on the grounds of human reasoning the Vedānta could not stand, but that it is supported by the Vedas. We are now surveying that fundamental support. I am anxious to get at your theory of the Veda before proceeding to examine it."

Āgamika.—"Well, hear patiently the proofs we adduce. I have already shown that the Śwetāśwatara, Kaṭha, and the Bṛhadāraṇyaka support the authority of the Vedas. The Muṇḍaka does the same. "From Him the Ṛk, Sāman, Yajus[9]."

Satyakāma.—"Go on, why do you stop short? Does not

the Upaniṣad specify the whole creation as a procession from him like the Vedas?"

Āgamika. – "It does."

"And who is the 'Him' here?" asked Satyakāma. "What is the antecedent of the *tasmāt*?

"The soul, or Male person, spoken of immediately before."

"That is a Male described as one of like passions with ourselves, becoming a father after the ordinary animal fashion, the description itself not being at all choice in point of decency of language. It is hardly consistent with the reverence due to God to identify Him with such a 'male,' and call him the author of the Vedas on the strength of this passage[10]."

"What is the use of such criticisms?" said Āgamika querulously. "Do you seriously mean that the Upaniṣads do not uphold the authority of the Vedas."

Satyakāma. – "I think you cannot deny that some of the texts you have quoted actually *disprove* your theory of Vedic inspiration. But suppose I waived that question for the present, and allowed that the Vedas support the authority of the Vedas. What then? *Not even a dexterous person can ride on his own shoulder*[11]."

Āgamika. – "What do you mean?"

Satyakāma. – "As you are impatient of cross-questioning on the Vedas, you had better ask what Sāyana means by introducing that remark, for it is not mine. The remark means that the Vedas cannot prove their own authority, any more than a man support himself on his own shoulders."

Āgamika. – "I am astonished at your still calling the authority of the Vedas in question. At the marriage assembly you quoted Gotama against Tarkakāma in order to prove that if all evidence were denied there would be an end of discussion. You are now acting against the spirit, if not the letter, of that Sūtra of the Nyāya. You are calling in question the authority of that which everybody allows is the word of God. Really I feel now the wisdom of Manu's ordinace that those who vilify the Vedas ought to be banished from Society."

Satyakāma. – " You may banish me, if you like; but you must remember, I have not wantonly said anything against the Vedas. On certain questions of vital importance you contend that the authority of the Veda should be binding on all. You say that it is the repository of infinite wisdom. I ask only for proof. If your point can be established by satisfactory evidence, I cannot fail to be highly edified. Your summary appeal to Manu does not augur well for the strength of your position. Nor is it just to the great interests at stake. The Vedas are now appealed to as the only support of the Vedāntic doctrine, which appears to be much at variance with reason and conscience. Before I can consent to this appeal, I am anxious to examine the authority of our judge. Is the Veda the inspired word of God? Let the question be dispassionately discussed. You can gain nothing by hastily asserting its authority, if it really have none. Nor can I gain any thing by disproving its authority. Before we can once for all surrender our Reason, it is necessary to sift the pretensions of that which challenges implict obedience.

"Besides, continued Satyakāma, it is somewhat out of place now to decline discussion on the authority of the Vedas, when some of our eminent scholars long ago condescended to cite objections against their genuineness and inspiration, and undertook to answer them. Indeed it is impossible to conceive stronger objections against the authority of a Śāstra than those which Jaimini, Sāyana, Gotama, Kaṇāda, and Kapila have themselves cited. If they could but have refuted them with any success, the cause of the Vedas would have been entirely triumphant. You need not be afraid of condescending too much to sceptical cavillers, when such authorities attempted to answer the objections to which I refer. Allow me to bring some of them to your notice. Sāyana notices the following objections as to the authenticity of the Vedas.

1. The four Vedas are named in several texts. Is not that proof[12]? 'No, says he, for those texts being contained in the Vedas, their admission would amount to a satisfaction with mere self-dependence. Not even a dexterous man can support himself on his own shoulders.

2. But the Smṛti bears testimony to the Vedas. 'This is nothing, because the Smṛti itself depends on the Vedas.'

3. 'As to the popular opinion in favour of the Vedas, though it prevail universally, it may be as erroneous as the notion that the sky is blue.' If such objections, added Satyakāma, have been noticed by so many condescending sages, perhaps it may not be beneath your dignity to resolve my doubts."

Āgamika. – "But Sāyana has satisfactorily replied to those objections and disposed of them. You have yourself said you can conceive no stronger objections. You should accordingly declare yourself satisfied."

Satyakāma. – "If Sāyana's reply to those objections were at all satisfactory, I should never have troubled you with my doubts. But he has left the objections quite intact. He says[13], 'with reference to the authenticity of the Vedas, proofs as mentioned, founded on the Vedas, on Smṛti, on popular opinion, may be seen. As it is not absurd that the sun, moon, and other luminaries should have the quality of self-manifestation, though pots, clothes, and other substances cannot manifest themsevles; so there may be in the extra-ordinarily powerful Vedas, the quality of proving themselves, as they have that of proving other substances, though it may be impossible for men to ride on their own shoulders.'

"This, I submit, added Sātyakāma, is no demonstration. The argument comes too late after the entertainment of the objections already mentioned. The entertainment of the objections shows that the proposition was not, in the conception of Sāyana, self-evident; for no sane man would seriously entertain an objection against a self-evident proposition, such as the existence of the sun and moon though a blind man might question it. The blind man would in such a case be simply *nigraha-sthāna, i.e.,* not fit to be argued with on that question. But it would be a mockery to think of satisfying a man by an assertion of which he was not capable of judging for himself."

Āgamika.—"But if you were called upon to prove the existence of the sun, what would you say? You would only wonder, would you not at the question? My feeling is, and I have no doubt Sāyana's also was, the same, at this question on the authority of the Vedas."

Satyakāma.—"It is not for me to contradict you in what you describe as a matter of feeling. But Sāyana could not have been possessed with such a feeling : for then he would not have so elaborately cited objections, or tendered replies. Nor does any other sage appear to have partaken of your wonder at the question, for we find Jaimini, Vyāsa, Gotama, Kaṇāda, Kapila, Śaṅkarācārya all undertaking to establish the authority of the Veda, by the refutation of arguments adduced by infidels. They could not therefore have considered it as clear as the sun or moon. If the omniscient wisdom contained in the Vedas were of this self-evidencing description, you could not have staggered at the conclusions of the Vedānta. It is because they were *prima facie* opposed to the dictates of reason and conscience, because they were not as clear as the sun or moon, that you appeal to the positive authority of the Vedas. However brilliant the Vedas may be in other respects, here is the Vedāntic doctrine hanging over it as a cloud. Here we have Indra's achievements, as a chief god, enthusiastically celebrated as acts performed under the influence of liquor[14]. Here we have Brahma, declared to be all-vice, no less than all-virtue. Here we have the Creator pronounced to be a sort of conjurer, deliberately deluding rational souls, by the projecting of illusory appearances[15]. Here we have the very author of the Vedas described as an ordinary male, with animal propensities, producing a large offspring. Here we have elaborate lectures on the most obscene subjects, which even profligate men would think it beneath the dignity of human nature to realize in practice[16]. Are we to be silenced by the assertion that the divine authority of such books is as apparent as the sun or moon? If you have any explanations to offer on these revolting descriptions, we may give you the patient hearing due to your learning and character. But if you wish to persuade us that the Vedas are of divine authority, you must prove your position by evidence. You must show by external proofs that they are possessed of such authority, or we must draw the natural inference, to which the offensive descriptions I have just mentioned, would lead us. There is no use therefore in screening them from a critical examination. Jaimini himself never did so. He noticed numerous objections against those works."

Āgamika.—"And has answered them too. Are you not satisfied with his replies?"

Satyakāma.—"Satisfied! No, on the contrary, I am confirmed in my doubts."

A.—"How?"

S.—"Jaimini notices an objection to the eternity of the Vedas, founded on their containing names of persons and places. 'From connection with non-eternal objects the Mantras are vain'. On this Sūtra the commentator remarks, In the Mantra, what do they in Kikaṭa, there is mention made of the country Kikaṭa. So are other uneternal objects mentioned, such as the town Naichāśākha, the king Pramangada. This being the case, it follows that the Mantra could not have existed before Pramangada[17].' The answer to the objection is obviously inconclusive. It can refer only to those names after which any portions of the Vedas are called. 'The names, says the philosopher, 'from reading'[18]. Different sections were styled after different men who first read them. This does not at all meet the question regarding the names which historically occur in the narratives. Another answer is therefore attempted, but that is a mere reference to a previous Sūtra in which a similar objection was noticed. That objection concerned a text wherein mention was made of 'Babara, son of Prāvāhaṇi.' The question was how could the Veda be eternal when non-eternal objects are named in it. Jaimini replied that the words may be otherwise interpreted, and the commentator makes out, ingeniously enough, that Prāvāhaṇi may be tortured to do duty for the 'wind' and Babara may serve as the imitation of its sound[19]. This explanation is not only unsatisfactory; it is something more. It recoils against the Vedas. A sad plight such as this shows how much the philospher must have been straitened. Is it possible to explain away by this violent artifice all the passages that one can adduce containing narratives concerning men? Is it to be pretended that no persons, places, or human actions are historically named in the Vedas? The very supposition is preposterous. What for instance is the Kaṭhopaniṣad—but a series of lectures given by Yama to Nuchiketas? Are not Sanatkumāra, Śwetaketu, Yājnavalkya, Uddālaka, Gotama, my own namesake, persons of Vedic notoriety? How could the Vedas be composed before the persons mentioned in them were born? The objection recoils with redoubled force after such an ineffectual attempt to refute it. Had Jaimini never undertaken the refutation of objections against the Vedas, my doubts on their divine authority could hardly have been so strong as now they are. When a philosopher of his intelligence is driven to the necessity of *spelling out* a fanciful meaning from a well-known word (Prāvāhaṇi), the cause must be bad indeed. This subtle interpretation is however impossible with scores of proper names that occur in the Vedas. You cannot volatilize the whole army of Ṛṣis celebrated in those wrtings. Are Indra's exploits against Vṛtra also to be dissolved into the 'wind'? Even Jaimini's shift therefore must fail. You cannot reconcile with your theory of Vedic eternity the existence of historical narratives in the Vedas.

"Again the Vedas themselves refer to times anterior to their own age. How could there be a period before eternity? In the very first *Sūkta* of the Ṛg-Veda there is mention made of *old* and *new* Ṛṣiṣ. The Śwetāśwatara speaks also of former periods of gods and Ṛṣis[20]. The *Kena,* or as it is otherwise called the *Talavakāra,* similarly speaks of *old* teachers, from whom was derived its mysterious doctrine[21]. The *Iśa,* or *Vājasaneya,* repeats the same idea in two different places, only substituting the word *wise* for *old*[22]. The *Kaṭha* describes the doctrine delivered to Nuchiketas as so subtle that even the gods had doubts about it in *olden* times[23]. The Muṇḍaka says that Atharva *in the days of yore* revealed the science of Brahma to Aṅgir[24]. Again, that Aṅgiras declared it of *old* to Saunaka[25]. The Taittirīya Brāhmaṇa says 'the Vajaśravases knew this Brāhmaṇa of old[26].' Thus the Vedas themselves testify against your theory of their eternity."

Āgamika. – "Well, but have not Gotama, Kaṇāda, Vyāsa, Śaṅkarācārya, and Kapila defended the authority of the Vedas. To begin with Vyāsa and Śaṅkara :– they explain the anachronisms you complain of by declaring that there are *eternal species of gods, men,* and other beings, and that it is with the species that words are connected, and not with individuals, for as the latter are infinite, such a connection would in their case be impossible. But as species are eternal (though individuals begin to exist) no contradiction is discoverable in the case of such word as *cow,* etc. In the same way it is to be remarked that though we allow that the individual gods, etc., have commenced to exist, there is no contradiction [to the eternity of the Vedic word] in the [existence of the] words *Vasu,* etc. [which denote those individual gods], since species are eternal. And the fact that the gods, etc., belong to particular species may be learned from this, that we discover their corporeality and other attributes in the hymns and *arthavādas* (explanatory remaks in the Vedas), etc[27].' In truth it was by means of the eternal words of the Vedas, as prototypes of things, that the Creator formed the universe. Thus the Veda says, at (or with) the word *etc (these)* Prajāpati created the gods; at *asṛgram (they were poured out)* he created men; at *indavah (drops of soma)* he created the *pitris; at tirah pavitram (through the filter)* he created the planets; at *āśavah (swift)* he created hymns; at *viśvāni* (*all*) he creted praise; and at the words *abhi saubhagā (for the sake of blessing)* he created the other creatures. And in another place it is said 'with his mind he produced speech, as *a mate.*' (Bṛ. Ār. Up. p. 50.) By these and other such texts the Veda declares that creation was prceded by the word. And when the Smṛiti says, 'At first a divine voice, eternal, without beginning or end, formed of the Vedas, was uttered by Svayambhū, from which all activities [proceeded] the expression *utterance* of the voice, is to be regarded as employed out of deference to the customary pharseology, since it is inconceivable that a voice which was without beginning or end,' could be uttered in the same sense as other sounds. Again, we have this other text. In the beginning Maheśvara created from the words of the Veda the names and forms of creatures, and their several modes of action;' and again, He created in the beginning the several names, functions, and conditions of all creatures from the words of the Veda.' And it is a matter of common observation to us all, that when any one is occupied with any end which he wishes to accomplish, he first calls to mind the word which expresses it, and then proceeds to effect his purpose. So, too, in the case of Prajāpati the creator, we conclude that before the creation the words of the Veda were manifested in his mind, and afterwards he created the objects which resulted from them. Thus the Vedic text which says, 'uttering *bhūr,* he created the earth (*bhūmi*), etc.,' intimates that the different worlds, earth and the rest, were manifested, *i.e.*, created from the words *bhūr*, etc., manifested in his mind[28].'

"Those eminent expounders of the Veda have also shown that the world being in reality without beginning, there is no absurdity in the supposition of all worldly events being only repetitions of the same things in other ages. There can be no such thing, therefore, as past or future. What is past is also future in reference to the next age in which it will re-appear. What is future is also past in reference to the last age in which it had already occurred once. There is no room for an argument founded on a charge of anachronism.

"Gotama has also noticed certain objections preferred by unthinking heretics, complaining of the failure of Vedic promises, of mutually conflicting texts, and of tautologies. He answers them quite effectually by contending that the failure of the promised fruit may be owing to defects in the performance of ceremonies; that the conflicting texts may be reconciled by the supposition that they refer to different times and places, and that tautologies are useful in the inculcation of doctrine.

"This defence is unanswerable. Men ought not to charge on the Vedas the consequences of their own neglect in the performance of ceremonies, nor ought they to be so narrow-minded as not to perceive that differences of time and season may occasion differences of description and injunction : and, instead of murmuring, they ought to be thankful for tautologies, for they may thereby have better chances of understanding the mysteries of truth.

"Kaṇāda too contends for the authority of the Vedas. 'The composition of sentences, says he, in the Vedas is according to reason.' 'In the Brāhmaṇas the occurrence of names is the characteristic (of omniscience.)' How could the Vedas contain the names of all things if they were not inspired?

Again 'the rules of alms-giving are also after reason.' Accordingly Kaṇāda begins and ends his work with the declaration of the authority of the Vedas as HIS word[29].

"Kapila, too, notwithstanding his many eccentricities and his denial of the eternity of the Vedas, avows that no person could have fabricated them; for, of free or bond, none was competent to produce them[30]."

Satyakāma. – "You have produced a formidable array of witnesses in support of the Vedas. Do not think I am wanting in respect for any of them; but you must remember that it is no disrespect to a witness to subject him to a cross-examination. I will do nothing more than test their assertions by that logical touchstone which they have themselves supplied.

"Let us first classify the questions under discussion. They may be considered as fourfold :

1. How can the Vedas be eternal when they not only contain narrations of events that occurred in time, but also speak of periods previous to themselves?

2. What proofs are there of their eternity, or of their inspiration by God?

3. What are the Vedas?

4. What are their own claims?

"In answer to the first question you refer to Vyāsa and Śaṅkarācārya, who maintain that there are eternal *Species* of men and gods, and that when the Vedas speak of names which appeared in time, they refer really to those eternal species, the individual members of which were manifested in the transactions of the world. They also maintain that the universe was created after the words contained in the Vedas. As those words arose in the Creator's mind, he formed the things indicated by them. They likewise contend that the world, being in reality without beginning, is revolving in continued cycles, so that the Vedas are only speaking of past events, namely those which happened in the previous age, when they refer to what appears to be posterior to the production.

"On this explanation of the difficulty contained in the first question, I have only to make three remarks. *First,* the explanation is founded on a gratuitous hypothesis of the existence of eternal species, for which no proof is offered other than a few sentences of the Vedas. This reason is vitiated by the fault of *self-dependence. Secondly,* assuming the existence of eternal species, and the unceasing revolution of worlds with the same personal manifestations and events, you may still be called upon to account for the singular fact that the Vedas make allusion only to such incidents as happened before a certain definable era, but are totally silent on all affairs that belong to a later date. *Thirdly,* Śaṅkara quotes the text that the Supreme Being settled 'the names, functions, and conditions of *all creatures* from the *words of the Vedas?'* If the fact were so, the Vedas would be a real *śabda-kalpa-druma,* or a cyclopaedia of every thing conceivable by any body. But the fact is not so, and we may meet the extravagant affirmation with a direct negative. For the Vedas have no terms, no names, for multitudes of things which are either of modern discovery, or were unknown in India in times of yore. If the creation of the universe was after the words of the Vedas suggesting ideas to the Creator's mind, how is it that there is an endless variety of things for which there are no terms in the Vedas, but of the creation of which we have nevertheless ocular evidence?"

Āgamika. – "I do not quite comprehend what you mean."

Satyakāma. – "In the first place the supposition of eternal species is altogether gratutitous. What is the meaning of *species* before the existence of individuals? Or supposing that *ākṛti* means form, and *vyakti* its manifestation, what is the meaning of a *form* before its manifestation? Assuming however that such eternal forms are possible, how is it that the Vedas only allude to forms of such things as may have appeared in India down to a certain ascertainable period? Again, the Vedas speak not of names only, as the *vyakti* of the *ākṛti,* but also of *acts* performed in time. How can the theory of eternal species account for the narration of *events,* in books supposed to have been completed before the creation of the universe? Is there for instance an eternal form of a drunken Indra when he kills Vṛtra[31], of a sober Indra when awe-stricken, with folded hands, before a more powerful god, and of a profligate Indra in the company of the *Apsarases*[32]? If you refer, in reply, to the theory of an eternal succession of world, I must then ask again, how is it there is no mention of any incident of an age posterior—say—to that of Yudhiṣṭhira. You hear of certain anecdotes of Śwetaketu, of Sanatkumāra, of Uddālaka, of Vaśiṣṭa; but you never meet with any accounts of Vikramāditya, Kālidāsa, Ghatakarpara, Bhāskarācārya, Śaṅkarācārya, Ādiśūra, Bullalsen;—not to mention characters still nearer to our times. How is it that some old manifestations of forms only are given, but there is profound silence concerning events later than the time of Yudhiṣṭira, or transpiring elsewhere than in India?

"If again the whole creation was regulated by the words of the Vedas, how is it that there are multitudes of created things of which there is no intimation to be found in them? How many plants and animals are there, how many organic and inorganic substances, how many things noticed in the different physical sciences and in natural history, are there, for which we have no term, no name, in the Vedas? Their *śabdas* are only indicative of some Indian produce of a date anterior to the age of Yudhiṣṭira. Why are you obliged to use foreign words when you apply to the sub-assistant surgeon for a little *quinine,* or ask Tarkakāma to decide a question of conscience, as to whether you can take a little *tea,* or *coffee,* as a remedy against cold? And if with our limited knowledge we are acquainted with so many things of which there are no traces in the Vedas, if we who have never travelled beyond the boundaries of our native land know more *śabdas* than are found in those writings, how much greater still must be the range of things, which men of larger experience must miss in their pages?

"As to the second question of proofs of Vedic inspiration, nothing that Gotama, Kaṇāda, or Kapila has advanced on the subject is worth a moment's consideration. Gotama says that its authority is deduced from the infallible person who (as the commentator adds) made the Vedas.[33] The *Sādhya,* or point to be proved, is, in other words, cited as its own *hetu* or reason! Who would doubt for a moment that the Vedas were of authority, if once convinced of their infallible original? That the very philosopher who discriminated so clearly between true and false reasons, in the explanation of his topics, should himself offer a proof, exactly corresponding to his own definition of the false reason, styled *Sādhyasama,* leaves little room for doubting that the cause, which drove him to such a departure from his own logical principles must be piteously weak."

Āgamika. – "Not exactly so, for Gotama says that the infallibility of the Veda is proved like that of Mantras (spells) and the Āyurveda (the medical treatise)."

Satyakāma. – "That only removes the difficulty one step. For what are spells? Nothing! At any rate we cannot connect the Most Holy, that governs according to rule and moral law, with *spells* that profess to be independent of rule, and make no discrimination of right and wrong. None but the vulgar practise them, none but the vulgar repose confidence in them, and certainly none can prove any thing about them. If spells be true, then it must be idle to talk of morals or of religion, then must we surrender reason and conscience to the freaks of the profligate men that deal in those unmeaning things. And as to the medical treatise, I need hardly remind you that the Medical College of Calcutta has served to throw it very much into discredit. I believe few in our days would trust a cholera patient to an adept in the Āyurveda.

"Kaṇāda's pleas for the authority of the Vedas are little better than Gotama's. His assertion in the third and last Sūtras is a mere confession of faith. 'The Veda is of authority, because it is His (God's) word'! This reason, almost identical with that which Gotama urged, is likewise *Sādhya-sama,* being scarcely different from the inference. Two other reasons, given by him, resemble the vicious arguments by which he himself exemplifies false reasoning. 'The composition of sentences and the rules of alms-giving contained in the Vedas are according to reason.' If the premises be admitted, the argument is an antitype of the one, *It has horns, therefore it is a cow*[34]. Many human compositions are reasonable, though not divine; just as many animals are horned, though not cows. But the premises are by no means certain, if not positively untrue. This very appeal to the authority of the Vedas is caused by the fact of their teaching not being according to reason, and as to the rules of alms-giving which they inculcate, they are based on *class prejudices* rather than on *reason.* Witness the passage cited by Kaṇāda's own commentator, though it is on alms-*taking* rather than alms-*giving,* but the two are treated as one subject by the author. 'On the seventh (day of going without food) he may steal Śūdra's food : on the tenth, the Vaiśya's : on the seventeenth, the Kṣatriya's : in peril of life, or for the preservation of himself or a relative, the Brāhmin's[35].' Excellent instance of reasonable jurisprudence! The above arugment for the Vedas rather resembles the other exemplar of false reasoning; *it has horns, therefore it is an horse*[36]!

"There is a fourth reason adduced by Kaṇāda, but that is identical with one of Śaṅkarācārya's, already noticed, viz., that the Vedas contain names of all things.

"You have cited Kapila, too, as a witness for the divine authority of the Veda. How a person that disbelieves the existence of the Deity, can bear testimony to His *word* is a problem which it is impossible to solve. But Kapila's attempt to prove the authority of the Veda gives us an insight into a theory which most of the shcools held on this point, but which is now little thought of by their followers. They looked upon it as a talisman,—a charm. Kapila grounds the authority of the Veda on the perfect knowledge of its utterers, and on its practical success, as in the *āyur-veda,* or the medical treatise. But he denies the possibility of its having an author of any kind. His reasoning on this point is analogous to that which he used in denying the existence of a Supreme Being. He says it could not be the production of any personal being, because there could be no personal being competent for the task of composing it. A person must either be free or in bondage. A free person *would* not, and one in bondage *could* not, compose it. A free person *would* not, because, (as Vijñāna Bhikṣu[37] expounds the last sūtra cited by yourself) not being subject to a motive, he would not impose on himself the task of composing such a work with its 'thousand ramifications,' and one in bondage could not, because he had not the omniscience necessary for the office. The fact of the first personal being having uttered it, does not constitute it his work; for it is only essays[38] intelligently and elaborately composed, that may be called an author's work. But the Vedas issued from the self-existent by the power of adṛṣta, like breath, without any deliberation on his part. And the self-existent himself is no God on Kapila's theory. The Vedas therefore are destitute of any external authority, and it is only their internal self-evidencing virtue[39], by force of which they challenge our obedience.

"Kapila is not singular in his view of the authority of the Veda. Vyāsa, Śaṅkarācārya, Jaimini, Sāyana, and others hold substantially the same opinion. But Kapila disavows the doctrine of its eternity[40]. He calls it a product. And here we have an extraordinary theory of a work, which is neither eternal, nor the composition of any person, divine or human, bond or free.

"But Kapila's theory cannot astound us more than that of a large and influential class of the followers of Jaimini, the author of the Pūrva Mīmāṅsā. Jaimini contendes for the paramount authority of the Vedas, and the universal obligation of Dharma, or the sacrificial works enjoined in their texts. Now religious injunctions can only have their authority from the sanction of God's will. To say that there can be a religion without God, is to say there can be a law without a law-giver, or a verdict without a judge. Jaimini however says nothing about a God. We are to be bound by words of which there was no intelligent utterer. Some of this followers have gone the length of denying the possibility of an original utterer, a First cause of the Vedas, ridiculing the idea, as if it were hunting after a rabbit's horn—sheer impossibility.

"It is the school of Prabhākara that talk in this bold and audacious way. 'An injunction, they say, implies a saying that moves to action. Hence is the authority of the Veda only in regard to acts. How then do we learn about objects, or existent substances? By the explanatory remarks and the mantras, (hymns or incantations). The Veda does not teach any thing liable to contradiction : hence there can be no fear of there being any incongruity in it[41].' This implies that the Vedas have nothing to do with existent substances which cannot be established for certain. There are no objective truths taught in them. You have only to follow out their injunctions and perform the established ceremonies. 'What is good? That which leads to supreme felicity, such as the performance of the *jyotiṣṭoma* and other sacrifices. What is evil? That which leads to ruin, such as theft[42].' As to the origin of the Vedas, one is to restrain his curiosity. The doctrine amounts to this that we *can* know of no being that could have composed them. If you talk of deducing the authority of the Veda from an author, the question will recur, and whence the authority of that author? Such authority, again, can only be settled by a text, and hence there will be a vicious circle. The Veda you see; its author you do not see. You have ocular proof of the existence of the Veda. You have no proof of the existence of its author. Nor is there any necessity for speculating about an author, for the un-beginning or eternal tradition of society is quite enough. The following extracts will show how some of the staunchest advocates for the Vedas argued on these points.

'Persons use language in order to communicate to others something which they know. But that which is not apprehended (on proof) cannot be known, hence a person's words ought to be supported by some other proof. Therefore it is said that a person cannot know any thing without a text (of the Veda). But why should we say 'without a text,' when we ought to say 'without some other proof'? And even though the aim [of the assertion] be some act, still ought not texts to have a personal utterer? [No!] Without a text (the utterance could not be proved). * * Thus Dharma is established as derived from age to age without any other proof. How is this established? In consequence of the futility of other proof than traditional instruction, it is impossible to introduce any prompter [of Dharma.]

Observation is everywhere a proof with us. A work that is seen is independent of any person's exertion, because no person could be proved (as its author). It is dependent when it is not known at the first application, and is known at another application. If the injunction does not teach (or persuade) at the first hearing, what is the meaning of its being an author's work? If again an author's work may be not of time, that is only establishing an established point, for the meaning of those who speak of the śabda [Veda] as proof is precisely that it is independent of any person's exertion or of any other aid.

Now relation is that by which the sense is known when a word is known. * * But is there not another relation than this of a name and its object? That is an unreasonable saying, for even then the relation between the thing to be apprehended and the causer of the apprehension is of the same character as that of the name and its object. But why [the Mīmāṅsaka asks] is this objection? Because, [the opponent of Jaimin's theory replies], as before explained, it (the Veda) has an author. Hence we believe that the Vedas were composed by some person who had settled the relation of the words with their meaning. And thus are they dependent.' To this now it is replied. It has been proved, that because of the relation not being caused by any person, the old usage of society is without a beginning. How is this? On this question the reply is, because of the want of a person to create the relation. The reply is not to the purpose. It is. The object is to exclude that which is opposed to the no-beginning theory. But why do you fear that it is opposed to your theory? Yes, we fear, because though it has been proved that the sense of words is determined by the un-beginning usage of old, yet if an author were allowed, then a beginning must come per force, like the vṛddhi of certain vowels after *a* (in grammar). Therefore the idea of an author must be excluded.

The Veda cannot be proved [to be an author's work] by the first kind of inference, because the old usage of society is without beginning. It cannot be established either by perception, or inference *ā priori*.'

Even if it could be shown that the Veda has fallen into oblivion, still we could not, without further proof, establish any other relation. In the case of an existing substance missing, we could not, without proof, fancy it to be a rabbit's horn. Suppose oblivion were established, what is the object forgotten? The very thing that we desire to demonstrate? Well then, it itself is a proof, the oblivion.

If, [says the opponent of Jaimini] non-perception were only possible of existent things, then who can say there is no rabbit's horn? But [replies the Mīmāṅsaka] we do not adduce oblivion or non-perception as proof, we only bring it forward to refute the absurdity of assigning a cause to an object established by perception. Because there may be a non-perception (or missing) of perceived objects, like pots, you cannot for that reason imagine the existence of the rabbit's horn. The non-perception of a perceived object is dependent on another cause, but the non-perception itself is simply the non-perception of a non-perception.

But how is it, [asks the opponent of Jaimini] that the author of the relation is not inferable from the non-understanding of the sense after the first hearing?

If on the first hearing, [replies the Mīmāṅsaka] the sense is not comprehended, what do you get from it of an author of the relation? If Devadatta is not found at home, what does it prove of his being without?

But does not conversancy itself presuppose that it is a work? How? Thus, that such a one is its utterer. But there can be no inconclusiveness in that which is seen. We see in the case of boys that the sense of words is arrived at by mere practice. Therefore of an object which is seen by perception, it is not consistent to sepculate about an author. This is another reason for excluding an instrument [or originator] of the practice. Even if the relation [of words with their meaning] were itself [an author's] work, its production by gods, who are themselves unseen, would be excluded by the impossibility of the case. The relation being therefore eternal, it is proved to be independent.

This notion of an effect is owing to the expansion of similarity (with the cause). But here dissimilarity being perceived, there can be no proof (of a cuase). If you say there can be no production without dissimilarity, it only establishes your inconsistency. By this very reasoning, an author, his desire and recollection, are all refuted.

Pleasure and other feelings being mere material affections can only be described as properties of matter. Now one that has no quality or property cannot affect that which has.'

Other adepts in Brahma (Vedāntists) say that from the word author, from remembrance, from desire, they find the existence of a spirit different from the material body and its organs. Hence they conclude there is an existent spirit as author. But [the Mīmāṅsaka asks] is he not also described as without work or agency? Thus the illustrious commentator [Prabhākara] refutes those reasons for taking that to be a spirit [or reality] which is no-spirit (or unreal).

Without a sensuous perception of the spirit itself, there cannot be this inference [of a spirit].

Perception can only be allowed as a proof in the establishment of the Supreme [Spirit]. It is useless to talk of inference.

If the adepts in supreme Brahma (Vedāntists) come to the conclusion that what is perceived is untrue, the real is not perceived, then we would simply bid them adieu with a bow.

If there be nothing but knowledge, then knowledge itself would be disproved.

If the spirit is to be known, then the instrument of the knowledge and the knower cannot be said to be excluded.[43]

"I need not multiply these extracts, but the passages already given show that Kapila was not the only *nirīśwara,* or atheistic, teacher among the Brāhmins. A large body of the followers of Jaimini openly inculcated the same idea. Indeed they went a good many paces beyond the author of the Sāṅkhya. For they contended that since the existence of a soul, as distinct from physical orgnanization, is not an object of sensuous perception, it could not be one of Inference, either. Thought and feeling they considered to be affections of our corporeal members. And it was with a view to defend the paramount authority of the Vedas that they were led to this atheism and materialism.

"I cannot say that the principles on which they based

their reasoning are peculiar to themselves. All schools of Brāhminical philosophers considered the mind, the instrument of thought and feeling, as a sort of material organ, which can only co-exist with the body. But they recognized an *ātmā,* or spirit, as the owner or director of the mind and other organs. The school of the Prābhākara Mīmāṅsā appear to deny such a director, and to assign all mental phenomena to the physical organization. And yet they are staunch defenders of the Vedas.

"*Thirdly,* therefore, I ask, what can the Vedas possibly be in the conception of Brāhminical philosophers? Not the word of God, not a revelation of His will, such as you justly say is needed for our guidance under bewildering circumstances, but something which, certain of them affirm, mechanically issued from Brahma, like smoke from burning fuel, something which, others declare, was educed from the elements, something which others again tell us, is eternal and independent of a cause. But what that thing is, it is impossible to gather from them, unless it be a charm or a talisman. They talk of it as articulate sound, but what is articulate sound without a sounder, an utterer? And they all identify it with the Ṛk, Yajush, Sāman, and Atharvan. Singularly enough, they know nothing about the date or circumstances of these compositions. It is clear, however, that whatever the eternal sound of the Veda may have been, it could not have been committed to writing without a fresh revelation from God—without the direct inspiration of His Spirit. Such revelation must be impossible on the theory of the atheistical writers I have noticed. And as to those that were theists, they do not pretend to give us any account of such a repeated revelation. They all talk indeed of tradition, but you will admit that tradition cannot be trusted as an infallible guide.

"Again I ask, what are the Vedas? In the Śatapatha Brāhmaṇa, it is said, He (Prajāpati) brooded &c. over [*i.e.* infused warmth into] these three worlds. From them, thus brooded over, three lights were produced,—fire, this which purifies (*i.e. pavana,* or the air), and the sun. (He brooded over these three lights. From them so brooded over, the three Vedas were produced,—the Ṛgveda from fire, the Yajur-veda from air, and the Sāmaveda from the sun. He brooded over these three Vedas. From them so brooded over, three seeds [or essences] were produced,—*bhūr* from the Ṛg-veda, *bhuvah* from the Yajur-veda, and *svar* from the Sāma-veda[44].'

"What were these productions? Mere sounds, or writings on paper, or palm leaf? In either case how could they be generated by brooding over fire and the sun? What again is the meaning of the production of *bhur, bhuva, svar* by brooding over the Vedas? The Chāndogya and Manu speak in a similar way of the origin of the Vedas. (See the passages in Dr. Muir's Sanskrit texts) Kulluka Bhatta, in explanation of the difficulty we have stated, says, The same Vedas which [existed] in the previous mundane era (*Kalpa*) were preserved in the memory of the omniscient Brahma, who was one with the supreme spirit. It was those same Vedas that, in the beginning of the [present] *Kalpa,* he drew forth from fire, air, and the sun : and this dogma which is founded upon the Veda is not to be questioned, for the Veda says, 'The Ṛg-veda comes from fire, the Yajur-veda from the sun.'

Another commentator on Manu, Medhātithi, explains this passage in a more rationalistic fashion, by remarking that the Ṛg-veda opens with a hymn to fire, and the Yajur-veda with one in which air is mentioned[45].'

"Manu adds, Prajāpati also milked out of the three Vedas the letters *a, u,* and *m,* together with the words *bhūr, bhuvah,* and *svar.* The same supreme Prajāpati also milked from each of the three Vedas one of the [three]lines of the text called *sāvitrī* [or *gāyatrī*], beginning with the word *tat*. The three great imperishable particles (*bhūr, buvah, svar*) preceded by *om,* and the *gāyatrī* of three lines, are to be regarded as the mouth of Veda [or Brahma][46].'

"What in the name of common sense is the meaning of all this? What is milking of letters or words from Veads? The explanation of Medhātithi only shows that the difficulty had occurred to him, but it does not at all remove it—for not only is nothing said as to the signification of the extraction of the Sāman from the sun, but the explanation about the Ṛk and the Yajush too is very unsatisfactory.

"The Śwetāśwatara Upaniṣad, however, gives a different story of the origin of the Vedas. The Supreme Being is there set forth as its imparter to Brahmā[47], and the Harivaṅśa says, "For the emancipation of the world, Brahmā, sunk in contemplation, issuing in a luminous form from the region of the moon, penetrated into the heart of Gāyatrī, entering between her eyes. From her there was then produced a quadruple being, lustrous as Brahmā, indistinct, and eternal, undecaying, devoid of bodily senses or qualities, distinguished by the attribute of brilliancy, pure as the rays of the moon, radiant, and embodied in letters. The god fashioned the Ṛg-veda, with the Yajush, from his eyes, the Sāma-veda from the tip of his tongue, and the Atharvan from his head. The Vedas, as soon as they are born, find a body (*xetra*). Hence they obtain their character of *Vedas,* because they *find (vindanti)* that abode. These Vedas then create the pre-existent eternal Brahmā (sacrifice or ceremonial,) a being of celestial form, with their own mind-born qualities[48].'

"In the Ṛg-veda, again, we have another story, 'In the 9th verse of the Puruṣa Sūkta, the three Vedas are said to have been derived from the mystical victim, Puruṣa. From that universal sacrifice were produced the hymns called Ṛk and Sāman, the metres, and the Yajush[49].'

"The Atharva Veda says, 'From time the Ṛk verses sprang, the Yajush sprang from time.' The Bhāgavata Purāṇa says, 'From these three letters the divine and unborn being created the various letters of the alphabet, distinguished as inner (*y, r, l, v*), *ushmas (ś, sh, s, h),* vowels, long and short, and consonants. With this [alphabet] the omnipresent Being, desiring to reveal the functions of the four classes of priests, [created] from his four mouths the four Vedas with the three sacred syllables and the *oṁkāra*'[50]. Again, 'There was formerly only one Veda, the sacred mono-syllable *om,* the essence of all speech; only one god, Nārāyaṇa; only one Agni, and [one] caste. From Purūravas came the triple Veda in the beginning of the Tretā age[51].'

"The learned Ṛṣis who propounded these theories of the production of the Vedas must have calculated on the permanence of a state of popular ignorance in the country. They could hardly have expected criticism or cross questioning from their readers. For even this *meteoric* origin of their śāstra is related in a slovenly manner without any regard to consistency. At times we hear of the Gāyatrī being the mother of the Veda which was produced from it; at times, again, the Gāyatrī appears to be the child of the Vedas, having itself been milked from them!

"Now before we can absolutely submit to the guidance of the Vedas, is it not a solemn duty to ponder these unmeaning, incoherent, and inconsistent descriptions of their nature and origin? I cannot at all gather from any of these descriptions what the substance, called Veda, was at its production, and certainly it could not be eternal, without falsifying some of these accounts."

Āgamika.—"The substance, called Veda, must at first have been *sound,* or words uttered, but not written down."

Satyakāma.—"What can be the meaning of producing words from fire, air, and the sun, or of extracting bhur, bhuvah, svar from words or sounds? Elsewhere, the Vedas are said to have been breathed out. What is meant by this? Brahmā, or whoever was the producer, emitted the sounds or words at beginning, for that is what most Śāstras say. Was there any person present to hear those sounds?"

Āgamika.—"There was no person present when the sounds were uttered, but the same words were afterwards written down by the persons to whom they were revealed."

Satyakāma.—"What evidence have you of that? How do you know they were revealed to the writers in question, and not produced from their own imaginations? The story of their original extraction from the elements, even if it could be made intelligible, can have no practical use in determining their authority, because we have no means of knowing any thing beyond what is written, and what we require is evidence of the writers' inspiration.

"But the writers in many instances claim their writings as their own productions, and not as communications of pre-existing sounds. And this leads me to the fourth question, what are the claims set up by the Vedas themselves? The following are but a few among many passages which have been cited by Dr. Muir to show that the Ṛṣis claimed their compositions are the products of their own minds :—

"This hymn, conferring wealth, has been *made* to the divine race, by the sages, with their mouth [or in presence of the gods]."

"Grow, O Agni, by this prayer which we have *made* to thee through [or according to] our power, or our knowledge."

"Thus, O Indra, yoker of steeds, have the Gotamas made for thee pure [or beautiful] hymns."

"These, your ancient exploits, O Aśvins, our fathers have declared. Let us, who are strong in bold men, *making a* hymn for you, O bountiful gods, utter our offering of praise."

"Nodhas, descendant of Gotama, *fashioned* this new hymn for [thee], Indra, who art of old, and who yokest thy steeds," etc.

"Desiring wealth, men have *fashioned* for thee this hymn, as a skilful workman [fabricates] a car, and thus they have disposed (*lit.* fashioned) thee to (confer) happiness."

"This reverential hymn, O divine Maruts, *fashioned* by the heart, has been presented by the mind [or, according to Sāyana 'let it be received by you with a favourable mind']."

"Thus, O hero, have the Gritsamadas, desiring succour, *fashioned* for thee a hymn, as men make roads." (Sāyana explains *vayāna* by "road;" but it generally means knowledge).

"We *generate* a hymn, like pure butter, for Agni Vaiśvānara, who promotes our sacred rites."

"I have *generated* a new hymn to Agni, the falcon of the sky; who bestows on us wealth in abundance."

"Indra, the wise ṛṣis, both ancient and modern, have *generated* prayers."

"The soma cheers not Indra unless it be poured out; nor do libations [gratify] Maghavan when offered without a priest. To him I *generate* a hymn such as may please him, that, after the manner of men, he may hear our *new* [song]."

"In like manner as I spread the sacrificial grass to the Nasatyas (Aśvins), so do I *send forth* to them hymns, as the wind [drives] the clouds; to them (I say), who bore off to the youthful Vimada his bride in a chariot which outstripped the enemy's host."

"The devout sage, deeply versed in sacred lore, *sends forth* his hymns to you, O Mitra and Varuṇa. You mighty gods, receive this prayers with favour, since ye fill [prolong?], as it seems, his autumns by your power."

Āgamika.—"I cannot deny the force of your arguments, Satyakāma, and yet I am far from being convinced. The result of our conferences hitherto has been to weaken the foundations of human belief, and foster a spirit of universal scepticism. There must be a grave error somewhere in all this. To disprove a certain position is not to find out the truth. And if there be no truth in the texts of the Vedas, or the aphorisms of philosophers, where are we to go in search of it. The characteristic of righteous men is to set forth *Faith*, as the poet says[52], not scepticism. Our studies, speculations, and discussions cannot be considered successful, if they end in the conclusion that there is no truth in the world. Our faculty of reason could never have been granted by the Almighty for *that;* it is doubtless intended to put us in possession of some definite and positive truth, to discover His will in nature and in His word, for it is preposterous to think of discovering His will for all practical purposes *without* His word. Surely He could not have left us in the dark destitute of a revelation of His will. Like yourself I find it difficult to believe that He would be deliberately deluding us by the projection of an illusion. But I cannot on the other hand understand that he would leave us, without an *āgama,* or revelation, to follow our own bewildering reason in things beyond its range, and thus, in another way, consign us to inevitable delusions. Hence my still cleaving to the hope that the Vedas may contain His word notwithstanding all you have said. We must have something on which to repose our faith, or our minds must be tossed to and fro by the waves of doubt and disputation, like a boat without a rudder on stormy waters. I cannot say that our conferences have at all tended to the discovery of that *something.*"

Satyakāma. – "I perfectly agree with you here, Āgamika. You are quite right in saying that belief, not scepticism, is the end of human study, but not belief of *every* kind. Bad as it is to be in a state of doubt, to believe in falsehood is still worse. To get rid of error is a most important step toward the discovery of truth. You will allow that he who removes rubbish in order to secure a good foundation, assists in raising the superstructure, as much as he that puts in layers of bricks. If the foundation of your house be radically bad, so that no supply of props or buttresses will save the building, you will doubtless be thankful to the man who points out the fact to you, and you will admit that your wisest course then is to dig it up. You dig up, however, only to build anew, and, in doing so, you do not recklessly throw away all the bricks and materials of the old edifice. Whatever is good you retain with pleasure, not only because that is the dictate of economy, but also because a stone that has stood the encroachments of time, uninjured, in a certain locality, has proved its adaptation to that locality, and must be preferable to one untried. Good stones of the old building may be depended upon more confidently than new ones."

Āgamika. – "I do not understand what you mean. You have certainly dug up the foundation by condemning the only revelation of God's will to which we looked for guidance. And as to bricks, I really do not know whether you have left any unbroken."

Satyakāma. – "I have only been condemning the Ṛk, Yajush, Sāman, and Atharvan. Their condemnation is not synonymous with the rejection of all revelation. A person does not disallow the true coin, merely because he refuses to accept a counterfeit one."

Āgamika. – "But where is your true coin? you are only finding fault with the Veda. We say that God communicated his will in the beginning. You say, No."

Satyakāma. – "I certainly do not say, No, to the idea of a primitive Revelation of God's will. If by talking of the eternal śāstra, you only mean that God gave an utterance to His will in the beginning, and if you do not insist on that utterance being recorded in the Ṛk, Yajush, Sāman, and Atharvan, I am sure we are both of the same opinion."

Āgamika. – "But if the revelation be not on record, of what use would it be?"

Satyakāma. – "You acknowledge that the primitive Revelation was not at the time committed to writing. It could only be transmitted by traditional instruction. It could not under such circumstances be recorded without direct inspiration from God,—in other words without a fresh revelation. You have no evidence to offer in favour of the Rich and others being such an after-revelation, and the books themselves purport in some places to be ordinary human compositions.

"I cannot join you in saying that an unwritten revelation is of no use. It serves the immediate object of its utterance, and, notwithstanding the mistakes and errors incident to human tradition, there is some utility in its oral transmission. Gold with alloy may still have some value. But I agree with you so far as to believe that revelation, thus transmitted, becomes mixed up with human errors, and gradually loses its influence. Unless it were recorded under divine inspiration it could not be a trustworthy guide for all ages.

"But that the oral transmission of unwritten revelation is not altogether useless is apparent from the fact that the Brāhminical systems, notwithstanding all their errors, have at least one great truth lurking in them all."

Āgamika.—"What truth do you allude to?"

Satyakāma.—"The fact of a primitive Revelation. No case has been made out for the Ṛk, Yajush, Sāman, and Atharvan, but the fact of a primitive Revelation from the Almighty can admit of little doubt, and the idea, almost universal in India, of an eternal Veda, may be accepted as an evidence of that great fact. The zealous apologist for the Vedas, the author of the Prior Mīmāṅsā, himself suggests some such consideration. His argument is that the Vedas are eternal, for sound is eternal. People may naturally wonder at the confidence with which this argument is broached. What especial connection, it may be asked, is there between the *Sādhya* and *hetu,* between the thing to be proved and the reason adduced. If the eternity of sound were admitted as a reason for the eternity of words, phrases, and sentences, all words, phrases, and sentences, and consequently all compositions must be eternal. How could a philosopher offer such a poor argument to his readers? How could he rely on its satisfying those who had reasoned so strongly against the Mantras and Brāhmaṇas?

"The mystery can only be explained on the supposition of some distorted tradition existing among the Brāhmins of a primitive revelation from God. By śabda, or sound, as an instrument of true knowledge, they meant the teaching of an infallible author. Those, who, like Jaimini, would not allow that the Vedas had an author, still understood śabda in the sense of an infallible teaching. When, again, they speak of śabda as eternal, they suggest the idea that there was an infallible teaching coeval with the creation of man. This is the only sense in which their language becomes intelligible, and, whether they understood their own minds or not, whether they were conscious of what they were propounding or not, we can find no difficulty in admitting that a great truth is couched in their words. The reason they give for their position is thus expressed : 'It is eternal, for its manifestation was for the benefit of others.[53]'

"Jaimini's theory, then, amounts to this, that there was an infallible teaching from the beginning for the benefit of others. This theory we may cordially accept as a testimony to the fact of a Primitive Revelation. We may well take for granted that an infallible teaching was available 'for the benefit of the others,' when sentient creatures were called into being. We can have no difficulty in believing that the Almighty made a communication of His will to our first parents when He created them. How dependent human beings are upon external aid for years after their birth, is known to all men. They are quite powerless as infants and children. They necessarily look to their parents and guardians for maintenance and education. But the first man could have had no earthly father to foster him. The inference is accordingly almost inevitable that He, who gave him being, furnished him at the same time with such directions as were necessary for his guidance. That which the first man thus heard from His Maker, was a śabda, an infallible teaching, intended for the benefit of others, *i.e.*, mankind, and co-eval with the commencement of human society.

"So far I see no reason for differing from Jaimini's aphorism, which certainly a theistic commentator may construe in our sense, whatever the author's own meaning may have been. But then he proceeds to identify that śabda, or infallible teaching, with the Veda. And, here, the double meaning attached to this word helped to introduce a great error. Veda is by some defined to be *Śabda rāśi*[54], or a collection of words, sounds, or infallible teachings. When Jaimini argued that the Veda is eternal, for sound is eternal, he was probably thinking of this definition. But if the word Veda be synonymous with sound, or infallible teaching, then the argument is a truism. If it signifies a *specific* collection of words, then the argument involves the false reasoning, *it has horns, therefore it is a cow.* Because there was some infallible teaching in the beginning, therefore the Ṛk, Yajush, &c.' are eternal! Assuming, however, that the word Veda stands simply for a collection of words, or infallible teachings, the aphorism, as we have interpreted it, only amounts to the assertion of a primitive Revelation, which, as I have already said, is more than probable in itself.

"But, as we know that Jaimini contends for the authorrity of the Ṛk, Yajush, Sāman, and Atharvan, the signification of the word Veda must shift from the *general* to the *particular* at same point in the argument. The moment however the word stands for the Ṛk and the other three, Jaimini's argument must be repudiated. Because some infallible teaching existed in the beginning, some collection of sounds was given, it does not follow that the Ṛk, Yajush, and others are eternal. To say that man was created in the beginning may be a truth, but to conclude from thence that Vikramāditya was co-eval with the creation is a gross error. Similarly, to say that some infallible teaching was received in the beginning may be a truth; to conclude from thence that the Ṛk and others were breathed out at that time is an error.

"The assertion of Jaimini, that the Ṛk, Yajush, Sāman, and Atharvan contain the primitive Revelation is not proved. No one knows when, where, or by whom, those four works were written, and consequently no one can pretend that they are a record of the primeval Sound. On the contrary a critical examination of their contents *disproves* their authority. As to the argument that the Vedas must have proceeded from the divinity because no human author can be shown to have produced it, it is not of much validity. If a stranger, or a man brought up as a foundling, came to you, and no one was able to give you an account of his paternity, you would not surely conclude that he was co-eval with the creation.

"And there is nothing in the general scope of the Vedas to justify the conclusion that they were revealed in the beginning. It is impossible to fancy what edification our first parents could derive from mere praises of the Sun, Moon, and Fire. If historical narratives were entirely excluded, the residuum would be mere invocations of the elements, and a few ceremonial injunctions."

Āgamika.—"But you have not answered my question, where is your true coin?"

Satyakāma.—"The true coin I believe to be the Bible. It has strong external evidences for its being composed under divine inspiration, and its contents are just what might be expected from a work intended for the spiritual instruction of mankind."

Āgamika.—"I have often heard of the Bible, but what I cannot fancy is the confidence with which you speak of the external evidences of the Bible, while you summarily reject those of the Vedas."

Satyakāma.—"You have no external evidences for the

Vedas. You have not the slightest idea of the time when, and the persons by whom, the Ṛk, Yajush, Sāman, and Atharvan were composed. There is a complete want of evidence here. As regards the Bible, it is, you must know, divided into two parts, the Old and New Testaments. The former was written by the prophets of the Jews, the latter by the apostles and followers of Jesus Christ, the Saviour of mankind. In both cases we have the evidence of miracles and prophecy; the evidence becoming, in the case of the New Testament, especially strong, because of its being confirmed by collateral and circumstantial proofs. Now to set your face against these evidences, simply because you have no external evidences for the Veda, would not be acting with the manliness of an inquirer after truth."

Āgamika.—"Well, what do you mean by the evidence of prophecy?"

Satyakāma.—"By the evidence of prohecy I mean the exact coincidence of events, as foretold long before their occurrence. There are in the Old and New Testaments, more especially the former, many predictions of events, far beyond the range of human sagacity, which were fulfilled, in some cases many centuries afterwards, exactly as they were uttered. The future condition of many nations of Asia and of Africa were thus accurately predicted long before the events. The circumstances attending the birth, death, and resurrection of Christ were in like manner foretold. Now since no man can obtain an insight into the future, beyond the ordinary range of *anumāna,* or guess, by natural sensation or reflection, the inference is inevitable that the writers of the Old and New Testaments obtained such knowledge by divine inspiration.

"To specify one instance of such predictions,—Moses, who lived fifteen hundred years before Christ, foretold the future sufferings of his own nation, which are still being realized in our days. At the time of the prediction, there was no *lakṣaṇa,* or sign, from which the prophet might have formed an idea of the calamities he was describing, especially since those calamities were, in some respects, without a parallel in the history of mankind. Consider now a few of those predictions, and the manner in which each was fulfilled.

"The following prophecies are taken from the 28th Chapter of the Book of Deuteronomy, and the statements representing their exact fulfilment, from a valuable work of a learned divine of the last century, Bishop Newton by name :

PROPHECY.

"The Lord shall bring a nation against thee from far, from the end of the earth, *as swift* as the eagle flieth; a nation whose tongue thou shalt not understand.'

FULFILMENT.

"This description cannot be applied to any nation with such propriety as to the Romans. They were truly brought *from far, from the end of the earth.* Vespasian and Adrian, the two great conquerors and destroyers of the Jews, both came from commanding here in Britain. The Romans too for the rapidity of their conquests might very well be compared to eagles, and perhaps not without an allusion to the standard of the Roman armies, which was an eagle : and their language was more unknown to the Jews than the Chaldee."

PROPHECY.

'A nation of fierce countenance, which shall not regard the person of the old, nor shew favour to the young :

'And he shall eat the fruit of thy cattle, and the fruit of thy land, until thou be destroyed : which *also* shall not leave thee *either* corn, wine, or oil, *or* the increase of thy kine, or flocks of thy sheep, until, he have destroyed thee.'

FULFILMENT.

Such also were the Romans : for when Vespasian entered

Gadara Josephus saith, that 'he slew all, man by man, the Romans showing mercy to no age, out of hatred to the nation, and remembrance of their former injuries.' The like slaughter was made at Gamala, 'For no body escaped besides two women, and they escaped by concealing themselves from the rage of the Romans. For they did not so much as spare young children, but every one at that time snatching up many cast them down from the citadel.'

PROPHECY.

'And he shall besiege thee in all thy gates, until thy high and fancy walls come down, wherein thou trustedst, throughout all thy land : and he shall besiege thee in all thy gates throughout all thy land, which the LORD thy God hath given thee.'

FULFILMENT.

So likewise the Romans, as we may read in Josephus's history of the Jewish war, demolished several fortified places, before they beiseged and destroyed Jerusalem. And the Jews may very well be said to have *trusted in their high and fenced walls,* for they seldom ventured a battle in the open field. They confided in the strength and situation of Jerusalem, as the Jebusites, the former inhabitants of the place, had done before them : insomuch that they are represented saying (Jer. XXI. 13). *Who shall come down against us? or who shall enter into our habitation?* Jerusalem was indeed a very strong place, and wonderfully fortified both by nature and art according to the description of Tacitus as well as of Josephus : and yet how many times was it taken? It was taken by Shishak king of Egypt, by Nebuchandezzar, by Antiochus Epiphanes, by pompey, by Sosius and Herod, before it final destruction by Titus."

PROPHECY.

'And thou shalt eat the fruit of thine own body, the flesh of thy sons and of thy daughters, which the Lord thy God hath given thee, in the siege and in the straitness, wherewith thine enemies shall distress thee :

'So that the man that is tender among you, and very delicate, his eye shall be evil toward his brother, and toward the wife of his bosom, and toward the remnant of his children which he shall leave :

'So that he will not give to any of them of the flesh of his children whom he shall eat : because he hath nothing left him in the siege and in the straitness, wherewith thine enemies shall distress thee in all thy gates.'

'The tender and delicate woman among you, which would not adventure to set the sole of her foot upon the ground for delicateness and tenderness, her eye shall be evil toward the husband of her bosom, and toward her son, and toward her daughter.

'And toward her young one that cometh out from between her feet, and toward her children which she shall bear : for she shall eat them for want of all *things* secretly in the siege and straitness, wherewith thine enemy shall distress thee in thy gates.'

FULFILMENT.

"And in the last siege of Jerusalem by the Romans there was a most terrible famine in the city, and Josephus hath given so melancholy an account of it, that we cannot read it without shuddering. He saith, particularly, that 'women snatched the food out of the very mouths of their husbands and sons of their fathers, and (what is most miserable) mothers of their infants :' and in another place he saith, that 'in every house, if there appeared any semblance of food, a battle ensued, and the dearest friends and relations fought with one another, snatching away the miserable provisions of life.'

* * And again it was fulfilled above 1500 years after the time of Moses in the last siege of Jerusalem by Titus, and we read in Josephus particularly of a noble woman's killing and

eating her own sucking child. Moses saith, *The tender and delicate woman among you, who would not adventure to set the sole of her foot upon the ground, for delicateness and tenderness* : and there cannot be a more natural and lively description of a woman, who was according to Josephus illustrious for her family and riches. Moses saith, *she shall eat them for want of all things :* and according to Josephus she had been plundered of all her substance and provision by the tyrants and soldiers. Moses saith, that she should do it *secretly :* and according to Josephus, when she had boiled and eaten half, she covered up the rest, and kept it for another time."

PROPHECY.

'And ye shall be plucked from off the land whither thou goest to possess it.'

'And the LORD shall scatter thee among all people, from the one end of the earth even unto the other;

'And among these nations shalt thou find no case, neither shall the sole of thy foot have rest : but the Lord shall give thee there a trembling heart, and failing of eyes, and sorrow of mind:'

'And thy life shall hang in doubt before thee; and thou shalt fear day and night, and shalt have none assurance of thy life:'

FULFILMENT.

"Now not to mention any other of the calamities and slaughters which they have undergone, there was in the last siege of Jerusalem by Titus an infinite multitude, saith Josephus, who perished by famine, and he computes, that during the whole siege, the number of those who were destroyed by that and by the war amounted to eleven hundred thousand, the pepole being assembled from all parts to celebrate the passover : and the same author hath given us an account of 1.240.490 destroyed in Jerusalem and other parts of Judea, besides 99.200 made prisoners; as Basange has reckoned them up from that historian's account. Indeed there is not a nation upon earth, that hath been exposed to so many massacres and persecutions. Their history abounds with them. If God had not given them a promise of a numerous posterity, the whole race would many a time have been extirpated.

They had come out of Egypt triumphant, but now they should return thither as slaves. They had walked through the sea as dry land at their coming out; but now they should be carried thither in ships. They might be carried thither in the ships of the Tyrian or Sidonian merchants, or by the Romans who had a fleet in the Mediterranean : and this was a much safer way of conveying so many prisoners, than sending them by land. It appears from Josephus that in the reigns of the two first Ptolemies many of the Jews were slaves in Egypt. And when Jerusalem was taken by Titus, of the captives who were above 17 years he sent many bound to the works in Egypt; those under 17 were sold : but so little care was taken of these captives, that eleven thousand of them perished for want. And we learn from St. Jerome, that 'after their last overthrow by Adrian many thousands of them were sold, and those who could not be sold were tansported into Egypt, and perished by shipwreck or famine, or were massacred by the inhabitants.'

They were indeed *plucked from off their own land,* when the ten tribes were carried into captivity by the king of Assyria, and other nations were planted in their stead; and when the two other tribes were carried away captive to Babylon; and when the Romans took away their place and nation; besides other captivities and transportations of the people. Afterwards, when the Emperor Adrian had subdued the rebellious Jews, he published an edict forbidding them upon pain of death to set foot in Jerusalem, or even to approach the country round about it. Tertullian and Jerome say, that they were prohibited from entering into Judea. From that time to this their country hath been in the possession of foreign lords and masters, few of the Jews dwelling in it, and those only of a low servile condition. Benjamin of Tudela in Spain, a celebrated Jew of the twelfth century, travelled into all parts to visit those of his own nation, and to learn an exact state of their affairs : and he hath reported, that Jerusalem was almost entirely abandoned by the Jews.

What people indeed have been scattered so far and wide as they? And where is the nation, which is a stranger to them, or to which they are strangers? They swarm in many parts of the East, are spread through most of the countries of Europe and Africa, and there are several families of them in the West Indies. They circulate through all parts, where trade and money circulate; and are, as I may say, the brokers of the whole world.

They have been so far from finding rest, that they have been banished from city to city, from country to country. In many places they have been banished, and recalled, and banished again. We will only just mention their great banishments in modern times, and from countries very well known. In the latter end of the thirteenth century they were banished from England by Edward I, and were not permitted to return and settle again till Cromwell's time. In the latter end of the fourteenth century they were banished from France (for the seventh time, says Mezeray) by Charles VI; and ever since they have been only tolerated, they have not enjoyed entire liberty, except at Metz where they have a synagogue. In the latter end of the fifteenth century they were banished from Spain by Ferdinand and Isabella; and according to Mariana, there were a hundred and seventy thousand families, or as some say eight hundred thousand persons who left the kingdom. Most of them paid dearly to John II for a refuge in Portugal, but within a few years were expelled from thence also by his successor Emanuel. And in our own time, within these few years, they were banished from Prague by the queen of Bohemia."

"That part of the prophecy which related to the dispersion of the Jews all over the world, is being still fulfilled before us. The fact is itself almost miraculous, and it is a standing evidence of Christian truth. There have been other people, dispossessed of their homes and banished from their country, but they have either been exterminated, or their nationality has been destroyed by amalgamation with strangers. The Jews, however, though long banished from their own country, still live as a separate people, with all their distinctive traditions and peculiar manners of old. They still live, not as emigrants in a new colony of their own, not removed in one body to any particular spot inhabiting it as another Judea, but they live, scattered over the whole world, 'present in all countries and with a home in none, intermixed and yet separated, and neither amalgamated nor lost : but like those mountain-streams which are said to pass through lakes of another kind of water and keep a native quality to repel commixture[55].' There is no land in the world which may now be called Jews' Land, and yet Jews are to be found, aliens, in all lands. They live under all governments, and yet have no government of their own. Such a fact has no parallel in history. It can only be looked upon as a wonder. He that could predict such a wonder, more than fifteen hundred years before the event, could only have done so under the inspiration of the Omniscient."

Āgamika.—"Are you not reasoning after a fashion for which even Gotama's category fails to find the proper terms? The eternity of the Veda, you say, is disproved by its recording events that transpired in time, and yet not only is the antiquity of Moses not disproved by his description of events that followed the capture of Jerusalem, but his prophetical authority is thereby actually established!"

Satyakāma.—"The Vedas, you must remember, my friend,

describe the events alluded to as by-gone facts, as past occurrences. The dialgoues between Yama and Nuchiketas, between Yājñavalkya and Maitreyī, between Uddālaka and Śwetaketu are recorded, not as prophecies of the future, but as narrations of the past. Hence we say that the naratives must have been written after the events. Moses, on the other hand, recorded the future sufferings of his countrymen as predictions. His writings existed before the Roman nation, 'of a fierce countenance,' which was, in the divine counsels, finally to inflict those chastisements on the Jews, was yet formed, or had obtained its name. These writings again were already translated into Greek above three hundred years before the destruction of Jerusalem, as a fact, is recorded by two of the most accurate of ancient historians. The alternative of assigning to Moses a date posterior to the events is not open in this case. It is precluded by the facts of the Septuagint translation and of the corruption of the Jewish language during the captivity. The Jews, you must know, were taken captives to Babylon about six hundred years before the Christian era, and, for seventy years, they remained exiles from their own country. There, by mixing with a strange nation, their language was very much corrupted. The five books of Moses must therefore have been written, at latest, before the captivity, while the destruction of Jerusalem and the dispersion of the Jews could not have taken place before the reign of the Emperor Vespasian.

"Judea, you must remember, had been brought under the subjection of the Romans some time before the catastrophe predicted by Moses. Roman historians, who, as Gentiles, could have had no motive in recording any thing from which a favourable inference might be drawn for the divine inspiration of prophets whom they despised, themselves inform us that one of their generals, Pompey, had forced himself into the temple of Jerusalem more than five hundred years after the captivity, which, as we saw, is the latest possible date that could be assigned to the Pentateuch, and about two hundred years after Moses had been translated into Greek. The temple, then, on the testimony of historians whose honesty was above suspicion, was in existence many hundred years after Moses, and it was destroyed in the regin of Vespasian, when the events gave accurate fulfilment to the predictions of Moses.

"In the above representation of the facts, I have confined myself to the testimony of enemies, and to the very extremes of historical possibilities. I have taken no account of the evidence which the Jewish writers themselves afford. As those writers again give a consistent account of the age of Moses and the time of his successors, we must consider the actual date of the Pentateuch as established, beyond doubt, by the cumulative evidence of Jews and Gentiles."

Āgamika.—"Is it certain that Moses lived long before the events described?

Satyakāma.—"I have just told you that Moses lived fifteen hundred years before Christ, and Jerusalem was destroyed seventy years after Christ. The works of Moses, originally written in Hebrew, were translated into Greek two hundred and seventy years before Christ, so that many persons unacquainted with Hebrew had also known, more than three hundred years before the event, what was coming on the Jews."

Āgamika.—"But is there no doubt of the events themselves?"

Satyakāma.—"The events are minutely described by Josephus and Tacitus, one writing in Greek, the other in Latin—the former a Jew, the latter a Roman, and both cautious, accurate, and faithful as historians. And we see with our own eyes the Jewish people dispersed all over the world, and without a country of their own."

Āgamika.—"But there are numerous prophecies in our own Purāṇas. May we not cite them as proofs of their authority?

The Rāmāyaṇa was written before Rāma was born."

Satyakāma.—"You cannot settle the age or paternity of any of the Purāṇas. How can you urge any thing as to the date of the predictions? The Upaniṣads say that the Purāṇas were breathed out from Brahma along with the Vedas at the time of the creation. The Purāṇas themselves claim Vyāsa for their author, and one of them goes the length of saying that it was composed for correcting the errors of the Vedas, while another pretends to be prior in point of time to the Vedas. Thus; 'That about which, venerable sage, you have enquired, is all known by me, the essence of the Purāṇas, the pre-eminent Brahma-vaivartta, which refutes the errors of the Purāṇas and Upapurāṇas and of the Vedas.' First of all the śastras, the Purāṇa was uttered by Brahmā. Subsequently the Vedas issued from his mouths[56].'

"Learned critics, again, are forced to assign a much more recent date to all the Itihāses and Purāṇas that are extant in our days. What trust-worthy evidence can you possibly have of any prophecy having been delivered? Or even of the facts (supposed to have been predicted), having really occurred? We do not know of any contemporaneous historian that recorded them. Nay the writing of history does not appear to have been undertaken by any Brāhminical authors, either in prose or poetry. Prose writers have chiefly treated of speculative subjects, and as to poetry, it is a recognized rule in rhetoric that poetry must be *rasātmaka,* or full of striking ideas and sentiments, and that *iti vṛtta,* or a mere narrative, is a defect in poetry.

"As to the Rāmāyaṇa, the popular saying about its composition before the events, may be a bold effort of fancy, but it cannot stand the test of historical criticism. Vālmīki is said to have been a contemporary of Rāma. Whether that be an authenticated fact or not, is not now the question, but what evidence can be possibly adduced under such a circumstance of his writing the whole epic before the recovery of Sitā, and the conqueror's return to Ayodhyā?"

Āgamika.—"You said that the Bible was attested by miracles as well as prophecies. What have you to say on the question of miracles?"

Satyakāma.—"As prohecy is a sign of divine knowledge, so are miracles proofs of divine power. Numerous miracles of that description were publicly performed by Christ, and they were recorded by men who had ample opportunities for obtaining correct information, and whose honesty as historians has been established by irrefragable proofs.

"Miracles of course require to be authenticated by stronger evidence than ordinary facts. We must have the testimony of contemporaries, and the witnesses must prove their competency and their integrity. Proof of competency is required as a safeguard against mistakes founded on their ignorance, and proof of integrity is necessary to prevent impositions. A learned divine says, 'the strength and validity of every *testimony* must bear proportion with the *authority* of the *testifier;* and the *authority* of the *testifier* is founded upon his *ability* and and *integrity : his ability* in the knowledge of that which he delivereth and asserteth; his *integrity* in delivering and asserting according to the knowledge. For two several ways he which relateth or testifieth any thing may deceive us; one, by being ignorant of the truth, which in itself is false, and so deceive himself and us; or if he be not ignorant, yet if he be dishonest or unfaithful, that which he knows to be false he may propound and assert to be a truth, and so, though himself be not deceived, he may deceive us. And by each of these ways, for want either of *ability* or *integrity* in the *testifier,* whose grounds his *assent* unto anything as a truth, upon the testimony of another, may equally be deceived. But whosoever is so *able* as certainly to know the truth of that which he delivereth, and so *faithful* as to deliver nothing but what and as he knoweth, he, as he is not deceived, so deceiveth no man[57]."

"Both these characters of credible evidence are prominent in the testimony on which we receive the miracles of Christ. Those who have testified to them were his own disciples, who constantly kept company with him and had every opportunity of knowing the truth of what they declared to others. And their honesty was unimpeachable. In the first place, they had nothing to gain by false testimony. Men are known in the world to pervert facts only from interested motives. No one tells a lie where he has nothing to gain. When we are satisfied that a person is disinterested, we never doubt his testimony. And so from the obvious disinterestedness of the disciples of Christ, their testimony is beyond suspicion. In the second place, their honesty was proved by the severest ordeal to which a human witness could possibly be subjected. Judea was at that time under the government of the Romans who, being idolaters, were bitterly opposed to the teaching of Christ. That teaching was also hateful to the Jews who had contracted the strongest prejudices against the Saviour. His disciples had therefore to encounter the severest persecutions both from Jews and Gentiles for their proclaiming the doctrines and miracles of Christ. They were reviled and reproached, imprisoned and beaten, and most of them were finally put to cruel deaths because of their unflinching honesty in declaring what they had seen and heard.

"The miracles, thus attested, were also numerous and stupendous. They could not otherwise have been such satisfactory credentials of divine commission. A single isolated act, however wonderful, might fail as an evidence of religious truth. It might be a deception, or a delusion. But Christ's miracles were both numerous and stupendous. The eye or the ear might have been deceived in a single instance. It could not be so in a multiplicity of instances, or in cases in which persons, born blind, were cured in an instant, or dead men were raised to life.

"The miracles of Christ, again, had nothing in them, militating with our conceptions of God's goodness and majesty.

They were exhibitions of the divine benevolence no less than the divine power."

Āgamika.—"But there are numerous miracles recorded in our Itihāses and Purāṇas. Why may we not cite them also as instances of divine power?"

Satyakāma.—"Because of failure of evidence and because of their militating with our conceptions of the divine perfection. Where nothing is known as to the age, circumstances, and character of the writers, how can the least confidence be placed in their sayings? The descriptions again are unworthy of the Godhead. The alleged miracles were in many instances performed by the most immoral personations and for improper purposes.

"The Christian miracles are in these respects totally different. The performer, Christ, was in his life a perfect pattern of holiness and moral virtue. It would be literally impossible for the disciples of Christ to have composed such an exemplar of perfection from their own heads.

"And the Bible, thus attested by external evidences, teaches in point of doctrine and precept precisely such things as might be expected from the teaching of God, and throws light on many points on which we were perplexed by doubts and dificulties. The internal evidence thus confirms the external, and leaves no possible room for doubt."

Āgamika.—"What are the points on which the Bible throws light?"

Satyakāma.—"Some of the very points on which we have been conversing for some days of late. As regards the external universe, it tells us, 'In the beginning God created the heavens and the earth,' thus showing that the Nyāya, Sāṅkhya, and Vedānt were all right and all wrong. They rightly apprehended the turth, as regarded their opposition to each other's systems. The Vedānt was right in its protest against the eternal atoms of the one, and the unintelligent creative prakṛti of the other; and the Nyāya and Sāṅkhya were euqally right on their part in inveighing against the doctrine of the world's identity with God. But they were all wrong in regard to their positive doctrines—the Nyāya in its theory of eternal atoms, the Sāṅkhya in that of creative Prakṛti, and the Vedānt in its denial of a duality of substance. The universe is neither an illusion nor self-formed, but was called into being, out of nothing, by the one only Eternal and Supreme Intelligence, the author of all things in heaven and in earth. All perplexing difficulties are thus cleared.

"As regards the chief end of human existence, again, we learn, that the soul is a created substance but immortal,neither eternal or self-existent, nor again a mere compound of physical organs; born in time but to endure for ever, neither *swayambhu,* nor *anitya* in the sense of perishable. It has neither independent nor *terminable* existence. Being a creature, it can never be promoted to the dignity of the Creator, but it has an eternity *before it,* to look forward to. It may strive to approach Him—it may aspire after communion with Him, but it can never be unified with its Creator. There may be spiritual communion, but not physical identity. Since, however, the human soul is become tainted with sin, it must be cleansed and purified before it can look for that communion. It is impossible there can be any fellowship between the most holy God and impure sinners, before the latter have been redeemed and freed from sin. But the sinner, could not compass his own redemption, and therefore Christ came into the world for the salvation of helpless man.

"Thus, Āgamika, we have a clearing up of those points on which philosophers had so long debated unprofitably. And in the doctrine of Christ's atoning sacrifice for the sins of men, we have an explanation of a point which had certainly often puzzled me, and, I dare say, you too. The followers of Jaimini you know are all most forward in exhorting men to perform the sacrificial rites enjoined in the Veda. The only way to the realms above, they say, is by means of sacrifices. Now it is singular that Jaimini never talks of God; and, as we have just seen, a large and influential class of Mīmāṅsakas set aside altogether the idea of a Supreme Creator and moral Governor of the universe. Works and worlds, they say, mechanically follow one another in eternal succession. There was no more necessity, in the opinion of the atheistic Mīmāṅsakas, for a Supreme Being to create the universe, than there was, in the opinion of the whole shcool, for a *puruṣa,* or personal author, to compose the Vedas, or for an intelligent Governor to direct the distribution of *fruits*. And yet they all say, he that desires heaven must perform sacrifice. I do not know whether the question ever struck you, but I have often asked myself, what could they possibly mean by performing sacrifices, when they did not acknowledge a Supreme Divinity?

"The difficulty is cleared up in the Bible. We there learn that in the inscrutable wisdom of God, there could be no remission of sin apart from sacrifice, that Christ was revealed in the primitive age of the world as the great sacrifice for the sins of men, and that immolation of animals was ordained at an early period as typical of that great sacrifice. On the dispersion of the families of men, the institution must have extended wiedely over the suface of the globe. But while the ceremonial performance of the rite was kept up, probably every where, its object and intention were gradually forgotten or lost sight of in many countries. The practice, no doubt, came down to our ancestors from their immediate progenitors, but its signification appears to have fallen into oblivion before the formation of our literature. The zeal and assiduity with which it was maintained in our country is accounted for by its transmission from age to age as an immemorial primitive practice, but the inability of our ancestors to give the least intelligent explanation of the rite, and the want of any information in the oldest of the Vedas on its connexion with the celestial fruits of which it was believed to be invariably productive, are enigmas which can only be understood by the light of Biblical history. Viewed as an institution originally appointed of God to represent the future sacrifice of Christ, and transmitted from father to son in every age as a most important ceremony connected with the eternal happiness of mankind, the external observance of the rite would, we can easily comprehend, be religiously maintained, even though the doctrine typified by it might be forgotten. Without the light which the Biblical account affords, one can find no adequate explanation of the difficulty. Why should the writers of the Vedas tell us abruptly that the only way to the felicity of heaven is the regular observance of certain sacrifices? What again could those advocates for rites and ceremonies possibly mean, who either doubted or actually denied the existence of God, and yet contended for the necessity of offering sacrifices?"

"Oh!" said I, "this is what you meant by the Great Sacrifice for sin of which you spoke the other day. Now I understand your meaning."

Āgamika.—"I have sometimes been perplexed, I must confess, by the zeal with which persons have contended for the importance of sacrificial ceremonies who were perfectly indifferent, if not absolutely opposed, to the very foundation of all religion, the doctrine of a Suprme Being, the creator and moral governor of the world.

"But I have always consoled myself with the idea that even atheists might by a happy inconsistency be animated by the sentiment contained in the following formula of adoration to Viṣṇu; 'Obeisance to the sovereign God, the benefactor of Brāhmins and kine. Obeisance, O 'obeisance! to Kṛṣṇa, even Govinda, the benefactor of the world. I am sin, my works are sin, my spirit is sin, my origin is sin. Save me, O thou lotus-eyed Hari, who art the Lord of all sacrifices. None such a sinner as myself, none such a destroyer of sin as thyself, taking this, O God, into consideration, do what is proper.' Sentiments such as these give some insight into the meaning of our ancient practice of animal sacrifices.[59]"

Satyakāma. – "That is however a formula of very recent origin. It was unknown to those who composed the Vedas and enjoined the sacrifices. There are reasons for suspecting that the idea contained in the formula you have quoted is derived from an exterior source."

Āgamika. – "What are those reasons?"

Satyakāma. – "In the first place, the doctrine of Kṛṣṇa, as a distinct object of worship, identical with the Supreme Being, appears to be quite modern. Professor Wilson, whom all Brāhmins respected for his profound Sanskrit learning and who was never suspected of having ever done the least injsutice to our national Śāstras, says :

'The whole of this book is dedicated to the biography of Kṛṣṇa. Many of the Purāṇas omit this subject altogehter, or only allude to it occasionally. In others, it is equally prominent. The Brahma P. gives the story exactly in the same words as our text : which has the best right to them may be questioned; but as it is usually met with, the Brahma P. is a very heterogeneous compilation. The Hari Vaṅśa has a narrative more detailed than that of the text, with additions and embellishments of its own. The Brahma Vaivarta throughout celebrates the acts of Kṛṣṇa; and one portion of it, the Kṛṣṇa Janma Khaṇḍa, especially describes his boyhood and youth. The incidents are the same in general as those in the text, but they are lost amidst interminable descriptions of Kṛṣṇa's sports with the Gopis and with his mistress Rādhā, a person not noticed elsewhere; the whole is in a style indicative of a modern origin. The Agni P. and Padma P. (Uttara Khaṇḍa) have accounts of Kṛṣṇa, but they are mere summaries, compiled evidently from other works. The principal authority for the adventures of Kṛṣṇa is the

Bhāgavata, the tenth book of which is exclusively devoted to him. It is this work which has, no doubt, mainly extended the worship of Kṛṣṇa, as its popularity is evinced by its having been translated into all the spoken languages of India professing to have a literature. The Prem-sāgar, its Hindi version, is well known; but there are also translations in Mahratta, Telugu, Tamil, &c. It does not seem likely, however, that the Viṣṇu Purāṇa has copied the Bhāgavata; for although its greater conciseness may sometimes look like abridgment, yet the descriptions are generally of a more simple and antiquated character. Here, as usual, the Mahābhārata is no doubt the earliest extent authority; but it is not the earliest, for whilst it omits to narrate most of his personal adventures unconnected with his alliance with the Pāṇḍavas, it often alludes to them, and names repeatedly his capital, his wives, and his progeny. It also devotes a section, the Mausala P., to the destruction of the Yādavas. The story of Kṛṣṇa, the prince and hero, must have been complete when the Mahābhārata was compiled. It is doubtful, however, if Kṛṣṇa the boy, and his adventures at Vṛindāvan, were not subsequent inventions. There are no allusions to them in the poem, of an unsuspicious nature. The only ones that I have met with are contained in a speech by Śiśupāla, Sabhā P., in which he reviles Kṛṣṇa; but they may easily have been interpolated. There may 'be others scattered through the poem, but I have not observed them.

"As a warrior and prince he is always on the scene; but he is repeatedly called an Aṅśa, or portion of Viṣṇu; whilst in a great number of places he is identified with Viṣṇu Nārāyaṇa, and is consequently 'all things.' This latter is his character, of course, amongst the Vaiṣṇavas, agreeably to the Bhāgavata; कृष्णस्तु भगवान् स्वयं। Kṛṣṇa is "the lord (Viṣṇu) himself.[60]' "

"Professor Wilson is of opinion that the Śrī Bhāgavata was composed in the twelfth century of the Christian era, or about seven hundred years ago. The worship of Kṛṣṇa as identical with the Supreme Being cannot then be much older than that.

Āgamika.—"Surely the *Nārada-pañca-rātra* speaks of Kṛṣṇa's sports with the Gopis and with Rādhā, magnifying his glory as the Supreme Brahma. And that work is older than the Śrī-Bhāgavata."

Satyakāma.—"I have no objection to allow that the Pañca-rātra was prior to the Bhāgavata in point of time, notwithstanding its express mention of the Bhāgavata in one of its chapters. That mention I think is an interpolation. The Pañca-rātra must have been written before Śaṅkarācārya, for he not only refers to it by name, but controverts some of its doctrines. I believe it was the Nārada-Pañca-rātra that first invested Kṛṣṇa with the dignity of the Supreme Godhead, and celebrated his youthful freaks as something mystically divine. I have my theory of the reasons which led the author of that work to exhibit as adorable what I believe had before been held to be at best only tolerable in a prince and a warrior. But we cannot possibly have any reasons for assigning to the doctrine of 'Kṛṣṇa the lord of sacrifices' any date anterior to the Pañca-rātra which was written probably in the eighth or ninth century. The formula which affords you an insight into the doctrine of sacrifices cannot accordingly be of an older date than the eighth or ninth century. Now we have strong evidences for believing that the doctrine of the Great Sacrifice for sin, of which I have been speaking, had been introduced before that period into some parts of India, not far from the scene of the literary labours and theological discussions of the age. It was in the South of India that the Brāhminical genius was in those days most active, as is apparent from the history of Śaṅkarācārya, Rāmānuja, and their respective followers, and it was also in the South of India that large congregations of Christians, calling themselves after the name of St. Thomas, had, for some centuries before the formation of Vaiṣṇava sects, been maintaining the doctrine of the Great Sacrifice for sin. It is not at all improbable that some enterprising Brāhmins had fallen in with them, and, struck by the doctrine in question, made use of it in giving a more imposing character to their popular god Kṛṣṇa."

Āgamika. – "But what is your theory of the reasons which led to the deification of Kṛṣṇa in the Pañcarātra and the Śrī-Bhāgavata?"

Satyakāma. – "I do not know whether I can explain myself in a few words, but I will make the attempt. Kṛṣṇa, you must remember, is a great character in the Mahābhārata, as the friend of the Pāṇḍavas,. He must have been admired from the beginning for the abilities he displayed both on the field of battle and in the hall of consultation. He was feared and honoured as an extraordinary person, perhaps a god. But though celebrated as a hero, there is no record of his youthful irregularities being held as adorable. Public morals had not as yet become so low. We need not consider the reproaches which Śiśupāla cast on him as an interpolation. There may have been reports of his having, as a boy, led a very dissolute life. Most princes in our country still do the same. But we have no reason for taxing the age of which we are speaking with recounting those irregularities as *divine* acts. If the hero was deified, it was only by throwing the mantle of pious charity over the infirmities of the body.

"Indeed the Brāhmins were so much opposed in those days to the recounting of the foibles of deified persons, that one entire canto of a popular poem was suppressed or expunged because of its containing an indelicate description of a god's dalliance with his own wife. Kālidāsa who seems to have taken peculiar delight in such descriptions had given a very indecent representation of Śiva's uxoriousness in the last canto of the last canto of the Kumāra-sambhava, and the horror of the Brāhmins at such an impious exposure of a god's infirmities has thrown that canto into utter oblivion.

"The moral constitution of the Brāhminical mind must therefore have undergone a radical change when poems like the Nārada-pañca-rātra and Śrī-Bhāgavata were composed. These works not only recounted as divine, acts on the part of Kṛṣṇa, far worse than those which Kālidāsa had described of Śiva, but they attached a peculiar religious merit to the constant hearing, uttering, and contemplating of those acts. And these impure descriptions have not only been received with favour, but that which is the more circumstantial of the two, I mean the Śrī-Bhāgavata, has been classed among the sacred writings, and translated, more or less freely, into most of the vernacular dialects of the country. What can be the cause of this moral revolution in the Brāhminical mind? What inducement could there be for selecting, as objects of religious worship, the most ugly traits in a character who had before been conspicuous in the traditions of the country only as a skilful prince and warrior. Above all, what could be the motive for exhibiting such a character as higher than all other gods, and identical with the Supreme Being?"

Āgamika.—"I never thought of this point; but I see that the deification of Bāl Kṛṣṇa is an event that may require to be accounted for. What do you think was the motive of our ancestors in setting up such an object of worship?"

Satyakāma.—"I have only a *theory* on the subject. I think it will afford an explanation of the moral phenomenon of the change in the Brāhminical mind, but since there is a total absence of historical evidence, I cannot propound it as absolutely true. The Pañca-rātra was written after the overthrow of Buddhism. What was the meaning of that overthrow? Only that its leaders were silenced or expelled. The great body of the people still entertained their veneration for the character of Buddha. They—more especially the Śūdras—had found in that personation an object of reverence and adoration, such as had never been supplied to them by the Brāhmins. Indeed the Brāhmins had denied them the privilege of engaging in religious exercises of any kind, and even punished such acts on their part as were indicative of the least aspiration after celestial blessings.[58] Buddha however had allowed them to participate freely in religious acts and meditations. He had so far emancipated the Śūdras. The Brāhmins saw, on regaining their supremacy after the fall of the rival school, that it would be impossible to enlist the popular sympathy in their favour without some concessions to the Śūdras. They accordingly pitched on the well-known, and perhpas already deified, character of Kṛṣṇa, and set it up as an object of universal worship. And in order to make it the more fascinating to the popular mind, and to give that mind a strong impulse in a direction the very opposite of Buddhism, they invested their new god with those infirmities of the flesh from which Śākya Muni is said to have been somewhat unnaturally free. The rude mind of the populace, devoid of education, is easily led in the direction of sensuality, and whereas Buddha had observed rigid chastity in the midst of several thousand damsels resident in his own palace, Kṛṣṇa was represented as the very antithesis of Buddha, deliberately going about to seek, seduce, carry off, or procure by other means many thousands of females from different parts of the country. The moral perversion of the Brāhminical mind was accordingly brought about by the reaction against Buddhism. The Brāhmins had found no difficulty in adopting the speculative principles of that system, but, as regarded practical devotion, they were desirous of setting up a character the very opposite of Śākya, with a view to wean the popular mind from Buddhism.

"Under the impulse of the reaction in their own minds the Brāhmins set up their popular god as the Supreme Brahma, allowing all castes freely to wroship him, taking care only to maintain their ministerial importance as *gurus,* or spiritual guides of other classes. Whatever ideas, expressive of the divine majesty, they could themselves imagine, and whatever sentiments, borrowed from other quartes, struck their fancies as suitable for a popular system, they freely received in the construction of their new idol. And thus the very character which had injured so many husbands and stained the purity of so many households, was otherwise described as the Lord of sacrifices, the greatest destroyer of sin, and the deliverer of the world. If a man had only faith in that pre-eminent divinity, he would obtain excellence whatever his caste or race[59]. The Śūdras carried the dogma to greater lengths than was intended by the Brāhmins. Sects arose afterwards which conferred the dignity of *gurus* on eminent members of their bodies without distinction of caste or colour.

"I need hardly add, Āgamika, that Kṛṣṇa, invested with the attributes of a Saviour from sin, presents only the picture (to use the fabulist's illustration) of a jackdaw in peacock's plumes. The picture looks unnatural, and you have no hesitation in saying that the plumage is borrowed. And yet the fact has some value in it. The jackdaw that borrows the peacock's plumes testifies thereby that the plumes are beautiful. And so the character of Kṛṣṇa proves that, in the conception of its framers, human salvation could only proceed from the free grace of Him who was the Lord of sacrifices, 'in whom,' to quote a text from the Bible, 'we have redemption through His blood, the forgiveness of sins, according to the riches of His grace.'"

Āgamika.—"But I am told that the Christian religion which you are now advocating speaks of a plurality of gods, three gods."

Satyakāma.—"Not three gods, nor a plurality of gods, but a plurality of persons in the unity of the Godhead. This doctrine you can find no great difficulty in acknowledging, (1) because it is inculcated in the Bible which, as we have seen before, is attested by miracles and prophecies, and (2) because the Brāhminical śāstras themselves bear some confirmatory testimony to its truth."

Āgamika. – "How?"

Satyakāma. – "The Brāhminical śāstras speak of a triad of divinities, Brahmā, Viṣṇu, and Śiva. They speak of it, as *one form and three gods.* They tell us that they are mystically united in One Supreme Being. But the doctrine appears incongruous, and quite out of place in their system. The gods are frequently represented, not as different personal manifestations of the same Godhead ought to be, but as impure characters and antagonistic gods, wrangling and fighting with one another. Śiva fights and punishes Brahmā,[60] and Viṣṇu humbles Śiva[61]. The votaries of Viṣṇu anathematize those of Śiva[62], and the votaries of Śiva anathematize those of Viṣṇu. And all three are, again, pronounced to be transient and perishable[63]. The doctrine represents an idea which is quite foreign to the Brāhminical system, and we can only unravel the mystery by supposing it to be a relic of some primitive revelation, of which a distorted tradition had probably reached our ancestors."

Āgamika. – "These appear to be strange and novel views of things, and yet I certainly cannot gainsay them. Well is there any other point on which you can collect evidence from our śāstras in behalf of Christianity?"

Satyakāma. – "The doctrine of Christ's incarnation for the redemption of the world, involved in the primitive revelation of a future Saviour, receives some confirmation from detached expressions in several portions of the Brāhminical śāstras. The idea propounded in the Bhagavadgītā and other works that Viṣṇu descends in human form for the relief of the world, whenever it is oppressed with sin and wickedness, is ill in keeping with the acts attribute to his alleged incarnations, of which Kṛṣṇa is declared to have been the fullest and most conspicuous. I need not offend your ears by a description of his character. You will admit that from such a character it would be preposterous to expect any relief from sin. The idea was apparently derived by tradition from the primitive revelation of a future Saviour, and it was eagerly entertained owing to the necessities of sinful human nature, incapable of helping itself, and panting for reconciliation with God.

"But the ineffectual rites and ceremonies of the Brāhminical system and the adoration of its imitation gods and pretended incarnations of Deity, have never succeeded in administering anything like solid or enduring peace and consolation to the human mind. The people want something better, and it was no doubt with a view to the satisfaction of this craving that the transcendental and mystic systems were propounded. How barren they are of anything really good, we have already seen. They labour to tranquillize the soul by simply telling it there is no hope for tranquillity but in the cessation of sentient existence or the destruction of individual consciousness. It is however a mere mockery to speak of happiness without sentient existence or individual consciousness."

Āgamika.–"But what is the great duty and what the chief end inculcated in the Christian religion."

Satyakāma.–"The great duty is devotion to God, through Christ, in consideration of the great sacrifice for sin. 'I beseech you, therefore, brethren, says an inspired apostle, by the mercies of God, that ye present your bodies a living sacrifice, holy, acceptable unto God, which is your reasonable service. And be not conformed to this world : but be ye transformed by the renewing of your mind, that ye may prove what is that good, and acceptable, and perfect will of God.' The chief end of human nature is to escape the evils of this corrupt and deceitful world,–this vanity of vanities, which though not a nullity, can still give no satisfaction,–and to enjoy God, not by identification with Him, nor by absorption in His essence to the destruction of separate individualities, but by communion with His Holy Spirit, and by being filled with all the fullness of God.

"The philosopher talks of *mukti,* and the Vedāntist speaks of unification with God. I do not know whether either of them had any traditionary knowledge of the fact that man was created in the image of God. Not that an essentially formless Being can have a corporeal image, but man was made in the likeness of His Spirit. The Vedāntic conception of the human soul being a reflection of the Supreme, like that of the sun or moon in the waters, is not correct, but the human soul is certainly an image, a likeness, and, in that sense of the term, a reflection of the Supreme Spirit. The likeness has been disfigured by the introduction of sin. The reflection partakes of the mirror's impurity, but the chief end of human existence is so to cleanse and polish the mirror of the soul by personal holiness that it may present an unspotted likeness of its God and Saviour, and be fully restored to the image in which it was originally made. The restoration of that image implies perfect release from all those corruptions which the Brāhminical philosopher dreaded most, but it does not involve destitution of sentient existence or loss of individual consciousness. Christianity animates us with the hope of positive happiness and glory. Far from involving a destitution of sentient existentce or loss of individual consciousness, the ineffable bliss we look for, signifies the full sanctification of our sense, and the unceasing contemplation of the divine perfections without the least abatement of individual consciousness. We do not seek to fall into a state of irreparable insensibility, but we seek for an eternal life of perfect sentiency, that we may live for ever, intelligently and consciously to laud and magnify the goodness and mercy of God. We wish our passions and affections, not to be destroyed, but to be brought in subjection to God, and to continue as immortal trophies of His omnipotent grace."

Āgamika. – "Many ideas are suggested by what you say. I shall not ask any more questions now. It is so late in the day, and I must first of all think more maturely of what you have already advanced. I shall probably call upon you soon for further information. I certainly feel that if there be truth in the world, it must be found in the Christian Scriptures."

*Satyakām*a.—"Since there is a God, the author and director of all things, there must also be a corresponding TRUTH. And if we seek it in dependence on Him, we shall no doubt find it, and the truth shall make us free, shall give us real *Mukti*."

References

1. वाक्यार्थविचारणाध्यवसाननिर्वृत्ताहि ब्रह्मावगतिर्नानुमानादिप्रमाणान्तरनिर्वृत्ता सत्सुतु वेदान्तवाक्येषु जगतो जन्मादिकारणवादिषु तदर्थग्रहणदार्ढ्यी-यानुमानमपि वेदान्तवाक्याविरोधि प्रमाणं भवन्ननिवार्य्यते ॥

   Com. Vedānt I. i. 2.

2. न हीदृशस्य शास्त्रस्य ऋग्वेदादिलक्षणस्य सर्वज्ञगुणान्वितस्य सर्वज्ञादन्यतः सम्भवोऽस्ति। Ibid. I. i. 3.

3. यो ब्रह्माणं विदधाति पूर्वं यो वैवेदांश्च प्रहिणोति तस्मै। तं हदेवमात्मबुद्धिप्रकाशं मुमुक्षुर्वै शरणमहं प्रपद्ये। Śwetāśwatara.

4. सर्वे वेदा यत्पदमामनंति तपांसि सर्वाणि च यद्वदन्ति। Kaṭha.

5. अरेऽस्य महतो भूतस्य निश्वसितमेतद्यदृग्वेदः। Bṛhadāraṇyaka.

6. स यथार्द्रेन्धाग्नेरभ्याहितात्पृथग्धूमा विनिश्चरन्त्येवं वा अरेऽस्य महतो भूतस्य निश्वसितमेतद्यदृग्वेदो यजुर्वेदः सामवेदोऽथर्वाङ्गिरस इतिहास पुराणं विद्या उपनिषदः श्लोका सूत्राण्यनुव्याख्यानानि व्याख्यानान्यस्यैवैतानि सर्वाणि निश्वसितानि। *Bṛhadāraṇyaka*.

7. तदाशङ्कानिवृत्त्यर्थमिदमुक्तं पुरुषनिश्वासवदप्रयत्नोत्थितत्वात्प्रमाणं वेदोन यथान्योग्रन्थ इति। *Śaṅkara*.

8. स वा अयमात्मा ब्रह्म मनोमयः प्राणमयश्चक्षुर्मय श्रोत्रमयः पृथिवीमय आपोमयो वायुमय आकाशमयस्तेजोमयोऽतेजोमयः काममयोऽकाममयः क्रोधमयोऽक्रोधमयो धर्म्ममयोऽधर्म्ममयः सर्व्वमयः। *Bṛhadāraṇyaka.*

9. तस्मादृचः साम यजूंषि *Muṇḍaka.*

10. पुमान् रेतःसिञ्चति योषितायां वह्वी प्रजाः पुरुषात् सम्प्रसूताः तस्मादृचः साम यजूंषि। *Muṇḍaka.*

11. न खलु निपुणोऽपि स्वस्कन्धमारोढुं प्रभवेदिति ॥

Sāyana in Max Muller's Ṛg-Veda.

12. न तस्यापि वाक्यस्य वेदान्तःपातित्वेनात्माश्रयत्वप्रसङ्गात् न खलु निपुणोपि स्वस्कंधमारोढुं प्रभवेदिति वेदएव द्विजातीनां निश्रेयसकरः पर इत्यादि स्मृतिवाक्यं प्रमाणमितिचेन्न तस्याप्युक्तश्रुतिमूलकत्वेन निराकृतत्त्वात् वेदविषया लोकप्रसिद्धिः सार्वजनीनापि नीलं नभ इत्यादिवद्भ्रान्ता। Ibid.

13. प्रमाणान्यपि यथोक्तानि श्रुतिस्मृतिलोकप्रसिद्धिरूपाणि वेदसद्भावे द्रष्टव्यानि यथाघटपटादिद्रव्याणां स्वप्रकाशत्वाभावेऽपि सूर्य्यचंद्रादीनां स्वप्रकाशत्वमविरुद्धं तथामनुष्यादीनां स्वस्कंधारोहासंभवेऽप्यकुंठितशक्तेर्वेदस्येतरवस्तुप्रतिपादकत्ववत्स्वप्रतिपादकत्वमप्यस्तु ॥

14. यस्मान् मायी सृजते विश्वमेतत् ॥

15. See the last section but one of the Bṛhadāraṇyaka Upaniṣadpp. 1077-1089. Bibliotheca Indica Vol. ii. No. 18. We cannot make up our minds to reprint such a long obscene passage.

16. अनित्यसंयोगान्मंत्रानर्थक्यमिति किंते कृणवन्ति कीकटेष्विति मन्त्रे कीकटो नाम जनपद आम्रातः तथानैचाशाखं नाम नगरं प्रमगंदो नामराजेत्येतेर्था अनित्या आम्नाताः तथाच सति प्राक् प्रमगंदान्नायं मंत्रोभूतपूर्व इति गम्यते ॥

17. आख्या प्रवचनादिति। Jaimini quoted in Max Muller's Ṛg-Veda.

18. नतु तत्रानित्यो बबराख्यः कश्चित्पुरुषो विवक्षितः किंतु बबर इति शब्दानुकृतिः तथा सति बबरेति शब्दं कुर्वन्वायुरभिधीयते सच प्राबाहणिः प्रकर्षेण वहनशीलः एवमन्यत्राप्यूहनीयं।

Jaimini quoted in Max Muller's Ṛg-Veda.

19. ये पूर्वदेवा ऋषयश्च तद्विदुः॥

20. इति शुश्रुम पूर्वेषां ये नस्तद्व्याचचक्षिरे॥

21. इति शुश्रुम धीराणां ये नस्तद्विचचक्षिरे॥

22. देवैरत्रापि विचिकित्सितं पुरा नहि सुविज्ञेयमणुरेष धर्म्मः॥

23. अथर्वा तां पुरोवाचाङ्गिरे ब्रह्मविद्यां॥

24. तदेतत् सत्यमृषिरङ्गिराः पुरोवाच॥

25. एतद्वै ब्राह्मणं पुरा वाजश्रवसा विदामक्रन्॥

26. Dr. Muir's Sanskrit Texts, Part iii, p. 70.

27. Ibid. pp. 71, 72.

28. बुद्धिपूर्वा वाक्यकृतिर्वेदे। ब्राह्मणे सज्ञांकर्म्मसिद्धिर्लिङ्गम्। बुद्धिपूर्वोददातिः। तद्वचवनादाम्नायप्रामाण्यं। तद्वचनादाम्नायप्रमाण्यं॥

29. न पौरुषेयत्वं तत्कर्तुः पुरषस्याभावात्। मुक्तामुक्तयोरयोग्यत्वात्॥

30. त्रिकद्रुकेष्वपिवत् सुतस्यास्य मदे अहिमिन्द्रोजघान॥

Max Muller's Ṛg-Veda. ii. p. 487.

31. नारदो नन्दनेऽपश्यत् पुंश्चलीगणमध्यगं। शक्रं सुराधिराजानं तन्मुखासक्तलोचनं॥ Mārkaṇḍeya Purāṇa.

32. मंत्रायुर्वेदवच्च तत्प्रामाण्यमाप्तप्रामाण्यात्। आप्तस्य वेदकर्तुः प्रामाण्यात् यथार्थोपदेशकत्वात् वेदस्य तदुक्तत्वमर्थाल्लब्धं।

33. यस्माद्विषाणी तस्माद्गौः।

34. शूद्रात्सप्तमे वैश्याद्दशमे क्षत्रियात्सप्तदशे ब्राह्मणात् प्राणसंशये क्षुधापीड़ितमात्मानं कुटुंवं वा रक्षितुं सप्तदिनान्याहारमप्राप्य शूद्रभक्ष्यापहारः कार्य्यः एवं दशदिनान्याहारमप्राप्य क्षत्रियात् प्राणसंशये ब्राह्मणात् भक्ष्यापहरणं न दोषायेत्याहुः।

35. यस्माद्विषाणी तस्मादश्वः।

36. जीवन्मुक्तधुरीणो विष्णुर्विशुद्धसत्त्वतया निरतिशयसर्वज्ञोपि वीतरागत्वात् सहस्रशाखवेदनिर्माणायोग्यः। अमुक्तस्त्वसर्वज्ञत्वादेवायोग्य इत्यर्थः॥

37. यस्मिनदृष्टेपि कृतबुद्धिरूपजायते तत् पौरुषेयं ॥ San. Sut. v. 50.

न पुरुषोच्चारितमात्रेण पौरुषेयत्वं श्वासप्रश्वासयोः सुषुप्तिकालीनयोः पौरुषेयत्वव्यवहाराभावात् किन्तु बुद्धिपूर्वकत्वेन। वेदास्तु निःश्वासवदेवा-दृष्टवशादबुद्धिपूर्वका एव स्वयम्भुवः सकाशात् स्वयं भवन्ति ॥ Vij-Bhik.

38. निजशक्त्यभिव्यक्तेः स्वतः प्रामाण्यं ॥

39. न नित्यत्वं वेदानां कार्य्यत्वश्रुतेः ॥

40. चोदनेति क्रियायाः प्रवर्त्तकं वचनमाहुरिति कार्य्यार्थे वेदस्य प्रामाण्यं दर्शयति कार्य्य एव अर्थे वेदस्य प्रामाण्यं। कथं तर्हि भूताद्यर्थावगतिः। मन्त्रार्थवादेषु। * * वेदे पुनर्बाधकज्ञानाभावात् अर्थासंस्पर्शिता शङ्कापि नास्ति ॥

41. पुनरपि प्रश्नपूर्व्वकमिदमुक्तं कोर्थ। योनिश्रेयसाय ज्योतिष्टमादिः। कोनर्थः। यः प्रत्यवायाय स्त्येनादि ॥

42. ज्ञातं हि अर्थं परस्मै प्रतिपादयितुं पुरुषाः प्रयुज्जते वाक्यानि नचाप्रतीतोऽर्थो ज्ञातो भवतीति प्रमाणान्तरसंवादिना पौरुषेयेण वचनेन भवितव्यं तदिदमुक्तं अशक्यं हि तत् पुरुषेण ज्ञातुमृते वचनात् इति ननु अशक्यं हि तत् पुरुषेण ज्ञातुमृते प्रमाणान्तरादिति वक्तव्ये ऋते वचनादिति कोभिप्रायः उच्यते ननु च कार्य्यार्थत्वेपि पौरुषेयतयैव वचसः प्राप्नोतीत्यस्त्यपरिहारार्थमिदमुच्यते ऋते वचनादिति ॥

अतः पुरुषपरम्परायामपि न प्रमाणान्तरगोचरो धर्म्म इति कथं पुनरिदं सिध्यति पुरुषपरम्परोपदेशान्यथानुपपत्त्या किमप्युपलम्भकमस्तीति न शक्यते कल्पयितुं ॥

सर्व्वत्र नो दर्शनं प्रमाणमिति दृष्टं हि कार्य्यं पुरुषप्रयत्नानपेक्षं पुरुषानुपलब्धेः सापेक्षञ्च प्रथमप्रयोगानवगतेः प्रयोगान्तरे चावगमात् यदि प्रथमः श्रुतो न प्रत्याययति कृतकस्तर्हि कोभिप्रायश्चोदकस्य यदि तावते कृतकः कार्यो न सामयिक इत्यभिप्रायः ततः सिद्धं साध्यते पुरुषान्तरप्रत्ययानन्तरानपेक्षता शब्दं प्रमाणमिति वदतोभिप्रेता ॥

ननु चासौ संज्ञासंज्ञिसम्बन्धः तस्मादन्य एवायं सम्बन्ध इति मन्यते तदयुक्तं तत्रापि प्रत्याय्यस्य प्रत्ययाकस्य च संज्ञासंज्ञिसम्बन्धलक्षणः सम्बन्ध इति स एवायं ज्ञाप्यज्ञापकलक्षणः सम्बन्ध उक्तः ॥

कुत एतत्। कृतक इति पुर्व्वोपवर्णितेनैवाभिप्रायेणोक्तं तस्मान्मन्यामहे केनापि पुरुषेण शब्दानामर्थैः सह सम्बन्धं कृत्वा संव्यवहर्तुं वेदाः प्रणीता इति सापेक्षत्वमपसंहृतं तादिनीमुच्यते। अपौरुषेयत्वात् संवन्धस्य सिद्धमिति वृद्धव्यवहारस्यानादितोपन्यासः। किमिदं तर्हि प्रश्नोत्तरं कथमिति पृष्टे पुरुषस्य सम्बन्धुरभावादित्युत्तरमयुक्तं अनादिप्रतिपक्षनिरासायेदमुच्यते कथं पुनरिदं प्रतिपक्षतया शङ्क्यते अनादिनापि वृद्धव्यवहारेण शब्दार्थावगमसिद्धौ यत्र कृर्तोपलभ्यते अत्रादिमत्तैव वलात् प्राप्नोति वृद्धिरादैजिति वत् तस्मात् कर्त्तुरपलम्भो निराकरणीयः॥

तत्राद्यं केवलानुमानागमप्रमेयता तावन्न सम्भवति अनादौ वृद्धव्यवहारे प्रत्यर्थिनि। तस्मात् प्रत्यक्षं तत्पूर्व्वकंच्चागमानुमानं निरसनीयमिति तस्मादुपपन्नमुत्तरं॥

यद्यपि च विस्मरणमुपपद्यते तथापि न प्रमाणान्तरेण सब्धन्धान्तरं प्रतिपद्येमहि यथा पिद्यमानस्यानुपलम्भो भवतीति नैतावता विना प्रमाणेन शशविषाणं प्रतिपद्येमहि यद्यपि च विस्मरणमुपपद्यते इति किं विषयमिदं विस्मरणमुपन्यस्तं यदि तावत् साध्यविषयं तदिदमेव प्रमाणं यदुत विस्मरणोपपत्तिः॥

यदि विद्यमानस्यैवानुपलब्धिः केन वा शक्यते वक्तुं शशविषाण नास्तीति॥

नैवेयं प्रमाणतयोपन्यस्यते विस्मृतिरनुपलब्धिर्वा किन्तु उपलब्धस्यार्थस्य कारणदोषनिराकरणायेदमुच्यते यथा घटादेरुपलब्धस्यानुपलब्धिरस्तीति नैतावता शशविषाणस्यास्तित्वं शक्यते वक्तुं उपलब्धिविषयस्यानुपलधिः-कारणान्तरमपेक्षते अनुपलब्धेः पुनरनुपलब्धेरेवानुपलब्धिः॥

ननु सम्बन्धस्य कर्ता कथं पुनरसौ नोपपद्यते प्रथम श्रवणोर्थानवगतेः॥

यदि प्रथमश्रवणेर्थोन प्रतिपद्यते किमायातं सम्बन्धस्य कर्त्तुरेवं तर्हि यदि गृहे देवदत्तो नोपलभ्यते किमायातं वहिर्भावस्य॥

ननुच व्युत्पत्तिरपि कार्य्यतामपेक्षते एव। कथं। अयमस्य वाचक इति॥

नहि दृष्टेनुपपन्नं नामव्यवहारमात्रादेवहि बालानामवगर्तिदृष्टा तस्मात् प्रत्यक्षदृष्ट एव उपपद्यमानेर्थे न कर्त्तुः कल्पोनोपपद्यते। इदमपरं व्यवहारानौपयिकं। कृते हि सम्बन्धे अदृश्यमानस्यार्थस्य देवादेः संबन्धकरणं अशक्तिस्तूपवार्य्येतैव तस्मात् औत्पत्तिकत्वात् सिद्धं अनपेक्षत्वं॥

अतः सभावसन्ततिहेतकमेवेदं कार्य्यज्ञानं नात्र विसृदशोपलब्धौ प्रमाणमस्तीत्यपसंहृतं। यदि च विसभागादृते नोत्पत्तिः स्यात् अव्यवस्थैव स्यात्, अनयैव युक्त्या कर्त्तृशब्दार्थ इच्छास्मृतिश्च प्रत्युक्ताः॥

येपि सुखादय उपन्यस्ताः तेपि भूतविकारहेतुत्वात् भूतगुणा एव शक्यन्त नह्यगुणो गुणिनं विकर्त्तुमुत्सहते॥

अथापरे ब्रह्मविदः कर्त्ताभिधानात् स्मृतेरिच्छातश्च महदादिभूतपर्य्यन्ता-च्छरीरादतिरिक्तमात्मानमुपलभामह इति प्रतिपन्नाः तस्मात्सिद्ध आत्मा कर्तृभूतः नन्वसौ निष्क्रय इत्युभ्युपगतं॥

तस्मादनात्मन्यात्मबुद्धिहेतवोमी निराकरणीयतयोपन्यस्ता भगवता भाष्यकारेण॥

स्वयमात्मानं प्रत्यक्षेणानुपलभ्य नेदमनुमानं प्रवर्त्तते॥

अथ परस्यापि प्रतिपत्तौ प्रत्यक्षमेव प्रमाणमिति मतं अनुमानोपन्यासो निरर्थकः॥

यदि परंब्रह्मविदामेष निश्चयः यदुपलभ्यते तदसत्यं नोपलभ्यते तत्तत्वमिति नमस्तेभ्यः॥

यदि विज्ञानादन्यं नास्ति विज्ञानमपास्यतं।

ज्ञेयत्वे ह्यात्मनो ज्ञानज्ञातृणी न व्यतिरिक्ते शक्यते वक्तु॥

Indrācārya Sarawati.

43. Dr. Muir's Sanskrit Texts.
44. Ibid.
45. Ibid.
46. See Endnote No. 21 of Dialogue IX.
47. Dr. Muir's Sans. Texts.
48. Ibid.
49. Ibid.
50. Ibid.
51. बभौच सा तेन सतां मतेन श्रद्धेव साक्षाद्विधिनोपपन्ना।

52. नित्यस्तु स्याद्दर्शनस्य परार्थत्वात् ॥18 ॥ जैं सूं ॥

53. वेदशब्देन तु सर्व्वत्र शब्दराशिर्विवक्षितः ॥ Śaṅkara on the Māṇḍukya.

54. Davison on Prophecy.

55. Dr. Muir's Sanskrit Texts, Part iii.

56. Pearson on the Creed.

57. नमो ब्रह्मण्यदेवाय गोब्राह्मणहिताय च . जगद्धिताय कृष्णाय गोविन्दाय नमो नमः॥ पापोहं पापकर्म्मांहं पापात्मा पापसम्भवः। त्राहि मां पुण्डरीकाक्ष सर्व्वयज्ञेश्वरो हरिः॥ मत्समः पातकी नास्ति त्वत्समो नास्ति पापहा। इति कृत्वा मतिं देव यथा योग्यं तथा कुरु॥

58. Note, Translation of the Viṣṇu Purāṇa, pp. 491, 492.

59. See above page 45.

60. ब्राह्मणः क्षत्रियो वैश्यः शुद्रो वा यदि वेतरः। विष्णुभक्तिसमायुक्तो ज्ञेयः सर्वोत्तमश्च सः॥ Kāśī Khaṇḍa in Wilson on the Religious Sects of the Hindus.

61. प्रजानाथं नाथ प्रसभमभिकं स्वां दुहितरं गतं रोहिद्भूतां रिरमयिषु मृव्यस्य वपुषा। धनुष्पाणेर्यातं दिवमपि सपत्राकृतममुं त्रसन्तं तेद्यापि त्यजति नमृगव्याधरभसः॥

62. See above p. 270.

63. रजस्तमोगुणोद्रिक्तौ विधीशानौ सुरोत्तमौ। शप्तौ मया न पूज्यौ तौ विप्राणामृषिसत्तमाः॥ शुद्धसत्वमयोविष्णुः कल्याणगुणसागरः। नारायणः परं ब्रह्म विप्राणां दैवतं हरिः॥

Pādma, uttara Khaṇḍa, in Dr. Muir's Mata *Parīkṣā*, Part 1.